RESEARCH METHODS IN HUMAN RIGHTS

HANDBOOKS OF RESEARCH METHODS IN LAW

Series Editors: Jan Smits, *Maastricht University, the Netherlands and University of Helsinki, Finland* and Nuno Garoupa, *University of Illinois at Urbana-Champaign, College of Law, USA*

The Handbooks of Research Methods in Law series provides definitive overviews of how research methods are used within, and affect, key fields of law – including European Law, Environmental Law, IP Law, Contract Law, Corporate Law and many others. Offering a deeper reflection, each volume focuses primarily on the prospects and challenges of different methodologies within a given topic.

Each Handbook consists of original contributions from leading authors, including perspectives from multiple appropriate disciplines, and forms a highly original research tool. As well as contributing to the debate on the role of methodology in legal research, these Handbooks will be an invaluable guide to students embarking on a research degree and to researchers moving into a new subject area.

Research Methods in Human Rights
A Handbook

Edited by

Bård A. Andreassen

Norwegian Centre for Human Rights, University of Oslo, Norway

Hans-Otto Sano

Danish Institute for Human Rights, Denmark

Siobhán McInerney-Lankford

The World Bank, USA

HANDBOOKS OF RESEARCH METHODS IN LAW

 Edward Elgar
PUBLISHING

Cheltenham, UK • Northampton, MA, USA

Published by
Edward Elgar Publishing Limited
The Lypiatts
15 Lansdown Road
Cheltenham
Glos GL50 2JA
UK

Edward Elgar Publishing, Inc.
William Pratt House
9 Dewey Court
Northampton
Massachusetts 01060
USA

Paperback edition 2018

A catalogue record for this book
is available from the British Library

Library of Congress Control Number: 2016959929

This book is available electronically in the **Elgar**online
Law subject collection
DOI 10.4337/9781785367793

Printed on elemental chlorine free (ECF)
recycled paper containing 30% Post-Consumer Waste

ISBN 978 1 78536 778 6 (cased)
ISBN 978 1 78536 779 3 (eBook)
ISBN 978 1 78897 638 1 (paperback)

Typeset by Servis Filmsetting Ltd, Stockport, Cheshire
Printed and bound in the USA

Contents

Figures

Tables

Contributors

Edward Anderson, School of International Development, University of East Anglia, Norwich, UK

Bård A. Andreassen, Norwegian Centre for Human Rights, University of Oslo, Oslo, Norway

Hilde Bondevik, Institute of Health and Society, University of Oslo, Oslo, Norway

Inga Bostad, Norwegian Centre for Human Rights, University of Oslo, Oslo, Norway

Roland Burke, Department of Archaeology and History, La Trobe University, Melbourne, Australia

Anna-Luise Chané, Leuven Centre for Global Governance Studies – Institute for International Law, KU Leuven, Leuven, Belgium

Laura Ferguson, Institute for Global Health, University of Southern California, Los Angeles, USA

Anne Hellum, Department of Public and International Law, University of Oslo, Oslo, Norway

Steven L.B. Jensen, Danish Institute for Human Rights, Copenhagen, Denmark

Daniel Kacinski, Center for Human Rights and Global Justice, New York University School of Law, New York, USA

Malcolm Langford, Department of Public and International Law, University of Oslo, Oslo, Norway

Tomas Max Martin, Dignity Institute against Torture, Copenhagen, Denmark

Siobhán McInerney-Lankford, World Bank, Washington, DC, USA

Sally Engle Merry, Department of Anthropology, University of New York, New York, USA

Dimitrina Petrova, Equal Right Trust, London, UK

Hans-Otto Sano, Danish Institute for Human Rights, Copenhagen, Denmark

Margaret Satterthwaite, Center for Human Rights and Global Justice, New York University School of Law, New York, USA

Martin Scheinin, European University Institute, Florence, Italy

Arjun Sharma, Leuven Centre for Global Governance Studies, KU Leuven, Leuven, Belgium

Kirsteen Shields, Dundee Law School, University of Dundee, Dundee, UK

George Ulrich, Riga Graduate School of Law, Riga, Latvia

Simon Walker, Office of the High Commissioner of Human Rights, Geneva, Switzerland

1. Human rights research method
Bård A. Andreassen, Hans-Otto Sano and
Siobhán McInerney-Lankford

INTRODUCTION

In the contemporary world, international human rights discourse has grown in prominence at international, national and local levels. At the same time, human rights are challenged and violated throughout the world every day, but nowhere can they be said to lack relevance for human life and interaction, or for social, cultural, institutional and economic change. Human rights inform political debates, social movements, rule-making and international relations in a variety of ways. Yet how robust is our knowledge of human rights, and of the role of human rights in the formation and transformation of societies? How do we construct human rights knowledge? What approaches and methods do researchers use to document the enjoyment of particular human rights, interpret human rights norms, identify the 'real content' of rights, ensure their effective realization across policy contexts or develop tools for reliable human rights measurement and research? How do different academic disciplines formulate and approach human rights issues within, but also increasingly across, disciplines? These are some of the questions addressed in this volume.

To some extent, the methods applied to human rights research reflect an understanding of the values and aims of the human rights discourse itself, and these methods are key to advancing an understanding of human rights in a variety of contexts and disciplines. The concern with methods is common to several disciplines engaged in human rights. Clarity on the methods advanced within each discipline is key to an understanding of the human rights discourse overall and to ensuring its normative promise. This volume departs from a premise that there is a lack of comprehensive, intelligible and accessible reference volumes on human rights methods. Consistent with the rapid growth of interdisciplinary academic research on human rights, this volume looks beyond disciplinary boundaries, drawing on research that moves across such boundaries.

The volume distinguishes between methodology and methods. Methodology is the generic term for choice of approach, sometimes connected to theoretical understandings and conceptual paradigms. For instance, the choice between an objectivist and a phenomenological understanding would represent a methodological choice. Method, on the other hand, refers to the specific approach selected, such as quantitative or qualitative methods along with particular analytical tools, such as data generation and analysis. The conceptual hierarchy employed here is, therefore, (a) methodology, (b) methods and (c) tools, where methodology occupies the stage between the theoretical understanding and the specific research design. Thus, Mikkelsen's outline of the research cycle includes the stages that connect to theory, models and concepts.[1] These would represent a methodological paradigm, whereas the ensuing steps of operationalization of the research, the development of indicators and instruments for observation and data collection, relate to the method of research.

Human rights research has been accused of methodological sloppiness. Coomanns et al. (2009) drew on an informal survey to infer a low degree of methodological interest among a surveyed group of human rights law researchers.[2] Although the survey itself may not have been robust in terms of its own methodological rigour to allow the authors to draw such firm conclusions, it did highlight a laxness with respect to methodology and methods among human rights researchers. There has not in fact been any systematic research on the subject but the claim that 'anything goes' because of an assumption about the 'good and benevolent' nature of human rights research is widely acknowledged to merit serious scrutiny.

For some human rights researchers, the very purpose of their human rights research has been to advance the practical implementation of human rights norms, and not to undertake research to pursue a critical investigation of the constitution, functioning and role of human rights in societal and institutional contexts. The practical orientation of human rights research has, however, sometimes resulted in insufficient attention being devoted to its methodological shortcomings and challenges. The purpose of this volume is to advance methodological awareness, competence and rigour, and thereby contribute to a greater understanding of the role and impact of human rights in context.

---

[1]   See Britha Mikkelsen, *Methods for Development Work and Research. A New Guide for Practitioners* (Sage 2005) 154. See also Bruce L. Berg, *Qualitative Research Methods for the Social Sciences* (Pearson International 2009) chapters 1 and 2. We have titled this book 'Research Methods' because the challenges in focus in the volume confronting human rights scholars are rather methodical than methodological.

[2]   Eva Brems, 'Methods in Legal Human Rights Research' in Fons Coomanns, Fred Grünfeld and Menno T. Kamminga (eds), *Methods of Human Rights Research* (Intersentia 2009).

Human rights research has evolved through distinct phases, with new disciplines having gradually entered the field over time. In the 1970s and 1980s, human rights research was primarily a legal field with a predominantly normative-legal underpinning. It maintained a strong focus on the elaboration and interpretation of human rights standards, and on building new international human rights institutions to monitor and enforce those standards. The methods used were usually interpretative, driven by the normative ambition of constructing, expanding and deepening our understanding of human rights norms and standards. Human rights academics contributed to the development of new conventions and declarations, with some becoming members of international human rights monitoring bodies. Following the 1986 Declaration on the Right to Development and landmark events such as the 1993 Vienna Declaration and Program of Action, the links between human rights and development began to be forged. During the early 1990s, social scientists, in particular in the field of development research, began to take an interest in human rights as a normative foundation for development and societal change.

Within legal research fields, legal anthropology emerged as a new field of human rights inquiry. Linking development and human rights opened analytical space for social scientists and anthropologists and the role of human rights in local processes of societal change. The analytical focus was often comparative and anthropological; it was frequently connected with regime change analysis or local/contextual analysis, or with conflicts between local versus universal norms.

During this period development economists were also beginning to engage with human rights, offering models and practical guidance for development policies conducive to human rights requirements. While patently political in their initial orientation, human rights-based approaches to development later emphasized the need for operational methods for assessing causal analysis of the human rights performance of development actors (e.g. UNICEF's model for human rights programming).[3]

In the 2000s, historians entered the human rights research arena, undertaking critical enquiries into the historically contingent nature of the modern human rights doctrine.[4] In the past decade the growing number of academic journals dedicated to human rights reflects the increasing engagement of new disciplines: human rights law journals have been

---

[3]   Urban Jonsson, 'A Human Rights-based Approach to Programming' in Paul Gready and Jonathan Ensor (eds), *Reinventing Development? Translating Rights-Based Approaches from Theory to Practice* (Zed Books 2005).

[4]   Samuel Moyn, *The Last Utopia. Human Rights in History* (Harvard University Press 2010); and see Jensen and Burke, Chapter 6 in this volume.

complemented by interdisciplinary journals and by journals from the fields of sociology, anthropology, development studies and economics. This has been accompanied by a strong interest in critical empirical research and evidence-based methodologies. From the mid-2000s a growing body of work has emerged on human rights indicators, including work led by the UN, helping to deepen and enrich the understanding of particular human rights, and build indexes and databases that allow larger quantitative and empirical analyses of human rights performance. This empirical social science research seeks to understand and explain variations and differences in human rights respect, protection, promotion and fulfillment across social contexts, cultures and political regimes. Yet the turn towards evidence-based and empirically grounded research requires appropriate methodological skills and competence. A key purpose of this volume is to advance knowledge in this area within higher education and research institutions.

This volume presents a variety of methodological departures and analytical methods used in a range of disciplines. Methods vary within and certainly across disciplines. Moreover, disciplinary traditions are important in linking the choice of methods to a theoretical or ontological approach. For instance, discussions about methodology may be more explicit in the social sciences. Methods consist of rules, procedures and practices for addressing and solving analytical problems and puzzles. When a puzzle is identified and a research question asked or a hypothesis suggested, the researcher must make choices about the analytical approach (generally to decide if the purpose is to explain, understand or interpret, or a combination of these) and identify the most suitable techniques and tools to collect information, and process and organize the data according to rules and procedures. Among generally recognized methods, no single method is 'better' than others, although disagreement about the robustness of results arising from different methods certainly exists. The choice of methods depends on the research question posed. Training in methods is essentially about building skills to develop robust research questions and make good choices about which method or methods to use, and how to apply the methods effectively once chosen. It also entails training in understanding how those choices relate to particular paradigms, values or theoretical premises. In making methodological choices, the researcher also usually acknowledges and explores underlying premises, value commitments and theories.

Human rights research commonly takes the international human rights legal framework as a starting point and foundation. This potentially limits the scope of the research, but it needs not. Human rights research should not be constrained by overt or implicit requirements to 'promote' and not criticize human rights. That is not to say that human rights research should not support or promote human rights, but rather that a critical approach to institutional or political solutions may ultimately be more effective. Indeed, that an unquestioning acceptance of the premises or assumptions underpinning human rights or human rights violations is both unhelpful and intellectually disingenuous. Human rights research should be assessed according to the methods applied, the reliability and validity of the data used, and if results can be controlled and tested by other research.

The interdisciplinary nature of human rights also calls for applying mixed methods in addressing and analysing research puzzles. Human rights are not only the subjects of legal obligations, they are also moral norms, with political content and social, cultural, anthropological and economic implications. Thus, for instance, political scientists can learn from and apply case law (judgments) in their analysis of human rights understanding and explanation, while anthropologists can use case law to criticize narrow or anachronistic interpretations of universal human rights norms and help interpret human rights standards in local and cultural contexts. The more recent 'turn to metrics' also calls for mixed methods, combining quantitative large-N studies with contextual analysis of 'deviant cases', which may have significant informational value.

So why is this volume necessary? The application of thorough analytical methods is indispensable for independent, high-quality and critical academic research. Human rights researchers sometimes cut short their research or approach it selectively because they seek a 'constructive' and positive approach to prevail in their research outputs. Consistent with this, human rights research often avoids a critical assessment of certain of its core normative assumptions and its practical uptake; instead it is frequently accompanied by a list of recommendations that may serve 'promotional' purposes, but do not advance methodologically reliable human rights research, and may ultimately do a disservice to the advancement of human rights implementation.

Methodology and Methods in this Volume

There exists only limited literature dedicated to human rights methods and methodology.[5] The approaches introduced in this volume represent a broad spectrum of approaches to both methods and methodology on human rights from quantitative and qualitative works to hermeneutics and law. The

---

[5] The most recent comprehensive relevant work is Fons Coomans, Fred Grünfeld and Menno T. Kamminga (eds), *Methods of Human Rights Research* (Intersentia 2009).

volume provides a comprehensive treatment of approaches and disciplines, providing theoretical and conceptual overviews emerging from disciplines of the social sciences and the humanities such as economics, history, law, political science and anthropology as well as case studies and local studies. The call for greater awareness about methodology and methods in the human rights field is not new. As early as 1992, Jabine and Claude published *Human Rights and Statistics. Getting the Record Straight*, which addressed two principal questions: how are human rights data developed and classified, and how can the data be analysed?[6] The book represented a rare contribution to human rights research, focusing on quantitative research and data analysis. The application of such methods has advanced significantly in human rights research, as a number of the chapters in this book make clear, but the prevailing pattern in human rights academic literature is still characterized by the absence of a focus on methods and a lack of methodological proficiency.

Does human rights research have a common core of methodological premises? According to a 2012 study conducted by Kristin Reed and Ausra Padskocimaite from the School of Law, University of California, semistructured interviews and case studies prevail when human rights researchers are asked to select one or more methods applicable to their human rights studies. The majority of respondents in a survey they conducted defined their disciplinary background in legal studies. It is therefore likely that, if the respondents had been asked about legal interpretation being part of the applied methodologies, many would respond in the affirmative.[7] Sano and Thelle looked at the references of articles published in *Human Rights Quarterly and Netherlands Quarterly* between 2005 and 2007, and found that, on average, over the three years analysed, 45% of the references were in secondary literature, 17% related to legal documents and 16% referred to organizational literature. About 0.6% referred to primary qualitative data, while less than 0.1% made references to quantitative data. Based on this, the authors concluded that human rights research published by these two journals over a three-year period tended to draw on international conventions, and on UN organizational reports and administrative documents, while the evidence-based research in the articles was very modest.[8]

---

[6]   Thomas B. Jabine and Richard B. Claude, *Human Rights and Statistics. Getting the Record Straight* (University of Pennsylvania Press 1992).

[7]   Kristin Reed and Ausra Padskocimaite, *The Right Toolkit. Applying Research Methods in the Service of Human Rights* (Human Rights Center, UCLA 2012). The study was conducted with a limited number of respondents.

[8]   Hans-Otto Sano and Hatla Thelle, 'The Need for Evidence-based Human Rights Research' in Fons Coomans, Fred Grünfeld and Menno T. Kamminga (eds), *Methods of Human Rights Research* (Intersentia 2009).

How do the authors in this volume approach human rights research methodology and methods? First, consistent with trends in contemporary human rights research, a number of chapters emerge from economics, anthropology, ethics, history and institutional studies. In fact, more recent engagement on human rights in these disciplines has created a new momentum for methodological reflection and the use of more sophisticated methodical instruments like social network analysis. However, as this volume also reflects, it is clear that legal interpretation still constitutes a cornerstone of human rights research methodology given the legal anchoring of human rights in international and domestic law (although the limitations of existing legal approaches emerges also as an important subject). Several chapters examine and criticize legal approaches, and draw on other social sciences to address themes and issues that cannot be adequately addressed in legal approaches.

Table 1.1 illustrates some of the major concerns raised in the book. We distinguish between methodological and methodical angles addressed in the various chapters. Some chapters will incorporate both perspectives. In between these entry points we have included a column highlighting 'blind spots' in human rights research identified by the authors.

While the methodological aspects of the volume address challenges of analytical premises and concepts in need of clarification, including in current research practice, those aspects of the volume concerned with methods focus more on opportunities, whether in terms of identifying potential areas of application or providing 'how to' guidance. Thus, as reflected in Table 1.1, many of the book's chapters contain 'how to' guidance, reflecting its instructive and practical purpose, and a number of the chapters consider opportunities for employing specific methods.

Part I of the book includes chapters emanating from specific disciplines. The focus is either on the particular challenges for methodology and methods in specific disciplines like law, or on the opportunities offered from disciplines like ethnographic research. Chapters on history and economics present perspectives and potential mutual gains in subject areas where human rights discourse have relatively recently been integrated in disciplinary discussions.

Martin Scheinin provides an in-depth analysis of the interpretation of human rights law, arguing that rigorous methodology is essential for the proper interpretation of international law, including human rights law, drawing on both treaties and custom. Scheinin reflects on the distinction between identification, interpretation and application of human rights norms, and on whether human rights treaties enjoy a special position among international treaties. He opines that human rights treaties do possess special characteristics that must be reconciled with interpretative

Table 1.1 Methodological and methodical issues raised in this volume

Methodological clarification	Examination of current practices	Blind spots — Issues not addressed in human rights research	Methodical application — Potentials of specific methods	How to research x?
Examination of challenges and valid normative designs	Practices of interdisciplinary research	The issue of trade-offs in implementing human rights	The potential of ethnographic methods and of multi-sited research	How to research discrimination
Law as a scientific discipline. Challenges of legal interpretation of human rights treaties	Practices of human rights measurement and monitoring	Research on duty-bearer's motivation for integrating human rights in their policies	The potentials of comparative methods	How to conduct interdisciplinary and mixed methods research
The tendency of human rights lawyers to assume the validity of the norms underpinning human rights	Transnational human rights history as an emerging practice	The relative lack of reference to institutional theory	The potential of social network analysis	How to measure and monitor human rights
Human rights legal research as a lawyer internal domain	The lack of dialogue between economists and human rights scholars	The relative ignorance of historical human rights research during the 1950s and 1960s	The potential of agency-oriented human rights historical research	How to research duty-bearers
Ethical accountability and human rights research	The tendency to conceptualize ethics as a negative proposition		Human rights and the social welfare approach in economics	How to address a plurality of legal orders
Conceptual challenges of measurement			The relevance of human rights assessment in the health sector	How to address ethical accountability
Human rights historiography				How to conduct social network analysis
				Methods available to address human rights in health
				Methods of monitoring the right to food

rules derived from the Vienna Convention on the Law of Treaties. Scheinin concludes that a proper legal methodology for the interpretation of human rights treaties does indeed exist and the interpretive activity of scholars, judges and practicing lawyers can be assessed for the rigour of its methodology and the correctness of the answers it yields.

Siobhán McInerney-Lankford examines the challenges and opportunities of human rights legal research. The chapter analyses 'internal' and 'external' methodological challenges: the first relates to the depth and critical quality of mainstream human rights legal research and the tendency of human rights lawyers to assume the validity of the norms underpinning human rights law and to be insufficiently aware and critical of the values or choices these embody. The second challenge relates to the breadth and orientation of human rights law, emphasizing the sources of law at the expense of the impact and policy uptake of human rights norms. The chapter concludes by exploring the implications of these critiques for human rights legal methodology as well as offering some cautionary notes from a legal positivist perspective highlighting the distinct features of human rights discourse.

Hilde Bondevik and Inga Bostad offer an introduction to the method of philosophical hermeneutics based on Gadamer's concept of understanding and the process of dialogical interplay. The chapter introduces concepts of hermeneutics that may be employed in the interpretation of legal texts and in the interpretation of human rights principles and treaties, addressing those that may be used in applied research, as well as in theoretical analyses of human rights issues. The chapter posits that the hermeneutic tradition may serve as a basis for a critical and socially engaged approach to human rights.

The chapter by Edward Anderson contributes a much needed account of the dialogue between economists and human rights scholars. Anderson stresses that the mutual scepticism prevailing in both camps may be overstated. Within economics scholars may share the same concerns as human rights researchers; for instance, issues of resource constraints have become increasingly prominent in human rights research. Apart from addressing conceptual misunderstandings, Anderson also considers elements of causal analysis in economics and its relevance in the human rights domain.

Steven L. B. Jensen and Roland Burke explore how the discipline of history has entered the field of human rights research over the last decade. They argue that the most significant contribution history can make to the field is to facilitate a shift from the normative sphere to transnational dynamics. The chapter discusses the methods of history research on human rights from three complementary perspectives: (a) representation, periodization, and intent-based narratives; (b) sources and evidence; and

(c) key methodological approaches. The authors do not argue for an abandonment of the normative, but rather for a change in emphasis, implying a repositioning of the normative in human rights research, in order to provide more representative, agency- and time-sensitive accounts of the global human rights dynamics, and thereby facilitate a more constructive and accurate interaction between past and present.

Sally Engle Merry's chapter on the potential of ethnographic methods for human rights researchers introduces three sections drawing on qualitative methods. Merry discusses human rights documentation based on reports of individual cases and situations and the tendency to dismiss such narratives as 'anecdotal' and therefore not reliable. The author claims, however, that in order to understand the effect of human rights ideas and laws in local communities, it is essential to examine local ideas, experiences and practices. Merry therefore explores the potential of ethnography to inform such research since ethnography not only looks at individual behaviour but also at patterns of behaviour and their structural conditions. The chapter traces the understanding of gender-based violence as a human rights violation and compares the way non-governmental organizations in four sites appropriate global ideas about women's rights in collaboration with international scholars. The chapter underscores the significance of using ethnographic approaches to understand the human rights norms in practice.

From a focus on specific disciplines, Part II of the book brings together perspectives on human rights research methods which go across disciplines.

Malcolm Langford examines the growing body of interdisciplinary scholarship and reflects on how specific disciplinary approaches engage with human rights research. He offers a typology of human rights research considering how normative, empirical and evaluative approaches give rise to interdisciplinary approaches. The chapter discusses single-method approaches as well as multiple methods, whether these are mixed methods or what is defined as 'trans-methods'. He concludes that human rights constitutes a natural field for methodological heterogeneity, but that human rights researchers need to improve institutional collaboration and become better at linking research questions to solid methodological reflections.

George Ulrich also addresses an issue of cross-cutting relevance: research ethics for human rights researchers. Ethical issues may arise as human rights research will involve groups who are at imminent risk of being abused if exposed. Research ethics addresses scientific conduct, i.e. compliance with scientific and professional standards. Relevant for human rights research is the principle of 'do no harm', but relevant ethical concerns also comprise the quality of interaction with the groups researched and conflicts of interest; moreover, ethical accountability is exercised by monitoring bodies, but is also an integral feature of real-life communicative interaction and research methodology.

A number of chapters cut across qualitative and quantitative perspectives, such as Andreassen's chapter on comparative analyses of human rights performance and Sano and Martin's chapter on research methods inside organizations.

Bård A. Andreassen discusses key features of the comparative method and their importance for, and application in, recent human rights research. In this chapter, the centrality of comparison in human rights research and reporting is addressed and the purposes of comparing discussed. The chapter explores key methods of comparative human rights research and argues that comparison is essential in explaining human rights situations and the effectiveness, or weakness, of human rights advocacy strategies and policies.

Hans-Otto Sano and Tomas Max Martin start from the fact that very little human rights research has been conducted inside state organizations on motivations of state duty-bearers to integrate human rights in their policies. Given the importance of state actor-led human rights change, this is a particularly important lacuna. The agency and role of state actors are largely a *terra incognita*. The authors suggest that applying institutional theory in human rights research may be a useful starting point for defining research agendas within public agencies. The methodical implications of such theoretical premises are discussed and the chapter concludes with a discussion of elite interviews as a tool for assessing institutional dynamics within state, and inter-state, organizations.

Several scholars in the volume contribute political and social science perspectives to human rights studies with a quantitative orientation. Margaret Satterthwaite and Daniel Kacinski provide reflections on quantitative methods in advocacy-oriented human rights research, reporting a turn towards quantitative methods. A range of methods have been used in this regard, including randomized sample surveys and events-based data collection as two tools of documenting human rights infringement and violations. They also provide useful insights into other analytical techniques, such as the use of 'big data'.

Simon Walker's chapter describes the challenges of human rights measurement starting with methodical tools necessary for human rights research. Walker outlines the contours of a sound methodological approach from norm identification and specification to operationalization to the provision of 'scores' for human rights indicators – the last step in effect constituting actual human rights measurement. Walker suggests four principal approaches to measuring human rights: (a) an events-based approach; (b) an expert-scoring approach; (c) an official data approach;

and (d) the opinions and perception survey approach. Walker points to a series of challenges to human rights measurement and concludes with a series of recommendations and proposals.

Kirsteen Shields considers methods related to the measurement and justiciability of human rights through the example of the right to food. Shields' chapter provides a thorough assessment of existing methods to monitor the right to food. The chapter explains the problems associated with monitoring rights, both in general and in relation to the right to food, and considers the use of indicators as well as the relationship between indicators, monitoring and the definition of the right to food itself. Shields analyses the Food and Agriculture Organization (FAO) Guidelines on the right to food, inquiring as to whether these address the identified challenges of monitoring, including the challenges related to methodology: she assesses who and what is monitored and what is *not* monitored using the FAO Guidelines. Shields concludes with practical recommendations to advance methodological approaches to monitoring the right to food.

Under quantitative methods, social network analysis is particularly useful in identifying underlying patterns of social phenomena. Anna-Luise Chané and Arjun Sharma elucidate how they have used social network analysis in an analysis of the engagement of the European Union with the UN Human Rights Council. The network analysis allowed Chané and Sharma to assess the ability of the EU to advance its human rights goals while taking into account how other countries or country groups influence the EU. While a conventional documentary study of resolutions would have shown the level of cohesiveness of the EU's agenda, the broader network approach instead revealed processes of contestation and relative isolation of the EU agenda, thus providing a more comprehensive and complex mapping of the norms and processes underlying Human Rights Council resolutions.

Dimitrina Petrova's chapter offers a thoroughgoing review of researching discrimination, beginning with fundamental questions about the nature of discrimination and the norms that protect equality and non-discrimination, and surveying the legal instruments that provide for the right to non-discrimination and affirmative action. The chapter describes research methodologies within the study of discrimination, such as researching individual discrimination cases, direct observation and review of records, face-to-face interviews, researching patterns of discrimination, researching perceptions of discrimination and normative research on protection frameworks and researching discrimination jurisprudence. Petrova concludes with a succinct discussion of methodological risks common to all methods in researching discrimination.

Laura Ferguson analyses human rights in public health laws, contrasting human rights and public health approaches and highlighting the methodological challenges inherent in assessing the impact and effectiveness of interventions at the intersection of health and human rights. She underscores the importance of evidence-based methodology in public health, which goes beyond the legal imperatives, norms and obligations underpinning human rights-based approaches. Ferguson points to the need to translate international human rights commitments into public health action and to test the assumption that compliance with international human rights law also improves health outcomes, which itself relies on assessment based on both quantitative and qualitative data.

In the final chapter Anne Hellum explores how legal pluralities promote or constrain human rights and how this can be studied in local contexts. Case studies of three localities in Zimbabwe illustrate how an analytical approach which sees law as a multi-tiered and a semi-autonomous social field may be used to explore how legal pluralities impact on the realization of human rights. The chapter demonstrates the marginal role of the human right to water in the Zimbabwean Water Act compared with the influence of local customary norms. The chapter illustrates the importance of making human rights analysis contextually specific and sensitive to different layers of legal norms. Human rights analysis must also be cognizant of the interaction between these different types of legal norms and sensitive to the ways in which they may conflict.

PART I

HUMAN RIGHTS RESEARCH METHODS INSIDE DISCIPLINES

2. The art and science of interpretation in human rights law
Martin Scheinin

This chapter will address one of the most important questions for the methodology of human rights law, both as a social practice and as a scholarly discipline: how to interpret, i.e. give specific and concrete meaning to, the provisions of human rights treaties, many of which are seemingly vague or open-ended as texts. Is interpretation of human rights treaties subjective and unpredictable, or is it governed by clear rules and a rigorous methodology? The author defends the view that there is a proper methodology for this activity, and that even if different scholars or different lawyers may sometimes end up defending differing interpretations, often also related to their worldviews or who they happen to represent in a case, the interpretive activity of each of them can be assessed for the correctness of its methodology and ultimately also for the correctness of the answer arrived at.

IS IT AN ART OR A SCIENCE?

There is a saying, repeated in some of the most authoritative works on the topic, that the interpretation of international treaties is 'more an art than a science'.[1] The main purpose of this chapter is to demonstrate that this statement is wrong, or at least a gross exaggeration. As far as law is a scientific discipline, it is also capable of addressing and resolving issues concerning the interpretation of international treaties, as far as the question is about finding a legally correct answer through a methodology that meets the requirements of a scientific undertaking.

There are several reasons why some well-informed practitioner-lawyers and even occasional academic legal scholars feel a temptation to sign the 'more an art than a science' statement. The most important ones of them are the following:

---

[1] See, e.g., Anthony Aust, *Modern Treaty Law and Practice* (2nd edn, Cambridge University Press, 2007) 230.

(1) There is a great degree of variation between national legal systems in the issue of rules governing the interpretation of national law. Just to give one example, some legal traditions see the role of courts merely as executors of laws passed by parliament, while in other legal systems judge-made law is recognized as welcome and valid. As a consequence, the roles given to preparatory works for legislation and for judicial decisions vary greatly what comes to their respective weight in the process of interpreting statutes. International lawyers may feel perplexed by the differences between national legal systems and therefore unwilling to insist on any firm rules concerning interpretation of international treaties.

(2) As a legal system, international law is relatively weak. There are rarely mechanisms for independent international-level enforcement of the rules of international law. Much more often, including under human rights treaties, there are independent authoritative procedures to establish what the law says, even if enforcement must rely on the will of states to comply with the law and to compel also other states to comply. Often states themselves are the interpreter-enforcers of international law. All this contributes to the perceived indeterminacy of international law, particularly in the eyes of so-called 'relativists' for whom conduct by states is the ultimate criterion for what is regarded as law and what is not.

(3) A third explanation for scepticism in respect of methodological rigour in treaty interpretation is the popularity of the 'toolbox' metaphor: an international lawyer is praised for one's ability to address different situations when always defending his or her government's position while at the same time remaining a lawyer. This results in a lawyer shifting from one argumentative tool to another between different cases. The same lawyer may resort to strictly textual interpretation today, tomorrow emphasize teleological interpretation based on the 'object and purpose' of a treaty, and on the day after tomorrow insist on the importance of preparatory works as evidence of what the parties intended when they were drafting and adopting a treaty.[2] Even if there are lawyers who as counsel adopt this ad hoc approach

---

[2]   The dilemma of the conflicting expectations faced by a professional international lawyer is captured in Martti Koskenniemi, *From Apology to Utopia: The Structure of International Legal Argument* (Finnish Lawyers' Publishing Company, 1989) where Koskenniemi's solution famously is that the lawyer struggling between apology and utopia should be 'normative in the small'. From the perspective of this chapter, this means to stick to the proper methodology of treaty interpretation, even when being selective when representing a party.

it is, however, to be noted that judges and scholars must strive for better consistency from day one to the future, so that the 'tools' of the toolbox each have their proper place and proper usage in crafting the proper line of argument for resolving an interpretive question.

While the current author defends the idea of international law scholarship as a science and is dismissive of the 'artistic' approach of some authors, it needs to be pointed out that a middle ground also exists. For instance, Ulf Linderfalk is of the view that the interpretation of treaties is neither an art nor a science but a structural framework for rational decision-making that however also allows considerable free discretion, including not to follow the idea of rational decision-making.[3]

WHAT IS BEING INTERPRETED?

One could address the issue of interpreting international treaties from a philosophical perspective, by looking into hermeneutics as a branch of philosophy focusing on theories of interpretation and building upon the classics, starting from Aristotle, or on the modern theories by Martin Heidegger and Hans-Georg Gadamer, among others.

However, when speaking about interpretation in international law, the most important preliminary observation is that what can be interpreted is *language*, or other *symbols*, or even *action* that carries a meaning (and therefore is a symbol for that meaning). Interpretation is an exercise in trying to understand the meaning, what in some sense is located 'behind' what is immediately visible. In law, interpretation is an effort to find and understand the legal norm that is expressed in writing in a legal text, such as a statute of national law or an international treaty, or – much less frequently – in human action that is taken as an expression of an underlying legal norm.

International treaties are one of the main 'sources' of international law, as recognized in Article 38 of the Statute of the International Court of Justice.[4] The interpretation of a treaty is an exercise in trying to find the true

---

[3]   Ulf Linderfalk, 'Is Treaty Interpretation an Art or a Science? International Law and Rational Decision Making' (2015) 26 European Journal of International Law 169.

[4]   Accoding to a standard reading of Article 38 (1) of the Statute of the International Court of Justice, the three main sources of international law are (a) international treaties, (b) 'international custom, as evidence of a general practice accepted as law', and (c) 'the general principles of law recognized by civilized

normative meaning that has been expressed in the linguistic formulation of a treaty provision. The legal norm, which defines what is permitted, obliged or prohibited, is 'behind' the text, and is expressed in the text which often is the primary evidence of the content of the norm. Through interpreting a treaty text properly, a qualified scholar or legal practitioner is expected to be able to say with great certainty what exactly is obliged, permitted or prohibited by the legal norm that has been expressed in the text – perhaps burdened by the imperfections that always characterize human action.

Contrary to what is suggested by many authors, what is being interpreted is not the legal norm but an expression of the legal norm, such as the linguistic formulation consolidated in a treaty provision, in an effort to understand and perhaps reformulate with greater precision the legal norm that hides behind its linguistic expression in a treaty text. In short, instead of a norm of international law we are seeking to interpret a *source* of law, a treaty text. Towards the end of this chapter we will get to the question of whether also other sources of international law, particularly *custom*, can be interpreted.

IDENTIFICATION – INTERPRETATION – APPLICATION?

Much of legal human rights research is centred around the process of identifying the applicable human rights norms, their legal nature and scope of application, and their correct interpretation. The chapter will focus on the last phase or element, interpretation, in the context provided by the other ones. The phase of interpretation is, however, not entirely separate from the other phases, as for instance defining the scope of application of a norm may entail a question pertaining to the interpretation of the norm itself. One may also speak of one more phase after the interpretation of a norm, namely its application in a concrete case, situation or issue. This final phase of application would relate to a norm that has already been interpreted, as to both its contents and its scope of application. In this author's view a strict separation between the interpretation and application of a treaty provision would be artificial, as any factors related to the situation in which a norm will be applied also unavoidably affect its interpretation.

---

nations'. The same provision also identifies 'as subsidiary means for the determination of rules of law' judicial decisions and 'the teachings of the most highly qualified publicists of the various nations'.

The task of interpreting human rights norms requires an understanding of the sources of international law, including human rights law. A natural point of departure is offered by the Statute of the International Court of Justice which in Article 38 provides an authoritative list of the sources of international law. Next, the inquiry will need to move to Articles 31 and 32 of the Vienna Convention of the Law of Treaties that provide, respectively, for a 'general rule' of interpretation, consolidating a catalogue of primary means of interpretation, and then a second set of 'supplementary means' of interpretation. However, these two obvious first steps represent just the beginning of a journey. There is considerable flexibility, or even ambiguity, in determining a proper methodology for the interpretation of human rights law. The current author, however, takes the view that such hesitations should not discourage a scholar or a practitioner from striving for the best possible, indeed correct, interpretation.

THE VCLT AND THE MEANS OF INTERPRETATION

International lawyers tend to believe that the authoritative rules concerning the interpretation of international treaties can be found – where else – in an international treaty about international treaties. This treaty is the 1969 Vienna Convention on the Law of Treaties (VCLT), drafted by the International Law Commission of the United Nations, adopted by a UN Conference on the Law of Treaties in 1969,[5] and since then ratified by many but not all states.[6] According to its own provisions, the VCLT applies to treaty relationships between two states when both of them became parties to the VCLT before they entered the other treaty in respect of which the VCLT is to be applied.[7] Further, as the VCLT is not hierarchically superior to other international treaties, it is as *lex generalis* (general law) subsidiary in relation to more specific rules (*lex specialis*) perhaps enshrined in other treaties of for instance in the issue of interpretation. While technically these limitations would result in a fragmented and almost arbitrary application of the VCLT to some but not all treaty relationships between states, even under one and the same treaty, legal doctrine accepts

---

[5]   United Nations Treaty Series, vol. 1155, p. 331.

[6]   As of June 2016, there were 114 states parties to the VCLT, see <https://trea ties.un.org/pages/ViewDetailsIII.aspx?src=TREATY&mtdsg_no=XXIII-1&chap ter=23&Temp=mtdsg3&lang=en>. This is clearly less than what is the case for instance for most of the major UN human rights treaties. States that are not party to the VCLT include, for instance France, Norway and the United States.

[7]   VCLT Article 4.

a more prominent role for the VCLT by explaining that it reflects norms of *customary international law*, both because many of them pre-existed the VCLT and because VCLT itself has contributed to the further evolution of customary international law where that was not the case. Yet even customary international law is subsidiary in relation to any specific rules based on a particular treaty. Therefore, it would be wrong to apply the VCLT as a dogma, a straitjacket that constrains the application and interpretation of a treaty according to its own rules and procedures.[8]

There is a complicated relationship between the VCLT and the rules applied in interpreting human rights treaties. On the one hand human rights scholars and human rights courts and treaty bodies tend to refer to the provisions of the VCLT, to demonstrate that their interpretive activity is in line with international law, sometimes perhaps just to strengthen the legitimacy of the outcome of their interpretation. On the other hand the VCLT is manifestly insufficient in answering questions that arise when interpreting human rights treaties. Perhaps most clearly so because it is completely silent on the interpretive authority of a court, tribunal or treaty body established under a treaty – as if for instance judgments by the European Court of Human Rights had no role in the interpretation of the European Convention on Human Rights. The reason for this silence is simple: the VCLT was drafted with one *ideal type* of international treaty in mind, namely treaties between states, without third-party beneficiaries and without any international-level monitoring mechanisms. The VCLT is primarily a toolbox intended for *states*, helping them to find a methodology for amicably resolving disputes between states.

The VCLT contains three articles in a specific section devoted to the interpretation of treaties.[9] The first one of them (Article 31) carries the ambitious title 'General rule of interpretation', while another provision seemingly addresses second-rate issues (Article 32 on 'supplementary means of interpretation') and the third one (Article 33) the special case of treaties that have been adopted in more than one authentic language. This

---

[8]   See Martin Scheinin, 'Impact on the Law of Treaties' in Menno Kamminga and Martin Scheinin (eds), *The Impact of Human Rights Law on General International Law* (OUP 2009) 23–36.

[9]   VCLT Articles 31–33; see also Aust (n 1) 233–255; Richard Gardiner, 'The Vienna Convention Rules on Treaty Interpretation' in Duncan B. Hollis (ed.), *The Oxford Guide to Treaties* (OUP 2012) 475–505; Ian Sinclair, *The Vienna Convention on the Law of Treaties* (2nd edn, Manchester University Press 1984); Marc Villiger, *Commentary on the 1969 Vienna Convention on the Law of Treaties* (Martinus Nijhoff 2009). For a review essay on books about treaty interpretation, see Michael Waibel, 'Demystifying the Art of Interpretation' (2011) 22 European Journal of International Law 571.

seemingly simple logic is however shattered by two factors, namely that Articles 32 and 33 will also affect the application of Article 31, and that the 'general rule' in Article 31, even if carrying this title in the singular form, consists of no less than four paragraphs, two of them further divided into several subparagraphs.

The obvious point of departure for an effort to apply the VCLT in an undertaking of interpretation is Article 31 (1) that reads:

> A treaty shall be interpreted in good faith in accordance with the ordinary meaning to be given to the terms of the treaty in their context and in the light of its object and purpose.

The provision encapsulates the most important elements that jointly constitute the 'general rule', however, without establishing an order of priority between its elements. The terms of the treaty (i.e. the text) is where one starts, seeking to understand the terms used in their ordinary meaning and in good faith, but also placed in their context and in the light of the object and purpose of the treaty.

Article 31 (2) is subsidiary in respect of Article 31 (1), as it then defines what is to be taken as the 'context' against which individual treaty provisions are to be understood. It lists the whole text of the treaty (including also its preamble and annexes), as well as any separate agreements or instruments that were adopted or accepted simultaneously with the treaty by the same states. Any treaty provision is hence to be understood according to its own linguistic expression but also taking into account that all other provisions in a treaty (and other texts adopted in parallel to it) will affect how that linguistic expression is to be understood. A single provision is hence subject to systematic interpretation, as it is taken in its context.

There are no similar definitions of *good faith,*[10] *ordinary meaning* or *object and purpose.* Instead, VCLT Article 31 (4) confirms the primacy of natural language (ordinary meaning) in understanding treaty texts through establishing a presumption that a term in a treaty shall be given a special meaning (only) when it can be established that the parties so intended. Article 33 on the interpretation of treaties that were concluded in more than one language further supports and elaborates the primacy of natural language, inter alia through a presumption that the terms used in the different language versions are presumed to have the same meaning. It is

---

[10]   See, however, VCLT Article 26 which establishes the most foundational rule of the law of treaties, namely that international treaties are legally binding for their states parties that must comply with them 'in good faith'.

not uncommon that interpretive exercises start with presenting dictionary definitions of the relevant terms used in a treaty.

Somewhat surprisingly, the 'general rule' provision of Article 31 also includes a complex paragraph 3 that has no direct connection with paragraph 1. According to this provision, the following factors are to be taken into account together with the context: (a) 'subsequent agreement' between the same states; (b) 'subsequent practice' that establishes the agreement of the parties, and, most expansively; and (c) 'any relevant rules of international law applicable in the relations between the parties'. While Articles 31 (3) (a) and (b) can be read as broadening the understanding of what counts as 'context', subparagraph (c) clearly goes beyond the context of a specific treaty and establishes a principle of coherence-based understanding of any provision of international law which through this interpretive operation is seen more as a legal system than as a mere matrix of separate bilateral relationships between pairs of two states. Here, the reader is reminded that this principle of systemic integration[11] is still part and parcel of the general rule enshrined in Article 31.

For reasons that will be explained below, in the interpretation of human rights treaties one of the most important questions relates to the notion of *subsequent practice* in VCLT Article 31 (3) (b). Before moving to that issue it is however necessary to address the Article 32 provision on supplementary means of interpretation. Both the title of the provision and its own terms – understood in their ordinary meaning – make clear that the additional means of interpretation mentioned in this provision are secondary in nature, as they according to the provision itself are resorted to when an effort under Article 31 has left the meaning of the treaty provision to be interpreted as 'ambiguous or obscure', or has led to a 'manifestly absurd or unreasonable' result. Only two supplementary means of interpretation are mentioned in the provision, but with a wording that clearly shows that the list of two is not exhaustive: 'including the preparatory work of the treaty and the circumstances of its conclusion'. Here, 'circumstances of its conclusion' refers to other statements or events related to the conclusion of the treaty than those already included under 'context' in Article 31 (2). The subsidiary nature of these factors is easy to understand, as what is covered by context and its extensions in the earlier provisions represents agreement

---

[11]   See Campbell McLachlan, 'The Principle of Systemic Integration and Article 31 (3) (c) of the Vienna Convention' (2005) 54 ICLQ 279; Martti Koskenniemi, 'Conclusions of the work of the Study Group on the Fragmentation of International Law: Difficulties arising from the Diversification and Expansion of International Law', *2006 Yearbook of the International Law Commission*, vol. II, Part Two. For the principle of systemic integration see para. 17 et seq.

between the parties of a treaty, while here for instance 'statements' may refer to the expressed opinion of some but not all participating states.

The reference to preparatory works (*travaux preparatoires*) also being of supplementary nature is to be approached much more carefully, as even if the ordinary meaning of the wording of Article 32 suggests that they would be consulted only exceptionally, it is unavoidable that preparatory works will be relied upon also under Article 31, for instance to establish in good faith what the object and purpose was, or how the ordinary meaning of the terms of the treaty was understood at the time it was drafted. Hence, *travaux preparatoires* as a supplementary means of interpretation should be understood as giving them a decisive role when an interpretive effort has failed under Article 31, not as excluding arguments derived from preparatory works already when applying the general rule.

All in all, Articles 31–33 of the VCLT provide a frame of reference – or a 'toolbox' as is often said – for the interpretation of treaties. However, as the list of relevant elements is lengthy and partly open-ended, and as there is no clear priority order between the different elements, mere reliance on the VCLT provisions will rarely resolve an interpretive disagreement.

SPECIAL NATURE OF HUMAN RIGHTS TREATIES?

From time to time, discussion emerges whether human rights law is a self-contained regime, or if human rights treaties are a special category, so that the normal rules of the law of treaties would not apply or they would at least need to be modified.[12] Some of the features of human rights treaties that are seen as supporting the special nature thesis are:

(1)   Human rights treaties are not merely about reciprocal relationships between states but they also create legally binding rights to third-party beneficiaries, individuals and sometimes groups.
(2)   Human rights treaties routinely create international monitoring mechanisms that protect the beneficiaries in respect of states, also by shifting the centre of gravity in treaty interpretation from states to an international court or treaty body.
(3)   Among the well-established means of treaty interpretation, the object and purpose of a human rights treaty to create real and effective

---

[12]   See, e.g. Jonas Christoffersen, 'Impact on General Principles of Treaty Interpretation' in Kamminga and Scheinin (n 8) 37–62; Başak Çali, 'Specialized Rules of Treaty Interpretation: Human Rights' in Hollis (n 9) 525–548.

rights will have in comparative terms more weight than, say, textual interpretation or preparatory works. In other words, teleological interpretation appears to a more extensive degree justified under human rights treaties than under some other treaties.

(4)   Largely as a consequence of the relative emphasis on object and purpose and of the role of international courts or treaty bodies in their interpretive practice, the interpretation of human rights treaties tends to be more dynamic and evolutive than what is the case for many other categories of treaties.

Even if it is true that these four features all apply to human rights treaties, various combinations of them also apply to other categories of international treaties, such as those related to international humanitarian law, environmental law, investment law, international criminal law, treaties to avoid double taxation, etc. Hence, we may not be addressing an exceptional case of human rights treaties but much more general shortcomings of the VCLT to take into account the rich and evolutive landscape of the phenomenon of international treaties. The claim of human rights treaties being a special category can be turned around by recognizing that it is actually the VCLT that for its wording reflects a special category of international treaties, namely the ideal type for which the VCLT was written: treaties that regulate the reciprocal relationships between sovereign states as beneficiaries and duty bearers, where no third parties are affected and no international monitoring bodies involved and where interpretive activity will solely or primarily be reserved for the same states. Many or all of the challenges posed by human rights treaties to the mechanical application of the VCLT rules are present also with other categories of international treaties that do not represent the 'ideal type' which preoccupied the drafters of the VCLT.[13]

Rather than claiming that human rights treaties are a special category for which the VCLT rules, including those on interpretation in Articles 31–33, would not apply, the current author sees it as advisable to pursue a reconciliation approach. The four typical features of human rights treaties listed above in this section do affect the interpretation of human rights treaties but they can also be reconciled with the provisions of the VCLT, provided one is willing to reject a strict positivist approach and a dogmatic approach to the VCLT and recognize that it was written with one ideal

---

[13]   This is demonstrated by Catherine Brölmann, 'Law-making Treaties: Form and Function in International Law' (2005) Nordic Journal of International Law 383.

type of international treaty in mind. The VCLT may be relevant for the interpretation of human rights treaties but only through adopting a reconciliation approach to the relationship between the VCLT and human rights treaties.[14]

RELATIONSHIP BETWEEN 'SOURCES' AND 'MEANS OF INTERPRETATION'?

It is a matter of particular importance for the interpretation of human rights treaties that there appears to be an inconsistency between the means of interpretation referred to in the VCLT and the question of what are the sources of international law. For example, judicial decisions by international courts or tribunals constitute a source of law under Article 38 of the Statute of the International Court of Justice but find no explicit recognition in the VCLT, in Articles 31–33 or elsewhere. Even when a court has been specifically established to interpret one treaty – as the European Court of Human Rights interprets the European Convention on Human Rights and its Protocols – the VCLT seemingly gives no place for the judgments of this court in the interpretation of the treaty in question.

For the methodology of legal human rights research the consequences of this omission are huge. Much of the legal study and discussion on human rights law focuses on case law by the European Court of Human Rights, other regional human rights courts or United Nations human rights treaty bodies. Their judgments and decisions in individual cases and other outcome documents from the monitoring mechanisms established under various human rights treaties constitute 'case law' that is relied upon when presenting informed opinions on what is the correct interpretation of a particular treaty provision.

To take an example, Article 8, paragraph 1 of the European Convention on Human Rights (ECHR) reads: 'Everyone has the right to respect for his private and family life, his home and his correspondence'. This is how the human right in question is formulated as a matter of treaty law. Paragraph 2 of the same article then authorizes restrictions upon the right(s) and defines the permissible scope of such limitations. In today's world, 70 years since the adoption of Article 8, it would be absurd for a legal human rights scholar or practising lawyer to try to argue a matter simply on the basis of the wording of Article 8. It has proven to be perhaps the most dynamic

---

[14]   Reference is made to my chapter in Kamminga and Scheinin (n 8) where the various competing approaches to the VCLT are presented and discussed.

of all ECHR provisions, given rise to fine-tuned and yet constantly evolving jurisprudence in a wide range of issues ranging from abortion to euthanasia, from relationships between parents and children to the legal recognition of transsexual identity, or from defamation to surveillance. It is therefore plain common sense that any effort to interpret Article 8 must be cognizant of the body of case law by the European Court of Human Rights.

Yet, we are facing a paradox here. 'Common sense' is not a valid canon of interpretation in law, in international law, or in human rights law. Therefore, we will have to identify the doctrinal basis for the interpretive authority of the European Court of Human Rights (ECtHR) and other judicial and quasi-judicial bodies established under human rights treaties. Why would their interpretations carry more weight or authority than, say, the opinion of a government lawyer working at the Foreign Ministry of his or her country, or the outcome of a discussion in a PhD seminar convened by an eminent human rights law professor with a group of excellent emerging scholars?

In order to answer this question, four competing doctrinal constructions need to be considered. Looking into them will demonstrate that the paradox identified above is not a trivial one, as still today there is no settled answer to this simple doctrinal question. A second-order paradox can be seen in the fact that, in order to engage in a discussion between the competing doctrinal constructions, we will have to embark on the journey of interpreting international treaties.

Construction No. 1

Interpretive decisions by the ECtHR are authoritative only to the extent they are legally binding, and decisions by UN human rights treaty bodies are not at all authoritative because they are not binding as a matter of law. This construction is based on an *e contrario* reading of ECHR Article 46 (1), according to which participating states 'undertake to abide by the final judgment of the Court in any case to which they are parties'. ECtHR judgments would have legally binding effect only in respect of the state that was a party to a specific case. No similar clause can be found in UN human rights treaties which therefore could be fended off as mere 'opinions' without any actual legal consequences. This construction results in the fragmentation of human rights law – as every state would have separate and different legal obligations, to indeterminacy and ultimately to a denial of the rights that were promised by the treaty. In short, this construction leads to outcomes that are contrary to the object and purpose of human rights, namely to provide real and effective rights to individuals.

Construction No. 2

Irrespective of how the rules concerning interpretation operate in inter-state relationships, as captured in the VCLT for treaties where there is no international monitoring mechanism, whenever a judicial or quasi-judicial body is created to monitor state compliance with the treaty, it will possess the *inherent power* to interpret the treaty at the level of international law and hence with considerable authority in respect of individual states that are legally bound by the treaty. Sometimes, such as under the ECHR, this power is not merely inherent but actually *explicitly* provided by the treaty. According to Article 19 of the ECHR, the ECtHR is entrusted with the function 'to ensure the observance' of the Convention, and according to Article 32 (1), the 'jurisdiction of the Court shall extend to all matters concerning the interpretation and application of the Convention and the Protocols thereto'. The mere use of the word 'interpretation' in the last-quoted provision will mean that the ECHR is *lex specialis* in the application of the *lex generalis* of the VCLT. Under other human rights treaties the same conclusion would flow from the construction of inherent powers of a monitoring body created through a treaty, the interpretive function of it unavoidably affecting the applicable rules of interpretation.

Construction No. 3

A third option is to accept the omission of judicial or quasi-judicial decisions as means of interpretation in the text of VCLT Articles 31–33 and instead acknowledge to them independent status as a *source* of law. As Article 38 of the Statute of the International Court of Justice proclaims that judicial decisions constitute a subsidiary source of international law, they would need to be given authority in the application of a treaty, these judicial decisions being themselves a result of the process of interpreting the treaty provisions, presumably through the application of the means of interpretation listed in VCLT Articles 31–33. This construction appears quite problematic, as it separates the main actual interpretive practice of human rights treaties – the practice emanating from the courts or treaty bodies established under them – from what apparently would be acknowledged as interpretation, namely the arguments presented by states concerning how they think the treaty should be interpreted.

Construction No. 4

As was mentioned above, Article 31 (3) (b) of the VCLT acknowledges 'subsequent practice' as a primary means of treaty interpretation, provided such practice is capable of establishing the agreement of the parties. There are many good reasons to accept that ECtHR judgments and more generally institutionalized practices of interpretation under human rights treaties do count as subsequent practice that establishes the correct interpretation of the provisions of the treaty in question. Under the ECHR the agreement of the parties to the practice generated through the case-law of the ECtHR has been established proactively and *in abstracto* in ECHR Article 32 (1) that grants the ECtHR jurisdiction to interpret the ECHR. This agreement is constantly renewed *in concreto* through the role of the participating states in the Committee of Ministers of the Council of Europe, to supervise the execution of ECtHR judgments, as provided by ECHR Article 46 (2).

The current author is prepared to reject constructions 1 and 3 and to opt for constructions 2 and 4, or a combination of the two, as appropriate efforts to explain the role of human rights courts and treaty bodies in the interpretation of human rights treaties. Within the framework of the VCLT this outcome is supported by the foundational *pacta sunt servanda* provision of VCLT article 26: 'Every treaty in force is binding upon the parties to it and must be performed by them in good faith'.

ARE NORMS OF CUSTOMARY INTERNATIONAL LAW SUBJECT TO INTERPRETATION?

This chapter is about the legal methodology of interpreting human rights treaties. Some readers may however wonder whether the issue of 'interpretation' merely relates to one of the three main sources of international law, namely the written texts of international treaties between states (or between states and international organizations),[15] or do exactly the same, similar or different issues of interpretation arise in the context of other sources of international law, such as norms of customary international law or general principles of law derived as norms of national law from the legal systems of a wide range of states? Somewhat separately, one can also ask whether the rules and principles applied when interpreting treaties also apply when interpreting other 'instruments', i.e. written normative international texts that do not take the form of a treaty, such as United

---

[15]   For the three main sources of international law as acknowledged in Article 38 (1) of the ICJ Statute, see n 4, above. For a classic discussion of the sources of international human rights law, see Bruno Simma and Philip Alston, 'The Sources of Human Rights Law: Custom, Jus Cogens and General Principles' (1988–89) 12 Australian Yearbook of International Law 82.

Nations Security Council resolutions, or judicial decisions by international or regional courts, or even so-called 'soft law' documents?

A short and probably incomplete answer is that the rules and principles that govern the interpretation of treaties can without great difficulty be extended, and where needed adjusted, to aid the interpretation of other international legal texts, for instance UN Security Council resolutions.[16] Such texts represent supranational legislation that carries many of the same features as treaties between states, except that they are adopted by an organ of an international organization pursuant the powers it possesses under an international treaty – the constituent instrument of the international organization in question – as delegated to it by the member states of the organization. The outcome is a legally binding and publicly available text that addresses the legal obligations of states. Even if it is not issued in the form of an international treaty, it is fairly unproblematic to state that the rules and principles that govern treaty interpretation will guide the process of interpreting these texts as well.

The same approach can be applied also in respect of textual formulations that seek to capture an unwritten norm of customary international law or a general principle derived from national legal systems. Here, however, one has to be careful and notice that what is being interpreted is not the (unwritten) legal norm of international law itself. Rather, this kind of interpretation of a text would relate as a second-degree interpretation to a preceding interpretive activity, the effort of someone else – such as a scholar or a judge – to formulate in a textual form his or her understanding of what the unwritten legal norm is. For both customary norms of international law and general principles of law derived from the legal systems of the world this second-degree interpretive activity is inseparable from the identification of a norm of international law: by formulating as text a norm of international law that falls into one of these two categories the scholar or practitioner at the same time seeks to identify a valid legal norm and to provide a meaning for (interpret) that norm.

Focusing now specifically on customary international law, a reference to its interpretation can mean two very different things.

(1) Primarily, we would be speaking about interpreting *texts* that seek to capture an underlying unwritten legal norm. As above, we are speaking of a second-degree interpretation immediately focusing on textual

---

[16] See Alexander Orakhelashvili, *The Interpretation of Acts and Rules in Public International Law* (OUP 2008). What is said in the text primarily relates to Security Council resolutions adopted under Chapter VII of the UN Charter, as they will be legally binding for all member states.

expressions that are aimed at identifying, formulating and interpreting an unwritten customary norm of international law. Here, one
could interpret the language used for instance in a judicial decision
or in the writings of an eminent scholar, accepting them as best available efforts to formulate a norm of customary law. Unavoidably one
part of that exercise would be to question the text, as to whether it
is a true reflection of the customary law norm that it seeks to formulate. Hence, the interpreter would need to move beyond the second-
degree interpretation and address also the question whether the first
interpreter correctly identified the underlying unwritten norm. To
take an example, it is generally understood that a prohibition against
torture is not only a norm of international treaty law, based on the
Convention Against Torture and other human rights treaties. It is
also acknowledged as a norm of customary international law, the
validity of which is not dependent on how many states or whether a
particular state has ratified the said Convention. A judicial decision
may identify the prohibition against torture as a norm of customary
international law, at the same time seeking to capture the norm in a
textual formulation that unavoidably also entails interpretation. In
the famous case of *Filartiga v. Pena-Irala*, the US Court of Appeals
formulated the norm of international customary law as follows:
'we hold that deliberate torture perpetrated under color of official
authority violates universally accepted norms of the international law
of human rights, regardless of the nationality of the parties'.[17] While
this formulation of a norm of customary international law is itself a
result of an interpretive process,[18] it will unavoidably also be subject
to interpretation itself: What is the meaning of the word 'torture'
here? And are the references to the 'deliberate' nature of torture and
to 'official authority' qualifying elements of the norm of customary
law, or do they merely represent the application of the norm in the
context of the specific factual circumstances of the case? These questions pertain to the interpretation of customary law as second-degree
interpretation of an earlier text that seeks to capture the unwritten
norm.

(2)   Interpretation of customary norms of international law can, however,
also relate to something very different. Instead of a text, one would

---

[17]   United States Court of Appeals, Second Circuit, *Dolly M.E. Filartiga and
Joel Filartiga v. Norberto Pena-Irala*, 630 F.2d 876 (1980).
[18]   Ibid., where endnotes 4, 11 and 15 of the judgment demonstrate, through
their references to scholarly works and international instruments, how the court's
formulation of a norm of customary international law was an interpretive exercise.

be interpreting *conduct* – primarily by states – that relates to an accepted or claimed norm of customary international law, in order to determine whether that conduct is merely a habitual practice by states or *qualified* practice in the sense that it is driven by a sense of being bound by a legal norm. Only such qualified practice will serve as a source of law, giving rise to a norm of customary international law. Indeed, it is to be noted that Article 38 of the Statute of the International Court of Justice refers to custom as a *source* of law, not as legal norms as such.[19] Mere conduct by states is not custom in the meaning of a source of international law (a customary norm of international law), and one task for the interpreter is to assess whether that conduct represents an acknowledgment of it being based on a legal obligation, i.e. an expression of *opinio juris*. As this second type of interpretation in respect of customary law ultimately is a matter of interpreting practice, it is *not* a methodological error that there is a huge overlap between the two constitutive elements of customary law, namely state practice and *opinio juris*. It is the same actions by states that are being interpreted, both as to whether they actually constitute a habitual practice and as to whether they represent acceptance of a legal obligation. Critiques of 'double counting'[20] of the same conduct as evidencing both elements are hence mistaken. Again, this can be illustrated by a reference to the prohibition against torture as a norm of customary international law. An interpreter seeking to derive the content of the norm from the conduct of states would not simply ask what kinds of potentially torturous practices official authorities are involved in in different parts of the world, such an exercise perhaps

---

[19]   The wording of Article 38 (1) (b) of the ICJ Statute identifies custom as a source of law by using the following formulation: 'international custom, as evidence of a general practice accepted as law'. The required two distinct elements of actual practice ('general practice') and *opinio juris* ('accepted as law') are clearly visible in the wording.

[20]   For a critique of 'double counting', i.e. the high degree of overlap between the two elements of customary law formation (state practice and *opinio juris*), see John Tasioulas, 'Custom, Jus Cogens, and Human Rights' in Curtis A. Bradley (ed.) *Custom's Future: International Law in a Changing World* (CUP 2016) 95–116. For the very high degree of overlap in mainstream accounts, resulting in almost identical parallel lists for the two elements and seemingly justifying the critiques, see Michael Wood, 'Second Report on Identification of Customary International Law' in *Report on the Work of the Sixty-sixth Session (2014) by the International Law Commission*, UN document A/69/10, chapter X. The answer to the problem of 'double counting' is that the same conduct will indeed need to be interpreted for two different purposes, once as to whether it has become a practice and a second time to assess whether it was based on an acknowledgment of a legal obligation.

giving rise to a simplistic conclusion that physical beatings and sleep deprivation administered upon terrorism suspects do not constitute torture as prohibited by a norm of customary international law (or that there is no customary law norm at all).[21] Rather, an interpreter would look at such state practice that is capable of demonstrating acknowledgement of a legal norm, and here relevant practice would include official government denials of any ill-treatment occurring and official condemnation of such practices by other states. Do states that are accused of torture routinely deny that they torture? Is that practice indicative of these states being aware that international law prohibits them from torturing? As both answers are affirmative, this kind of conduct has become a practice and represents *opinio juris*, even when the police officers of the same government secretly engage in acts of torture.

Interpretation of state practice for the purpose of determining whether it involves an understanding that the practice is regarded as a matter of legal obligation (*opinio juris*) is a task that is very different from the task of interpreting international treaties or other texts that seek to capture an unwritten norm. Therefore, in the context of the current chapter this issue has to remain at the level of this conceptual clarification.

INTERPRETATION BY SCHOLAR, JUDGE, LAWYER

As a matter of principle it is important to note that if law seeks to be a scientific discipline, its methodology in identifying the pertinent sources in order to capture the applicable legal norms, and in engaging to interpretation of texts or conduct as a part of that process is one and the same for all members of the legal community. Different lawyers may propose different solutions in a dispute or to a legal problem, but they should all share a commitment to the same methodology and a professional expectation that they will be able to convince each other of the correctness of one's own proposed solution. It is of course a fact of life that, particularly in a legal dispute, a lawyer representing a party will pick and choose both issues and arguments, in the hope of convincing the judge (or other neutral arbiter)

---

[21]   See Amnesty International, *Torture in 2014: 30 Years of Broken Promises* (ACT 40/004/2014) 10: 'Between January 2009 and May 2013, Amnesty International received reports of torture and other ill-treatment committed by state officials in 141 countries, and from every world region'.

that in all or at least some issues the party that one represents should win the case. That said, counsel who serves his or her client by being dishonest or manipulative will not succeed in convincing the judge. Therefore, even when representing opposing parties to a dispute, qualified professional lawyers should be able to share some common ground and focus on disagreeing where there is good justification for more than one answer – including in issues of interpretation.

Despite the principal answer given above, there will be genuine and legitimate differences between lawyers when they address the same legal question. These differences can be based on the different roles different people play within the legal profession, or also on differing extra-legal normative commitments. As a non-exhaustive list of reasons why lawyers may legitimately come to different answers, the following five can be presented:

(1) A lawyer representing a party in a dispute is allowed to be selective but not dishonest, while both judges and scholars are expected to identify and address all relevant issues.
(2) That said, the applicable legal framework may constrain the judge (or other arbiter) to address only sources and arguments invoked by the parties, while a scholar of course is free of such procedural constraints.
(3) Further, a judge is usually bound by the rule of having to avoid situations of *non liquet*, i.e. statements that there is no law in the issue which therefore cannot be resolved through interpretation. A scholar can legitimately come to that sort of a conclusion, while a judge usually has to give a ruling, even on the basis of weak or conflicting law.
(4) Particularly within academia but also in disputes within international law – for instance in human rights cases – also extra-legal normative commitments may affect the way a lawyer in good faith seeks an answer that in his or her view is the best legal answer. A lawyer may be critical or conventional, conscious of the societal consequences of a case or ignorant of them, or he or she may as a lawyer allow expressions of one's progressive, conservative or revisionist worldview. A conventional and conservative scholar may favour a particular interpretation of a treaty because 'this is what the drafters intended' or 'this is how things have been decided before', while a critical and progressive scholar will emphasize changes in society that call for the adaptation of the old treaty text to new and unforeseen circumstances. The same differences in worldview may be reflected in how lawyers argue in a legal dispute, again typically also in human rights cases where counsel to the alleged victim of a human rights violation

will often adopt a more critical and dynamic line of argument than the lawyer who represents the respondent state.

(5) Finally, while explicit references to extra-legal normative commitments affecting the answer will almost always be avoided in a legal dispute, it is not as rare that legal scholars engage in a moral assessment of the outcome that emerges from a strictly legal analysis. One would however expect that a good scholar will always make it clear to the reader when he or she is moving between different spheres of normativity, so that extra-legal normativity is relied upon in assessing the outcome of the legal analysis, rather than blending it into it.

CONCLUSION

The way a lawyer conducts a task concerning the interpretation of a treaty, be that lawyer a scholar, a judge or counsel, distinguishes a good professional from a bad one. Even where a lawyer represents a party to a dispute and is selective in presenting only those arguments that support the case of his or her client, he or she must keep in mind that only good and relevant arguments will be convincing to a judge. Everyone seriously engaging in treaty interpretation with the intention to say something meaningful about what a treaty provision means, whether it is applicable in a given situation or case, and whether the conduct at issue constituted a violation of human rights law or not, will need to master the methodology of treaty interpretation. Efforts to resolve an issue of interpretation through wrong or bad arguments will only harm the credibility and legitimacy of what one is suggesting.

This chapter has demonstrated how the interpretation of human rights treaties is governed by a set of rules and principles that are also reflected in the VCLT. As human rights treaties nevertheless possess a number of special characteristics that are not present for the 'ideal type' of an international treaty that only addresses the reciprocal rights and duties of states in respect of each other and for which the VCLT was written, there is a need for reconciliation between the VCLT rules and the special characteristics of human rights treaties. In the view of this author there is a proper legal methodology for the interpretation of human rights treaties. Hence, the interpretive activity of scholars, judges and practising lawyers can be assessed for the correctness of its methodology and ultimately also of the answer arrived at.

REFERENCES

Amnesty International, *Torture in 2014: 30 Years of Broken Promises* (ACT 40/004/2014)

Aust, A., *Modern Treaty Law and Practice* (2nd edn CUP 2007)

Brölmann, C., 'Law-making Treaties: Form and Function in International Law' (2005) Nordic Journal of International Law 383

Çali, B., 'Specialized Rules of Treaty Interpretation: Human Rights' in Duncan B. Hollis (ed.), *The Oxford Guide to Treaties* (OUP 2012) 525–548

Christoffersen, J., 'Impact on General Principles of Treaty Interpretation' in Menno Kamminga and Martin Scheinin (eds), *The Impact of Human Rights Law on General International Law* (OUP 2009) 37–62

Gardiner, R., 'The Vienna Convention Rules on Treaty Interpretation' in Duncan B. Hollis (ed.), *The Oxford Guide to Treaties* (OUP 2012) 475–505

Hollis, D.B. (ed.), *The Oxford Guide to Treaties* (OUP 2012)

Kamminga, M. and Martin Scheinin (eds), *The Impact of Human Rights Law on General International Law* (OUP 2009)

Koskenniemi, M., *From Apology to Utopia: The Structure of International Legal Argument* (Finnish Lawyers' Publishing Company 1989)

Koskenniemi, M., 'Conclusions of the work of the Study Group on the Fragmentation of International Law: Difficulties arising from the Diversification and Expansion of International Law', *2006 Yearbook of the International Law Commission*, vol. II, Part Two

Linderfalk, U., 'Is Treaty Interpretation an Art or a Science? International Law and Rational Decision Making' (2015) 26 European Journal of International Law 169

McLachlan, C., 'The Principle of Systemic Integration and Article 31 (3) (c) of the Vienna Convention' (2005) 54 International and Comparative Law Quarterly 279

Orakhelashvili, A., *The Interpretation of Acts and Rules in Public International Law* (OUP 2008)

Scheinin, M., 'Impact on the Law of Treaties' in Menno Kamminga and Martin Scheinin (eds), *The Impact of Human Rights Law on General International Law* (OUP 2009) 23–36

Simma, B. and Philip Alston, 'The Sources of Human Rights Law: Custom, Jus Cogens and General Principles' (1988–89) 12 Australian Yearbook of International Law 82

Sinclair, I., *The Vienna Convention on the Law of Treaties* (2nd edn Manchester University Press 1984)

Tasioulas, J., 'Custom, Jus Cogens, and Human Rights' in Curtis A. Bradley (ed.) *Custom's Future: International Law in a Changing World* (CUP, New York 2016) 95–116

Villiger, M., *Commentary on the 1969 Vienna Convention on the Law of Treaties* (Martinus Nijhoff 2009)

Waibel, M., 'Demystifying the Art of Interpretation' (2011) 22 European Journal of International Law 571

Wood, M., 'Second Report on Identification of Customary International Law' in *Report on the Work of the Sixty-sixth Session (2014) by the International Law Commission*, UN document A/69/10, chapter X

3. Legal methodologies and human rights research: challenges and opportunities
*Siobhán McInerney-Lankford**

INTRODUCTION

A premise of this chapter is that human rights legal research is essential for upholding human rights norms and ensuring the realization of human rights. A second premise is that human rights legal research should develop its own methodology, as opposed to borrowing from social sciences or methods from related schools such as law and society or legal anthropology.[1] The chapter assumes the inherent value of legal research and the importance of human rights legal research methodology[2] to the foundation, strength and legitimacy of human rights norms and to refining our understanding of those norms. It is then from a baseline standpoint of the worth and value of human rights legal research that this chapter critically assesses its quality. Considered from a normative perspective, human rights legal research boasts a robust body of literature. Assessed from a methodological perspective, however, it is argu-

* Senior Counsel, World Bank Legal Department. This chapter reflects the personal views of the author and should not be attributed to the World Bank. The author thanks Jordi Agusti-Panareda, Varun Gauri, Kirsteen Shields, Hans-Otto Sano, two anonymous reviewers and the participants of the 2015 Oslo authors workshop for comments on earlier drafts of this chapter. Responsibility for any errors or omissions remains with the author.

[1] While the term 'legal anthropology' defies precise definition, it is broadly understood to refer to interdisciplinary studies in anthropology and law which may cover areas such as the clash of non-Western and Western cultural beliefs and related legal structures (including the interaction of formal and informal systems); legal pluralism in multicultural settings; human rights including the rights of minorities and religious groups and indigenous peoples (the latter to include claims related to land and intellectual property); and alternative methods of dispute or conflict resolution.

[2] A broad definition of this term is used here. The term 'human rights legal research methodology' is understood to mean the method or methods self-consciously employed to study, define and interpret human rights law and norms, as well as the method or methods that might be used to measure, elaborate, assess, evaluate and implement human rights law and norms and their application.

ably weaker,[3] especially when compared with the research methodology underpinning certain social science.[4] This methodological deficit may be attributable to a number of elements, among them the general lack of emphasis on methodology in legal research and the failure to be explicit about legal method or go beyond the legal methodology itself. As Thérèse Murphy rightly observes, 'It is true that human rights method has been a non-topic, at least in legal circles – a matter disregarded rather than studied'.[5] It is also arguably linked to the nature and purpose of human rights law scholarship, which is often undertaken by human rights activists, driven by laudable moral purpose and political convictions,[6] and a belief that human rights law research contributes to the protection or promotion of human rights.[7]

This chapter will argue that methodology ought to be a far more important element in human rights legal research for both normative and instrumental reasons. Given the legal protection provided by human rights law and the fact that the strength and credibility of the human rights discourse is rooted in its foundation in international legal norms, 'engagement with human rights legal method is essential'.[8] Indeed, the need to address the methodological deficit is made all the more urgent by the fact that, at least

---

[3]   In tackling the research hypothesis of this chapter it is also apposite – if not crucial – that the premise behind the hypothesis be itself critically assessed. It is submitted that, based on the research undertaken for the chapter, the dearth of literature on human rights legal research methodology was itself evidence of a neglect of methods in this field and therefore symptomatic of the weakness of this aspect of human rights legal research. In assessing whether this has changed or evolved over time, it is further submitted that there has not been a significant growth in human rights legal research related to methods, which is indeed an important part of the impetus behind this book project (see Introduction). I am indebted to Malcolm Langford for raising this important point.

[4]   'Legal academics, in my experience at least, seldom appear to talk about methodology in the context of their research, whereas other, social scientists often place particular importance on methodological issues'. C. McCrudden, 'Legal Research and the Social Sciences' (2006) 122 LQR 632–650, 646. See also F. Coomans, F. Grunfeld and M. Kamminga, 'A Primer' in F. Coomans, F. Grunfeld and M. Kamminga (eds), *Methods of Human Rights Research* (Intersentia 2009) 12.

[5]   T. Murphy, *Health and Human Rights* (Hart 2013) 9.

[6]   F. Coomans, F. Grunfeld and M. Kamminga, 'Methods of Human Rights Research: A Primer' (2010) 32(1) Human Rights Quarterly 179–186.

[7]   E. Brems 'Methods in Legal Human Rights Research' in F. Coomans et al. (n 4) 86.

[8]   T. Murphy (n 5) 8.

since the 1980s,[9] legal scholarship has dominated human rights, such that the neglect of method on the part of legal scholars has particularly serious implications for human rights scholarship.

This chapter analyses the state of legal human rights research and addresses two interconnected methodological challenges illustrative of the deficit afflicting human rights legal research along two separate vectors – one internal and the other external.

(1) The first challenge relates to the *depth and critical quality* of mainstream legal research methodology. It charges that human rights legal research often assumes the validity of the normative baselines it employs; that it is insufficiently critical of the norms themselves, relying excessively on textual articulations and not going beyond them.

(2) The second challenge looks to the *breadth and orientation* of human rights legal research focuses on the 'what', but neglects the 'how'. Further, it neglects *impacts* of legal norms on the ground and places insufficient emphasis on policy uptake and contextual relevance. It is insufficiently interdisciplinary and is not open to social sciences.

These challenges address the need to interrogate the power of human rights law and discourse: to go beyond assumptions and investigate its normative baselines and its practical impacts. They relate to the observation that human rights legal research has become 'a combination of sloppy humanitarian arguments and overly formal reliance on textual articulations which are anything but clear or binding'.[10] In a similar vein, others have charged that 'wishful thinking and sloppy legal analysis tend to be too common in international human rights law'.[11] This chapter is a call to reassess and reinforce human rights legal methods, arguing that its legitimacy and effectiveness hinges on such methodological rigour. It is also a call for examining human rights legal methods to see whether and how human rights law achieves its purpose.[12]

---

[9] Philosophy may have held sway before law, but since at least the 1980s most would agree that legal scholarship has dominated human rights research. Some note that that dominance is now on the decline with social science scholarship establishing an increasingly strong presence in the human rights arena.

[10] D. Kennedy, *The Dark Side of Virtue: Reassessing International Humanitarianism* (Princeton University Press 2004) 27.

[11] J. Crook, 'The International Court of Justice and Human Rights' (2003) 1 NW Journal of International Human Rights 2, 8.

[12] See generally, D. Kennedy (n 10).

These challenges are both most evident in the dominant model of traditional doctrinal scholarship, which concentrates on legal coherence, black letter law[13] and the maintenance of an 'internal approach'.[14] An internal approach is characterized by some as the analysis of legal rules and principles taking the perspective of an insider in the system.[15] It denotes a more traditional, and presumptively introspective, approach to legal research, where legal scholars are writing almost exclusively for other legal scholars.[16] H.L.A. Hart employed a similar distinction between 'internal' and 'external' aspects of the law:[17] the former recognizes the characteristic normativity of the law, while the latter focuses on its social efficacy in terms of publicly observable behaviour.[18] Taking an internal perspective is not equated with neglecting methodology, but it may tend toward making assumptions about the importance, influence and legitimacy of the law, and as a result, underestimating the importance of methodological considerations, since it is lawyers speaking to lawyers about the law. Thus human rights legal researcher may be less likely to appreciate the need to go beyond the powerful normative system that constitutes international human rights law and critically assess the impact methods may have on outcomes.

Having explored these two interconnected challenges in detail, the chapter will conclude with some basic suggestions for what Meg Satterthwaite and Justin Simeone call 'investigative principles' and 'methodological standards'[19] to help researchers more effectively navigate human rights law.

---

[13]   The term 'black letter law' is a term sometimes used in common law systems to refer to purportedly well-established or entrenched legal rules or norms that are both well known and arguably no longer subject to dispute or contestation.

[14]   C. McCrudden (n 4) 633.

[15]   Ibid.

[16]   F. Muger and C. Seron, 'Critical Legal Studies vs. Critical Theory: A Comment on Method' (1984) 6 Law and Policy 257, 258.

[17]   For an insightful argument articulating an approach to international law that would accommodate both internal and external dimensions of the law in a single more complex analysis, see J. Holtermann and M. Rask Madsen, 'European New Legal Realism and International Law: How to Make International Law Intelligible' (2015) 28(2) Leiden Journal of International Law 211.

[18]   H.L.A. Hart, *The Concept of Law* (OUP 1994) at 91.

[19]   M. Satterthwaite and J. Simeone, 'An Emerging Fact-finding Discipline? A Conceptual Roadmap for Social Science Methods in Human Rights Advocacy' in *NYU School of Law Public Law and Legal Theory Research Paper Series –* Working Paper No. 14-33 (July 2014) 1.

ASSUMPTIONS ABOUT THE VALIDITY OF HUMAN RIGHTS LAW NORMS

Legal research is defined by the study of doctrine and therefore centred on individual cases statutes and rules.[20] This has a number of implications.

First, the primordial focus of the individual case, statute or rule explains the strength of more localized individual case analysis and its comparative weakness in broader systemic, contextual or institutional analysis.

Second, the prioritization of doctrine means that departures from that focus must be justified and may be viewed with suspicion. For instance, Muger and Seron argue that when legal scholarship moves beyond the examination of doctrine it does so for one purpose: the substantiation of a preconceived position about the meaning of the doctrine under study.[21]

Third, a contention of this chapter, and a potential reason for the weakness of human rights legal research methodology, is its excessive emphasis on sources of law, sometimes failing to distinguish sources from methods or confusing what has been investigated with how it has been investigated.[22] 'Public international lawyers devote an inordinate amount of time and effort to trying to explain the sources of the law that they claim to teach or practice. That is not the case in other fields of law where the sources are more or less clear and not seriously questioned'.[23] It may be that similar observations could be made of human rights law[24] and indeed the need for human rights law to defend itself as international law just like international trade law or environmental law may explain the emphasis on sources and perhaps the reluctance to be more self-critical. Criticisms of the validity and legitimacy of human rights law abound and challenges as to its international law pedigree are well known. These factors may explain international human rights lawyers' defence of the doctrine and their relative neglect of methodological dimensions.

In sum, human rights legal research appears at times to assume the validity, coherence, legitimacy and objectivity of the normative baselines underpinning human rights law. Relying on Hart's distinction between

---

[20]   F. Muger and C. Seron (n 16) 258.
[21]   Ibid. 261.
[22]   F. Coomans et al. (n 6) 184.
[23]   M. Wood, 'International Organizations and Customary International Law', Jonathan J. Charney Distinguished Lecture in Public International Law (2015) 48 *Vanderbilt Journal of Transnational Law* 609, 611.
[24]   The point pertains more obviously to international human rights, law but similar arguments may also be made of human rights norms at the domestic or local level.

internal and external aspects of the law,[25] human rights legal research can be argued to overemphasize the internal aspect, to the neglect of the external aspect. Clearly, the fact that there is no articulation of a methodological analysis or the choice of norms does not mean that there is no valid method being used,[26] but it does indicate that the choices are not explicit and may suggest that insufficient attention has been placed on the norms themselves. As a result, human rights legal research methods are often insufficiently critical of the norms, their political content and their value biases (whether implicit or explicit), and fail to articulate the operating assumptions or organizing principles underpinning them.[27]

Choices and Values Underpinning Norms

All human rights scholars make normative statements in their work, yet there is no agreed way of framing or legitimizing such statements. In the absence of such an agreed 'validation framework', greater attention must be paid to the choices and values implied in human rights legal research and the normative claims it makes, as well as the values and assumptions it bases those upon. Forsythe charges that lawyers are often uncritical about international human rights law, too focused on treaty language and court cases, and insufficiently focused on soft law and extra-legal factors.[28] He urges that human rights lawyers should be contrarians, willing to challenge the conventional wisdom of the law and its unexamined assumptions. Forsythe argues that existing norms, whether developed through legislatures or courts, should no longer be taken as the starting points of analysis but that researchers should go to the level of agents to focus on substance.[29] In some senses this critique addresses the question of what values underpin a particular right or theory of rights and what makes the right important. It may look also at how the significance and application of a right depends on context and may vary according to social or political setting and according to local structures.[30] At issue too are the pitfalls

---

[25]   Supra n 16.

[26]   E. Brems, 'Methods in Legal Human Rights Research' in F. Coomans et al. (n 4) 89.

[27]   F. Coomans et al. (n 6) 182.

[28]   D. Forsythe, 'Human Rights Studies: On the Dangers of Legalistic Assumptions' in F. Coomans et al. (n 4) 59.

[29]   Ibid. 62.

[30]   See, D. Brinks, V. Gauri and K. Shen, 'Social Rights Constitutionalism: Negotiating the Tension between the Universal and the Particular' (2015) 11 Annual Review of Law and Social Science 289.

of using human rights as moral trumps: human rights center on a moral argument that cannot (or at least need not) be empirically proven and is (or should be) accepted on faith.[31]

By definition, this critique applies more to refining and strengthening doctrinal legal analysis, widely viewed as the chief method for legal scholarship, and pertains more to 'internal' approaches than to externally focused interdisciplinary legal analysis. However, the essential recommendation is as follows: go to substance, investigate the values and assumptions, interrogate their cogency, legitimacy, and consequences and address 'the "softness" (some might say "mushiness") of the conceptual grounding of human rights'.[32] Some scholars note the need for a theory of rights[33] or even a theory of justice to better make the case for rights than arguing for them directly in the way their proponents currently do.[34] Arguing for a theory of justice in the context of socioeconomic rights, Jeremy Waldron opines: 'a theory of justice necessarily brings together with the consideration of socioeconomic rights a consideration of all the claims and principles with which such rights might be thought to compete or conflict'.[35] Such theories are therefore essential to defending the legitimacy and coherence of international human rights norms.

> If it is known that the case for a right like that in the ICESCR Article 11 (1) has been made without proper consideration of competing claims, then the alleged right is easy to discredit, easy to dismiss as naïve and unrealistic. If, however, the alleged socioeconomic right has been properly defended in the context of a theory of justice, then it may be presented more confidently and more effectively in political and philosophical argument. Its presentation can be associated with a sense that competing claims (to property, desert or whatever) have been fairly considered in a way that takes their normative aspirations seriously.[36]

In this sense, the human rights law researcher has the capacity and perhaps

---

[31]   D. Forsythe, 'Human Rights Studies: On the Dangers of Legalistic Assumptions' in F. Coomans et al. (n 4) 62.

[32]   A. Sen, 'Elements of a Theory of Rights' (2004) 32(4) Philosophy and Public Affairs 315.

[33]   Jeremy Waldron has written in defence of a theory of justice over a theory of rights on the basis that 'theories of rights do good work when it comes to explaining why each right is important but they are notoriously bad at thinking about conflict or competition among rights or among claims that aspire to be treated as rights'. J. Waldron, 'Socioeconomic Rights and Theories of Justice', NYU School of Law Public Law and Legal Theory Research Paper Series; Working Paper No. 10-79 (November 2010) 5.

[34]   Ibid.

[35]   Ibid.

[36]   Ibid. 6.

the responsibility to articulate such theories to mount a vigorous defence of the norms and framework which are so often under attack.

The foregoing recommendations can be applied along a number of different dimensions.

Choice of Norm

One dimension is that there should be a critical assessment of the choice of governing norm and its source, as well as the choice of interpretative rule(s) and the source and quality of data and indicators drawn upon make an interpretation. Indeed, as Christopher McCrudden points out, even in the more internal approaches adopted in doctrinal legal analysis the decision about what constitutes an appropriate source of norms for legal analysis is contested, and the relative weight and cogency of norms is also debated.[37] This requires a more thoroughgoing appraisal of whether legal rights alone are sufficient to fulfill their announced purpose,[38] and a more self-critical assessment of whether legal rights are the basic instruments of human freedom and welfare.[39]

Pedigree of Norms

Another dimension requires that human rights legal methodology include an examination of the 'pedigree' of the norms underpinning human rights law, the implicit preferences, world view or values they reflect,[40] as well as the social and political orientation of the institutions that monitor and enforce them. Borrowing from the Critical Legal Studies tradition,[41] it may

---

[37] D. Forsythe, *Human Rights in International Relations* (3rd edn, CUP 2012) 30.

[38] E. Sparer, 'Fundamental Human Rights, Legal Entitlements and the Social Struggle: A Friendly Critique of the Critical Legal Studies Movement' (1984) 36 Stanford Law Review 509, 514.

[39] Ibid. 512, describing a key tenet of the Critical Legal Studies scholarship connected with the general critique of liberalism.

[40] See D. Kennedy (n 10) discussing claims about the 'tainted origins' of human rights and the potential usefulness of downplaying universal claims and look for parallel developments in other cultural traditions.

[41] Critical legal studies defines itself as a theory that challenges accepted norms and standards in legal theory and practice. Proponents believe that logic and structure attributed to the law result from societal power relationships and that law exists to support the interests of the party or class that forms it: law is politics and it is not neutral or value free. Critical legal studies began in the late 1970s as a movement in legal theory and a network of US leftist legal scholars that include Roberto Unger, Morton Horwitz, Duncan Kennedy and Katharine MacKinnon.

demand that legal researchers consider or acknowledge the constructed nature of what is taken to be objective,[42] potentially uncovering the indeterminacy of legal reasoning as well as the influence of power relations and issues such as gender or race.[43] It means that human rights law scholars need to be prepared to expose the potential for rights to legitimate powerful interests, serve the purposes of the market or insulate the economy such that existing distinctions of wealth, status and power can seem more legitimate once rights have been legislated.[44] Others have charged that rights potentially bolster bureaucratic institutions as the institutional setting of liberalism,[45] or 'defend a liberty that is only anxious privatism and a legal quality that conceals practical domination'.[46]

Contestation of Norms

This threshold critique calls for an acknowledgment of the inherent contestation of legal norms since law, including human rights law, is often about balancing conflicting normative priorities and interests.[47] Conflict of norms is the essence of normatively based scholarship,[48] and nowhere is this more evident, or more important, than in human rights legal scholarship

---

[42]   J. Singer, 'The Player and The Cards: Nihilism and Legal Theory' (1984) 94 Yale LJ 1, 12–13; D. Kennedy, 'Legal Formality' (1973) 2 Journal of Legal Studies 351, 351–354; and R. Unger, 'The Critical Legal Studies Movement' (1983) 96 Harvard Law Review 561, 571.

[43]   This has been the subject critical feminist scholarship see C. MacKinnon, *Feminism Unmodified: Discourses on Life and Law* (Massachusetts: Harvard University Press 1987). It has also been the subject of critical race theory, see K. Crenshaw, N. Gotanda, G. Peller and K. Thomas (eds), *Critical Race Theory: The Key Writings That Formed the Movement* (The New Press 1996). For a pre-eminent example of scholarship that addresses the intersectionality of race and gender, see e.g., K. Crenshaw. 'Mapping the Margins: Intersectionality, Identity Politics, and Violence Against Women of Color' in M. Albertson Fineman and R. Mykitiuk (eds), *The Public Nature of Private Violence* (Routledge 1994) 93–118.

[44]   D. Kennedy (n 10) 11.

[45]   A different but related argument posited by David Kennedy is that human rights bureaucracy is itself part of the problem (n 10) 26–27.

[46]   P. Gabel 'Book Review (reviewing Ronald Dworkin, Taking Rights Seriously)' (1977) 91 Harvard Law Review 302, 315.

[47]   See e.g. J. Waldron, 'Rights in Conflict' (1989) 99 Ethics 503; and F.M. Kamm, 'Conflicts of Rights' (2001) 7 Legal Theory 239.

[48]   J. Smits, 'Redefining Normative Legal Science: Towards an Argumentative Discipline' (Intersentia 2007), <http://ssrn.com/abstract=1411716> 50, citing E.L. Rubin, 'The Practice and Discourse of Legal Scholarship' (1988) 86 Michigan Law Review 1835–1905; and see also *The Mind and Method of the Legal Academic* (Edward Elgar Publishing 2012).

where the balance between rights lies at the heart of the discourse. Such a balance may have to be struck between rights and with collective interests, between competing rights within a society (right to freedom of expression vs right to privacy or right to religious freedom vs right to education), or between rights claimed by different countries (right to a clean and healthy environment versus right to development).

Implications for Human Rights Legal Methodology

In concrete terms the forgoing critique requires that human rights law scholarships include a self-critical method. Human rights legal scholars ought therefore to include as a standard part of their methodology some consideration of the origin and history of the relevant norms under consideration, as well as their relative applicability and legitimacy in particular contexts. Such analysis should integrate consideration of the legal, political, institutional and historical contours of the norm and the right(s) it grounds. This would require that the contested history and contextualized interpretation and application of the international human rights law framework be acknowledged as a standard methodological starting point for mainstream doctrinal legal research. It would require that human rights legal researchers articulate a theory of human rights, as Amartya Sen put it – or offer something that grounds the human rights norm and its associated legal and political claim in robust terms.

INSUFFICIENT FOCUS ON THE IMPACT OF HUMAN RIGHTS LEGAL NORMS

The forgoing argument about the insufficiently critical approaches used by human rights legal scholars with respect to human rights norms challenges us to assess and defend human rights in the social, political and legal contexts in which they must be implemented. This relates to the content and legitimacy of human rights norms while a distinct challenge calls for investigation of the impacts that human rights norms have on the lives of those they are supposed to protect. Both challenges implicitly question the power of human rights, calling for scholars to go beyond assumptions.[49]

---

[49]　S. Hopgood, *The Endtimes of Human Rights* (Cornell University Press 2013) 172, challenging the power human rights discourses in global institutions, norms, law, courts, trials, conditional aid, international campaigns funding – charging that they assume in their own right whatever their impact on the ground.

This second challenge requires that 'attention is drawn to the importance of a law "of everyday life" a form of law that does not shirk structural injustice or assume that law and legalization leave only to justice, never to unintended, unwanted or unexpected side effects.'[50] From a methodological perspective, therefore, it requires going beyond theoretical assumptions about impact, and acknowledging, if not addressing, the empirical challenges of measurement and assessment. This relates also to the recurrent questions surrounding effectiveness and the weakness of human rights monitoring and enforcement mechanisms.[51]

Beyond Legal Constructs

At another level, it demands not taking for granted the relevance, applicability or legitimacy of legal norms in particular contexts and that the principle of universality be assessed in a critical light.[52] Few would deny that law is central to human rights, but likewise few would deny that there is a need to go beyond the law, legal text and legal reasoning.[53] As Therese Murphy noted: 'there is more to human rights than human rights law'; she went on to observe that 'rights are more than a legal construct; they are more than formal entitlements and freedoms'.[54] Murphy argues that human rights legal method, if it is to be plausible, must be able to accommodate this. This second challenge targets the need to go beyond legal norms and address and measure impact and results. Human rights legal scholars tend to neglect the empirical dimension of the law, its practical ramifications and actual impact in social, economic, institutional and political terms, as well as its relevance to the areas of power relations and policy evaluation.[55] Human rights scholars have tended to neglect studying the implementation of human rights standards and the global politics[56] that are determinative of whether they

---

[50]   T. Murphy (n 5) 11.

[51]   A. Bayevsky, *The UN Human Rights Treaty System: Universality at the Crossroads* (Kluwer Law International 2001); and E. Posner, *The Twilight of Human Rights* (OUP 2014) 104.

[52]   See legal realists' first attempt to open up legal scholarship by demanding that law be analysed as part of a socio-political institution – challenging legal formalism. Formalism typically asserts the autonomy of the juridical form in relation to the social world while instrumentalism conceives of law as a reflection or a tool in the service of dominant groups. P. Bourdieu, 'The Force of Law: Toward a Sociology of the Juridical Field' (1987) 38 Hastings Law Journal 805, 814.

[53]   D. Forsythe (n 37) 61.

[54]   T. Murphy (n 5) 10.

[55]   D. Forsythe (n 37) 61.

[56]   Ibid. 33–37.

are respected or not: such political factors may ultimately be more influential than legal factors in the struggle for human rights.[57] Writing in 1994, Jack Donnelly complained of the lack of comparative empirical studies and the inattention to the particularities of implementation. Donnelly was critical of inadequate investigation of the details of human rights problems or their impacts, the lack of progress on implementing economic, social and cultural rights, and insufficient attention on how cultural diversity impedes progress on implementation of universal rights.[58]

This challenge is rooted also in an internal approach to legal research and a view of the law as relatively autonomous and not in need of empirical buttressing or justification. It is connected with the tendency to treat legal rules and text as operating in a social, economic and political vacuum, and with inadequate attention being paid by human rights legal researchers to social science and political theory methods. Indeed, some scholars have gone as far as to state that the 'proper method for a normative legal science consists primarily of the methods of sociology, psychology and economics'.[59] This goes to the heart of the evolving nexus of human rights law and social sciences, which has caused some to question the very possibility of a political science of human rights since – in very basic terms – human rights have a primarily normative content and natural law pedigree, while social sciences have their roots in nineteenth-century, "value-free" positivism, methodological rigour and descriptive, empirical findings.

Responding to this critique demands that the traditional 'internal approach'[60] associated with doctrinal legal analysis[61] be oriented 'outward' and supplemented by other 'external' perspectives, including instrumental and empirical approaches. This would strengthen human rights legal research methods by going beyond a purely normative analysis. A distinct, but related, issue associated with the internal approach is the temptation to extrapolate broader conclusions and recommendations from individual cases: human rights legal research tends to be stronger in the analysis of individual cases or examples, and less effective at institutional or systemic

---

[57]   M. Freeman, 'Is a Political Science of Human Rights Possible?' 19 (2001) Netherlands Quarterly of Human Rights 123, 138.

[58]   J. Donnelly 'Post War Reflections on the Study of International Human Rights' (1994) 8 Ethics and International Affairs 97.

[59]   J. Hage 'The Method of a Truly Normative Legal Science' (2010) 4 Maastricht Working Papers – Faculty of Law 1.

[60]   Christopher McCrudden would contrast this with an external approach of law in practice and at work in institutions and society; C. McCrudden (n 4) 640–641.

[61]   C. McCrudden (n 4) 633.

analyses, which take into account a range of external contextual factors including social and political ones to enable general lessons to be drawn.[62]

A Focus on Impacts

This second critique targets the insufficient focus on *impacts* on the part of human rights scholars.[63] Human rights lawyers and legal researchers are good at setting the norms and elaborating the rules; they are also trained to design legal systems, legal processes and normative frameworks. However, as David Kennedy notes, lawyers tend to place an excessive focus on legal process to the exclusion of other factors, neglecting impacts and the results of that process.[64] Lawyers are less good at predicting and assessing how the norms and systems will apply, especially in fluid, multi-tier contexts or where formal and informal systems exist together. In the context of public health, Stephen Marks has observed that 'Human rights studies tend to provide rigourous of norms and institutions for their furtherance, but often make unsubstantiated generalizations about what impact human rights-based policies and practices might have on populations.'[65]

Another approach is to ask what Forsythe termed the 'so what?' question. Does the law make any difference to public policy and human behaviour?[66] What is the implementation process and what are its results? As some scholars have noted, the best approach to the vindication of rights and protection of human dignity is not always to emphasize legal approaches, underscore rights and prosecute under the law.[67] For instance, some argue that the now defunct UN Human Rights Commission was largely ineffective, but that nothing in the legal analysis of reports of the Commission would reveal this. Thus, the focus on impacts confronts the possibility that the effectiveness of legal obligations is greatly overstated.[68]

---

[62]   D. Forsythe (n 37) 69.

[63]   Ibid. 70.

[64]   However, drawing from the human rights and development literature, one can point to the emphasis on process as precisely one of the distinct contributions that human rights law and principles, as well as a human rights based approach to development, may offer development: going beyond just ends and outcomes to scrutinize means and processes.

[65]   S. Marks, 'The Evolving Field of Health and Human Rights: Issues and Methods' (2002) 30(4) The Journal of Law, Medicine and Ethics 739, 748.

[66]   D. Forsythe (n 37) 64.

[67]   Ibid. 69.

[68]   E. Posner, 'The Case Against Human Rights', *The Guardian*, 4 December 2014.

Social Science Research on International Human Rights Law

The challenge also relates to the need for human rights legal scholarship to 'catch up' with the growing body of social science and empirical research on international human rights,[69] which tackles the international human rights law framework in empirical terms.[70] The work of Varun Guari,[71] Oona Hathaway[72] and Beth Simmons[73] on the impacts of human rights treaty ratification is well known,[74] and a growing body of literature employs social science methodology to challenge assumptions of the effectiveness of human rights treaties in terms of fulfilling their promise.[75]

It is true that in the past decade the human rights community, including human rights legal researchers, has placed greater emphasis on empirical approaches, including metrics and human rights measurement, which have yielded significant advances in the development of human rights indicators. Indeed 'the demand for and use of indicators in human rights are part of a broader process of systematic work to implement, monitor and realize human rights.'[76] Beyond the standards themselves, however, some have argued that a more appropriate approach to human rights measurement is based on theories of development, rather than some aggregate notion of human rights and that 'quantitative studies purporting to demonstrate causal relationships between human rights and other variables should

---

[69]   V. Gauri, 'The Cost of Complying with Human Rights Treaties: The Convention on the Rights of the Child and Basic Immunization' (2011) 6 *Review of International Organizations* 33.

[70]   G. Schaffer and T. Ginsburg, 'The Empirical Turn in International Legal Scholarship' (2012) 196 Am J Int'l Law 1; E. Hafner-Burton, D. Victor and Y. Lupu 'Political Science Research on International Law: The State of the Field' (2012) 106 Am. J. Int'l Law 47; A. Chilton and D. Tingly, 'Why the Study of International Law Needs Experiments' (2013–2014) 52 Columbia J. Transnational Law 176; and Y. Lupu, 'Evidence: The Role of International in Domestic Legal Enforcement of International Human Rights Agreements' (2013) 67 Int Orgs 469.

[71]   V. Gauri (n 69) 33–56.

[72]   Oona A. Hathaway, 'Do Human Rights Treaties Make a Difference?' (2002) 111 Yale LJ 1870; and Beth A. Simmons, 'Why Do Countries Commit to Human Rights Treaties?' (2007) 51(4) The Journal of Conflict Resolution 588.

[73]   B. Simmons, 'Treaty Compliance and Violation' (2010) 13 Ann Rev Pol Sci 273; and Beth A. Simmons, *Mobilizing for Human Rights* (CUP 2009).

[74]   E. Neumayer, 'Do International Human Rights Treaties Improve Respect for Human Rights?' (2005) 49(6) Journal of Conflict Resolution 925.

[75]   E. Hafner-Burton and K. Tsutsui, 'Justice Lost! The Failure of International Human Rights Law to matter Where Needed Most' (2007) 44(4) Journal of Peace Research 407.

[76]   Office of the High Commissioner for Human Rights (OHCHR), *Human Rights Indicators, A Guide to Measurement and Implementation* (2012) 12.

be treated with methodological caution and political suspicion'.[77] It is moreover essential to articulate the purpose or aim of measuring human rights and to be clear about what distinct functions such measurement may fulfill.[78] However, human rights law scholars have some way to go to respond to this growing scholarship and match it in methodological terms. Indeed, the scholarship related to human rights law by non-lawyers offers yet another reason to be interested in human rights legal method.[79]

However, many human rights law researchers rightly caution that 'human rights performance is not easily measurable',[80] and quantitative methods may be more difficult to use for economic and social rights than for civil and political rights.[81] Nevertheless, the advances in quantitative methodology for human rights demonstrate: (a) the potential for a more concerted focus on methods in human rights scholarship; and (b) the potential that exists for human rights legal research to connect the norms, language and institutions of human rights with the data and empirics of economics, sociology and development. This, in turn, can help make the case for human rights in strategic and instrumental terms, and strengthen human rights uptake in policy contexts. This emphasis on methods is therefore essential to explaining the 'value added' of human rights in a variety of contexts, where the moral case alone is not sufficient or where human rights are not accepted on faith. It can also be instructive where human rights approaches or the application of human rights norms and principles yields less than optimum results or even harm, and where identifying pitfalls and limitations as well as negative impacts is essential.

Implications for Human Rights Legal Methodology

In concrete terms, therefore, it is suggested that human rights law researchers should be open to the influences of social sciences in terms of how they approach methodology, even if they do not radically alter their methods. As Michael Freeman has argued, there is a need to break the grip of legal scholarship on the study of human rights law and get the balance

---

[77]   R. Lawrence Barsh, 'Measuring Human Rights: Problems of Methodology and Purpose' (1993) 15 Human Rights Quarterly 87, 121.

[78]   See T. Landman, 'Measuring Human Rights' (2004) 26(4) Human Rights Quarterly 906, 909.

[79]   T. Murphy (n 5) 11.

[80]   E. Neumayer (n 74) 934.

[81]   F. Coomans et al. (n 4) 185. Yet, see *contra* Malcolm Langford and Sakiko Fukuda-Parr (Guest Editors), 'Quantifying Human Rights – Special Issue' (2012) 30(3) Nordic Journal of Human Rights 222.

right between law and politics for effective human rights policy-making.[82] Freeman also argues that a legalistic approach to human rights may distract the attention of human rights scholars and activities from the political, social, economic, and cultural causes of human rights violations.[83]

Interdisciplinary and Multidisciplinary Approaches

Relatedly, there have been calls for a more interdisciplinary approach and for broadening the scope of human rights legal research, if not to use empirical approaches. Others have urged for an openness to the influence of empirical analysis in order to support or test doctrinal and theoretic models by drawing on social science-influenced information,[84] embracing the pluralism of methodological approaches.[85] In practical terms, it would encourage the human rights legal scholar to assess how much popular support a particular right or set of rights has in a given country or community, and to ascertain how the government interprets, supports or promotes the realization of the particular right. It would encourage the human rights legal scholar to ensure that when she goes beyond doctrine she incorporates social science findings, constructs or theories for a reason other than as evidence to support conclusions grounded in existing legal doctrine.[86] Notwithstanding the potential value of such an approach, it is worth noting a lawyer's caution against stretching human rights legal research beyond what it is designed to do or capable of doing, pushing for multidisciplinary and interdisciplinary approaches that may compromise its quality and leave it insufficiently doctrinal.

Human Rights as Part of a Social Process

The approach proposed here supplements doctrinal analysis with the insights of practical application. It goes beyond the norm to the outcome, state or condition in reality.[87] A key benefit of such an assessment or

---

[82]   M. Freeman (n 57) at 138.
[83]   Ibid.
[84]   McCrudden (n 4) 645.
[85]   Ibid. 642.
[86]   F. Muger and C. Seron (n 16) 261.
[87]   Such as through human rights measurement or the use of human rights indicators. The OHCHR defines human rights indicators as 'specific information on the state or condition of an object, event, activity or outcome that can be related to human rights norms and standards and that addresses and reflects human rights

empirical validation is that it forces human rights legal methodology to view human rights norms as part of a social process,[88] and not a static fact. 'Human rights as law cannot succeed without social processes . . . rights should never be cabined within a juridical cage'.[89] It necessarily views practice as a method of testing the strength and validity of doctrinal constructs.[90] It encourages factoring in a less than perfect acceptance of the normative underpinning of the right in question. It accepts the basic precept that treaties – either standing alone or alongside other acknowledge sources of international law – are not the whole story of human rights law'.[91]

The approach would require the legal human rights researcher to assess with realism the nature of the legal and political transposition of a human rights norm, as well as its practical limitations and the prospects for the implementation of the right in question. Examples of scholarship that acknowledges the interaction of legal and political norms, and that emphasizes the interaction between states and domestic actors, includes the transnational legal process model, which analyses the process through which state actors internalize norms codified in international treaties.[92] For instance, Goodman and Jinks analyse the process of acculturation, which points to interaction rather than persuasion as the sources of cognitive and social pressures for state actors to conform with treaty norms.[93] This type of scholarship focuses on the actual uptake of human rights norms beyond the parameters of human rights treaty regimes, such as an empirical assessment of the convergence of international human rights in domestic constitutions.[94] Some of it contends that the domestication of rights should

---

principles and concerns; and that can be used to assess and monitor the promotion and implementation of human rights'. OHCHR (n 76) 16.

[88]   T. Murphy (n 5) 11.

[89]   Ibid., quoting H. Charlesworth 'International Law: A Discipline of Crisis' (2002) 65 Modern Law Review 377, 391.

[90]   Muger and Seron (n 16) 261.

[91]   T. Murphy (n 5) 9.

[92]   See generally, H. Koh (1997) 'Why Do Nations Obey International Law? Review Essay of *The New Sovereignty: Compliance with International Regulatory Agreements* by Abram Chayes and Antonia Handler Chayes Cambridge: Harvard University Press, 1995 and *Fairness in International Law and Institutions* by Thomas M. Franck, Oxford: Clarendon Press, 1995', Yale Law School, Yale Law School Legal Scholarship Repository; Faculty Scholarship Series 1-1-1997.

[93]   R. Goodman and D. Jinks, *Socializing States: Promoting Human Rights through International Law* (OUP 2013).

[94]   Z. Elkins, T. Ginsburg and B. Simmons, 'Getting to Rights: Treaty Ratification, Constitutions Convergence and Human Rights Practice' (2013) 54(1) Harvard International Law Journal 61.

be seen as a global model of rights, with its own distinctive modes of reasoning,[95] while other work analyses the 'democratic iteration'[96] or 'vernacularization of international human rights law.'[97] Ultimately, this body of work acknowledges that the 'struggle to realize social rights is a political one, grounded and pursued through local structures of demand.'[98]

Human Rights and Regime Interaction

Human rights law must be shown to have instrumental not just normative value in order to be taken seriously within non-human rights regimes, and there may be a role for human rights legal methods in advancing this. Human rights legal research methods may be useful in the translation of human rights norms across international regulatory regimes. They may help articulate the logic within which each regime (including the international human rights regime) operates, explaining how their various institutions and regulatory mechanisms process information from outside and from other regimes as well as how other regimes employ each other's norms and principles.[99] The principle of international policy coherence may therefore support researchers in broadening their scope of inquiry and explore how human rights legal research may influence or be influenced by other regulatory regimes.

Compliance Challenges

This approach would also force the human rights legal researcher to confront the relative weakness of compliance with human rights treaty law compared with that of say finance or trade regimes.[100] Acknowledging the reality of weak enforcement may encourage scholars to articulate other functions fulfilled by human rights law beyond strict compliance, such as generating political concern in low-standard countries, communicating the intensity of preferences among regime members, or legitimating technical aid to improve capacity to comply with norms. It may also compel the

---

[95]   T. Murphy (5) 9.

[96]   K. Moller, *The Global Model of Constitutional Rights* (OUP 2012).

[97]   S. Benhabib, *Dignity in Adversity: Human Rights in Troubled Times* (Polity Press 2011).

[98]   D. Brinks, V. Gauri, K. Shen (n 30).

[99]   See e.g. how an investment or trade arbitral panel might approach or interpret a reference to human rights in a free trade agreement or in a bilateral investment treaty.

[100]   E. Neumayer (n 74) 926.

human rights law researcher to inquire into the determinants of ratification and/or the reasons for non-compliance (the malevolent nature of a regime, the lack of capacity, resource constraints or the fact that compliance is a long term process with a far more extended timeframe than most human rights scholars acknowledge, and leaving human rights scholarship open to a range of criticisms). Essentially, it demands that the human rights legal researcher acknowledge the ambiguity, complexity and messy reality of impact, such that in answering a question about whether international human rights treaties improve respect for human rights, the legal scholar might join the social scientist engaged in quantitative analysis and state that 'the answer is more complex than a simple yes or no'.[101]

CAUTIONARY NOTES ON HUMAN RIGHTS LAW OBLIGATIONS AND UNDEREMPHASIZING LEGAL POSITIVISM

A number of cautionary notes are apposite: these critiques should not obscure the distinct nature of legal scholarship or detract from the unique features of the international human rights framework. Human rights law is and should remain a central plank of human rights method.[102] A central motivation in emphasizing human rights legal methodology is the fact that legal obligations matter and legal rules are worthy of attention. Indeed, 'the development of international legal rules has been the central collective project to address human rights for the past 60 years'.[103]

Human Rights Law Obligations are a Legal Reality

Law has a normative content, and where international human rights law emanates from an openly normative project, it is nevertheless manifest in positive legal rules. In this way, human rights treaty obligations are about what ought to be,[104] but they are also a legal reality. Human rights are backed by the force of international legal obligations, which are voluntarily undertaken by all states parties to human rights treaties. Put simply, human rights obligations matter because they are the law. It is therefore

---

[101]   Ibid. 950.

[102]   T. Murphy (n 5) 15.

[103]   B. Simmons (n 73) 6.

[104]   According to Smits, legal reasoning tries to answer the normative question of what out to be. J. Smits (n 48) 49.

appropriate for human rights legal method to foreground obligations,[105] so that neither the existence of human rights obligations nor the significance of their ratification be denied, even in the face of violations.[106] As Philippe Sands has observed, 'we should remember that the bigger story is that the international rules outlasted the Bush administration. The idea (if not reality) that individuals have basic human rights under international law seems to have been reinforced, not replaced'.[107]

Rights Imply Duties

Human rights are ultimately about accountability[108] and at the international level they are about international legal accountability. They are backed by the force of a legal commitment and the principle of *pacta sunt servanda*,[109] where 'compliance is the normal organizational presumption'.[110] Human rights are about limits on public power: 'human rights serve as a check on (the abuse) of power'.[111] They are also about assigning responsibility (mostly to states) for particular processes and outcomes. They regulate the relationship between the right holder and duty bearer, where the right holder (account holder) is the one affected by the act or omission of the duty bearer (or power wielder).[112] They regulate not only the horizontal relationships between state parties, but crucially,

---

[105]   T. Murphy (n 5) 14.

[106]   See case of *Hamdan v. Rumsfeld*, 548 U.S. 557 (2006), in which the US Supreme Court held that military commissions set up by the Bush administration to try detainees at Guantanamo Bay lack 'the power to proceed because their structures and procedures violate both the Uniform Code of Military Justice and the four Geneva Conventions signed in 1949' (Common Article 3 of the Geneva Conventions).

[107]   P. Sands, *Human Rights Under International Law*, FT.com, 20 February 2015. A separate discussion should assess the degree to which these reinforced rights have been altered by the process of challenges and violations, and whether they have survived intact.

[108]   P. Alston, 'What's in a Name: Does it Really Matter if Development Policies Refer to Goals, Ideals or Human Rights?', in H. Helmich (ed.), *Human Rights in Development Co-operation* (OECD Development Centre and Netherlands Institute of Human Rights, Externe Publikationen 1998); and J. Brunnée, 'International Legal Accountability Through the Lens of the Law of State Responsibility' (2005) 36 Netherlands Yearbook of International Law 3.

[109]   Translated from Latin as 'Agreements are to be kept and honoured'.

[110]   A. Chayes and A. Handler Chayes, 'On Compliance' (1993) 47(2) International Organization 175 at 176–179.

[111]   A. Vandenbogaerde, *Towards Shared Accountability in International Human Rights Law: Law, Procedures and Principles* (2016) (Intersentia 22).

[112]   A. Vandenbogaerde (n 111) 24.

the vertical relationship between a state and its citizens, and do not allow sovereignty to act as a shield against scrutiny of what a government does within its own territory.[113]

Designating something a right effects an important qualitative difference:[114] there is something fundamentally different between an education policy goal and the right to education because a right implies a duty.[115] As Jack Donnelly put it, quoting Feinberg, 'claiming a right can "make things happen"'.[116] Duties inhere in rights and are connected with them as correlatives,[117] and duties are transposed in positive law as legal obligations. It is through establishing that standard that rights uphold accountability; from this human rights law also requires information and a sanction or consequence.[118] 'Having and arguing with and for human rights as law are crucial moves. They take us from need, charity, "doing good" humanitarianism and the like towards freedom, entitlement and obligation. In so doing, they establish both claimants and duty-bearers giving agency to both'.[119] As such, an emphasis on rights brings with it a corresponding emphasis on duties and legal obligations, which remain the core, if not exclusive, focus of doctrinal human rights legal research.[120] Addressing the challenges outlined above must not overburden human rights law scholarship to the point of having it abandon its doctrinal moorings or losing sight of its essentially normative purpose. Nor should it be read as directing lawyers to undertake social science analysis or use empirical methods in which they may have no training. Human rights lawyers, including researchers, are rightly preoccupied primarily with the normative. As Amartya Sen observed, 'The

---

[113]   B. Simmons (n 73) 3.

[114]   P. Alston 'Ships Passing in the Night: The Current State of the Human Rights and Development Debate seen through the Lens of the Millennium Development Goals' (1993) 27(3) Human Rights Quarterly 755. OHCHR, *Claiming the MDGs* (2008); and UNDP, *Beyond the Midpoint: Accelerating Support for MDG Achievement* (2009).

[115]   B. Saul, 'In the Shadow of Human Rights: Human Duties Obligations and Responsibilities' (2001) 32(2) *Columbia Human Rights Law Review* 565, 585.

[116]   J. Donnelly, *The Concept of Human Rights* (St Martin's Press 1985) 8, citing J. Feinberg *Rights, Justice and the Bound of Liberty: Essays in Social Philosophy* (Princeton University Press 1980) 150.

[117]   A. Eide 'Economic Social and Cultural Rights as Human Rights' in A. Eide, C. Krause, A. Rossas (eds) *Economic, Social and Cultural Rights* (Martinus Nijhoff 2001) 21–40, 22.

[118]   A. Vandebogaerde (n 111) 26–27.

[119]   T. Murphy, 'An Argument for Method' in T. Murphy, *Health and Human Rights* (n 5) 10.

[120]   L. Trakman and S. Gatien, *Rights and Responsibilities* (University of Toronto Press 1999) 10.

invoking of human rights tends to come mostly from those who are concerned with changing the world rather than interpreting it'.[121]

Human rights legal research methodology should acknowledge these distinctive features of the human rights discourse while remaining self-critical of how rights and duties are constructed and how they play out in context. While methodological rigour and self-critical approaches should be pursued consistently, it is nevertheless acceptable, even appropriate, for human rights law methods to be self-consciously normative since 'human rights under international law is a project in changing consciousness and the basic rules' and that 'the essential change remains a vital one: the idea that power of the state[122] is limited, the constraints might exist under external (international) law, and that the individual has a cherished place'.[123]

CONCLUSIONS

This chapter has argued for legal human rights scholars to proceed with fewer assumptions about the norms they are analysing,[124] to be more aware of implementation and application of the norms in context,[125] and to be more open to tackling empirical and methodological challenges. All of the foregoing points to the importance of interdisciplinary research methods for effective human rights research and the need to encourage these methods, while maintaining a balance between 'internal' and 'external' approaches, both of which are valid and have a key role. The critiques above, particularly the second, speak to what human rights legal research can learn from social sciences and interdisciplinary or multidisciplinary approaches.[126] However, these insights on the legal reality of human rights norms also point to the possibility for legal research and law to

---

[121]   A. Sen, 'Elements of a Theory of Rights' (2004) 32(4) Philosophy and Public Affairs 317.

[122]   While an analysis of who the duty bearers are under international human rights law lies beyond the scope of this chapter, this quotation discusses limits on the power of the state but the point might equally be applied to non-state actors. See e.g., A. Clapham, *Human Rights and Non-State Actors* (Edward Elgar Publishing 2013).

[123]   P. Sands, 'Human Rights under international law', FT.com, accessed 20 February 2015.

[124]   F. Muger and C. Seron (n 16) 261, commenting on how doctrinal legal analysis is inaccessible to members of other professions leaving the theoretical and behavioural assumptions in legal scholarship unlikely to undergo scrutiny.

[125]   Ibid. 261.

[126]   In support of multidisciplinary approaches, see F. Coomans et al. (n 4) 186.

influence the social sciences – and ensure that the calls for interdisciplinary approaches result in a two-way influence.[127]

Overall, the chapter has argued for methodological rigour to help reinvigorate and ultimately strengthen human rights legal research and doctrinal methodology. A preferred approach may still acknowledge the primacy of critical reasoning around an authoritative text,[128] but may call for it to be viewed in context and supplemented by other information and analysis. It has therefore argued for the importance of balancing legal and social science methods in human rights legal scholarship. Yet it has also cautioned against losing sight of the distinct and powerful nature of human rights as an inherently normative enterprise. Human rights are unique and have a special quality, not only as the subjects of obligation, but also because their central aim is to protect human dignity.

This chapter calls for scrutiny of the inbuilt normative and political assumptions of the human rights framework and a broadening of the methodological scope of work precisely to help advance the human rights project and see human rights obligations fulfilled in a range of legal and policy contexts. Ultimately, the emphasis on legal methods must remain at the service of the normative project of human rights: the relevance of the former hinges on the intrinsic value of the latter.

REFERENCES

Alston, P., 'What's in a Name: Does it Really Matter if Development Policies Refer to Goals, Ideals or Human Rights?', in H. Helmich (ed.), *Human Rights in Development Co-operation* (OECD Development Centre and Netherlands Institute of Human Rights 1998) 95–106

Alston, P., 'Ships Passing in the Night: The Current State of the Human Rights and Development Debate seen through the Lens of the Millennium Development Goals' (2005) 27(3) Human Rights Quarterly 755–829

Bayevsky, A., *The UN Human Rights Treaty System: Universality at the Crossroads* (Kluwer Law International 2001)

Benhabib, S., *Dignity in Adversity: Human Rights in Troubled Times* (Polity Press 2011)

Bourdieu, P., 'The Force of Law: Toward a Sociology of the Juridical Field' (1987) 38 Hastings Law Journal 805, 814

Brems, E., 'Methods in Legal Human Rights Research' in F. Coomans, F. Grunfeld and M. Kamminga (eds), *Methods of Human Rights Research* (Intersentia 2009) 89

Brinks, D., V. Gauri and K. Shen, 'Social Rights Constitutionalism: Negotiating the Tension Between the Universal and the Particular' (2015) 11 Annual Review of Law and Social Science 289–308

Brunnee, J., 'International Legal Accountability Through the Lens of the Law of State Responsibility' (2005) 36 Netherlands Yearbook of International Law 3–38

---

[127]   C. McCrudden (n 4) 650.
[128]   J. Smits (n 48) 46 citing Christopher McCrudden.

Charlesworth, H., 'International Law: A Discipline of Crisis' (2002) 65 Modern Law Review 377, 391

Chayes, A. and A. Handler Chayes, 'On Compliance' (1993) 47(2) International Organization 175–205, 176–179

Chilton, A. and D. Tingly, 'Why the Study of International Law Needs Experiments' (2013–2014) 52 Columbia J. Transnational Law 176

Clapham, A., *Human Rights and Non-State Actors* (Edward Elgar Publishing 2013)

Coomans, F., F. Grunfeld and M. Kamminga, 'A Primer' in F. Coomans, F. Grunfeld and M. Kamminga (eds) *Methods of Human Rights Research* (Intersentia 2009) 12

Coomans, F., F. Grunfeld and M. Kamminga, 'Methods of Human Rights Research: A Primer' (2010) 32 Human Rights Quarterly 179

Crenshaw, K., 'Mapping the Margins: Intersectionality, Identity Politics, and Violence Against Women of Color' in M. Albertson Fineman and R. Mykitiuk (eds), *The Public Nature of Private Violence* (Routledge 1994) 93–118

Crenshaw, K., N. Gotanda, G. Peller and K. Thomas (eds), *Critical Race Theory: The Key Writings That Formed the Movement* (The New Press 1996)

Crook, J., 'The International Court of Justice and Human Rights' (2003) 1 NW Journal of International Human Rights 2, 8

Donnelly, J., *The Concept of Human Rights* 8 citing J. Feinberg *Rights, Justice and the Bound of Liberty: Essays in Social Philosophy* (Princeton University Press 1980) 150

Donnelly, J., 'Post War Reflections on the Study of International Human Rights' 8 Ethics and International Affairs (1994)

Eide, A., 'Economic Social and Cultural Rights as Human Rights' in A. Eide, C. Krause and A. Rossas (eds), *Economic, Social and Cultural Rights* (Martinus Nijhoff 2001) 21–40, 22.

Elkins, Z., T. Ginsburg and B. Simmons, 'Getting to Rights: Treaty Ratification, Constitutions Convergence and Human Rights Practice' (2013) 54(1) Harvard International Law Journal 61

Forsythe, D., 'Human Rights Studies: On the Dangers of Legalistic Assumptions' in F. Coomans, F. Grunfeld and M. Kamminga (eds) *Methods of Human Rights Research* (Intersentia 2009) 59

Forsythe, D., *Human Rights in International Relations* (3rd edn, CUP 2012) 30

Freeman, M., 'Is a Political Science of Human Rights Possible?' (2001) 19 *Netherlands Quarterly of Human Rights* 123, 138

Freeman, M., 'Is a Political Science of Human Rights Possible?' (2001) 19 *Netherlands Quarterly of Human Rights* 123, 138

Gabel, P., 'Book Review (reviewing Ronald Dworkin, Taking Rights Seriously) (1977) 91 *Harvard Law Review* 302, 315

Goodman, R. and D. Jinks, *Socializing States: Promoting Human Rights through International Law* (OUP 2013)

Guari, V., 'The Cost of Complying with Human Rights Treaties: The Convention on the Rights of the Child and Basic Immunization' (2011) Review of International Organizations

Hafner-Burton, E. and K. Tsutsui, 'Justice Lost! The Failure of International Human Rights Law to matter Where Needed Most' (2007) Journal of Peace Research 44(4) 407–425

Hafner-Burton, E., D. Victor and Y. Lupu, 'Political Science Research on International Law: The State of the Field' (2012) 106 Am J Int'l Law 47

Hage, J., 'The Method of a Truly Normative Legal Science' (2010) 4 Maastricht Working Papers – Faculty of Law 1

Hart, H.L.A., *The Concept of Law* (OUP 1994) 91

Hathaway, O., 'Do Human Rights Treaties Make a Difference?' (2002) 111 Yale L.J. 1870; 'Why Do Countries Commit to Human Rights Treaties?' (2007) 51(4) The Journal of Conflict Resolution 588–621

Holtermann, J. and M. Rask Madsen, 'European New Legal Realism and International Law: How to Make International Law Intelligible' (2015) 28(2) Leiden Journal of International Law 211–230

Hopgood, S., *The End Times of Human Rights* (Cornell University Press 2013)

Kamm, F.M., 'Conflicts of Rights' (2001) 7 Legal Theory 239

Kennedy, D., 'Legal Formality' (1973) 2 Journal of Legal Studies 351, 351–354

Kennedy, D., *The Dark Side of Virtue: Reassessing International Humanitarianism* (Princeton University Press 2004)

Koh, H., 'Why Do Nations Obey International Law?' Yale Law School; Yale Law School Legal Scholarship Repository; Faculty Scholarship Series Yale Law School Faculty Scholarship 1-1-1997 (1997)

Landman, T., 'Measuring Human Rights' (2004) 26 *Human Rights Quarterly* 906, 909

Lupu, Y., 'Evidence: The Role of International in Domestic Legal Enforcement of International Human Rights Agreements' (2013) 67 Int Orgs 469

Langford, M. and Sakiko Fukuda-Parr (Guest Editors), 'Quantifying Human Rights – Special Issue' (2012) 30(3) Nordic Journal of Human Rights 222–400

Lawrence Barsh, R., 'Measuring Human Rights: Problems of Methodology and Purpose' (1993) 15 Human Rights Quarterly 87, 121

Lupu, Y., 'Evidence: The Role of International in Domestic Legal Enforcement of International Human Rights Agreements' (2013) 67 Int Orgs 469

MacKinnon, C., *Feminism Unmodified: Discourses on Life and Law* (Harvard University Press 1987)

Marks, S., 'The Evolving Field of Health and Human Rights: Issues and Methods' (2002) 30(4) The Journal of Law, Medicine and Ethics 739, 748

McCrudden, C., 'Legal Research and the Social Sciences' (2006) 122 LQR 632–650, 646

Moller, K., *The Global Model of Constitutional Rights* (OUP 2012)

Muger, F. and C. Seron, 'Critical Legal Studies vs. Critical Theory: A Comment on Method' (1984) 6 Law and Policy 257, 258

Murphy, T., 'An Argument for Method' in T. Murphy, *Health and Human Rights* (Hart 2013) 10

Murphy, T., *Health and Human Rights* (Hart 2013) 9

Neumayer, E., 'Do International Human Rights Treaties Improve Respect for Human Rights?' (2005) 49(6) Journal of Conflict Resolution 925–953

OHCHR, *Claiming the MDGs* (2008)

OHCHR, *Human Rights Indicators, A Guide to Measurement and Implementation* (2012) 12

Posner, E., *The Twilight of Human Rights* (OUP 2014) 104

Posner, E., 'The Case against Human Rights', *The Guardian*, 4 December 2014

Rubin, E.L., 'The Practice and Discourse of Legal Scholarship' (1988) 86 Michigan Law Review 1835–1905

Sands, P., *Human Rights Under International Law*, FT.com, 20 February 2015

Satterthwaite, M. and J. Simeone, 'An Emerging Fact-Finding Discipline? A Conceptual Roadmap for Social Science Methods in Human Rights Advocacy' NYU School of Law, Public Law and Legal Theory Research Paper Series – Working Paper No 14–33 (July 2014) 1

Satterthwaite, M. and Justin Simeone, 'a conceptual roadmap for social science methods in human rights fact-finding', in Philip Alston and Sarah Knuckey (eds), *The Transformation of Human Rights Fact-Finding* (Oxford University Press, 2015) 321

Saul, B., 'In the Shadow of Human Rights: Human Duties Obligations and Responsibilities' (2001) 32(2) Columbia Human Rights Law Review 565–624, 585

Schaffer, G. and T. Ginsburg, 'The Empirical Turn in International Legal Scholarship' (2012) 196 Am J Int'l Law 1

Sen, A., 'Elements of a Theory of Rights' (2004) 32(4) Philosophy and Public Affairs 315

Simmons, B., *Mobilizing for Human Rights* (CUP 2009) 6

Simmons, B., 'Treaty Compliance and Violation' (2010) 13 Ann Rev Pol Sci 273

Singer, J., 'The Player and The Cards: Nihilism and Legal Theory' (1984) 94 Yale LJ 1, 12–13

Smits, J., 'Redefining Normative Legal Science: Towards an Argumentative Discipline' (Intersentia 2007) <http://ssrn.com/abstract=1411716>

Smits, J., *The Mind and Method of the Legal Academic* (Edward Elgar Publishing 2012)

Sparer, E., 'Fundamental Human Rights, Legal Entitlements and the Social Struggle: A

Friendly Critique of the Critical Legal Studies Movement' (1984) 36 Stanford Law Review 509, 514

Trakman, L. and S. Gatien, *Rights and Responsibilities* (University of Toronto Press 1999) 10

UNDP, *Beyond the Midpoint: Accelerating Support for MDG Achievement* (2009)

Unger, R., 'The Critical Legal Studies Movement' (1983) 96 Harvard Law Review 561, 571

Waldron, J., 'Rights in Conflict' (1989) 99 Ethics 503

Waldron, J., 'Socioeconomic Rights and Theories of Justice' NYU School of Law Public Law and Legal Theory Research Paper Series; Working Paper No. 10–79 (November 2010) 5

Wood, M., 'International Organizations and Customary International Law', International Organizations and Customary International Law 2014 Jonathan J. Charney Distinguished Lecture in Public International Law (2015) 48 Vanderbilt Journal of Transnational Law 609, 611

Cases

Hamdan v. Rumsfeld, 548 U.S. 557 (2006)

APPENDIX – METHODOLOGICAL PROPOSAL (TABLE)

Given the foregoing critiques, and the argument in favour of a more balanced and open methodological approach to human rights legal research, what might a more rigourous approach consider? What are the key elements and what would they require in terms of analytical approach to a human rights norm underpinning a particular right or group of rights? The following table contains a list of methodological issues or challenges and some possible sequential questions that could be used to address those with more rigour in human rights legal research.

Table 3A.1   Proposal for research questions to guide human rights legal methodology

Proposal for questions guiding human rights legal methodology	Challenge/issue	Research question(s) to answer
1	Insufficient clarity around the research question – threshold question	What is the legal research question being tackled?
2	Type/level of norm and locus of transposition	What are the applicable norms? What level is being addressed: international, regional, domestic, customary or informal?
3	Sources of law/norm	What is the regulatory framework that governs? What is the source of the applicable norms: treaty, statute, court judgment?
4	Nature of the norm	Is the norm binding or non-binding in formal legal terms? How 'binding' is it considered in informal, cultural, political, and social terms?
5	Genesis/pedigree of the norm	What is the theory of the human rights norm? What is source of the norm in legal and cultural terms?

Table 3A.1   (continued)

Proposal for questions guiding human rights legal methodology	Challenge/issue	Research question(s) to answer
		What is the history of the applicable norms? What values does it purport to embody? What values, norms or choices have critics charged it as embodying? Is it contested? If so, where, why and by whom?
6	Norm interpretation	How has the norm been interpreted and/or enforced by the relevant compliance body or monitoring body? What of universal or regional special procedures? What of international or domestic jurisprudence?
7	Transposition/influence of the norm – fragmentation and international policy coherence	What is the relevance of the norm in other, non-human rights spheres, e.g. trade, investment, environment, development, security? Does the norm translate? Does it have any influence in other regulatory regimes?
8	Acceptance of the norm	What is the level of acceptance of the norm – is it contested, controversial, the subject of multiple reservations, and derogations?
9	Formal acceptance of the norm Compliance/enforcement of the norm	What is the record of implementation, compliance, and enforcement of that norm (UN Human Rights

Table 3A.1   (continued)

Proposal for questions guiding human rights legal methodology	Challenge/issue	Research question(s) to answer
		Council, international courts or tribunals, domestic law, and international law?)
10	Structural analysis of the right	Having identified the norm/right – apply the analysis of respect, protect, fulfill
11	Identifying the right-holder	Who is/are the rights holder(s)? How do they relate to or interpret the norm? What is/was their role in identifying/ratifying/interpreting it?
12	Identifying the duty- bearer	Who is/are the duty-bearer(s)? How does the duty-bearer relate to or perceive the norm? What is/was their role in identifying/ratifying/interpreting it?
13	Relationship of the right-holder and duty-bearer	What is the relationship between the right-holder(s) and duty-bearer(s)? How would one characterize the power balance between them? How is this relationship reflected in legal, political and cultural terms?
14	Nature of the corresponding obligations	What is the nature of the obligation? What action (or restraint) does the norm require on the part of duty-bearer(s)? How does it relate to the nature of the right and to the answers to questions 5–10 above?
15	Prospective developments	Consider future directions for the right/norm

Table 3A.1   (continued)

Proposal for questions guiding human rights legal methodology	Challenge/issue	Research question(s) to answer
16	Legal recommendations	Areas of improvement; refinement or reform; strengthening of the norms
17	Tools, indicators and data	Sources of relevant assessment tools, human rights impact assessment and due diligence, human rights indicators

4. Core principles in argumentation and understanding: hermeneutics and human rights

Hilde Bondevik and Inga Bostad

What types of argumentation strategies can be seen as valid and relevant for studies in human rights? How can one argue in favor of what is relatively acceptable and what is regarded as universal or globally accepted? Hermeneutics is a theory of interpretation that has descended from ancient Greek philosophy. It addresses how humans may understand and interpret each other across time and culture. In the field of human rights, the core principles of hermeneutics have a two-fold function; they clarify and distil the argument's validity, as well as playing a critical role in presenting a theory of an argument's limitations of interpretations in general.

This chapter gives an introduction to the method of philosophical hermeneutics based on Gadamer's concept of understanding and the process of dialogical interplay. The prejudicial character of understanding implies that whenever we understand, we are involved in a dialogue that encompasses both our own self-understanding and our understanding of the matter at issue. Gadamer claims that hermeneutic experience is itself universal,[1] and this is a fruitful starting point for our argumentation. In this chapter, we will provide an introduction to the concepts of hermeneutics that can be used in the argumentation and interpretation of legal texts and human rights principles and treaties, in applied research, as well as in theoretical analyses of human rights issues. Hermeneutics expresses something important and fundamental about our ability to understand and interpret. It finds favor with the field of human rights and in situations where we need to understand and communicate across different social groups and cultures. Referencing Gadamer, we seek to bridge the traditional gap between the humanities and legal science, which have often been regarded as two fundamentally different disciplines with distinctive theoretical and methodological approaches. We will also use Seyla

---

[1]   Hans-Georg Gadamer, *Philosophical Hermeneutics* (University of California Press 1977) 10; and Hans-Georg Gadamer, *Truth and Method* (2nd rev. edn, Continuum 2003) 351.

Benhabib and Martha Nussbaum as representatives of human right hermeneutics, that is, a philosophical pluralism concerning issues of justice, contemporary social issues and gender. These fields rely on Gadamer's hermeneutics but also set the boundaries for the relevance of hermeneutics. In this chapter, the case of the 'burqa bans'[2] or the ban on face covering will be applied as a case study. In the case, *S.A.S. v. France* (2014),[3] the European Court of Human Rights ruled that the French law prohibiting face covering in public does not violate international human rights instruments. We will discuss how this conflict can be addressed and dealt with within a hermeneutic perspective. As a human rights case, the burqa ban ruling elucidates how hermeneutics addresses the way in which a court of judges interprets a variation of opinions and norms (by the applicant, the state and different non-state actors).

THE HISTORICAL BACKGROUND OF HERMENEUTICS

Different methods in the field of humanities and social sciences may have relevance for studies of human rights, using either qualitative or quantitative, inductive or deductive, casuistic or apodictic methods. They start from simple facts and figures, meaningful material, general principles or laws. Hermeneutics as an epistemological approach is more fundamental than other methods, focusing on interpretation and understanding as a human activity, always in need of self-reflection. However, hermeneutics can be operationalized in its own way as a fruitful and practical tool that may provide insights as well as offering a stepwise path to current human rights dilemmas. Hermeneutics can also supplement other methods, but it is important to emphasize that the hermeneutical method does not aim at quantifiable generalizations and statistical causality. Accordingly, it differs from both the natural and the social sciences.

---

[2] Eva Brems questions the use of the word 'burqa ban' and suggests instead 'face veils', because the word for 'burqa' is used for 'clothing that covers the whole body as well as the face', which is rarely used in Europe. In Europe, it is more common to use the 'niqab', a cloth that covers the face, and may or may not cover the eyes (see Eva Brems, 'Face Veil Bans in the European Court of Human Rights: The Importance of Empirical Findings' (2014) 22(2) Journal of Law and Policy 517–551). We are aware of this distinction and will primarily use 'face veil' in this chapter; in the French case, the word 'voile integrale' is used, which could be translated to face veil. However, in the specific case against France we will keep to the use of the word 'burqa'.

[3] *S.A.S. v. France* [GC], App no. 43835/11 (ECHR, 1 July 2014).

The word 'hermeneutics' derives from the Greek word 'hermeneuein', which means to express or pronounce, construe or explain, translate or interpret. From antiquity, societies have needed to understand and convey key documents, such as religious writings and legal texts. Hermeneutics was long synonymous with the art of interpretation and eventually led to the formation of specific rules for discourse. These rules were developed especially in conjunction with the interpretation of documents related to theology, classical philology and jurisprudence and had a normative status within these fields.

Modern hermeneutics revolves around more than normative rules for interpretation of various texts and laws. It is rather a general theory of interpretation. It was the German theologian and philosopher Friedrich Schleiermacher (1768–1834) who, in 1805, began to question the dogmatism of historical hermeneutics and its rules of interpretation. He eventually devised a universal theory of hermeneutics.[4] The central question was: How should we understand a text? Modern hermeneutics is also dominated by two other pivotal names, namely, Wilhelm Dilthey (1833–1911) and Hans-Georg Gadamer (1900–2002), both German philosophers. While Dilthey was particularly concerned with the humanities and the interpretation and understanding of different life experiences expressed in texts, documents, laws and works of art, Gadamer concentrated on how the understanding of a text is related to its application. According to Gadamer, hermeneutics can be extended to anything whatsoever that is understandable. We shall return to Gadamer and his major work from 1960, *Wahrheit und Methode* (*Truth and Method*), where he also discusses the relationship between legal hermeneutics and general hermeneutics, and here only summarize what follows from these works.

The objects of hermeneutics are often referred to as a *meaningful material*, i.e. that which has a meaningful dimension and the actual meaning. The meaningful dimension is concrete, material and observable, such as the different national constitutions, the Universal Declaration of Human Rights and the European Convention on Human Rights. The actual meaning or content may consist in how a particular law should be understood and interpreted. The fundamental idea is that we understand something using a number of assumptions. While the significant methodological issue in the practice of hermeneutics consists of how understanding may be achieved, the philosophical question relates to what characterizes understanding. These issues are of course interrelated, and in this chapter we will not make clear distinctions between them. Central concepts in

---

[4]   Gadamer (n 1, 2003) 188.

hermeneutics are the *horizon of understanding, pre-understanding* or *prejudice, the hermeneutical circle* and not least *life-world*.[5] We will examine them in depth and apply them throughout this chapter. We begin with the one that is constituent for all understanding and interpretation and which is fundamentally connected to the other concepts.

THE HORIZON OF UNDERSTANDING

According to Gadamer,[6] every human being is constituted by a specific historical background. It is not possible to free oneself of this ever-present horizon of understanding; it is an ontological condition. Our prejudices are aspects of our past, and, as such, are sources that we should not be forced to overcome. Rather, we should seek to be conscious of the present situation as part of our history. 'To be historical', writes Gadamer, 'means that one is not absorbed into self-knowledge'.[7] The existence of prejudices will always remain a part of our understanding; however, the understanding of a specific text comes about at a particular time in history and must be seen as a mediation of past and present, neither as a repetition of the past nor as objective or detached from history.

A much used concept is the hermeneutical circle. The word 'circle' illustrates the priority that hermeneutic scholars give to the process of self-reflection and that every human being finds herself in a circle when trying to reach some kind of understanding. All efforts to gain more insight into understanding develop in a loop where the whole is interpreted in light of the single elements, and the elements in light of the circle. Simultaneously, the general historical horizon of understanding is always present, in a more or less conscious and conceptualized form. The more elements that are put into the circle, the more it grows, encompassing the new elements.

One example of the hermeneutical nature of understanding is the reading of a legal judgment for the first time. The expectations and pre-understanding that the reader has are often complex and unclear, for instance, when a student of human rights tries to grasp the different elements of the judgment against France in the European Court of Human Rights regarding the prohibition of the face covering. The student already

---

[5] We have written more on these concepts in Hilde Bondevik and Inga Bostad, *Tenkepauser. Filosofi og vitenskapsteori* [Pauses of Thinking. Philosophy and Theory of Science] (Akribe 2003).

[6] Gadamer (n 1, 1977).

[7] Ibid. 68.

has some assumptions about the judgment – primarily that a judgment has been rendered and what consequences it has on the subject matter, that it is about religious garments and freedom of religion and the security needs of society. In addition, she may have an expectation that this represents aspects of the complex position of women in a modern democracy, as well as a whole range of conscious and subconscious opinions, feelings and experiences regarding the issue of women wearing face veils in public.

The student may have an expectation that the matter will be time-consuming as well as interesting in terms of the media coverage of the case, and she has chosen this particular issue because she finds it difficult to have a definite opinion about religious headgear. All this helps to characterize the student's expectations, but in addition, having an expectation is a prerequisite for achieving any kind of understanding. Without expectations there will be no understanding. Our pre-understanding consists of languages, beliefs, cultural conditions, social norms and personal perceptions. In engaging themselves in a specific case, students may experience that their expectations prove erroneous, that is, prejudices about a particular case, whether negative or positive, conscious or unconscious, are always present.

ON INTERPRETATION

To interpret someone or something is part of everyday life. It is precisely in this way that we can orient ourselves, interact with each other and gain knowledge. Nevertheless, it is frequently the case that the meaning of something is unclear to us, and that we must strive for it to become clear. The fact that the interpretation of meaning in most situations is seen as fixed or indisputable is connected to common biological and physiological aspects of human beings and the cultural and social conditions we share, such as language, gender identity and other cultural and social norms. However, it is of vital importance to be conscious of why and how interpretations – and subsequently, understanding – may still vary from person to person, and this may prevent problems, at least in a scholarly context. 'a person who understands, understands himself, projecting himself upon his possibilities'.[8]

Mastering the mechanisms of understanding may be described as facing the unknown. What is pre-understood comes to light, and the very struggle to put into words, reasoning in a just and fair manner, enlightens the basic

---

[8]   Gadamer (n 1, 2003) 260.

structures of interpretation; it is a gap between experiencing something through a complex set of emotions, opinions and presuppositions in a context, and the descriptions of the same experience. The core of hermeneutics comes to life through alienation, according to Gadamer.[9] When we are confronted with art, the distinction between the immediate experience and our aesthetic judgment is a kind of alienation. If we turn to the legal sciences (law), this will involve a kind of alienation perceived as a form of distance between what is immediately obvious in a case and the decisions that must always be taken through interpretations. The concept of alienation can be used to illustrate that there is a difference or distance between an immediate experience of something and its interpretation in terms of a plea or verdict.

However, trying to understand what we experience tends to be assisted by an intuitive ideal of gaining some kind of objectivity: that our understanding qualifies for reaching or experiencing something that is 'true', and that we cannot but grasp the full picture. The search for understanding in Gadamer's philosophy is seen as a basic structure of all human activity. All theoretical understanding therefore originates in the life-world of meaning in which humankind lives, every human lives in his or her life-world, which of course includes relations to other persons and their life-world. At the same time, Gadamer claims that traditional hermeneutics has an unrealistic ideal of understanding. According to Gadamer, an unresolved conflict exists between the ideal of objectivity and the concept of historical experience as a basis for hermeneutical understanding.[10] We have to accept that we can never free ourselves from our own insights, from our own horizon of understanding with our own prejudices. Total objectivity, from a scientific perspective, is not a norm or ideal. For instance, there is no neutral vantage point from which we can accept or reject the selection of our pre-judgments, prejudices and foreknowledge. Therefore, we cannot reconstruct objectively a text written in a different historical era or another culture or for that matter by any other persons in our own time. According to Gadamer, one must, in other words, abandon the hermeneutics of reconstruction of the past as an objective fact in favor of a universal and philosophical hermeneutics. Gadamer formulates an important requirement for the interpreter to attempt to see her/his own historical situation.

When we interpret a text, we have virtually to test our pre-judgments and expectations of it. During this process, according to Gadamer, some kind of fusion or overlap between the text and the interpreter's precognition

---

[9]   Gadamer (n 1, 1977).
[10] Gadamer (n 1, 2003) 174.

will emerge, even if the circle of understanding never disappears; understanding never arrives at closure or completeness.[11] To achieve this type of fusion of understanding, it is a necessary condition that we as interpreters are benevolent toward the author and the text, which means that we are open to it, that we think that the author, the text or the lawmaker has a notable and meaningful message.

Interpretations are, however, always subjectively constructed. This is transferable to a variety of situations, such as meeting with people from other cultures. If I wish to understand another person's actions and motives, I must be open so as to be influenced by the other person. However, Gadamer does not argue in favor of seeing the two horizons, before and after being influenced by the other person, as one and the same. Yet the 'new' one differs from the 'old'. What has happened is a kind of transformation of my primary horizon so that my references, my background of foreknowledge, has changed and been transformed or expanded.

It has been argued that Gadamer accepts authority (as political, philosophical, and so on) and traditions (social and cultural conventions) all too easily, and that his thinking is located within a harmonizing and not a critical model. As a consequence there is, for example, no way of knowing if or when we have arrived at the author's understanding, or when various types of oppression have taken place. We can only say something about how we understand a text, and clarify why we understand a text as we do. One who has criticized Gadamer for his conservative orientation is the German philosopher Jürgen Habermas (1929–). He is, however, particularly concerned with the interests and ideology behind apparently neutral institutions of society, 'the heritage of philosophy issue is the critique of ideology'[12]), and will show that these interests lead the research and society in specific directions. What may be perceived as economic and structural necessities, such as an unequal balance of power in a society between the unemployed and the government, may prove to be cultural conditions and constructions. Habermas argues for political freedom and change,[13] which is not the issue for Gadamer, who, as mentioned above, is particularly concerned about the ontological features of understanding. Habermas appears to believe that the interpreter can understand the

---

[11]   Shaun Gallagher, *Hermeneutics and Education* (University of New York Press 1992) 61.

[12]   Jürgen Habermas, *Knowledge and Human Interest* (Suhrkamp 1968) 63.

[13]   Ibid. Habermas presents the concepts of ideology to show how language is dominated by social power, and that interest, instead of prejudices, explains that there is no such thing as pure knowledge, every disinterested knowledge hides a form of interest (p. 196).

social actor better than he can understand himself, while Gadamer stresses that we cannot free ourselves from our prejudices as they constitute our understanding as such. Habermas's position thus points toward what has been called 'critical hermeneutics', or more specifically 'the hermeneutics of suspicion', a position that may also have valuable input in our context.

THE HERMENEUTICS OF SUSPICION

Critical hermeneutics focuses on the ideological, structural and political aspects of our culture and society that emerge in understanding something, and how this unconsciously affects each of us, aiming at liberating people from suppression and subordination. Conditions that are connected to different power relations, such as political influence, money, gender, property and education, are essential in the tradition of critical hermeneutics. We have no access to part of our pre-knowledge, therefore we cannot adapt many of the ideas and beliefs we have. The problem is that a number of these conceptions and perceptions appear to be independent and unaffected by culture and society – almost as if they were about actual and natural truths.

The concept of 'hermeneutics of suspicion' stems from French philosopher Paul Ricoeur (1913–2005) and can be described as the systematic search for hidden intentions of the counterparty, whether ideological, ethical or political vested interests, whatever is relevant in our context.[14] We see this search for hidden intentions as one of the main reasons why debates on human rights are often politically misplaced. Thinkers like Marx, Nietzsche and Freud are all said to have contributed to the development of a 'hermeneutics of suspicion', but there are several reasons to be critical of this perspective. It is essential to strive for some kind of objectivity or neutrality in the sense of not allowing suspicion, distrust or deliberate assumption that the other is hiding something to be part of the analysis – for then the counterpart has already lost and is unable to converse with you. On the other hand, as mentioned above, Gadamer is criticized for being too harmonizing and conservative. In Habermas's view, Gadamer leaves little room for critical judgment. Thus, according to Habermas, hermeneutics has to be completed by a critical theory of society to serve the purpose of emancipation and social liberation.[15]

---

[14] Paul Ricoeur, *Freud and Philosophy: An Essay on Interpretation* (Yale University Press 1970) 27.

[15] Jürgen Habermas, A Review of *Truth and Method* (Trans. Fred R. Dallmayr and Thomas McCarthy, Ormiston and Schrift 2000) 213–244; Bjørn Ramberg and

Such liberation has its ideal model in a dialogue between two parties where each should initially be equal, and ideally no one should come to the table with a biased suspicion that the other has hidden intentions. However, no one holds a neutral position when claiming something, as in doing so one also has some kind of expectation of truth. Rather, what you argue is more true and valid for you than for the other person. This is perhaps the most important insight in hermeneutics, namely the value of having well-founded arguments (as it also is in legal and human rights thinking and practice), which in turn involves others and their right to have other (more or less) well-founded claims. In a communicative community of this kind, therefore, there exists both common standards[16] of what we should approve as valid reasoning and assumptions that this involves ways of being together which apply to everyone.

If we revert to our initial question on the universality of human rights, one could say that in the tradition of hermeneutics of suspicion there is an opening for the variety within the individual: to maintain diversity as a consequence of the singular is taken care of by the rules of dialogical interplay. The primary challenge is to create this in everyday places – such as ideal meetings.

According to Gadamer, however, it is not a commonality of concepts or minds, nor a fixed yardstick, that points to correct answers, clear rules of the game or the dialogical interplay, but rather a potential of reaching a deeper understanding of the counterpart through empathy with the life situation of others.[17] The concept of *sensus communis* (common sense) is closely related to the concept of power of judgment[18] in that well-founded power of judgment is dependent on the individual having sound discretion or well-developed 'common sense'. Power of judgment implies an ability to see what is particular, a certain experience or a specific situation, in light of what is general or in a larger and more general context.

At the same time, the concept of power of judgment has an elitist aspect:

Kristin Gjesdal, *Hermeneutics. Stanford Encyclopedia of Philosophy* (2005) <http://plato.stanford.edu/entries/hermeneutics/>.

[16]   Habermas argues that to engage in communicative actions you have to (1) utter something understandable, (2) give (the hearer) something to understand, (c) make himself thereby understandable and (4) come to an understanding of another person (Habermas n 13).

[17]   Gadamer (n 1, 2003) 43.

[18]   According to Gadamer (*Truth and Method* (2nd rev. edn, Continuum 2003) 56), the humanities are characterized by the humanist ideal of a common sense or *sensus communis*, with the aim of bringing people up to create a good and just society, a concern for community and a sympathy for fellow humans which is closer to the 'heart' than to the 'head' (ibid. 50).

assigning power of judgment cannot be isolated from the societal, cultural and economic framework – for instance, education and the use of concepts and references, and the way people dress ('power-dressing' or 'solidarity-dressing'), all are related to status and power relations, and may have a major impact in a variety of contexts.

THE THIRD WAY

How can we conceive of the dialogical impetus of hermeneutics as a possible resource for resolving certain contemporary social and political human rights challenges in our world today? We will argue that there might be a fruitful methodological path available for human rights scholars that neither appeals to prior, transcendent, eternal truths, nor devolves into incommensurability, but rather forges a third way 'beyond objectivism and relativism'.[19] We will use the Turkish-American philosopher Seyla Benhabib (1950–) and her communicative ethics as a representative of this third way, which is a philosophical pluralism with regard to justice, contemporary social issues and gender that could be elucidated by Gadamer's hermeneutics. Yet it simultaneously pinpoints the limits of hermeneutics.

Benhabib has some critical arguments against using hermeneutics in general and Gadamer more specifically. She believes that this will strengthen a liberal-individualistic approach focusing on the individual's understanding of a work of art or an academic journal article. Such an understanding is a process which may overshadow the deeper layers of our history and culture and is often inaccessible to historical and philosophical analysis as well as the role of a public dialogue in constituting public institutions and citizens.[20] At the same time, it may be argued in favor of Gadamer that the process of understanding is first and foremost participation of a historical individual in a moral and aesthetic reflection.

Other arguments against Gadamer are to be found in Benhabib's work, explicit in her key concept of a 'post-metaphysical interactive universalism'.[21] The core issue is to reformulate a moral point of view as an achievement contingent on an interactive form of rationality – inspired

---

[19] Richard J. Bernstein, *Beyond Objectivism and Relativism. Science, Hermeneutics, and Praxis* (University of Pennsylvania Press 1983).
[20] Meili Steele, 'Three Problematics of Linguistic Vulnerability – Gadamer, Benhabib and Butler' in Lorraine Code (ed.), *Feminist Interpretations of Hans-Georg Gadamer* (Pennsylvania University Press 2003) 338.
[21] Seyla Benhabib, *Situating the Self. Gender, Community and Postmodernism in Contemporary Ethics* (Routledge 1992) 6.

BOX 4.1   A THEORY OF JUSTICE

The American moral and political philosopher John Rawls offers a useful theoretical justification of social democratic principles of justice – a theory that is appropriate because it systematizes a particular sense of justice.[22] Rawls argues that the principles of justice are principles that rational men would choose if they had to choose, under defined constraints, in an original position of social contract. It was in his *A Theory of Justice* (1971) that he introduced what he called the 'original position' as a thought experiment. The original position is a hypothetical situation, of which the parties select principles that will determine the basic structure of the society they will live in. The choice is made from behind a veil of ignorance, which would deprive participants of information about their particular characteristics, such as his or her ethnicity, social status, gender and religion. However, it has been argued that 'the choice that Rawls imputes to his contractors' reflects a specific socialization – one dominant in Western democracies. Thus, critics have claimed that Rawls's theory is in no sense a universal theory.

by Habermas's way of addressing a citizen of the world and its striving for independence and autonomy. Benhabib emphasizes rules and procedures before and during a dialogue or public discourse. She puts forward an ideal that rules of impartiality will provide a greater degree of universalism than referring only to the content or matter to be discussed. Unlike a liberal model of individual rights and rules for how these must be protected, she seeks to elaborate an alternative, that of a public discourse that is more or less a rational debate that exists between members of society, institutions, and policy instruments. In particular, Benhabib discusses and criticizes universalism in ethical rights theories, and one of the main philosophers she is arguing against is John Rawls (1921–2002) and his well-known contract theory of justice, outlined and discussed in *A Theory of Justice* from 1971.

According to Benhabib, the universalistic theories express how a particular group of subjects defines their own experiences as universal. They consequently ignore questions related to the concrete others.[23] The exclusion of the concrete other has to do with the historical division of labor we have had in modern Western society, which has had a special focus on gender and rights and the position of women. She argues that we need

---

[22]   John Rawls, *A Theory of Justice* (Oxford 1972).

[23]   According to Benhabib (1992), there are two types of moral orientations that are interconnected. She calls these the *concrete* and *generalized others*. The caring perspective is related to the concrete others, while the rights perspective is related to the generalized others.

both orientations in the understanding of interpersonal relationships as a basis for moral and political questions.

In Benhabib's hermeneutically inspired philosophical discussion, she argues for a reconstruction of an alternative principle of morality. We have to transcend the boundaries traditionally drawn between care and justice, partiality and impartiality, particularity and universality, emotion and reason. Benhabib believes that we have to overcome such dichotomies within a context where they are not mutually exclusive, but rather interconnected.

In her book *Situating the Self*, Benhabib poses one central argument. If the universal theory of justice is to face its promises of liberty and equality for all, we must reconstruct some of the core concepts that this theory is based on. She criticizes the theory as being 'gender blind' and neglecting differences between individuals and groups. A major problem in this context is that justice is related to what is traditionally defined as the public sphere in society. The public was, and to some extent still is, defined in opposition to the private, and is thus opposed to activities and experiences that have traditionally been linked to women. The concrete others are perceived as a contrast to the generalized others, and excluded. Benhabib concludes that the concrete others have to be assumed in universal ethics. She also claims that to have a notion of dignity in the first place, we have to start with the concrete identity of others. Ethics, in other words, has to cover both justice and questions about quality of life and values, both the generalized and the concrete other. 'In the democratic polity, the gap between the demands of justice, as these articulate principle of moral rights, and the demands of virtue, as these defines the quality of our relations to others in the lifeworld', Benhabib writes, 'can be cultivating qualities of civic friendship and solidarity'.[24] This leads us to our specific example – the case of the so-called French burqa ban.

THE CASE OF THE BURQA[25] BANS

How can hermeneutics be used to solve the case of the burqa bans? The answer to this is, first of all, that the interpreter of the case is always self-reflecting, that is, in a position of trying to balance between the interpretation of the context of the case and the interpretation of the case.

In recent years, there have been several discussions in European coun-

---

[24]   Benhabib (n 21) 11.
[25]   See earlier clarifications on the use of the word 'burqa' versus 'face veil', n 2.

tries related to the use in the public space of clothing that covers the face, but only Belgium and France have banned the full-face veil in public. Face coverings are therefore already subject to legal prohibition in those countries. As we have mentioned earlier, confusion exists regarding the three different garments involved in cases of face veils. First there is the *hijab*. This is a traditional veil that covers the woman's head and chest, worn by some Muslim women beyond the age of puberty. It is worn in the presence of adult males outside of their immediate family and, according to some interpretations, in the presence of adult non-Muslim females outside of their immediate family. The second garment is the *niqab*. This is much like the hijab, but additionally the niqab also covers part of the face, leaving only the eyes visible. Thirdly there is the *burqa*. This type is the least common and covers the whole body as well as covering the face with mesh, so that the eyes are not visible.

The hijab is generally worn by Muslim women all over the world, while the niqab and burqa are more common in specific regions, such as in India, the Middle East and Afghanistan. The different types of veil are often confused in the debates. It is not obligatory for a Muslim woman to dress in one of the above ways in front of other women. What is considered a religious practice and a religious norm when it comes to garments is interpreted differently in different Islamic cultures. According to Blaker Strand, there are various interpretations of the putative Koranic ban enjoining the use of full face covering.[26]

THE FRENCH CASE

In July 2014, the European Court of Human Rights ruled that the French law prohibiting face-covering in public is not a violation of the European Convention on Human Rights (ECHR) – the case of *S.A.S v. France*. The complainant was a Muslim woman who wore the burqa and niqab in accordance with her religious beliefs, culture and personal convictions.[27] She stressed that neither her spouse nor other family members exerted any pressure on her to wear these garments. She used them both privately and in public, but not all the time. Hence, she wanted to be able to wear them whenever she wanted. She was born in Pakistan and her family belongs to a Sunni cultural tradition in which it is customary and respectful for

---

[26]   Vibeke Blaker Strand, *Diskrimineringsvern og religionsutøvelse* [The Protection of Discrimination and Exercise of Religion] (Gyldendal 2010) 245.
[27]   *S.A.S. v. France* (n 3).

women to wear a full-face veil in public. She claimed to have suffered a serious infringement of the exercise of her rights under the ECHR (articles 3, 8, 9–11 and 14 of the ECHR). Further, she held that the ban prohibiting Muslim women from wearing the full-face veil in public places in France prevented her from manifesting her faith, from living by it and from observing it in public (*S. A. S. v. France*).

If found in violation of the ban, women could be fined up to EUR 150 and could also be required to attend citizenship courses. The complainant was of the opinion that the legislation violated her rights under the Convention and brought the case before the court. The case was submitted to the court in chambers, which relinquished jurisdiction in favor of the Court Grand Chamber.[28]

The complainant alleged violation of article 3 (ECHR, article 3 – Prohibition of torture: 'No one shall be subjected to torture or to inhuman or degrading treatment or punishment'), referring to the risk that she could be subjected to degrading treatment if she wore such garments in public. Furthermore, the complainant alleged that the prohibition entailed a violation of articles 8–11, alone and in conjunction with article 14 (article 8 – 'Right to respect for private and family life'; article 9 – 'Freedom of thought, conscience and religion'; article 10 – 'Freedom of expression'; article 11 – 'Freedom of assembly and association'; and article 14 – 'Prohibition of discrimination').

Before we address the legal case according to hermeneutical concepts and reasoning, we will reflect upon the deeper conflicts that surround this case and the genuine human rights dilemmas that it brings to light. On one hand, this case is a question about religion and religious practice, as enshrined in article 9.1 in ECHR:[29] 'this right includes freedom to change his religion or belief and freedom, either alone or in community with others and in public or private, to manifest his religion or belief, in

---

[28] The domestic remedies had been exhausted.

[29] Which relates to article 18 of the Universal Declaration of Human Rights (Adopted by General Assembly Resolution 217 A(III) of 10 December 1948): 'Everyone has the right to freedom of thought, conscience and religion. This right includes freedom to change his religion or belief, and freedom either alone or together with others and in public or private, to manifest his religion or belief in teaching, practice, worship and observance'. Also expressed in UN Convention on Civil and Political Rights, 16 December 1966, United Nations, Treaty Series, 999, p. 171, article 18: 'Everyone shall have the right to freedom of thought, conscience and religion. This right shall include freedom to have or to adopt a religion or belief of his choice, and freedom, either individually or in community with others and in public or private, to manifest his religion or belief in worship, observance, practice and teaching'.

worship, teaching, practice and observance'. On the other hand, the use of a solid garment that also covers the face may be regarded as an obstacle to security, communication and an open society. Finally, there is the question of whether discrimination against women might be an element in this case as well.

The French rationale for the introduction of the ban on full-face veils in public consisted of three main arguments that were used to introduce a ban. The first argument referred to state security and the risks of unidentified people in public spaces. This argument was not regarded by the Court as sufficient for a general ban against using the burqa/niqab in public places:

> As regards the question of necessity in relation to public safety, within the meaning of Articles 8 and 9 (see paragraph 115 above), the Court understands that a State may find it essential to be able to identify individuals in order to prevent danger for the safety of persons and property and to combat identity fraud. It has thus found no violation of Article 9 of the Convention in cases concerning the obligation to remove clothing with a religious connotation in the context of security checks and the obligation to appear bareheaded on identity photos for use on official documents . . . However, in view of its impact on the rights of women who wish to wear the full-face veil for religious reasons, a blanket ban on the wearing in public places of clothing designed to conceal the face can be regarded as proportionate only in a context where there is a general threat to public safety. The Government has not shown that the ban introduced by the Law of 11 October 2010 falls into such a context . . . It cannot therefore be found that the blanket ban imposed by the Law of 11 October 2010 is necessary, in a democratic society, for public safety, within the meaning of Articles 8 and 9 of the Convention.[30]

Secondly, France referenced the need for gender equality and for integration of women into French society; and thirdly, the State held that the need to maintain a secular state was the rationale behind introducing a ban.[31] The Court, however, concluded in their judgment that,

> A State Party could not invoke gender equality in order to ban a practice that was defended by women – such as the applicant – in the context of the exercise of the rights enshrined in those Articles, unless it were to be understood that individuals could be protected on that basis from the exercise of their own fundamental rights and freedoms. Moreover, in so far as the Government thus sought to show that the wearing of the full-face veil by certain women shocked the majority of the French population because it infringed the principle of

---

[30]   Premise 139 in the judgment in the case of *S. A. S. v. France* (n 3).
[31]   *S. A. S. v. France* (n 3).

gender equality as generally accepted in France, the Court referred to its reasoning (below) as to the other two values that they had invoked.

However, interestingly, French feminists did not agree about the outcome of the case. As Spohn has argued, some of the feminists view the ban as an important achievement in the struggle for women's rights. Others regard it as a violation of women's rights. Despite the fact that both camps use human rights as a shared normative basis, they arrived at different conclusions regarding the ban.[32] However, the argument that the Court regarded as sufficient was the conditions of living together: to 'protect a principle of interaction between individuals' (*S.A.S. v. France* 153).[33] *S.A.S. v. France*, sentence 157, states that: 'Consequently, having regard in particular to the breadth of the margin of appreciation afforded to the respondent State in the present case, the Court finds that the ban imposed by the Law of 11 October 2010 can be regarded as proportionate to the aim pursued, namely the preservation of the conditions of "living together" as an element of the "protection of the rights and freedoms of others"'.

However, it has been argued that the face covering bans in all public spaces could be regarded as a violation of religious freedom under ECHR article 9. Wearing a face veil could be considered a religious expression, which enjoys protection through the right to freedom of religion. It could therefore be argued in the light of the ECHR's relatively broad understanding of freedom of religion in article 9, according to which the wearer's subjective perception of the religious significance of various garments is essential, that the introduction of a face coverings ban would be a human rights violation.

Køhler-Olsen argues that the question of whether a ban on the niqab and burqa discriminates against children is a question of how it is experienced as such by the individual.[34] The difference in treatment can be justified on the grounds of gender equality and education. The right of parents to raise children according to their own faith is likewise restricted by the consideration of the child's right to equality and education. In the French case, the right to privacy and the right to freedom of belief and

---

[32] Ulrike Spohn, 'Sisters in Disagreement: The Dispute Among French Feminists about the "Burka Ban" and the causes of their Disunity' (2013) 12 Journal of Human Rights 145–164.

[33] *S.A.S. v. France* (n 3), 153 regards the General principles concerning article 9 of the Convention, that is freedom of thought, conscience and religion.

[34] Julia Franziska Køhler-Olsen, 'Forbud mot niqab og burka i den offentlige skolen' [Prohibition against niqabs and burqas in public schools] (2010) 49 Lov og rett: Norsk juridisk tidsskrift [Law and Justice: Norwegian Legal Journals].

religion are seen as infringed upon, but not violated. The verdict also refers to what is needed to legitimize intervention – that is, public safety and protection of the rights and freedom of society as a whole. Two of the judges (Judges Nussberger and Helena Jäderblom) in the case expressed a partly dissenting opinion on this matter. In their opinion, the judgment sacrificed individual rights to abstract principles, and they found it hard to conceive that the rights protected outweighed the rights infringed. 'Even if we were to accept that the applicant's rights under Articles 8 and 9 of the Convention could be balanced against abstract principles, be it tolerance, pluralism and broadmindedness, or be it the idea of "living together" and the "minimum requirements of life in society", we cannot, in any event, agree with the majority that the ban is proportionate to the aim pursued' (C.2.15).

Furthermore, it is interesting to note that the basic argument of the plaintiff in *S. A. S. v. France* was her wish to wear the face veil whenever she wanted, and in whatever situation she wanted. It could, however, be argued that this is in conflict with the traditional practices of wearing face veils and that her description of her life as a young Muslim and her generation of young female Muslims opposes the traditional religiously grounded practices.

THE BAN ON FACE COVERING IN A HERMENEUTICAL CONTEXT

Here we arrive at how to interpret and apply a hermeneutical approach to the French case, and how to develop tools for interpretations on these and similar cases. According to Gadamer, it is a common understanding that the humanities and law are two different disciplines and that their methods differ. However, in line with Gadamer's argumentation,[35] we see that there are fruitful similarities and connections: 'The jurist understands the meaning of the law from the present case and for the sake of this present case'.[36] The law exists, but has to be interpreted separately from the case in hand. A legal historian has no actual case as his motive, but seeks to gain an understanding of the essence of the law as a product of quite different historical applications. In other words, the hermeneutical interpreter seeks to create a balance or mediate between the original application and the present application of the law.

---

[35]   Gadamer (n 1, 2003) 324.
[36]   Ibid., 325.

A fundamental question in the *S.A.S. v. France* case was the following: could the ban be considered proportionate, or could it be regarded as intrusive, especially since it affects only a few women? The judges argued that a ban may have a negative effect on these women, and many human rights organizations were critical of a ban.[37] A ban could in this respect trigger hate speech against religious practices. However, more important than this are public safety and protection of the rights and freedoms of all French citizens. As such, the ban could be said to be directed not toward a religious garment, but toward any kind of solid facial garment. According to Brems, this is a somewhat more complex issue:[38] 'Feminist critiques . . . recognize that while the veil has often, although not always, been a symbol of patriarchal oppression, the veil, and hijab, at least for some women who wear it, can also be a visible symbol of political positionality and an expression of resistance to and contesting of Western foreign policy'. Benhabib is especially concerned with Muslim women who immigrate into democratic liberal states and how their understanding and experience of religious practice, as well as the duties of being a citizen, is debated. 'Benhabib herself speaks of the *chador* (head scarf) as a sign of a woman's "private faith and identity" but admits that such an interpretation represents a "protestantization of Islam" – in other words, the transformation of Islam from a communal submission to divine law into a personal confession of conscience'.[39] Brems argues that the seemingly neutral legislation is in fact targeted at a specific group, namely Muslim women who wear a face veil, and could therefore be interpreted as indirect discrimination. The European Court of Human Rights recognizes that 'a general policy or measure that has disproportionately prejudicial effects on a particular group may be considered discriminatory notwithstanding that it is not specifically aimed at that group'.[40]

According to Brems,[41] there is a trend throughout (Western) Europe to ban 'face coverings' in public spaces, which targets women who wear the Islamic face veil. Formally, these bans apply to 'face covering' in general. Yet both the parliamentary debates and the political discourse surround-

---

[37] *S.A.S. v. France* (n 3).

[38] Eva Brems (ed.), *The Experiences of Face Veil Wearers in Europe and the Law* (CUP 2014) 291.

[39] Seyla Benhabib, *The Rights of Others* (CUP 2004), quoted in Michael S. Kochin, 'Where Rawls was Right' (2006) 24 (Spring) Azure 142, 145 <http://azure.org.il/download/magazine/1823az24_Kochin_review.pdf>.

[40] Brems (n 2).

[41] Ibid. 519.

ing their adoption, as well as the practice of their implementation, indicate that in fact these bans target only Islamic face veils.

Bans were adopted nationwide in France, and since 2010, there has been a general prohibition against face coverings 'in spaces open to the public, (to) wear a garment that has the effect of hiding the face'.[42] In addition to this, the penalty for wearing a burqa is relatively lenient.

According to Nussbaum,[43] we have to acknowledge others' right to do what we wish to do for ourselves, that is, the right to practice our religion or beliefs. At the same time, the increasing fear of foreign cultures and religions underpins frequent abuse of that freedom. Is the fear of the burqa best understood as a fear of difference and otherness and the unknown? Nussbaum argues that religious hostilities are increasing, and that this is the key factor behind the ban on face veils in Europe. According to Pew Forum, the number of countries with a very high level of social hostilities involving religion reached a peak in 2012.[44] A third of 198 countries experienced a surge in the high level of religious hostilities, from 20% in 2007 to 29% in 2011. 'Certain types of religious hostilities have driven this rise: abuse of religious minorities, violence or threat of violence, harassment of women over religious dress, mob violence related to religion, religion-related terrorist violence, and sectarian violence'.[45]

Nussbaum argues further that we need to cultivate '"the inner eyes", the imaginative capacity that makes it possible for us to see how the world looks from the point of view of a person different in religion and ethnicity'.[46] However, as we have seen, in the case of France, other arguments are used, such as the need for a secular state and that the best way to avoid conflict – and enhance the pluralistic society – is to eliminate any use of religious symbols in the public sphere. These arguments have to be

---

[42]   Ibid. 520; and Law 2010–1192 of October 11, 2010 on the Prohibition of Concealing the Face in Public Space, Journal official de la republique Francaise [J.O.] [OFFICIAL GAZETTE OF FRANCE], Oct. 12, 2010, 18344. Article 1 states, 'No one may in spaces open to the public wear a garment that has the effect of hiding the face'. Exceptions apply when 'clothing [is] prescribed or authorized by legal or regulatory provisions', when the clothing 'is justified by reasons of health or professional motives', or when the clothing is 'part of sports activities, festivities or artistic or traditional manifestations'.

[43]   Martha Nussbaum, *The New Religious Intolerance* (Harvard University Press 2012).

[44]   Lena Larsen, 'The New Religious Intolerance. A Book Review' (2014) 34(4) Nordic Journal of Human Rights 406.

[45]   Ibid.

[46]   Nussbaum (n 43) 3.

seen as a whole, especially since acts of religious hostility have increased.[47] As Larsen argues, Nussbaum underlines the need to balance 'the principle of equal respect for persons . . . (that). . . requires equal religious liberty, . . .(but). . . it does not require personal approval of all religious practices'.[48]

Not only has the debate and knowledge about the face veil hitherto been absent, not least in light of the extensive discussion on the headscarf, but it has also been marked by a disturbing consensus.[49] What is primarily needed is more insight and empirical studies into women's (the face-veil wearers') situation, to qualify the legal and human rights discourse. However, it is worth noting that the results of interviews with women who wear religious headgear have strong similarities. First, it is not about those women who are first-generation immigrants. Instead, it concerns women who were born or are otherwise long-term residents in Europe, including many who have recently converted to Islam. Secondly, the interviews show that the vast majority of those who use the face veil do so of their own free will. Thirdly, they give no impression of wanting to withdraw from society.[50] At the same time, they experience harassment and abuse that calls for a greater degree of participation and representation in the community.

Brems[51] applies indirectly the hermeneutical method by presenting empirical data and interviews with these women and puts them forward for academics. In her next step, scholars, who had no prior empirical knowledge, were invited to write about the face veil debates after familiarizing themselves with this data. Their task was to imagine what it must be like to live wearing a face veil. The result was that each author adopted 'a different angle, in line with her or his expertise and previous work on the matter'.[52] The fact that all authors opposed a general prohibition is of subordinate interest to this discussion, but that their arguments were different and the conclusion similar is interesting in our context; it points to the fact that data is always to be interpreted in context, and that using imagination, empathy and cultural and social experience, colors your arguments as well as your use of data. In addition to this, Brems[53] shows that the report by

---

[47] Brems (n 2); and Pew Research, *Religious Hostilities Reach 6 Year High* (2014) (accessed 6 August 2014) <http://www.pewforum.org/2014/01/14/religious-hostilities-reach-six-year-high/>. The claim of the report is based upon The Social Hostility Index, which measures acts of religious hostility by private individuals, organizations, or groups in society.

[48] Larsen (n 44) 408.

[49] Brems (n 38).

[50] Ibid. 13.

[51] Ibid.

[52] Ibid. 14.

[53] Brems (n 2) 517.

the Parliamentary Commission of Inquiry in France before the ban on face veils was adopted[54] could be criticized for lacking data and empirical knowledge in addition to not actually listening to the women who wore the face coverings. The report consisted of 32 members representing all parliamentary groups and it heard about 200 witnesses and experts and sent out questionnaires to several French Embassies. However, the commission had not planned to hear a single woman who actually wore a face veil. The only person whom they did interview who wore a face veil, Kenza Drider, was only heard upon her own request.[55]

The aggregate social context is the nation state. At the same time, countries in Europe use quite different arguments, based more on national experiences (what is near to home) and less on arguments of principle and universal rights.[56] The general argument is that the case of the burqa ban shows that the human rights conventions need to be interpreted by the nation states and that these interpretations are often vague and in need of some 'necessary objectivity that distance prevails'.[57] For example, in 2013, the Norwegian Parliament argued that a ban should be rejected, primarily because Norway risked being found guilty of a human rights violation by the ECHR.[58] One way to understand the Norwegian reasoning perspective is that it expresses a compromise between pragmatic and democratic considerations.

Another argument that has been raised in the Norwegian public is related to the general moral norms. For example, the Norwegian scholar Lena Larsen has argued that, when many Norwegians react negatively toward the niqab, it is not because they necessarily hate Muslims or are racists. It is a completely different mechanism that takes effect in peoples' heads, namely general Norwegian moral judgments. As Larsen writes, 'in Norway it is considered important to show your face and to look at the

---

[54]   a. grin, assemblè nationale no. 2262, rapport d'information fait en application de l'article 145 du règlement au nom de lamission d'information sur la pratique du port du voile integral sur le territoire national (2010).

[55]   Brems (n 2) 518.

[56]   Judge Spano, *Torkel Opsahl lecture*, University of Oslo, 28 November 2014.

[57]   Ibid.

[58]   Decision 542. Document 8:91 S (2012–2013) – suggestions from the members of Parliament Siv Jensen, Morten Ørsal Johansen, Per Sandberg, Gjermund Hagesæter and Åge Starheim to not allow the use of burqas, niqabs or other all-encompassing solid garments in public spaces – is not endorsed. [Vedtak 542. Dokument 8:91 S (2012–2013) – representantforslag fra stortingsrepresentantene Siv Jensen, Morten Ørsal Johansen, Per Sandberg, Gjermund Hagesæter og Åge Starheim om ikke å tillate bruk a, niqab eller andre heldekkende plagg i det offentlige rom – bifalles ikke].

person you are talking to. Openness and eye contact in communication is considered to be an important moral value. That means you do not have anything to hide'.[59] Here one could also add that many citizens might feel that using face-covering could be an obstacle to social activities and dialogue.

We conclude that there are arguments for the right to wear a face covering and, additionally, arguments in favor of developing rules on the practice of face-covering; to show the face in certain situations is necessary to ensure public safety. On the other hand, a ban is a clear interference in the individual's religious practice. A preferable approach might be to work to change the attitudes and values that cause some women to want to cover their faces. The conclusion in the judgment of the case S.A.S. v. France was that 'A general policy or measure that had disproportionately prejudicial effects on a particular group might be considered discriminatory even where it was not specifically aimed at that group and there was no discriminatory intent'.[60]

> The Court reiterates that 'This is only the case . . . if such policy or measure has no "objective and reasonable" justification, that is, if it does not pursue a "legitimate aim" or if there is not a "reasonable relationship of proportionality" between the means employed and the aim sought to be realised (ibid., § 196). In the present case, while it may be considered that the ban imposed by the Law of 11 October 2010 has specific negative effects on the situation of Muslim women who, for religious reasons, wish to wear the full-face veil in public, this measure has an objective and reasonable justification for the reasons indicated previously'.[61]

Although the European Court of Human Rights concluded that no breach of the Convention took place, the Court sends important signals to other member states: a ban is not necessarily the best way to go.[62] Alia Al-Saji argues that the Western representations of veiled Muslim women are not simply about Muslim women themselves. Rather than representing Muslim women, these images fulfill a different function: they provide the foil or negative mirror in which Western constructions of identity and gender can be positively reflected.[63]

---

[59] Lena Larsen, 'Ansiktsslør er problematisk' [Face Veils are problematic], *Aftenposten*, 24 June 2006.

[60] *S.A.S. v. France* (n 3) 161.

[61] Ibid.

[62] Ibid. 149.

[63] Alia Al-Saji, 'The Racialization of Muslim Veils: A Philosophical Analysis' (2010) 36(8) Philosophy and Social Criticism 875.

THE PRIMACY OF DIALOGUE

How should this case be interpreted concluded from the perspective of hermeneutics? If we return to Gadamer and the hermeneutical principles, we see that the fundamental insights of hermeneutics are about achieving understanding through a dialogical approach to a text or a case: 'the hermeneutic phenomenon too implies the primacy of dialogue and the structure of question and answer. That a historical text is made the object of interpretation means that it puts a question to the interpreter'.[64] In other words, this means that understanding a case involves knowing not only what questions are to be posed by the person who will understand, but also what questions and dilemmas the case itself puts forward to be solved. One could say that every case deserves to be listened to. What you hear when you listen to a case depends not only on your pre-knowledge, your horizon of understanding, but also your own engagements in the case, including your own biography.

Therefore, to understand a case, according to Gadamer, primarily involves knowing these questions, which again requires placing oneself within the hermeneutical horizon of understanding. To understand a case is thus to interpret it in response to some underlying issues, and how these in turn are linked with other questions. However, this 'horizon of the question' shows that there may be other possible answers with regard to what is right, well founded or applicable to the law. In this vein, an essential question would be: does the hermeneutic method therefore lead to a form of relativism? Is it the case that we can only arrive at a suitable tool for interpretation of the matter, but never reach the actual substance of a case and be able to decide or make a true judgment?

There is always something that constitutes facts, for example, that a law exists, that historical events have happened, and that statements have been recorded. Yet to make a direct inference from what *is* to what *ought to be* is not legitimate. In other words, none of these facts necessarily lead to a normatively based judgment. The various facts can be clarified as far as possible, be collected and be prepared as objectively and comprehensibly as possible so as to draw the most qualified normative conclusion or decision. The judgment itself it not to be seen, heard or sensed *in* the facts available as a direct result of what is presented. The jurist has to 'take account of the change in circumstances and hence define afresh the normative function of the law', as Gadamer writes.[65]

---

[64]   Gadamer (n 1, 2003) 369.
[65]   Gadamer (n 1, 2003) 327.

To come to a decision therefore requires prudence, self-assessment, empathy and so on. However, if the individual defense counsel or judge goes too far in immersing her/himself in the personal side of the case, the court and the moral order risk losing their legitimacy. It is also important to emphasize that the facts are constructed, for example, that what is said by a witness can be repeated so often that it eventually becomes a 'truth' or is perceived as a fact.

Hermeneutics has been described as the art of avoiding misperception.[66] However, we might rather say that, when successfully attempting to understand a 'foreign' text or action, we always understand that text or action differently. As we have mentioned earlier, it is not primarily our decisions that shape us, but our prejudices.[67]

A HERMENEUTICS-INSPIRED MODEL

Based on the case of the French burqa ban, we shall draw some concluding remarks on how we can use hermeneutics as a model to obtain an overview, analyze a case and develop arguments to help the individual interpreter. These can be characterized as 'hermeneutical phases', which is not very different from the methods used in the field of law. The identification, interpretation and exposition of concepts are central to this process.

(1)   First, try to get an overview of all the facts that are relevant in this particular case and the fundamental values that are involved. Listen to the questions that are raised in the case as well as in yourself. How could the different questions be interpreted? Would it be possible to rank the values?

(2)   Secondly, ascertain the right laws and apply them to the case. Lawyers look for statutory meaning in light of the case. The lawyer should become familiar with the act's original meaning.

(3)   Thirdly, try to understand what kind of climate the law was originally formulated within and what signifies its later development.

(4)   Fourthly, try to situate the case both in the present context and in our historical situation, and ask yourself the following questions: why is this case relevant now, why does this matter right now? What is at stake? What characterizes the different dilemmas and interests that are at stake?

---

[66]   Gadamer (n 1, 1977) 7.
[67]   Ibid. 9.

(5)   Finally, on the basis of the mapping of facts, values involved, laws, the historical as well as the present contexts, your interpretations of the different elements of and reflections on the overall mapping, you may have a basis for developing good arguments and drawing some cautious preliminary conclusions. Then you have to discuss these and test your interpretations and arguments within the relevant context. A hermeneutical conscious community may serve as a reference and measurement point for legal arguments in the field of human rights.

CONCLUDING REMARKS

How can we argue for the universality of human rights, while at the same time accepting that the world consists of cultural and religious variations that must also be respected? What are the trade-offs and how should we deal with them? In what way could the methods of hermeneutics help to approach and clarify these topics?

When we ask questions such as 'How can human rights be justified globally?' we are involving several discourses. The same applies when we ask: 'How can we understand and incorporate cultural diversity and the right to autonomy in relation to international human rights?' According to Gadamer, legal hermeneutics has been exemplary for the significance of hermeneutics in the humanities, which was concerned with literary and historical texts. According to Peter Kemp, legal hermeneutics does not aim at understanding texts as such but at providing legal aid as means of the shortcomings of the dogmatic legal system.[68] The relationship between listening and being critical characterizes the hermeneutical method. To engage in hermeneutics is not only to clarify how we debate and promote, interpret, protect, fulfill and practice human rights differently in different cultures, religions, historical time and place, but it expresses a deeper insight as well. To do research on the method of interpretation and understanding elucidates the very core of human rights principles: how to live together while protecting the right to differ on political, religious and social issues. Universal does not mean accepted or honored everywhere – or eternally valid – but applicable to all humans. The value of hermeneutics lies primarily in that it offers a set of concepts that clarify linguistic misunderstandings, and as an extension of this, we can also discover ourselves. As

---

[68]   Peter Kemp, 'Tolkningsbakgrunn' [The Background for Interpretation] in Erik Boe (ed.), *Veien til rettsstudiet* [The Path to the Study of Law] (Tano-Aschehoug 1996).

Jan Fridthjof Bernt has argued, the opinion on what is current law is ultimately a hermeneutical process of cognition in which jurisprudence has a crucial importance and responsibility to balance between the preservative, the system bias or tradition, and the critical, dynamic aspect.[69] According to Bernt, a purely descriptive approach to legal phenomena is of limited interest to the users of the discipline – the lawyers themselves – and will not be able to give a complete answer to questions about current or future application of the law.[70] The lawyers in their various professional roles are always inside the power apparatus that justice constitutes, and the task is to expound or interpret these standards and have a conversation about what is the right understanding of the legal rule. According to Bernt, legal methodology is a set of meta-norms that define how we can gain knowledge, justify, discuss and, possibly, verify claims about interpretation of legal questions. The basic questions that legal methodology should address are: how do we determine disagreement on interpretations of jurisprudence; and how do we gain knowledge about the norms that determine jurisprudence? Different narratives may lead to different conclusions.[71]

Thus, Gadamer and the hermeneutic tradition may serve as a basis for a critical and socially engaged approach to human rights. In this way the hermeneutical inspired perspectives may contribute in regarding the study of human rights as a discursive arena or interpretation community for a persistent and critical review of established and new allegations. To interpret something is therefore not only an external conception, but is rather to engage in the conditions of that which is being interpreted.

---

[69]   Jan Fritjof Bernt, 'Det juridiske fortolkningsfellesskap som referanseramme for avgjørelse i juridiske tvilsspørsmål' [Using the Legal Interpretation Community as a Framework in Legal Decisions Concerning Doubt], in H. Aune, O.K. Fauchald, K. Lilleholt and D. Micahelsen (eds), *Arbeid og rett. Festskrift til Henning Jakhellns 70-årsdag* 31–43 (Cappelen forlag 2009).

[70]   Ibid. 33.

[71]   Hans Petter Graver, *Judges Against the Law* (Springer 2015); Hans Petter Graver, *Rett, retorikk og juridisk argumentasjon – Keiserens garderobe og andre essays* [Law, Rhetoric and Legal Argumentation – The Emperor's Wardrobe and Other Essays] (Universitetsforlaget 2010).

5. Economics and human rights
Edward Anderson

INTRODUCTION

There is undoubtedly much skepticism, and relatively little dialogue, between economists and human rights scholars. Economists have often viewed human rights, particularly economic and social rights, as vague and impractical.[1] Human rights scholars often view economists as being preoccupied with economic growth and other aggregate social outcomes, without due consideration for the rights of vulnerable groups. At the heart lies a perceived fundamental conceptual difference between the consequentialist approach of economics and the deontological approach of human rights.[2] Economists are concerned with the maximization of social welfare, measured by indicators such as gross domestic product; human rights play, at best, an instrumental role. Human rights scholars are concerned with respect for human dignity and the moral restrictions and obligations which follow from this, irrespective of the consequences.

Yet the skepticism and the fundamental differences can be overstated. Human rights scholars do recognize the resource constraints to the fulfillment of many human rights and have made considerable efforts in trying to take this into account.[3] At the same time, economics is a broad field and there are many within the discipline who share the concerns expressed

---

[1]   Varun Gauri, 'Social Rights and Economics: Claims to Health Care and Education in Developing Countries' (2004) 32 World Development 465.

[2]   Ibid.; Dan Seymour and Jonathan Pincus, 'Human Rights and Economics: The Conceptual Basis for their Complementarity' (2008) 26 Development Policy Review 387; and Sanjay Reddy, 'Economics and Human Rights: A Non-conversation' (2011) 12 Journal of Human Development and Capabilities 63.

[3]   See e.g. Robert E. Robertson, 'Measuring State Compliance with the Obligation to Devote the "Maximum Available Resources" to Realizing Economic, Social, and Cultural Rights' (1994) 16 Human Rights Quarterly 693; Scott Leckie, 'Another Step Towards Indivisibility: Identifying the Key Features of Violations of Economic, Social and Cultural Rights' (1998) 20 Human Rights Quarterly 81; and Stephen Holmes and Cass R Sunstein, *The Cost of Rights: Why Liberty Depends on Taxes* (WW Norton 1999); Eitan Felner, 'Closing the "Escape Hatch": A Toolkit to Monitor the Progressive Realization of Economic, Social, and Cultural Rights' (2009) 1 Journal of Human Rights Practice 402.

by human rights scholars. A number of recent papers have shown how and why the two disciplines can work together,[4] and there are several examples of novel, important collaborative work between economists and human rights scholars, the recent work by Sakiko Fukuda-Parr, Terra Lawson-Remer and Susan Randolph being one prominent example.[5]

This chapter is an attempt to review and add to the literature highlighting the differences – but also the complementarities between – the disciplines of economics and human rights. It focuses, in particular, on methodological issues and gives examples of areas in which methods used in human rights research overlap quite closely with research methods used in economics and where similar challenges are faced. The chapter is divided into three main sections. The second section begins by discussing concepts and particularly the ways in which the traditional 'social welfare' approach on which economists tend to rely for making normative judgments can be extended to incorporate human rights. The next section then turns to issues of measurement. Here there are clear overlaps and complementarities between the two disciplines, both in terms of the measurement of human rights outcomes and in the assessment of human rights performance. The fourth section moves on to discuss methods of causal analysis, particularly multiple regression analysis, and again identifies a number of areas in which similar approaches are being used by both disciplines and where similar challenges are faced. The final section concludes.

CONCEPTS

The Limitations of Neoclassical Welfare Economics

As pointed out by Dan Seymour and Jonathan Pincus, neo-classical welfare economics remains the dominant normative approach used by

---

[4] See e.g. Gauri (n 1); Seymour and Pincus (n 2); Radhika Balakrishnan, Diane Elson and Raj Patel, 'Rethinking Macro Economic Strategies from a Human Rights Perspective' (2010) 53 Development 27; Reddy 2011 (n 2); and Nicolaj Sonderbye and others, *Human Rights and Economics: Tensions and Positive Relationships* (The Nordic Trust Fund and the World Bank 2012).

[5] Sakiko Fukuda-Parr, Terra Lawson-Remer and Susan Randolph, 'An Index of Economic and Social Rights Fulfilment: Concept and Methodology' (2009) 8 Journal of Human Rights 195; Susan Randolph, Sakiko Fukuda-Parr and Terra Lawson-Remer, 'Economic and Social Rights Fulfillment Index: Country Scores and Rankings' (2010) 9 Journal of Human Rights 230; and Sakiko Fukuda-Parr, Terra Lawson-Remer and Susan Randolph, *Fulfilling Social and Economic Rights* (OUP 2015).

economists to assess public policies.[6] It has its roots in utilitarianism, and the idea that actions should be judged on the basis of the sum total of utility or happiness created. Neo-classical welfare economics departs from strict utilitarianism however, because it assumes that there is no objective way of making inter-personal comparisons of utility; it is not possible therefore to calculate the sum total of utility.[7] Instead, policies can only be judged by two possible criteria. The first is the Pareto criterion, according to which a policy can be recommended if it makes at least one person better off, without making any one else worse off. The second is the Hicks–Kaldor criterion, according to which a policy can be recommended if it is possible for the winners to compensate the losers, even if this compensation does not occur in practice.[8]

Of these two ways of justifying public policy decisions, the Pareto criterion is considered the stronger, but it is limited in terms of applicability: most policies involve winners and losers. The Hicks–Kaldor criterion is therefore more widely relied on and forms the basis for the standard approach to cost–benefit analysis.[9] The Hicks–Kaldor criterion has been widely challenged however, both from within and from outside the economics profession, as 'either unconvincing or redundant'.[10] The idea that negative impacts of policies on some individuals can be justified on the basis of hypothetical compensation, which may not be forthcoming, is also pretty much 'anathema' to a human rights-based approach.[11]

Within welfare economics, the alternative to relying on the Pareto or Hicks–Kaldor criterion is the social welfare approach. This approach involves the use of a social welfare function, which states that the welfare of society as a whole depends on (and only on) the welfare or utility of each individual member. The social welfare function is written in algebraic terms as:

$$SW = f(w_1, w_2, \ldots, w_n)$$

where SW stands for social welfare, $w_1, w_2, \ldots, w_n$ stand for the welfare levels of each individual in society, and $f(\ldots)$ stands for 'is a function of'.

---

[6]   Seymour and Pincus (n 2).

[7]   Amartya Sen, *On Ethics and Economics* (Blackwell 1988).

[8]   See e.g. Anthony E. Boardman and others, *Cost Benefit Analysis: Concepts and Practice* (4th edn, Pearson Education 2010); Sen (n 7); Amartya Sen, 'The Discipline of Cost Benefit Analysis' (2000) 29 The Journal of Legal Studies 931.

[9]   The standard approach to cost–benefit analysis states that a government policy or project is worth doing if the total benefits exceed the total costs, and where benefits and costs are measured in terms of individuals' willingness to incur the benefits or avoid the costs; see Boardman and others (n 8).

[10]   Sen (n 7) 13.

[11]   Sonderbye and others (n 4) 8.

The precise form of the social welfare function is left indeterminate, but it can accommodate utilitarianism, where social welfare is the sum total of each individual's welfare, as well as 'Rawlsian' views, according to which the welfare of society is equal to the welfare of the worst off individual.[12] However, once the form of the social welfare function has been agreed on, it is possible to judge public policies according to whether they raise or lower overall social welfare.

The social welfare approach is often criticized for arbitrary normative judgements, and economists do not agree on what form the social welfare function should take.[13] Nevertheless, it does at least allow for more explicit treatment of distributional issues. The form of social welfare function may itself place a value on equality, in the distribution of individual utilities. It may also value greater equality in the distribution of individual incomes, on the grounds that this leads to a larger total sum of social welfare, given diminishing marginal utility of income. Nevertheless, the social welfare approach is still based on the idea that policies should be judged only by their impact on individuals' welfare and not on any other considerations – such as their rights, freedoms or agency.[14] This clearly represents a fundamental difference from a human rights-based approach.

For economists who are prepared to go beyond the social welfare framework, and adopt a broader normative framework which incorporates human rights, a natural first question to ask is whether human rights should be viewed as goals or as constraints. More specifically, do human rights represent constraints on the actions that a government may take in order to raise social welfare? Or are they goals that a government is required to pursue, in addition to or perhaps instead of higher social welfare? Debate around this question goes back at least four decades, and has continued to attract comment in more recent years.

---

[12]   See e.g. Richard W. Tresch, *Public Finance: A Normative Theory* (Academic Press 2002) 81. The Pareto principle is incorporated into the social welfare function by the additional assumption or restriction that the marginal social welfare weight for each individual, defined as the partial derivative of social welfare with respect to each individual's welfare, is greater than zero.

[13]   See e.g. Prasanta K. Pattanaik, 'Social Welfare Function' in Steven N. Durlauf and Lawrence E. Blume (eds), *The New Palgrave Dictionary of Economics* (Palgrave Macmillan 2008).

[14]   See e.g. Amartya Sen, 'Utilitarianism and Welfarism' (1979) 76 Journal of Philosophy 463; Amartya Sen, 'Consequential Evaluation and Practical Reason' (2000) 97 Journal of Philosophy 477; and Amartya Sen, *The Idea of Justice* (Allen Lane 2009).

Human Rights: Goals or Constraints?

In 1974, Robert Nozick argued in favor of viewing rights as moral 'side constraints' that must not be violated. In particular: '[t]he rights of others determine the constraints upon your actions ... The side-constraint view forbids you to violate these moral constraints in the pursuit of your goals'.[15] His argument was put forward on the grounds of the inviolability of the individual: there are certain ways in which persons may not treat others, and these must be prohibited, not simply kept to a minimum. Applied to the realm of public policy, a side constraint can be defined as a restriction on the permissible range of one of the government's policy instruments.[16]

A slightly different approach is to view rights not as side constraints but as 'outcome constraints', i.e. outcomes which must be attained by all individuals, irrespective of what this might imply for overall social welfare. Martha Nussbaum, for example, has argued in favor of viewing human rights as basic capabilities which 'should be secured to people no matter what else we pursue'.[17] Applied to a public policy framework, an outcome constraint differs from a side constraint in that it applies to individual outcomes, over which the government has some control, rather than the government's policy instruments, over which it has full control.

The alternative to viewing human rights as constraints is to view them as goals that a government is required to pursue. This perspective has been set out most clearly by Amartya Sen, who introduced the concept of a 'goal rights system': an approach in which the 'fulfilment and non-realization of rights are included among the goals, incorporated in the evaluation of states of affairs, and then applied to the choice of actions through consequential links'.[18] Applied to public policy, the basic requirement is that the realization of human rights is included among the government's objectives, alongside social welfare, and therefore among the set of criteria according to which policy options are evaluated. It is not necessary that

---

[15]   Robert Nozick, *Anarchy, State and Utopia* (Basic Books 1974) 29.

[16]   See e.g. Jean Drèze and Nicholas Stern, 'Chapter 14: The Theory of Cost–Benefit Analysis', *Handbook of Public Economics*, Vol. 2 (Elsevier 1987) 912. These authors define side constraints as 'any further limitations on the selection of [policy instruments] by the planner – e.g. permissible tax rates may be restricted.' Side constraints can arise for various reasons, of which human rights are only one.

[17]   Martha Nussbaum, 'Capabilities and Human Rights' in Pablo De Greiff and Ciaran Cronin (eds), *Global Justice and Transational Politics: Essays on the Moral and Political Challenges of Globalization* (MIT Press 2002) 143.

[18]   Amartya Sen, 'Rights and Agency' (1982) 11 Philosophy and Public Affairs 3, 15.

non-right objectives be ruled out, nor that rights be considered higher priority than non-right objectives; the 'crucial issue is the inclusion of fulfilment and non-fulfilment of rights rather than the exclusion of non-right considerations'.[19]

There are, however, other versions of the 'rights as goals' perspective which go beyond this basic requirement. One possible extension views human rights not simply as goals but as 'high priority' goals.[20] The term 'high priority' can be interpreted in different ways, but if interpreted in a lexicographic sense, the implication is that human rights always prevail over non-right considerations, in the event of a conflict. This has much in common with the view, advocated by Ronald Dworkin, that rights are best viewed as 'trumps'.[21] In Dworkin's terminology, a right which is a goal but not a high-priority goal is classified as an 'abstract' right. Such a right would only become 'concrete' if it were clearly specified as being higher priority than at least some (not necessarily all) other non-right considerations, in at least some circumstances.[22] Another possible extension rules out trade-offs among human rights. The reluctance of human rights theorists to allow trade-offs between different rights is stressed by Dan Seymour and Jonathan Pincus and has been linked to the principles of inviolability and non-retrogression.[23] Another possible extension requires that basic or essential aspects of human rights be given priority over other government objectives, including the achievement of non-essential aspects of those rights. This has been referred to as a government's 'minimum core obligation'.[24]

---

[19] Sen (n 18) 15.

[20] See e.g. Gauri (n 1); see also James W. Nickel, *Making Sense of Human Rights* (2nd edn, Blackwell 2007).

[21] Ronald Dworkin, *Taking Rights Seriously* (Harvard University Press 1977).

[22] Ibid. 93. In particular, 'an abstract right is a general political aim the statement of which does not indicate how the general aim is to be weighted or compromised in particular circumstances against the other political aims'.

[23] Seymour and Pincus (n 2). See e.g. Arjun Sengupta, 'The Human Right to Development' (2004) 32 Oxford Development Studies 179, ff.14: 'th[e] principle of inviolability . . . rules out the possibility of a trade-off between rights, even when some drop in the realization of a right might be compensated by an increase in the realization of another right'. The idea of 'non-retrogression' is generally taken to imply that a government may not take deliberate steps which cause a decline in the level of realization in a human right; see e.g. UN Committee on Economic, Social and Cultural Rights, General Comment No. 3: The Nature of States Parties' Obligations (Article 2, Para. 1, of the Covenant), 14 December 1990, E/1991/23, para 10.

[24] Katharine Young, 'The Minimum Core of Economic and Social Rights: A Concept in Search of Content' (2008) 33 Yale Journal of International Law 113.

Which of these two ways of viewing rights is more appropriate, namely, as goals or constraints? Many economists might be concerned about viewing rights as outcome constraints, on the grounds that such constraints may not be feasible, owing to resource constraints. For example, Varun Gauri has argued that '[g]overnments in developing countries cannot provide or assure adequate levels of health care and education'.[25] Similarly, Wiktor Osiatynski writes that '[e]ven when social and economic rights are recognized as human rights, there is no doubt about their character as aspirations'.[26] For this reason, economists would appear more inclined to the rights as goals view. By contrast, many human rights scholars doubt whether human rights viewed as goals really can be described as human rights at all. For example, James Nickel has argued that 'rights-like goals' are not 'rights in a strict sense', since they lack the mandatory character of fully fledged claim rights, and do not directly imply actions or responsibilities for particular persons or agencies.[27] It is arguably for similar reasons that authors such as Maurice Cranston have considered economic and social rights to fall into a different 'logical category', on the grounds of their goal-oriented, aspirational nature.[28]

In many situations, however, the difference between viewing a right as a

---

[25]   Gauri (n 1) 468.

[26]   Wiktor Osiatynski, 'Needs-based Approach to Social and Economic Rights' in Shareen Hertel and Lanse Minkler (eds), *Economic Rights: Conceptual, Measurement and Policy Issues* (CUP 2007) 58. Note that some arguments made by economists relating to the 'problem' of economic and social rights refer not to their feasibility but to their potential adverse consequences. For example, Varun Gauri argues that guaranteeing anti-retroviral therapy for HIV patients might, at least to some extent, 'encourage risky behaviour and reduce the effectiveness of prevention efforts'; see Gauri (n 1) 27. Such arguments are of course relevant, but they are of a different nature, relating to the potential trade-offs between economic and social rights and other social goals, rather than the more basic question of whether the full realization of those rights is feasible. Moreover, there are likely to be many beneficial consequences of economic and social rights fulfillment which may offset the negatives. Thus Gauri also recognizes that declaring anti-retroviral therapy to be a right to be guaranteed to all may generate moral pressure to lower the prices charged by manufacturers of the treatment; see Gauri (n 1) 27. See also Andy McKay and Polly Vizard, *Rights and Economic Growth: Inevitable Conflict or Common Ground?* (Overseas Development Institute 2005); Kaushik Basu, 'Human Rights as Instruments of Emancipation and Economic Development' in Shareen Hertel and Lanse Minkler (eds), *Economic Rights: Conceptual, Measurement and Policy Issues* (CUP 2007).

[27]   James W. Nickel, 'Goals and Rights: Working Together?' in Malcolm Langford, Andy Sumner and Alicia Ely Yamin (eds), *The Millennium Development Goals and Human Rights: Past Present and Future* (CUP 2015) 40, 44–45.

[28]   Maurice Cranston, *What are Human Rights* (Bodley Head 1973).

constraint and viewing it as a goal may be quite small. The overall effect in each case is to restrict the range of permissible actions that a government may take, one of the key features of a human rights-based approach.[29] If this is true, the case for placing rights-like goals into a different logical category is less clear. Yet there is a key difference between viewing rights as a constraint as opposed to a goal. In the latter case, there is no longer a direct link between level of realization of a right and the extent to which the right is being respected or violated. How can we establish whether a government is making sufficient efforts to realize the human rights of individuals, alongside other objectives? More generally, how can we establish whether it is giving sufficient priority to human rights, alongside other objectives such as social welfare? This relates to the issue of measurement, to which we now turn.

MEASUREMENT

There is now a very large and expanding literature on the measurement of human rights.[30] Here we highlight two measurement issues, which have clear overlaps with the economics discipline and clear potential for collaboration between economists and human rights scholars. The first is the measurement of the realization of economic and social rights; the second is the assessment of government performance in realizing economic and social rights, subject to available resources.

The Realization of Economic and Social Rights

Many of the indicators used by development economists to measure and compare levels of human development around the world can be used, and have been used, as proxies for the extent of realization or 'enjoyment' of human rights, particularly economic and social rights.[31] For example, the

---

[29] Radhika Balakrishnan and Diane Elson, 'Auditing Economic Policy in the Light of Obligations on Economic and Social Rights' (2008) 5 Essex Human Rights Review 1; and Reddy (n 2).

[30] See e.g. Todd Landman, 'Measuring Human Rights: Principle, Practice and Policy' (2004) 26 Human Rights Quarterly 906; and Todd Landman and Edzia Carvalho, *Measuring Human Rights* (Routledge 2010).

[31] Landman (n 30); and Kate Raworth, 'Measuring Human Rights' (2006) 15 Ethics and International Affairs 111. The level of realization of a right is typically defined as the extent to which rights-holders – in this case, individuals – have the object of that right. This is also referred to as the level of enjoyment of a right.

proportion of school-aged children enrolled in school is one possible proxy indicator of the right to education; a situation in which less than 100% of children are enrolled in school indicates that the right to education is not being realized.[32] Other examples include daily per capita calorie supply as a proxy measure of the right to food and infant mortality rates as a proxy for the right to health.[33] Most recently, Sakiko Fukuda-Parr, Terra Lawson-Remer and Susan Randolph have identified 13 key indicators of the human rights to education, health, food, housing and work.[34]

This overlap between indicators used by development economists and human rights scholars means that there is clear potential for on-going synergies in the search for better indicators – of human development on the one hand and human rights enjoyment on the other. For example, it is widely recognized that the primary school enrolment rate fails to capture what children actually learn in school. Indicators that capture educational attainments, such as the primary school completion rate, the youth literacy rate or average test scores should be used in their place wherever possible.

The overlap is not perfect however, and there are likely to be some differences between indicators of human development and indicators of human rights enjoyment. For example, human rights scholars may place greater emphasis on indicators that reflect the proportion of the population achieving a particular threshold, such as the primary school completion rate, or the proportion of households with access to 'improved' sources of water and sanitation, rather than indicators reflecting average well-being, such as gross domestic product per capita and life expectancy, often favored by development economists.[35] More importantly, measures of the enjoyment of human rights constitute just one part of human rights measurement: what Kate Raworth calls the 'enjoyment' approach.[36] The other part is what Raworth calls the 'obligations approach': the measurement and assessment of whether governments and other duty-holders are meeting their obligations to respect and promote human rights.[37]

Here the terms enjoyment and realization are used interchangeably; no distinction is made between them.

[32] Raworth (n 31).

[33] Landman (n 30).

[34] Fukuda-Parr, Lawson-Remer and Randolph 2009, 2015 (n 5); and Randolph, Fukuda-Parr and Remer (n 5).

[35] Fukuda-Parr, Lawson-Remer and Randolph 2015 (n 5) 70.

[36] Raworth (n 31) 116.

[37] Ibid.

Human Rights Performance Subject to Available Resources

It is widely accepted that the promotion of many human rights – particularly economic and social rights, but also many civil and political rights – requires the use of scarce resources. This is recognized in article 2(1) of the International Covenant on Economic, Social and Cultural Rights (ICESCR),[38] according to which governments have an obligation to ensure the progressive realization of economic and social rights, to the maximum of their available resources.[39] As has been well documented, monitoring compliance with this obligation poses a number of challenges.[40] In particular, while we might be able to measure the level of realization of an economic or social right, and the increase in the realization of a right over time, how are we to determine whether these represent what a state party is able to achieve, given its available resources?

The main approach to this challenge proposed in the literature involves the use of benchmarks. In this context, a benchmark is simply the level of a rights indicator that a state party is considered able to achieve, given its available resources. By comparing the benchmark with the actual level of the indicator, it is possible to assess whether the state party is using its maximum available resources.

One example of this sort of approach is the 'IBSA' procedure, which stands for indicators, benchmarks, scoping and assessment.[41] In this approach, the benchmarks are levels of economic and social rights indicators considered achievable by the end of a five-year period, and are determined through a process of dialogue between the state party and the UN

---

[38] International Covenant on Economic, Social and Cultural Rights (adopted 16 December 1966 entered into force 3 January 1976) UNTS Vol. 993, p. 3.

[39] The precise obligation on each state party is 'to take steps individually and through international assistance and co-operation, especially economic and technical, to the maximum of its available resources, with a view to achieving progressively the full realization of the rights recognized in the present Covenant' (article 2(1), ICESCR, n 38). See Philip Alston and Gerard Quinn, 'The Nature and Scope of States Parties' Obligations under the International Covenant on Economic, Social and Cultural Rights' (1987) 9 Human Rights Quarterly 156.

[40] See e.g. Robertson (n 3); Leckie (n 3); Felner (n 3); and Edward Anderson and Marta Foresti, 'Assessing Compliance: the Challenges for Economic and Social Rights' (2009) 1 Journal of Human Rights Practice 469.

[41] Paul Hunt, 'State Obligations, Indicators, Benchmarks and the Right to Education' (1998) 4 Human Rights Law and Practice; Eibe Riedel, 'New Bearings to the State Reporting Procedure: Practical Ways to Operationalize Economic, Social and Cultural Rights – the Example of the Right to Health' in Sabine Schorlemer (ed.), *Praxishandbuch UNO: Die Vereinten Nationen im Lichte globaler Herausforderungen* (Springer 2003).

Committee for Economic, Social and Cultural Rights. If actual levels of the relevant indicators turn out to be below the benchmarks, and this is not considered to be the result of factors outside the state party's control, the state party may be criticized for not adequately complying with article 2(1).

More recently, development economists and human rights specialists have been using statistical analysis to calculate economic and social rights benchmarks. One example is provided by David Cingranelli and David Richards.[42] These authors use a country's physical quality of life (PQLI) score as a proxy for the level of realization of economic and social rights, and a country's gross domestic product (GDP) per capita as a proxy for its available resources.[43] They then measure the government's effort in realizing economic and social rights as the difference between the actual level of the PQLI index and the predicted level of the index, given the country's GDP per capita.

The approach is shown graphically in Figure 5.1. Two countries are shown, Tanzania and South Africa. In 2000, the actual level of the PQLI index in Tanzania was above the level predicted by its level of GDP per capita (see Figure 5.1). The country therefore had a positive score for government effort for that year. In contrast, the level of the PQLI index in South Africa was below the predicted level; the country therefore had a negative score for government effort in that year (see again Figure 5.1). Figures for other countries, calculated in exactly the same way, can be used to provide a ranking of all governments in the world by their effort to promote economic and social rights in any one particular year.

Another version of this approach has been provided by Sakiko Fukuda-Parr, Terra Lawson-Remer, and Susan Randolph.[44] These authors use statistical analysis to calculate an index of economic and social rights fulfillment, based on the concept of an 'achievement possibilities frontier' (APF). The APF is designed to reflect the best a country can do in terms of the fulfillment of economic and social rights, at any given level of resource availability. It is constructed by producing a scatter plot between an

---

[42]   David Cingranelli and David Richards, 'Measuring Government Effort to Respect Economic and Social Human Rights: A Peer Benchmark' in Shareen Hertel and Lanse Minkler (eds), *Economic Rights: Conceptual, Measurement and Policy Issues* (CUP 2007).

[43]   The PQLI is a composite of three indicators: the infant mortality rate, life expectancy at age one, and the adult literacy rate. GDP is the most common measure of economic output. More specifically, it is market value of all the final goods and services produced within a country's borders within a given period of time (typically a year). GDP per capita is GDP divided by population.

[44]   Fukuda-Parr, Lawson-Remer and Randolph 2009, 2015 (n 5); and Randolph, Fukuda-Parr and Remer (n 5).

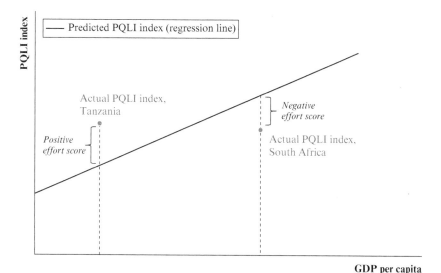

Source: Based on results in Cingranelli and Richards (2007) (see n 42), Table 10.1.

Figure 5.1   Measuring government effort to realize economic and social rights

indicator of the enjoyment of an economic and social right and GDP per capita, then identifying the observations on the outer edge of this plot, and finally using econometric techniques to fit a curve that runs through these outer observations.[45] A country's level of fulfillment of that right is then equal to the actual level of enjoyment as a percentage of the maximum achievable level, as indicated by the APF. This is shown in Figure 5.2. The weighted average level of fulfilment across all economic and social rights gives a country's overall SERF index.

The SERF index provides a quantitative measure of the fulfillment of economic and social rights which is comparable across countries with different levels of available resources.[46] The results of the analysis suggest that the enjoyment of economic and social rights remains a lot lower than could be achieved.

However, there are a number of challenges with this sort of approach. Measuring the enjoyment of economic and social rights is clearly difficult,

---

[45]   Fukuda-Parr, Lawson-Remer and Randolph 2015 (n 5) 43.
[46]   Fukuda-Parr, Lawson-Remer and Randolph 2015 (n 5) 216.

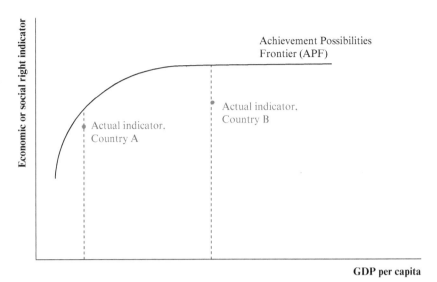

Note: In this case, Country A will have a higher level of fulfillment of the right than country B, despite a lower level of enjoyment, since the level of enjoyment is closer to the maximum achievable level, as indicated by the APF.

Source: Based on Fukuda-Parr, Lawson Remer and Randolph (2015) (see n 5), Figure 3.1.

Figure 5.2   Measuring the fulfilment of economic and social rights

as has already been discussed; measuring available resources is equally, if not more, so. GDP per capita is widely used as a measure of resource availability, but this measure has certain drawbacks. For example, it ignores the amount of income that countries receive from abroad (e.g. foreign aid, remittances), which should arguably be added to any measure of available resources. It also omits income that countries pay out abroad (e.g. profits from foreign multinational corporations, payments on foreign debt), which should in theory be subtracted. A further problem is that low GDP may sometimes be at least partly caused by poor government policy, and therefore not a true reflection of what resources really could be available if appropriate policies were in place. Fukuda-Parr, Lawson-Remer and Randolph do, however, find that their results differ little when using other measures of domestic resource availability, such as gross national income per capita, or when including foreign aid. They also argue that their results do not change markedly when allowing for the effects of government policies on GDP.

Another potential problem is that the ease with which domestic resources can be translated into rights enjoyment can differ across countries, for reasons which are outside the government's control. For example, in countries with low population density, or large rural populations, the costs of providing health and education services might be higher, so that a higher level of GDP per capita is needed to attain the same level of enjoyment of the rights to health and education. Edward Anderson and Malcolm Langford also find that state capacity to realize the right to water and sanitation depends on a wide range of structural factors, rather than GDP per capita alone.[47] This suggests the need for indicators that reflect not only resource availability but also the cost or difficulty of translating resources into rights enjoyment.

Despite these challenges, it is clear that recent collaborative work of this nature between economists and human rights scholars has advanced the debate significantly, opening up a range of new issues and areas for continued collaboration. The results clearly also have important implications for human rights monitoring in practice.

CAUSAL ANALYSIS

Economists make extensive use of multiple (or 'multivariate') regression analysis to test relationships predicted by economic theory; this is the field of econometrics. Human rights scholars are also increasingly making use of such methods, and although the outcomes of interest are often very different, the methods themselves are often very similar.

As conventionally applied, multiple regression analysis starts by focusing on a particular outcome or 'dependent variable', and then identifying the factors or 'explanatory variables' which may in theory have a causal effect on that outcome. For example, if the variable of interest is the rate of growth in a country's GDP per capita, the explanatory variables would include things like investment, education, governance, political stability, openness to trade, and so on (see Figure 5.3).

Given data on each variable included in the model, regression analysis is able to calculate the quantitative effect of each explanatory variable on the dependent variable, holding all other factors constant. The analysis also indicates which effect is statistically significant – in the sense that we can be reasonably sure, at a certain level of confidence, that the effect is not simply due to chance – as well as the proportion of variation in the dependent

---

[47] Edward Anderson and Malcolm Langford, *A Distorted Metric: The MDGs and State Capacity* (University of Oslo 2013).

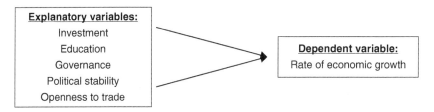

Figure 5.3   Determinants of economic growth

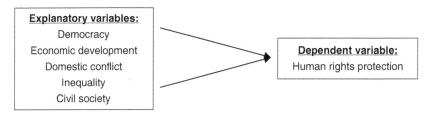

Figure 5.4   Determinants of human rights outcomes

variable which is explained by the variables included in the model (the so-called '*R*-squared').

There is a large literature using multiple regression analysis to explain variation in human rights violations around the world. Much of this focuses on civil liberties and personal integrity rights.[48] The factors considered to affect the extent of violations of these rights include the level of democracy, economic development, income inequality, ethnic fragmentation, conflict and the strength of civil society, among others (see Figure 5.4). This type of analysis is referred to as 'secondary analysis' by Todd Landman. It is argued to play an important role in testing hypotheses about human rights violations, which can in turn have important policy implications.[49]

---

[48]   See e.g. Steven C. Poe and C. Neal Tate, 'Repression of Human Rights to Personal Integrity in the 1980s: A Global Analysis' (1994) 88 The American Political Science Review 853; Steven C. Poe, C. Neal Tate and Linda Camp Keith, 'Repression of the Human Right to Personal Integrity Revisited: A Global Cross-National Study Covering the Years 1976–1993' (1999) 43 International Studies Quarterly 291; Todd Landman, *Protecting Human Rights: A Comparative Study* (Georgetown University Press 2005); and Todd Landman and Marco Larizza, 'Inequality and Human Rights: Who Controls What, When, and How' (2009) 53 International Studies Quarterly 715.

[49]   Landman (n 30) 909.

One limitation with simple regression analysis is the assumption that a change in any one explanatory variable always has the same effect on the dependent variable. It is relatively straightforward, however, to allow for the possibility of more complex relationships. For example, development economists test the 'Kuznets hypothesis' – the idea that income inequality first rises and then falls with economic development, following an inverse-U shaped pattern – through a regression that includes both GDP per capita and GDP per capita squared among the explanatory variables.[50] Non-linear relationships have also been tested in this way in the human rights literature, for example by Todd Landman and Marco Larizza with respect to the relationship between ethnic fractionalization and violations of civil and personal integrity rights.[51]

It is also straightforward to allow for the possibility that the effect of some explanatory variables may be conditional on other explanatory variables. This is done through the use of 'interaction terms': explanatory variables that are calculated by multiplying two other explanatory variables together. The coefficient on the interaction term indicates whether, and if so how, the effect of one explanatory variable differs according to the level of the other. A good example of this type of approach in the human rights field is provided by Eric Neumayer, who looks at whether the ratification of human rights treaties has any effect on the extent to which human rights are protected in practice.[52] Initial empirical work on this issue pointed towards a weak positive or even negative correlation.[53] Neumayer extends these earlier studies by testing whether the effect of ratification differs across countries, according to either the level of democracy or the strength of civil society. He does this by adding two interaction terms to the regression, one given by the product of the ratification measure with the democracy measure, and the other equal to the product of the ratification measure with the civil society measure. The results of his analysis suggest that ratification of human rights treaties can lead to better human rights protection, but only in more democratic countries, with relatively strong civil society. This shown in Figure 5.5.

---

[50] See e.g. Sudhir Anand and S.M.R. Kanbur, 'Inequality and Development: A Critique' (1993) 41 Journal of Development Economics 19; and Robert J. Barro, 'Inequality and Growth in a Panel of Countries' 5 Journal of Economic Growth 5.
[51] Landman and Larizza (n 48).
[52] Eric Neumayer, 'Do International Human Rights Treaties Improve Respect for Human Rights?' (2005) 49 Journal of Conflict Resolution 925.
[53] See e.g. Linda Camp Keith, 'The United Nations International Covenant on Civil and Political Rights: Does it Make a Difference in Human Rights Behavior?' (1999) 36 Journal of Peace Research 95; and Oona Hathaway, 'Do Human Rights Treaties Make a Difference?' (2002) 111 Yale Law Journal 1935.

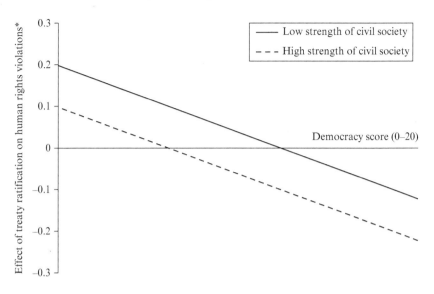

Notes: * More specifically, the effect of ratification of the Torture Convention on violations of personal integrity rights. Democracy is measured by the Polity measure, which varies between 0 and 20; the strength of civil society is measured by the number of international non-governmental organizations with domestic participation.

Source: Based on results in Neumayer (2005) (see n 52), Table 2, Column 1.

Figure 5.5   The conditional effect of ratification on human rights protection

Multiple regression analysis has also been applied to explain variations in levels of economic and social rights. A good example is the study by Shawna Sweeney, which explains cross-country variation in government respect for women's economic rights.[54] Compared with the large literature on civil, political and personal integrity rights, however, there are fewer studies in this case, partly because violations of economic and social rights are harder to measure.[55] Yet there is a very large empirical literature, carried out mainly by development economists, explaining variation in levels of human development around the world, as measured by things

---

[54]   Shawna E. Sweeney, 'Government Respect for Women's Economic Rights: A Cross-national Analysis, 1981–2003' in Shareen Hertel and Lanse Minkler (eds), *Economic Rights: Conceptual, Measurement and Policy Issues* (CUP 2007).

[55]   Landman (n 30).

like infant mortality rates, school enrolment rates, and so on.[56] Since these same indicators can be (and often have been) used as proxies for the enjoyment of economic and social rights, this literature is of clear relevance to human rights scholars. It serves to highlight the many factors that affect the enjoyment of economic and social rights, including, but by no means limited to, a country's level of GDP per capita. Work is also beginning to look at the factors that explain differences in government effort to realize economic and social rights. For example, Fukuda-Parr, Lawson Remer and Randolph find that their measure of the fulfillment of economic and social rights tends to be higher in countries with more robust democratic accountability, and in countries with legally enforceable rights guarantees in domestic law.[57]

Although widely used, multiple regression analysis is subject to a number of drawbacks. The first issue relates to the use of cross-national data. The most common measures of human rights outcomes used in cross-country research are 'standards-based' measures: typically, ordinal scales based on expert judgements, designed to provide comparable measures of the extent of human rights violations across countries and over time.[58] The use of such measures poses specific challenges for regression analysis, which must be addressed through the use of specialized techniques, such as ordered probit models.[59] A broader question is whether such measures are able to capture the complex reality on the ground. Eric Posner, for example,

---

[56]   Examples of studies in this area include Sudhir Anand and Martin Ravallion, 'Human Development in Poor Countries: On the Role of Private Incomes and Public Services' (1993) 7 The Journal of Economic Perspectives 133; Lant Pritchett and Lawrence H. Summers, 'Wealthier is Healthier' (1996) 31 The Journal of Human Resources 841; Lucia Hanmer, Robert Lensink and Howard White, 'Infant and Child Mortality in Developing Countries: Analysing the Data for Robust Determinants' (2003) 40 Journal of Development Studies 101; Richard G. Wilkinson and Kate E. Pickett, 'Income Inequality and Population Health: A Review and Explanation of the Evidence' (2006) 62 Social Science and Medicine 1768; Susanna Wolf, 'Does Aid Improve Public Service Delivery?' 143 Review of World Economics 650; Andrew Sunil Rajkumar and Vinaya Swaroop, 'Public Spending and Outcomes: Does Governance Matter?' (2008) 86 Journal of Development Economics 96; Brian Biggs and others, 'Is Wealthier always Healthier? The Impact of National Income Level, Inequality, and Poverty on Public Health in Latin America' (2010) 71 Social Science and Medicine 266; and Bernadette O'Hare and others, 'Income and Child Mortality in Developing Countries: A Systematic Review and Meta-analysis' (2013) 106 Journal of the Royal Society of Medicine 408.
[57]   Fukuda-Parr, Lawson-Remer and Randolph 2015 (n 5) 175–180.
[58]   Landman (n 30).
[59]   See e.g. Neumayer (n 52).

questions the use of a simple dichotomous 'dummy' variable to measure religious freedom, which is either 0 (restrictive) or 1 (free).[60]

Another issue relates to the distinction between correlation and causation. Although regression analysis aims to measure the causal effect of each explanatory variable on a dependent variable, there are often good reasons for expecting the direction of causality to run in both directions. For example, Todd Landman and Marco Larizza discuss how higher levels of income inequality might lead to the abuse of personal integrity rights, on the grounds that the wealthy in such cases have a stronger incentive to resort to violence.[61] They also recognize, however, that the abuse of personal integrity rights can lead to higher income inequality, if for instance the use of violence by economic elites suppresses collective action in support of redistributive policy measures. A standard multiple regression analysis cannot, by itself, distinguish between these two possibilities.

More advanced methods are available which can work around this problem. One example is the method of instrumental variables (IV) estimation. This requires the researcher to identify additional 'instrumental' variables, which are correlated with the explanatory variable of interest but are themselves clearly unaffected by the dependent variable. If such variables can be identified, they can be used to infer the true causal effect of the relevant explanatory variable. For example, in a widely cited paper, Daron Acemoglu, Simon Johnson and James Robinson use data on the mortality rates of European settlers during the late nineteenth century as an instrumental variable for the quality of institutions (e.g. secure property rights, absence of corruption) in different countries around the world today.[62] This allows the authors to estimate the causal effect of institutional quality on economic performance, controlling for the possibility of reverse causation. Landman and Larizza also used an IV approach in their analysis of the effects of income inequality on personal integrity rights.[63] However, the IV method cannot always be used, since it depends on suitable instruments being available, which is not always the case.

A further issue is omitted variable bias. This refers to a situation in which the estimated effect of an explanatory variable differs from its true

---

[60]   Eric Posner, 'Some Skeptical Comments on Beth Simmons's Mobilizing for Human Rights,' (2012) 44 New York University Journal of International Law and Politics 819.

[61]   Landman and Larizza (n 48).

[62]   Daron Acemoglu, Simon Johnson and James A. Robinson, 'The Colonial Origins of Comparative Development: An Empirical Investigation' (2001) 91 American Economic Review 1369.

[63]   Landman and Larizza (n 48).

effect, as a result of being correlated with other variables that also affect the dependent variable but which are omitted from the model. The omission may be due to oversight on the part of the researcher, or it may simply be that data are not available; whatever the reason, the result is a misleading inference. For example, Eric Posner has challenged the results of studies looking at the effect of human rights ratification on human rights outcomes, on the grounds that both variables are likely to be the result of an underlying process of democratization and domestic mobilization.[64] The correlation between the two variables may therefore be entirely spurious, with no causal effect in either direction.

Once again, there are ways of dealing with omitted variable bias. The first and most important is simply to make sure that all relevant explanatory variables are included in the regression model. Beyond this, however, options are more limited. One approach is so-called 'fixed effects' estimation, which controls for any unobserved influences on the dependent variable which are country specific and time invariant. This approach was used by Neumayer in his study of the effects of ratification on personal integrity rights, but it also has drawbacks, not least in terms of higher data requirements and also greater computational and modeling complexity.[65]

To summarize, economists and (increasingly) human rights scholars make substantial use of multiple regression analysis to investigate relationships of interest, often, although by no means exclusively, using cross-country data. Although the outcomes of interest are often quite different, in some cases they overlap quite closely: school enrolment or adult literacy rates for example, which are proxies for the realization of the human right to education, as well as of the level of human development. Both groups also face very similar methodological challenges, in terms of dealing with the limitations of national-level data, distinguishing causation from correlation, and avoiding the pitfalls of omitted variable bias.

CONCLUSION

This chapter is an attempt to review and add to the literature highlighting the differences but also the complementarities between the disciplines of economics and human rights. Despite the skepticism and relative absence of dialogue, economists and human rights scholars share much in common.

---

[64]   Posner (n 60).
[65]   Neumayer (n 52).

The second section showed that the social welfare approach on which economists tend to rely for making normative judgments can be augmented, without too much difficulty, to include the realization and fulfillment of human rights. Further discussion and debates about the precise way of doing this – that is, as goals or constraints, and what type of goal or constraint – would help clarify the implications of human rights principles for public policy decision making in practice and resolve many apparent conflicts with economic principles.

The third section then showed how development economists and human rights scholars have been working together to assess the extent to which governments are doing as much as they can to progressively realize economic and social rights, given available resources – an issue which has troubled human rights scholars for many years. Collaborative work in this area has advanced the debate forward significantly and opened up new issues and areas for continued collaboration. Finally, the fourth section showed that economists and (increasingly) human rights scholars both make substantial use of multiple regression analysis to investigate relationships of interest. Although the outcomes of interest are often quite different, in some cases they overlap quite closely: school enrolment or adult literacy rates, for example, are proxies for the realization of the human right to education, as well as of the level of human development. Both groups also face very similar methodological challenges in terms of dealing with the limitations of national-level data, distinguishing causation from correlation and avoiding the pitfalls of omitted variable bias. This also raises the potential and scope for fruitful collaboration.

REFERENCES

Acemoglu, D., S. Johnson and J.A. Robinson, 'The Colonial Origins of Comparative Development: An Empirical Investigation' (2001) 91 American Economic Review 1369

Alston, P. and G. Quinn, 'The Nature and Scope of States Parties' Obligations under the International Covenant on Economic, Social and Cultural Rights' (1987) 9 Human Rights Quarterly 156

Anand, S. and S.M.R. Kanbur, 'Inequality and Development: A Critique' (1993) 41 Journal of Development Economics 19

Anand, S. and M. Ravallion, 'Human Development in Poor Countries: On the Role of Private Incomes and Public Services' (1993) 7 The Journal of Economic Perspectives 133

Anderson, E. and M. Foresti, 'Assessing Compliance: the Challenges for Economic and Social Rights' (2009) 1 Journal of Human Rights Practice 469

Anderson, E. and M. Langford, *A Distorted Metric: The MDGs and State Capacity* (University of Oslo 2013)

Balakrishnan, R. and D. Elson, 'Auditing Economic Policy in the Light of Obligations on Economic and Social Rights' (2008) 5 Essex Human Rights Review 1

Balakrishnan, R., D. Elson and R. Patel, 'Rethinking Macro Economic Strategies from a Human Rights Perspective' (2010) 53 Development 27

Barro, R.J., 'Inequality and Growth in a Panel of Countries' 5 Journal of Economic Growth 5

Basu, K., 'Human Rights as Instruments of Emancipation and Economic Development' in S. Hertel and L. Minkler (eds), *Economic Rights: Conceptual, Measurement and Policy Issues* (CUP 2007)

Biggs, B. and others, 'Is Wealthier Always Healthier? The Impact of National Income Level, Inequality, and Poverty on Public Health in Latin America' (2010) 71 Social Science and Medicine 266

Boardman, A.E. and others, *Cost Benefit Analysis: Concepts and Practice* (4th edn, Pearson Education 2010)

Cingranelli, D. and D. Richards, 'Measuring Government Effort to Respect Economic and Social Human Rights: A Peer Benchmark' in S. Hertel and L. Minkler (eds), *Economic Rights: Conceptual, Measurement and Policy Issues* (CUP 2007)

Cranston, M., *What are Human Rights?* (Bodley Head 1973)

Drèze, J. and N. Stern, 'Chapter 14: The Theory of Cost–Benefit Analysis' in *Handbook of Public Economics*, Vol. 2 (Elsevier 1987)

Dworkin, R., *Taking Rights Seriously* (Harvard University Press 1977)

Felner, E., 'Closing the "Escape Hatch": A Toolkit to Monitor the Progressive Realization of Economic, Social, and Cultural Rights' (2009) 1 Journal of Human Rights Practice 402

Fukuda-Parr, S., T. Lawson-Remer and S. Randolph, 'An Index of Economic and Social rights Fulfilment: Concept and Methodology' (2009) 8 Journal of Human Rights 195

Fukuda-Parr, S., T. Lawson-Remer and S. Randolph, *Fulfilling Social and Economic Rights* (OUP 2015)

Gauri, V., 'Social Rights and Economics: Claims to Health Care and Education in Developing Countries' (2004) 32 World Development 465

Hanmer, L., R. Lensink and H. White, 'Infant and Child Mortality in Developing Countries: Analysing the Data for Robust Determinants' (2003) 40 Journal of Development Studies 101

Hathaway, O., 'Do Human Rights Treaties make a Difference?' (2002) 111 Yale Law Journal 1935

Holmes, S. and C.R. Sunstein, *The Cost of Rights: Why Liberty Depends on Taxes* (WW Norton 1999)

Hunt, P., 'State Obligations, Indicators, Benchmarks and the Right to Education' (1998) 4 Human Rights Law and Practice

Keith, L.C., 'The United Nations International Covenant on Civil and Political Rights: Does it Make a Difference in Human Rights Behavior?' (1999) 36 Journal of Peace Research 95

Landman, T., 'Measuring Human Rights: Principle, Practice and Policy' (2004) 26 Human Rights Quarterly 906

Landman, T., *Protecting Human Rights: A Comparative Study* (Georgetown University Press 2005)

Landman, T. and E. Carvalho, *Measuring Human Rights* (Routledge 2010)

Landman, T. and M. Larizza, 'Inequality and Human Rights: Who Controls What, When, and How' (2009) 53 International Studies Quarterly 715

Leckie, S., 'Another Step Towards Indivisibility: Identifying the Key Features of Violations of Economic, Social and Cultural Rights' (1998) 20 Human Rights Quarterly 81

McKay, A. and P. Vizard, *Rights and Economic Growth: Inevitable Conflict or Common Ground?* (Overseas Development Institute 2005)

Neumayer, E., 'Do International Human Rights Treaties Improve Respect for Human Rights?' (2005) 49 Journal of Conflict Resolution 925

Nickel, J.W., *Making Sense of Human Rights* (2nd edn, Blackwell 2007)

Nickel, J.W., 'Goals and Rights: Working Together?' in M. Langford and others (eds), *The Millennium Development Goals and Human Rights: Past Present and Future* (CUP 2015)

Nozick, R., *Anarchy, State and Utopia* (Basic Books 1974)

Nussbaum, M., 'Capabilities and Human Rights' in P. De Greiff and C. Cronin (eds), *Global Justice and Transational Politics: Essays on the Moral and Political Challenges of Globalization* (MIT Press 2002)

O'Hare, B. and others, 'Income and Child Mortality in Developing Countries: A Systematic Review and Meta-analysis' (2013) 106 Journal of the Royal Society of Medicine 408

Osiatynski, W., 'Needs-based Approach to Social and Economic Rights' in S. Hertel and L. Minkler (eds), *Economic Rights: Conceptual, Measurement and Policy Issues* (CUP 2007)

Pattanaik, P.K., 'Social Welfare Function' in S.N. Durlauf and L.E. Blume (eds), *The New Palgrave Dictionary of Economics* (Palgrave Macmillan 2008)

Poe, S.C. and C.N. Tate, 'Repression of Human Rights to Personal Integrity in the 1980s: A Global Analysis' (1994) 88 The American Political Science Review 853

Poe, S.C., C. N. Tate and L.C. Keith, 'Repression of the Human Right to Personal Integrity Revisited: A Global Cross-national Study Covering the Years 1976–1993' (1999) 43 International Studies Quarterly 291

Posner, E., 'Some Skeptical Comments on Beth Simmons's Mobilizing for Human Rights' (2012) 44 New York University Journal of International Law and Politics 819

Pritchett, L. and L.H. Summers, 'Wealthier is Healthier' (1996) 31 The Journal of Human Resources 841

Rajkumar, A.S. and V. Swaroop, 'Public Spending and Outcomes: Does Governance Matter?' (2008) 86 Journal of Development Economics 96

Randolph, S., S. Fukuda-Parr and T. Lawson-Remer, 'Economic and Social Rights Fulfillment Index: Country Scores and Rankings' (2010) 9 Journal of Human Rights 230

Raworth, K., 'Measuring Human Rights' (2006) 15 Ethics and International Affairs 111

Reddy, S., 'Economics and Human Rights: A Non-conversation' (2011) 12 Journal of Human Development and Capabilities 63

Riedel, E., 'New Bearings to the State Reporting Procedure: Practical Ways to Operationalize Economic, Social and Cultural Rights – the Example of the Right to Health' in S. Schorlemer (ed.), *Praxishandbuch UNO: Die Vereinten Nationen im Lichte globaler Herausforderungen* (Springer 2003)

Robertson, R.E., 'Measuring State Compliance with the Obligation to Devote the "Maximum Available Resources" to Realizing Economic, Social, and Cultural Rights' (1994) 16 Human Rights Quarterly 693

Sen, A., 'Utilitarianism and Welfarism' (1979) 76 Journal of Philosophy 463

Sen, A., 'Rights and Agency' (1982) 11 Philosophy and Public Affairs 3

Sen, A., *On Ethics and Economics* (Blackwell 1988)

Sen, A., 'Consequential Evaluation and Practical Reason' (2000a) 97 Journal of Philosophy 477

Sen, A., 'The Discipline of Cost Benefit Analysis' (2000b) 29 The Journal of Legal Studies 931

Sen, A., *The Idea of Justice* (Allen Lane 2009)

Sengupta, A., 'The Human Right to Development' (2004) 32 Oxford Development Studies 179

Seymour, D. and J. Pincus, 'Human Rights and Economics: The Conceptual Basis for their Complementarity' (2008) 26 Development Policy Review 387

Sonderbye, N. and others, *Human Rights and Economics: Tensions and Positive Relationships* 2012)

Sweeney, S.E., 'Government Respect for Women's Economic Rights: A Cross-national Analysis, 1981–2003' in S. Hertel and L. Minkler (eds), *Economic Rights: Conceptual, Measurement and Policy Issues* (CUP 2007)

Tresch, R.W., *Public Finance: A Normative Theory* (Academic Press 2002)

Wilkinson, R.G. and K.E. Pickett, 'Income Inequality and Population Health: A Review and Explanation of the Evidence' (2006) 62 Social Science and Medicine 1768

Wolf, S., 'Does Aid Improve Public Service Delivery?' 143 Review of World Economics 650

6. From the normative to the transnational: methods in the study of human rights history

Steven L.B. Jensen and Roland Burke

INTRODUCTION

History is not neutral territory to navigate, either for human rights research or in human rights practice. This recognition has too rarely been the subject of adequate elaboration, even if the use of history has been part and parcel of the evolution of human rights. The rhetoric of 'tradition' and debates over origins, for example, have been particularly powerful and often include problematic representations of this historical evolution.

If history from the outset was a companion to the contemporary developments in the field of human rights, fuller and more systematic, reflective and critical contributions from history are a more recent development. In the last decade the discipline of history has in a substantive way entered the field of human rights research. New questions have been asked about the evolution of human rights. New interpretations have been put forward – some of which have already gained traction or been the subject of critique across other disciplines.[1] The new body of human rights historiography is worthy of methodological reflection, including on what lessons it may offer the wider research field. We argue that one of the most significant contributions that history can make to the field is facilitating a shift from the confines of the normative – a space that can never be abandoned but can be handled in a more creative way – into a greater appreciation of its transnational dynamics.

The chapter starts by situating history and historical narratives in the context of existing human rights scholarship. It also highlights some of the intellectual and ethical pitfalls that may be a factor when other disciplines apply history in their human rights research. There are relevant lessons to capture here in order to refine the use of historical methods and the use of

---

[1] See e.g. Samuel Moyn *The Last Utopia. Human Rights in History* (Harvard University Press 2010).

history in human rights scholarship.[2] The chapter speaks to the practice of method in human rights history and also aims to explore some interfaces on how other disciplines may consider handling the role of history in human rights research.

The traditional focus of historical method is on how to work with primary sources and other forms of evidence. We have chosen to explore the question of methods from what we see as three complimentary perspectives. The first perspective identifies some blind spots in human rights research focusing on representation, periodization and intent-based narratives. These blind spots have shaped how human rights research has been conducted – partly because of the tendency to limit methodological reflection – and they deserve greater attention across disciplines. Historical method can help shape the response needed to address these. This is where the two other perspectives fit in. They focus respectively on sources and evidence as well as on key methodological approaches, such as transnational history, that may help us shift from the standard historical narratives to capturing the evolution of human rights with greater nuance, complexity and richness and thereby inform the wider field of scholarship. Transnational approaches allow us to approach, with greater nuance, the dynamics of the processes – across time and space – that shaped the historical evolution of human rights.

HISTORY AND HUMAN RIGHTS – AN OVERVIEW

The recent human rights historiography is not without precedent. Since the 1980s, several important historical works have been published. While these do represent pioneering studies and may represent useful lessons for assessing historical methods, they are too scattered to represent a full body of historiography. These works did, however, serve as precedents for a professionalization of human rights history.

---

[2] As historians of human rights, we have mainly focused on the post-1945 period with an emphasis on qualitative, empirical history based on multi-archive, and multi-national studies. We will therefore rely mainly on the post-1945 era to exemplify our points in what follows. For two insightful articles with a much longer timeframe (pre-twentieth century) that combines reflections on historiography and methodological approaches, see Reza Afshari 'On Historiography of Human Rights Reflections on Paul Gordon Lauren's the Evolution of International Human Rights: Visions Seen' (2007) 29(1) Human Rights Quarterly 1; and Stefan-Ludwig Hoffman (ed.), 'Introduction: Genealogies of Human Rights' in *Human Rights in the 20th Century* (CUP 2011).

Much of the focus of these earlier historical works involved the construction of genealogies, often intricate, spanning centuries of time and
continents of geography.[3] These works posed substantial philosophical
questions attendant to all intellectual history, involving a relatively clear
set of assumptions about what constitute the defining features of 'human
rights' and how these were apparent in assorted precursor movements.
Creation of genealogies – be they long or, in more recent historiography,
'short' – inevitably involves a fairly strong set of normative assumptions
when observing the emergence and proliferation of terms like 'human
rights' (and/or related terms) without much by way of evaluation as to
their specific context and meaning.

Historical study of human rights tends to produce a distinctive kind
of understanding of the concept, whatever the ideological orientation
of the scholar. As a discipline that defaults to narrative, and organizes
via chronology, its methods encourage at least a degree of linearity, and
a profound concern with evolution over time, be it gently continuous or
wrenchingly disruptive. With an analytical axis aligned to time, and generally less so to space, even the finest recent studies are necessarily written in
a diachronic mode. While much recent work is explicitly transnational, and
increasingly sensitive to, and inclusive of, voices outside the articulate core
of Western juridical and diplomatic elites, this inherently temporal frame
necessarily diminishes the kind of precision it can accord to any particular
moment. This was especially so in the initial, formative works of human
rights history, which sought to produce a grand synthesis account of
human rights over a vast expanse of time and inevitably traded precision
in the process. The proliferation of work in the past decade has begun to
moderate this single, sweeping narrative of human rights evolution – with
key recent works acutely sensitive to competing ideas of rights and the
diversity of how they have been understood. Insights from the most recent
scholarship have begun to transition a 'human rights history' toward a
constellation of 'human rights histories', with complementarity of global,
regional and thematic accounts. Historical work is now a mosaic of scales
and sites, albeit one that invariably privileges time as an organizational
prism for its analysis.

Both the trends of expansive genealogies versus historically sensitive
context and meanings and the seduction of textual formalism necessitate
bringing reflections on methodology to the forefront of scholarly prac-

---

[3]   Paul Gordon Lauren, *The Evolution of Human Rights: Visions Seen* (University
of Pennsylvania Press 1998); Micheline Ishay, *The History of Human Rights. From
Ancient Times to the Globalization Era* (University of California Press 2004).

tice – something that is not always a habit in human rights research. Within the discipline of history, scholarly reflections on practice tend to coalesce around historiographical overviews and debate and not discussions on method in human rights history. Some of the historiographical debate does have implications for historical method, but there is hardly any stand-alone work on the latter, at least in its traditional sense. In this sense, history resembles other disciplines engaged in human rights research as identified by the editors of this volume.[4]

The complex relationship between historical evolution and the notion of universality also necessitates greater attention to methodological practice. Universalism, at least to some extent, presumes that the philosophical content is fixed and immutable. French and American revolutionaries described rights, in their eighteenth century iteration, in terms of 'eternal principles' that lived in the heart. The powerful exhortation of the 1948 Universal Declaration spoke of 'a common standard for all peoples and all nations' – were it so, then rights would be profoundly more constrained in their emancipatory potential.

As human rights historiography has recently become dramatically finer in its granularity it has wandered closer to generating a kind of knowledge with the capacity to compromise the notion of universality that subtends its power. A historiography more attentive to the plurality of meanings with the term 'human rights', and the shifts in those meanings over time, has necessarily complicated and problematized universality. Histories that are less triumphalist, more inclined to draw distinctions between particular usages of human rights and differentiate between various emancipatory campaigns that operated under the banner of rights, may well sit in tension with universality. They reveal that the idea was, to at least some extent, less universal across both time and space.

Universalism, however, can also be a dynamic concept. The emerging history of human rights, vastly more detailed and complex than that which preceded it, can certainly also be marshalled to support universality. Fortunately, the principal measure of prophylaxis against its misuse by states is intrinsic to good history. A richly contextualized history of what human rights meant, when and to whom has its own latent ethical facility. Readers can decide for themselves which usages hold legitimacy and which were flags of convenience or frank attempts at subversion. In this, the discipline of history may have something substantial to offer both to our understanding of the universality of human rights and to the wider research field.

---

[4]   Bård A. Andreassen, Hans-Otto Sano and Siobhán McInerney-Lankford (eds), 'Human Rights Research Method', Chapter 1 in this volume.

History has a layered presence in human rights practice, which should inform how we approach it. We may look at historical developments in the field and changes over time. This takes the form of a chronological and forward-looking view. History also comes in a retrospective and presentist form, namely through the use of history in political debates, activism or social mobilization. For the historically oriented there is also a third form: human rights debates often reference contemporary developments. It is part of what provides their dynamism. However, when looking at sources from the past, the contemporary turns into the historical. The researcher must consider the level of knowledge required to navigate the referencing to what is now historical events, sort them for relevance and address them with adequate understanding. There is a richness in this dimension on its own, but it must be managed depending on the type of study design, research problem, historical context and timespan that is the focus of the researcher's endeavor.

Human rights struggles and movements have almost always conceived of themselves in historical terms as operating within a much grander, longer and greater enterprise. They may self-fashion their movements as heirs to an animating spirit traced through the sixteenth-century priest Bartolomé de Las Casas and abolitionist Frederick Douglass, women's rights advocate Olympe Des Gouges and suffragette Sylvia Pankhurst, to Nelson Mandela and Argentinean human rights defender Emilio Mignone. For many activists, there is a productive tension between drawing upon, and placing themselves within, a long tradition of preceding emancipation struggles, while simultaneously claiming the authority of principles that are notionally ahistorical and transcendent. The course of human rights has been one with an incremental, narrative logic, of each increment of greater freedom inducing the struggle for the next. This evolution of rights and rights bearers over time is exquisitely suited to the kind of investigations proposed by history.

In brief, it seems that, despite pretending to being outside history, a key rhetorical and philosophical feature of the human rights movement, broadly speaking, has been locating a particular struggle and activism within a continuous genealogy, or at least a genealogy of lineage presumed to be continuous, of a centuries-long march of justice, equality and freedom. From the imagined 'Ancient Liberties' of early modern England, to the invented freedoms of free men invoked in 1776, rights have paradoxically claimed universality and temporal transcendence by appeals to a past, be it mostly fantastical, mostly real or, more often, a mix of expedient myth and history. As a consequence, human rights activists are, by necessity, historians of a kind. They recover a usable past upon which to found the legitimacy of their crusades, a narrative within which to place the battles of the present. This then, becomes part of the historian's navigational challenge.

BLIND SPOTS: SOME CHALLENGES WITH THE STANDARD HISTORICAL NARRATIVES

Human rights research and practice have for a long time relied heavily on drafting histories as the main accounts of the post-1945 evolution of human rights. While drafting histories hold value as, for instance, legal commentary, they tend to represent accounts too narrow to understand how human rights – or a sub-theme thereof – evolved and amassed such social and political significance on a global scale.[5] These drafting histories have been important in constituting and reproducing what has been labeled as the 'textbook narrative'.[6] This refers to a narrative that has largely remained an unchanged standard account, while the rest of the human rights research field and the world has significantly evolved over the decades.

This narrative represents a very instrumental view of history that most likely emanates from the close connection to the discipline of law that human rights had from the outset. The legal approach to history, sometimes derived from the position of legal positivism, may be an explanatory factor here when it comes to the methodological conservatism and the limited scopes of interest, including some practices of exclusion, that have affected the research field. This has led to three noteworthy blind spots when it comes to understanding the relationship between history and human rights dynamics. By blind spots are meant distinct methodological angles or challenges that have somehow been left out of sight. They are an important factor in achieving an understanding about this relationship and scholars should strive to overcome blind spots with a more reflexive use of historical method.

Human rights research has – overall – been surprisingly loyal to the human rights project. This does not necessarily imply that the research has

---

[5]   At their best, these drafting histories can provide an excellent account of the philosophical roots and hidden meanings behind the normative standards that were included in human rights declarations and conventions. Johannes Morsink, *The Universal Declaration of Human Rights. Origins, Drafting and Intent* (University of Pennsylvania Press 1999).

[6]   Miia Halme Tuomisaari and Pamela Slotte (eds), 'Revisiting the Origins of Human Rights: Introduction', in *Revisiting the Origins of Human Rights* (CUP 2015).

always been uncritical. The point is rather that there has been a great deal of loyalty and lack of questioning of the parameters that were laid out for the human rights project from the outset. The project, as it was defined in the 1940s, focused on developing the International Bill of Rights. This consisted of the 1948 Universal Declaration of Human Rights and what became the 1966 Human Rights Covenants that, with their measures of implementation, only entered into force in the mid-1970s. This posits civil, political, economic, social and cultural rights as the foundations for the human rights project, no matter what else transpired during the 30-year period from the initial conception to the entry into force of these international legal norms.

The story of the human rights project remains a powerful structuring 'textbook narrative', but it relies on an intent-based narrative where later developments are deemed to have remained 'loyal' to 1940s plans. There was a clear intent in the 1940s as to how the human rights project should unfold, namely through the elements of the International Bill of Rights. This is the first blind spot because a global process evolving over three decades does not necessarily follow the same development stages as those defined at the outset. Global political developments, including mid-twentieth-century decolonization that certainly was a defining and transformative historical development with worldwide ramifications, were deemed to have had no autonomous impact on the chronology, substance and precedents in the evolution of human rights. This illustrates well the gap between standard human rights accounts and the historical record. The intent-based narrative has undergirded a progressive narrative for human rights and overdue attention to a 'canon' of human rights sources linked to the Universal Declaration of Human Rights and the Human Rights Covenants.

An illustrative example of this blind spot is the fact that the 1950s and 1960s were until very recently largely ignored. We have to the contrary previously argued that the 1950s and 1960s are critical to understanding the nature and evolution of the international human rights project.[7] This project was in fact fundamentally re-defined in 1962 around race and religion by key and newly independent states from the Global South. This new formula shaped key human rights developments – including the legal breakthrough for international human rights – until the mid-1970s when civil, political, economic, social and cultural rights again reclaimed

---

[7]   Roland Burke, *Decolonization and the Evolution of Human Rights* (University of Pennsylvania Press 2010); and Steven L.B. Jensen, *The Making of International Human Rights. The 1960s, Decolonization and the Reconstruction of Global Values* (CUP 2016).

their structuring power in the human rights field. This 1962 redefinition was accompanied by several other developments that, during the 1960s, created a whole new momentum for human rights with rather far-reaching effects.[8]

Methodologically, a first step may be to find the most suitable ways to question the parameters set for the human rights project because the reliance on this type of 'original intent' has helped sustain two other blind spots. One relates to the question of periodization. The other relates to the question of representation. The blind spot regarding periodization of human rights history may not represent an absolute one, but at a minimum what is exhibited is a highly asymmetric distribution of vision. Three chronological spans have been addressed with excellent acuity: the period of Enlightenment; the 1940s, most especially the immediate post-war years; and the 1970s. Those years in between the two latter periods in particular, have borne witness to a marked indifference to the dynamics of the project; consigned to marginalia and subject to much more limited historical attention.

Certainly, historical research should be sensitive to notions of ruptures and discontinuities. Yet human rights research has been, at least in the contemporary twentieth-century version, somewhat addicted to the notion of breakthroughs and 'human rights moments' and has paid less attention to historical processes and trends over time.[9] Connecting, or for the more revisionist scholars, disconnecting the dots in time and space has been less important than characterizing the nature of the idealism manifest in these 'human rights moments'. The point is not that these time periods are unimportant; often they have been selected for emphasis because they were transformative in some way. Rather, the problem is that this approach has tended to prevent the pursuit of richer and more complex understandings of the evolution of human rights in the global domain, and in turn, our understandings of their proliferation or expansion. The recent historiography has therefore faced the paradoxical task of historicizing human rights history.

The elevated emphasis on the above-mentioned periods has had the distinct effect of privileging Western agency and perspectives in the historical narratives on human rights. These three periods work on a 'Western historical time' so to speak or have at least been presented this way. The

---

[8]   Jensen, ibid.

[9]   Robert Brier, 'Beyond the Quest for a "Breakthrough", Reflections on the Recent Historiography on Human Rights' (2015) 16 Jahrbuch für Europäische Geschichte/European History Yearbook 155.

human rights story has been constructed as a markedly more Western story than the historical record merits and this has become the default narrative in both academic and popular contexts. The problems with this should be self-evident. The effects on human rights research have been amplified because they have been accompanied by a form of perspective blindness linked to representation. It is therefore important to ask: what stories are told? What forms of agency do we acknowledge? What forms of agency do we ignore?

What has been ignored is how significant and, equally important, how varied Global South agency was in the historical evolution.[10] One can begin to address this omission by shifting focus to how the intervening periods were pivotal to the broader developments and by offering more contextualized global histories of human rights, sensitive to historical contingencies, to challenge the standard applications of history. There should be a greater emphasis on shifting the narrative vantage points that determine from which perspectives the human rights story is told. The comprehensive source materials produced by the United Nations do enable this to some extent owing to the global, and historically changing, composition of actors and contributors to international debates. Furthermore, the United Nations has always functioned not only as a site for normative and political debates – whether constructive or stale – but also as a kind of feedback mechanism reflecting external developments. UN sources can therefore serve as a starting point and guide the researcher toward other types of sources and other archives in a variety of geographical settings, although at points, the proceduralism through which these sources operate is an opaque window to encounter the wider world. This is where another

---

[10]   Burke (n 7). Before the most recent historiography, there have been a number of pioneering attempts to address this gap. This has probably been done best by the American political scientist Susan Waltz. In a selection of articles, she studied the contribution by Global South actors in the UN human rights standard setting processes during the 1940s and 1950s. These are informative studies that certainly have broadened perspectives. However, they also clearly present themselves as drafting histories operating within the intent-based narrative and focused on UN negotiations without expanding the perspectives beyond the multilateral forum into what larger political developments shaped the positions taken by representatives from the Global South countries that were active in the human rights diplomacy. See Susan Waltz, 'Universalizing Human Rights: The Role of Small States in the Construction of the Universal Declaration of Human Rights' (2001) 23(1) Human Rights Quarterly 44; Susan Waltz, 'Reclaiming and Rebuilding the History of the Universal Declaration of Human Rights' (2002) 23(3) Third World Quarterly 437; and Susan Waltz, 'Universal Human Rights: The Contribution of Muslim States' (2004) 26(4) Human Rights Quarterly 799.

aspect of the question of historical methods becomes critically important: the way we perceive of and work with sources can help to address and overcome the blind spots.

SOURCES AND EVIDENCE

History furnishes the kind of disciplinary tools for pursuing some of the most significant questions in the study of human rights. This includes a means to approach the plasticity of an idea that tends to claim fixed, crystalline, normative content. The same tools also enable us to better appreciate how human rights were understood at specific moments, by particular actors and movements, and the context and purpose of their invocation. There may also be a unique virtue in the kind of knowledge generated by historical inquiry. Part of the virtue lies in the potential to facilitate an escape from abstraction, compared with narrow disquisitions on international law and philosophical knowledge, both of which are typically unable to access the actual operation of rights, and the contexts which have generated human rights ideas. This may have very practical manifestations.

In a way, the most powerful human rights tool has been a historical one – that of meticulously documented and narrated testimony, exemplified by the earliest humanitarians, Roger Casement and Edmund Dene Morel. Their work took place in Congo at the beginning of the twentieth century, and this approach continued through the relentless documentary synthesis of Amnesty International's research staff, and is now practiced as the mainstay of non-governmental organization (NGO) activity. At the juridical level, documentation and narration of abuses resides at the heart of measures of international accountability. The Hague provides an attentive audience for history. There is much historical inquiry in established human rights practice or in key institutions of international law.[11] Yet there exists a considerable gap between historical inquiry as an established practice and the historical narratives that underpin our broader understandings of human rights. This gap is very much shaped by the blind spots identified

---

[11]   For a critical exploration of this point see Richard Ashby Wilson, *Writing History in International Criminal Trials* (CUP 2011). See also Christian Axboe Nielsen, 'Can We Salvage a History of the Former Yugoslav Conflicts from the Milošević Trial', in Timothy Waters (ed.), *The Milošević Trial: An Autopsy* (OUP 2014). For a state-of-the-art overview of fact-finding as a field of human rights practice, see Alston, Philip and Sarah Knuckey (eds), *The Transformation of Human Rights Fact-Finding* (OUP 2016).

above and the way that connections have been drawn between historical sources in time and geographical space to shape these narratives.

The historian Jean Quataert has eloquently captured the problem of the blind spots and what is at stake. In a review article from 2013, Quataert observed that Aryeh Neier's *The International Human Rights Movement: A History* was not fully successful in delivering upon its promise of 'international'.[12] Neier, an eminent American lawyer, and co-founder of the international NGO Human Rights Watch, held an extremely well-established record of global human rights activism. While he had sought to write an international history of the human rights movement, Neier tended to reproduce the standard narrative. The nature of the problem, as Quataert identified it, goes to the core of historical method:

> It is not, as Neier has it, to label an argument suspect because the idea originated in Europe or the West. What validates a notion of Eurocentrism in human rights debates about origins is more precise, specific, and readily documented: It is about evidence and sources – who the agents in the study are and whose voices the historian consults and allows to be heard. International human rights history cannot be written credibly from sources that are exclusively and narrowly limited to Western thought and thinkers.[13]

Much more attention should be paid to the voices that are consulted, an insight that is well appreciated in those disciplines that reside more heavily in the present, but less practiced by human rights historians. After an admittedly problematic start in the 1940s, anthropology has engaged in this kind of human rights research in a contemporary setting. While the need for an equivalent effort on the part of human rights historians is widely recognized, it remains a challenge – one that faces substantial impediments, most notably, a less visible and accessible set of identified archives. In the synchronically oriented disciplines, a detailed appreciation for the recovery and synthesis of plural perspectives constitutes almost common practice – and an animating imperative in some fields of research. This has not necessarily been applied when it comes to diachronic approaches – even if its importance and value is not contested. This is both an intellectual and an ethical difficulty. It also highlights a problem with

---

[12] Aryeh Neier, *The International Human Rights Movement: A History* (Princeton University Press 2012).

[13] Jean Quataert, 'A Review of "The International Human Rights Movement: A History"' (2013) 13(4) Journal of Human Rights 537, 538. See also her own contribution to the field, Jean Quataert *Advocating Dignity. Human Rights Mobilizations in Global Politics* (University of Pennsylvania Press 2009). See also Lynn Hunt, *Writing History in the Global Era* (W.W. Norton 2014) 71.

method and why the shift from the normative to the transnational remains a principal challenge on the horizon for historians.

Sally Engle Merry's contribution to this volume illustrates well how ethnographic methods have worked to address this area of comparative deficiency. While history draws on different methodology, the discipline can learn from the arguments presented by Engle Merry when she argues in favor of 'multi-sited ethnography'. Recognizing that 'human rights ideas travel and come to ground in a variety of contexts and situations' and that it is 'in the micro-processes of human rights discourse, practice and consciousness that its effects become visible', multi-sited ethnography as a methodological approach has 'emerged as a way to grapple with the important intersections between the local and the global'.[14] This implies that fieldwork is undertaken both at the global UN policy-making level and at local levels where these decisions are translated, or maybe untranslated, into implementation processes.[15] These observations reflect a reality that affects all disciplines engaged in human rights research. This reality should guide historical methodology toward the multi-national, multi-actor and multi-archive approaches.

Resolving, or less ambitiously, mitigating, the artifacts and elisions in historical writing is conceptually straightforward. Much of the strategy is the kind of self-reflexivity on what is being undertaken that has already been incorporated, or at least, aspired to, in almost all fields of history for many decades. The first step could be to look at one's research questions and ask: why have these blind spots, fractional perspectives and exclusions proliferated, and why do they persist? What can be done, within the constraints of sources and sheer practical and logistical reality, to overcome these limitations? What constitutes a representative account, or, at least, how can there be a more explicit recognition of silences and limits in the account?

Historians engaged in human rights tend to be more naturalistic in methodological disposition. Extensive and self-conscious reflection on study design runs counter to the felicity of language and narrative that is one of the assets of the field. Yet more deliberate attention to research design is time and effort well spent. It allows a fuller reflection on the

---

[14]   Sally Engle Merry, 'The Potential of Ethnographic Methods for Human Rights Research', Chapter 7 in this volume.

[15]   Engle Merry calls this process *vernacularization* of human rights. It is an analytical concept that is also sensitive to 'how circulation and translation evolve over time'. See Peggy Levitt and Sally Engle Merry, 'Vernacularization on the Ground: Local Uses of Global Women's Rights in Peru, China, India and the United States' (2009) 9(4) Global Networks 441.

research inquiry to be undertaken and prevents any confusion as to what kind of human rights history, precisely, is being told. The next set of questions become less abstract and seek to translate methodological aspiration into archival and narrative reality. What type of sources and what forms of evidence should be explored? How and where can they be accessed? This is where the scope of the research project should be considered. There is little doubt that the multi-archival and multi-national approaches that have come forward as part of the new human rights historiography have helped tremendously in creating a dynamic field and moving research agendas forward. This works well for projects with the scale and resource to traverse the world. Avenues for down-scaling this sort of grand endeavor to granules that can be managed in less grand scope is not always obvious.

A partial avenue for smaller-scale works, those that can be quantized at a level less than the globe, is a retreat from a master narrative toward a distributed, multi-resolution history. By avoiding the pretense of full inclusion and full expansiveness, and stating candidly the limits of the study in terms of their representativeness, modest sized histories, bounded by geography, period, theme, movement or cohort, can be tessellated into place. Each identifies where it resides and what it seeks to represent, and draws its sinews to other studies, finding complementarity and contrast. None, or very few, will aim for equilateral coverage or representation. Yet assembled together, they will constitute the kind of mosaic of human rights histories where knowledge arrives in increments of greater inclusion, wider representation and diversity of emphases. Although more partial in each tile, the assembled accounts, together, will allow plurality. Synthesis between them will allow a kind of index human rights history narrative, built on the sheer scale of its constituent sub-histories.

Human rights is a subject of enquiry that has left a voluminous documentary record. The empirical basis for human rights scholarship spans the full spectrum, from elite juridical and political actors through to those normally excised from historical agency. Such abundance and variegation bring their own challenges, not least of which is the seduction of textual formalism and the assumption of a comprehensive record. The problem with textual formalism is partly that human rights can be too narrow a keyword to study human rights, although it generates enough source material from the outset. The meaning and connotations of the subject under study come in other conceptual disguises and this variability must be handled. A too literal approach to the historical study of human rights can become a problem. The fate or trajectory of human rights may be determined through other terminology or different processes than those traditionally assigned to human rights debates. For example, the first organizational efficiency review conducted by the United Nations in 1950 and 1951 questioned whether the

UN Human Rights Commission should be discontinued (at least after it had completed the UN Covenants, which the Commission eventually did in 1954) alongside the Commission on the Status of Women and other bodies that dealt with human rights issues. In reality, this was not a question of organizational efficiency but a politically charged issue about the nature of international organization and to what extent this should include the social and human rights fields. This process, had the outcome been different, could have had a significant impact on international human rights.

It reflected conflicts over deeper meanings related to global politics and international organization at a decisive time. The research field has tended to focus on the standard fora for human rights debates and has not considered, for example, UN efficiency review processes as a site for human rights contestation. This example is mentioned to highlight the need for a greater awareness and openness toward what may constitute important sources. It might cause logistical challenges owing to the scope of sources to consider, but, from our perspective, these contestations over meaning and changes herein should remain at the core of historical analysis. It was key countries from the Global South who, in the immediate aftermath of the 1948 Universal Declaration of Human Rights, protected the social and human rights-focused work at the United Nations against attempts from the United States and the UK to severely curtail or even abandon this field of international diplomacy and standard-setting. In terms of sources and evidence, this example shows that some basic factors still matter greatly, such as: who speaks; and who speaks when in what context; and, fundamentally, to what extent do their contributions exert influence?

The other problem with textual formalism is the belief that what we can readily access is representative of the historical record. This is where the legal approach may have played tricks on the research field because sometimes research questions pre-determine research outcomes. Legal conventions are an obvious subject of study and discretely bounded processes seeking to crystallize particular human rights ideas. This is why drafting histories have featured so strongly as de facto histories of human rights. They addressed a demand for knowledge and juridical context, and this may have been sufficient for addressing certain research questions. Furthermore, a relatively clear and distinct trail of source materials were generated known as *Travaux Preparatoire*, which are relatively straightforward to access and analyze.[16] This relatively easy accessibility may be

---

[16]   The *Travaux Preparatoire* are often pre-identified for example by UN staff or other scholars and hence are easier to access without having to patiently trawl through sources from a much larger range of UN debates and other processes.

deceiving because there is an inherent risk that convention histories can easily become conventional histories. The history of economic and social rights is not well represented through writing a history of the Covenant covering these rights, but in many ways it is what we have settled for. The history of human rights conventions, an important sub-set of human rights history, has been confused with the wider story. The way that larger political processes and social transformations shaped international law may not be adequately considered if the focus is merely on the processes of how standards were drafted and how they are later implemented in the development of human rights jurisprudence.[17] This is not the best path to achieve nuanced and contextualized histories, and it certainly has allowed the methodological and interpretative blind spots to proliferate. Allow us to illustrate how this becomes a problem through the example of race and religion referred to above.

As mentioned earlier, the international human rights project was in important ways redefined in 1962 around race and religion. The Convention on Elimination of All Forms of Racial Discrimination from 1965 is a well-known legal instrument and counts as one of the major human rights conventions. It is anchored institutionally with a treaty body and has served as an important reference point for later norm-setting. There is plenty of research dealing with this Convention. The Convention on Elimination of All Forms of Religious Intolerance, developed between 1962 and 1967, was the most significant attempt in the twentieth century to make religion a subject of international law, but it has had no status and hardly any references in the whole human rights research field. The obvious explanation is that the attempt failed to materialize because the full draft convention collapsed at the United Nations in 1967 in the aftermath of the Six-Day War. There are no established and ratified legal standards to interpret and apply in legal or diplomatic settings.[18] In the absence of a convention, there has been an absence of the political history to which it was coupled.

---

[17] A very thoughtful analysis on these aspects and how to study law as an 'imaginary' before law manifests itself in courts and other legal institutions can be found in Paul Kahn, *The Cultural Study of Law. Reconstructing Legal Scholarship* (Chicago University Press 1999). Also of relevance in a human rights context, Kahn writes on p. 36, 'The rule of law is a social practice: it is a way of being in the world. To live under the rule of law is to maintain a set of beliefs about the self and community, time and space, authority and representation'. On p. 6 he writes, 'The issue is not whether law makes us better off, but rather what it is that the law makes us'.

[18] Jensen (n 7).

This is where the shortcomings to the legal approach are revealed. History may assist in addressing this imbalance, not by abandoning conventions, but by putting them within a broader world – one which does not terminate at the walls of a committee or commission chamber. From the historian's perspective, projects that failed may be of equal interest compared with processes with successful legal outcomes as long as the former had some form of political significance and importance relating to what is being researched. It is of course the responsibility of the historian to document the claim that a failed project had significance but these projects are legitimate subjects for study. The Convention on Religious Intolerance certainly had such importance as the race–religion axis proved to be an important Cold War formula to transform both Eastern and Western engagement with international human rights during this pivotal period. Brokered by a group of key states from the Global South, a number of Western countries, including the UK, started changing their policies as the convention began a process which produced a much stronger acceptance of human rights as a legitimate issue of international concern. The focus on racial discrimination led an opportunistic Communist bloc much further into the field of international human rights diplomacy and lawmaking than they actually wanted to go. This created new political opportunities that laid the foundation for the human rights developments in the 1970s, including the Helsinki Final Act.[19]

From a methodological perspective, the main point is that it is comparatively easy to write a history of the convention on racial discrimination because there is a negotiation process with a start date and a clearly defined outcome. The companion story on religion is much more blurred. It has remained largely forgotten for decades. There is no clear outcome and the failed convention appears not to have left a mark on human rights developments. Apart from the fact that it did. It just requires a very different methodological approach to capture this story, and to appreciate the significance of a notional failure.

It requires a multi-national, multi-organizational, and multi-archive approach to piece together the elements of this parallel story. In reality, the history of the Convention on Elimination of all Forms of Racial Discrimination merits the same approach. It is just that the distinct drafting process and the ready availability of sources has functioned as a siren song for limiting the scope of analysis to drafting histories and legal commentaries. Ease and visibility of a very straightforward narrative have preferentially drawn interest that otherwise might have been more

---

[19]   Ibid.

widely apportioned and disbursed to the grander movement of which the Convention was but a single, significant, product. The limited methodological reflection has served as an obstacle to fully explore how, for example, the international negotiation process over racial discrimination interacted with and mutually influenced concurrent national and local developments related to the politics of race in different places around the world.[20] It is in these transnational connections that we may be able to develop the richer, contextualized human rights histories that will allow us a fuller understanding of how things unfolded and evolved, and what their significance has been past and present.[21] This is where it becomes relevant to explore what transnational history means as an approach to studying human rights.

Before reaching this point, it is worth mentioning that social science methods focusing on collection of quantitative data have not really featured in human rights historiography. Histories of rights have had a distinct emphasis on qualitative approaches, but the absence of quantitative approaches and social science methods also reflects under-explored areas of human rights history. The whole sub-field related to the histories of economic, social and cultural rights and also economic histories of human rights has barely been addressed, although indications are that the focus of human rights historiography is moving toward these critical areas as well. If research here expands, it is more than likely that historical method will be complemented by social science methods in the histories of human rights.

There is ample space for using data to inform research approaches as long as source criticism is consistently applied. This ranges from simpler uses of available data to more elaborate explorations of how data collection can bring new insights forward. When we have known for decades that there was a 10-fold increase in the number of speeches that African states delivered on human rights at the United Nations from 1960 to 1967, and that the term 'human rights' during this period shot up the ranks of most important political themes for those states in this influential multilateral

---

[20] There are of course scholarly works addressing national and local developments in mid-twentieth-century politics but human rights research has not done much in terms of connecting its approach with these stories.

[21] The application of the concept of 'connections' should in itself invite methodological reflection. The historian Sebastian Conrad has presented an insightful analysis of the meaning of 'connections' in the practice of global history. Conrad argues that global history should also look at integration and structural transformations. His highly recommended analysis can be found in Sebastian Conrad, *What is Global History?* (Princeton University Press 2016) esp. 64–79.

forum, we should maybe not have ignored the 1960s as an irrelevant decade or have hesitated when hearing that the Third World was only interested in racial discrimination.[22] Should this type of data and knowledge at least not have sparked curiosity?

The Social Network Analysis – explained by Anna-Luise Chané and Arjun Sharma in this volume – is a method that could also be relevant for historical analysis.[23] This quantitative approach – strongly reliant on the documental record – could be used to capture in greater detail the nature of networks in international human rights diplomacy that were important in shaping the evolution of human rights after 1945. It could subsequently inform more qualitative studies of how these networks operated, how they shaped human rights discourse and the motivations and political developments that determined the engagement in terms of support, critiques and obstructions.[24]

METHODOLOGICAL APPROACHES

The fact that human rights have evolved in the global domain with a strong emphasis on their universality sits well with the 'transnational turn' in historical scholarship over the last decade. Human rights historiography has even been described as a 'paradigmatic site for the new transnational history'.[25] Transnational history comes with methodological and theoretical insights that shape how it is applied in scholarship on the evolution of human rights. It also entails methodological practices and lessons from which historical research can inform other disciplines engaged in human rights research.

Conceptually, transnational history is connected to international history and world history. Whereas the notion of the 'international' is connected to the domain of states, world history often deliberately moves away from engaging with the nation state as a historical entity in world system approaches. This leaves a gap for the transnational with its understanding

---

[22] David Kay, 'The Impact of African States on the United Nations' (1969) 23(1) International Organization 20.

[23] Anna-Luise Chané and Arjun Sharma, 'Social Network Analysis in Human Rights Research', Chapter 15 in this volume.

[24] See e.g. Roland Burke, 'Human Rights Day after the "Breakthrough": Celebrating the Universal Declaration of Human Rights at the United Nations in 1978 and 1988' (2015) 10(1) Journal of Global History 147.

[25] Devin O. Pendas, 'Toward a New Politics? On the Recent Historiography of Human Rights' (2012) 21(1) Contemporary European History 95, 96.

that 'the destinies of individuals, institutions and countries are closely interrelated' and its willingness to 'draw out the varied, multi-textured forces which shape them'.[26] This can serve as an inspiration to adapt to the dynamics of the historical processes themselves and shift analytical perspectives when sources point toward new horizons. This is in itself an important recognition that can help crack open the standard narratives and lay them open to be challenged.

Transnational history has broadly been defined as the links and flows that connect or create relationships between 'people, ideas, products, processes and patterns that operate over, across, through, beyond, above, under, or in-between polities and societies'.[27] This is an intimidatingly broad definition, but it does signify an important shift in perspective for history as a discipline. The nation-state and national histories were for a very long time the defining features in historical scholarship. The transnational approach invites a more dynamic reflection that can shed new light on the strengths and weaknesses of the nation-state, while at the same time connecting local histories with global history and understanding their relationships. It opens up new approaches to studying time and space in a given historical enquiry and can reconfigure periodization and chronologies compared with approaches dominated by more nationally determined historiographies. As Patricia Clavin has argued, 'the value of transnationalism lies in its openness as an historical concept'.[28] This is an important part of the appeal of transnational history.

It also helps unsettle established categories such as the Third World, the Global South or Africa and bring greater sensitivity to individual agency and difference between the entities that constitute these very broad and general categories. As it happens, it is actually helpful in order to understand the global human rights dynamics of the mid-twentieth century. For example, it may help to have an understanding of the nuances in the foreign policies of the West African states of Ghana, Liberia, Nigeria and

---

[26] Patricia Clavin, 'Defining Transnationalism' (2005) 14(4) Contemporary European History 421.

[27] This definition originates with Akira Iriye and Pierre-Yves Saunier, *The Palgrave Dictionary of Transnational History* (Palgrave Macmillan 2009).

[28] Patricia Clavin (n 26) 438. Clavin also argues 'If a focus on connectivity can blur, if not usurp, standard chronologies, the transnational and international frame also sharpens the claim to novelty or distinction of any given event or phenomenon'. See Patricia Clavin, 'Time, Manner, Place: Writing Modern European History in Global, Transnational and International Contexts' (2010) 40(4) European History Quarterly 624, 629. See also Sarah B. Snyder, 'Bringing the Transnational In: Writing Human Rights into the International History of the Cold War' (2013) 24 Diplomacy & Statecraft, 100–116.

Guinea and how they enacted these nuances at the United Nations, or to be sensitive to the political trajectories of key diplomatic actors from the Global South in international policy-making fora.[29] Admittedly, this may seem like a very specialized example, but it is meant to illustrate how greater sensitivity to agency can help enlighten our understanding of more mainstream global human rights developments.

Transnational approaches can, if applied, function well with the diplomatic and social movement histories that have been the main modes of writing the history of human rights. There certainly are signs that these approaches are embraced in the new human rights historiography.[30] In fact, the new human rights historiography has also proven quite adept at mixing genres of sources that in traditional terms could be said to have originated from diplomatic, intellectual or social movement history.

More concretely, one may inquire how these approaches can be translated into the human rights field. In an extensive review essay from 2013, Philip Alston presented a wide-ranging reflection on writing human rights history.[31] Alston elaborated a framework for analysis by identifying six criteria or ways that human rights manifest themselves and which need to be considered in writing this type of history. Alston's criteria were human rights as: (a) an idea; (b) an elaborated discourse; (c) a social movement; (d) a practice or an institution; (e) a national or international legal regime; or (f) a system to promote respect for the rights of individuals and groups.[32]

All of these categories speak both to the international and the transnational. They all represent important elements, but there is one important omission: human rights as a field of international diplomacy. The field of human rights diplomacy has its own autonomous dynamic that complements and ties together all the elements in Alston's framework. It also connects human rights with a range of other issues in the global domain with mutual influencing taking place, notably broader legal diplomacy, development, trade and economic issues, and security and conflict, as well as specific issues related to geographic contexts. Diplomacy was crucial to the evolution of human rights at various stages and in various fora. It is

---

[29]   Jensen (n 7); and Roland Burke, *Decolonization and the Evolution of International Human Rights* (University of Pennsylvania Press 2010).

[30]   Jan Eckel, *Die Ambivalenz des Guten. Menschenrechte in der internationalen Politik seit den 1940ern* (V&R 2014); and Patrick W. Kelly, 'The Chilean Coup and the Origins of Transnational Human Rights Activism' (2013) 8(1) Journal of Global History 165, 165–186.

[31]   Philip Alston, 'Does the Past Matter: On the Origins of Human Rights' (2013) 126(7) Harvard Law Review 2043.

[32]   Ibid. 2078.

a multi-faceted field of practice, and for this exact reason it is a necessary analytical component to understanding this historical evolution. It therefore deserves to be an independent part of such an analytical framework.

It also underpins the importance of another factor to consider which Alston's framework only alludes to but provides insignificant weight to: the role of international organizations in transnational dynamics. International organizations provide an important structure for the above elements identified by Alston. The study of these organizations and their forms of governance has been significant for transnational history because they operate as meeting points for many different national, regional and global processes. This is one reason why the United Nations and other international organizations remain an important forum for the new human rights history and indeed for all human rights-related research. With this, there most certainly is a common starting point for human rights research across the disciplines, which makes the cross-disciplinary nature of the field more interesting to explore.

While, this chapter has argued in favor of transnational approaches to the study of human rights history, for reasons outlined above, our views should not be mistaken as considering this approach as imperative or the only available option. There is still value in other approaches such as histories of human rights in national contexts, as these studies may fill important gaps in our knowledge. Jan Eckel has argued, persuasively, that, 'Africa and Asia are deplorably under-researched regions in this global story' of human rights.[33] In addressing gaps of this nature, in-depth national histories can make novel contributions to the much broader field.[34] Scholarly works of this kind are not necessarily dependent on transnational history to be of value. However, it remains highly valuable to consider the specific questions presented throughout this chapter and to reflect more deeply on the blind spots, underlying assumptions and preconceived notions, as well as on the possible limitations caused by one's research questions and design as part of the methodological thinking that underpins a research project within human rights history. The recent expansion in human rights historiography allows ample opportunity to take on these challenges as part of a stimulating dialogue with scholarship and thereby refine one's method in the process.

---

[33]   Jan Eckel, 'The Rebirth of Politics from the Spirit of Morality: Explaining the Human Rights Revolution of the 1970s' in Jan Eckel and Samuel Moyn (eds), *The Breakthrough. Human Rights in the 1970s* (University of Pennsylvania Press 2014), 238.

[34]   For a promising example see Jennifer Johnson, *The Battle for Algeria. Sovereignty, Health Care, and Humanitarianism* (University of Pennsylvania Press 2016).

CONCLUDING REMARKS

Human rights research will by its nature continue to engage with the normative. This chapter has not argued for an abandonment of this engagement but for a shift in emphasis. By highlighting a shift toward the transnational, we have tried to explain one of the major contributions that human rights history can make to the human rights research field and how this can be approached. This does, however, imply a repositioning of the normative in human rights research. The aim is to provide more representative, agency- and time-sensitive accounts of the global human rights dynamics and in the broader research context a more constructive and accurate interaction between past and present. History alone cannot make this happen. It must also be part of the ambition by other research disciplines in order to come to fruition.

There are opportunities for other disciplines to draw on and learn from the finer granularity of the transnational human rights histories that is currently expanding the scope of and knowledge produced by human rights research. Just to mention a few examples, the subtle and refined work by scholars such as Linde Lindkvist on the deeper meanings – and changes herein – that led to article 18 on freedom of thought, conscience and religion in the 1948 Universal Declaration, Eleanor Davey's account of the changes in global political and ideological outlooks that facilitated the rise of humanitarian movements and its intersections with human rights forming part herein, and Daniel J. Whelan's history of the notion of indivisibility from the 1940s to present day have all enriched human rights historiography while having clear relevance for other disciplines engaged in human rights research.[35] Other examples could be given as this contribution looks set to continue.

This chapter has tried to offer relevant perspectives on some of the questions of method faced by human rights history. There are other relevant perspectives that space has not allowed exploration of, such as methods used in intellectual history or in the 'history of concepts' approach. Both of these build on interesting methodological approaches that can be useful to capture the strong normative – but still historically contingent and changing – content of human rights.[36]

---

[35] Linde Lindkvist, *Religious Freedom and the Universal Declaration of Human Rights* (CUP 2017); Eleanor Davey, *Idealism Beyond Borders. The French Revoluti onary Left and the Rise of Humanitarianism, 1954–1988* (CUP 2015); and Daniel J. Whelan, *Indivisible Human Rights. A History* (University of Pennsylvania Press 2010).

[36] For an example of this is Samuel Moyn's study of the concept of dignity in Christian thought in the 1930s and 1940s and how this concept played a role in

As already mentioned, human rights history has become a dynamic and expanding field. As such, it is likely that it will in new ways inform and inspire other disciplines and even other but related thematic areas of research in the years to come. This could include histories of exclusion and discrimination, which are equally valid subjects for human rights history compared with those focusing on their emergence or evolution. This reveals something more profound on what historical approaches to human rights can contribute. Human rights history allows the charting of the renovation of the architecture of freedom and who has been permitted to inhabit it and who has not. This ability alone makes the endeavors to refine the use of historical methods a worthwhile challenge.

REFERENCES

Afshari, Reza, 'On Historiography of Human Rights Reflections on Paul Gordon Lauren's the Evolution of International Human Rights: Visions Seen' (2007) 29(1) Human Rights Quarterly 1

Alston, Philip, 'Does the Past Matter: On the Origins of Human Rights' (2013) 126(7) Harvard Law Review 2043

Alston, Philip and Sarah Knuckey (eds), *The Transformation of Human Rights Fact-Finding* (OUP 2016)

Andreassen, Bård A., Hans-Otto Sano and Siobhán McInerney-Lankford (eds), 'Human Rights Research Method' in Bård A. Andreassen, Hans-Otto Sano and Siobhan McInerney-Lankford (eds), *Research Methods in Human Rights* (Edward Elgar Publishing 2017)

Brier, Robert, 'Beyond the Quest for a "Breakthrough", Reflections on the Recent Historiography on Human Rights' (2015) 16 Jahrbuch für Europäische Geschichte/European History Yearbook 155

Burke, Roland, *Decolonization and the Evolution of International Human Rights* (University of Pennsylvania Press 2010)

Burke, Roland, 'Human Rights Day after the "Breakthrough": Celebrating the Universal Declaration of Human Rights at the United Nations in 1978 and 1988' (2015) 10(1) Journal of Global History 147

Chane, Anna-Luise and Arjun Sharma, 'Social Network Analysis in Human Rights Research' in Bård A. Andreassen, Hans-Otto Sano and Siobhan McInerney-Lankford (eds), *Research Methods in Human Rights* (Edward Elgar Publishing 2017)

Clavin, Patricia, 'Defining Transnationalism' (2005) 14(4) Contemporary European History 421

Clavin, Patricia, 'Time, Manner, Place: Writing Modern European History in Global, Transnational and International Contexts' (2010) 40(4) European History Quarterly 624

Conrad, Sebastian, *What is Global History?* (Princeton University Press 2016)

Davey, Eleanor, *Idealism Beyond Borders. The French Revolutionary Left and the Rise of Humanitarianism, 1954–1988* (CUP 2015)

Eckel, Jan, *Die Ambivalenz des Guten. Menschenrechte in der internationalen Politik seit den 1940ern* (V&R 2014)

Eckel, Jan, 'The Rebirth of Politics from the Spirit of Morality: Explaining the Human

the post-1945 emergence of human rights. Samuel Moyn, *Christian Human Rights* (University of Pennsylvania Press 2015).

Rights Revolution of the 1970s' in Jan Eckel and Samuel Moyn (eds), *The Breakthrough. Human Rights in the 1970s* (University of Pennsylvania Press 2014), 226

Hoffman, Stefan-Ludwig (ed.), 'Introduction: Genealogies of Human Rights' in *Human Rights in the 20th Century* (CUP 2011)

Hunt, Lynn, *Writing History in the Global Era* (W.W. Norton 2014)

Iriye, Akira and Pierre-Yves Saunier, *The Palgrave Dictionary of Transnational History* (Palgrave Macmillan 2009)

Ishay, Micheline, *The History of Human Rights. From Ancient Times to the Globalization Era* (University of California Press 2004)

Jensen, Steven L. B., *The Making of International Human Rights. The 1960s, Decolonization and the Reconstruction of Global Values* (CUP 2016)

Johnson, Jennifer, *The Battle for Algeria. Sovereignty, Health Care, and Humanitarianism* (University of Pennsylvania Press 2016)

Kahn, Paul, *The Cultural Study of Law. Reconstructing Legal Scholarship* (Chicago University Press 1999)

Kay, David, 'The Impact of African States on the United Nations' (1969) 23(1) International Organization 20

Kelly, Patrick W., 'The Chilean Coup and the Origins of Transnational Human Rights Activism' (2013) 8(1) Journal of Global History 165

Lauren, Paul Gordon, *The Evolution of Human Rights: Visions Seen* (University of Pennsylvania Press 1998)

Levitt, Peggy and Sally Engle Merry, 'Vernacularization on the ground: local uses of global women's rights in Peru, China, India and the United States' (2009) 9(4) Global Networks 441

Lindkvist, Linde, *Religious Freedom and the Universal Declaration of Human Rights* (CUP 2017)

Merry, Sally Engle, 'The Potential of Ethnographic Methods for Human Rights Research', in Bård A. Andreassen, Hans-Otto Sano and Siobhan McInerney-Lankford (eds), *Research Methods in Human Rights* (Edward Elgar Publishing 2017)

Morsink, Johannes, *The Universal Declaration of Human Rights. Origins, Drafting and Intent* (University of Pennsylvania Press 1999)

Moyn, Samuel, *The Last Utopia. Human Rights in History* (Harvard University Press 2010)

Moyn, Samuel, *Christian Human Rights* (University of Pennsylvania Press 2015)

Neier, Aryeh, *The International Human Rights Movement: A History* (Princeton University Press 2012)

Nielsen, Christian Axboe, 'Can We Salvage a History of the Former Yugoslav Conflicts from the Milošević Trial', in Timothy Waters (ed.), *The Milošević Trial: An Autopsy* (OUP 2014)

Pendas, Devin O., 'Toward a New Politics? On the Recent Historiography of Human Rights' (2012) 21(1) Contemporary European History 95

Quataert, Jean, *Advocating Dignity. Human Rights Mobilizations in Global Politics* (University of Pennsylvania Press 2009)

Quataert, Jean, 'A Review of "The International Human Rights Movement: A History"' (2013) 13(4) Journal of Human Rights 537

Snyder, Sarah B., 'Bringing the Transnational In: Writing Human Rights into the International History of the Cold War' (2013) 24 Diplomacy & Statecraft, 100

Tuomisaari, Miia Halme and Pamela Slotte (eds), 'Revisiting the Origins of Human Rights: Introduction', in *Revisiting the Origins of Human Rights* (CUP 2015)

Waltz, Susan, 'Universalizing Human Rights: The Role of Small States in the Construction of the Universal Declaration of Human Rights' (2001) 23(1) Human Rights Quarterly 44

Waltz, Susan, 'Reclaiming and rebuilding the history of the Universal Declaration of Human Rights' (2002) 23(3) Third World Quarterly 437

Waltz, Susan, 'Universal Human Rights: The Contribution of Muslim States' (2004) 26(4) Human Rights Quarterly 799

Whelan, Daniel J., *Indivisible Human Rights. A History* (University of Pennsylvania Press 2010)

Wilson, Richard Ashby, *Writing History in International Criminal Trials* (CUP 2011)

7. The potential of ethnographic methods for human rights research
*Sally Engle Merry**

Human rights documentation frequently relies on reports of individual cases and situations. Yet there is a tendency to dismiss such narratives as 'anecdotal' and therefore not reliable. Ironically, however, in order to understand how human rights ideas and laws are having an effect in local communities, it is essential to examine local-level ideas, experiences and practices. Individual cases and situations provide valuable insight. It is in the micro-processes of human rights discourse, practice and consciousness that its effects become visible. This requires attention to the use of human rights language, to practices of activism and network creation among advocates working on different issues, and to the conditions under which individuals adopt a sense of self that includes the entitlements and rights offered in the human rights system.

Human rights reports rely on individual narratives, but presenting these stories alone, without context, is not the same as analyzing micro-processes ethnographically. The discipline of anthropology has developed ethnography as a systematic method for examining these processes by focusing on interactions and actors as well as the structural, social, cultural and historical context of action. Ethnography looks not only at individual behavior but also at patterns of behavior and the structural conditions within which they occur. An ethnographer examines what people do routinely – practices – the way they talk about their social world – meanings and modes of discourse – and the social structures within which they live and work – social networks and institutions. Understanding individual action requires embedding it within these larger frameworks of structure and meaning.

Moreover, an ethnographer examines individual behavior in the context of more general patterns of action. The individual is located within a context which enables the ethnographer to judge if his actions are typical.

* This research was generously supported by the National Science Foundation Cultural Anthropology Program and the Law and Social Sciences Programs, #BCS-9904441 as well as the National Science Foundation Law and Social Sciences Program, #SES-0417730 and the Wellesley College Faculty Research Fund.

She asks questions such as: is this action typical or does it appear abnormal in the eyes of the group? How do groups differ in what they consider normal? How do practices, discourses and networks differ among groups, nations and regions? These are a few of the fundamental questions that form the basis of ethnographic research. They are answered by observations and conversations with people who participate in small groups that have some level of common understanding.

Can an ethnographic approach that looks at small places examine the way the human rights system works in practice? Ethnography's genius is the examination of micro social spaces in context. Yet in order to do ethnographic work on human rights, it is essential to work at both the local and the global levels. Over the last 20 years, anthropologists have developed ethnographic methods that can be used to study things that exist in global and local spaces and move back and forth between them, crossing national and local boundaries. Two important approaches are multi-sited ethnography and the study of deterritorialized social systems. This chapter discusses these two innovative approaches to ethnographic research.

Multi-sited ethnography has emerged as a way to grapple with the important intersections between the local and the global and to examine micro social spaces in both settings. It adapts ethnography to the global world. In this analytical framework, what constitutes a 'site' ranges from an expert-group meeting in UN headquarters in Geneva to a small non-governmental organization (NGO) project in India, to a conference on human rights reporting in New York. While ethnography is resolutely focused on small sites of social interaction, this method applies to phenomena that circulate transnationally. Ethnography can illuminate social scenes that exist only in international space or that are deeply local but embedded in national and transnational systems of meaning and practice. Wherever it is practiced, multi-sited ethnography focuses on forms of discourse and meaning, everyday practices and habits, and systems of actors, networks and institutional frameworks. Deterritorialized ethnography examines unified social systems that exist in multiple locations yet share common discourses, practices and social networks, such as professional associations or UN activities.

Analyzing a micro-social situation within its larger social context provides a valuable methodology for examining how international human rights work in local situations. This chapter begins with an example of ethnographic research within a human rights context, then describes both multi-sited and deterritorialized ethnographic research, using examples from research on human rights, to demonstrate their potential as a way of understanding human rights in practice.

ETHNOGRAPHY IN A GLOBAL MICRO-SPACE

The distinctive feature of ethnographic research is its focus on a particular site where the researcher can observe interactions, see who is present, observe who speaks, note whose ideas are influential and record what is said. She focuses on what is happening in this site and how it is embedded in a larger context as one way to uncover social networks, context, meanings and discourse. For example, I attended an expert group meeting in Geneva in 2009 working to develop human rights indicators. There were about 20 people present, by invitation only. It was the sixth in a series of meetings tasked with developing a set of indicators of human rights to be used in country reports to treaty bodies. The project was sponsored by the Office of the High Commissioner of Human Rights (OHCHR) at the request of the human rights treaty bodies. One of the questions I asked myself was, who was present at this meeting and who was not there who might have been included? Those present included north European human rights lawyers, US academics, representatives from treaty bodies, a representative from a national human rights institution in Uganda, two European statisticians, a person working on development indicators at an NGO in Spain, and, on a drop-in basis, a representative from UNICEF and other UN agencies. A development economist and statistician were the staff members developing the indicators, both of whom said they had no particular knowledge of human rights. Who was not there? Human rights abuse victims, government leaders, prominent members of OHCHR, the Special Rapporteur on Violence against Women for the discussion of the indicator on this topic, and the representative of the UN Statistical Division, even though he had been invited. Few of the participants were from the Global South. The shape of the conversation was clearly influenced by who was present and what other interested parties were not.

Given this group around the table, a second important question is who speaks and who is heard? Those who took leadership roles in speaking and seemed to have the most influence in terms of uptake by others were primarily white male lawyers from Northern Europe. When the female representative from Uganda spoke, there was little response. The treaty body representatives also said little, and when asked if they thought their treaty bodies would be supportive of this system of human rights, said that they did not represent their treaty bodies. On the other hand, the economist who created the system was very forceful and assertive with his ideas, and tended to resist major changes to the template he had created. When meeting participants offered suggestions that were substantial, such as the idea that the whole system was too complicated to use, they received little response. Small suggestions were welcomed. The suggestions of one woman, a US human rights academic who had been involved in the project since the beginning, were generally ignored. Thus, observing who speaks and who is listened to provides valuable insight into how new ideas are generated and which ones prevail in such a setting.

A third important question is, what do such groups talk about? What frameworks do they use to organize information? Where do these frameworks come from? In this case, the human rights indicators are framed by a template appropriated from the fields of economic development and health, not human rights. Each human right is measured in terms of structure, process and outcome, with the assumption that, with structures and processes in place, the outcome will appear. Structures referred to laws and institutions while processes include government programs and policies. This framework, like that of economic development more generally, assumes that the path to desired outcomes can be drawn in a similar way for all countries. The template articulates an implicit theory of social change. However, as Rosga and Satterthwaite point out, the path may differ for different countries.[1] In contrast, the widely used human rights framework of respect/protect/fulfill developed in the 1980s measures human rights compliance in terms of the extent to which states respect human rights, protect them from other actors and seek to fulfill human rights obligations. The structure/process/outcome framework focuses less on the role of the state in protecting rights from its own actions and from those of other entities, and more on the necessary steps for states to take in order to produce human rights-compliant outcomes. Thus, the new framework is potentially more useful but is also less flexible under differing national conditions. It is, I argue, a shift from a legal framework to one more compatible with development economics.[2]

The ethnographic perspective encourages interpreting such scenes to make their principles and practices visible. For example, my interpretation of the meeting was that the North European lawyers dominated the process and the Global South representatives had far less influence. The treaty body representatives seemed very ambivalent about the indicators. Although the OHCHR was behind it, it was not a major concern for the agency, nor were other UN agencies particularly interested. Overall, the development economist and statistician staff members had the greatest influence in structuring the indicators. They adopted a new template

---

[1]   AnnJanette Rosga and Margaret L. Satterthwaite, 'The Trust in Indicators: Measuring Human Rights' (2009) 27 Berkeley Journal of International Law 253.
[2]   Sally Engle Merry, *The Seductions of Quantification: Measuring Human Rights, Gender Violence, and Sex Trafficking* (University of Chicago Press 2016).

that converted the legal framework of human rights into one familiar to developmental economists, an agenda that they acknowledged in the final report.[3] This framework incorporated an implicit theory of how human rights compliance could be achieved.

Observing the actors, interactions, discourses and social networks enables the ethnographer to trace the production of new forms of knowledge and to tease out relations of power even when they are not obvious or articulated. An analysis should attend to these micro-level processes as well as the context in which they occur. In this case, there was a preexisting crisis in treaty body costs and time, highlighting the need to streamline the process, along with the growing popularity of quantitative measures of performance. The wider context is the overarching UN system with its tensions between state sovereignty and international control and its ideology of equal participation juxtaposed to vastly unequal power among countries. Another dimension of the larger context is global inequality in statistical expertise, resources for data collection and experience with producing and using indicators. These features of context, as well as the history of the human rights conventions and treaty bodies, are essential ingredients in the interpretation of the event.

MULTI-SITED ETHNOGRAPHY

The previous example shows how ethnography works in any micro-space, including a global one. Understanding such spaces is essential for understanding how human rights work. Multi-sited ethnography is also valuable in human rights research. It focuses on the way ideas and practices circulate among local situations. We know that human rights ideas travel and come to ground in a variety of contexts and situations. They must be translated into terms that make sense in particular situations, a process I have called 'vernacularization'.[4] Conversely, human rights activists who work in particular situations must translate in the opposite direction.[5] When they write human rights reports, they convert particular situations into the more globally recognizable terms and categories of human rights

---

[3] UN OHCHR (Office of the High Commissioner of Human Rights), 'Human Rights Indicators: A Guide to Measurement and Implementation' (2012) HR/PUB/12/5.

[4] Sally Engle Merry, *Human Rights and Gender Violence: Translating International Law into Local Justice* (University of Chicago Press 2006).

[5] Sally Engle Merry, 'Transnational Human Rights and Local Activism: Mapping the Middle' (2006) 108 American Anthropologist 38.

law. In order to study human rights, it is essential not only to study micro spaces, even in New York or Geneva, but also to study the circulation of ideas and practices across such distinct spaces.

Multi-sited ethnography examines both the immediate social space of an individual or group and the larger system within which it exists. This way of doing ethnography is particularly appropriate for understanding the influence of the human rights system since its discourses and practices simultaneously act in local spaces and circulate globally. Indeed, the influence of human rights in local spaces depends on the awareness in these spaces that human rights are rooted in global ones. Multi-sited ethnography examines not only the circulation of human rights, but also the travels of ideas, people, money and things.

The idea of multi-sited ethnography was first articulated by George Marcus in 'Ethnography in/of the World System'.[6] He begins with the difficulty and challenge of studying the world system using insights provided by interdisciplinary studies such as anthropology and media, science and technology, and cultural studies. This approach moves out of the single, deeply contextualized site to one embedded in the world system, to 'examine the circulation of cultural meanings, objects, and identities in diffuse time–space'.[7] His perspective is that 'This mobile ethnography takes unexpected trajectories in tracing a cultural formation across and within multiple sites of activity that destabilize the distinction, for example, between life world and system, by which much ethnography has been conceived'.[8] The point of ethnography is 'to discover new paths of connection and association by which traditional ethnographic concerns with agency, symbols and everyday practices can continue to be expressed on a differently configured spatial canvas'.[9] To do multi-sited ethnography, he says, one should follow the *people* (migrants, diasporas), follow the *things* (commodities, gifts, intellectual property, money), follow the *ideas*, or, as he puts it, signs, symbols and metaphors, follow the *narrative* or the plot, story, or allegory and the myths or stories people tell about their everyday situations, and follow the *conflict*. In the past, this meant attending to disputes, but increasingly it includes wars and civil conflicts as well.

There are several interesting features to Marcus's approach. It is framed in world system theory, which moved anthropology away from its long

---

[6]   George Marcus, 'Ethnography in/of the World System: The Emergence of Multi-Sited Ethnography' in *Ethnography through Thick and Thin* (Princeton University Press 1998).

[7]   Ibid. 79.

[8]   Ibid. 80.

[9]   Ibid. 82.

tradition of studying small social spaces to more transnational and global ones. It is inspired by postmodernity, by a focus on fractures and gaps rather than coherence and order. It is concerned with understanding the subaltern, following an understated Marxist analytical framework. It draws on the work of anthropologists in media studies, science studies and development. It was in these ways a response to the theoretical and political problems of the 1990s: the impact of postmodernism on grand narratives such as Marxism or capitalist expansion; the emergence of the world system as a central analytic; the replacement of a more robust Marxist theory by a more contingent understanding of society; and the need to theorize the global and the local. This methodological move was shaped by all of these trends.

Twenty years later, there are new issues for which this methodology is relevant: the role of experts and forms of global knowledge production, the nature of democracy and human rights emerging after the demise of Marxism, forms of conflict such as genocide and global and local efforts to ameliorate them through humanitarianism and transitional justice, and of course the increasing power of international institutions such as the UN and its peacekeeping mechanisms, international NGOs, international criminal tribunals, development agencies and globally funded as well as local humanitarian and refugee organizations. We now see a new and rapidly expanding array of actors beyond the nation state, typically highly mobile both in space and in consciousness. New groups of highly mobile experts and helpers follow paths already laid down by the imperial reformers of the Global North. At the same time, migrant populations are moving from the Global South to the North, both the desperate undocumented poor and increasingly affluent and powerful diaspora populations. The latter sometimes intervene in political and military struggles in their homelands. This is a period of anxiety about population movements, about porous borders, and about flexible and ambiguous membership in states and communities. These anxieties are manifested in anti-immigrant sentiments, mobilization against trafficking and new forms of racism and exclusion, as well as the persistence of growing numbers of undocumented residents and refugee camps, some now coalescing into major urban centers along international borders. These are all social formations on the move that require multi-sited research.

One example of multi-sited research on the practice of human rights is my study of the way gender violence became defined as a human rights issue during the 1980s and 1990s and flourished in the 2000s.[10] In order to

---

[10]   Merry (n 4).

trace this historical transformation, I focused on the global circulation of ideas about gender violence both in the international institutions, where it was being defined as a human rights violation, and in a series of places where local and national movements were working to redefine gender violence as a crime and draw attention to its severity and pervasiveness. I did ethnographic observations of activists and local social movements in the USA, Fiji, China and India to understand their efforts to constitute gender-based violence as a criminal offense that warranted state intervention. These activists were already part of transnational exchanges of ideas and practices even before the turn to a human rights framework. I was intrigued by the similarity of approaches to gender violence in each of these countries despite significant differences in history, culture and social organization. Activists in each country I studied began with surveys of the frequency of gender violence and developed shelters, hotlines, laws targeting domestic violence and rape, systems of restraining orders and campaigns to improve the response of criminal justice systems. I traced how these ideas moved, who carried them, the direction of movement and the circulation of funding to support these campaigns over a period of 30 years. Clearly, by the 1980s, there were already international networks developing among anti-violence activists who shared ideas and approaches to the problem. While many ideas moved from the Global North to Global South, there were also important exchanges among both North countries and among South countries.

Only after the transnational movement was well underway did a campaign to define gender-based violence as a human rights violation emerge. The 1993 Vienna Conference on Human Rights provided a critical platform for introducing this idea, which was reinforced and strengthened at the 1995 Fourth World Conference on Women in Beijing and its outcome document, the Platform for Action. The addition of the human rights framework facilitated the circulation of ideas, practices, and funding about gender-based violence by reframing the issue into terms more broadly recognizable. Through this translation, the movement gained greater visibility and new allies. It also acquired an international platform through UN recognition and its incorporation into international mechanisms for fact finding, debate and resolutions. Mechanisms such as a Special Rapporteur on Violence against Women established in 1994, the inclusion of violence against women in the mandate of the Convention on the Elimination of all forms of Discrimination against Women (CEDAW) in 1992, the focus on violence against women in the agreed conclusions of the Commission on the Status of Women (CSW), and the Secretary-General's report on violence against women in 2006 are all important steps in raising the visibility of violence against women as a human rights violation.

Studying the movement of the issue into the human rights system requires ethnography, but here of local spaces within the international system. It means attending conferences and meetings in New York and Geneva as well as interviewing individuals who are central to this transformation. Since the movement of the issue into the human rights system was supported and pushed by NGOs, it also means interviewing and studying the role of the prominent organizations carrying out the transition. Here again, the key focus is circulation: the movement of ideas, people and funds through a variety of institutions as well as into broader publics as the visibility of the issue increases. It is necessary to trace the circulation of ideas and practices from local and national movements that are connected horizontally to global institutions and their subsequent journeys back to the local movements, now with a new framework. In order to understand the impact of this new global awareness and activism about violence against women, it is essential to see how these ideas and approaches are appropriated by local actors.[11]

This study of the circulation of ideas and practices of human rights and gender violence highlighted the processes of translation that are essential to the localization of human rights. An important form of translation is 'vernacularization': the reconfiguration of global human rights ideas into terms that are relevant and coherent within local life worlds. Local spaces are embedded within transnational systems, but are also distinctive. For example, an NGO working in a local community with international funding using a human rights framework must figure out how to translate the global framework into terms that resonate with local understandings.[12]

The advantage of this focus on circulation is that it reveals how ideas, conflicts, resources move, travel and can come to ground in various ways, and recognizes the connectedness of local places. However, the drawback is that it is difficult with this approach to carry out a detailed ethnographic study of a small space and the knowledge of any local site is inevitably more superficial. In depth ethnographic research takes time and money. There is clearly a trade-off between a multi-sited approach and an in-depth study of a particular situation.

Recognizing this dilemma, in a subsequent study Peggy Levitt and I examined how local organizations adopted global ideas of human rights in their campaigns against gender-based violence.[13] My initial

---

[11] Merry (n 5).
[12] Merry (nn 4 and 5).
[13] Peggy Levitt and Sally Engle Merry, 'Vernacularization on the Ground: Local Uses of Global Women's Rights in Peru, China, India and the United States' (2009a) 9 Global Networks 441; and Peggy Levitt and Sally Engle Merry,

study had examined the use of human rights language in the USA, Fiji, India and China, but in order to develop a clearer idea of the process of vernacularization, Peggy Levitt and I focused on the way local women's rights NGOs in four cities used human rights language in their everyday practices.[14]

Local/global interconnections were central to this study. We examined the movement of human rights ideas from global spaces to local ones and back again to global ones. The research focused on how ideas and practices concerning women's human rights were vernacularized by two women's organizations in each of four large cities that vary by region, religion, and history of human rights activism: Baroda in India, Beijing in China, Lima in Peru, and New York City in the USA.[15] All the organizations were committed to using a human rights approach to help women. However, they carried out this mission quite differently. Each selected a set of issues and strategies from those promoted by local and national women's movements, national traditions of human rights, and the texts and practices of human rights law. As actors and organizations move across local, national and international fields of power and meaning, they forge moral and instrumental strategies to promote their organizational goals within the constraints of funding, community support, and North/South power relations. They remake international human rights in the vernacular.

Human rights vernacularization is a process of translation within context. How various ideas are redefined or rejected varies across countries and settings. NGOs select how to use women's human rights according to their funders' preferences, their allies' interests and their clients' support. They adapt them to local meanings of human rights, formed by the political and historical experience with human rights in the country. Where human rights ideas are central to political movements and have a long history, as

---

'Vernacularization in Action: Using Global Women's Human Rights Locally' (2009b) Special Issue 9 Global Networks.

[14]   Ibid.; Peggy Levitt and Sally Engle Merry, 'Making Women's Human Rights in the Vernacular: Navigating the Culture/Rights Divide' in Dorothy Hodgson (ed.), *Gender and Culture at the Limit of Rights* (Series: Studies in Human Rights, University of Pennsylvania Press 2011); Sally Engle Merry, Peggy Levitt, Mihaela Serban Rosen and Diana H. Yoon, 'Law from Below: Women's Human Rights and Social Movements in New York City' (2010) 44 Law and Society Review 101; and Peggy Levitt, Sally Engle Merry, Rosa Alayza and Mercedes Crisostomo Meza, 'Doing Vernacularization: The Encounter between Global and Local Ideas of Women's Rights in Peru' in Gulay Caglar, Elisabeth Prugl and Susanne Zwingel (eds), *Feminist Strategies in International Governance* (Routledge 2013).

[15]   Levitt and Merry 2009a (n 13), 2009b (n 13) and 2011 (n 14).

in Peru,[16] framing women's claims to equality or freedom from violence in rights terms evokes greater public support than where human rights seem to be new and threatening, as in China. In general, enthusiasm for human rights discourse depends on its historical and cultural resonance in particular locales. This study retained the multi-sited focus on small spaces understood within larger structures and patterns of circulation.

From 2005 to 2009, we studied the circulation and localization of women's human rights ideas and practices.[17] In each site, we compared two or three NGOs working to implement women's human rights to see how they translated global concepts into local terms. We asked what women's human rights look like in the day-to-day work of these organizations and why organizations translate these concepts in different ways. Each university collaborator hired and supervised a graduate student to carry out intensive ethnographic research on two to three organizations over a one to two year period.[18] Each team wrote its own analysis.[19] Merry was the primary supervisor for the New York City team and Levitt worked more intensively with the Peru team. Levitt and Merry developed the overarching research questions and raised the funds from the National Science Foundation, but the detailed research strategies and questions for each site emerged through collaborative discussions. We traveled twice to each study site and organized two conferences which were attended by all of the members of the research teams as well as by other regional experts, ensuring an active intellectual exchange among all of the researchers. Thus, this research is itself an international collaboration in which we all learned from one another. We worked to translate ideas about research, about the questions we asked, and about the meanings of our results from one national context to another.[20]

In each country, we compared two women's NGOs. All were selected because they had an explicit commitment to women's human rights. Each team interviewed the leaders of each organization, its trustees and its staff members, observed staff/client interactions, determined caseload information and traced the history of the organization. They each did

---

[16] See Levitt et al. 2013 (n 14).

[17] This study was a collaboration with professors Liu Meng at the Department of Social Work, National Women's University in Beijing, N. Rajaram at the Department of Sociology, M.S. Univ. of Baroda in India, M. Rosa Alayza at the Escuela de Graduados, Pontífica Universidad Católica del Perú in Lima, Peru.

[18] The graduate students were Mercedes Crisóstomo in Peru, Vaishali Zararia in India, M. Liu, Y.H. Hu and M.L. Liao in China, and Diana Yoon and Mihaela Serban in the USA.

[19] Levitt and Merry 2009b (n 13).

[20] See Levitt and Merry 2009b (n 13); and Merry et al. 2010 (n 14).

ethnographic work in the organizations. There are clearly differences in how each team carried out this process, despite collective work on questions and issues for investigation. Although Merry and Levitt visited the sites, interviewed the leaders and met the staff, we relied on the language skills, background knowledge and analytic insights of each team.

In each site, NGOs cobbled together a collection of discourses and approaches to implementing women's human rights. Each NGO focused on particular issues and kinds of services, such as providing legal aid to battered women or advocating for better treatment in court for battered women seeking custody of their children. Each adopted a communication technology to get out a message about gender equality and women's rights. Some used conventional practices such as street plays while others turned to techniques such as personal testimonials. All shared to varying degrees what we call the global values package of women's human rights.[21] This package is premised on ideas of equality and freedom from discrimination, as articulated in CEDAW,[22] the major women's human rights convention. Article 1 of CEDAW defines discrimination against women as 'any distinction, exclusion or restriction made on the basis of sex which has the effect or purpose of impairing or nullifying the recognition, enjoyment or exercise by women, irrespective of their marital status, on a basis of equality of men and women, of human rights and fundamental freedoms in the political, economic, social, cultural, civil, or any other field'.[23] This global values package, premised on an essentialized understanding of 'woman',[24] was shaped by world-wide events such as the end of the Cold War, the decline of socialism and communism, the rise of neoliberalism, and the promotion of democracy and the rule of law. When elite women lawyers in China, with a history of socialist revolution, adopt this values package, however, they use it differently than do neighborhood leaders in Peru with a tradition of liberation theology.

In order to understand how and when these organizations translated

---

[21]   See Amrita Basu, 'Introduction' in Amrita Basu (ed.), with the assistance of C. Elizabeth McGrory, *The Challenge of Local Feminisms: Women's Movements in Global Perspective* (Westview Press 1995).

[22]   UN General Assembly, *Convention on the Elimination of All Forms of Discrimination Against Women*, 18 December 1979, United Nations, Treaty Series, vol. 1249 p. 13.

[23]   CEDAW (n 22), article 1.

[24]   See Inderpal Grewal, 'On the New Global Feminism and the Family of Nations: Dilemmas of Transnational Feminist Practice', in Ella Shohat (ed.), *Talking Visions: Multicultural Feminism in a Transnational Age* (MIT Press and New Museum of Contemporary Art 1998); and Inderpal Grewal, *Comment on Human Rights and Gender Violence* (American Anthropologist 2008).

women's human rights into terms relevant to their work, we examined the issues each organization tackled, the way it communicated its ideas and its modes of organization and funding. The importance of human rights in the choice of issues and communication strategies varied a good deal, depending on how receptive the local community was to human rights ideas, the value that a human rights frame added to working on local issues and the extent of external funding that valued human rights. Thus, this ethnographic approach allowed us to examine individual NGOs in depth and at the same time to focus on the larger cultural and structural context within which they worked. Attention to circulations of people, money, ideas and things (such as program brochures and websites) helped to understand how NGOs operated and the constraints they faced in choice of issues and approaches.

The focus on circulation included attention to the role of donors and funding in the work of these NGOs. The power of rich donors over poor recipients and the need to tailor and frame work in ways that elicit donations was dramatic, although it varied significantly among NGOs and countries. Some organizations refused to take foreign funds or speak English and resisted participating in global events. They drew on national and local agendas for women's reform, often explicitly rejecting international frameworks. Others relied heavily on international funding and ideological support, forcing them to conform to the agendas of their funders. Yet we found that those reliant on local funding tended to focus on more locally resonant issues, while those with international funding chose less resonant ones with perhaps greater difficulty of acceptance but at the same time a more radical potential for change.

An important methodological dimension of this research was its focus on local cultural understandings and practices. Vernacularization is a process of translating between cultural fields. A key dimension of vernacularization is what we call the 'resonance dilemma'. The more extensively a human rights issue is defined to be concordant with existing cultural frameworks, the more readily it will be adopted, but the less likely it is to challenge existing modes of thinking. The less extensively the human rights idea is vernacularized, the less likely it is be adopted but the more likely it is to challenge existing social structures. For example, one NGO we studied in India focused on familiar women's issues such as female infanticide and domestic violence and had widespread support, while another sought to improve the rights of LGBT individuals, a far more radical idea in the mid-2000s, and had limited uptake from individuals or other women's organizations. The extent to which any translator, particularly those embedded in NGOs, can promote new ideas that are only somewhat resonant with local issues depends on organizational autonomy and funding sources.

In sum, multi-sited ethnography has considerable potential as a way to study human rights in practice. This approach explores micro-situations in their larger context and at the same time follows the way ideas, persons, money and things circulate. It offers a promising way to do research on both the production and the implementation of human rights. Multi-sited ethnography examines social structures such as networks and institutions as well as cultural meanings and everyday practices. It considers how actors, ideas and things move and adapt as well as the ways they are appropriated, redefined or rejected.

DETERRITORIALIZED ETHNOGRAPHY

Another qualitative method valuable for studying human rights is deterritorialized ethnography. Instead of looking at things that circulate, this approach looks at social systems that exist in multiple locations but are the same wherever they are. They are not territorially bounded but represent one social system in several locations. Actors typically circulate among sites and form into social networks. These are generally large institutions existing in several locations. I noticed this first at UN conferences, commission meetings and treaty body hearings where I encountered the same procedures, ways of papering over differences with polite speech, practices of producing documents and the uses of particular phrases and ideas. The same people often inhabited these different spaces. A deterritorialized social system is marked by shared ideologies, practices and expertise. For example, my observation of UN deterritorialized cultural space suggested that there are some cultural practices, ideas and discourses shared in its multiple locations. Here are a few examples:

(1)   Representation of countries on committees and commissions is based on establishing equal regional representation.
(2)   Diplomatic protocol dominates conversational style, with debates over wording used to cover over significant differences.
(3)   Work focuses on generating documents that can be agreed on by consensus, such as treaties concerning climate change or arms control or agreed conclusions from Commission on the Status of Women (CSW) and resolutions from the Human Rights Council. This approach provides an aura of agreement despite significant differences.
(4)   Discussions at UN meetings focus on the performance of country identity and assertions of national accomplishments. Both in country reports and in statements at UN events, a country's reputation on this global stage seems to matter.

(5)   Discussions use a shared set of terms and ideas, such as best practices, lessons learned, political will and the need for flexibility and sensitivity when a country is criticized. English is the dominant language, despite translation into six official languages, and is the language used for informal exchanges and for wordsmithing during the production of collective documents.
(6)   An ongoing tension exists between monitoring state actions according to global standards and respecting the sovereignty of individual countries. This tension appears in the monitoring of compliance with human rights treaties and in the Universal Periodic Review process. Countries must agree to accept international supervision by, for example, ratifying a human rights treaty.
(7)   Although both states and NGOs participate in the deterritorialized space of human rights creation and monitoring, their interests are often sharply divided and mutual suspicion is common.

The international human rights system is hardly the only transnational, deterritorialized organization with shared practices, discourses and ways of doing things. Universities, multinational corporations and global law firms, are only a few examples of organizations that create cultural systems that exist in a variety of locations. The use of indicators for global governance also takes place in a transnational space of shifting actors and locations marked by shared expertise and cultural practices. In my current research, I examine how quantitative measurements of complex social phenomena, such as human rights compliance or trafficking interventions, are developed and disseminated ethnographically.[25] I examine sites such as expert group meetings, UN conferences and treaty body meetings as well as documents, reports and summaries of meetings in various parts of the world. There are clearly shared ideas of quantification, categorization and the nature of statistical knowledge traversing these sites despite significant regional differences in experience and resources. Statistical techniques and templates are similar.[26]

The space for indicator creation is also marked by shared cultural practices and expertise. This is a global space, but not one that incorporates the world equally. It builds on quantitative and social science expertise grounded in the cosmopolitan elites of the Global North and some parts

---

[25]   See Levitt and Merry 2011 (n 14); Sally Engle Merry 'Firming Up Soft Law: The Impact of Indicators on Transnational Human Rights Legal Orders', Chapter 11 in Terence C. Halliday and Greg C. Shaffer (eds), *The Theory and Dynamics of Transnational Legal Orders* (Cambridge University Press 2015); and Merry (n 2).
[26]   Merry (n 2).

of the Global South. An ethnographic tracing of this differential participation and input into indicators reveals the politics and inequalities in the
production of 'objective' truth through quantification.[27]

CONCLUSIONS

There are multiple ways of doing ethnography of the global, all of
which provide insights but are also inevitably partial. I have tried several
approaches: tracing the development of a global idea, such as gender
violence as a human rights violation; comparing the way NGOs in four
sites appropriate global ideas about women's rights in collaboration with
international scholars; and developing a network of scholars working
on indicators and global governance in a variety of locations, building a
shared theoretical orientation. The network approach was developed in a
collaborative research project on indicators and global governance with
Benedict Kingsbury, Kevin Davis and 14 US and international scholars,
published as an edited volume in 2015.[28]

There is currently a trend to use quantitative approaches alone to study
global phenomena; to ignore the insights of an ethnographic approach.
This may be because ethnography seems unsuited to understanding global
phenomena, but an ethnographic approach is clearly possible as a way to
understand global phenomena, such as the practice of human rights. It
provides valuable insights not accessible in other ways. Moreover, qualitative work improves quantitative work by developing better categories for
counting and theories for analyzing data. My own work on global governance in the field of human rights offers an ethnographic approach to the
process of quantification.[29] It shows how the production of indicators for
global governance is shaped by those who have the power to define the
terms of measurement, to pay for data collection and analysis and to disseminate the findings. Some organizations that create indicators are even

---

[27]   See also Kevin Davis, Angelina Fisher, Benedict Kingsbury and Sally Engle
Merry (eds), *Governance by Indicators: Global Power through Classification and
Ranking* (Oxford University Press 2012); Kevin Davis, Benedict Kingsbury and
Sally Engle Merry, 'Indicators as a Technology of Global Governance' (2012) 46
Law and Society Review 71; and Sally Engle Merry, 'Human Rights Monitoring
and the Question of Indicators' in Mark Goodale (ed.), *Human Rights at the
Crossroads* (Oxford University Press 2012).

[28]   See Sally Engle Merry, Kevin Davis and Benedict Kingsbury (eds), *The
Quiet Power of Indicators: Measuring Governance, Corruption, and Rule of Law*
(Cambridge University Press 2015).

[29]   Merry (n 2).

able to attach rewards and penalties to compliance. Thus, an ethnographic approach reveals inequalities in the power to influence how indicators are formed. It shows that quantification can be a powerful technology of management, control and reform, yet one that is not equally available to all.

REFERENCES

Basu, Amrita, 'Introduction' in Amrita Basu (ed.) with the assistance of C. Elizabeth McGrory, *The Challenge of Local Feminisms: Women's Movements in Global Perspective* (Westview Press 1995)

Davis, Kevin, Angelina Fisher, Benedict Kingsbury and Sally Engle Merry (eds), *Governance by Indicators: Global Power through Classification and Ranking* (Oxford University Press 2012)

Davis, Kevin, Benedict Kingsbury and Sally Engle Merry, 'Indicators as a Technology of Global Governance' (2012) 46 Law and Society Review 71

Grewal, Inderpal, 'On the New Global Feminism and the Family of Nations: Dilemmas of Transnational Feminist Practice', in Ella Shohat (ed.), *Talking Visions: Multicultural Feminism in a Transnational Age* (MIT Press and New Museum of Contemporary Art 1998)

Grewal, Inderpal, *Comment on Human Rights and Gender Violence* (American Anthropologist 2008)

Levitt, Peggy and Sally Engle Merry 'Vernacularization on the Ground: Local Uses of Global Women's Rights in Peru, China, India and the United States' (2009a) 9 Global Networks 441

Levitt, Peggy and Sally Engle Merry 'Vernacularization in Action: Using Global Women's Human Rights Locally' (2009b) Special Issue 9 Global Networks 441

Levitt, Peggy and Sally Engle Merry 'Making Women's Human Rights in the Vernacular: Navigating the Culture/Rights Divide' in Dorothy Hodgson (ed.), *Gender and Culture at the Limit of Rights* (Series: Studies in Human Rights, University of Pennsylvania Press 2011)

Levitt, Peggy, Sally Engle Merry, Rosa Alayza and Mercedes Crisostomo Meza 'Doing Vernacularization: The Encounter Between Global and Local Ideas of Women's Rights in Peru' in Gulay Caglar, Elisabeth Prugl and Susanne Zwingel (eds), *Feminist Strategies in International Governance* (Routledge 2013)

Marcus, George 'Ethnography in/of the World System: The Emergence of Multi-Sited Ethnography' in *Ethnography through Thick and Thin* (Princeton University Press 1998). Merry, Sally Engle *Human Rights and Gender Violence: Translating International Law into Local Justice* (University of Chicago Press 2006a)

Merry, Sally Engle 'Transnational Human Rights and Local Activism: Mapping the Middle' (2006b) 108 American Anthropologist 38

Merry, Sally Engle 'Human Rights Monitoring and the Question of Indicators' in Mark Goodale (ed.), *Human Rights at the Crossroads* (Oxford University Press 2012)

Merry, Sally Engle 'Firming Up Soft Law: The Impact of Indicators on Transnational Human Rights Legal Orders', Chapter 11 in Terence C. Halliday and Greg C. Shaffer (eds), *The Theory and Dynamics of Transnational Legal Orders* (Cambridge University Press 2015)

Merry, Sally Engle *The Seductions of Quantification: Measuring Human Rights, Gender Violence, and Sex Trafficking* (University of Chicago Press 2016)

Merry, Sally Engle, Kevin Davis and Benedict Kingsbury (eds), *The Quiet Power of Indicators: Measuring Governance, Corruption, and Rule of Law* (Cambridge University Press 2015)

Merry, Sally Engle, Peggy Levitt, Mihaela Serban Rosen and Diana H. Yoon 'Law from Below: Women's Human Rights and Social Movements in New York City' (2010) 44 Law and Society Review 101

Rosga, AnnJanette and Margaret L. Satterthwaite 'The Trust in Indicators: Measuring Human Rights' (2009) 27 Berkeley Journal of International Law 253

UN OHCHR (Office of the High Commissioner of Human Rights) 'Human Rights Indicators: A Guide to Measurement and Implementation' (2012) HR/PUB/12/5

PART II

HUMAN RIGHTS
RESEARCH METHODS
ACROSS DISCIPLINES

8. Interdisciplinarity and multimethod research
*Malcolm Langford**

INTRODUCTION

The last few decades have witnessed an explosion of interest in both inter-disciplinary scholarship and multimethod research. Such eclecticism is not only fashionable; it has gained a certain respect. In late modernity, the challenges of complexity and epistemology have necessitated the erosion of disciplinary barriers. Singular approaches to disciplinarity risked being too rooted in 'what is already known'[1] and mono-methodism fostered needless 'paradigm wars', the most entrenched being the battle between the positivist 'quantitative purists' and the constructivist 'qualitative purists'.[2] The consequence of the (partial) withering of disciplinary boundaries has been the spawning of intellectual synergies and new approaches to knowledge accumulation, methodological frameworks and institutional organization,[3] even if there are natural limits to disciplinary pluralism.[4]

The study of human rights is no exception to this development. While temporal disciplinary monopolies and methodological paradigm wars have marked the field, human rights research has gradually embraced the pluralistic turn. More than a quarter of online publications in English mentioning both 'human rights' and 'multimethod', 'mixed method' or 'interdisciplinary' were published in 2014 and 2015 alone. Indeed, human rights constitutes a natural field for interdisciplinary endeavour and methodological heterogeneity. It is neither a discipline nor delimited by a single discipline; and it is both a *research subject* (internally determined) and

---

* This chapter was partly prepared during the author's time at the Norwegian Centre for Human Rights, University of Oslo.

[1] C.W. Mills, *The Sociological Imagination* (OUP, 1959) 204.

[2] R.B. Johnson and Omwuegbuzie, 'Mixed Methods Research: A Research Paradigm Whose Time has Come' (2004) 33(7) Educational Researcher 14–26, 14.

[3] J. Braithwaite, 'In Praise of Tents: Regulatory Studies and Transformative Social Science' (2014) 10 Annual Review of Law and Social Science 1–17.

[4] M. Nissani, 'Ten Cheers for Interdisciplinarity: The Case for Interdisciplinary Knowledge and Research' (1997) 34(2) The Social Science Journal 201–216, 212; G. Grant and D. Reisman, *Perpetual Dream* (Chicago University Press 1978) 35.

research object (externally observed). This applies to academic scholarship but also to research in human rights practice.

Yet, while a new generation of students in different disciplines are beginning to partly master this new research modus, it is not yet clear how far such pluralism has penetrated the core of the human rights research community. This applies to both academic scholarship and applied human rights research. In the latter, despite the absence of formal disciplinary boundaries, monodisciplinarity tends to thrive and survive – often through internalization.

Against a backdrop of interdisciplinarity, this chapter takes up the topic of the use of mixed methods. It asks: how can we use different disciplines in framing research questions and locating methods? What do we mean by a multimethod approach? And how are pluralistic approaches best advanced in research?

The chapter proceeds as follows. The next section examines the benefits and risks of interdisciplinarity and methodological pluralism. Then I chart the contours of interdisciplinarity and multimethodism in human rights. The section begins by discussing relevant disciplines, the common and cross-disciplinary forms of human rights research, and the common faultlines or paradigm wars in this field. Next I set out a framework of multimethod research which would apply to different research modalities and potentially address some of the key faultlines. Illustrations are provided from research within and outside academia. The final section concludes.

WHY INTERDISCIPLINARITY?

Why embrace interdisciplinarity in human rights research? Why should we consider the research objects, methods and traditions of neighbouring or far-flung disciplines? In his article, 'Ten cheers for interdisciplinarity', Nissani[5] lists a host of reasons:

1. Creativity often requires interdisciplinary knowledge. 2. 'Immigrants' often make important contributions to their new field. 3. Disciplinarians often commit errors which can be best detected by people familiar with two or more disciplines. 4. Some worthwhile topics of research fall in the interstices among the traditional disciplines. 5. Many intellectual, social, and practical problems require interdisciplinary approaches. 6. Interdisciplinary knowledge and research serve to remind us of the unity-of-knowledge ideal.

---

[5]   Nissani (n 4) 202.

7. Interdisciplinarians enjoy greater flexibility in their research. 8. More so than narrow disciplinarians, interdisciplinarians often treat themselves to the intellectual equivalent of traveling in new lands. 9. Interdisciplinarians may help breach communication gaps in the modern academy, thereby helping to mobilize its enormous intellectual resources in the cause of greater social rationality and justice. 10. By bridging fragmented disciplines, interdisciplinarians might play a role in the defense of academic freedom.

These are all important but in my view three particular reasons stand out in the case of human rights. The first is the advancement of *research frontiers*. It is arguable that some of the most significant breakthroughs in rights thinking have emerged at the boundaries of disciplines. Even in the most expressly mono-disciplinary human rights articles and reports, one can find assumptions, findings or logics that have earlier jumped a disciplinary divide. Many core doctrinal concepts in human rights law owe their heritage to work in philosophy, politics, critical theory, social psychology and social mobilization. For example, the notion of the 'minimum essential level' in social rights traces itself back to German philosophy and sociology at the turn of the twentieth century. In 1951, it was judicialized by the German Federal Constitutional Court[6] and was later imported into the well-known jurisprudence and conceptual apparatus of the UN CESCER and domestic courts such as the Colombian Constitutional Court.[7] As the cannibalization of concepts from elsewhere has been long a trademark of law, such borrowing will continue to be necessary in solving new research puzzles and challenges in the face of complexity.

Contrariwise, human rights law itself has helped reshape theories of rights in philosophy and even ideas of citizenship and social change in the social sciences. For example, the philosopher Beitz[8] amongst others takes a point of departure in the post-1945 international human rights regime. He defends his choice *empirically* by pointing to the startling omnipresence of global human rights practice and *instrumentally* as its 'norms seek to protect important human rights interests against threats . . . which we know from historical experience are real and can be devastating when

---

[6] BVERFGE 1, 97 (104), 1 BvR 220/51 (1951) (Federal Constitutional Court of Germany).

[7] See *General Comment 3, The Nature of States Parties' Obligations* (fifth session, 1990), U.N. Doc. E/1991/23, annex III at 86 (1991), para. 10; and M. Sepúlveda, 'Colombia: The Constitutional Court's Role in Addressing Social Injustice', in M. Langford (ed.), *Social Rights Jurisprudence: Emerging Trends in International and Comparative Law* (CUP 2008), 144–162.

[8] C. Beitz, *The Idea of Human Rights* (OUP 2009).

realised'.[9] Human rights law has provided equally an engine for human rights practice that is now the subject of study in the social sciences.

Second, many of the *present and burning questions* in human rights cannot be answered within the confines of a single tradition or method. Whether it is parsing the contested meanings of a specific right, determining the impact of the international rights regime, measuring the general realization of rights, assessing the legitimacy of human rights policies, proving the existence of discrimination or engaging with the emerging challenges of biotechnology, eclecticism is essential. Put simply, important research questions do not correlate neatly with disciplinary boundaries.

In the face of such disciplinary uncertainty, the scholarly temptation is to retreat to known methodologies and methods. Yet crossing disciplinary boundaries increases the likelihood of finding more plausible answers, even if the effort is greater. Let us take the example of assessing the impact of legalized rights. The trait of good studies in this field is that researchers take time to familiarize themselves with the relevant *legal* aspects but also select an *empirical* method that best suits the question and context. For example, Helfer and Voeten[10] analyse the material impact of the LGBT judgments of the European Court of Human Rights. Through a careful attention to law (tracing the jurisprudence, identifying relevant national laws, contextualizing the Court's role) and the use of both standard and sophisticated political science techniques (hypotheses, baselines, multivariate analysis, robustness checks), the authors offer a convincing story of the specific conditions under which the European Court has contributed to the realization of these rights and provide, in effect, some practical guidance on how advocates can best use the court to foster social transformation. This empirical approach is just one of many. Other impact studies have used qualitative methods, comparative methods, experimental methods, quantitative content analysis methods and mixed methods from a range of disciplines.[11] Importantly,

---

[9]   Ibid. 11.
[10]   L. Helfer and E. Voeten, 'International Courts as Agents of Legal Change: Evidence from LGBT Rights in Europe' (2014) 68(1) International Organization 77–110.
[11]   B. Simmons, *Mobilizing for Human Rights: International Law in Domestic Politics* (CUP 2009); Basak Cali and Alica Wyss, *Why Do Democracies Comply with Human Rights Judgments? A Comparative Analysis of the UK, Ireland and Germany* (Working Paper 2011); Rodríguez Garavito, César and Diana Rodríguez-Franco, *Radical Deprivation on Trial: The Impact of Judicial Activism on Socioeconomic Rights in the Global South* (CUP 2015); Vincent Vecera, 'The Supeme Court and the Social Conception of Abortion' (2014) 48 Law & Society Review 345–375; D. Brinks and V. Gauri, 'The Law's Majestic Equality?

such diverse approaches have not only contributed to a deeper understanding of the extent of and conditions for impact, they have widened and problematized what we mean by impact. Different disciplines understand the concept differently. They frame and privilege its material, symbolic, political, psychological, legal, discursive and aesthetic dimensions differently.

Third, a key contribution of interdisciplinarity is *theory and method*. Each discipline tends to act as an incubus for intellectual developments and toolboxes that soon become relevant elsewhere. Indeed, the two dominant disciplines in human rights today, law and social science, have been thoroughly shaped by philosophy, theology and hermeneutics (in the case of law) and the natural sciences and history (in the case of the social sciences). Today, the movement of theory and methods across disciplines happens at a remarkable pace. In some cases, it is a case of theoretical fetishism and method mania, but for the most it is arguably a form of intellectual cross-border pollination that improves the development, framing and answering of research questions.

In the case of human rights, the broader transdisciplinary movements have made their mark across human rights in terms of both theory and method. One only needs to think of the discursive turn that has given attention to language and its underlying structural power; the new institutional theories from economics, sociology and history that help us make sense of the rights-relevant political and legal institutions; quantitative and network analysis methods that embrace the immense research material from rights realization through to the proliferation of institutions and explosion of doctrinal jurisprudence; qualitative and experimental methods that better get at questions of causation and archival methods that have opened a wealth of new material; the affective turn that allows the study of emotion in human rights; critical gender and race theory that has deepened theories of discrimination; or political philosophy and sociology that have given us the tools to negotiate the new questions of legitimacy surrounding human rights and predictions of its demise. One can only imagine the poverty of human rights research if it were isolated from these broader intellectual movements.

To be sure, interdisciplinarity is as risky as it is promising. Pluralistic research in human rights is accompanied by all the standard dilemmas. First,

The Distributive Impact of Judicializing Social and Economic Rights' (2011) 12(2) Perspectives on Politics 375–393; M. Langford, B. Cousins, J. Dugard and T. Madlingozi (eds), *Socio-Economic Rights in South Africa: Symbols or Substance?* (CUP 2014).

one risks *dilettantism* by rising above a single discipline yet failing to master the multiple disciplines covered.[12] One of the critiques of many interdisciplinary research programmes is that they end in a stodge of pure descriptivism or sloppy method. All of these risks are present and evident in human rights.

This does not mean that interdisciplinary research must always reach the standard required by some commentators, namely a contribution or impact in two or more disciplines. In my view, it can simply mean the use of one discipline to enhance or advance another, without any reciprocity. Otherwise, interdisciplinarity would be too much of a straightjacket. Indeed, such an approach underestimates the massive one-way flows across disciplines: e.g. rational choice approaches were exported from economics to political science, while economics imported the idea of social status from sociology. Both were profound but entirely separate and unidirectional interdisciplinary movements.

Instead, a commitment to genuine interdisciplinarity often means a willingness to learn and use another discipline at *some* level. It does not require full mastery although there is a (welcome) tendency to take additional graduate education. Instead, basic literacy, general familiarity or mastery of specific areas/methods in another discipline may be sufficient for the task at hand. Alternatively, one can collaborate with others from other disciplines. Such approaches are particularly common with quantitative methods in both scholarly and applied research but also in the use of other methods across disciplines. Over time, both approaches tend to be synergistic: collaborations improve one's own capacities, while the journey of self-learning opens new fields with potential collaborators.

Second, interdisciplinarity risks becoming *stale and naive* if it becomes 'cut off from fresh infusions of disciplinary knowledge'.[13] This dilemma is often unavoidable. Sub-disciplines and specialist research programmes are common offspring of interdisciplinarity but participants risk becoming unaware of broader and ongoing developments. In the case of human rights, it is possible that the proliferation of specialist human rights research centres around the world has closed off many researchers from major developments, critical perspectives and new methods, particularly in the social sciences and regulatory/critical theory. In my view, an important corrective is to ensure the presence of insiders and outsiders (or a core and periphery) on any interdisciplinary journey – whether it be a project, a programme, a centre, an NGO, a foundation, a conference, a society. Outsiders help insiders avoid the perils of excessive introspection.

---

[12]   Nissani (n 4) 212.
[13]   Grant and Reisman (n 4) 35.

Third, the weaker methodological moorings of interdisciplinarity leave it vulnerable to excessive and under-specified *normativism*. Assumptions, methodological choices and interpretive bias can go easily unchecked.[14] With its transformative impulse, human rights scholarship risks especially sliding uncritically over disciplines, drawing on their inherent weaknesses as much as their towering strengths. Thus, any interdisciplinary human rights endeavour needs to be well armed with participants who are willing to be both self-critical and critical of others.

INTERDISCIPLINARITY AND HUMAN RIGHTS

Relevant Disciplines and Implications

In thinking about the role of different disciplines in human rights research it is useful to identify which disciplines we are discussing. In my view, a broad approach is conducive but care should be taken in treating different disciplines in a similar fashion.

What are disciplines? The answer to this question varies over time. The very idea of a discipline is, of course, a construction, a recent and modern invention. Before their rise in the mid-nineteenth century, along with modern university departments, interdisciplinarity and multidisciplinarity comprised the standard modus of research. While many disciplines solidified during the course of the twentieth century, their boundaries continue to defy easy identification.

Any definition must therefore be flexible. Disciplines can be thus defined as a 'self-contained and isolated domain of human experience which possess its own community of experts'.[15] The definition is broad with its (1) weak substantive requirement of internal logic and (2) the general institutional requirement of an identifiable body of adherents. This 'broad church' approach allows one to paper over claims that certain fields (such law or anthropology) might not qualify as disciplines since they lack a strong core (in terms of methodological diversity or ability to resist incursions from other disciplines).[16] It also welcomes those disci-

---

[14] D. Kennedy, 'The International Human Rights Movement: Part of the Problem?' (2001) 15 Harvard Human Rights Journal 99–126.

[15] Nissani (n 4) 203.

[16] On the latter, see D. Westbrook, 'Creative Engagements Indeed! Open "Disciplines," The Allure of Others, and Intellectual Fertility' (2014) 3(2) Journal of Business Anthropology 170–179.

plines whose agenda is strongly coloured by the training and influencing of professionals (such as law, social work, theology and medicine). However, adopting an inclusive approach also means that it is often challenging to distinguish between a discipline and an inter-disciplinary field at a point in time. As we shall see, today's interdisciplinary collaboration is tomorrow's discipline.

Broadly speaking, we can categorize the relevant human rights disciplines into the social sciences and the humanities. The *social sciences* share a common bond with their 'empirical' focus on human behaviour and institutions. In economics, political science, sociology, social psychology, geography and anthropology we find similar repertoires of research, even if their object of interest is different (money, power, relations, thought/emotion, space, culture) and methodological preferences vary. Each engages in description; almost all privilege causal explanation (anthropology is the exception); some seek prediction (particularly economics and partly political science and social psychology); and many seek to influence public policy and socio-economic relations.

The empirical dimension of the social sciences does not mean that theory is irrelevant. Most social sciences are heavily theory-driven in trying to understand the world; theory is mobilized to solve empirical puzzles. Normativism and moral theory is also deeply present in all social sciences despite the valiant attempt to hive it off. The boundary between empiricism and normativism is often contested and unclear and, from the 1970s, conflation was increasingly welcomed.[17] Yet, and at risk of gross generalization, social sciences still foreground empiricism – it is their *raison d'etre*. In human rights research, this is often their distinct contribution. The social sciences help us understand the discourse, institutions, politics, norms, trade-offs, cultures, effects and origins of human rights.

In the past few decades, the borders of each social science have become increasingly blurred. Multiple sub-disciplines have emerged, such as political psychology, economic sociology, organizational studies, social geography, social work and public policy to name a few. Moreover, interdisciplinary collaborations between the *natural* and *life sciences* have produced relevant sub-disciplines to human rights. These include public health, evolutionary psychology, and political ecology. However, what is notable about all these interdisciplinary projects (with many of them now

---

[17]   W. Eastman and J. Bailey, 'Crossroads – Mediating the Fact-value Antinomy: Patterns in Managerial and Legal Rhetoric, 1890–1990' (1998) 9(2) Organization Science 231–245.

recognized disciplines) is that they bear the key hallmarks of their parental disciplines.

This disciplinary comparability breaks down once we move into what I will broadly define as the *humanities*. Empiricism loses ground as normativism and narrativism gain greater ascendancy. Here we find singular disciplines like philosophy or hybrid disciplines such as law, history, theology, education and linguistics. Philosophy largely eschews empirical methods while the hybrid disciplines combine an emphasis on text with either empiricism and/or normativism. For instance, law is a peculiar fusion of doctrine and hermeneutics (which it shares with theology, literature and linguistics), normative evaluation (which it shares with philosophy and ethics) and institutional/discursive analysis and regulatory theory (which resonates with the social sciences even if it is often methodologically limited).

Like the social sciences, the approach to human rights research in the humanities diverges on questions of different research objects and methods and the role of normativism. However, the differences between the disciplines are often paradigmatically deeper both as to how scholarship is understood and done. This makes interdisciplinary dialogue more challenging but sometimes richer.

As to philosophy, it is clearly a human rights relevant discipline, particularly the fields of political theory, ethics and critical theory. Its methods are valuable in clarifying concepts, exposing logical irregularities and implicit biases, and deconstructing established norms and frames.[18] At the same time, the philosophy of human rights itself is in need of interdisciplinarity. For example, some philosophical critiques of human rights law proceed on the basis that there is no legal jurisprudence or custom surrounding and clarifying these provisions;[19] some assumptions of actor behaviour appear unrealistic in light of what we know from social science and political behaviour: see, e.g. the assumptions in Waldron;[20] and both human rights advocates and democracy theorists often avoid difficult questions of trade-offs. On the latter,

---

[18]   See, e.g. T. Pogge, 'The First United Nations Millennium Development Goal: A Cause for Celebration?' (2004) 5(5) Journal of Human Development 377–397; R. Cox, 'Social Forces, States and World Orders: Beyond International Relations Theory' (1981) 10(2) Millennium – Journal of International Studies 126–155.

[19]   J. Griffin, *On Human Rights* (OUP 2008); O. O'Neill, 'The Dark Side of Human Rights' (2005) 81 International Affairs 427–439.

[20]   J. Waldron, 'The Core of the Case Against Judicial Review' (2006) 115 The Yale Law Journal 1346–1406.

Nickel[21] and Fung[22] respectively show that in most (if not all) contexts it is difficult to implement the full range of human rights or diverse forms of democracy (representative, participatory, deliberative). Likewise, while critical theory provides a useful corrective on the hubris and ambitions on human rights, and critical race and gender theory provides a deep conceptual apparatus for understanding discrimination, its normative thrusts sometimes lead it to ride roughshod over the nuances and diversity of human rights practice.[23]

The *hybrid disciplines* in the humanities offer an especially significant contribution to human rights research. Law, history, education, theology and linguistics offer empirical insights into the functioning of human rights; their textual focus sharpens our ability to understand the meaning of human rights; and their explicit normative drive (history and linguistics exempted) provide a powerful motor for both advancing and restricting the march of human rights. Yet these strengths can be equally weaknesses. The empirical focus can be quite limited (lawyers tend to mostly obsess with courts and legislation); there is a tendency to treat texts in isolation from politics, economics and culture; and the normative enterprise makes some recommendations for action blind to the world of unintended consequences and the riddles of human and institutional behaviour. Articles in law and fact-finding mission reports are perhaps most notorious for offering sets of recommendations which take no account of institutional alternatives, political feasibility, economic cost or psychological reception.

The humanities have also experienced a mushrooming of sub-disciplines of particular relevance to human rights. Some of these are internal to the humanities (critical race theory, critical gender/queer theory, liberation theology). Others intersect with the social or natural sciences: criminology, historical sociology, legal sociology, law and economics, legal anthropology, law and neuroscience, etc. All of these sub-fields have dealt with human rights in different ways. Some have even gained a specific human rights moniker with a highly defined cluster of researchers and advocates: e.g. 'human rights education'.

This broad approach to disciplinary choice signals the potentially wide

---

[21]   J. Nickel, 'Rethinking Indivisibility: Towards a Theory of Supporting Relations between Human Rights' (2008) 30 Human Rights Quarterly 984–1001.

[22]   A. Fung, 'Democratic Theory and Political Science: A Pragmatic Method of Constructive Engagement' (2007) 101(3) American Political Science Review 443–458.

[23]   See discussion in M. Langford, 'The New Apologists: The International Court of Justice and Human Rights' (2015) 28(1) Retfærd 49–78.

number of relevant disciplines to human rights research. It also suggests that caution should be exercised in privileging a single discipline outside the context of a particular research question or policy problem. Thus, the notion of human rights introduced by the editors of the book is problematic. A broad approach could not accept, *a priori*, the 'internationally recognized human rights norms, institutions and procedures as the principal reference points' for human rights research. Such a focus may reflect or usefully orient the book's contents, but is not desirable from an interdisciplinary perspective. First, it represents a methodological choice in itself which excludes other definitions of what constitutes human rights.[24] Second, it excludes bottom-up, domestic and subaltern conceptions of human rights which are the object of study in various disciplines, particularly critical theory, historical and political sociology, geography and anthropology, archival history and comparative law.[25,26] These perspectives are especially critical to anyone in trying to understand the role and impact of international human rights law.[27] Third, it affirms implicitly the highly problematic big-bang definition of human rights by Samuel Moyn[28] that whitewashes human rights out of history.[29] Finally, it glosses over the symbiotic and dynamic development of international human rights law. Most internationally accepted understandings of rights have a particular-

---

[24] Cf. P. Alston, 'Conjuring Up New Human Rights: A Proposal for Quality Control' (1984) 78 American Journal of International Law 607; M.-B. Dembour, 'What Are Human Rights? Four Schools of Thought' (2010) 32(1) Human Rights Quarterly 1–20.

[25] T. Halliday and L. Karpik (eds), *Lawyers and the Rise of Western Political Liberalism: Europe and North America from the Eighteenth to Twentieth Centuries* (OUP 1998); N. Fraser, 'Rethinking Recognition' (2000) 3 New Left Review 107–120; M. Tushnet, *Weak Courts, Strong Rights: Judicial Review and Social Welfare Rights in Comparative Constitutional Law* (Princeton University Press 2008); P. Jones, *Aids Treatment and Human Rights in Context* (Palgrave MacMillan 2009); T. Madlingozi, 'Post-Apartheid Social Movements and Legal Mobilisation' in M. Langford, C. Rodríguez-Garavito and J. Rossi (eds), *Symbols or Substance? The Role and Impact of Socio-Economic Rights Strategies in South Africa* (CUP 2014).

[26] However, one chapter in this book has been included to reflect this view.

[27] A. Guzman and K. Linos, 'Human Rights Backsliding' (2014) 102(3) California Law Review; S. Robins, *Revolution to Rights in South Africa: Social Movements, NGOs and Popular Politics after Apartheid* (Boydell and Brewer 2008); S.E. Merry, *Human Rights and Gender Violence Translating International Law into Local Justice* (Chicago University Press 2006).

[28] S. Moyn, *The Last Utopia: Human Rights in History* (Belknap Press of Harvard University Press 2010).

[29] S.L.B. Jensen, *The Making of International Human Rights – The 1960s, Decolonization, and the Reconstruction of Global Values* (CUP 2016).

ist origin and the nature of their formation often carries their historical pedigree.[30] One only has to to read the International Covenant on Civil and Political Rights and the International Covenant on Economic, Social and Cultural Rights to mark that the formulation of some rights emerges from situated historical experiences. A failure to appreciate their origins can skew interpretation or critique.[31] Thus, the first step in an inter-disciplinary approach to human rights is to be reflexive as to what we mean by the very concept. Like learning a new language, it requires a certain readiness to accept that the world can be perceived and described in different ways.

Forms of Human Rights Research

Drawing back from specific disciplines also allows us to see the broader modalities in human rights research – that are shaped by specific research questions and suggest different sets of methods. Human rights research can be divided into three general forms: normative, evaluative and empirical. The boundaries between each are not always clear and one could also include standard analytical techniques such as conceptualization (to which there corresponds entire sub-disciplines, i.e. onotology and conceptual history). However, in thinking about the fusion of disciplines and the use of multimethodism, it is useful to isolate these modalities.

Normative approaches are concerned with how things ought to be, how to value them, which things are good (or bad) and which actions are right (or wrong). This 'should'-based approach often leads to questions such as what are human rights, what is their content, how should we interpret them, what is the best way to implement and enforce them. Such questions are predominant in philosophy, law and applied rights work but are also surprisingly common across the social sciences. While the type of methods employed and degree of empiricism obviously vary across disciplines, it should be noted that even in philosophical work empirics can play a central role.[32]

---

[30] L. Henkin, 'Introduction' in L. Henkin and A. Rosenthal (eds), *Constitutionalism And Rights: The Influence of the US Constitution Abroad* (Columbia University Press 1989).

[31] M. Langford, 'Socio-Economic Rights: Between Essentialism and Egalitarianism', in J.K. Schaffer and R. Maliks (eds) *Moral and Political Conceptions of Human Rights: Implications for Theory and Practice* (CUP 2017).

[32] M. Walzer, *Thick and Thin: Moral Argument at Home and Abroad* (University of Notre Dame Press 1994); B. Williams, *In the Beginning was the Dead* (Princeton University Press 2006); C. Taylor, 'Conditions of an Unforced Consensus on Human Rights' in J. Bauer and D.A. Bell (eds), *The East Asian Challenge for Human Rights* (CUP 1999); Beitz (n 8); T. Pogge, *World Poverty and Human Rights: Cosmopolitan Responsibilities and Reforms* (2nd edn, Polity Press 2008).

Empirical approaches focus on human rights as an object. The aim is to describe, explain and/or predict relevant human or institutional behaviour – treating them as contingent historical phenomena, social facts, a cultural practice. The inclinations of each discipline to tackle all three types of empirical questions vary dramatically. As noted earlier, some disciplines such as anthropology and law express a decided preference for only description/interpretation, a few reach for prediction (particularly economics but also political science and psychology); most see explanation as a sufficient holy grail (sociology, political science, social psychology, education); and most draw on some theory explicitly (or implicitly) in framing the research. Full-throttled empirical approaches are the most recent entry to human rights research with researchers tracking the origins, functioning, construction and effects of rights and associated movements, institutions, backlash with a wide array of methods, etc.[33]

Evaluative approaches seek to determine the degree of compliance or conformity of actor behaviour with a human rights norm (legal or non-legal). They are very much a combination of the normative and empirical. Such approaches are implicitly interdisciplinary since they involve methods to establish a norm, identify facts and assess those facts against the norms. This approach is typical of much applied and lawyerly work in human rights. Interestingly, some organizations such as Human Rights Watch have increasingly employed journalists on the basis they are comparatively better at data collection and analysis than lawyers, which is often the most demanding aspect of such research. However, evaluative approaches are also quite common in the social sciences as part of 'transformative' approaches to research, which 'give primacy to the value-based and action-oriented dimensions of different inquiry traditions'.[34] The

---

[33]   See e.g. Simmons (n 11); B.A. Andreassen and G. Crawford, *Human Rights, Power and Non-Governmental Action: Comparative Analyses of Rights-based Approaches and Civic Struggles in Development Contexts* (Routledge 2013); D. Chong, *Freedom from Poverty: NGOs and Human Rights Praxis* (Pennsylvania University Press 2010); T.M. Keck, 'Beyond Backlash: Assessing the Impact of Judicial Decisions on LGBT Rights' (2009) 43(1) Law & Society Review; P. Gready, 'Reasons to be Cautious about Evidence and Evaluation: Rights-based Approaches to Development and the Emerging Culture of Evaluation' (2009) 1(3) Journal of Human Rights Practice 380–401; L. Hunt, *Inventing Human Rights* (W.W. Norton 2007); Langford et al. (n 11); H.-O. Sano, 'Evidence in Demand: An Overview of Evidence and Methods in Assessing Impact of Economic and Social Rights' (2015) 32(4) Nordic Journal of Human Rights 387–402.

[34]   J.C. Greene and V.J. Caracelli (eds), *Advances in Mixed-method Evaluation: The Challenges and Benefits of Integrating Diverse Paradigms* (Jossey-Bass 1997).

recent explosion of human rights indicators is testament to a concern with trying to improve the evaluative capacity of human rights.[35]

Methodological Faultlines

It is equally useful to think about common faultlines in human rights research. These may signal the relevance of interdisciplinary and multi-method approaches but also potential resistance. For the moment, I will focus on divides that possess a particular methodological character even if these divides are often discussed in disciplinary terms. These are the (a) lawyer–nonlawyer, (b) activist–observer and (c) quantitative–qualitative rifts. To be sure, there are many others. Most notable are the substantive divides in human rights research, e.g., consequentialist vs non-consequentialist, maximalist vs minimalist, universalist vs particularist, constructivist vs rationalist. These may also be susceptible to better resolution through multimethod research but they also are based on deeply held (but often unexpressed) values. For now, I will focus on a subset of discipline and method-based faultlines.

Legal vs non-legal

In recent decades, the *legal vs non-legal* divide has been most prominent in human rights research. I have lost count of how many multistakeholder and multidisciplinary workshops and conferences have begun with participants clarifying whether they are lawyers or not lawyers. Such confessionalism is remarkable and speaks to the recent hegemony of legal methodology: non-lawyers have had to justify their presence, perspective and approach. The result is that lawyers have secured a certain legitimacy in human rights research. They could freely assert that their methods were particularly well suited to normative and evaluative questions and partly or largely avoid inquisitions over their choice of research object/subject, methodical repertoire, interpretive bias, conflicts of interest or the empirical grounding of their recommendations. They have been relatively free to describe institutions, actors, the costs and benefits of certain policy choices, the impact of human rights and so forth.[36] Yet they have done

---

[35]   M. Langford and S. Fukuda-Parr, 'The Turn to Metrics' (2012) 30(3) Nordic Journal of Human Rights 222–238; A. Rosga and M. Satterthwaithe, 'The Trust in Indicators: Measuring Human Rights' (2009) 27(2) Berkeley Journal of International Law 253–315; T. Landman, 'Measuring Human Rights: Principles, Practice and Policy' (2004) 26(4) Human Rights Quarterly 906–931; Satterthwaithe in this volume.

[36]   For some examples see M. Pieterse, *Can Rights Cure? The Impact of Human Rights Litigation on South Africa's Health System* (PULP 2014); M. Dennis and

so without any awareness that in the social sciences these types of questions demand an explicit and rigorous methodology and that personal experience and anecdotes, while invaluable, do not necessarily constitute evidence in and of themselves.

However, this hegemony is fast crumbling. The rise of social sciences in human rights had increased the tension in the reverse direction. Lawyers have found that other disciplines will not accept their conclusions easily without greater attention to normative argument (e.g. philosophy, economics) and empirical evidence (most social sciences, education and history) Notably, lawyers are now pushing back with assertions that legal scholarship has something particularly unique to contribute, including in traditional domains of social science.[37] Such tensions and disciplinary politics are largely positive. They bring disciplinary consciousness and methodological choices to the fore. In my view, multimethod approaches are often ideally suited to answering questions that fester on this legal vs non-legal divide.

Activist vs observer

The *activist vs observer* divide is only partly disciplinary driven. Within each discipline, there exists a debate over the extent to which the transformative pull of human rights should inflect research questions, design and analysis. It is evident in philosophy, in debates over the catalogues and scopes of rights, in law, over teleological and dynamic interpretation of human rights treaties, and in the social sciences, history and medicine, over frames and methods that bias findings towards a sympathetic treatment of human rights.

However, it also crosses disciplines with assumptions that certain disciplinary approaches to human rights are inherently activist. Curiously, it goes in all directions. For instance, the philosopher[38] is suspicious of lawyers who dress up normative positions with 'precedent, texts, and interpretation', while the lawyer[39] exhibits frustrations with the 'conflicting

---

D. Stewart, 'Justiciability of Economic, Social, and Cultural Rights: Should There Be an International Complaints Mechanism to Adjudicate the Rights to Food, Water, Housing, and Health?' (2004) 98 American Journal of International Law 462–515; P. Alston, 'Against a World Court of Human Rights' (2014) 28(2) Ethics and International Affairs 197–212; J. Kozma, M. Nowak and M. Scheinin, *A World Court of Human Rights: Consolidated statute and commentary* (Neuer Wissenschaftlicher Verlag 2010).

[37] R. Howse and R. Teitel, 'Beyond Compliance: Rethinking Why International Law Really Matters' (2010) 1(2) Global Policy 127–136.

[38] Waldron (n 20) 1353.

[39] Alston (n 24) 608.

ideologies, cultures and interests' that have pervaded philosophical debates and argues that, on some issues, international law has provided a 'final arbiter'. One can repeat the same sorts of accusations between the social sciences and law/philosophy. This issue is not unique to human rights research and has been arguably exacerbated by the value-turn in scholarship since the late 1960s, in which there is 'an avowal and reliance on the controversial quality and values of disciplinary reason'.[40]

Resolution or moderation of this activist–observer tension can be achieved sometimes through standard methodological and analytical techniques. A researcher can be pressed to reveal their normative assumptions or positions, frame questions in an open manner and examine fairly counter-arguments or hard cases. However, a conscious multimethod approach can also provide an opportunity to cross this divide. Methods from different disciplines can be used to test the 'robustness' of different types of conclusions. While this approach is common in mixed methods research within the social sciences, it is gradually making an appearance in law and philosophy. For instance empirically driven sociological assessments of legitimacy can be used to test more deductive normative legitimacy approaches.[41] Even a narrow doctrinal question in law might be reasonably served by rigorous comparative and quantitative approaches to assessing prior jurisprudence and the constituent factual elements of doctrine (think for example of the doctrine of emerging consensus in the European Court of Human Rights or significant harm in the UN Human Rights Committee).

Quantitative vs qualitative
Finally, the traditional *quantitative vs qualitative* divide has fully reared its head in human rights research. This is partly a result of the shock in legal circles upon the use of quantitative methods in their territory. One exchange is typical of the many I have witnessed in multidisciplinary conferences, conversations and journal rebuttals. In a 2005 study, Posner and de Figueiredo[42] found that permanent judges on the International Court

---

[40]   W. Eastman and J. Bailey, 'Crossroads – Mediating the Fact-value Antinomy: Patterns in Managerial and Legal Rhetoric, 1890–1990' (1998) 9(2) Organization Science 231–245.

[41]   D. Bodansky, 'The Legitimacy of International Governance: A Coming Challenge for International. Environmental Law?' (1999) 93(3) American Journal of International Law 596–624; J. Gibson, G. Caldeira and V. Baird, 'On the Legitimacy of National High Courts' (1998) 92(2) American Political Science Review 343–358; E. Voeten, 'Public Opinion and the Legitimacy of International Courts' (2013) 14(2) Theoretical Inquiries in Law 411–436.

[42]   E. Posner and M. de Figueiredo, 'Is the International Court of Justice Biased?' (2005) 34 Legal Studies 599, 623–624.

of Justice are more likely to vote for a disputing state that shares a similar level of democracy and economic development and to a lesser extent with shared religion and language. According to the authors, these statist correlations explain a remarkable 60–70% of variance amongst individual judicial votes. In a response, the international lawyer Calliess[43] chafes if not explodes at the use of numbers: 'I am not convinced by the hypothesis' and 'doubt that there can be constructed a viable relationship'.[44]

The divide is also an extension of existing debates in social science into new research on human rights. For instance, Hafner-Burton[45] observed the paradox that qualitative and quantitative researchers came to radically divergent conclusions over the impact of human rights treaties – the former more positive and the latter decidedly negative with the exception of Neumayer.[46] Interestingly, it was the mixed methods approach of Simmons[47] that led to a more moderate but significant set of results and helped reshape the framework for ongoing research.

Nonetheless, the quantitative–qualitative divide is fairly deeply dug and drawn in empirical research. The table in Appendix 1 presents a typical dichomotization of 10 different features of both methods.[48] The first two are perhaps the most central. Qualitative approaches are more focused on individual cases with a quest to find necessary and sufficient conditions. Quantitative approaches are often concerned with the average effects and seek the probabilistic contribution of each independent factor. This usefully explains the different cultures behind each method. Some of the mixed methods literature goes even further in sharpening the differences, assuming that qualitative methods are exploratory rather than explanatory.[49]

However, the differences identified in the Appendix also illustrate the

---

[43] Calliess, 'Judicial Independence and Impartiality in International Courts: A Comment on Posner's Institutional Theory of the ICJ's Decline' in S. Voigt, M. Albert and D. Schmidtchen (eds), *International Conflict Resolution* (Mohr Siebeck 2006).

[44] Towards the end of the response Calliess partly concedes the point and makes various proposals to ensure the Court is 'statistically unbiased': judges should be more 'homogenous' or possess a distinctly 'cosmopolitan' or universalistic outlook.

[45] E. Hafner-Burton and J. Ron, 'Human Rights Institutions: Rhetoric and Efficacy' (2007) 4(4) Journal of Peace Research 379–383.

[46] E. Neumayer, 'Do International Human Rights Treaties Improve Respect for Human Rights?' (2005) 49(6) Journal of Conflict Resolution 925–953.

[47] Simmons (n 11).

[48] J. Mahoney and G. Goertz, 'A Tale of Two Cultures: Contrasting Quantitative and Qualitative Research' (2006) 14 Political Analysis 227–249.

[49] J.W. Creswell, V.L. Plano Clark, M.L. Gutmann and W.E. Hanson, 'Advanced Mixed Methods Research Design' (2003) *Handbook of Mixed Methods*

potential for mixed methods by drawing on two different approaches to our understanding of causes and consequences. Moreover, the differences are sometimes over-drawn. The boundary is not always clear. Experimental methods, quantitative/qualitative content analysis methods and some survey methods share features of both quantitative and qualitative approaches. Moreover, simplistic assumptions slide over the fact that a significant body of qualitative research is explanatory oriented, including in the human rights field.[50]

The quantitative–qualitative debate is equally divisive in evaluative and normative driven human rights research. From one perspective, there is a desperate need for quantitative methods here. Qualitative methods for evaluation often elicit the complaint that the evidence is too *ad hoc*, inadequate in establishing systematic patterns of violations, identifying clear failures by duty-bearers to fulfil their positive obligations or motivating systemic reform.[51] At the heart of quantification is aggregation and replication. A broader swathe of events and experiences can be captured, represented and compared across time and space (e.g. localities, countries, regions, etc.), which provides particularly information on the magnitude and source of problems. Establishing seemingly neutral, scaleable and externally verifiable methods seems ideal for human rights. In an environment characterized by accountability relations, distance between actors, and mutual distrust, 'audit'-like tools such as indicators can provide a mutually acceptable means for actors to assess and communicate with each other.[52]

Quantification is also driven by attempts to substantiate certain normative arguments and overcome resistance to them. Researchers have sought to demonstrate that human rights do not generate negative externalities but instead provide verifiable benefits, whether it is peace, economic growth, improved health, democratic deliberation, etc.[53]

---

in Social and Behavioural Research (Reprinted in the Mixed Method Reader (Sage) 159–196) 209–240; Johnson and Omwuegbuzie (n 2).

[50]   Langford et al. (n 11); Halliday and Karpik (n 25); S. Gloppen, 'Courts and Social Transformation: An Analytical Framework' in R. Gargarella, P. Domingo and T. Roux (eds), *Courts and Social Transformation in New Democracies: An Institutional Voice for the Poor?* (Ashgate 2006); Chong (n 33).

[51]   Langford and Fukuda-Parr (n 35).

[52]   Rosga and Satterthwaithe (n 35).

[53]   R.L. Barsh, 'Measuring Human Rights: Problems of Methodology and Purpose' (1993) 15 Human Rights Quarterly 87–121; S. Randolph and P. Guyer, 'Tracking the Historical Evolution of States' Compliance with their Economic and Social Rights Obligations of Result: Insights from the Historical SERF Index' (2012) 30(3) Nordic Journal of Human Rights 297–323; J. Heymann, M. Barrera,

However, the problems of using quantitative human rights in evaluative and normative work are regularly pointed out by qualitative researchers. The first is the definition and choice of indicators. The criteria for creating an indicator may not match the relevant human rights standard and the problem of ill-fitting proxies does not stop at the phase of constructing, processing and interpreting data. It is also a reflexive process whereby an indicator reshapes its parent norm. As Davis, Kingsbury and Merry put it, indicators embody a 'theoretical claim about the appropriate standards for evaluating actors' conduct'.[54] If an indicator is loosely matched with a standard or simply achieves prominence, it can quickly take on a normative life of its own.[55] The second challenge is the reliability of data. Recorded observations may not be an accurate reflection of the complex reality that a measuring instrument is trying to capture.[56] One particular challenge for many civil rights indicators is that recorded violations – particularly those concerning violence, death or displacement – may actually increase as the state improves compliance. The third challenge is aggregation. Higher levels of aggregation do not provide adequate detail and differentiation and data truncation is a particular problem with global datasets.[57] The fourth challenge is action-orientation and perverse incentives. Many are sceptical as to the relevance of global data for country-focused assessments[58] while actors might prioritize actions that are quantitatively measurable rather than those intended to meet the objective

---

I. Vincent and N.D. Guzman, 'Data-Based Accountability Mechanisms for Human Rights: Testing a New Methodology' (2012) 30(3) Nordic Journal of Human Rights.

[54]   K. Davis, B. Kingsbury and S.E. Merry (eds), *Governance by Indicators: Global Power through Classification and Rankings* (OUP 2012) 9.

[55]   T. Pogge, *Millions Killed by Clever Dilution of Our Promise* (CROP Poverty Brief, August 2010); A. Fischer, 'The Political within the Depoliticised: Poverty Measurement, Implicit Agendas and the MDGs' in M. Langford, A. Sumner and A.E. Yamin (eds), *The MDGs and Human Rights: Past, Present and Future* (CUP 2013).

[56]   A.E. Yamin and K. Falb, 'Counting What We Know; Knowing What to Count: Sexual and Reproductive Rights, Maternal Health, and the Millennium Development Goals' 30(3) (2012) Nordic Journal of Human Rights.

[57]   For a discussion in the context of human rights, see Barsh (n 53) 102–103 and Landman (n 35) 923.

[58]   A. Wilde and J. Nahem, 'UNDP and Democratic Governance Assessments' in UNDP (ed.), *Making the State Responsive: Experience with Democratic Governance Assessments* (UNDP 2011); M. Orkin, C. Naval, J.R. Suesser and R.S.D. Miguel, 'Towards the Democratic Monitoring of Governance: The Metagora Experience' in UNDP (ed.), *Making the State Responsive: Experience with Democratic Governance Assessments* (UNDP 2011).

behind the indicator.[59] The final challenge is interpretation and publicity: what indicators 'actually communicate, and to whom, may not be what their producers and promulgators sought to communicate'.[60] Judgments may be too light or harsh because of problems in the data or method rather than reality.

In this context, mixed methods that use both quantitative and qualitative methods are being recognized as particularly important in creating sounder policy arguments and providing more trustworthy pictures of human rights performance.

MULTIMETHOD RESEARCH DESIGN

How should we think about multimethod approach in the context of human rights? In my view, we need to pay greater attention to the nature of research questions and research design and exhibit more methodological rigour or humility in articulating assumptions, hypotheses and recommendations.

Research Questions

The importance of specifying research questions varies across disciplines. Disciplines that are primarily or exclusively in the 'narrative' tradition (law, anthropology, history, literature) rather than the 'analytical' tradition tend to regard question specification as of slightly less importance. This might be accounted for by the prominence of descriptive analysis or the emphasis on style, text and exploration. One needs to be careful of stylistic or methodological imperialism! There are different traditions of knowledge production. However, in the field of law, this de-emphasis is striking. While carefully structured questions are the driving force behind judging and legal advocacy/practice,[61] one often strains to find a precisely specified research question in reading legal scholarship. One is sometimes left at the end of an article trying reconstruct what the author was setting out to achieve. A similar conundrum exists in history, which often sets out to identify causal relations.

---

[59]   R. Black and H. White (eds), *Targeting Development: Critical Perspectives on the Millennium Development* (Routledge 2004); S. Fukuda-Parr and A.E. Yamin, *The MDGs, Capabilities and Human Rights: The Power of Numbers to Shape Agendas* (Routledge 2015).

[60]   S.E. Merry, *Human Rights and Gender Violence Translating International Law into Local Justice* (Chicago University Press 2006).

[61]   L.H. Carter and T.F. Burke, *Reason in Law* (8th edn, Longman 2010).

Table 8.1 Research questions and methods

	Monodisciplinary question	Multidisciplinary question
Single method	I. Monomethod	III. Parallel methods
Multiple methods	II. Mixed methods	IV. Multimethod/transmethod

Table 8.1 classifies research questions according to four basic options across a disciplinary and methodological axes. In Quadrant 1, we find a *single discipline* and a *single method*. Such research questions are often highly specific in the use of an adjective as well as conditioning nouns. For example, we might ask: is there a legal right to same-sex marriage under the American Convention on Human Rights; what is the moral case for a free right to migration; or what is the psychological impact of torture? All of these questions can be reasonably answered within a single discipline even if broader interdisciplinary perspectives might be helpfully introduced.

For some questions, however, multiple methods within a single discipline may be critical or very important. See Quadrant II. Here the adjectives tend to be more open in a research question. In practice, many research questions fall into this category although they are often incorrectly specified as single discipline/method. A reflexive practice of reviewing research questions is critical.

For Quadrant II, let us take an example from rights in asylum law. If we ask the question of whether asylum seekers from Ethiopia have a right to asylum, whether in Canada, Switzerland or the USA, a plausible answer cannot be obtained with the singular use of doctrinal, quantitative or qualitative methods. A doctrinal approach will foreground legally the grounds for asylum and permissible considerations from human rights law, and factually the general political conditions in Ethiopia and the risk of persecution for an individual or class of applicants. However, we know from quantitative studies that the likelihood of being granted asylum is also dependent on the political ideology of an adjudicator, particularly their express or imputed views on migration and foreign policy.[62] Other quantitative studies of judicial behaviour show the importance of judicial background,[63] interaction

---

[62] Christopher J. Fariss and Andy J. Rottman, 'The Political Economy of Decision Making Bias: An Analysis of Asylum Merit Hearings in US Immigration Court' (2009) Available at SSRN 2080286; D. Hangartner, B. Lauderdale and J. Spirig, *Refugee Roulette Revisited: Judicial Preference Variation and Aggregation on the Swiss Federal Administrative Court 2007–2012*, Conference on Empirical Legal Studies, Amsterdam, 21–22 June 2006.

[63] Voeten (n 41).

effects between panel members,[64] considerations of judicial reputation[65] and the remarkable importance of blood sugar levels for high-volume case processing – i.e. whether a judge ate a sufficient breakfast![66] Yet even this is not sufficient. Qualitative methods help understand the prevailing culture and history within an asylum tribunal or court,[67] the mediating influence of tribunal appointments, and the importance of the structure of decision-making (e.g. sequential and concurrent decision-making in panels).[68] Taken in isolation, each one of these methods cannot answer the question as to whether there is a right to asylum for Ethiopian asylum seekers. The question can be framed sensibly within law but cannot be plausibly and fully answered with law (or for that matter political science or sociology). A doctrinal approach cannot capture these broader probabilistic factors; a quantitative approach cannot capture the nuances of the legal and cultural conditions; and a qualitative approach cannot tell us anything about the magnitude of different factors, including law and ideology.

A similar pattern emerges if we flip disciplines and method. Identical research questions can be asked in different disciplines but a single method may be justifiable: Quadrant III. Here the adjectives and nouns may line up perfectly but a methodological choice can be freely made. Let us take the research question: should issues of human rights be decided by referendum? The question is clearly a normative question, i.e. 'should'. However, it is possible to construct a full and reasonable research project (or at least article/short report) that is confined to a single discipline. The political philosopher might examine the moral case; the lawyer might examine the arguments in light of jurisprudence; the political scientist might examine the effects of such referendums; the historian may provide the *longue duree*, etc. Obviously no discipline can provide a holistic answer to the question(!). However, each discipline can provide a coherent answer within their discipline. This is to be contrasted with the asylum question where no discipline could purport to provide a full answer, as the question was *framed*.

Finally, some (or many) questions that cross disciplines also require

[64]   Jonathan P. Kastellec, 'Racial Diversity and Judicial Influence on Appellate Courts' (2013) 57(1) American Journal of Political Science 167–183.

[65]   L. Epstein and J. Knight, 'Reconsidering Judicial Preferences' (2013) 16 Annual Review of Political Science 11–31.

[66]   See S. Danziger, J. Levav and L. Avnaim-Pesso, 'Extraneous Factors in Judicial Decisions' (2011) 108(17) PNAS 6889–6892.

[67]   K. Whittington, 'Once More Unto the Breach: Post-Behavioralist Approaches to Judicial Politics' (2000) 25(2) Law and Social Inquiry 601–634.

[68]   Hangartner et al. (n 62).

multiple methods: Question IV. For example, if we ask how should we best address balance concerns of terrorism and the right to privacy, no discipline or method has a monopoly on the answer. While the 'should' invokes the normative traditions across different disciplines (as in the Quadrant III example), the addition of 'best' not only introduces considerations of both consequentialism and values, but also signals that the solution has to engage with the real world. It thus foregrounds the rationales of public policy, which particularly open for multiple disciplines and every imaginable method in social sciences and the humanities. Any plausible answer would thus have to engage with questions of social values, legal constraints, security risks, economic and crime consequences, political fallout and social trust. The methods could include interviewing security officers and victims, undertaking large-N studies of different techniques and effects, doing experimental studies of citizen values and decision-making under uncertainty or examining different legal and regulatory regimes and the underlying rights and security law framework.[69]

Indeed, such questions are often similar to the recommendations discussed at the end of many human rights articles, reports and monographs. However, as noted earlier, lawyers and many others often fail to draw on the insights from public policy/policy science. This includes identifying the common requirements for reform (moral, efficiency, feasibility) and the elements of policy: agenda setting/problem definition; alternatives; policy formulation/adoption; implementation; and monitoring/evaluation.[70] Moreover, the failure of human rights philosophers, advocates, courts and activists to consider from an interdisciplinary perspective the nature, extent and reception of their recommendations and their psychological and political reception has come under increasing scrutiny.[71]

---

[69] For some of these methods, see C. Lum and L. Kennedy (eds), *Evidence-based Counterterrorism Policy* (Springer 2011); R. van der Hilst, 'Putting Privacy to the Test: How Counter-terrorism Technology is Challenging Article 8 of the European Convention on Human Rights', PhD Thesis, University of Oslo, 2013.

[70] H.D. Lasswell, *Power and Personality* (Transaction Press 1948); C. Weible, T. Heikkila, P. deLeon and P. Sabatier, 'Understanding and Influencing the Policy Process' (2012) 45 Policy Sci 1–21, 3–4.

[71] H. Burke, 'Political Theorists as Dangerous Actors' (2010) 15(1) Critical Review of International Social and Political Philosophy 41–61; P. Alston, 'The Challenges of Responding to Extrajudicial Executions: Interview with Philip Alston' (2010) 2(3) Journal of Human Rights Practice 355–373; C. Rodríguez-Garavito, 'Beyond the Courtroom: The Impact of Judicial Activism on Socioeconomic Rights in Latin America' (2011) 89 Texas Law Review 1669–1698; V. Baird and D. Javeline, 'The Persuasive Power of Russian Courts' (2007) 60(3) Political Research Quarterly 429–442.

Mixed Methods

We now turn to multimethodism and mixed methods. We might distinguish between three types of approaches with only the last fully meeting the requisite definition. A *contextual* approach is the thinnest approach to mixed methods and would not qualify under many definitions of mixed methods. It is simply the use of other disciplines as a departure point or source material. The social scientist borrows for a hypothesis; the philosophers appropriates for a puzzle; and the lawyer steals for a concept or exception. However, the method remain singular – it is just contextualized by connecting with other disciplines and methods. A *programmatic* approach is a broader research agenda, centre, edited collection or association that seeks to trigger or encourage multiple methods for a general objective or overarching research questions. However, such a programme might allow all its participants to engage in monomethodism with its leaders or editors synthesizing the results. Again, it is a thin or weak approach as it does not encourage singular research design that incorporates more than one method. A *project* approach meets the definition of multimethodism fully as mixed methods are required within the confines of a single research design. It is this approach I will focus on for the remainder of the subsection although the other two are of course welcome and legitimate.

Mixed methods approaches emerged in the social sciences but in my view they can also include the humanities. We can graft contemporary mixed methods discussions in the social sciences, medicine and history on to the broader palette of multidisciplinary human rights research. Thus, we should be open too for the use of mixed methods from law, history, linguistics or philosophical research.[72] However, I am less sure about speaking of different methods within the humanities (with the exception of education and linguistics). To take law, it is possible to discuss different legal methods in international and national law, public and private law, federal and local law; or deductive vs inductive vs abductive approaches to interpretation. However, the underlying methodological logic is startlingly similar and all of these elements have their parallels in quantitative approaches or qualitative approaches. Thus, I remain unconvinced that the dominant doctrinal approach in law is more than one method. It is better to think of sub-methods within law.

---

[72]   Some might argue that philosophical methods are often meta-methods. I am less sure given their sophistication and the implicit and explicit use of mathematics in philosophy. In any case, for an empirical sub-question in a philosophical inquiry, such mixed methods would be of relevance: J. Nickel, *Making Sense of Human Rights* (Blackwell 2007).

Table 8.2 is adapted from Creswell, Plano Clark, Gutmann and Hanson.[73] The key distinction is between sequential and concurrent forms of mixed methods. The former concerns the use of methods that build on each other to answer a question while concurrent approaches seek to answer a single question independently of each other. For the moment, it follows the customary quantitative vs qualitative distinction but this can also incorporate doctrinal and archival methods. Most archival and doctrinal approaches would be included under qualitative unless they were being used to generate numeric data, which would place them under quantitative. This underlines the point that quantitative and qualitative are large categories. As can be also seen, mixed methods thinking has also incorporated research design that is guided by normative or evaluative concerns (often called 'transformative'). This term is used for research within social sciences and medicine but could equally apply to all the other disciplines discussed in this chapter.

However, there is one important caveat to be made in the use of the table. In my view, it is possible to take a multimethod approach within and not just between different quantitative and qualitative traditions. This is not to excuse sloppy research but rather recognize that there are strong and distinct methodological traditions under these banners that can be fruitfully combined. Indeed, leading mixed methods scholars now prefer to speak of a continuum of approaches, even if it means somewhat contradicting their earlier frameworks: 'Mixed methodologists have repeatedly placed mixed methods on a continuum that includes qualitative, quantitative, and mixed approaches rather than using the dichotomy of qualitative or quantitative'.[74]

This spectrum-based approach is well represented in human rights research. For example, Linos and Twist[75] use a concurrent nested approach with two different quantitative methods: embedding experimental design in a standard panel survey instrument on the effects on public opinion of two US Supreme Court decisions. In a volume on South Africa,[76] I used

---

[73]   Creswell et al. (n 49).

[74]   J.W. Creswell and A. Tashakkori, 'Editorial: Exploring the Nature of Research Questions in Mixed Methods Research' (2007) 1(3) Journal of Mixed Methods Research 207–211, 211.

[75]   K. Linos and K. Twist, 'Endorsement and Framing Effects in Experimental and Natural Settings: The Supreme Court, the Media and the American Public' (2013) UC Berkeley Public Law Research Paper No. 2223732.

[76]   M. Langford, 'Housing Rights Litigation: Grootboom and Beyond' in M. Langford, B. Cousins, J. Dugard and T. Madlingozi (eds), *Socio-Economic Rights in South Africa: Symbols or Substance?* (CUP 2014).

Table 8.2 Mixed methods research design by criteria

Type	Form	Order	Priority	Integration stage	Value-driven or element
Sequential	Explanatory	Quantitative then Qualitative	Usually quantitative, but can be equal or qualitative	Interpretation	Maybe
Sequential	Exploratory	Qualitative then Quantitative	Usually qualitative, but can be equal or quantitative	Interpretation	Maybe
Sequential	Transformative	Either	Any	Interpretation	Yes
Concurrent	Triangulation	Concurrent collection of data	Preferably equal	Interpretation or analysis phase	Maybe
Concurrent	Nested	Concurrent collection of data	Quantitative or qualitative or equal	Analysis	Maybe
Concurrent	Transformative	Concurrent collection of data	Quantitative or qualitative or equal	Usually analysis; can be interpretive	Yes

two qualitative methods sequentially (case study and comparative case method) in order to understand the impact of the *Grootboom* judgment on housing rights. Schaffer[77] argues that the rise of 'political' approaches to human rights in philosophy involves mixed methods, combining in effect qualitative methods from law and philosophy, while Young[78] goes further in her theory of social rights, which fuses rational (largely essentialist), legal (largely deliberative) and socio-political practice into a single normative theory. Thus, while mixed methods approaches should strongly encourage a meeting of the quantitative and qualitative traditions, there is much space for other method mixing.

Sequential approaches
Turning to Table 8.2, sequential approaches have represented the traditional form of mixed methods in human rights. Researchers begin with one method and adopt a second in order to test, confirm, deepen or extend the findings. One recent and notable example is Beth Simmons's *Mobilizing for Human Rights*.[79] Not only does the book provide a powerful argument for reconceiving theoretically how we understand the impact of human rights treaties (by drawing together theories of commitment and compliance), but it also provides multivariate quantitative analysis across a range of human rights treaties and in-depth studies to test the quantitative findings: namely that human rights treaties work most by affecting domestic politics and this effect is most significant in transitional middle-income countries.

A similar approach but with different methods is an analysis of human rights in ethics and social studies textbooks in South Korea.[80] The authors begin with a longitudinal quantitative content analysis which is followed by semi-structured interviews with key actors in the field. Similarly, Satterthwaite's[81] rights-based analysis of the humanitarian response after the Haiti earthquake begins with an online survey in 2010 that was followed by two dozen semi-structured interviews as well as on-site visits

---

[77] J.K. Schaffer, 'A Pluralist Approach to the Practice of Human Rights' in J.K. Schaffer and R. Maliks (eds) *Moral and Political Conceptions of Human Rights: Implications for Theory and Practice* (CUP 2017).

[78] K. Young, *Constituting Economic and Social Rights* (OUP 2012).

[79] Simmons (n 11).

[80] J. Moon and J-W. Koo, 'Global Citizenship and Human Rights: A Longitudinal Analysis of Social Studies and Ethics Textbooks in the Republic of Korea' (2011) 55(4) Comparative Education Review 574–599.

[81] M. Satterthwaithe, 'Indicators in Crisis: Rights-based Humanitarian Indicators in Post Earthquake Haiti' (2011) 43 N.Y.U. J. Int'l L. & Pol. 865–964.

in 2011. This approach sought to 'harness' the power of indicators by 'transcending' them with mixed methods.

Sequential approaches that begin with qualitative methods and end with quantitative approaches are slightly less common but still present. A pertinent example is Gauri and Brinks's[82] edited collection *Courting Social Justice*, which analyses the impact of social rights judgments in Nigeria, India, Brazil, South Africa and Indonesia. The analysis by the participating authors is largely of a qualitative nature but was sufficient for the project leaders to develop a database for comparative quantitative analysis. This allowed them to estimate more precisely the numbers of people who benefitted from judgments, and in a later paper the distribution of such benefits amongst different income classes.[83]

Concurrent approaches
Concurrent approaches are clearly present in a new generation of mixed methods approaches. What is often common is medium-N analyses (50–300 respondents) in which interviews or focus groups are nested or conducted separately (i.e. triangulation). The advantage of these approaches is that a partial aggregative picture is combined with a deeper descriptive and casual information. However, care should be taken that this does not become the only form of concurrent mixed methods study. In any case, there are also instances of very different mixed methods approaches emerging with large-N, infoscience and experimental methods being used in conjunction with qualitative methods: see Box 8.1 for an example.

Concurrent triangulated models are the most common form. A recent example is a measurement of the health impact of human rights violations related to Australian asylum policies and practices. A cross-sectional survey was conducted with 71 Iraqi *Temporary* Protection Visa (TPV) refugees and 60 Iraqi *Permanent* Humanitarian Visa (PHV) refugees; these quantitative results were triangulated with semi-structured interviews with TPV refugees and service providers. The results found that 46% of TPV refugees compared with 25% of PHV refugees reported symptoms consistent with a diagnosis of clinical depression (statistically significant at the 1% level). The qualitative data revealed that TPV refugees generally felt socially isolated and lacking in control over their life circumstances, which was due to both their experiences of detention and the temporary nature of their visa. A similar study was conducted in Eastern Democratic

---

[82]   Varun Gauri and Daniel Brinks, *Courting Social Justice: Judicial Enforcement of Social and Economic Rights in the Developing World* (CUP 2008).
[83]   Brinks and Gauri (n 11).

BOX 8.1   CONCURRENT METHODS: GEOGRAPHIC INFO
SCIENCE AND QUALITATIVE METHODS

In this project by Madden and Ross, the authors combined qualitative data of
personal narratives with geographic information science (GIScience) technologies to explore the potential for critical cartography in the study of mass atrocity.[84]
The place was northern Uganda, where millions have been affected by physical
violence and hardship, displacement and fear. Web-based virtual globes provided
a ready source of imagery for remote areas and derived spatial data imported to
geographic information systems (GIS) provided quantified data that complemented
testimonials and other qualitative data from the field. Cartographic functions, geo-
visualization and spatial analyses available in GIS were used to extract information
from high-resolution remote sensing images documenting internally displaced
persons camps and quantifying evidence of crimes against humanity. These techniques explored spatial relationships and communicated results on the extent and
impact of the atrocities in northern Uganda.

Republic of Congo on experiences of female survivors of sexual violence.
A non-random sample of 255 women attending a referral hospital and
two local NGOs were surveyed, which was followed by focus groups of 48
women survivors.

Nested approaches are less common. They require a single research
technique which mixes both quantitative and qualitative methods. A recent
example is the investigation of the criminalization of homelessness in Oslo,
Norway.[85] The team began with a doctrinal analysis of the proportionality,
discrimination and cruel and degrading treatment law in light of European,
international and comparative law that was followed by a mixed methods
survey of 81 persons living on the streets of Oslo. Amongst the quantitative findings, the report found that non-Norwegians were more than twice
as likely to be evicted and persons of Roma and African descent were three
times more likely to report property confiscation. Qualitatively the report
uncovered the varying relations between police and homeless persons
but also the significant divergences in behaviour between police officers.
The latter finding revealed that the variations in experience of racist and
abusive behaviour by police was not necessarily context or chance; rather
they were due to the attitudes of the individual police officers.

---

[84]   M. Madden and A. Ross, 'Genocide and GIScience: Integrating Personal
Narratives and Geographic Information Science to Study Human Rights' (2009)
61(4) The Professional Geographer 508–526.
[85]   NCHR, *Criminalisation of Homelessness in Oslo: An Investigation*
(Norwegian National Institution for Human Rights 2015).

CONCLUSION

Human rights constitutes a natural field for interdisciplinary endeavour and methodological heterogeneity. While it has been subject to waves of disciplinary hegemony in recent years (philosophy and then law), interdisciplinarity has now found a solid foothold in research in the social sciences, humanities and beyond. Not only does it allow researchers the opportunity to reconceive, reimagine and refine research questions, it provides access to the smorgasbord of methods across disciplines to better answer those questions. Moreover, the paradigmatic rise of multimethodism offers a framework in which to better mix disciplinary perspectives and the full range of quantitative and qualitative methods, including doctrinal, archival and even philosophical methods. However, as this chapter has argued, there are many dangers along the path. Human rights researchers need to improve institutional collaboration,[86] develop better interdisciplinary literacy, avoid simple cherrypicking of data and theory from other disciplines,[87] foster the courage and humility to subject work to multidisciplinary peer review and develop new forms of educational instruction. They will also need to take new steps to embrace new disciplines and methods beyond the social sciences and humanities, particularly in the burgeoning medical sciences.[88]

---

[86] Braithwaite (n 3).

[87] Nissani (n 4).

[88] D. Church, 'Neuroscience in the Courtroom: An International Concern' (2012) 53(5) William and Mary Law Review 1824–1854; O. Jones, J. Schall and F. Shen, *Neuroscience and the Law* (Aspen 2014); C. Dawes, P. Loewen, D. Schreiber, A. Simmons, T. Flagan, R. McElreath, S. Bokemper, J. Fowler and M. Paulus, 'Neural Basis of Egalitarian Behavior' (2012) 109(17) PNAS 6479–6483.

APPENDIX: CONTRASTING QUALITATIVE AND QUANTITATIVE RESEARCH

	Criterion	Qualitative	Quantitative
1	Approaches to explanation	Explain individual cases; 'causes-of-effects' approach	Estimate average effect of independent variables; 'effects-of-causes' approach
2	Conceptions of causation	Necessary and sufficient causes; mathematical logic	Correlational causes; probability/statistical theory
3	Multivariate explanations	INUS causation; occasional individual effects	Additive causation; occasional interaction terms
4	Equifinality	Core concept; few causal paths	Absent concept; implicitly large number of causal paths
5	Scope and generalization	Adopt a narrow scope to avoid causal heterogeneity	Adopt a broad scope to maximize statistical leverage and generalization
6	Case selection practices	Oriented toward positive cases on dependent variable; no (0,0,0) cases	Random selection (ideally) on independent variables; all cases analysed
7	Weighting observations	Theory evaluation sensitive to individual observations; one misfit can have an important impact	All observations are a priori equally important; overall pattern of fit is crucial
8	Substantively important cases	Substantively important cases must be explained	Substantively important cases not given special attention
9	Lack of fit	Nonconforming cases are examined closely and explained	Nonsystematic causal factors are treated as error
10	Concepts and measurement	Concepts centre of attention; error leads to concept revision	Measurement and indicators centre of attention; error is modelled and/or new indicators identified

9. Research ethics for human rights researchers
George Ulrich

INTRODUCTION

The fact that human rights research is conducted in pursuit of a good cause in no way exempts practitioners from ethical scrutiny and accountability. To the contrary, it is often the case that the capacity to do good is matched by a corresponding risk of inadvertently inflicting harm or otherwise violating the integrity of research participants – and hence the need for ethical awareness and scrutiny is all the greater.

Research in the area of human rights, like human rights practice, invariably concerns issues that in one way or another are sensitive and charged. It may involve population groups whose lives are in jeopardy or who are exposed to imminent risks of abuse. It may involve recently traumatized individuals and communities, or it may touch upon issues that are deeply contentious and politically divisive.

That said, the academic contexts and methodologies of human rights research vary widely, and so do the ethical implications. Doctrinal legal analysis is less likely to pose immediate risks of harm than field research involving living human beings, yet both may be ethically charged in their long-term effects. In some cases the line is blurred between academic analysis and fact finding about particular instances of human rights abuse, thus raising the ethical stakes even further. Research methodologies such as critical policy analysis or archive-based historical research may not have direct consequences for identifiable individuals but may be sensitive and controversial in terms of their social and political implications.

Research ethics is a branch of professional ethics that addresses scientific conduct.[1] In addition to commonly applicable ethical standards, it is premised on values of scientific integrity, honesty and contributing to

---

[1] For a general overview of what research ethics is about, see, e.g. David Resnik, 'What is Ethics in Research and Why is it Important?' (2011) 8 National Institution of Environmental Health Sciences <http://www.niehs.nih.gov/research/resources/bioethics/whatis/> accessed 20 May 2016. See also A. Shamoo and D. Resnik, *Responsible Conduct of Research* (2nd edn, OUP 2009).

the public good through the pursuit of knowledge (which in the present context may imply providing a knowledge base for the advancement of human rights).

There are a multitude of sources of ethical guidance available to researchers. Some have been adopted by professional organizations to guide scientific conduct within particular academic disciplines, some have been elaborated by funding agencies and some apply specifically to researchers undertaking their work in a particular institutional context. Some ethics guidelines are purely instructive in nature, whereas others are obligatory in a given context. The present chapter will make reference to some such ethics resources of relevance to research in the area of human rights.[2]

The main focus of the chapter, however, is on the *issues* in need of attention. The author presents an analytical framework which distinguishes between five primary levels of ethical consideration. This provides a basis for scholars to identify the ethical implications of their proposed or on-going research and take appropriate measures in response to the relevant ethical concerns. In a wider sense, the aim of the chapter is to contribute to ethical awareness-raising within the community of human rights researchers and facilitate discussion about ethical dilemmas and challenges in an open and proactive fashion.

Ideally, the focus on ethics should be viewed as an integral aspect of research methodology. While it cannot be excluded that ethical considerations from time to time will run counter to a given methodological approach, and may be experienced as inhibiting scientific expediency, the general presumption of the chapter is that ethics and good science usually go hand in hand. A high level of ethical compliance is generally conducive to positive research outcomes, and it is incumbent upon researchers to pursue synergies, or at least consistency, in this regard.

This is particularly relevant in a normatively defined context such as human rights research. A natural source of guidance for research in this area can be found in the international human rights framework itself.

---

[2]   Ethics codes and reference documents that have inspired the present discussion include: Council for International Organizations of Medical Science (CIOMS), *International Ethical Guidelines for Biomedical Research Involving Human Subjects* (2002); American Anthropologist Association, 'Statement on Ethics' <http://ethics.americananthro.org/category/statement/> accessed 20 May 2016; National Committees for Research Ethics in Norway, *Guidelines for Research Ethics in the Social Sciences, Law and the Humanities* (2006); and Nuffield Council on Bioethics, *The Ethics of Research Related to Healthcare in Developing Countries* (2002).

While this first and foremost obligates states, it also entails important 'horizontal obligations' for social actors at different levels, including scientists and other professionals. A further aim of this chapter will be to elaborate specific implications of the 'ethos of human rights' and demonstrate how this resonates with core principles of research ethics. This is a dimension of research ethics that so far has not been well illuminated in the literature.

A final question addressed in this chapter has to do with enforcement and accountability. In keeping with the overall aim to contribute to ethical awareness-raising and discussion within the community of human rights researchers, the focus in this regard will be on a notion of situated, 'soft' accountability rather than on the quasi-judicial enforcement of a narrow set of rigidly defined norms.

ANALYTICAL FRAMEWORK: WHAT IS ETHICS ABOUT?

An important first step towards enhancing ethical standards of conduct within a profession, including among scientists, consists in raising awareness about the issues in need of attention and supplying practitioners with the tools to identify and analyse the possible ethical implications of their proposed or on-going practice. This can be framed in terms of an inquiry into how we conceptualize the realm of ethics. What types of issues are perceived as ethically significant, and is there a shared perception of this not only among practitioners/scientists but also with the communities within which professional practice and research is carried out? Experience shows that it is often more fruitful, especially when working in a cross-cultural context, to seek to develop a common conceptual language and typology of ethical issues than to immediately seek to articulate binding norms.

The pertinent standards of professional conduct can to a large extent, if not exhaustively, be articulated with reference to a limited number of basic normative considerations and commitments.[3] Specifically, it is proposed

---

[3]   Various basic approaches have been advanced in this regard. Bernard Gert, among others, has developed a rule-based approach to medical ethics whereas Tom Beauchamp and James Childress are associated with a principle-based approach. See, respectively, B. Gert, *Morality: A New Justification of the Moral Rules* (OUP 1988); B. Gert, C.M. Cluver and K.D. Clouser, *Bioethics: A Return to Fundamentals* (OUP 1997); and T. L. Beauchamp and J. F. Childress, *Principles of Biomedical Ethics* (6th edn, OUP 2008). The present author's own approach as presented in the following is partially inspired by both schools of thought.

that there are five main categories of ethical issues that together delineate the field of professional ethics.[4] These are:

(1) *no-harm issues* (about how one's actions and decisions affect others, *what* one does to others – directly or indirectly, physically, materially or psychologically, immediately or in the longer term, by commission or by omission, etc.);

(2) communication issues/issues concerning *recognition* and *respect* (relate to the quality of our interaction, *how* one relates to others, recognition of the competence and autonomy of participants in research, negotiating expectations of reciprocity);

(3) issues having to do with *beneficence* and *justice* (about doing good for others, promoting a greater good, maximizing available scarce resources, ensuring a fair distribution of burdens and benefits, preventing and redressing wrongs, addressing needs);

(4) issues related to *collaboration* and possible *conflicts of interest* (about correct conduct and fairness in the negotiation of vested interests); and

(5) issues of compliance with *scientific and professional standards* and institutional policies.

In what follows, the underlying rationale and core ethical commitments at each level of consideration will be elaborated with particular attention to their application to scientific conduct. At each level, the author will

---

[4] The considerations presented in the following are to a large extent based on the author's direct experience of working with ethical problems and challenges in the fields of overseas medical research, social anthropology, international development cooperation, and international human rights field operations. A particular source of inspiration for the author was a study conducted in the mid-1990s on behalf of the Danish Council for Development Research on ethical challenges of donor-sponsored research in developing countries. This involved extensive field work in research environments in East Africa. Findings of the study were presented in the project report *Globally Speaking: Report on the Ethics of Research in Developing Countries* (Copenhagen 1998) and in numerous subsequent publications, including G. Ulrich, 'Optimum Ethical Standards', in 'Proceedings Seminar on Health Research Ethics in Africa' (January 2001) 78 (Supp. 1) Acta Tropica 1; G. Ulrich 'Charges and Counter-charges of Ethical Imperialism: Towards a Situated Approach to Development Ethics' in Ph. Q. van Ufford and A.K. Giri (eds), *A Moral Critique of Development: In Search of Global Responsibilities* (EIDOS, Routledge 2003); and G. Ulrich, 'Elucidating Ethics in Practice – Focus on Accountability' in P.W. Geissler and S. Molyneux (eds), *Evidence, Ethos and Experiment: The Anthropology and History of Medical Research in Africa* (Berghahn Books 2011).

attempt a provisional mapping of the ethical dilemmas and challenges that may arise in connection with human rights research. Where relevant, linkages will be made with the implicit ethos of human rights and reference will be made in an illustrative fashion to applicable ethics codes and guidelines.

It should be noted that many characteristic ethical dilemmas present themselves at the intersection between two or more levels of consideration, typically in the form of a tension or conflict between competing ethical commitments. Paternalism, for example, denotes a prioritization of one's commitment to doing good for others over the obligation to respect their capacity for self-determination. Utilitarian reasoning, which typically prioritizes the third parameter indicated above, raises questions about the degree to which particular risks of harm are justified by the prospect of a greater good. Cross-cutting issues of this nature will be thematized in an ongoing fashion along the way.

NO-HARM ISSUES

The injunction not to expose individuals or groups affected by one's professional engagements to harm is widely recognized as a foundational principle of professional ethics – also known as the principle of *non-maleficence*. In the context of scientific practice this implies that scientists have a primary responsibility towards research participants irrespective of any greater good that is expected to result from the research.

The principle of *non-maleficence* has been regarded as a guiding principle of medical ethics since antiquity.[5] In a contemporary context, it features centrally in virtually every code of ethics.[6] This echoes a legacy

---

[5]   Non-*maleficence* is one of four primary ethical principles recognized in the seminal textbook by Beauchamp and Childress (n 3). Within the medical profession, the maxim *primum non nocere* is commonly associated with the Hippocratic Oath. It does not in fact appear explicitly in this ancient text, but has throughout the ages served as a cornerstone of medical ethics. See C.M. Smith, 'Origin and Uses of Primum Non Nocere – Above All, Do No Harm!' (2005) 45(4) J Clin Pharmacol 371ff. For a more narrative account of the complexities and personal challenges involved in honouring the no-harm principle, see Henry Marsh, *Do No Harm: Stories of Life, Death and Brain Surgery* (Weidenfeld & Nicolson 2014).

[6]   It thus also applies to the human rights profession and features prominently in the *Statement of Ethical Commitments of Human Rights Professionals* that the present author has taken part in drafting; see G. Ulrich, 'The Statement of Ethical Commitments of Human Rights Professionals: A Commentary' in M. O'Flaherty

of scandal whereby vulnerable human beings – typically members of discriminated groups – have been callously exposed to abuse in the name of science. The experimentations conducted by Mengele in the concentration camps during World War II and the infamous Tuskegee syphilis experiments conducted in the United States from 1932 to 1972 are two of the most important recent examples.[7] The former led to an express reference to research ethics being included in the ICCPR article 7,[8] and the latter to the establishment of an elaborate system of institutional review boards in the US and around the world.

Analytically, the no-harm principle concerns what one does *to* others, how one's actions affect the well-being of others. This is largely a matter that is within one's own control – at least in the sense that any manifest risk or incident of harm should lead to revising or terminating the given activity. In other words, it is a principle that is largely commensurable with the agency of the practitioner, and hence the injunction not to do harm (in contrast to many other ethical principles) has an absolute character. To operationalize the principle, two important points need to be considered: first, *how to qualify harm* and, secondly, *what types of obligations* the no-harm principle entails.

---

and G. Ulrich (eds), *The Professional Identity of the Human Rights Field Officer* (Ashgate 2010). The ethics code of the OHCHR §11 similarly states that '[OHCHR staff shall]: Refrain from endangering, by way of their words or action during or after their service with the OHCHR, the safety and privacy of the people with whom they come into contact and their own safety . . .;' see OHCHR, Code of Conduct for OHCHR staff, Directive No. 2 (1999). Reproduced in 'Norms Applicable to UN Human Rights Officers and Other Staff', *Training Manual on Human Rights Monitoring*, (OHCHR, 2001), pp. 449–464. For an insightful discussion of the application of the no-harm principle to the area of humanitarian assistance and peace building, see M.B. Anderson, *Do No Harm: Supporting Local Capacities for Peace Through Aid* (Local Capacities for Peace Project, Collaborative for Development Action 1996).

[7] See, e.g. G.L. Posner and J. Ware, *Mengele: The Complete Story* (McGraw-Hill 1986); and S.M. Reverby, *Examining Tuskegee: The Infamous Syphilis Study and its Legacy* (University of North Carolina Press 2009). See also A.R. Jonson, *A Short History of Medical Ethics* (OUP 2000).

[8] International Covenant on Civil and Political Rights (ICCPR), G.A. res. 2200A (XXI), 21 U.N. GAOR Supp. (No. 16) at 52, U.N. Doc. A/6316 (1966), 999 U.N.T.S. 171, entered into force 23 March 1976. By stipulating that 'no one shall be subjected without his free consent to medical or scientific experimentation', ICCPR article 7 *prima facie* accentuates another foundational ethical principle, namely, that of autonomy. However, the fact that this is directly linked with a prohibition against torture and other cruel, inhuman or degrading treatment or punishment makes it clear that informed consent is intended and understood as a means of (self-)protection against harm.

In terms of qualifying the concept of harm, it is relevant to distinguish between:

- physical, mental and material harm;
- direct and indirect harm;
- immediate harm and harm that only becomes manifest in the long term (with delayed effect);
- harm by commission and harm by omission;
- intentional and unintentional harm.

All dimensions of the concept are relevant, which is to say that researchers need to be concerned not only about immediate and direct effects of their actions, but also about harm perpetrated by others as an indirect, sometimes long-term, consequence of research. It is rare that serious harm is inflicted deliberately or even knowingly by scientists. When it occurs, it is (almost always) an unintended consequence of activities that are undertaken with good intentions. The essential ethical requirement, therefore, is to exercise foresight and diligence in ascertaining the possible adverse consequences of one's proposed and on-going research.

The three main obligations incumbent upon researchers are to *anticipate*, *monitor* and *react to* risks of harm. In the clinical testing of pharmaceuticals, a very rigorous attention to risks of harm is built into the progression of phase I, II and III trials, which in essence requires researchers to test and monitor toxicity before beginning to test efficacy. Being less invasive, other areas of science are also less exacting in terms of ethical vigilance, but for research involving human subjects it is as a general rule reasonable to require project descriptions and research protocols to include:

- an explicit and comprehensive detailing of the risks of harm that have been identified as possible outcomes of the proposed research;
- a statement on how such risks will be monitored and managed; and
- a statement on what remedial measures will be taken in case things go wrong (e.g. termination of research, counselling, protection measures, insurance).

In the case of research involving more than a trivial risk of harm or other identifiable inconveniences to research participants, it may also be appropriate to include:

- a statement to the effect that the given risks and inconveniences are proportionate to the expected benefits deriving from the research and therefore justifiable on balance;

- an account of why the envisioned research outcomes cannot be achieved without the given risks and inconveniences (i.e. an explanation of why the risk factor is necessary); and
- an assurance of an equitable distribution of burdens and benefits, such that the individuals or communities who are exposed to risk and sustain inconvenience also have a realistic prospect of sharing in the anticipated benefits of the research.

Professional ethics recognizes a number of additional requirements and principles which, while motivated by a rationale of their own, are related to the no-harm principle. The principle of *confidentiality* in effect marks a requirement to protect clients and individuals in one's care from the physical, mental or material harm that might derive from the disclosure of sensitive personal information. The requirement to obtain *voluntary and informed consent* (which will be further discussed below), similarly, is widely conceived as a means to empower research participants to protect themselves against harm. Some ethics codes, moreover, include an elaborate set of provisions related to decision-making on behalf of minors, the mentally disabled and other persons who are not fully competent to safeguard their own interests.[9] This too can be understood as a direct extension of the no-harm principle.

Application in Relation to Human Rights Research

The next step of our analysis consists in undertaking a provisional survey of ways in which research in the area of human rights, despite good intentions, may entail risks of inflicting harm. Given the diversity of the research area, this will be far from exhaustive.

Risks of indirect harm

In situations of conflict, social tension or repressive government, there is an immediate risk of exposing research participants to harm perpetrated by others. This can notably happen by sensitive and personalized data getting into the wrong hands. In some cases the mere association with foreign researchers may be a cause of suspicion and possible retaliatory action, as the human rights agenda may be regarded as a treat to local privileges and power structures or to particular groups of local actors. In such situations, researchers carry a heightened responsibility to protect informants and

---

[9]   The CIOMS Guidelines (n 2) are an important case in point; cf. guidelines 9–10 and 13–15.

ensure confidentiality, undertake data collection in a discrete and protective manner, anonymize and carefully guard research data and interview recordings, etc. Considerations of this nature are particularly relevant in connection with applied research (e.g. post-conflict fact finding or research with direct implications for resource allocation) and research undertaken in contexts of on-going human rights abuse, repression and extreme disparities of wealth and social access.

Risks of direct harm

Human rights research is rarely physically invasive and does not involve 'experimentation' in the sense foreseen in ICCPR article 7. It may however be associated with direct mental harm. Some forms of inquiry may, for example, rekindle traumatic experiences and trigger angst and dysphoria, or they may place research participants in inherently embarrassing and compromising situations leading to severe stress, social exposure, or both.[10] It is often ambiguous whether researchers should be able to anticipate adverse consequences of this nature, but the matter should be given careful consideration in the design of research projects and planning of how interviews and other forms of data gathering are to be conducted. In case of severe dysphoric reactions, it is incumbent on the researcher to immediately terminate or revise the given data collection procedures and seek qualified assistance (with adequate local knowledge) to address the underlying issues. In practice, it is often beyond the capacity of researchers – in particular individual researchers working in meagerly funded academic contexts – to effectively respond to complex social and psychological reactions on the part of research participants. It is for this reason all the more important to pay close attention to risks of mental harm in advance of a given research initiative.

Delayed effect

The issue of adverse consequences of research is not only a concern in the immediate interaction with research participants. There may also be long-term harmful consequences as a result of the manner in which individuals and populations implicated by the research are subsequently

---

[10]   Stanley Milgram's (in)famous experiments on obedience to authority figures in the early 1960s have been widely criticized for placing research participants in a profoundly compromising situation and were on this account influential in drawing attention to the issue of mental harm in the context of research ethics. For a detailed account of the legacy of these experiments, see G. Perry, *Behind the Shock Machine: The Untold Story of the Notorious Milgram Psychology Experiments* (The New Press 2013).

portrayed, as this may be perceived to be humiliating and offensive and may have a lasting impact. Questions related to the ethics of representation overlap in many regards with the ethical considerations related to *communicative interaction*, as shall be further examined below, but may also be thematized as a question of mental harm, at times bordering on outright defamation.[11]

The publication of research findings may also be linked with long-term physical or material harm in cases where the findings are intrinsically unfavourable to particular parties in a given social situation, perhaps an on-going conflict or a situation involving competing claims to scarce resources. This is of particular relevance in connection with applied research and studies that have immediate policy implications. The possible adverse outcomes for certain parties in divisive situations need not imply that the research itself was biased, but simply that the results cannot be regarded as neutral.

Harm by omission
Issues of *harm by omission* typically involve a failure to intervene in situations where researchers encounter severe deprivation or witness blatantly harmful or hazardous practices. Health professionals recognize an obligation to take action when confronted with medical malpractice and acute health crises. Human rights professionals, by analogy, may be expected to react when encountering evidence of imminent or grave and persistent human rights abuse. This may, in exceptional cases, entail taking direct personal action, but more frequently the appropriate ethical response will consist in directing the attention of competent authorities to the given concerns.

In practice, the notion of harm by omission is often associated with ambiguity. To shed light on the nature of the ethical obligations to which it gives rise, it is relevant to distinguish between situations that involve a categorical obligation to take action, which by omission would constitute

---

[11] Problems related to the ethics of representation have been an important point of concern within the discipline of social anthropology at least since Colin Turnbull's seminal publication of a monograph (*The Mountain People* (Simon & Schuster 1972)) on an indigenous population that he found inherently unlikable. James Clifford and George Marcus's *Writing Culture: The Poetics and Politics of Ethnography* (University of California Press 1986), which draws inspiration from Edward Said's *Orientalism* (Vintage Books 1979), exposes the constructions and power dynamics at play in ostensibly objective and neutral scientific representations. Issues related to the ethics of representation are also, from a different point of view, central to journalistic ethics and media ethics.

a breach of ethics, and situations that merely involve a perceived respon-sibility to do good, which one may feel strongly motivated to honour but which conceptually has more of an optional character. One's sense of obligation in the latter scenario may be reinforced by the persistence of local expectations, which often relate to exigencies that fall outside the scope of one's professional engagement and which in a cumulative sense may vastly exceed one's capacity to address. Medical scientists conducting research in deprived communities, for example, are continuously con-fronted by requests for medical attention that is unrelated to the subject of their research. They may feel a profound sense of personal and profes-sional obligation to respond to such requests, to the best of their ability, but the failure to do so, and indeed the need to draw limits, can hardly be construed as a matter of inflicting harm. In human rights research, simi-larly, the witnessing of deprivation, oppression and continuous low-level or indeed serious abuse may spur the researcher to campaign for change in all manners possible, but outside a narrow range of situations in which researchers in virtue of their professional status and privileged access to sensitive information are in a position to affect immediate change, the failure to remedy or prevent abuse cannot be construed as harm by omis-sion. Reference to the notion of harm by omission, therefore, should be used sparingly.

Exposing human rights violators to harm?

The possibility of witnessing human rights violations in conjunction with research also gives rise to uncertainty regarding *to whom* the researcher's ethical obligations pertain. This is especially pressing in cases where research from the outset is intended to address unlawful activities and/or involve the participation of identified human rights violators and actors who may be complicit in human rights violations, e.g. by propagating extremist views. Such research may obviously be justified by an overarch-ing interest in understanding the perceptions, motivations, and modes of operation of perpetrators, but publishing research findings and disclosing the identity of informants may seriously expose individuals with whom one has interacted in good faith to harm. Not to do so, conversely, may be construed as a matter of tacitly endorsing human rights violations or failing to prevent future transgressions and thereby contributing to harm by omission. The resolution of this dilemma will typically depend on the severity of the issues at stake and the ability or lack of ability of the researcher(s) to meaningfully contribute to a cessation of the identified abuses. The matter, in any case, remains complicated and requires careful ethical scrutiny in a suitable public or semi-public forum.

COMMUNICATION ISSUES

The inquiry into ethical perceptions in everyday life (the 'phenomenology of ethics') shows that ethics is commonly perceived not only as a matter of *what we do to and for one another*; it is also, importantly, about the manner of *how we interact*. This is reflected in expectations of being recognized and treated with respect and, conversely, in the hostile reaction that people everywhere display when feeling slighted, misled, humiliated, perhaps even used. For the present purposes this class of ethical issues may be grouped under the heading 'communication issues', as it involves expectations of reciprocity, openness, honesty and transparency that are implicit in our communicative interaction.

In comparison with the injunction against inflicting harm, this level of ethical consideration does not feature prominently in formal ethics codes and review procedures.[12] This may be because the underlying issues are assumed to be 'soft' in nature, i.e. indeterminate and not easily subject to regulation. They are, however, perceived as highly relevant by people on the ground and are particularly sensitive and charged in situations characterized by disparities of knowledge, access and power – which often apply in relation to professional conduct. Issues of recognition and respect also demand special attention in cross-cultural settings, where they from the outset are tenuous and fraught with ambiguity.

The present author's examination of ethical practices in donor-sponsored research in developing countries revealed a persistent and widespread perception that researchers come to 'the field' to collect data for reasons that are not properly explained, i.e. neither intelligible nor immediately relevant from a local perspective. The researchers then simply disappear, attending to their own objectives and interests and leaving the host community with a feeling of having been taken advantage of. Despite promises to come back to the participants with a report on research outcomes, this rarely happens.[13] While it cannot be assumed that such misgivings are indicative of research practices in other contexts, they do underscore the ethical importance of communicative interaction with research participants.

---

[12] It does, however, feature as a central aspect of two out of four core ethical principles in the Nuffield Council on Bioethics' report (n 2) pp. 47ff.

[13] Frustrations related to substandard communication are not always openly articulated but are rather expressed in the form of indirect misgivings and rumours attributing illicit motives to the researchers. See, e.g. P.W. Geissler and R. Pool, 'Popular Concerns about Medical Research Projects in sub-Saharan Africa – A Critical Voice in Debates about Medical Research Ethics' (July 2006) 11 in Tropical Medicine and International Health 975ff.

The primary expression of this dimension of ethics in formal ethics codes is found in the principle of *voluntary informed consent*. Other well-established norms that are relevant in the present context are *anti-harassment* norms and norms related to the protection of *confidentiality*. Both are commonly interpreted as means of preventing harm but also fundamentally concern respectful interaction and the fostering of trust.

Beyond the formally defined standards, there is a range of underlying and less precisely defined commitments that are essential to a genuinely ethical approach to research. These include:

- treating research participants and host communities with respect;
- being open and transparent about research aims, methods and implications of participating in research;
- respecting the right of research participants to freely determine the nature and extent of their involvement;
- displaying sensitivity to the life situation of research participants, including possible vulnerabilities and experience of abuse;
- treating sensitive information with discretion;
- displaying respect for the values and life choices of interlocutors;
- displaying sensitivity to how individuals and groups contributing to or affected by research are portrayed in the presentation of results; and
- a reasonable degree of follow-up and feedback on research outcomes to the involved participants.

Application in Relation to Human Rights Research

Projecting an ethos of human rights
The ethics of communicative interaction resonate strongly with core human rights principles such as *participation, non-discrimination, social inclusion* and *respect for the dignity of the human person*. The commitments listed above are therefore immediately relevant in the context of human rights research. It is a central premise of the present publication that human rights research, irrespective of disciplinary context and choice of methodologies, must be committed to a high standard of openness and accountability and should be explicit about the value commitments, baselines and judgments that inform and guide the research. This serves as a means of exposing oneself to external scrutiny and as an incentive to being reflexive about impacts of the research.

Displaying sensitivity

When working with traumatized, vulnerable and exposed individuals or groups, there is a particular need for sensitivity in the manner in which research participants are engaged. Researchers may in some situations find themselves torn between urgently documenting and drawing attention to human rights violations that otherwise remain ignored and treating human suffering with sensitivity and discretion, which may require a less invasive and assertive approach. Such dilemmas should as a general rule be resolved in a manner that prioritizes respect for the dignity of individual research participants. It is by the same token ethically incumbent on researchers to beware of reinforcing stereotypes and portraying identifiable individuals or groups in a derogatory or humiliating manner. This applies both while conducting research and in the presentation of findings.[14] When working in conflict and post-conflict situations and among divided populations, there is an onus on researchers to avoid contributing to a further escalation of hostility by projecting preferences for one party in the given conflict at the expense of others.

Broaching value differences

A characteristic dilemma has to do with how to react to non-human rights-compliant values and practices. The notion of respect for human dignity implies an obligation, implicit in our everyday communicative interaction, to recognize the competence of the Other to form and assert independent value judgments, also when such values conflict with one's own. This, however, does not imply an obligation to remain silent. When confronted with extreme views or patterns of abuse, passive acceptance and inactivity can be construed as a moral failure. The ethical imperative in such situations may be to speak out or take remedial action in other ways.

It is a common experience, conversely, that the values and agendas projected by human rights research are openly or implicitly contested in the local context by certain interlocutors. This may be due to an opposition to the concept and practice of human rights as such. Or it may be due to feelings of mistrust and threats associated with the practical outcomes of research, as is particularly a concern in relation to consultancies, evaluation and monitoring assignments, research involving an explicit advocacy component, and other forms of applied human rights research.

In all such cases, the essential challenge for the researcher lies in broaching differences in a candid but respectful manner and in striking a balance between being transparent about one's own value commitments and giving

---

[14]   This overlaps with the question of mental harm; cf. n 11.

space for the articulation of conflicting views, thereby setting the contestation of norms and objectives on a constructive track. This is a challenge with far-reaching practical implications, as human rights practice at every level involves a contestation of norms which reflexive interaction in the research setting may help to illuminate.[15]

Informed consent

Since the Nuremberg Code of 1947, the principle of *voluntary informed consent* has been attributed an absolutely central role in medical research ethics. Increasingly, it is recognized as a core standard in other branches of professional ethics. It *prima facie* reflects a commitment to respect the autonomy and capacity for self-determination of prospective research participants. Upon examination, it is actually a complex principle. *Voluntary informed consent* comprises a right to be properly informed about research methods and aims; a right to freely determine the scope and nature of one's involvement; and, in a wider sense, a right to protect oneself against externally inflicted harm or risks of harm (as discussed above). In practice, these objectives are not always well served by formal consent procedures. Subsequent surveys often show that the information provided in conjunction with the consent procedure was not fully intelligible to research participants and that many elements of direct or indirect coercion come into play in decisions about participation.[16] Formal consent procedures are therefore at best only partially effective in empowering research participants to protect themselves against excessive risks of harm. Being structurally modelled on a legalistic, contractual relation, they are not necessarily conducive to continued reciprocal and respectful interaction. The upshot of such considerations, in the present author's view, is not that informed consent should be abandoned as a core standard of research ethics. Rather, ethically responsible researchers need to keep sight not only of formal requirements but also of the underlying rationale of the principle and of the wider range of ethical issues related to communication.

---

[15]   For a discussion of the role of contestation in human rights diplomacy and human rights practice more generally, see G. Ulrich, 'Framework for the Analysis of Human Rights Diplomacy' in M. O'Flaherty, Z. Kedzia, A. Müller and G. Ulrich (eds), *Human Rights Diplomacy – Contemporary Perspective* (Martinus Nijhof/Brill 2011).

[16]   Cf. G. Ulrich 2001 and 2003 (n 4). See also C.S. Molyneux, N. Peshu and K. Marsh, 'Understanding of Informed Consent in a Low-income Setting: Three Case Studies from the Kenyan Coast' (December 2004) 59 Soc Sci Med. 2547ff; and P.A. Marshall, *Ethical Challenges in Study Design and Informed Consent for Health Research in Resource-poor Settings*, WHO Special Topics No. 5, TDR/SDR/SEB/ST/07.1 (WHO 2007).

It is from time to time questioned whether the requirement for informed consent applies in connection with research that is non-invasive and associated with only minimal risks of harm. In other words, are some research areas exempt from the standard of informed consent? A related set of questions has to do with the application of methodologies that are premised on detracting attention from the research situation and that therefore are deemed to be incompatible with explicit consent procedures. While there is no single authoritative answer to these questions, it may be suggested that the standard of informed consent should as far as possible be acknowledged as a mandatory requirement for all research involving the participation of human subjects, but that it in some circumstances may be justified to allow for a certain degree of flexibility with regard to the formality of application.[17]

Covert research
Special complications arise in connection with covert and contested research, i.e. in situations where researchers in effect are dissimulating, disguising or deflecting attention from the fact that they are conducting research. The two most common reasons for doing this are that the research agenda is expected to be met with opposition by participants or by authorities competent to grant research permission, and that the awareness of contributing to research is assumed to affect the manner in which research participants act and respond to questions and therefore to hamper the ability to obtain untainted and reliable research data. This is above all a concern in the behavioral sciences and in some social sciences as well as in research involving illegal or morally/socially controversial practices. In such situations, researchers sometimes seek to bypass informed consent procedures and may argue that the standard is not applicable. Or they may tailor the description of research methodologies and objectives to the given context and seek to disguise elements that might meet with opposition. A common motivation behind such dissimulation is a profound sense of mistrust towards authoritative review bodies and a concomitant sense of the importance of one's research and superiority of one's own moral integrity.

Such impulses should be approached with great caution. If standard consent and/or approval procedures are exceptionally to be waived in a

---

[17] In the article 'Informed Consent, We Are Not Exempt' ((1994) 53 Human Organization 1), Carolyn Fluehr-Lobban argues against the characteristic adversity among social anthropologists to embrace the principle of informed consent on account of its apparent incompatibility with the method of participant observation, but she concedes that it may be legitimate to attain consent 'without forms'.

given context, then two supplementary conditions must in the present author's view obtain. First, the research proposal and methodology must be reviewed and approved by a competent audit body in another setting – which is to say, in other words, that professional ethics cannot be construed merely as a matter of exercising private conscience. Secondly, the researchers should, as emphasized above, be attentive to the underlying rationale of the principle of informed consent and ensure that this is respected to the maximum degree possible in the given situation through complementary means.

DOING GOOD

Perhaps the most common connotation of the notion of ethics is to reach out and do good for others. The technical term for this is *beneficence*. Alongside the injunction not to do harm (*non-maleficence*) and the requirement to treat others with dignity and respect, the principle of beneficence must be recognized as a core parameter of ethical consideration. It features in one form or another as central to most schools of moral philosophy, notably utilitarianism, which in effect reduces all ethical reasoning to this single formula.

The sense of obligation to do good for others applies in immediate face-to-face relations and across vast distances (as when we feel obliged to contribute to disaster relief after natural disasters in faraway places), at a general societal level and in a more abstract sense to humanity at large. Some schools of thought, often associated with the notion of an 'ethics of care', recognize special responsibilities towards individuals with whom we are personally related (such as parents towards their children), but this is not a primary concern in the context of professional ethics where relations as a point of departure are anonymous. In everyday social interaction, the inclination to do good is associated with sentiments such as empathy, compassion and social responsibility. Conceptually, the act of doing good for others can be thematized as something *optional*: something we elect to do as a gesture of benevolence and charity, or it may have an *obligatory* character and be interpreted as a matter of responding to pre-existing moral or legal entitlements. In the latter sense it is intrinsically linked with notions of *social justice*.

Either way, beneficence is always at best an imperfect approximation of an ideal, as the good we can accomplish pales in comparison with existing needs. This is particularly true when it comes to large-scale need, mass violence, systemic deprivation and impoverishment – all of which pose requirements that vastly exceed the capacity and agency of any individual actor. The fulfillment of the obligation not to expose others to harm, by contrast, largely falls within our own control. While seemingly closely related and overlapping in many regards, the principles of beneficence and non-maleficence are therefore structurally and logically very different. The commitment to do good marks a positive rather than a negative aspiration. It is relative rather than absolute in nature, and the obligations deriving from it tend to be imprecisely defined.

Its inherent ambiguities notwithstanding, the principle of beneficence defines an essential point of inquiry in the context of research ethics. The capacity to conduct research as well as the access to infrastructure and data that this presupposes must be conceived as a public good and hence entail an obligation to make adequate use of available scarce resources and return something to society. It is, moreover, reasonable to insist that if a certain element of risk is to be accepted as an inevitable feature of research, then there had better be compelling positive reasons for accepting this – in other words reasonably well defined, likely positive outcomes of a given enterprise. A purist might argue that individual harm beyond a certain point is never justifiable by reference to a greater good, but as one can never be certain of outcomes, the weighing of probable risks and benefits is a standard element in virtually all *ex ante* ethical assessments.

The essential questions to ask at this level of ethical consideration in relation to research are:

- What are the expected benefits of the research?
- In what ways does the research contribute to scientific knowledge, and does it have foreseeable practical applications?
- Are the inconveniences and possible risks of harm proportionate with the benefits anticipated to be accrued from the research?
- Do the probable benefits justify the investments of time and resources in the proposed research? Are scarce public resources being used in a responsible manner?
- How are favourable outcomes likely to be distributed? Will they benefit the general public/humanity at large, or will they rather be reserved for particular communities, groups or individuals?

In probing such questions, it is relevant to distinguish between benefits that are *intrinsic* to the research and those which might be considered *incidental* outcomes. In terms of intrinsic benefits, research must as a point of departure always be expected to contribute to the enhancement of scientific knowledge. The research should be situated in a well-defined academic context, and it is incumbent on the researcher to elaborate specifically how the proposed study may enhance our understanding of the given subject matter. Further to this, research often aims at achieving practical outcomes in the form of technological advances or an improved ability to solve human and societal challenges.

Incidental beneficial outcomes, by comparison, may include raising awareness of pressing issues and advantageous practices, linking up people, developing capacity to tackle societal problems and, importantly, building local research capacity and laying the foundation for further studies in the same area.[18] Researchers, moreover, are often requested to assist people in the areas where research is being conducted in ways that are unrelated to the research itself. This may be a source of high, sometimes unrealistic, expectations and may place the researcher in an awkward dilemma in terms of how far to extend oneself beyond one's core engagements – as discussed above in connection with the notion of 'harm by omission'. It will often be deemed reasonable to make some returns to individual participants and host communities for their contribution to the given research, but to offer outright compensation for research participation should be approached with great caution as it may function as an undue incentive to research participation and hence as a source of implicit coercion which runs counter to the principle of free and voluntary consent. This is particularly a problem in connection with research in low-income countries or communities.[19]

Application in Relation to Human Rights Research

A characteristic feature of human rights research is that it sheds light on otherwise neglected problems and addresses the concerns of disadvantaged and marginalized social groups. This may in and of itself be regarded as an intrinsic benefit – an expression of the universalistic ethos of science in the context of social injustice.

In applying the general formula of beneficence to research in the area of human rights, a natural point of inquiry is to ask: *does the proposed research contribute to the promotion and protection of human rights?* It should of course not be assumed that human rights researchers subscribe

---

[18]   Hampering the possibilities to conduct future research in a given area, conversely, must be conceived as a matter of long-term harm. This is a not infrequent side effect of substandard research practice.

[19]   The Commentary to CIOMS Guideline (n 2) number 7 contains a detailed and perceptive discussion of this issue, as does the Nuffield Council report (n 2), chapter 6. See also C.S. Molyneux, S. Mulupi, L. Mbaabu and V. Marsh, 'Benefits and Payments for Research Participants: Experiences and Views from a Research Centre on the Kenyan Coast' (2012) 13 BMC Med Ethics 1.

uncritically to any agenda associated with human rights. Good science presupposes a propensity for self-criticism and a healthy dose of scepticism *vis-à-vis* established doctrine. This must be applied to the human rights idiom itself and should to some extent inform all human rights research. However, even so, the international human rights framework, while open to contestation, is the closest one can come to a universal authoritative standard for qualifying the general good, and in this sense it constitutes a relevant point of reference for all professional activity, including research. This, indeed, may be seen as a primary example of how the human rights paradigm in important ways can inform and enhance the general discourse on professional ethics.

COLLABORATION ISSUES

In professional contexts related to civil service,[20] public administration and legal practice,[21] among others, the notion of ethics tends to be narrowly associated with an obligation to not abuse office.[22] This applies, for example, in relation to procurement and employment practices or when lawyers and judges recuse themselves from involvement in cases in which they may be partial or may be suspected of having a conflict of interest. The essential requirement, which in fact applies to anyone with significant professional decision-making responsibilities, is to disclose any possible conflicts of interest and avoid unduly benefitting from decisions taken in one's professional capacity or privileging individuals to whom one is related.

It is important to underline that this general requirement does not imply a ban on self-interested conduct. Quite the contrary, the presumption governing professional ethics is that it is normal and legitimate to pursue personal interests. The ethical requirement is merely that this must be done in a transparent fashion and without unduly compromising the interests

---

[20]   See, e.g. *Standards of Conduct for the International Civil Service*, adopted by the International Civil Service Commission (1954, most recently revised in January 2002) <http://icsc.un.org/resources/pdfs/general/standardse.pdf> accessed 20 May 2016.

[21]   See, e.g. the American Bar Association *Model Rules of Professional Conduct* (1983, most recently revised in February 2013) <http://www.americanbar.org/groups/professional_responsibility/publications/model_rules_of_professional_conduct.html> accessed 20 May 2016.

[22]   Interestingly, the UN Ethics Office's resources materials on 'Ethics Advice and Guidance' are almost exclusively devoted to issues of this nature <http://www.un.org/en/ethics/standvalue.shtml> accessed 20 May 2016.

of others. This level of ethical consideration, therefore, is fundamentally about managing and negotiating vested interests while ensuring transparency, propriety and equity (or fairness) in professional conduct. The same basic outlook is reflected in anti-corruption and good governance agendas at the societal level.

In the academic arena, the issue of equity notably arises in relation to questions about how relations of collaboration are defined, who gets credit for research results and recognition of authorship and the degree to which different parties benefit materially and professionally from their involvement in the given scientific endeavour. Most research is in one sense or another a collaborative effort, and upon examination it is not uncommon to find that some members of a research team harbour misgivings about being misrecognized and unfairly treated, perhaps outright discrimination. Implicit tensions related to the terms of collaboration may be further fuelled by the fact that most research is embedded in hierarchical structures and shaped by differences in title and status, differences in experience and understanding of the given subject matter, differences in access to funding and research permission, and, on account of all of these differences, disparities in recognition and reward.[23] Such disparities may be ethically justifiable, but to establish this they are subject to a test of non-discrimination, equity and a reasonable degree of openness and inclusiveness in the negotiation of terms – even when set in markedly hierarchical structures. In effect, this means applying a high standard of communication ethics within the research team itself, which in turn may be expected to enhance the prospect of successful scientific outcomes.

Given that this level of ethical consideration applies to professional conduct irrespective of the subject area, it has no special implications for research in the area of human rights. It may be noted, however, that the principles of equity and non-discrimination, like the related principles of transparency and good governance, are integral to the ethos of human rights and should be rigorously honoured in this research context.

---

[23]   When conducting fieldwork on ethical problems in donor-sponsored research in developing countries (cf. n 3), the present author was repeatedly confronted with the perception that foreign researchers, owing to their privileged funding access, lead in developing research protocols and perception of superior scientific competences, unfairly privilege their own agendas and in effect treat local collaborators as inferior. Whether or not fully justified, such perceptions are indicative of an ethical issue in urgent need of attention. However, it is only very sporadically addressed, if at all, in most ethics guidelines. The Norwegian *Guidelines for Research Ethics in the Social Sciences, Law and the Humanities* (n 2) touch upon ethical considerations related to research collaboration in Section D of the guidelines.

PROFESSIONALISM AND GOOD SCIENTIFIC CONDUCT

A fifth and final parameter of ethical consideration has to do with compliance with standards of good scientific conduct. This includes anti-plagiarism norms, academic honesty and a general requirement for methodological stringency, accuracy in the recording of research data, caution about generalizing findings pertaining to particular cases, and ensuring that empirical findings can be tested and verified or falsified, as the case may be.

Such norms can in most cases be linked with another level of ethical consideration. The falsification of research findings may thus be an immediate cause of harm; plagiarism, in a generalized sense, violates norms of equity in research cooperation; and sloppy methodology detracts from the ability of research to enhance scientific knowledge and contribute to a greater social good, etc. It nevertheless makes sense to group them together under a separate heading, as they reflect a general requirement to conduct oneself in accordance with the knowledge base and established procedures of the profession and (unless there are compelling reasons to the contrary) in compliance with the fundamental values, procedures, and objectives of the employing entity.[24]

ETHICS IN THE RESEARCH CYCLE

Taking into account the full range of relevant considerations as elaborated in the present chapter, the question of ethics requires attention throughout the entire research process. The following paragraphs provide an indication, summarized in Table 9.1, of the types of issues that typically need to be considered at different stages of research.

Planning the Research

Research proposals in some academic disciplines are required to include an explicit and detailed ethics section. It is suggested that this standard should be adopted for all human rights research irrespective of academic discipline.

---

[24]   The *Code of Conduct for OHCHR staff* (n 6), thus places strong emphasis on compliance with organizational rules and procedures and on displaying allegiance to the objectives of the UN. The same ethos characterizes the *Standards of Conduct for the International Civil Service* (n 20).

Table 9.1 Ethics in the research cycle

	Initial phase Project planning and design	Preparation phase	Implementation phase Data collection and analysis	Completion phase Dissemination and operationalization of results
No harm issues	Identify risks of harm. Plan for how to react in case of negative developments.	Alert research collaborators and participants to possible risks of harm, including harm perpetrated by others as a consequence of research activities.	Carefully monitor effects of the on-going research activity with regard to direct and indirect harmful outcomes.	Monitor reactions to the publication of results. Beware of long-term adverse consequences of published research findings.
Communication issues	Adopt policy on informed consent and plan for how research aims and methodologies will be communicated to stakeholders.	Communicate research methodologies and aims to prospective research participants and other relevant stakeholders. Obtain informed consent, as required.	Maintain respectful interaction with research participants. Monitor and respect willingness of research participants to continue their involvement. Treat sensitive information with discretion.	Ensure adequate feedback on research outcomes to individuals and groups who have contributed to the research. Beware of humiliating or degrading portrayal of individuals or groups implicated by the research.

Beneficence issues	Elaborate expected benefits of the research. Ensure proportionality between likely beneficial outcomes and any risks of harm or other inconveniences linked with the research.	Negotiate incidental benefits with participants and stakeholders.		Seek, as far as possible, to maximize the impact and benefits of the research and ensure equitable access to research outcomes.
Collaboration issues	In collaborative research, be as inclusive as possible in defining methodologies and objectives, responsibilities and authorship, etc.	Openly discuss and reach agreement on terms of collaboration within research team.	Monitor perceptions of equity within the research team; broach issue as required.	Ensure equitable recognition for research outcomes.

215

The development of a research initiative should as a matter of course involve taking stock of and making a statement about ethical implications, including possible risks of harm and anticipated benefits, whether and how informed consent will be obtained, and safeguards in case of unforeseen complications. Such an *ex ante* ethics analysis serves a dual purpose. It provides assurance that the relevant ethical considerations have been taken into account in the planning of the research and it may subsequently serve as a point of reference for ethical monitoring and accountability.[25]

Obtaining Research Permission

Research proposals may be subject to multiple levels of review: initially by funding agencies and the home institution(s) of the lead researcher(s) and subsequently by review boards in the location or locations where the research will be conducted. The authority of each such review body should in principle be respected and given equal weight. However, complications arise in cases where a given research agenda is supported by the sponsoring institution(s) but is for one reason or another considered controversial in the context in which the research is to be carried out. This may prompt researchers to adapt the manner in which methodologies and objectives are described and in some cases submit alternative versions of their project description to the different review bodies – sometimes even with the tacit knowledge of the funding agency. This is typically justified by the greater good that the research is committed to advancing. While partially understandable, such dissimulation is fundamentally problematic, not least because it undermines the authority and effectiveness of local review structures. It moreover runs counter to the commitment to honesty and openness that ought to characterize human rights research.

---

[25]   It may be noted that the request for an ethical assessment prior to commencing research bears a close affinity to what in the context of project planning is known as *ex ante Human Rights Impact Assessment*, and likewise to the notion of *Human Rights Due Diligence* as envisioned in the UN *Guiding Principles on Business and Human Rights*, prepared by John Ruggie and adopted by the Human Rights Council in 2011 (A/HRC/17/31, 21 March 2011) <http://www.ohchr.org/Documents/Publications/GuidingPrinciplesBusinessHR_EN.pdf> accessed 20 May 2016. The fact that these compliance mechanisms have gained widespread support within the human rights community should serve as impetus to also subscribe to a rigorous ethical review standards for research in the area of human rights.

Preparation Phase

The initial stage of planning and setting up the research is typically the moment when relations of collaboration are defined. This should be taken as an opportunity to broach potentially divisive, competing claims to recognition and reward. A candid ethics discussion at this stage may also help research collaborators to develop a common perspective on key ethical decisions, policies and issues in need of subsequent attention. In conjunction with the preparation of eventual field visits and interviews, a plan should be made for how research objectives, methodologies, and possible risks or other inconveniences will be communicated to the relevant stakeholders.

Implementation Phase

Once up and running, most scientific engagements (except when entirely restricted to desk research) will involve an important element of interaction with individuals and groups contributing to the research in different capacities. This requires attention to the common standards of respectful interaction; attentiveness to tensions, sensitivities and vulnerabilities in the given area; and a careful monitoring of effects and consequences of the research, in particular with regard to possible direct or indirect harm. Sensitive research data must be carefully protected and confidentiality safeguarded. On-going cooperative research should also involve an intermittent stocktaking of how the terms of collaboration are being perceived by the parties involved.

Completion Phase

Upon completion of a given scientific engagement, it is ethically incumbent on the lead researcher(s) to ensure a reasonable degree of follow up with the involved parties; to award credit and recognition of authorship to collaborators, as appropriate; to refrain from stereotyping and unwarranted derogatory portrayals of particular individuals or groups; to remain attentive to possible long-term harmful impacts; and, on a more positive note, to actively disseminate results and seek to maximize possible benefits accruing from the research while striving, as far as possible, to ensure equity in the enjoyment of beneficial outcomes.

A CONCLUDING PERSPECTIVE: CONTEXTUALIZING ACCOUNTABILITY

The overriding focus of the present chapter has been on identifying ethical considerations of relevance to research and articulating specific obligations at each level of consideration. Against this background it is naturally asked, how are the relevant ethical norms enforced and what can be done to ensure a reasonable degree of ethical accountability?

To broach these questions, it must be noted that different norms are subject to different forms of monitoring and enforcement. Norms related to the prevention of harm, formal consent procedures and the avoidance of blatant conflicts of interest, for example, may be monitored by externally appointed review boards and are in many cases subject to formal appraisal in advance of commencing the research. Other norms, such as the obligation to display sensitivity to the life situation of research participants or to ensure proportionality between contributions and benefits deriving from the research, require attention throughout the research cycle and in the concrete settings in which the research is conducted. They tend to be less precisely defined and cannot be 'cleared' in advance of the research in the manner of a checklist approach.

This speaks to the question of how to understand accountability.[26] At one level ethical accountability is exercised by monitoring bodies that have been established with a mandate to oversee scientific and professional practice and with the ability to impose sanctions in the case of serious compliance failures. Ethical accountability on this interpretation has a quasi-judicial character. In another (complementary) sense, accountability must be recognized as an integral feature of real-life communicative interaction, and hence also as integral to the research process itself. In this sense it involves responding to uncertainties and legitimate concerns on the part of a broad range of stakeholders involved in or affected by the research.[27] These two basic modalities of accountability may be described, respectively, as *hard* and *soft* accountability. Ethics requires an element of both. Some issues are so grave that they call for external monitoring with adequate enforcement power, but not all relevant ethical requirements are

---

[26]   For a wider discussion of accountability in research ethics, see G. Ulrich 2011 (n 4).

[27]   Robert Gibbs's *Why Ethics? Signs of Responsibilities* (Princeton University Press 2000) contains a highly insightful and challenging analysis of the concept of *responsibility* and its inherent affinity to a readiness to respond to legitimate concerns in face-to-face interaction with interlocutors and (by implication) parties affected by professional conduct.

amenable to enforcement through coercive means. They rather display an interactive, reciprocal character.

Accountability does not flourish in a vacuum. It is by its very nature always *situated*, i.e. embedded within determinate structures which may be characterized as 'sites of accountability'. Ethics review boards at both national and institutional level naturally fulfill this function, but so do a range of other entities such as funding agencies, publishing houses, the public media, and self-appointed watchdog agencies. An element of ethical monitoring and accountability also continually unfolds in relations among peers and in the interaction between scientists and research participants or between scientists and the local communities hosting research.

To strengthen ethical standards in a given research area, scientists need to engage constructively with demands for both hard and soft account-ability in multiple contexts. This requires not only goodwill but also that the relevant accountability structures are functional. Scientists, in other words, must be met with qualified and credible requests for an elabora-tion of the ethical implications of their proposed or on-going activities and must be held responsible in an appropriate and meaningful fashion when things go wrong. Where requests for accountability are lacking, insufficiently informed or governed by extraneous motives, the respect for ethical review procedures tends to atrophy. Requests for accountability are then perceived as a vehicle of external control and practitioners naturally gravitate towards treating ethics first and foremost as a matter of personal conscience.[28] This undermines the standing of professional ethics as a legitimate and crucially important public concern.

What is essential in the present author's view is to frame an approach to ethics that does not from the outset focus on misconduct, thereby placing researchers in a defensive position *vis-à-vis* requests for accountability. If the very fact of encountering ethical problems is treated as an indication of acting irresponsibly and in bad faith, then scientists and other profes-sionals will naturally resist any form of situated accountability and per-ceive ethics as an unwelcome interference with their otherwise important and well-intended activities. To overcome such resistances, an element of ambiguity and candid disagreement about what constitutes the correct course of action in a given situation needs to be accepted as an integral dimension of healthy ethical discourse. Only in exceptional cases do ethical

---

[28] For a discussion of this and related issues, see P. Pels, 'Professions of Duplexity: A Prehistory of Ethical Codes in Anthropology'; and G. Ulrich, 'Comment to Peter Pels "Professions of Duplexity"' (1999) 40 Current Anthropology 101, 126–127. See also M. Strathern (ed.), *Audit Cultures: Anthropological Studies in Accountability, Ethics and the Academy* (Routledge 2000).

failures genuinely compromise the character and professional integrity of the protagonist. For the most part, uncertainties are legitimate and in fact indicative of a reflexive approach to one's research and a sincere commitment to responsible professional conduct. The forging of spaces to address such uncertainties will help to foster 'good science' in both a normative and an academic sense.

REFERENCES

American Anthropologist Association, 'Statement on Ethics' <http://ethics.americananthro.org/category/statement/> accessed 20 May 2016

American Bar Association, *Model Rules of Professional Conduct* (1983, revised February 2013) <http://www.americanbar.org/groups/professional_responsibility/publications/model_rules_of_professional_conduct.html> accessed 20 May 2016

Anderson, M.B., *Do No Harm: Supporting Local Capacities for Peace Through Aid* (Local Capacities for Peace Project, Collaborative for Development Action 1996)

Beauchamp, T.L. and J.F. Childress, *Principles of Biomedical Ethics* (6th edn, OUP 2008)

Clifford, J. and G. Marcus, *Writing Culture: The Poetics and Politics of Ethnography* (University of California Press 1986)

Council for International Organizations of Medical Science, *International Ethical Guidelines for Biomedical Research Involving Human Subjects* (2002)

Fluehr-Lobban, C., 'Informed Consent, We Are Not Exempt' (1994) 53 Human Organization 1

Geissler, P.W., and R. Pool, 'Popular Concerns about Medical Research Projects in sub-Saharan Africa – A Critical Voice in Debates about Medical Research ethics' (July 2006) 11 Tropical Medicine and International Health 975ff

Gert, B., *Morality: A New Justification of the Moral Rules* (OUP 1988)

Gert, B., C.M. Cluver and K.D. Clouser, *Bioethics: A Return to Fundamentals* (OUP 1997)

Gibbs, R., *Why Ethics? Signs of Responsibilities* (Princeton University Press 2000)

International Civil Service Commission, *Standards of Conduct for the International Civil Service*, adopted by the United Nations General Assembly (1954, revised 2013) <http://icsc.un.org/resources/pdfs/general/standardse.pdf> accessed 20 May 2016

Jonson, A.R., *A Short History of Medical Ethics* (OUP 2000)

Marsh, H., *Do No Harm: Stories of Life, Death and Brain Surgery* (Weidenfeld & Nicolson 2014)

Marshall, P.A., *Ethical Challenges in Study Design and Informed Consent for Health Research in Resource-poor Settings*, WHO Special Topics No. 5, TDR/SDR/SEB/ST/07.1 (WHO 2007)

Molyneux, C.S., N. Peshu and K. Marsh, 'Understanding of Informed Consent in a Low-Income Setting: Three Case Studies from the Kenyan Coast' (December 2004) 59 Soc. Sci. Med. 2547ff.

Molyneux, C.S., S. Mulupi, L. Mbaabu and V. Marsh, 'Benefits and Payments for Research Participants: Experiences and Views from a Research Centre on the Kenyan Coast', (2012) 13 BMC Med Ethics 1

National Committees for Research Ethics in Norway, *Guidelines for Research Ethics in the Social Sciences, Law and the Humanities* (2006)

Nuffield Council on Bioethics, *The Ethics of Research Related to Healthcare in Developing Countries* (2002)

O'Flaherty, M. and G. Ulrich (eds), *The Professional Identity of the Human Rights Field Officer* (Ashgate 2010)

O'Flaherty, M., Z. Kedzia, A. Müller and G. Ulrich (eds), *Human Rights Diplomacy – Contemporary Perspective* (Martinus Nijhof/Brill 2011)

Pels, P., 'Professions of Duplexity: A Prehistory of Ethical Codes in Anthropology' (1999) 40 Current Anthropology 101

Perry, G., *Behind the Shock Machine: The Untold Story of the Notorious Milgram Psychology Experiments* (The New Press 2013)

Posner, G.L. and J. Ware, *Mengele: The Complete Story* (McGraw-Hill 1986)

Resnik, D., 'What is Ethics in Research and Why is it Important?' (2011) 8 National Institution of Environmental Health Sciences <http://www.niehs.nih.gov/research/resources/bioethics/whatis/> accessed 20 May 2016

Reverby, S.M., *Examining Tuskegee: The Infamous Syphilis Study and its Legacy* (University of North Carolina Press 2009)

Said, E., *Orientalism* (Vintage Books 1979)

Shamoo, A. and D. Resnik, *Responsible Conduct of Research* (2nd edn, OUP 2009).

Smith, C.M., 'Origin and Uses of Primum Non Nocere – Above All, Do No Harm!' (2005) 45(4) J Clin Pharmacol 371ff

Strathern, M. (ed.), *Audit Cultures: Anthropological Studies in Accountability, Ethics and the Academy* (Routledge 2000)

Turnbull, C., *The Mountain People* (Simon & Schuster 1972)

Ulrich, G., 'Comment to Peter Pels "Professions of Duplexity"' (1999) 40 Current Anthropology 126–127

Ulrich, G., 'Optimum Ethical Standards', in 'Proceedings Seminar on Health Research Ethics in Africa' (January 2001) 78 (Supp. 1) Acta Tropica 1

Ulrich, G., 'Charges and Counter-Charges of Ethical Imperialism: Towards a Situated Approach to Development Ethics' in Ph. Q. van Ufford and A.K. Giri (eds), *A Moral Critique of Development: In Search of Global Responsibilities* (EIDOS, Routledge 2003)

Ulrich, G., 'The Statement of Ethical Commitments of Human Rights Professionals: A Commentary' in M. O'Flaherty and G. Ulrich (eds), *The Professional Identity of the Human Rights Field Officer* (Ashgate 2010)

Ulrich, G., 'Framework for the Analysis of Human Rights Diplomacy' in M. O'Flaherty, Z. Kedzia, A. Müller and G. Ulrich (eds), *Human Rights Diplomacy – Contemporary Perspective* (Martinus Nijhof/Brill 2011a)

Ulrich, G., 'Elucidating Ethics in Practice – Focus on Accountability' in P.W. Geissler and S. Molyneux (eds), *Evidence, Ethos and Experiment: The Anthropology and History of Medical Research in Africa* (Berghahn Books 2011b)

United Nations, 'International Covenant on Civil and Political Rights', G.A. res. 2200A (XXI), 21 U.N. GAOR Supp. (No. 16) at 52, U.N. Doc. A/6316 (1966), 999 U.N.T.S. 171, entered into force 23 March 1976

United Nations, OHCHR, Code of Conduct for OHCHR staff, Directive No. 2 (1999). Reproduced in 'Norms Applicable to UN Human Rights Officers and Other Staff', *Training Manual on Human Rights Monitoring* (OHCHR, 2001), pp.449–464

United Nations, *Guiding Principles on Business and Human Rights*, prepared by John Ruggie and adopted by the Human Rights Council in 2011 (A/HRC/17/31, 21 March 2011) <http://www.ohchr.org/Documents/Publications/GuidingPrinciplesBusinessHR_EN.pdf> accessed 20 May 2016

10. Comparative analyses of human rights performance
Bård A. Andreassen

INTRODUCTION

Human rights protection and monitoring inevitably entail comparison. When international human rights bodies discuss human rights performance in single countries or across countries, they apply comparative approaches to receive reliable understandings of the state of affairs. To start out with an illustration, human rights reports and studies often refer to the 'implementation gap'. In spite of official proclamations of the opposite, actual respect and implementation on the ground can be serious and dismal. The 'implementation gap' statement is comparative and points to the variation of a declared ideal state of affairs of full human rights respect, and a less-than-ideal situation on the ground, with human rights violations. This gap between 'rights in principle' and rights in 'practice' can be compared across countries,[1] or within a country over time by use of time series data. Such comparison is a key method for constructing information about human rights trends within or variations between states, and helps to identify explanatory factors and conditions that can account for patterns of human rights violations within and across states.[2]

Another example is the human rights advocacy method of 'naming and shaming', and the more recent term 'knowing and showing' in business and human rights relations.[3] Although often used for polemic or political

---

[1] J. Foweaker and T. Landman, *Citizenship Rights and Social Movements: A Comparative and Statistical Analysis* (OUP 1997).

[2] The International Covenant on Economic, Social and Cultural Rights, 16 December 1966, United Nations, Treaty Series, Vol. 993, p. 3 asks states to include 'factors and difficulties affecting the degree of fulfilment of obligations' under the Covenant when preparing reports to the Committee Economic, Social and Cultural Rights, cf. article 17.2 of the Covenant. This is a provision that should be interpreted in light of article 2.1 where states are granted a leeway to 'achieving progressively the full realization of the rights' of the Covenant.

[3] According to the new discourse on human rights and business, companies are supposed to know what their human rights impacts are and show how they address them through human rights due diligence analysis and processes.

purposes, both of these descriptive models of criticising human rights performance rest on comparative assessment of a country or business, and address failures to comply with human rights standards.

This chapter argues that the comparative approach is a key method for analysing state human rights compliance. The comparative approach can be used in examining variation between states and between non-state actors, for instance between commercial entities, or the impact of non-governmental organisations on human rights protection.[4] However, in human rights studies, most comparative analyses have focused on variation and similarities between states. The essence of the comparative method is contrasting, whether with a view to identifying differences or similarities.[5] Based on comparative research questions and research design, comparative studies explore variables that may help explain variation in human rights, respect, protection and fulfilment between countries. In recent years, a number of comparative studies of human rights compliance or non-compliance by states have been published, attempting to explain and understand conditions and factors that may account for variation in human rights realization or violations.[6] By examining methods of comparing countries, the chapter aims to encourage the use of comparative approaches and techniques in human rights research. The focus of the chapter is on comparative analysis of two or more countries, which I shall refer to as external comparative analysis. I shall also refer to single case studies, and in-country human rights assessment of change over time.

Comparison of two or more countries may be synchronic in the sense that it studies variation in human rights records between countries at a particular time. In contrast, diachronic or temporal, internal comparative analysis examines cases where a country's performance, the status of civil and political rights and freedoms at one point in time, is compared with the state of affairs at an earlier point in time. Internal case comparison is much used in human rights studies and gives analytical opportunities for in-depth contextual understanding of human rights situations and conditions. The

---

[4]   Thomas Risse, Stephen C. Ropp and Kathryn Sikkink (eds), *The Power of Human Rights. International Norms and Domestic Change* (CUP 1999); Foweaker and Landman (n 1); Beth Simmons, *Mobilizing for Human Rights. International Law and Domestic Politics* (CUP 2009); and Bård A. Andreassen and Gordon Crawford (eds), *Human Rights, Power and Civic Action. Comparative Analyses of Struggles for Rights in Developing Societies.* (Routledge 2013).

[5]   Charles C. Ragin and Lisa M. Amoroso, *Constructing Social Research. The Unity and Diversity of Method* (Sage 1994).

[6]   Risse, Ropp and Sikkink (n 4); Foweaker and Landman (n 1); Simmons (n 4); and Andreassen and Crawford (n 4).

diachronic approach is an underlying feature of human rights and related governance and development indexes that measures how a country improves or deteriorates according to a set of variables and indicators. It is often referred to as trend analysis, and has been used to map out the direction of change in a state's human rights record from one point in time to another.

The first section identifies some key features of comparative analysis, and asks what comparison is; the second section discusses the purpose and objects of comparing. In the third section, we ask *how* to compare in human rights research, drawing on old and new examples of comparative human rights research.

WHAT IS COMPARISON IN HUMAN RIGHTS RESEARCH?

To compare is a common way of handling information. In everyday activities we look at how people make similar choices, or make different priorities. We compare ourselves with others and explain why we are more or less similar or differ in opinions, choices and behavior. We talk about 'larger' or 'smaller' or 'more' or 'less' of something, students compare themselves with their fellow students, and political parties compete for votes by emphasizing what makes them different from other parties. We form opinions by comparing. In political science, the comparative method is a major approach for *systematic* comparison, but other sub-disciplines of social sciences, including law, apply comparative approaches as well. Comparative human rights law, for instance, compares legal protection of human rights across various jurisdictions in the world, and asks, *inter alia*, why one or some jurisdictions are more able and effective in protecting freedom of association, than others: can various degrees of protection be explained by variations in the effectiveness of courts, or perhaps by the constitutional status of human rights provisions? Or is the legal system being used by non-democratic regimes to harass and suppress political and civic dissent? The latter question indicates the need for crossing the borders of social science disciplines: while the lawyer observes bias and problems in court rulings, the sociologist and political scientist help explain why such bias or influence occur, using role and power analysis. The 'fragmentation' discourse of international human rights law asks if there is a trend of treating singular human rights, for instance freedom of speech, differently across international and regional human rights treaty bodies.[7]

---

[7]   Marjan Ajevski, 'Fragmentation in International Human Rights Law – Beyond Conflicts of Laws' (2014) 32(2) Nordic Journal of Human Rights 87–98.

BOX 10.1   ARISTOTLE'S METHOD OF COMPARISON
DEVELOPED ON POLITICS, CAN BE OUTLINED
AS FOLLOWS:

1. Formulation of problem (causes of political stability and instability
2. Collection of cases
3. Classification of cases
   3a. by number of rulers; monarchy, oligarchy, democracy
   3b. by mode of operation – oligarchic or democratic
   3c. by class structure and distribution of power among classes
4. Correlation of 3a–3c with relative stability or instability
5. Analysis – which types are most stable and why?

Peter H. Merkl (n 16)

These are research questions that require elaboration of an appropriate research design requiring that the object of study is being described in detail (what is court effectiveness in upholding freedom of association; what are the observed differences between courts in the interpretation of the freedom of expression?). It also requires the development of a research model that establishes relationships between the phenomenon to be explained (e.g., variation in court effectiveness) and factors and variables that explain the variation.

Comparing entails establishing knowledge that allows for some degree of generalization but, as we shall return to below, there are different degrees of generalization. Comparing also implies searching for answers to questions based on theory or theoretical guidance offered by reasonable hypotheses; and to collect and systematize information by using indicators that can be applied to compare different cases, and that are reliable and open to replication, that is, external validity.[8]

The main emphasis of this chapter is comparative political studies of human rights. The primary purpose is to present key entries to systematic and analytical approaches to human rights comparison in contrast to 'anecdotal' information.[9] An essential feature of comparative political analysis is the construction of a realistic research design based on empirical

---

[8]   Paul Penning, Hans Keman and Jan Kleinnijenhuis, *Doing Research in Political Science. An Introduction to Comparative Methods and Statistics* (Sage 2006) 5.

[9]   This does not dismiss anecdotal information as such, but such information often expressed as narratives require systematic and contextual processing and analysis. Cf. Chapter 7 by Sally Engle Merry in this volume.

research questions about human rights events or performances, and where observation of a relationship between dependent and independent variables can be analyzed and inferences drawn. This, in a nutshell, is the logic of comparative empirical research, that is, the mode of constructing systematic and reliable research-based knowledge.

Comparison can be made between two or many cases. A distinction is made between research designs that compare many cases (large-*n* comparison), few cases (small-*n* comparison) or one-case studies. Put simply, large-*n* comparison (sometimes referred to as global comparison or statistical comparison) aims at statistical analysis and explanatory generalizations, that is, statements and inferences about a large number of units. Comparative approaches, however, should be distinguished from multivariate regression. While the purpose of multivariate regression analysis is to explain co-variation in one variable with another among a very large number of cases, the purpose of the comparative approach is to identify patterns and to *explain* these patterns of similarities and differences (diversity patterns). Some case comparisons aim at in-depth descriptive and contextual explanatory analysis, for instance the paired comparison used in Risse, Ropp and Sikkink (1999)[10] that set out the empirical ground for development of the 'Spiral model' of human rights change.

Why the single case studies should be grouped under comparative social science studies is not intuitively intelligible. Single case study design is frequently used in human rights research, and aims at in-depth analysis of individual cases. They may be seen as the foundation of comparative analysis, and may give, as we shall return to, opportunities for falsifying a hypothesis by contextual description and analysis of a particular case. Comparisons are often built into case studies, and we learn from making these explicit.[11]

All three comparative research strategies have their logics of inquiry and strengths and limitations. Yet, despite limitations, the purpose of comparison is to establish explanations about real-world events, the relationship between a measureable phenomenon, for instance an increase in reported violations of freedom of assembly in a country, and the variables that explain it.

Comparative human rights research examine social, cultural, economic and political conditions for human rights compliance or neglect on scales that can be empirically measured, compared and assessed. After discussing

---

[10]   See n 4.
[11]   David Collier, 'The Comparative Method' in Ada W. Finifter (ed.), *Political Science: The State of the Discipline II*. (American Science Association 1993) 115.

why comparative approaches are important in empirical studies of human rights in the next section, the three models of comparative research strategies are discussed.

THE PURPOSE OF COMPARISON

Comparative analysis does not have a particular subject of inquiry; it offers methods for comparing – it is a set of methodological principles, procedures and techniques for comparing a wide range of issues and phenomena, by using quantitative or qualitative data and research designs or through mixed methods combining quantitative and qualitative methods. As different academic disciplines in the social sciences address different objects of inquiry and ask different types of research questions, they compare according to their own themes, e.g. comparative law, comparative anthropology, comparative political and governance studies or, in our case, comparative human rights studies. Yet in spite of these different thematic foci, the 'art of comparing' follows some similar logics across sub-disciplinary borders.

In the political science tradition of comparative analysis, focus has been on variations between states. Lane and Ersson, however, suggest a broad definition of the comparative method that goes beyond a state focus: comparative analysis is 'a methodology for the study of any kind of social unit, for example, political parties or societies, diachronically or synchronically'.[12] While much focus has been on cross-country studies, this is, as we return to below, not the only subject of comparative inquiry. Comparative politics analyzes political events, processes, structures, etc. at the macro level in nation-states at governance level.[13] In micro-analysis it explores general propositions about factors affecting institutional development and individual political behaviour across countries.[14] Commenting on comparative microanalysis, Rokkan refers to Tingsten as one of the first to see the potential for applying comparative inquiry in micro-analysis. Tingsten applied micro-analysis to study the entrance of workers and women to the electorate when suffrage rights were extended

---

[12] Jan Erik Lane and Svante Ersson, *Comparative Politics. An Introduction and New Approach* (Polity Press 1994) 6.

[13] Ibid.

[14] Stein Rokkan, 'Dimensions of State Formation and Nation-building: A Possible Paradigm for Research on Variations within Europe' in Charles Tilly (ed.), *The Formation of National States in Western Europe* (Princeton University Press 1975) 15.

in the early nineteenth century. Tingsten used pioneering statistical data of comparative politics studies where he tested hypothesis about conditions affecting political choices of these new entrants to electoral politics, in new institutional settings, and across selected political systems.[15] Comparative political studies, in other words, are not limited to states, and comparative human right studies can be applied to a wide ('unlimited') variety of cases and phenomena. One does not need to study phenomena across national borders; it often addresses in-country sub-units, e.g. regional analysis of school performance, or voter turnout in elections.[16] As noted, recently international human rights institutions and human rights research have addressed the human rights impact of non-state actors, e.g. the impact of non-governmental organizations (NGOs) and commercial entities, in particular transnational business on human rights. With human rights entering the field of corporate social responsibility, studies are designed to compare how different companies move from commitment to compliance with human rights norms under certain conditions.[17]

Landman refers to four main objectives of systematic comparative studies. Although they often co-exist in an analysis, focus may vary according to the scholar's analytical intentions. The first purpose is contextual description. All good analysis relies on good description of the cases and the description has to be guided by the research objectives and research question of the analysis, that is, what is appropriate to address the research question. Here lies a problem in much analytical description, stressed by Landman: in comparative analysis, researchers are often studying countries that are foreign to them, and in order to avoid ethnocentrism, the country study is subject to excessive description, conscious or unconscious, by the researcher. Working with other societies than one's own, often in different regions and cultures, unavoidably challenges the comparativist with a constant danger of ethnocentrism. This makes it essential that the empirical description is sufficiently contextual to the research question, and the researcher reflexive of his or her 'analytical' cultural (and other) bias.

Two other purposes of comparison noted by Landman are *classification and testing of hypotheses*. To classify is to systemize and simplify. All analytical work aims at some sort of realistic, well-argued and sound simplification of a complex world, and to classify through development of

---

[15]   Ibid.

[16]   Peter H. Merkl, *Modern Comparative Politics* (Holt, Rinehart & Winston, 1970) 4.

[17]   Bård A. Andreassen and Vo Khanh Vinh (eds), *Duties Across Borders. Advancing Human Rights in Transnational Business* (Intersentia 2016).

concepts and typologies is an important task of comparative analysis. A well-established classification in comparative politics – and highly relevant for human rights research – is categorization of states into regime types.[18]

The third purpose of comparing is testing hypothesis, that is, to transform proposed theoretical relations between dependent and independent variables derived from the research question into testable propositions.[19] This emphasizes that comparative political studies are predominantly empirically grounded, striving at theoretical inferences. Hypotheses are derived from research questions that build on different theoretical perspectives. Comparing different countries by testing hypotheses allows us to rule out rival explanations, and build more comprehensive and robust theories. For instance, in *The Power of Human Rights* Risse, Kopp and Sikkink build their analysis of change in a country's human rights commitment through international norm diffusion on a theoretical framework of socialization. This framework combines rationality (rational choice) theories of strategic bargaining and state adaptation to pressure with communicative theories of conscious raising, argumentation, dialogue and persuasion. From this composite theory, they derive a number of propositions about how national and international human rights advocacy networks constitute 'necessary conditions'[20] for domestic human rights change by 'putting norm-violating states on the international agenda in terms of moral consciousness-raising'; by being able to 'empower and legitimate the claims of domestic opposition groups against norm-violating governments'; and by challenging norm-violating governments by creating a transnational structure pressuring such regimes simultaneously 'from above' and 'from below'. These propositions are deducted from theoretical reflection, and developed into dynamic models (research design) for empirical investigation (the *Spiral* and *Boomerang* models). The empirical chapters of Risse et al. examine these theoretically inducted propositions (hypotheses) on paired comparisons of countries in different geographical regions. Hence, this example demonstrates a comparative approach to theoretical hypothesis testing, and is a representation of the hypothetical-deductive method, that deduces testable hypothesis (propositions) from theory.[21]

---

[18] Regime classification goes – again – back to Aristotle's comparative constitution study, more specifically his distinctions between monarchy, aristocracy, polity, tyranny and democracy based with reference to critical institutional features such as the nature of the regime (good, bad) and the number of rulers (one, few, many).

[19] Penning et al. (n 8) 13.

[20] Risse et al. 1999 (n 6) 5.

[21] For a discussion of the advantages and weaknesses of paired comparison in political analysis, see Sidney Tarrow, 'The Strategy of Paired Comparison:

Another recent theory-driven study is Landman's *Protecting Human Rights. A Comparative Study.*[22] Landman undertakes 'comparative and quantitative analyses of the growth and effectiveness' of the global (post-World War II) human rights regime.[23] The study assumes that there are different, including mutual, relationships between the emergence of the international human rights regime, and the protection of human rights in different countries and regions. By using various variables (democracy, wealth, population, region, etc.) the study identifies relationships between human rights ratifications and protection of human rights and explains variations between types of political regimes. The research design is informed by theories about the relationship between the growth and effectiveness of the human rights regime and the actual protection of human rights on the ground. The purpose is not only to identify that relationships exist (correlation) but also to assess the explanatory strength and reasons for the relationship and how it varies between cases, referred to as 'global variation in human rights protection'.[24] The crux of the study is to examine human rights empirically and test theories of relationships between human rights law, norms and various types of power. The study finds, *inter alia*, support for a limited effect of human rights law on state practice; the gap between law in principle (ratification) and rights in practice (protection and implementation) has narrowed in the time period covered; democracies tend to ratify human rights instruments and respect them more than non-democracies; the spread of the human rights regime by institutions of global interdependency (NGOs, international NGOs) enhances rights practices; and internal conflict has a strong negative impact on rights protection.

Social Theory and Human Rights

Theory-driven research questions mean that research puzzles must be formulated as a point of departure for doing comparative analysis. This helps to systematize the structure of the study and to gather data to assess, analyse or evaluate the research question. The theoretical approach chosen by the researcher is framing the intellectual orientation of the research, that is to say, it shapes the types of questions asked, and influences the data gathered and the inferences that are drawn. The social sciences

---

Toward a Theory of Practice' (2010) 43 (Feb) Comparative Political Studies 230.

[22]   Todd Landman, *Protecting Human Rights. A Comparative Study* (Georgetown University Press 2005).

[23]   Ibid. 6.

[24]   Ibid. 5.

have developed different theoretical orientations and positions. They are not clear-cut as mutually exclusive positions, and they are often nested. Hybrid or nested positions can increase the validity of the research, combining insights from different theoretical traditions. Landman, with reference to Lichbach,[25] distinguishes between three groups or traditions in social theory that may be applied in human rights research – rationalism, structuralism and culturalism.[26] These theoretical traditions emphasise modes of explanation, that is, differing assumptions about human behaviour, and hence, the theoretical orientation of the propositions they make about variation in human rights promotion and protection across countries. Giddon's notion of *structuration* captures how theoretical traditions may be nested. Structuration acknowledges the significance of social structures and social relations that we need to describe and understand, but structures and relations are socially constructed – they are produced, reproduced and transformed by purposeful actors: 'human agency is undertaken within the context of pre-existing social structures and to some extent is constrained by them . . . such structures are continuously reproduced and changed through social action. In this sense, structuration is a bridge between structure and agency, between external reality and the thinking subject'.[27] Andreassen and Crawford applied this theoretical approach in the operationalization of a model of power in comparative analyses of how power constrain human rights agency in different political and social contexts.[28]

Alternatively, *inductive methods* of theory testing start out with observing and describing one or several cases and then choose which theories can explain the variation between the cases. The starting point is a few or many

---

[25]   M. Lichbach, 'Social Theory and Comparative Politics' in M. Lichbach and A. Zuckman (eds), *Comparative Politics: Rationality, Culture and Structure* (CUP 1997).

[26]   Todd Landman, *Studying Human Rights* (Routledge 2006) 36f.

[27]   Gordon Crawford and Bård A. Andreassen, 'Human Rights, Power and Civic Action. Theoretical Considerations' in Andreassen and Crawford (n 6) 9; M. Haugaard (ed.), *Power: A reader* (Manchester University Press 2002); and Anthony Giddens, *The Constitution of Society: Outline of the Theory of Structuration* (Polity Press 1984).

[28]   Andreassen and Crawford (n 6). Over recent years, the idea of constrained or *contingent agency* has been studied in different empirical and comparative studies in empirical analyses of how multidimensional power may constrain human rights advocacy by non-governmental organizations and social movements, and in the rapidly growing field of the business and human rights nexus, and the functioning of new forms of regulatory norms on commercial behaviour. Sury Deva, *Regulating Corporate Human Rights Violations. Humanizing Business* (Routledge 2012); Andreassen and Vinh (n 17).

case analysis and may entail a 'thick' few case description or be based on sample of 'thin' statistical data. The 'thick'–'thin' metaphor is somewhat misleading if it is interpreted as one being more robust and important than the other. They are used for different analytical purposes; while contextual ('thick') case description seeks the details of one or few cases, the statistical ('thin') description seeks to establish correlations that can be explained by statistical interpretation and analysis. Hypotheses are then derived from observed differences or unexpected similarities that trigger explanation by hypothesis formulation. Empirically observed differences and correlations are guiding the researchers, and the choice of method for trying to identify causal mechanisms.

Modes of Explanation and Strategic Comparative Calculation

Explanation, in principle, is a universal statement about causal relations between an event or state of affairs, and the conditions and causal mechanisms that bring about the situation. However, as our data for practical, economical and other reasons are constrained any explanation has some degree of uncertainty. When using comparative approaches we attempt to reduce uncertainty by 'identifying explanatory variables that are carefully defined, and relationships between them are demonstrated through comparison of empirical evidence'.[29] At the same time, the *explanatory power* of a hypothesis relies on a number of factors. Explanatory power is stronger if it accounts clearly for the data used (facts and observations), if the accuracy of contextual description is high, if it gives opportunity for falsification (by being testable by data observation), and if it is offering some predictive power. Hence, a causal relationship may give rise to prediction, that is, what we expect will happen if the conditions and causal relationships of the state of affairs established are established with relative similarity in future. Prediction, however, is again a difficult exercise in comparative political research, and usually takes the probabilistic form of 'likelihood under certain conditions'. For instance, on basis of the finding of *The Power of Human Rights* study that 'efforts of external actors to directly help, strengthen and support the domestic opposition and civil society' was essential for human rights progress (in the cases studied), the Spiral Model made a general conclusion with a clear prediction: '(p)ushing governments towards making tactical concessions almost always opens up political and discursive space in the society of the "target state" during

---

[29]   Todd Landman, *Issues and Methods in Comparative Politics: An Introduction* (Routledge, 2003) 29.

early phases of the change process'.[30] The probabilistic nature of the prediction, however, moderates its explanatory power and opens for alternative, possible or probable outcomes.

Hence, comparative analysis distinguishes between probabilistic and deterministic modes of explanation. Probabilistic explanations assume that a particular situation – say a violent crackdown on an opposition movement – can lead to a number of new and more or less likely situations (or outcomes): it may trigger installing authoritarian rule or a military coup but it may also mobilize democratic counterforces that help restore state respect for rights. In the early democratization process of the one-party state of Kenya after 1990, a number of outcomes were possible: a quick transition to multi-party democracy; a slow and violent situation of instability and conflict; or a return to authoritarian rule based on ethno-demographic control by an alliance of ethnic groups. To put our mind-set in a probabilistic mode is to ask why one of these paths occurred while other probable paths did not. There are always several probable paths ahead, but only one is pursued at the expense of others. By accepting that there were different possibilities, we avoid deterministic explanations that assume that a particular path *had* to be followed. Deterministic 'explanations' close our eyes for the 'openness' and indeterminism of social life, the unexpected and the possible unintended effects of choice-making. The possibility of unintended consequences reminds us that although human behaviour and social outcomes are purposeful and intentional, they are also uncertain. Pursuing a purpose as in normative human rights action, the search for possibilities is equally important. However, while *probabilism* is a mode of explanation of outcomes, the search for possibilities to realize goals is a mode of strategic calculation. Such future-oriented calculation is generally based on comparison of alternatives, and the assessment of pay-offs, costs and benefits.

Events, Sequencing and Relationships

Comparative politics has tended to generalize about recurrent events, recurrent sequences and recurrent relationships.[31] This is also reflected in the increasing comparative literature on human rights studies. The choice of any of these objects of inquiry depends on the research question and the theory one wants to examine and test. Typical examples of

---

[30]   Risse et al. 1999 (n 4) 276.
[31]   Charles Tilly (ed.), *The Formation of National States in Western Europe* (Princeton University Press 1976).

events for comparison are rights violations in times of internal conflict or war, the conduct of 'free and fair' elections, legal reforms to prevent gender discrimination, or social movements for peasants' rights. At the level of sequencing, there is a long tradition in political science of delineating standard stages of political development. This was a major effort of political science in the 1950s–1970s. One of the most renowned attempts in comparative politics is the nation-building and state-formation studies of Stein Rokkan, who explored possible standard sequencing of political-historical transformations through longitudinal phases for serial resolution of development challenges, or systemic crises of transformation: state penetration (control of territory and monopoly of power), cultural standardization (through unified language), participation and inclusion of the lower classes into the political system (extension of suffrage and organizational rights) and establishment of workable consensus for redistribution of resources and benefits.[32] In all these historical phases of a multi-dimensional model of institutional development of the European development, Rokkan's main geographical area of research, a key mechanism was the gradual extension of citizenship rights. In a work jointly authored with Reinhart Bendix, Rokkan states that 'a core element of nation-building is the codification of the rights and duties of all adults who are classified as citizens. The question is how exclusive or inclusive citizenship is defined'.[33]

In the structuring of social and political orders in the European region, there were many variations in the sequencing of state formation and national consolidation; still the 'master variables' of the model give some scope for 'constructing a corresponding grid of variables for the differentiation of sequences in the other regions of the world'.[34] From a cross-regional and comparative point of view, a paradigm for studying variation in sequencing in rights-based institutional development and system consolidation in Europe gave scope for analogous comparative studies of other regions (in twentieth-century post-colonial systems). Rokkan concludes that the European sequence cannot be repeated in other regions and countries, but learning can be made from European experience to breeding combinations of policies for institutional development (e.g. state formation and consolidation) in the 'new nations'.[35]

---

[32]   Rokkan (n 14).

[33]   Reinhart Bendix, *Nation-building and Citizenship. Studies of Changing Social Order.* (University of California Press 1977) 90. The quote is taken from a section, 'The Extension of Citizenship to the Lower Classes', chapter 3 in Bendix, 1977. Bendix refers in a footnote to the co-authorship with Rokkan.

[34]   Rokkan (n 14). 592.

[35]   Ibid. 600.

Hence, the search for sequences and patterns is immanent in comparative research. A main motivation of this search is inherent in this question: can comparison of countries detect structures, policy combinations and paths of development that can be of use for actual and contemporary political, social, economic, and not least human rights challenges in political systems? Comparison by looking for patterns may give insight for policy design and implementation. Over the last three decades a number of regime changes have given rise to debates about the sequencing of transitional politics: are early elections after a regime breakdown good or bad? When and how should institutional reforms of state institutions and the basic constitutional reforms be introduced? Under what conditions should transitional justice be 'sequenced in', and when is a transitional process better served with slow and gradual processes of justice in order to avoid destabilization and breakdown of a fragile process? Hence, search for sequences has spilled over to the field of human rights inquiry and policy-making. It rests on insights from comparative analysis.

One of the most comprehensive attempts at comparative sequencing of human rights implementation is the *Power of Human Rights* volume on socialization of international human rights norms in domestic practices, edited by Risse, Ropp and Sikkink.[36] A main argument of the volume is that domestication of human rights in the selected countries (mainly in the Global South and Eastern Europe) may happen through interactive diffusion processes among actors of domestic and transnational human rights networks. An important feature of these processes is that the networks are able to mobilize the Western public and Western governments to exercise pressure on norm-violating states. This networking and alliance-building among domestic and transitional organizations is essential for putting norm-violating states on the agenda, and alerting liberal Western states about their duty to pursue human rights values. Local actors in repressive states are protected by international exposure, and this support helps mobilize domestic opposition and social groups. This simultaneous pressure 'from below' and 'from above' limits the scope of norm-violating regimes, who are pulled into processes of policy change, described as processes of socialization. The causal mechanisms that make this change happen take place through 'processes of instrumental adaptation and strategic bargaining; processes of moral consciousness-raising, argumentation, dialogue and persuasion; (and) processes of institutionalization and habitualization'.[37]

---

[36] Risse et al. 1999 (n 4).
[37] Ibid. 5.

In the ideal model developed by the project, the diffusion of norms over time flows through five sequences where one follows the other: a situation of norm-violation and repression is followed by a process of *denial* from the repressive regime. Further mobilization of domestic and transnational networks by norm-promoting agents pushes the state to make *tactical concessions*, and possible political changes through a state where the regime accepts international human rights (*the prescriptive phase*) and begins a regime change to a state where it accepts and begins implementing human rights treaties and norms (*a new phase of rule-consistent behaviour*). These processes (or sequences) of change are much shorter in time than the larger historical processes discussed by Rokkan. *The Power of Human Rights* project concerns regime transitions through five phases over a period of a few years, yet these sequences can be rapid or slow depending on context and conditions. By applying this theoretical perspective to comparative empirical studies, the project concludes that the transnational networking represented a necessary but by no means a sufficient condition for norm-conducive diffusion (so-called snowballing effect).[38]

The paired comparison of countries was qualitative, emphasizing context, and the research model emphasized processes with the consequent use of process tracing in the case analyses. For the 11 countries studied the dependent variable – the outcome of a process of socialization towards state compliance with human rights – varied across the countries. Hence, the study examined both success and more problematic cases of norms diffusion and socialization and enabled discussion of conditions for different outcomes of processes of human rights change. Process-tracing as a method helped to identify causal mechanisms that led to different outcomes, and helped to move beyond 'correlational arguments about norm compliance in the human rights area that simply take note of the "convergence" of international norms and improved domestic human rights behaviour'.[39]

One of the main critiques of the *Power and Human Rights Project* was that the limited number of international human rights norms examined empirically by the project, that is, a narrow set of 'freedoms from' rights – like torture and disappearances, and civil liberties like freedom of association, expression, etc. – significantly weakened conclusions about systemic and sustainable regime change. Another methodological weakness is a failure to provide indicators (proxies) that provide empirical evidence about persuasion of state elites to change behaviour through

---

[38]   Ibid. 275.
[39]   Ibid. 271.

norm socialization, which indeed is an essential part of the theoretical model.[40]

In a recent study revisiting the analyses of the 1999 volume the authors adhere to these and other critiques, but claim that the dynamics of change of the spiral model stand up to scrutiny: the 'spiralling' or sequenced form of change is a valid research model, while they explore further the social mechanisms and modes of action that cause human rights change, and the scope conditions for such changes,[41] where more emphasis is put on regime type and degree of statehood that in the previous 1999 study.

In summary, from the studies examined above the primary task of empirical comparisons is to single out 'the most parsimonious configuration of variables required in the explanation of the differences on the given dependent variable'.[42] Early comparative politics was developed through geo-cultural region studies, comparing countries in political-cultural regions. A justification of regional studies was that the number of variables needed to explain differences is smaller if the cases have historical, institutional and cultural experiences in common: 'You need fewer variables to account for differences among the Nordic countries than for differences among all Protestant countries, fewer for an analysis of variation among Protestant countries than among all Christian countries, fewer for differences among Christian countries than among all political systems initially formed under the one of the world religions'.[43] This enables studies of the 'evidence–inference' logic, which is key to comparative analysis.

HOW TO COMPARE?

The main challenge of comparing is to strive for reliable information that allows some level of generalization about variation and similarities. In doing comparative research the starting point is to formulate a research question in order to decide units of analysis and methods of comparing. The next step is to develop a proper research design that makes it possible to translate research questions about real-life events into observations, and to analyse these systematically. The meaning of 'systematic' can certainly vary – it might be an explorative study that examines a case in detail and may lead to theory formation; or it might be explanatory and aim to test causal

---

[40] Jeffrey T. Checkel, 'Review of The Power of Human Rights: International Norms and Domestic Change' (2000) 33 Comparative Political Studies 1337.

[41] See n 4.

[42] Rokkan (n 14) 570.

[43] Ibid.

relationships in order to verify existing theories and develop these further.[44] The research design requires elaboration of the research object, a mode of analysis that clarifies the comparative nature of the analysis (the nature of comparison) and the elaboration of the empirical cases. Comparative analysis transcends pure description and seeks external validity – a level of generalization. It is also a basic requirement that research should be open to replication by other researchers, so-called internal validity; data produced should be stored and made available for other researchers.

Number of Cases and Case Selection

In principle, there is no one *preferred* method in comparative research. The methodological choices that any researcher has to make are informed by research questions, theories applied and the epistemological orientation of the researcher.[45] Comparative analysis has a high *level of abstraction* if it includes a high number of cases.[46] This implies that the analysis travels across very different contexts; it is conceptually complex. At a high level of abstraction we want to compare, for instance, violations of the prohibition against torture, inhuman and degrading treatment in democracies versus authoritarian states. At a less abstract and more complex level of analysis we may want to compare the prevalence of torture, inhuman and degrading treatment in European democracies, which would require a more fine-tuned classification of democracies, for instance between Northern and Southern European states, or between common law and civil law democracies.

This *epistemological orientation* varies along a continuum from 'thick' hermeneutical and context-sensitive analysis using a variety of qualitative techniques, e.g. participant observation (cf. Chapter 18) or in-depth interviews or ethnographic methods (cf. Chapter 7) to 'thin' or statistical analysis that aims at theory-driven inferences based on quantitative evidence (statistical data). The goal of such 'ideographic' contextual analysis is usually to understand the meaning of acts and behaviour and interpret a case in detail. Some scholars have referred to these methods as a-theoretical and interpretative, and of less value because they do not seek universal applicability and generalization.[47] Others argue that such analysis

---

[44]　Penning et al. (n 8) 8.

[45]　Landman (n 26) 58.

[46]　Ibid.; and Giovanni Sartori, 'Concept Misformation in Comparative Politics' (1970) 64(4) American Political Science Review 1033.

[47]　Arend Lijphart, 'Comparative Politics and the Comparative Method' (1971) 65(3) The American Political Science Review 682. Gabriel A. Almond, *Comparative Politics. A Theoretical Framework* (HarperCollins 1996) 682–693.

gives very important understanding of cases, not least in studies of human rights developments and changes in particular countries. These studies are at any rate inductive based on empirical evidence, while they do not draw inferences beyond the case.

Along the epistemological continuum, we find the theory-driven comparative analysis which combines quantitative and qualitative data and draws contingent inferences about generality. In the *Power of Human Rights study* paired comparison and single-case studies were combined, and gave evidence for testing out research questions. At a higher level of abstraction theory-driven and inductive statistical analysis based on quantitative evidence gives room for exceptions from the general explanation. We may identify 'outliers' of deviant cases in a statistical pattern that calls for explanation and represent interesting cases for further contextual examination. At the other end of the epistemological continuum, we find the purely theoretical and argumentative studies which are deductive and conclude after normative reasoning or based on theoretical reflection. They are theoretical constructions, but may help develop hypotheses and ideas for further studies.

The third factor influencing a comparative research design – in addition to level of abstraction and epistemological orientation – is the number of cases that the researcher wants to include, that is, the scope of units analysed. The number of cases is also often referred to as the 'property space'. In comparative research the number of cases involved suggests three research models: few case comparisons; many case comparisons; and one-case studies. Before going through each of them in some detail, we need to address what a case is, as the word is used with different meanings.

A case can be seen as a 'carrier of information' about the world. It can be empirically observed and measured, and is defined by space and time. Cases are units of observation that are logically connected to the research question posed. Thus, cases in comparative research are not just countries; cases may also be NGOs in studies of civic action, voters in studies of voting behaviour, companies in studies of corporate human rights responsibility, etc. Cases carry information about theoretical concepts, the state of freedom of assembly in a country, or a company's respect for labour law. Cases therefore refer to the units of observation that are compared.[48] If you study the compliance of a country's international obligations to implement the right to adequate food, the number of observed units is increased by looking at annual levels of implementations (variation) over a period of, say, 20 years. If performance every five years

---

[48] Penning et al. (n 8) 9.

is compared, the number of units observed is four, hence, there are four cases; it is a single case study with many observations.

Comparing Many Cases

Comparing many countries in comparative research is referred to as 'large-*n*' studies, while comparing a few cases is referred to as 'small-*n*' studies. Large-*n* studies are variable-oriented in the sense that they assess relationships between general features of different social structures considered as variables. Landman applies a large-*n*, global comparison to study if ratification of human rights treaty law enhances the protection of human rights in ratifying states, and to account for global variation.[49] In large-*n* studies, an underlying assumption is that human rights are being 'more or less' protected by states and that this can be measured and coded for statistical analysis. The study assembled national time series data for 193 countries for the period between 1976 and 2000, giving altogether 4825 observations,[50] and demonstrated that there is 'strong empirical support' for a limited positive effect of ratification of human rights conventions on state practice. Controlling for other variables, Landman concluded that this impact has to be seen as part of 'a larger set of socioeconomic changes' and the impact of democratic institutions was considerable. Using regression analysis, the study showed that democracies are more likely to ratify human rights instruments and protect human rights than non-democracies. Regression analysis also showed support for the 'lock in' theory that newly democratized regimes have a greater tendency to ratify new human rights treaties than old and established democracies: by ratifying such instruments the democratizers are trying to 'lock in' future generations to prevent them from undermining the democratic institutions. However, the impact of international law on practice is limited, and can partly be accounted for by a state's previous commitment to rights protection, and other intervening variables of the research model, that is, underlying political and social processes: democratization, economic development, global interdependence, the existence or not of internal or external conflict, population size and geo-political region.[51]

A main strength of global or statistical comparison is that by statistical control we may rule out alternative explanations, give evidence for strong inferences and theory-building, and identify 'deviant' cases or 'outliers',

---

[49]   See n 22.
[50]   Ibid. 35.
[51]   Ibid. 31.

that is, surprising or unexpected values on the dependent variable of the unit (country) given the value of the independent variable. Deviant cases may call for further analysis, where contextual analysis with qualitative techniques can help explain the case. For instance, it is commonly assumed that countries with democratic institutions and high levels of economic wealth score low on number of torture and inhuman and degrading treatment cases. Still, there are many countries with high levels of economic wealth and democratic institutions where torture is prevalent. Landman concludes that, while regression analysis 'confirmed that the level of democracy is an important explanatory variable for human rights protection . . . such protection is highest for old democracies, followed by third wave and fourth wave democracies'.[52] Still there are important outliers that regression identified, e.g. Columbia, being an old democracy but still with serious human rights violations, that call for further examination and explanation by contextual analysis.

Gilligan and Nesbitt[53] present a good example of the strength of large-*n* studies. These studies may help correct ill-founded yet intuitive conclusions. They ask if norms can prevent torture, and use the Convention against Torture (CAT) as the main reference for a large-*n* study on how the introduction of new norms, by a state's ratification of CAT, can affect and change state behaviour. Scholars have claimed, they assert, 'that states are constrained by norms of appropriate behaviour and furthermore that norms actually change . . . states' understanding of their own interests, thereby leading states to change their behaviour as they pursue these new interests'.[54] However, they claim that these theoretical assertions have not been subjected to rigorous empirical tests, and are based on a small number of 'nonrandomly selected case studies'.[55] They then test the claim that norms change state behaviour, that is, whether ratification in itself is effective in preventing torture, or whether other strategies should be explored. Contrary to common anticipation indicated by case studies, they conclude that spreading the norm not to torture through ratification of CAT did not have the expected effect – according to regression analysis with controls they find that torture in fact was becoming worse in the sample as a whole as the norms spread.[56] They address this counterintuitive result by discussing their measurement of torture and ask if torture before ratification was

[52]   Landman (n 22) 163.
[53]   Michael J. Gilligan and Nathaniel H. Nesbitt, 'Do Norms Reduce Torture?' (2009) 38(2) The Journal of Legal Studies 445.
[54]   Ibid. 446.
[55]   Ibid.
[56]   Ibid. 459.

underreported and ratification of CAT provided a context for more effective reporting. However, the authors assume that there is no fundamental measurement problem in the analysis. Rather, they explain the unexpected result by arguing that the ratification of CAT is in fact the ratification of a *deontological norm*, that is, a norm that prescribes certain rules and obligations. This should not be conflated with behaviour norms, that is, a norm that is immediately practiced: torture is practiced in spite of those responsible knowing that it is wrong.[57]

Dwelling on this study highlights both strengths and weaknesses of large-*n* studies. The empirical quantitative test of an intuitive assumption ('ratification of a treaty leads to less violation of rights') demonstrates how the assumption can be flawed. This is very important knowledge, not least because it may, as the authors allude to but do not address in detail, help discuss alternative, or better, complementary strategies to ratification. Follow-up few-*n* or single case studies may have revealed that there are different explanations for this weakness of norm effectiveness through ratification in different regimes and contexts. While one reason might be, as Gilligan and Nesbitt argue, that 'torture is a practice in which leaders engage even if they know it is wrong',[58] more plausible explanations might be suggested by analyses of the power and behaviour of duty-bearers in key state institutions; the police, security bodies and the public prosecutor.

A significant challenge of global, large-*n* comparison often referred to in human rights analysis is availability of relevant data, the high costs of collecting data and the fact that collecting data is time-consuming. However, these problems are increasingly reduced by the availability of new sets of data. While statistical analysis of human rights performance predominantly refers to a small selection of rights, such as political participation, extrajudicial killings, torture, political disappearances, etc., there is now increasing availability also in the area of economic and social rights. An important contribution is the Socio-economic Rights Fulfilment Index, which has developed a methodology for benchmarking a country's obligation for economic and social rights fulfilment that takes into account the country's resource capacity and constraints.[59]

A second challenge is the standard problem in social science of validity of the measures chosen. To choose indicators that are apt proxies to the phenomenon a researcher wants to measure (do they measure what was

---

[57]   Ibid. 467.

[58]   Ibid.

[59]   Susan Randolph and Patrick Guyer, 'Tracking the Historical Evolution of State's Compliance with their Economic and Social Rights Obligations of Result' (2012) 30(2) Nordic Journal of Human Rights 297.

expected) is critical, but often problematic. A typical problem is that of measuring poverty. While some apply a very narrow concept, for instance an income level of US$1.9 per day (The World Bank), others use a more composite and complex measure, and rely on Amartya Sen's concept of poverty as deprivation of capabilities. Other concepts greatly related to human rights analysis which are measured in different ways are democracy, authoritarianism and economic development. Yet another example is the right to food, which is (in human rights terms) expected to be adequate, affordable, available and culturally acceptable. What counts as adequate etc., may certainly differ between cultural contexts.

A related third challenge is also standard to quantitative analysis, that of reliability and replicability. This concerns the extent to which the indicators used can be given observations across systems, in different cultures and social systems, i.e. whether they are 'invariant' and 'universal'.[60] Sartori warned against the danger of 'conceptual stretching, and raised doubts about concepts capacity for global travel'.[61] A fourth challenge is data aggregation. Aggregation aims to produce terms that cover many cases and diverse situations in order to allow generalization; grouping together different cases in one category – again democracy is often used this way, or the 'welfare state' as another example – hides differentiations that may be important for a realistic and reliable analysis.

Hence, in spite of the growing interest in the metrics of human rights and the use of quantitative methods, there are several issues that need to be seriously examined. Variations among countries, in particular across cultural regions and economic levels of development, may be so significant that generalizations may not be universally valid. As the example on the effects of norms against torture demonstrates, there may be 'variable bias' where key variables (in that case institutional reforms) have not been adequately specified. Most importantly, in spite of its strengths, the difficulties of operationalizing many topics in human rights research at a high level of abstraction in large-*n* comparison has limits, and requires lower levels of analysis and techniques.[62]

---

[60] Adam Przeworski and Henry Teune, *Logic of Comparative Social Inquiry. Comparative Studies in Behavioural Science* (John Wiley and Sons 1970).

[61] Sartori (n 46).

[62] Todd Landman 'Comparative Politics and Human Rights' (2002) 24(2) Human Rights Quarterly 903.

Comparing Few Cases

Some of the challenges above are reasons why comparative human rights studies largely have approached a smaller number of countries. The few-cases comparison sometimes takes the form of regional or area studies, also referred to as 'focused comparison'.[63] The few-cases research design has been used in human rights comparative analysis for various reasons, some referred to above: availability of data, funding and even lack of quantitative training among human rights researchers. While few-cases comparison can draw on statistical evidence, it is generally more intensive and contextual than large-*n* comparison. It gives more space to the description and analysis of each case, and may also typically take a historical (longitudinal or short) perspective. A focus on differences and similarities of cases rather than differences in the relationship between variables, makes it 'case oriented' as opposed to the 'variable orientation' of large-*n* comparison.

How do we select cases (countries) for comparison, when we chose to approach just a few cases? In comparing few cases the selection is purposeful (non-random), and there are two basic research designs that the researcher applies: choosing relatively similar countries or relatively different countries. These two logics of inquiry[64] are *the most similar system design* (MSSD) and the *most different system design* (MDSD). Building on earlier works by John Stuart Mill,[65] a standard reference of these designs is Przeworski and Teune.[66]

The most similar system design compares countries that are similar on as many features as possible assuming that this provides the optimal sample for comparison. It is typically used in 'areas studies' where the area is defined in political or cultural terms, for instance Western Europe, Scandinavia or Sub-Saharan Africa. The focus is on similarities or differences between countries, where the common characteristics are seen as 'controlled' (for instance, legal system, political system, economic level of development and social stratification). An observed difference (the

---

[63]　Arend Lijphart, 'The Comparable Case Strategy in Comparative Research' (1975) 8(2) Comparative Political Studies 158.

[64]　Theodore W. Meckstroth, '"Most Different Systems" and "Most Similar Systems": A Study in the Logics of Comparative Inquiry' (1975) 8(2) Comparative Political Studies 132.

[65]　John Stuart Mill, *A System of Logic* (Longman 1843).

[66]　Przeworski and Teune (n 60). These logics go back to a comparable distinction made by John Stuart Mill between the method of difference and the method of agreement in Mill, 1843.

dependent variable) is then explained by a key factor that is different among the cases and hence explains a particular outcome.[67]

The MSSD manipulates the independent variables through purposeful case selection that 'neutralizes' most, but not all explanatory variables. As an example, the comparative project *Democracy in Developing Countries: Africa* applies largely the MSSD in comparing and explaining democratic failure and progress in six African countries.[68] The countries selected for in-depth case studies – Nigeria, Ghana, Senegal, Botswana, Zimbabwe and Uganda – all shared many major characteristics on colonial legacy, ethnic pluralism, political culture, political legitimacy and political leadership. In spite of similarities in such features, they differ in democratic outcome, because democracy can only work if it 'responds innovatively to each country's distinctive cultural traditions, political problems and social forces', and it 'responded' differently in the selected countries.[69]

The MDSD selects countries that share few common features apart from the political outcome to be explained, or one or two explanatory factors (independent variables) likely to explain the outcome. Often this strategy assumes that the phenomena to be explained reside at a lower level than the country level, that is, at micro or meso (group) levels, or a middle level of conceptual abstraction. It is also based on the testing of hypotheses that may eliminate explanatory causes more than 'finding positive relationships'.[70] The MDSD was applied in a study of *Human Rights, Power and Civic Action*, exploring how civic struggles in 'developing societies' are constrained by different forms of power, but at the same time are producing countervailing power by civic organization.[71] This was a six-country comparative study using qualitative techniques for data collection (including document analysis, interviews with key organizational staff and members, focus group discussions and non-participatory observations). The project was guided by research questions about power as constraining civic action, but also the options available for mobilizing civic actors in different contexts. The project compared six countries (Ghana, South Africa, Kenya, Zimbabwe, Cambodia and China), selected to reflect different political contexts with regards to degree of democratization and protection

---

[67]   Przeworski and Teune (n 60) 33.

[68]   Larry Diamond, 'Introduction: Roots of Failure, Seeds of Hope' in Larry Diamond, Juan J. Linz and Seymour Martin Lipset (eds), *Democracy in Developing Countries: Africa* (Lynne Rienner 1988).

[69]   Ibid.

[70]   Guy Peters, *Comparative Politics, Theory and Method* (New York University Press, 1998).

[71]   Andreassen and Crawford (n 4).

of political rights: 'Through comparative analysis of such *dissimilar cases*, it is anticipated that *similar outcomes* will be demonstrated in terms of opposition and resistance to rights claims by power-holders, although the specific nature of the constraints experienced by rights-promoting organizations will vary dependent on the particular context'.[72] The basic units of observation of the project were a selection of 19 NGOs (four in one case, three in the others), which were selected through contextual background studies of political context and the organizational landscape over the past 20–30 years, and organizational mapping of civil society in the respective countries. These background studies enabled a purposeful selection of cases. The project design, in other words, reflected the trust of the MDSD to explore how different political contexts entailed constraints by people in power to rights-promoting organizations. However, as these obstacles vary in different contexts, so do the opportunities to challenge such constraints by civic action and the opportunities for strategies to enhance the capacity of civic agents.[73] While different political dispensations represented structural constraints, the research explored how various forms of civic agency by NGOs explained the outcome of rights-promoting mobilization, albeit mobilization succeeded (in terms of producing countervailing power) to various degrees. The units of analysis were the NGOs studied; yet variation in degree of successful civic action was explored by different political contexts.

Case Studies

The case study method is much used in human rights research and advocacy. Depending on the theoretical ambition of the research and level of analysis, different one-case models are used. It entails single case analysis, cross-case analysis and within-case methods of analysis. It also encompasses ethnographic and narrative analysis (cf. Chapter 7). According to Campbell,[74] case studies are the basis of most comparative research, and this provides opportunities for falsifying hypotheses. Eckstein argues for *testing hypotheses* in case study analysis.[75] Hence, an important characteristic of one-case research is to make explicit the comparative nature of

---

[72]   Ibid. 15.

[73]   Ibid.

[74]   Donald T. Campbell, 'Degrees of Freedom and the Case Study' (1975) 8(2) Comparative Political Studies 178–193, 185.

[75]   Harry Eckstein, 'Case Study and Theory in Political Science,' in F.I. Greenstein and N.W. Polsby (eds), *The Handbook of Political Science* (Addison-Wesley 1975) 113–123.

case studies. Collier points out that examination of a critical case 'about which the analyst has particularly strong expectations that it will fit the hypothesized causal pattern', provides an opportunity for hypothesis falsification.[76] There are different techniques of case studies, and Collier refers to the 'congruence procedure' where the values of a dependent and an independent variable are compared with other cases to identify congruence, and 'process tracing', which is a careful processual examination of how a case unfolds over time. An example from human rights research is protection against child abuse measured by child labour in a particular location, and assessment of how a rights-based campaign against child labour may bring effects over time. Process tracing is a form of the wider concept of 'pattern matching' where description of a case is compared with a theoretical pattern to establish uniformity or congruence, and variation explained.

Case studies can be part of a broader few-case comparison as discussed in the previous section, but may also stand alone as a comparative case that helps building theoretical insight about a phenomenon. Previous hesitation with regard to case studies, notably in political science, has subsided and case studies are now broadly accepted as part of the comparative method.[77] The interest in theory-oriented case studies has increased, and it is acknowledged that they may provide opportunities for falsifying hypotheses, and that much comparison is built into country case studies. Although case studies can never establish generalizations, intensive studies of a case can give important contributions to development of general propositions and theory-building. In his seminal article 'Comparative Politics and the Comparative Method',[78] Lijphart distinguishes between six categories of case studies. Case studies may be atheoretical, interpretative, hypothesis-generating, theory-confirming, theory-infirming and may invite examination of deviant cases. The atheoretical case study is perceived to exist in a 'theoretical vacuum' and is purely descriptive (even if any description is implicitly informed by theoretical assumptions) and may have value in terms of intensive data-gathering and contribute to theory-building. Interpretative theories, moreover, while focusing on a single case, make use of theories to interpret the case. The remaining four one-case methods are to different degrees aimed at some level of theory construction. Theory-building cases, for instance, start out by hypothesis testing a case that

---

[76] Collier (n 11) 115.

[77] Lijphart (n 47), Collier (n 11), Landman (n 29) and Alexander L. George and Andrew Bennett, *Case Studies and Theory Development in Social Sciences* (MIT Press 2005).

[78] Lijphart (n 46).

subsequently may be applied to other cases and hence turned into a few case comparisons.

A case study encompasses the key elements of a research design: a research question, a proposition or hypothesis (if any), identification of the units of analysis, a theoretical framework, that is, the logic linking the data and the proposition, and criteria for interpreting the data.[79] So what is a case? At the basic level a case is an individual, a singular social entity, a country or a particular process. There is also a parallel here to 'case law' in legal studies. Legal cases are usually in-depth contextual descriptions of an act conducted by an individual, and a judgment entails references and comparisons of similarities or differences with similar cases. Often, legal case descriptions apply methods and reasoning from several social science disciplines, most typically psychology and for contextual description and understanding, sociology and political science. The legal case is embedded in a structuring social context.

The definition of the case is reflecting the research question and defines the type of data that are required. A case study of a democratic transition in a particular country may include transitional elections, the role of civil society, constitutional and institutional reforms and the role of leadership and political negotiations. A case of illustration, discussed by George and Bennett,[80] is Lijphart's classic study on why democracy was possible in the Netherlands between 1917 and 1967 in spite of the absence of conducive democratic conditions as postulated by pluralist theory. Lijphart contends that according to pluralist theory extreme pluralism is unfavourable to stable democracy. Stable democracy, the theory argues, requires secondary groups that disperse power, represent checks on the government and spur political freedoms and liberties. It also requires forms of communication across socio-cultural and other divisions. Lijphart demonstrates that stable and effective democracy was possible in the highly segmented society in Netherlands in spite of the lack of all the conditions assumed by pluralist theory. In explaining this phenomenon he focuses on an elaboration of the third of the elements listed and suggests that, in the Netherlands case, stable democracy can best be explained by the institutionalization of politics of accommodation. A major conclusion of Lijphart's study is that the Netherlands over time was able to develop and nurture an elite political culture that created rules and structures for accommodation of cultural differences and hence avoided mass-level

---

[79]   Robert K. Yin, *Case Study Research. Design and Methods* (Sage, 1994); and George and Bennett (n 77).

[80]   George and Bennett (n 77).

BOX 10.2

The usual disclaimer about the conclusions to be drawn from a case study are in order here. A case study may be able to disprove a generalization, but only if the generalization is stated in absolute terms and most of the general propositions in the social sciences are not universal but probabilistic in nature. A single case study can obviously not be the sole basis for a valid generalization. Case studies have a more modest function. In particular, deviant case analysis can lead to the identification of additional variables and the refinement of concepts and indicators.

(Lijphart (n 81) 181)

---

societal conflicts that would undermine democratic institutions.[81] Lijphart's[82] comment on the application of case study method is represented in Box 10.2.

Case studies are attractive to human rights research. One apparent reason is that human rights analysis often has a normative point of departure rather than a causal–explanatory starting point. The question often asked is whether or not one particular state is complying with its treaty-based human rights obligations, and not what explains why some countries adhere to, respect and protect human rights more than other countries. However, when case studies are designed within a comparative approach, focus should be on understanding and explanation of variation (theory development), rather than on assessment of a singular state and its human rights accountability at a given point in time. Yet, one-case studies can enable analysis of within-case comparative trend analysis, by using process tracing and historical institutional analysis. Although case studies may help to develop hypotheses or support or falsify hypotheses, causal explanations require comparative few-*n* or large-*n* analysis. The main strengths of such case studies is that they enable high conceptual validity, help derive new hypotheses through studying outliers or deviant cases, and enable detailed exploration of causal mechanisms.

CONCLUSIONS

A comparative approach to human rights may help human rights advocates, human rights institutions and human rights organizations to develop

---

[81]   Ibid. 293.
[82]   Arend Lijphart, *The Politics of Accommodation: Pluralism and Democracy in the Netherlands* (California University Press 1975).

insights and empirically grounded knowledge that helps explain human rights situations and conditions. Such analysis is useful in assessing and contrasting human rights policies and institutional development in comparable cases. Comparative research helps us understand and assess the effectiveness of strategies for human rights advocacy. It brings new insight for actors seeking human rights improvement.

Comparison is integral to most scientific analysis, and an essential approach to human rights research exploring causes for the gaps between human rights norms and their practical implementation. The comparative method is also used in mixed methods research design. While emerging data indexes allow for more statistical analysis of human rights performance of most individual human rights – civil, political, economic, social and cultural – the use of few-*n* approaches and single case studies will remain a major option for much human rights research. Qualitative comparison of few cases will continue to represent an important research strategy, but may be complemented more than in the past by large-*n* statistical analysis.

REFERENCES

Ajevski, Marjan, 'Fragmentation in International Human Rights Law – Beyond Conflicts of Laws' (2014) 32(2) Nordic Journal of Human Rights 87–98

Almond, Gabriel A., *Comparative Politics. A Theoretical Framework* (HarperCollins 1996)

Andreassen, Bård A. and Gordon Crawford (eds), *Human Rights, Power and Civic Action. Comparative Analyses of struggles for rights in developing societies* (Routledge 2013)

Andreassen, Bård A. and Vo Khanh Vinh (eds), *Duties Across Borders. Advancing Human Rights in Transnational Business* (Intersentia 2016)

Bendix, Reinhart, *Nation-building and Citizenship. Studies of Changing Social Order* (University of California Press 1977)

Checkel, Jeffrey T., 'Review of The Power of Human Rights: International Norms and Domestic Change' (2000) 33 Comparative Political Studies 1337

Collier, David, 'The Comparative Method' in Ada W Finifter (ed.), *Political Science: The State of the Discipline II* (American Science Association 1993)

Campbell, Donald T., 'Degrees of Freedom and the Case Study' (1975) 8(2) Comparative Political Studies 178–193

Claude, Richard P. (ed.), *Comparative Human Rights* (The John Hopkins University Press 1976)

Crawford, Gordon and Bård Anders Andreassen, 'Human Rights, Power and Civic Action. Theoretical Considerations' in Andreassen and Crawford (eds), *Human Rights, Power and Civic Action. Comparative Analyses of Struggles for Rights in Developing Societies* (Routledge 2013)

Deva, Sury, *Regulating Corporate Human Rights Violations. Humanizing Business* (Routledge 2012)

Diamond, Larry, 'Introduction: Roots of Failure, Seeds of Hope' in Larry Diamond, Juan J. Linz and Seymour Martin Lipset (eds), *Democracy in Developing Countries: Africa.* (Lynne Rienner 1988)

Diamond, Larry, Juan J. Linz and Seymour Martin Lipset (eds), *Democracy in Developing Countries: Africa.* (Lynne Rienner 1988)

Eckstein, Harry, 'Case Study and Theory in Political Science,' in F.I. Greenstein and N.W. Polsby (eds), *The Handbook of Political Science* (Addison-Wesley 1975) 113–123

Finfter, Ada (ed.), *Political Science: The State of the Discipline II* (American Science Association 1993)

Foweaker, J. and T. Landman, *Citizenship Rights and Social Movements: A Comparative and Statistical Analysis* (OUP 1997)

Gaventa, John, 'Finding the Spaces for Change: A Power Analysis' in (2006) 37(6) IDS Bulletin

George, Alexander L. and Andrew Bennett, *Case Studies and Theory Development in Social Sciences* (MIT Press 2005)

Giddens, Anthony, *The Constitution of Society: Outline of the Theory of Structuration* (Polity Press 1984)

Gilligan, Michael J. and Nathaniel H. Nesbitt, 'Do Norms Reduce Torture?' (2009) 38(2) The Journal of Legal Studies 445

Greenstein, F.I. and N.W. Polsby (eds), *The Handbook of Political Science* (Addison-Wesley 1975)

Haugaard, M. (ed.), *Power: A Reader* (Manchester University Press 2002)

Huntington, Samuel P., *The Third Wave. Democratization in the Late Twentieth Century.* (University of Oklahoma Press 1991)

Landman, Todd, *Issues and Methods in Comparative Politics: An Introduction* (Routledge 2003)

Landman, Todd, *Protecting Human Rights. A Comparative Study* (Georgetown University Press 2005)

Landman, Todd, *Studying Human Rights* (Routledge 2006)

Lane, Jan Erik and Svante Ersson, *Comparative Politics. An Introduction and New Approach* (Polity Press 1994)

Lichbach, M., 'Social Theory and Comparative Politics' in M. Lichbach and A. Zuckman (eds), *Comparative Politics: Rationality, Culture and Structure* (Cambridge University Press 1997)

Lijphart, Arend, 'Comparative Politics and the Comparative Method' (1971) 65(3) The American Political Science Review 682

Lijphart, Arend, 'The Comparable Case Strategy in Comparative Research' (1975) 8(2) Comparative Political Studies 158

Lijphart, Arend, *The Politics of Accommodation: Pluralism and Democracy in the Netherlands* (California University Press 1975).

Meckstroth, Theodore W., '"Most Different Systems" and "Most Similar Systems": A Study in the Logics of Comparative Inquiry' (1975) 8(2) Comparative Political Studies 132

Merkl, Peter H., *Modern Comparative Politics* (Holt, Rinehart & Winston 1970)

Mill, John Stuart, *A System of Logic* (Longman 1843)

Møller, Jørgen and Svend-Erik Skaaning, 'Regime Types and Democratic Sequencing' (2013) 24(1) Journal of Democracy 142–155

O'Donnell, Guillermo and Phillippe C. Schmitter. *Transitions from Authoritarian Rule: Tentative Conclusions about Uncertain Democracies* (Johns Hopkins University Press 1986)

Penning, Paul, Hans Keman and Jan Kleinnijenhuis, *Doing Research in Political Science. An Introduction to Comparative Methods and Statistics* (Sage 2006)

Peters, Guy, *Comparative Politics, Theory and Method* (New York University Press 1998)

Przeworski, Adam and Henry Teune, *Logic of Comparative Social Inquiry. Comparative Studies in Behavioural Science* (John Wiley and Sons 1970)

Ragin, Charles C. and Lisa M. Amoroso, *Constructing Social Research. The Unity and Diversity of Method* (Sage 1994)

Randolph, Susan and Patrick Guyer, 'Tracking the Historical Evolution of State's Compliance with their Economic and Social Rights Obligations of Result' (2012) 30(2) Nordic Journal of Human Rights 297

Risse, Thomas, Stephen C. Ropp and Kathryn Sikkink (eds), *The Power of Human Rights. International Norms and Domestic Change* (Cambridge University Press 1999)

Risse, Thomas, Stephen Ropp and Kathryn Sikkink (eds), *The Persistent Power of Human Rights* (Cambridge University Press 2013)

Rokkan, Stein, 'Dimensions of State Formation and Nation-building: A Possible Paradigm for Research on Variations within Europe' in Charles Tilly (ed.), *The Formation of National States in Western Europe* (Princeton University Press 1976)

Sartori, Giovanni, 'Concept Misformation in Comparative Politics' (1970) 64(4) American Political Science Review 1033

Simmons, Beth, *Mobilizing for Human Rights. International Law and Domestic Politics,* (Cambridge University Press 2009)

Tarrow, Sidney, 'The Strategy of Paired Comparison: Toward a Theory of Practice' (2010) 43(Feb) Comparative Political Studies 230

Tilly, Charles (ed.), *The Formation of National States in Western Europe* (Princeton University Press 1976)

Yin, Robert K., *Case Study Research. Design and Methods* (Sage 1994)

11. Inside the organization. Methods of researching human rights and organizational dynamics

Hans-Otto Sano and Tomas Max Martin

INTRODUCTION

An understudied subject in human rights research is the process by which state and interstate institutions decide to integrate human rights in organizational practices in order to respect, protect and fulfil the state's human rights obligations. There has been a greater quantity of systematic research into how bilateral donors and multilateral organizations integrate human rights in development cooperation than into how national state actors address human rights in policy implementation and execution of their core mandates. The agency and role of state actors – for instance, the interaction between civil servants or politicians – is largely terra incognita. Human rights typically represent political force as a counter-culture, imbued with an image rooted in opposition movements, but they are also becoming part of mainstream bureaucratic cultures embraced by powerful elites.[1] Despite this, evidence regarding the dynamics inside state agencies and between politicians and bureaucratic elites is scarce. As Gready and Vandenhole have noted, the path leading from an organization's decision to integrate human rights to the actual implementation of follow-up policies is rarely a straightforward one.[2] According to them, for some institutional actors, the integration of human rights provokes resistance and a fear of crude legalism; for other actors, human rights policies meet with half-hearted enthusiasm and a lethargic bureaucratic response.[3] Others again may see human rights as a welcome opportunity to reform and modernize organizations.[4]

---

[1] See George Ulrich, 'Epilogue: Widening the perspective on the local relevance of human rights' in Koen De Feyter, Stephen Parmentier, Christiane Timmerman and George Ulrich (eds), *The Local Relevance of Human Rights* (CUP 2011).

[2] Wouter Vandenhole and Paul Gready, 'Failures and Successes of Human Rights-based Approaches to Development: Towards a Change Perspective' (2014) 32(4) Nordic Journal of Human Rights 292–293 and 306–307.

[3] Ibid. 292.

[4] Nicolas Guilhot, *The Democracy Makers. Human Rights and the Politics of the Global Order* (1st edn, Columbia University Press 2005).

Much research on human rights change presupposes an external dynamic, i.e. pressure from civil society actors operating autonomously or in conjunction with other states. Hafner-Burton has referred to the latter practice using the term 'steward states'.[5] Her study of externally induced human rights change deals with how regimes transition from abusing human rights (especially civil and political rights) to a less violating situation. American political science has dominated these studies,[6] but scholars from other parts of the world have also contributed to studies of how pressure from outside the state may lead to positive human rights change.[7]

This chapter argues that there is a lack of knowledge in human rights studies of endogenous organizational dynamics and their impact on human rights, i.e. of the impetus for human rights change induced by forces within state (and interstate) organizations. This problem is compounded by the fact that human rights studies rarely pay much attention to organizational and institutional theory.

The chapter addresses this methodological deficit in the area of duty-bearers' agency. The main questions addressed are: what methods can be used to gain insights into how these duty-bearers strategize, implement, and make decisions regarding human rights? In what way can these methodological choices be guided by theoretical angles that take internal dynamics more adequately into account? By 'organizations' we refer to social units of people that are managed to meet a need or pursue collective goals. 'Institutions' are considered to be systems of established and prevalent social rules that structure social interaction.[8] Organizations

---

[5] Emilie M. Hafner-Burton, *Making Human Rights a Reality* (1st edn, Princeton University Press 2013). An important agent of change in the perspective of this book is the steward state, which through foreign policy and/or development assistance seeks to push human rights-abusing states in the direction of more positive policies.

[6] Margaret Keck and Kathryn Sikkink, *Activists beyond Borders: Advocacy Networks in International Politics* (1st edn, Cornell University Press 1998); Thomas Risse, Stephen C. Ropp and Kathryn Sikkink, *The Power of Human Rights: International Norms and Domestic Change* (1st edn, CUP 1999); Beth A. Simmons, *Mobilizing for Human Rights. International Law in Domestic Politics* (1st edn, CUP 2009).

[7] Jean Grugel and Enrique Peruzzotti, 'The Domestic Politics of International Human Rights Law: Implementing the Convention on the Rights of the Child in Ecuador, Chile, and Argentina' (2012) 34(1) Human Rights Quarterly 178–198; Alejandro Anaya Muñoz, 'Transnational and Domestic Processes in the Definition of Human Rights Policies in Mexico' (2009) 31(1) Human Rights Quarterly 35–58.

[8] Geoffrey Hodgson, 'What are Institutions' (2006) XL(1) Journal of Economic Issues 2. See also Charles Handy, *Understanding Organizations* (5th edn, Penguin 1999), part 1.

and institutions therefore overlap in that they establish a framework for social interactions and behavior, but organizations are vested with specific purposes and tend to have clearly demarcated boundaries distinguishing members from non-members. Organizations also embody principles concerning who is in charge, and incorporate chains of command that define responsibilities within the organization. In other words, a state institution such as a ministry is defined as an organization, whereas a more generalized structure for organizing relationships – e.g. marriage – is defined as an institution. When we refer to organizational dynamics we refer to processes within organizations that may change roles and responsibilities and incorporate new agendas.

Our assumption is that human rights policy has *to some degree* become a less politically sensitive domain owing to the significant proliferation of human rights after the end of the Cold War (often termed 'the age of human rights'),[9] but also owing to the gradual and uneven integration of social rights concerns in government reforms.[10] An implication is that changes in the field of human rights may occur in less dramatic fashion than, say, the major socio-political transitions in Latin American states during the 1980s. It should be recognized though that political dramas involving human rights do take place, as the Arab Spring has demonstrated.

The subject of human rights integration in duty-bearer organizations may concern at least four types of phenomenon: the efforts of organizational actors to redress abuse and to implement rule of law and human rights-based policy change; the technical and political debates within organizations on how human rights are to be transposed and translated into policies, law and procedures; efforts to weave human rights into organizational narratives and 'culture'; and efforts to link human rights to existing procedures and practices within organizations, for instance monitoring or measurement practices. The latter type of human rights integration may contribute to the reform of procedures and practices, for instance within the police, but it rarely implies a total overhaul of organizational norms and practices.

---

[9] Samuel Moyn, *The Last Utopia: Human Rights in History* (1st edn, Harvard University Press 2010).

[10] Anis A. Dani and Arjan Haan (eds), *Inclusive States. Social Policy and Structural Inequalities* (The World Bank 2008). See the following chapters in particular: Martín Hopenhayn, 'Recognition and Distribution: Equity and Justice Policies for Disadvantaged Groups in Latin America'; Lynn Bennett, 'Policy reform and Culture Change: Contesting Gender, Caste, and Ethnic Exclusion in Nepal'; and Siri Gloppen, 'Public Interest Litigation, Social Rights, and Social Policy'.

One consequence of the lack of thorough research into such organizational dynamics is that unrealistic assumptions tend to prevail among rights protagonists on the leverage that human rights law and policy may have.[11]

The need for more detailed examination of the specific process of human rights integration in state organizations arises in part owing to the stronger emphasis on the implementation of economic, social and cultural rights, but also as a result of the proliferation of human rights-based approaches to development. These trends entail complex organizational decision-making in terms of setting priorities, allocating resources, creating specific programming tools and enhancing measurement and evidence requirements. Recent work on human rights measurement has developed more precise notions of 'process indicators' and therefore also of the implementation efforts of duty-bearers.[12] Greater knowledge of the actual nature and consequences of these efforts is warranted, not least in terms of economic and social rights where human rights may be integrated in public service delivery.

We also posit that there is an urgent need to understand organizational dynamics in relation to a certain 'flipside' to the proliferation of human rights. The acceleration of the 'human rights project' has not only made human rights less of a sensitive issue – it has also made them increasingly vulnerable to attack. The response of states that perceive human rights as a threat has traditionally been one of denial in order to, as far as possible, avoid questions of human rights.[13] More recently, we have seen politicians

---

[11]   The second guideline of the UN Common Understanding of a Human Rights-Based Approach to Development stipulates that 'Human rights standards contained in, and principles derived from, the Universal Declaration of Human Rights and other international human rights instruments guide all development cooperation and programming in all sectors and in all phases of the programming process'. This can be seen as an example of the somewhat over-extended guidelines that many UN organizations have had difficulties in living up to. See more at the UN HRBA Portal, 'The human-rights based approach to development cooperation' <http://hrbaportal.org/the-human-rights-based-approach-to-development-cooperation-towards-a-common-understanding-among-un-agencies#sthash.Rv8vZoKo.dpuf>, accessed 25 March 2016. An example of an HRBA skeptic who contrasts planning and technocratic thinking with human rights holism from the vantage point of working inside UNICEF in Africa is Lauchlan Munro, 'The "Human Rights-based Approach to Programming": A Contradiction in Terms?' in Sam Hickey and Diana Mitlin (eds), *Rights-Based Approaches to Development Exploring the Potential and Pitfalls* (Kumarian Press 2012).

[12]   OHCHR, *Human Rights Indicators. A Guide to Measurement and Implementation* (Report 2012).

[13]   See, for instance, Stan Cohen, 'Government Responses to Human Rights Reports: Claims, Denials, and Counterclaims' (1996) 18(3) Human Rights Quarterly

whose national policies are challenged by international human rights law actively attack and denounce human rights as an outdated and undemocratic proposition. We suggest that the response of state bureaucracies to this regressive trend in the current history of human rights also requires analytical attention.

What are the potential drivers of change from the inside that we may identify and scrutinize? By 'inside' we mean the organizational dynamics within bureaucracies, interactions between decision-makers, internal debates and changes of policy and procedure inspired by human rights integration or its rejection. 'Insiders' refers to staff employed in these organizations, but may also mean independent researchers who assume the role of an insider as they are allowed in to observe, interview and immerse themselves institutionally. The latter category of 'insider researchers' may exhibit a more independent role relative to internal staff, as discussed below.

The following sections focus on human rights-related approaches to such organizational analysis and their methodical implications. The third section examines specific methods and practices of human rights-related scholarly work inside organizations.

TWO APPROACHES TO INSTITUTIONAL ANALYSIS

Institutional theory has seen significant developments in the last 40 years, spurred by the neo-institutionalist perspective. While previous studies embarked on comparative studies of formal organizational set-ups and their functions, the neo-institutional perspective emphasized historical, sociological, political and economic factors in examining what happened inside the 'black box' of formal institutions. Power relations, rules and procedures, behavioral responses and norm-affected actions are some of the principal research dimensions of the neo-institutional perspective, and institutions are thereby mostly seen to change as a result of exogenous shocks or impulse.[14]

517–543. The Asian Values debate may be an important exception: see Ole Bruun and Michael Jacobsen, *Human Rights and Asian Values: Contesting National Identities and Cultural Representations in Asia. Vol. 6* (Psychology Press 2000).

[14] For some economists and political scientists, rational choice offers an explanation for the strategic decisions of actors within institutional settings. For proponents of this school, institutions were created to reduce the uncertainty of collective action and to minimize transaction costs. According to rational choice thinking, institutions express solutions to collective action dilemmas, allowing actors to maximize utilitarian behavior. See Douglass North, 'Five Propositions

There is a pressing need for greater insight into the theory of how institutions change and the relevant research themes suggested by this theory when working from the inside of organizations. Reinforcing knowledge and analytical frameworks concerning the receptivity of duty-bearer organisations to human rights may well involve such theoretical thinking. Receptivity to human rights can mean the framing of policies according to human rights norms and laws as well as assessment frameworks that monitor and measure policy performance based on human rights impact. Two strands from neo-institutional theory that appear particularly relevant are historical and sociological institutionalism.

Historical Institutionalism

There are two insights in historical institutionalism that may be of benefit to human rights scholars. One is the notion that change may be incremental, deriving from internal power structures and competition and from collective action dilemmas. Within institutions, the top echelons will have more power than the bottom ones; this implies that internal mobilization for change will mostly be orchestrated from the top.[15] In proposing their theory of gradual institutional change, Mahoney and Thelen underline that compliance with the institutional template – i.e. norms and practices – is a variable that may or may not be subject to pressures dependent on existing political coalitions within the institution. According to them, for rational choice scholars compliance is a non-issue, precisely because compliance behavior is built into the definition of the institution. In the rational choice perspective, institutional actors operate in an equilibrium where each actor responds according to their own rational and optimal choice. Institutions do not therefore change owing to internal dynamics (as equilibria have already been established), but according to exogenous factors.[16] In contrast, in Mahoney and Thelen's theory, institutional change

---

about Institutional Change' in Jack Knight and Itai Sened (eds), *Explaining Social Institutions* (University of Michigan Press 1998); Kenneth Shepsle, 'Studying Institutions. Some Lessons from the Rational Choice Approach' [1989] 1 Journal of Theoretical Politics 131–149. See also Peter A. Hall, 'Historical Institutionalism in Rationalist and Sociological Perspective' in James A. Mahoney and Kathleen Thelen (eds), *Explaining Institutional Change. Ambiguity, Agency, and Power* (CUP 2010), 204–205. Also John A. Campbell, 'Institutional Reproduction and Change' in Glenn Morgan, John L. Campbell, Colin Crouch, Ove Kaj Pedersen and Richard Whitley (eds), *The Oxford Handbook of Comparative Institutional Analysis* (OUP 2010), 87–115.

15   Hall (n 14).

16   See James Mahoney and Kathleen Thelen, 'A Theory of Gradual Institutional

and non-compliance with norms and practices are explained by a dynamic created by the political context (endo- or exogenous), the characteristics of the institution itself and the change agents operating from within the institution.[17]

The other perspective offered by historical institutionalism is path-dependence. Path-dependence refers to the dynamics of self-reinforcing systems or feedback loops whereby initial effects trigger the recurrence of a pattern. Aberration from the pattern is often triggered by a critical juncture in macro-level institutions, such as processes of democratization in transitional regimes. However, institutional choices can be difficult to change once made, not because change is irrational according to the merits of the case itself, as for instance when embarking on a process in support of universal pension schemes, but because systems and expectations have been built around an existing framework – in this example, segmented pensions. Interest groups will often have multivariate preferences; for a political party to change its policy in a particular area, such as human rights, requires the conviction of the party leadership that the prevailing and interlocking interests of the voters will favor human rights change.[18] Change of an institutional arrangement in one area that appears justified on paper may affect other institutional arrangements negatively.

Institutional Sociology

According to institutional sociology, institutions create socializing scripts, directing actors to behave according to certain norms and practices, even when these are seemingly no longer effective or rational. Human action is driven less by preferences or knowledge of consequences than by a logic of appropriateness.[19] The self-reproducing scripts of institutions are to some sociological institutionalists cognitive in nature. Institutions are

---

Change' in James A. Mahoney and Kathleen Thelen (eds), *Explaining Institutional Change. Ambiguity, Agency, and Power* (CUP 2010).

[17]   Ibid. 23, 31, 32. Change agents may be insurrectionaries who seek to undermine the institution and its rules, symbionts who seek to preserve the institution but are not abiding by its rules, subversives who seek to undermine the institution while adhering to its rules, or opportunists who pursue strategies according to what may serve them best.

[18]   See David F. Suarez and Patricia Bromley, 'Institutional Theories and Levels of Analysis, History, Diffusion, and Translation' in Jürgen Schriewer (ed.), *World Culture Recontextualized* (Routledge 2015); Hall (n 14), 212–214.

[19]   James G. March and Johan P. Olsen, *Democratic Governance* (1st edn, The Free Press 1994) 28.

taken for granted and are beyond reflection,[20] while actors often reproduce the same script across various domains. Institutions or even organizations become isomorphic with other organizations, for instance, at the global level. Human rights integration can be seen as part of such isomorphic processes,[21] whereby states seek to comply with legitimate world models. The efforts to promote national human rights institutions are part of an isomorphic organizational effort in the human rights domain. Thus, when such processes are transposed from the global to the national level, what can often be observed is a decoupling of official policies from actual practice. However, institutional sociologists have also realized that such processes of diffusion give rise to substantial translation locally.[22] According to Suarez and Bromley, Scandinavian sociologists such as K. Sahlin and L. Wedlin have emphasized not only the isomorphic reconstruction of institutional norms and behavior, but also the concurrent and often competing co-construction, editing and reshaping of institutional structures that belong to similar global institutional arrangements yet are reshaped and adapted locally.[23] 'Bricolage' is a concept applied by some scholars to describe these productive processes.[24] To human rights scholars and actors operating across national boundaries and at different levels of societies, such processes of translation and editing are familiar and vital.

Implications of Institutional Theories: Research Themes Inside Organizations

What themes should scholars therefore consider when designing their research strategy within organizations in order to trace human rights integration? These theoretical interpretations offer a range of approaches.

The first option is to examine the formal organizational set-up and the functional roles of relevant administrative units within the organization. The problem with this type of analysis is, precisely, its formal approach. The result can be a static perception of the actual roles and real functions within the organization, ignoring the political groupings and

---

[20]   See Mahoney and Thelen (n 16) 5, quoting Berger and Luckmann.

[21]   Ibid.; Suarez and Bromley (n 18). See also John Clarke, Dave Bainton, Noémi Lendvai and Paul Stubbs (eds) *Making Policy Move: Towards a Politics of Translation and Assemblage* (Policy Press 2015).

[22]   Campbell (n 14) 96–97, uses the cross-national variation of EU member countries as an example of the translation processes at work.

[23]   Mahoney and Thelen (n 16).

[24]   See Campbell (n 14), 98–100.

power-holders within the organization that may be the significant drivers (or spoilers) of change.[25]

A second possibility is to consider the intra-institutional incentive frameworks: salary structures and promotional rewards, cost structures based on functional units, the costs of mobilizing members and the costs, including political ones, of inducing change. Included in such perspectives inspired by rational choice thinking could also be efforts to localize rent-seeking behavior and corruption.[26] These issues relate to power from within and corruption of power and may hold relevance for human rights scholars.

A third approach is to look for the institutional entrepreneurs and champions (or 'change agents' as suggested by Mahoney and Thelen above). Within human rights research, the notion of 'champions' forms part of the explanation for UNICEF's adoption of a human rights-based strategy.[27] A change of attitude was originally spurred by pressure from non-governmental organizations (NGOs) on UNICEF. However, according to Oestreich, the perceptions of principled actors among the staff and in the management of the organization were in fact more important. By involving itself in the drafting of the Convention of the Rights of the Child (CRC), the management of the organization worked in tandem with a group of 'true believers', internal proponents of principled ideas, as Oestreich terms them using a concept borrowed from Sikkink.[28] Notions of empowerment and non-discrimination, which the true believers thought would enhance the effectiveness of UNICEF's work, were instrumental in persuading internal staff to lend support to the drafting and subsequently the implementation of the convention under the banner of a human rights-based approach.

A complementary research theme within organizations is to look for blind spots, i.e. issues where human rights fail to become part of the intra-organizational discourse or script. This design will draw on the insights

---

[25]   Some of these issues are described and commented upon in J. Samuel Barkin, *International Organization. Theories and Institutions* (Palgrave Macmillan 2006); see in particular chapter 3.

[26]   According to Shepsle (n 14) the implications of introducing new institutional rules are often hard to predict, and the wedge of uncertainty can make leaders reluctant to introduce change. The economic and political costs of collective action and mobilization have been analyzed by Robert Bates, 'Contra Contractarianism. Some Reflections on New Institutionalism' (1988) 16(2) Politics and Society 387–401.

[27]   Joel E. Oestreich, *Power and Principle. Human Rights Programming in International Organizations* (1st edn, Georgetown University Press 2007).

[28]   Ibid. 5, 27–33.

from institutional sociology referred to above. An example from the human rights field is the research on indicators in which one of the authors of this chapter participated. This study focused on the formulation of indicators within the European Union and on the needs and perceptions of the civil servants who worked on them after the decision to mainstream human rights externally and internally.[29] One of the findings of the study was that the majority of the EU officials interviewed did not perceive themselves to be involved in human rights measurement, in all likelihood because the mandate of the various EU Directorate Generals did not explicitly cover human rights.[30] The interviews with EU officials who monitor poverty and social inclusion in the Social Protection Committee revealed that the indicators monitored derived originally from the 'Laeken indicators on poverty and social exclusion' established during the early 2000s as part of the Lisbon Strategy of the European Union. These indicators focused on economic growth and employment and were not human rights based.[31] Some of the civil servants had apparently never considered this. The mainstreaming objective did not reach this technical domain of the indicators with the result that economic and social rights were only monitored indirectly through lenses that were primarily economically conceived. In this case path-dependency prevailed, causing significant blind spots.

A final research theme inspired by institutional theory is the processes of translation and 'bricolage'. These processes are at play in sector ministries such as health ministries,[32] courts, parliaments, the policies and dialogues of national human rights institutions,[33] and in other state institutions' efforts to localize human rights.[34] A particular example of 'bricolage' is

---

[29]   Council of the European Union, 25 June 2012 11855/12, EU Strategic Framework and Action Plan on Human Rights and Democracy.

[30]   Klaus Starl, Veronika Apostolovski, Isabella Meier, Markus Möstl, Maddalena Vivona and Alexander Kulmer in collaboration with Hans-Otto Sano and Erik André Andersen, *Report on the Baseline Study of Uses and Objectives of Human Rights Indicators and EU Human Rights Indicator Schemes* (FRAME Fostering Human Rights Among European Policies, GA no. 320000, 2012).

[31]   See Hans-Otto Sano, 'Economic Factors' in Lassen et al., *Report on Factors which Enable or Hinder the Protection of Human Rights* (The Danish Institute for Human Rights, FRAME Fostering Human Rights Among European Policies 2014) 59–86.

[32]   See Flavia Bustreo and Paul Hunt, *Women's and Children's Health: Evidence of Impact of Human Rights* (WHO 2013). This work shows, for instance in the case of Nepal, how health authorities integrate and blend human rights-based health work with programming instruments such as conditional cash programs, a program intervention originally developed by the World Bank.

[33]   See Hafner-Burton (n 5).

[34]   See Feyter et al. (n 1).

the position of the World Bank on human rights. Oestreich argues that, in contrast to UNICEF, the World Bank's initial interest in human rights issues was a result of external pressures owing to the failure of structural adjustment programs, public relations disasters of large-scale projects, and external criticism of the Bank as a neo-liberal institution.

Galit Sarfaty conducted anthropological fieldwork within the Bank between 2002 and 2006[35] in order to explore why human rights remained marginal within the Bank despite these external pressures. Most observers have explained the Bank's reservations to human rights with reference to the legal mandate that prevents it from engaging in the political affairs of client countries. Sarfaty argues that this position underestimates the internal dynamics of the Bank's bureaucracy.[36] Human rights challenge the dominant economic regime of the Bank. During the mid-2000s, there was a persistent clash in the Bank between market rationality and social democratic liberalism, the latter implying a positive attitude towards human rights integration, according to Sarfaty. This clash was clear in the debates on the establishment of the Bank's Nordic Trust Fund, a human rights initiative promoted by Nordic governments during the mid-2000s. Although the pro-human rights lawyers in the Bank (only a fraction of the group of lawyers) feared the dilution of human rights, they decided to pursue a pragmatist course, Safarty argues. They translated human rights into an instrumentalist domain where the effectiveness of human rights was to be demonstrated in pilot projects to persuade the more powerful and skeptical economists that human rights could be made operational. The Bank would then, the lawyers' pragmatic argument went, assist governments in 'translating internationally agreed human rights standards into operational policy actions, thereby prioritizing support for those services that both contribute to economic and social development and constitute human rights obligations of the state'.[37] Sarfaty sees this as depoliticization – i.e. a desire to integrate rights into a bureaucratized logic whereby their political potential to challenge sovereignty and to bring about social justice was curtailed.[38] However, the Nordic Trust Fund was in fact first established during 2009, but with a knowledge and learning mandate – and not with operational tasks, except in countries where governments explicitly endorsed operational human rights work. Thus, bricolage in this case implied firstly that human rights were translated into an operational logic,

---

[35] Galit Sarfaty, *Values in Translation Human Rights and the Culture of the World Bank* (1st edn, Stanford University Press 2012).

[36] Ibid. 133.

[37] Ibid. 129.

[38] Ibid. 134.

and secondly that this logic was only allowed to rule in instances where states accepted it. However, the negotiations also resulted in the establishment of a specific human rights unit within the Bank with a mandate not only for knowledge and learning, but also to establish pilot human rights projects inside the organization.

SPECIFIC METHODS TO THE STUDY OF INSTITUTIONAL PROCESSES AND POLICY CHANGE

Determining Policy Change Externally Through Quantitative Analysis

Most of the research on human rights change has focused on violations and whether ratifications of human rights core instruments would contribute to the improvement of states' human rights records. This research originally focused on civil and political rights.[39] Contemporary research on the impact of ratification is more broadly founded on both of the covenants and on core conventions such as the Convention Eliminating all Forms of Violence against Women. A key example of such work is Beth Simmons's compliance theory, which argues that treaties may change politics in the ratifying country, however, with the greatest chance in transitional countries.[40] The data and method used in Simmons's analysis are quantitative, regressing treaty ratifications on state human rights practices – for instance, fair trial practices.[41]

While certainly important, such studies tell us little about duty-bearers' decision-making processes and about their motivation for change. According to these studies, the important drivers of change are situated outside the state. In Simmons's work, for instance, the drivers of change are the advocacy options of local NGOs and the rewards to be won by other external state actors for their own constituencies. These are persuasive arguments, but they may not reflect the whole story. Rights issues are not always the object of strong advocacy efforts, for instance in circum-

---

[39]   See, for instance, Eric Neumayer, 'Do International Human Rights Treaties Improve Respect for Human Rights?' (2005) 49(1) Journal of Conflict Resolution 925–953. See also the review by Hans-Otto Sano on part of this literature in: 'Evidence in Demand. An Overview of Evidence and Methods in Assessing Impact of Economic and Social Rights' (2014) 32(4) Nordic Journal of Human Rights 387–402.

[40]   Beth A. Simmons, *Mobilizing for Human Rights. International Law in Domestic Politics* (1st edn, CUP 2009) 113, 159–255.

[41]   See also Edward Anderson's overview of regression analysis in the present volume, Chapter 5.

stances where governments are seen to formally follow up on objectives of aligning policies with human rights.

Apart from the quantitative metrics used in regression analysis, social network analysis is another method used by human rights scholars to determine policy orientations and change.[42] Social network analysis examines the interaction of different actors through the flow of power, resources or ideas between them. By defining relations and patterns of behavior, this approach is particularly useful for understanding social dynamics in human rights fora, and can provide insights into the existence and nature of networks and trends.[43] However, this method may not enable a deeper understanding of the motivations for policy choices or the organizational dynamics that lead to change.

Analyzing Institutional Processes and Policy Change Through Documentary Studies

One of the most prevalent methods employed by human rights scholars is the use of documentary evidence. Yet it is also common for researchers not to consider documentary evidence an element in the method toolbox. Often a distinction is made between qualitative and quantitative methods, while details relating to the selection, use and interpretation of documentary sources are passed over in silence.[44]

One example of the use of documentary evidence to reveal intra-organizational policy change or rejection thereof is Joel Oestreich's book *Power and Principle.* We referred to Oestreich's work in the previous section with respect to his analyses of the institutional processes surrounding human rights in UNICEF and the World Bank.[45] He presents two observations on the drivers of change which relate to the theories of institutional change treated above. The first, particularly in the case of UNICEF, is that the process of changing policies in the organization to a human rights-based framework was mainly driven from the inside, motivated by the management's

---

[42]   See also Chané and Sharma in Chapter 15.

[43]   Ibid.

[44]   Hans-Otto Sano and Hatla Thelle, 'The Need for Evidence-Based Human Rights Research' in Fons Coomans, Fred Grünfeld and Menno T. Kamminga (eds), *Methods of Human Rights Research* (Intersentia 2009). The prevalence of documentary evidence in human rights journal articles is brought out in this chapter. For the observation that human rights research in some respects resembles historical research, see Jensen and Burke, Chapter 6.

[45]   Joel E. Oestreich, *Power and Principle. Human Rights Programming in International Organizations* (Georgetown University Press 2007).

interpretations of strategic gains for the organization. The executive director at the time became convinced, also because of the efforts of internal human rights proponents, that the CRC would help the organization in expanding its mandate in a way that would tally well with the objective of providing assistance to children in difficult circumstances. The executive board also pushed for an agenda that favored support for CRC. In the case of the World Bank, much of the debate was driven internally too, although the external pressures were quite pronounced. Secondly, in both cases, the main drivers of the internal debates were what Oestreich refers to as the 'true believers', the internal proponents of principled ideas and champions of human rights.[46] Internal strategic assessments, normative propositions, and internal translation processes, rather than a response to pressures from the member states of both organizations, were therefore the predominant drivers of change – or of a negotiated status quo, as in the case of the World Bank.

Oestreich is not very explicit about his sources. However, it becomes clear that the arguments are based on documentary evidence. The analysis of UNICEF is based on 18 internal UNICEF sources and published UN materials, from board meetings to workshop and training reports as well as reports interpreting the human rights-based approach from a UNICEF perspective. How these documents are employed is not clear, as specific references to them are not made in the text or notes. In addition to this documentary evidence, Oestreich also bases his analysis on mostly anonymous interviews. It is not clear, though, at what level the interviews are conducted. An interview guide is not available, and references to these interviews are not made in the text or notes.

The methods underpinning Oestrich's analysis are therefore not treated particularly thoroughly – a deficit inasmuch as some of the 'true believers' are not given a face or professional profile. While the book provides an informed and interesting perspective, the reader's impression is that an explanation of the method used is not important because the study is based primarily on documentary material.

Analyzing and Determining Change Through Observation

The analytical endeavor inside organizations that we encourage here will have consequences for the methods that may be used to explore organizational dynamics. Neo-institutional theory highlights how the organizational processes that impinge so fundamentally on the way organizations appropriate new norms and change or hold on to their 'scripts' manifest

---

[46]   Ibid. Chapters 2 and 3.

themselves empirically in the ever-present tension between official discourse and organizational practice. It is the local social actors within organizations – most often bureaucrats – who deal with this tension on an everyday basis. Thus, an exploration of organizational dynamics will need to unpack the agency of these actors and their disposition to change or consolidate their positions in the organization (and in their own lives), as they themselves see it.

It will be no surprise that ethnographic fieldwork – famously referred to as a quest to get 'the native's point of view'[47] – lends itself to exactly such an exploration.[48] Applying ethnographic methods to the study of organizational dynamics basically implies the use of observation and open-ended interviewing in the field as the primary means of data collection. Fieldwork based on methods of observation is a tenet of ethnography, whereby the researcher engages with the people under study, shares their everyday lives as far as possible and converses with them in order to generate data for a detailed description (an ethnography) of the social life of a particular place or institution.

Closeness

Fieldwork of the ethnographic type used here is more or less interchangeable with participant observation in the sense that it implies a composite engagement with people and places of the field through informal talks, observing, spectating, eavesdropping, collectively discussing, moving and sitting, mingling, tagging along and participating in activities where possible. The veteran scholar of institutional micro-sociology Erving Goffman defines observation as a technique of:

> subjecting yourself, your own body and your own personality, and your own social situation, to the set of contingencies that play upon a set of individuals . . . So that you are close to them while they are responding to what life does to them . . . and with your 'tuned-up' body and with the ecological right to be close to them (which you have obtained by one sneaky means or another), you are in a position to note their gestural, visual, bodily response to what's going on around them and you're empathetic enough – because you've been taking the same crap they've been taking – to sense what it is that they're responding to. To me, that's the core of observation.[49]

---

[47]   Bronislaw Malinowski, *Argonauts of the Western Pacific* (Routledge and Kegan Paul 1922).
[48]   See also Sally Engle Merry's article, Chapter 7.
[49]   Erving Goffman, 'On Fieldwork' (1989) 18(123) Journal of Contemporary Ethnography 123–132.

Observation is visceral and corporal. It is less about picking people's brains than about learning what happens by being physically and socially close. 'Closeness' enables a profound understanding of the organizational culture, the unwritten rules and the actual tactics of local actors. This form of observation is a particularly pertinent way to unpack the local effects of the strongly normative and universally 'self-explanatory' concept of human rights and to discern the local, unwritten, tacit road rules of practical norms that organizational actors draw on so extensively in order to govern bureaucracies in practice.[50]

It is important to note that the effort to observe the tension between claims of official discourse and organizational practice is *not* a crude exercise in exposing discrepancies between what people say and what they do. Observation is not investigation. As noted by Malkki, the role of 'the police detective discovering what is "hidden", assembling "evidence" to make a strong "case", relentlessly probing for more information' is not a fruitful fieldwork strategy.[51] The researcher gets caught up in her or his own quest to extract and adjudicate truth. Data collected in this manner tends to be contrived and attention is diverted from what people actually do and have to say, according to Malkki.

Observation is rather, as Goffman astutely puts it, a way to exercise an 'ecological right to be close'. Such closeness, Goffman suggests, enables the researcher to 'tune up', be 'empathic' and to 'sense' what is going on. In a more recent text, Schatz defines ethnography exactly as the combination of 'immersion' through participant observation[52] and the ensuing 'sensibility' to the 'meanings that the people under study attribute to their social and political reality'.

On the basis of an in-depth ethnographic investigation, one of the authors made a study of the appropriation of human rights in Ugandan prisons.[53] The Uganda Prison Service has gone through a much-applauded, human rights-based reform process and the prison system seems to be changing accordingly. The study argued that, while human rights reform

---

[50]   Jean-Pierre Olivier de Sardan, 'Researching the Practical Norms of Real Governance in Africa' (2008) Africa, Power & Politics 5 December, 1–23.

[51]   Liisa Malkki, *Purity and Exile. Violence, Memory and National Cosmology among Hutu Refugees in Tanzania* (University of Chicago Press 1995) 51.

[52]   Edward Schatz (ed.), 'Political Ethnography. What Immersion Contributes to the Study of Power' (University of Chicago Press 2009).

[53]   Tomas Max Martin, 'Reasonable Caning and the Embrace of Human Rights in Ugandan Prisons' (2014) 68 Focaal 68–82. See also Tomas Max Martin, 'The Importation of Human Rights by Uganda Prison Staff' (2014) 212 Prison Service Journal 45–51.

was being forcefully exported into Ugandan prisons, the powerful global discourse was significantly localized in the process. One example of this appropriation concerns actual changes in disciplinary practices. With the new Prison Act of 2006, corporal punishment was taken out of the disciplinary toolbox and prison managers and human rights advocates were adamant that disciplinary practices changed accordingly. In-depth analysis confirms that the prohibition against torture – a basic tenet of human rights in prison – affects disciplinary practices, but the persistent practice of caning has at the same time been re-invented in a new 'reasonable' form. 'Reasonable caning' was still seen as a pertinent response to infractions, administered moderately, for the purpose of correction and, staff repeatedly insisted, circumscribed by natural justice principles. As such, caning was in practice seen as distinct from the cruel, colonial and maiming practice of corporal punishment or the unlawful, injurious and capricious practice of torture. Brutality was devalued and violence against prisoners decreased, but unlawful physical violence still remained productive in practice in a more reasoned and pseudo-legalized form.

In this particular case, the 'closeness' offered insights about the volatility of everyday governance of Ugandan prisons. Prison staff had their eyes firmly fixed on making it through the day. Human rights reform was a threat, which expanded the power of formal rules – too often usurped by powerful superiors and capable prisoners – but it was also an opportunity to make the institutions they work in less insecure. For Ugandan prison staff, the embracing of human rights was an active aspiration to gain more purchase on legal technologies, reconceptualizations of propriety and humane imprisonment, and the new management practices that affected their lives. In that sense, micro-sociological methods helped to unpack the contradictions and indeterminacy of human rights reform and the interface between prescribed ideals, local contingencies and social actors' motivations and strategies.

Insiders

A method that has 'immersion' as an objective in order to bring about 'sensibility' towards the field under study is likely also to valorise the researcher's role as an 'insider'. By approaching an insider role, the researcher seeks to learn (and to some extent even embody) the social practices of the field. As Goffman bluntly puts it, one actively tries to 'take the same crap' as the organizational actors, whose positions and dispositions one is attempting to discern.

The role of an apprentice is often assumed by the fieldworker seeking to approach a situation of participation and to shorten distances between the self and others in the field.[54] Apprenticeship – even as an openly artificial way of taking up minor tasks – is a fruitful way to find a place to settle and work from when conducting fieldwork in a bureaucracy, where everybody else is explicitly tasked and mandated.[55] However, apprenticeship also opens up a slippery slope of identification and emotional attachment with actors in the field. In the case of prison ethnography, as conducted by one of the authors of this article, Rhodes for example notes the ethical problems of Fleisher's work,[56] who enrolled as correctional officer as part of his fieldwork strategy and ended up siding with his fellow guards' defense of maximum security imprisonment as a commendable means to create a peaceful prison environment.[57] This quest to understand and stay close is challenged by the threat of humiliation, exploitation, misuse of power and even physical violence, which call for distancing. Studying bureaucracies is typically also an essential aspect of 'studying up'[58] – a household term in anthropology for studying not its traditional subjects i.e. the poor, 'primitive' and marginalized, but rather the centrally placed wielders of (state) power. When studying up, identification with the people studied and defense of their interests is not self-evident.[59] However, the up-close nature of fieldwork entails a commitment to take seriously what one is told and attempt to 'be on the same wavelength' as the people in the field (Olivier de Sardan, 2008: 20).

The researcher who takes on an insider role must confront this dilemma. The most obvious solution is to maintain a degree of independence and remain as objective as possible. In many cases, researchers who write about organizational dynamics have a history of former employment or professional involvement with these organizations. A good example, which we have described above, is Sarfaty's analysis of the internal debates on the human rights policies of the World Bank. Such researcher-cum-employee analyses may raise concerns of bias, but they are also a good indicator of the researcher's thorough understanding of the organization – from the inside.

What we suggest here is that an objective and independent approach

---

[54]   Helle Bundgaard, 'Lærlingen: Den formative erfaring' in Kirsten Hastrup (ed.), *Ind i Verden. En grundbog i antropologisk metode* (Reitzel 2003).

[55]   Helle Max Martin, *Nursing Contradictions: Ideals and Improvisation in Uganda* (AMB Diemen 2009).

[56]   Mark Fleisher, *Warehousing Violence* (Sage 1989).

[57]   Lorna A. Rhodes, 'Toward an Anthropology of Prisons' (2001) 73 Annual Review of Anthropology 65–83.

[58]   Laura Nader, 'Up the Anthropologist: Perspectives Gained from Studying Up' (1972) ECRIS.

[59]   Peter Pels, 'Professions of Duplexity: A Prehistory of Ethical Codes in Anthropology', (1999) 40(2) Current Anthropology 101–136.

is not in fact the best way to solve the inherent dilemmas of being on the inside. The immersed and sensible researcher should rather seek to establish the validity of the analysis. Whether pursuing an insider role as a former employee, a covert researcher, an enthusiastic apprentice or a lab-coated fly-on-the-wall observer (good luck with that!), there are no better or worse positions to argue from in terms of objectivity. There are rather more or less convincing attempts to be explicit and reflexive about the researcher's position as a means to validate the argument.

As Flyvbjerg flatly states, '[l]ike other good craftsmen, all the researchers can do is use their experience and intuition to assess whether they believe a given case is interesting . . . and whether they can provide collectively acceptable reasons'.[60]

Such 'collective acceptability' can be directly derived from field feedback via concerted efforts to get reactions from informants and actors in context. Acceptability, of course, also comes from the convincing use of theory and thorough descriptions of the steps taken in the research process that invite the reader to accept, but also question, the data. Sanjek refers to this methodological move as a presentation of 'the ethnographer's path'.[61] Sanjek importantly stresses that the 'subjects of ethnography are more interesting than the authors', but he also argues that writing the researcher into the narrative is not just whimsical self-absorption;[62] rather, it opens up the text to further collective acceptability. What did you do, and why? Who did you talk to and learn from? What did you bring back to document it? This kind of reflexivity is a claim to validity and a way to explicate what Olivier de Sardan calls '"the anthropological pact", which confirms the reader in the idea that the researcher did not invent the discourse s/he relates nor dream up the description s/he proposes'.[63]

Analyzing and Determining Change Via Elite Interviews

If the black box of power relations and the motivation for changing policies around human rights are to be examined, i.e. if path-dependencies,

---

[60]   Bent Flyvbjerg, *Making Social Science Matter. Why Social Inquiry Fails and How it can Succeed Again* (CUP 2002) 80–81.

[61]   Roger Sanjek, 'On Ethnographic Validity' in R Sanjek (ed.), *Fieldnotes: The Makings of Anthropology* (Cornell University Press 1990).

[62]   Ibid. 413.

[63]   Jean-Pierre Olivier de Sardan, *La rigueur du qualitatif. Les contraintes empiriques de l'interprétation socio-anthropologique* – unpublished, translation into English by Antoinette Tidjani Alou, *Rigorously Qualitative. Epistemology, fieldwork and anthropology* (Academia-Bruylant 2008).

translation processes or bricolage are to be better understood, then interviews and participant observation are crucial methodical elements. In the section above, the ethnographic methods were discussed with a focus on participant observation. However, such interviews based on longer-term fieldwork inside organizations may not easily be conducted by political scientists, sociologists or lawyers who are not trained to use ethnographic methods and do not have the longer-term perspective traditionally employed by anthropologists.

Inside interviews conducted by the broader group of social scientists will mostly be qualitative. Another characteristic is that access to the decision-making powers in corporations or states is difficult to obtain. According to Adler and Adler, 'access' and 'resistance' are two features that characterize interviews with what they term the 'reluctant respondent'.

Certain scholars, mainly sociologists, have reflected on what is termed elite or specialized interviewing or simply interviewing reluctant respondents.[64] An initial observation is that the nature of methods used might well apply to specialized groups as well as to elites. Odendahl and Shaw, for instance, point out that the designating and defining of elites are tasks that require careful reflection on the part of the researcher. Dexter places any interviewee who is given a special, non-standardized treatment under the methodical heading of elite and specialized inquiry. In this regard, Adler and Adler refer to interviews with drug dealers where the researchers at one point acted as babysitters for the drug dealers whom they were going to interview.[65] Thuesen contrasts the interview with non-elites (the less powerful) with the elite interviews: while interviewers in the former, non-elite field may be wary of addressing overly intrusive questions to the informant, the elite interviewer must subject the respondent to demanding and intrusive questions in order to address accountability issues. Power distinctions and aspects of accountability, which ensue from the holding of power, determine the nature of the interview.[66] While Dexter adopts

---

[64]   Lewis Anthony Dexter, *Elite and Specialized Interviewing* (ECPR Press 2006). Patricia A. Adler and Peter Adler, 'The Reluctant Respondent' in Jaber F. Gubrium and James A. Hostein (eds), *Handbook of Interview Research. Context and Method* (Sage 2002) 515–535. Also Terese Odendahl and Aileen M. Shaw, 'Interviewing Elites' in Jaber F. Gubrium and James A. Hostein (eds), *Handbook of Interview Research. Context and Method* (Sage 2002) 299–316. Frederik Thuesen 'Navigating Between Dialogue and Confrontation: Phronesis and Emotions in Interviewing Elites on Ethnic Discrimination' (2011) 17(7) Qualitative Inquiry 613–622.

[65]   See Adler and Adler (n 64) 525; Dexter (n 64) 18; and Odendahl and Shaw (n 64) 301–302.

[66]   Thuesen (n 64) 619–620.

Table 11.1   Locating the decision-makers making strategic human rights decisions

Analytical category	Tools
External analysis	Documentary and secondary evidence. Interviews with observers outside the organization on who the agenda-setters are
Internal analysis	Extricating roles from the organizational hierarchy. Triangulating sources from internal interviews. Interviews with gate-keepers

an alternative position in this regard – leaving it to the elite informant to manage the interview and its directions – Odendahl and Shaw argue that the interviewer must establish his or her authority in order to ensure a productive exchange.[67]

A number of methodical recommendations for elite and specialized interviews are emerging from the literature and from experiences of such interviews. We shall categorize these according to three dimensions: *locating* the key decision-makers, *gaining access* to them, and *overcoming reluctance*. In the discussion below, we shall be referring to elite interviews within intra-state organizations, whether in central or in local governments, and also to elite interviews in intergovernmental organizations.

Table 11.1 shows how the process of researching the question 'Who decides on human rights?' might be undertaken from both outside and inside an organization. The main point is that identifying the key decision-makers in charge of particular human rights decisions may not be a straightforward process. Hence, triangulating sources from both outside and inside organizations may be necessary. The formal hierarchy may offer some guidance especially in public organizations bound by norms of transparency, but it may not tell the whole story. Secondly, key decision-makers will often be surrounded or protected by gatekeepers – staff, often operating in conjunction with the elite, who control access. These gatekeepers can also be helpful in locating the right decision-makers.[68]

A number of guidance recommendations are made with respect to *gaining access*, summarized in Table 11.2. Unlike corporate managers who are visible to their shareholders, decision-makers in public organizations are not always well known outside their organizations. However, they may

---

[67]   See Dexter (n 64) 18–19; Odendahl and Shaw (n 64) 311.
[68]   Odendahl and Shaw (n 64) 307.

Table 11.2 *Gaining access to the key organizational actors making strategic human rights decisions*

Analytical category	Tools
External approach	Letters of introduction. Research permits including formal appointments as researchers for the organization
Internal approach	Identification of the human rights champions. Being well-known and respected among organizational practitioners, i.e. having informal ties inside

be more accessible than their corporate counterparts as their managerial role in public organizations presupposes a certain level of accessibility. Nevertheless, it can be a challenge for researchers to get into contact with key decision-makers. When Muñoz, for instance, is capable of reporting in an informed manner on the human rights policy shifts of the Mexican government during the Zedillo and Fox regimes at the end of the last century and in the early 2000s, this is because he had access to key ministers and civil servants. These elite interviews allowed him to express himself with confidence about the motivation for policy change. The access that Muñoz had was facilitated by his acquaintance with the informants, which itself developed as a result of his role as a Mexican NGO representative in international fora during an earlier period.[69]

Thus letters of introduction, though important, may not be enough to ensure access. The fact that, in his research on EU indicator frameworks, one of the authors of this chapter was already part of an EU-financed research program facilitated access. However, in most cases research grants will be external to the organization under scrutiny. Allying oneself with the human rights champions within the organization may facilitate knowledge about the buttons to push to obtain access.

Having informal ties inside an organization is therefore crucial for gaining access in cases where research issues are politically sensitive. Rosalind Eyben, writing about her access inside aid organizations facilitated by her former status as a consultant and employee, quotes Weber who asserts that every bureaucracy will conceal its knowledge and operations unless forced to disclose them. The bureaucracy will therefore tend to represent researchers as having 'hostile interests' in order to protect themselves. In the case of aid agencies, they may morally blackmail researchers, arguing that their inquisitiveness may also hurt poor recipients of development assistance.[70]

---

[69] See Muñoz (n 7).
[70] Rosalind Eyben, 'Hovering on the Threshold. Challenges and Opportunities

Bureaucracies typically police their boundaries through rules, and it goes without saying that formalized authorization is important for access. As one of the authors of this article has written elsewhere,[71] a researcher aiming to get inside a bureaucracy will typically approach the field with due consideration. S/he will deliver a formal, concise presentation of her or his objectives, institutional affiliations, credentials and research clearances, and will make a conscious effort to avoid her or his requests for access being turned down by the management. This negotiation of access may be amicable. Bureaucracies are likely to be on the alert for bad press, but they also tend to invite committed and constructive attention. It is relatively rare for bureaucrats to be given an opportunity to explain themselves, and an interested researcher will not automatically be shut out. However, the negotiation of access is also a significant point of departure – what Bandyopadhyay refers to as a researcher's embarkation 'on a very conscious construction of the "self" in fieldwork'.[72] When one of the authors of this article negotiated access to a Ugandan prison, he was, like Bandyopadhyay, also consciously presenting 'a diminutive and restrained self'[73] and put on a patient, sometimes even docile and naive, air and mimicked modes of interaction in order to signal a willingness to submit to rules, surveillance, security and hierarchical power.

Characteristic of the bureaucratic setting is a tendency to expose the researcher to a constant fear of losing access.[74] The researcher is likely to continually sense a certain tension: a feeling that the rules and regulations that have been bent to facilitate access are just as capable of snapping back into place with equal force. In this sense, access is always conditioned, temporal and monitored. As boundary after boundary is negotiated and deeper access into the institutional landscape is gained, the researcher may experience the simultaneous impression that loss of access is also always imminent and that the damage would be increasingly irreparable. A researcher inside institutions has to be ready to cope with this.

---

for Critical and Reflexive Ethnographic Research in Support of International Aid Practice' in S. Hagberg and C. Widmark (eds), *Ethnographic Practice and Public Aid. Methods and Meaning in Development Cooperation* (University of Uppsala 2009).

[71] Tomas Max Martin, 'Witnessing and Accessing Ugandan prisons – Fieldwork within a Post-colonial Bureaucracy' in Deborah Drake, Jennifer Sloan and Rod Earle (eds), *Palgrave Handbook of Prison Ethnography* (Palgrave 2015).

[72] Mahuya Bandyopadhyay, *Everyday Life in a Prison: Confinement, Surveillance, Resistance* (Orient Black Swan 2010) 40.

[73] Ibid. 53.

[74] Ibid. 39.

Table 11.3   Overcoming the reluctance of the interviewee

Analytical category	Tools
Internal face-to-face interviews	Establishing the pay-off for the organization
	Carefully considering the location of the interview
	Being knowledgeable with regard to the interview's subject matter
	Being conscious of the underlying values of questions
	Pursuing a degree of informality for the interview and mastering cultural behavior
	Balancing detachment and involvement
	Balancing conversational dialogue with confrontation (phronesis)

The final category of recommendations is that of *overcoming reluctance.* Not all elite interviews will be in a setting where the interviewee will be outright hostile or resistant to divulging information. However, many respondents in such settings will be on their guard and may provide short answers when issues become sensitive. Thuesen explains how his interview with a trade union manager progressed smoothly until he started to ask questions about the human rights of ethnic minorities, relating this to discrimination in the labor market. At this point, the manager's responses became abrupt and restrained. Thuesen also describes a similar interview with an employer association executive that followed an identical pattern and degenerated into verbal wrestling as soon as the questions began to touch on ethnic discrimination.[75]

There are no detailed standard guidelines for conducting such sensitive interviews. Table 11.3 shows a number of tools developed by researchers who have systematically undertaken such interviews.

These simple guidelines relate to in-depth knowledge about the organization, its policies and its culture.[76] One challenge in such an interview is to obtain the respect of the respondent – and to make him or her see that even for the organization there can be benefits in participating (and risks in being too evasive). Researchers may reflect on the location of the interview in order to facilitate informality. Having morning coffee with

---

[75]   Thuesen (n 64) 616–617.

[76]   Odendahl and Shaw (n 64) 306–307. See also Steiner Kvale and Sven Brinkmann, *InterView. Introduction til et håndværk* (2nd edn, Hans Reitzel forlag 2009) [Danish edition of Steinar Kvale and Sven Brinkmann, *InterView*] (Sage 2008).

a respondent before normal working hours may generate a less formal atmosphere, but for most public sector organizations this may not be feasible.[77]

The fact that there are no specific or firm guidelines also reflects one of the clearest messages learned from research work in this domain: the need to rely on intuition and improvisation when conducting such interviews. Balancing detachment with involvement and confrontation with dialogue is also an approach that can help render the interview productive. According to some observers, there is a security perceived by the respondent in dealing with a neutral, observing and detached researcher, while others stress the importance of involvement and of forging trust through the use of personal and informal forms of communication.[78]

Thuesen argues that confrontational and conflict-causing interviews will produce knowledge and insights. However, one risk is that the researcher provoking emotions will be less attentive to details or to what is actually being communicated by the respondent. Thuesen also advocates, with Flyvbjerg, what he describes as phronesis, a practical reasoning approach that aims to piece together meaning and interpretation holistically from the social logic, emotions and values expressed in the specific interview. The approach balancing dialogue with confrontation should therefore be emotionally sensitive in situ. Faking friendship or subversive attitudes in the elite interview and then subsequently raising critiques of the respondent obviously has negative ethical implications. Respect for the dignity of the respondent should therefore be observed in order to uphold ethical professional norms.[79]

CONCLUSIONS

We have explored the methods that can be employed in researching how state institutions or duty-bearer organizations make strategic decisions on human rights policies. We have been motivated to do so by a deficit of knowledge in the area of duty-bearer agency in human rights research. Most studies that examine state or interstate strategizing or decision-making in the field of human rights do so using quantitative methods to delineate causal relations between changing human rights policies and ratifications of human rights conventions. Alternatively, studies have also related human rights policy change to enhanced civil society advocacy. In other words, few studies have

---

[77]   Adler and Adler (n 64) 528.
[78]   Ibid. 523.
[79]   See also Chapter 9, by George Ulrich.

approached state or interstate organizations using methods that explore motivations for human rights change in a detailed and qualitative manner.

We have argued that this deficit in research may be related to a lack of theoretical perspectives on institutions and organizations in human rights research. We maintain that there are links between the theoretical perspectives on these issues and methodological approaches, and that neo-institutional perspectives may enrich intra-organizational human rights research, especially perspectives on historical sociological institutionalism. Issues of path-dependency and of the translation mechanisms used by human rights actors inside organizations may throw light on how human rights become integrated within various organizational settings. The methods used in examining these processes of integration (or non-integration) are tools relevant for furthering an understanding of human rights change.

The methods that we outline for such research are documentary approaches and ethnographic fieldwork inside organizations, including methods of observation and elite interviews. Combinations of these methodological tools have, of course, been employed by researchers. Our review also indicates that apart from the explicitly ethnographic work where methodical awareness prevails, there is scant reflection in human rights research on the methodical choices available when working on the inside. This relates to the studies reviewed using documentary methods. With respect to elite interviews, we can only refer to one study in the human rights field (Thuesen n 64, cited above) containing more explicit reflections on this methodical choice and its foundations.

Research within organizations indicates that, in practice, they tend to give prominence to pragmatic voices and actors and to gravitate towards adaptive solutions, because this tactic enables organizational actors to translate new norms and technologies to institutional and political logics at the local level.

In sum, greater attention to organizational dynamics may also challenge the tendency to identify human rights change as a zero-sum game between a 'genuine conversion' of organizational actors and a mere 'opportunistic calculation' on their part.[80] Methodologically, by conducting research inside organizations it becomes possible to gain insight into the black boxes that harbour power relations and social agency, determining the path-dependencies, translation processes, blind spots and trade-offs that institutional theory encourages us to inspect.

The methods of studying human rights change from within organiza-

---

[80]   Migai Akech, 'Constraining Government Power in Africa' (2011) 22(1) Journal of Democracy 5.

tions is still uncharted territory, especially with respect to how state bureaucracies decide to integrate economic and social rights in policies relating to service delivery. In analyzing motivations for change among civil servants – an aspect that seems essential – long-term fieldwork, involving the 'ecological right to be close', is a suitable approach. However, the study of sensitive decision-making entails access to, and interviews with, key informants at the top level of organizations. Establishing this kind of access to the elites of organizations remains one of the key challenges in seeking a deeper understanding of the political economy of duty-bearer acceptance and the integration of human rights into governmental organizations.

REFERENCES

Adler, P. A. and P. Adler, 'The Reluctant Respondent' in Jaber F. Gubrium and James A. Hostein (eds), *Handbook of Interview Research. Context and Method* (Sage 2002)

Akech, M., 'Constraining Government Power in Africa' (2011) 22(1) Journal of Democracy 5

Bandyopadhyay, M., *Everyday Life in a Prison: Confinement, Surveillance, Resistance* (Orient Black Swan 2010)

Barkin, J.S., *International Organization. Theories and Institutions* (Palgrave Macmillan 2006)

Bates, R., 'Contra Contractarianism. Some Reflections on New Institutionalism' (1988) 16(2) Politics and Society 387–401

Bennett, L., 'Policy Reform and Culture Change: Contesting Gender, Caste, and Ethnic Exclusion in Nepal' in A. Dani and A. Haan (eds), *Inclusive States. Social Policy and Structural Inequalities* (The World Bank 2008)

Bruun, O. and M. Jacobsen, *Human Rights and Asian Values: Contesting National Identities and Cultural Representations in Asia. Vol. 6* (Psychology Press 2000)

Bundgaard, H., 'Lærlingen: Den formative erfaring' in K. Hastrup (ed.), *Ind i Verden. En grundbog i antropologisk metode* (Reitzel 2003)

Bustreo, F. and P. Hunt, *Women's and Children's Health: Evidence of Impact of Human Rights* (WHO 2013)

Campbell, J.A., 'Institutional Reproduction and Change' in G. Morgan, J.L. Campbell, C. Crouch, O.K. Pedersen and R. Whitley (eds), *The Oxford Handbook of Comparative Institutional Analysis* (OUP 2010)

Clarke, J., D. Bainton, N. Lendvai and P. Stubbs (eds), *Making Policy Move: Towards a Politics of Translation and Assemblage* (Policy Press 2015)

Cohen, S., 'Government Responses to Human Rights Reports: Claims, Denials, and Counterclaims' (1996) 18(3) Human Rights Quarterly 517–543

Council of the European Union, 25 June 2012 11855/12, EU Strategic Framework and Action Plan on Human Rights and Democracy

Dani, A. and A. Haan (eds), *Inclusive States. Social Policy and Structural Inequalities* (The World Bank 2008)

Dexter, L.A., *Elite and Specialized Interviewing* (ECPR Press 2006)

Eyben, R., 'Hovering on the Threshold. Challenges and Opportunities for Critical and Reflexive Ethnographic Research in Support of International Aid Practice' in S. Hagberg and C. Widmark (eds), *Ethnographic Practice and Public Aid. Methods and Meaning in Development Cooperation* (University of Uppsala 2009)

Fleisher, M., *Warehousing Violence* (Sage 1989)

Flyvbjerg, B., *Making Social Science Matter. Why Social Inquiry Fails and How It Can Succeed Again* (CUP 2002)

Gloppen, S., 'Public Interest Litigation, Social Rights, and Social Policy' in A. Dani and A.

Haan (eds), *Inclusive States. Social Policy and Structural Inequalities* (The World Bank 2008)

Goffman, E., 'On Fieldwork' (1989) 18(123) Journal of Contemporary Ethnography 123–132

Grugel, J. and E. Peruzzotti, 'The Domestic Politics of International Human Rights Law: Implementing the Convention on the Rights of the Child in Ecuador, Chile, and Argentina' (2012) 34(1) Human Rights Quarterly 178–198

Guilhot, N., *The Democracy Makers. Human Rights and the Politics of the Global Order* (1st edn, Columbia University Press 2005)

Hafner-Burton, E., *Making Human Rights a Reality* (1st edn, Princeton University Press 2013)

Hall, P.A., 'Historical Institutionalism in Rationalist and Sociological Perspective' in J.A. Mahoney and K. Thelen (eds), *Explaining Institutional Change. Ambiguity, Agency, and Power* (CUP 2010)

Handy, C., *Understanding Organizations* (5th edn, Penguin 1999)

Hickey, S. and D. Mitlin (eds), *Rights-Based Approaches to Development. Exploring the Potential and Pitfalls* (Kumarian Press 2009)

Hodgson, G., 'What are Institutions' (2011) XL(1) Journal of Economic Issues 1–25

Hopenhayn, M., 'Recognition and Distribution: Equity and Justice Policies for Disadvantaged Groups in Latin America' in A. Dani and A. Haan (eds), *Inclusive States. Social Policy and Structural Inequalities* (The World Bank 2008)

Keck, M. and K. Sikkink, *Activists beyond Borders Advocacy Networks in International Politics* (1st edn, Cornell University Press 1998)

Koskenniemi, M., 'The Effects of Rights on Political Culture' in Alston and others (eds), *The EU and Human Rights* (OUP 1999)

Kvale, S. and S. Brinkmann, *InterView. Introduction til et håndværk* (2nd edn, Hans Reitzel forlag, 2009) [Danish edition of S. Kvale and S. Brinkmann, *InterView*] (Sage 2008)

Mahoney, J. and K. Thelen, 'A Theory of Gradual Institutional Change' in J. Mahoney and K. Thelen (eds), *Explaining Institutional Change. Ambiguity, Agency, and Power* (CUP 2010)

Malinowski, B., *Argonauts of the Western Pacific* (Routledge and Kegan Paul 1922)

Malkki, L., *Purity and Exile. Violence, Memory and National Cosmology among Hutu Refugees in Tanzania* (University of Chicago Press 1995)

March, J. and J. Olsen, *Democratic Governance* (1st edn, The Free Press 1994)

Marslev, K. and H. Sano, 'The Nature and Consistency of Human Rights Integration in EU External Country Strategies' (FRAME Deliverable 2.2, 2015)

Martin, H., *Nursing Contradictions: Ideals and Improvisation in Uganda* (AMB Diemen 2009)

Martin, T., 'Reasonable Caning and the Embrace of Human Rights in Ugandan Prisons' (2012) 68 Focaal 68–82

Martin, T., 'The Importation of Human Rights by Uganda Prison Staff' (2014) 212 Prison Service Journal 45–51

Martin, T., 'Witnessing and Accessing Ugandan Prisons – Fieldwork within a Post-colonial Bureaucracy' in D. Drake, J. Sloan and R. Earle (eds), *Palgrave Handbook of Prison Ethnography* (Palgrave 2015)

Moravcsik, A., 'The Origins of Human Rights Regimes: Democratic Delegation in Postwar Europe' (2000) 54(2) International Organisation

Moyn, S., *The Last Utopia: Human Rights in History* (1st edn, Harvard University Press, 2010)

Muñoz, A., 'Transnational and Domestic Processes in the Definition of Human Rights Policies in Mexico' (2009) 31(1) Human Rights Quarterly 35–58

Munro, L., 'The "Human Rights-based Approach to Programming": A Contradiction in Terms?' in S. Hickey and D. Mitlin (eds), *Rights-based Approaches to Development Exploring the Potential and Pitfalls* (Kumarian Press 2012)

Nader, L., 'Up the Anthropologist: Perspectives Gained from Studying Up' (1972) ECRIS

Neumayer, E., 'Do International Human Rights Treaties Improve Respect for Human Rights?' (2005) 49(1) Journal of Conflict Resolution 925–953

North, D., 'Five Propositions about Institutional Change' in J. Knight and I. Sened (eds), *Explaining Social Institutions* (University of Michigan Press 1998)

Odendahl, T. and A. Shaw, 'Interviewing Elites' in Jaber F. Gubrium and James A. Hostein (eds), *Handbook of Interview Research. Context and Method* (Sage 2002)

Oestreich, J., *Power and Principle. Human Rights Programming in International Organizations* (1st edn, Georgetown University Press 2007)

OHCHR, *Human Rights Indicators. A Guide to Measurement and Implementation* (Report 2012)

Olivier-de-Sardan, J.P., 'Researching the Practical Norms of Real Governance in Africa' (2011) Africa, Power & Politics 5 December, 1–23

P. Pels, 'Professions of Duplexity: A Prehistory of Ethical Codes in Anthropology' (1999) 40(2) Current Anthropology 101–136

Rhodes, L., 'Toward an Anthropology of Prisons' (2001) 73 Annual Review of Anthropology 65–83

Risse, T., S. Ropp and K. Sikkink, *The Power of Human Rights International Norms and Domestic Change* (1st edn, CUP 1999)

Sanjek, R., 'On Ethnographic Validity' in R. Sanjek (ed.), *Fieldnotes: The Makings of Anthropology* (Cornell University Press 1990)

Sano, H., 'Economic Factors' in Lassen et al., *Report on Factors which Enable or Hinder the Protection of Human Rights* (The Danish Institute for Human Rights, FRAME Fostering Human Rights Among European Policies 2014)

Sano, H., 'Evidence in Demand. An Overview of Evidence and Methods in Assessing Impact of Economic and Social Rights' (2014) 32(4) Nordic Journal of Human Rights 387–402

Sano, H. and H. Thelle, 'The Need for Evidence-based Human Rights Research' in F. Coomans, F. Grünfeld and M. Kamminga (eds), *Methods of Human Rights Research* (Intersentia 2009)

Sarfaty, G., *Values in Translation. Human Rights and the Culture of the World Bank* (1st edn, Stanford University Press 2012)

Schatz, E. (ed.), *Political Ethnography. What Immersion Contributes to the Study of Power* (University of Chicago Press 2009)

Shepsle, K., 'Studying Institutions. Some Lessons from the Rational Choice Approach' (1989) 1 Journal of Theoretical Politics 131–149

Simmons, B., *Mobilizing for Human Rights. International Law in Domestic Politics* (1st edn, Cambridge University Press 2009)

Starl, K., V. Apostolovski, I. Meier, M. Möstl, M. Vivona and A. Kulmer, in collaboration with H. Sano and E. Andersen, *Report on the Baseline Study of Uses and Objectives of Human Rights Indicators and EU Human Rights Indicator Schemes* (FRAME Fostering Human Rights Among European Policies. GA no. 320000, 2012)

Suarez, D. and P. Bromley, 'Institutional Theories and Levels of Analysis, History, Diffusion, and Translation' in Schriewer J. (ed.), *World Culture Recontextualized* (Routledge 2015)

Thuesen, F., 'Navigating Between Dialogue and Confrontation: Phronesis and Emotions in Interviewing Elites on Ethnic Discrimination' (2011) 17(7) Qualitative Inquiry 613–622

Ulrich, G., 'Epilogue: Widening the Perspective on the Local Relevance of Human Rights' in K. De Feyter, S. Parmentier, C. Timmerman and G. Ulrich (eds), *The Local Relevance of Human Rights* (CUP 2011)

UN HRBA Portal, 'The Human Rights-Based Approach to Development Cooperation' <http://hrbaportal.org/the-human-rights-based-approach-to-development-cooperation-towards-a-common-understanding-among-un-agencies#sthash.Rv8vZoKo.dpuf> accessed 25 March 2016

Vandenhole, W. and P. Gready, 'Failures and Successes of Human Rights-based Approaches to Development: Towards a Change Perspective' (2014) 32(4) Nordic Journal of Human Rights 291–311

12. Quantitative methods in advocacy-oriented human rights research
Margaret Satterthwaite* and Daniel Kacinski

INTRODUCTION AND CORE DEBATES

Applied human rights researchers have turned to quantitative methods in recent years to systematize their knowledge and help answer questions about the scope, intensity, characteristics, responsibility for, and causes of human rights violations. Using data of widely varying type and provenance, a range of methods with different capabilities have been employed for a spectrum of purposes. These methods not only vary in their approach and capacity, but also relate to international human rights law in different ways. Thus, as Langford and Fukuda-Parr recommend in relation to quantitative methods in human rights, asking 'why', 'what' and 'how' are crucial to making an assessment of the role and impact of quantitative approaches.[1] Gruskin and Ferguson underscore the importance of asking the 'who' question as well when indicators are being used in the rights context, since 'a human rights perspective suggests querying the assumed neutrality of an indicator: we should think about who uses it, for what purposes and in what ways'.[2]

This chapter will provide some examples of how quantitative methods are used by researchers engaged in advocacy-oriented, real-world human rights work.[3] It is written as an introduction for researchers not trained

* Margaret Satterthwaite gratefully acknowledges support from the Filomen D'Agostino Research Fund at New York University School of Law. The authors also wish to acknowledge Hans-Otto Sano and Malcolm Langford for helpful comments on an earlier draft of this chapter.
[1] Malcolm Langford and Sakiko Fukuda-Parr, 'The Turn to Metrics' (2012) 30 Nordic J. Hum. R. 222, 223.
[2] Sofia Gruskin and Laura Ferguson, 'Using Indicators to Determine the Contribution of Human Rights to Public Health Efforts' (2009) 87 Bull. World Health Org. 714. Brian Root underscores the need to ask *who*, *why*, and *how* when using numerical data in the human rights context. See Brian Root, 'Numbers are Only Human: Lessons for Human Rights Practitioners from the Quantitative Literacy Movement' in Philip Alston and Sarah Knuckey (eds), *The Transformation of Human Rights Fact-Finding* (OUP 2015) 355.

in quantitative methods by authors trained in the law. It is therefore not meant to provide a how-to or an in-depth look at technical issues, but focuses instead on providing an overview of a growing field. It is also not meant to encompass all quantitative methods that are or could be used for human rights advocacy; it instead aims to highlight a few examples of approaches already applied in this context.

The methods discussed in this chapter can be split into two general categories: first, techniques focused on measurement and data collection; and second, methods that can be applied to transform and analyze data. Both categories of tools provide unique promise for human rights research, but also carry perils that practitioners must be aware of. These tools, when applied in the proper settings and for appropriate uses, can support knowledge that would otherwise be difficult, if not impossible, to attain, and can identify patterns, practices or trends that might otherwise be missed. Practitioners must be wary, however, of perils in application and fit: while applied human rights questions are similar in many ways to queries in social science – the origins of the methods discussed in this chapter – they may differ in their ethical dimensions and immediacy.[4] Further, there are dangers inherent in quantification itself, which – as Merry points out – may be especially acute in the human rights context, and so qualitative methods should always be considered alongside, or in lieu of, quantitative ones.[5] This chapter introduces some of the promises and perils in quantitative methods for applied human rights research.

---

[3]   For a discussion of other potential human rights applications of quantitative methods, see Margaret L. Satterthwaite and Justin C. Simeone, 'A Conceptual Roadmap for Social Science Methods in Human Rights Factfinding', in Philip Alston and Sarah Knuckey (eds), *The Transformation of Human Rights Fact-Finding* (OUP 2015) 340.

[4]   The distinction between advocacy-oriented research and social science research is not perfect and there is significant overlap. For example, much of what Cresswell, Clark, Gutmann, and Hanson label as 'transformational' social science – because it explicitly engages in normative assessment – could be included in the category deployed in this chapter. See J.W. Creswell, V.L. Plano Clark, M.L. Gutmann and W.E. Hanson, 'Advanced Mixed Methods Research Design', in *Handbook of Mixed Methods in Social and Behavioral Research* (Sage 2003) 209–240. However, this chapter focuses on such research approaches that have already been deployed for advocacy purposes. For a general discussion of the limitations of quantitative methods in human rights fact-finding, see Root (n 2).

[5]   Qualitative methods and the limits of quantitative approaches are discussed in this volume by Sally Merry in Chapter 7.

QUANTITATIVE METHODS FOR HUMAN RIGHTS RESEARCH

Measurement and Data Collection Techniques

Overview of illustrative techniques

Any quantitative approach to human rights research requires structured data, or methods to transform unstructured data into machine-readable formats. Because human rights relate to a broad spectrum of human endeavor and existence, a wide variety of data is relevant to human rights research. At the highest level of abstraction, data is relevant that sheds light on the respect for, protection of, or fulfilment of human rights, including civil and political, as well as economic, social and cultural rights. Some highly structured data exist that fits this definition. Administrative and demographic datasets, for example, contain information about things like water services, educational attainment, housing, wealth and income. Such data can be used as 'proxy measures for the progressive realization of social and economic rights' at an aggregate level,[6] or can be analyzed alongside qualitative data concerning government efforts to elucidate the adequacy of such endeavors.[7] Similarly, data recorded by agencies of the state, such as criminal justice, elections or immigration data can shed light on rights such as access to justice, the right to vote and the right to seek asylum. Despite the existence of troves of data relevant to some rights and populations, other rights and populations may be harder to measure and reach. Indeed, data about some violations are routinely not recorded, and are often denied or hidden – as with cases of torture or extrajudicial execution or enforced disappearance.[8] In addition, some populations – such as groups that are stigmatized or criminalized – may be hard to reach using traditional data-gathering techniques. As Brian Root has explained, human rights groups often seek information about individuals *outside the norm* by the very fact that they have experienced rights violations.[9]

Researchers have turned to methods more familiar to statisticians and

---

[6]   Todd Landman and Edzia Carvalho, *Measuring Human Rights* (Routledge 2010) 40.

[7]   For example, see the Center for Economic and Social Rights' OPERA Framework <http://cesr.org/section.php?id=179>.

[8]   This problem has been a concern of researchers examining human rights questions for decades. See Robert Justin Goldstein, 'The Limitations of Using Quantitative Data in Studying Human Rights Abuses' (1986) 8 Hum. Rts. Q. 607, 617.

[9]   Root (n 2).

social scientists to identify, collect and process standardized data in human rights-related contexts. The tools discussed below have been adopted by researchers to address one or more of the following challenges: the inability to generalize findings beyond those interviewed for a given investigation; the need to identify and correct biases in human rights data; and the desire to measure hidden and denied rights violations over time and across countries. Each approach poses potential risks and benefits: relying on previously collected data may, for example, be cheaper than conducting a new survey, but may restrict the specificity or even accuracy of any potential conclusions that could be drawn since the data were not gathered for rights analysis. Comparatively, conducting a survey may provide more relevant and tailored data, but may be limited by issues of scale, cost and technical expertise. Applied researchers must determine at an early stage which method is most suitable for their objectives and resources and be conscious that multiple techniques may need to be combined to obtain those research goals. Finally, it should be acknowledged that in some contexts, quantitative approaches may not be appropriate at all.

To provide an overview of measurement and data collection techniques, we discuss two specific measurement and data collection techniques used by advocacy-oriented researchers: events-based measures and randomized sample surveys (RSS). Events-based measures capture the individual-focused 'who did what to whom'[10] data at the center of much advocacy-oriented human rights research but in a sufficiently systematic manner to allow for quantitative analysis.[11] RSS is a technique that can allow human rights researchers to collect representative data through probabilistic sampling. This kind of data allows researchers to make estimates about the extent to which a given human right is respected or infringed at the level of the population of interest, and to conduct additional exploration concerning relationships among variables using inferential statistics.[12] There are numerous other techniques not covered in this chapter. For example, standards-based measures, which transform traditional (qualitative, narrative) human rights data into coded data at the country or specific allegation level, are used to assess relationships between human rights and large social, political or economic processes.[13] Another method

---

[10]   See Patrick Ball, 'Who Did What to Whom? Planning and Implementing a Large Scale Human Rights Data Project' (1996) <https://hrdag.org/whodidwhat towhom/contents.html>.

[11]   Landman and Carvalho (n 6), at 51.

[12]   Ibid. 91.

[13]   Standards-based measures are discussed in this volume in Simon Walker, Chapter 13. See also Margaret Satterthwaite, 'Coding Personal Integrity Rights:

emerging on the horizon but not addressed here is the use of randomized controlled trials (RCTs) in human rights settings. While RCTs – adapted from the medical sciences by economists and social scientists – have been in use in the development field for more than a decade, their adoption in the human rights context is thus far comparatively sparse.[14]

Illustrative Techniques

Counting violations: using events-based measures

Perhaps the most well-known type of quantitative data used in advocacy-oriented human rights is events-based measures of civil and political violations such as extrajudicial executions and disappearances. As Landman and Carvalho explain:

> Events-based data answer the important questions of what happened, when it happened and who was involved, and then report descriptive and numerical summaries of these events. Counting such events and violations involves identifying the various acts of commission and omission that constitute or lead to human rights violations, such as extra-judicial killings, arbitrary arrest, or torture.[15]

This type of structured data is generated through counting activities or coding qualitative materials that contain information about human rights violations such as the narrative reports of human rights organizations,[16]

Law, Advocacy, and Standards-based Measures of Human Rights' (2016) 48 N.Y.U. J. INT'L L. and POL. 513 (discussing the Cingranelli–Richards Human Rights Data Project and the Political Terror Scale); Courtenay R. Conrad, Jillienne Haglund and Will H. Moore, 'Disaggregating Torture Allegations: Introducing the Ill-Treatment and Torture Country-year Data' (2013) 14 Int'l Stud. Perspectives 199; and Landman and Carvalho (n 6) 64–90.

[14] RCTs have been used to test the effectiveness of interventions aimed at reducing certain kinds of human rights violations. For example, social science researchers are working with the UK Department for International Development to roll out an RCT in India assessing different interventions to reduce violence against women and girls. See Sally Neville, Lyndsay McLean Hilker, Macartan Humphreys, Sohail Husain, Sarah Khan and Summer Lindsey, 'Evaluation of the Madhya Pradesh Safe Cities Initiative: Baseline Study' (2014) <http://www.mac artan.nyc/wp-content/uploads/2015/08/20150603-MP-Baseline-Report-for-SEQAS. pdf>.

[15] Landman and Carvalho (n 6) 37.

[16] The major human rights NGOs explicitly eschew quantitative methods except the occasional use of basic descriptive statistics. As Amnesty International has written, its work is 'describing and trying to affect a complex and evolving situation using complex and evolving sources of information and analytical tools'.

media accounts of violations, witness statements provided to non-governmental organizations (NGOs) or truth commissions, and official records concerning specific events.[17] The latter category can include a wide variety of data, including morgue records, trial transcripts and police records.[18] The work of Patrick Ball, the American Association for the Advancement of Science and the Human Rights Data Analysis Group in the 1990s and early 2000s developed pioneering approaches to transforming 'found', often narrative, records into structured human rights data.[19] In recent years, a new set of sources for events-based data have emerged: crowd-sourced platforms and social media. Crowd-sourced platforms such as Ushahidi allow advocates and the general population to report human rights violations directly (and often anonymously) online. The resulting information can be used as a source for events-based analysis.[20] It should be noted that crowd-sourcing brings with it both new promise and new peril alike. While crowdsourcing can be seen as 'democratizing' fact finding[21] by giving those directly experiencing and witnessing violations an amplified voice in defining and reporting abuse, it can also magnify the problems associated with all 'found' human rights data (discussed below) when used for quantitative analysis. Similar issues arise when analyzing social media for events-based data. While scraping Twitter or Facebook posts can yield reports of relevant violations, those reports will suffer from the same bias as all data based on voluntary reporting.

Because this is an extremely time-consuming method that requires the existence of a variety of forms of information about violations, the 'who did what to whom' approach has most successfully been used to provide an historical record. Thus, truth commissions have been the primary consumers of this kind of data: transitional justice bodies in El Salvador,

---

Amnesty International's response to Andrés Ballesteros, Jorge A. Restrepo, Michael Spagat and Juan F. Vargas, 'The Work Of Amnesty International and Human Rights Watch: Evidence from Colombia', CERAC, Colombia, 21 February 2007.

[17]   Landman and Carvalho (n 6) 51–52; OHCHR, *Human Rights Indicators: A Guise To Measurement and Implementation* (2012) 51–54.

[18]   Landman and Carvalho (n 6) 51.

[19]   See Ball (n 10), and Patrick Ball, Herbert F. Spirer and Louise Spirer, 'Making the Case: Investigating Large Scale Human Rights Violations Using Information Systems and Data Analysis' (2000) <https://hrdag.org/wp-content/uploads/2013/MakingtheCase01/-2000-intro.pdf>.

[20]   OHCHR (n 17) 56.

[21]   Molly K. Land, 'Democratizing Human Rights Fact-finding' in Philip Alston and Sarah Knuckey (eds), *The Transformation of Human Rights Fact-Finding* (OUP 2015) 399–424.

Guatemala, Haiti and South Africa based their findings in part on events-based data developed for that purpose.[22] A secondary market for this kind of data is criminal tribunals seeking data about the crimes committed by alleged perpetrators.[23] Other growing consumers of this kind of data are human rights organizations and the media: as real-time data are sought by decision-makers, media outlets and NGOs have begun to rely on crowd-sourced events-based data in near real-time.

The main limit to this kind of data is its inherently biased nature. By definition, events-based data is drawn from convenience samples – the fruits of investigation by a human rights group, the voluntary reporting of cases to a truth commission, media reports on specific events or crowd-sourced case reports – instead of probability samples. This means that it is impossible to know how 'true' the data is as a reflection of reality. When the number of reported extrajudicial executions rises, for example, is this due to increased killings, or is it due to better documentation? When an urban province records double the number of cases of torture as a rural one, is this because more people were tortured in the first location, or because the main victims' service organization that records cases of torture was based in the urban province? Or is it simply because more people live in the second province? This kind of question is essential when working with events-based data, including crowd-sourced data. For this reason, a technique called 'multiple-systems estimation' (discussed later in this chapter) is sometimes used with events-based data as a way of overcoming, or at least reducing, the bias inherent in this kind of data.

Estimating prevalence: enabling inferential statistics using randomized sample surveys

Theoretically, randomized sample surveys could allow human rights researchers to accurately generalize whether a given human right is respected or infringed, and to what extent, on a local, provincial or national level. Researchers can also use randomized surveys to identify how these populations perceive human rights, and how closely the general perception aligns with the actual respect for rights.[24] Randomized sample surveys are a simple form of polling: individuals are selected and asked

[22]   Patrick Ball, Herbert F. Spirer and Louise Spirer, 'Making the Case: Investigating Large Scale Human Rights Violations Using Information Systems and Data Analysis' (2000) <https://hrdag.org/wp-content/uploads/2013/MakingtheCase 01/-2000-intro.pdf>.

[23]   Landman and Carvalho (n 6) 57–62.

[24]   For a discussion of surveys of opinions and perceptions, see Simon Walker, Chapter 13. See also, e.g., Landman and Carvalho (n 6) 38–39 (discussing rand-

to answer predefined questions about experiences or beliefs.[25] The key element of RSS is the scientifically valid random selection of participants: by selecting persons using a probability sample, random sample surveys provide results representative of the entire population under consideration.[26] This is in direct contrast to more targeted surveys or investigations in which individuals are selected on the basis of a specific trait, from which conclusions can only be drawn about that subset of the general population, or the study population itself, depending on the sampling method.[27] The most common approaches to sampling in human rights research for advocacy are convenience and purposive sampling, in which participants are selected on the basis of a specific experience, such as having survived a particular human rights violation, or because they are accessible to the researcher through an NGO or other trusted network. The findings of such investigations are not generalizable beyond the study population, although they may be crucial for identifying the dynamics and elements of particular abuses.[28] As with any method, RSS may not be best suited for all applications, but can produce relevant insights where it can be properly used.[29]

The greatest promise of RSS is that it permits conclusions to be drawn in relation to the whole population of which the sample is representative, increasing potential application and impact. RSS relies on the use of a randomized sample where each individual within the targeted population is equally likely to be surveyed.[30] This reduces the likelihood of results being skewed by intentional or unintentional bias, significant dangers that are present in traditional human rights research methods.[31] When sampling is done well, researchers may draw inferences about the prevalence of the measured condition within the general population.[32]

---

omized surveys of global human rights perceptions, but noting the high degree of subjectivity to such perception analyses).

[25]   Ibid. 91.

[26]   Catrien Bijleveld, 'On Research Methods for International Crimes – Methodological Issues in the Empirical Study of International Crimes', in Alette Smeulers (ed.), *Collective Violence and International Criminal Justice* (Intersentia 2010) 275, 277.

[27]   See, e.g., Jana Asher, 'Introduction', in Jana Asher, David Banks and Fritz J. Scheuren (eds), *Statistical Methods for Human Rights* (Springer 2007) 22.

[28]   For a discussion, see Root (n 2).

[29]   For a discussion of the limitations of RSS, see text accompanying notes 39–49.

[30]   Bijleveld (n 26).

[31]   Landman and Carvalho (n 6) 92.

[32]   Landman and Carvalho (n 6) 92; Root (n 2).

Perhaps the most common use of RSS in human rights research is to measure the enjoyment of economic and social rights.[33] The surveys used for this kind of analysis generally focus on factors which roughly correlate to the realization of certain rights, and are frequently conducted for other purposes, often by or with official state agencies. A survey inquiring about access to toilets, for instance, may be conducted to assess sanitary facilities and public health conditions, but it can yield data that human rights researchers can use to assess the extent to which a given population is enjoying the right to sanitation.[34] Human rights researchers frequently use data drawn from the UNICEF-funded Multiple Indicator Cluster Sample Survey (MICS),[35] the USAID-funded Demographic and Health Surveys (DHS),[36] or the World Bank-funded Living Standards Measurement Study,[37] all standardized household surveys aimed at gathering demographic, health, and wealth and poverty information, which are conducted periodically in cooperation with national statistical offices in developing countries.[38] The Office of the High Commissioner for Human Rights (OHCHR) identifies randomized sample surveys as a method for tracking the rights-related conditions experienced by specific populations.[39]

It is difficult – although not impossible – to design an RSS aimed at gathering information for more sensitive rights issues. Some scholars have suggested that RSS is often a poor tool among populations subject to

---

[33]   See Eitan Felner, 'Closing the "Escape Hatch": A Toolkit to Monitor the Progressive Realization of Economic, Social, and Cultural Rights' (2009) 1 J. Hum. Rts. Practice 402.

[34]   See Inga T. Winkler, Margaret L. Satterthwaite and Catarina de Albuquerque, 'Measuring What We Treasure and Treasuring What We Measure: The Promise and Perils of Global Monitoring for the Promotion of Equality in the Water, Sanitation, and Hygiene Sector' (2014) 33 Wisconsin J. Int'l L. 547.

[35]   See Felner (n 33).

[36]   See ICF International, 'The DHS: Demographic and Heath Surveys' <http://www.dhsprogram.com/>.

[37]   See World Bank, 'Living Standards Measurement Study' <http://econ. worldbank.org/WBSITE/EXTERNAL/EXTDEC/EXTRESEARCH/EXTLSMS /0,contentMDK:21610833~pagePK:64168427~piPK:64168435~theSitePK:33589 97,00.html>.

[38]   See UNICEF, 'MICS: Multiple Indicator Cluster Surveys' <http://mics. unicef.org/>.

[39]   'Monitoring and Protecting the Human Rights of Refugees and/or Internally Displaced Persons Living in Camps, in United Nations Office of the High Commissioner for Human Rights, Training Manual on Human Rights Monitoring' U.N. Doc. E.01.XIV.2 (2001) 167, 175.

ongoing or recent conflicts, because respondents may intentionally modify their answers to protect themselves or others, or unintentionally modify their answers owing to trauma or confusion.[40] For this reason, surveys are used with much less frequency to explore severe civil or political rights violations, although they have been used by researchers to ask a randomized sample of respondents about their experience with specific types of human rights violations.[41] In other cases, a particular sub-population is sampled to identify the extent to which specific types of violations are occurring within that group.[42] In other cases, such as in highly repressive environments or with stigmatized populations, RSS will not be a viable – or even ethical – option for collecting human rights data. In those cases, other methods must be chosen.

There are functional risks in using RSS in the human rights context as well. The 'sampling' element of RSS is at the forefront of these risks.[43] As Landman and Carvhalo note, some amount of bias may occur when using RSS to identify human rights violations.[44] Even in a population where conflict is occurring, the number of persons who have been exposed to such a violation is usually 'relatively small'.[45] Researchers conducting a study will therefore often choose a random sample from among a population understood as more likely than the general public to have experienced violations.[46] This targeting may undermine the representativeness sought

---

[40]   Meghan Foster Lynch, 'Collecting Data on Civilian Casualties: Scientific Challenges and Ethnographic Solutions' in Taylor B. Seybolt, Jay D. Aronson and Baruch Fischhoff (eds) *Counting Civilian Casualties: An Introduction to Recording and Estimating Nonmilitary Deaths in Conflict* (OUP 2013) 123–144.

[41]   See, e.g., Athena R. Kolbe and Royce A. Hutson, 'Human Rights Abuse and Other Criminal Violations in Port-au-Prince, Haiti: A Random Survey of Households' (2006) 368 The Lancet 864.

[42]   Ibid. at 102 (discussing Physicians for Human Rights use of random survey within population of internally displaced persons to investigate sexual violence).

[43]   Sampling, as a concept, is frequently misunderstood by researchers, both in terms of what it requires and what it 'tells' about a given population. Root (n 2), at 360, discusses frequent issues faced and proposes that practitioners need to develop a 'stronger understanding of the many different types of sampling'. Ibid. at 363.

[44]   Landman and Carvalho (n 6) 100.

[45]   Ibid.

[46]   See, e.g., Romesh Silva, Jeff Klingner and Scott Weikart (eds) 'Measuring Lethal Counterinsurgency Violence in Amritsar District, India Using a Referral-based Sampling Technique' 572 <http://www.amstat.org/sections/srms/proceedings/y2010/Files/306319_56256.pdf> (study of enforced disappearances combined a random survey with 'referral-based sampling', where some study participants were referred to the researchers, and required the assumption that 'the referral process was homogeneously reliable and exhaustive; [a]n assumption which is

when using RSS.[47] Further, the validity of RSS data depends on the quality of the design and implementation of the survey itself.[48] Such surveys are relatively easy to conduct in developed countries where sufficient background data exist about the target population to allow researchers to develop and implement the desired sampling frame, and infrastructure is such that less labor-intensive survey methods can be used.[49] However, the significant resource investments needed to conduct an RSS in an environment where basic census or population data is missing, or where infrastructure is very poor and conditions are unstable, may preclude the use of such survey techniques or, at least, require additional implementation considerations (see Box 12.1).[50]

DATA TRANSFORMATION AND ANALYSIS TECHNIQUES

Overview of Data Transformation and Analysis Techniques

Data, by themselves, mean very little. While great care is needed in relation to the methods used for data collection, it is equally important to attend to the methods used for processing and analyzing data. This is perhaps especially true when examining human rights-related questions. Applied researchers have therefore turned to techniques familiar to statisticians and social scientists for their analytical needs. This section presents three data transformation and analysis techniques: multiple-systems estimation (MSE) for analyzing incomplete human rights data; human rights-based analysis of development data; and the identification of rights-relevant patterns in Big Data.

MSE allows researchers to use multiple incomplete datasets to estimate

---

unlikely to be true in the best of times, let alone in a post-conflict rural society in Northern India').

[47] Cf. Root (n 2), at 361 (noting that data collected from an unrepresentative sample of the total target population can 'produce useful evidence to compliment qualitative research and provide insight into a human rights situation, even if it only represents the experiences of those interviewed').

[48] Landman and Carvalho (n 6) 105–106.

[49] See, e.g. Belden Russonello & Stewart, 'Human Rights in the United States', in *The Opportunity Agenda, Human Rights in the U.S.* (2007) 6 (showing use of telephone push poll conducted by traditional U.S. polling firm for survey about human rights) <https://opportunityagenda.org/pdfs/HUMAN%20RIGHTS%20 REPORT.PDF>.

[50] Landman and Carvalho (n 6) 101.

BOX 12.1   REAL-TIME HUMAN RIGHTS DATA: RSS IN POST-CONFLICT SETTINGS

The Harvard Humanitarian Initiative (HHI) has used RSS in numerous countries following conflict to gather data on people's experience of violence, its impact on their lives, and their opinions about the future of their country. These population-based studies have been carried out in countries including Burundi, Cambodia, Central African Republic, Colombia, Côte d'Ivoire, Democratic Republic of the Congo, Guatemala, Iraq, the Philippines, Rwanda, Timor Leste and Uganda. HHI reports that its researchers have interviewed more than 40,000 people.

For example, in the Democratic Republic of Congo, HHI conducts polls four times a year concerning security and access to justice in the Eastern region, producing real-time data for decision-makers. This RSS uses a sample of 5000 households surveyed in 2013 as its baseline. The periodic surveys use questions about exposure to specific forms of violence to collect data relevant to assessing improvements or deterioration in security. Since these surveys are administered to a randomized sample, the researchers are able to generalize their findings to the population, making their findings about the prevalence of violence particularly enlightening to decision-makers.

Source: Harvard Humanitarian Initiative, 'Peace and Human Rights Data', http://hhi.harvard.edu/research/peace-and-human-rights-data#intro.

the number of incidents that were not captured in any individual dataset.[51] This can provide a broader sense of the scope of a given problem, and it can be especially valuable in unstable environments or concerning sensitive subjects where surveys may be difficult or impossible to conduct.[52] However, owing to the nature of this estimation technique, only some human rights phenomena are suitable for MSE. Rights-based analysis of development data is increasingly performed. This is less a technique than an approach to using already-existing data collected for the purpose of assessing the progress of a population toward development-related goals. This approach, which was already in use during the era of the Millennium

---

[51]   Kristian Lum, Megan E. Price and David Banks, 'Applications of Multiple Systems Estimation in Human Rights Research' (2013) 67 Am. Statistician 191, 192.
[52]   See Jana Asher, 'Using Surveys to Estimate Casualties Post-Conflict: Developments for the Developing World' (discussing unstable environments) and Meghan Foster Lynch, 'Collecting Data on Civilian Casualties: Scientific Challenges and Ethnographic Solutions', at 123–143 (discussing sensitive subjects), in Taylor B. Seybolt, Jay D. Aronson and Baruch Fischhoff (eds), *Counting Civilian Casualties: An Introduction to Recording and Estimating Nonmilitary Deaths in Conflict* (OUP 2013).

Development Goals, is likely to increase significantly as the world pledges to 'leave no one behind' in pursuit of the Sustainable Development Goals. Finally, while 'Big Data' has not revealed itself to be centrally important in answering human rights questions, it is likely to become more prominent in the years to come.

Specific Techniques

Estimating violations: transforming incomplete samples using multiple systems estimation

Using randomization techniques with a population subject to human rights violations is often complicated and is sometimes impossible. In areas where human rights crises are occurring, security issues or resource limitations may preclude safe and complete data collection.[53] However, even in the midst of such crises, there are often multiple actors – from aid organizations, the media or NGOs – who may be recording data about these violations, frequently with the aim of bringing attention to the crisis or serving the population in distress. Typically, such groups gather their data independently, creating the potential for double counting or overlap.[54] What results is a hodgepodge of data collected by multiple actors for various and sometimes conflicting purposes. Researchers can address these challenges using MSE, which allows the use of these multiple incomplete data sources to better estimate the total scope of a given human rights violation.[55]

MSE generally refers to demographic methods to estimate the size of a selected population where multiple overlapping data sources are available.[56]

---

[53] See, e.g., Taylor B. Seybolt, Jay D. Aronson and Baruch Fischhoff, 'Introduction', in Taylor B. Seybolt et al. (eds), *Counting Civilian Casualties: An Introduction to Recording and Estimating Nonmilitary Deaths in Conflict* (OUP 2013) (Noting that in conflict situations '[i]t can be extraordinarily difficult . . . to gather accurate information about the number and identity of people who are killed and injured').

[54] One major area where these problems arise is where researchers are attempting to estimate casualty numbers from armed conflicts. Multiple actors produce 'casualty lists' but these are generally 'prone to incomplete registration, be it for institutional, financial, geographical or political reasons'. Daniel Manrique-Vallier, Megan E. Price and Anita Gohdes, 'Multiple Systems Estimation Techniques for Estimating Casualties in Armed Conflicts', in Taylor B. Seybolt et al. (eds), *Counting Civilian Casualties: An Introduction to Recording and Estimating Nonmilitary Deaths in Conflict* (OUP 2013) at 165.

[55] See generally Lum et al. (n 51) (describing the general methodology of multiple systems estimation).

[56] This chapter will provide an very brief overview of multiple systems estimation techniques, but will not discuss in depth the different MSE models or the

The technique assumes that, although data sources are incomplete, a certain number of incidents will probably be recorded in more than one set, creating duplicate records that should overlap between the different data sources.[57] Through a process of de-duplicating[58] the over-counted incidents, a 'capture pattern' emerges, revealing the probability that any given event will have been counted.[59] Using this pattern, it is possible to estimate the number of incidents that were not recorded in any source, producing an overall estimate that more comprehensively covers the incidence of a given violation.[60]

The most common application of MSE by human rights researchers is to develop more accurate accounts of human rights atrocities by ensuring that undercounted victims are not missed and that reporting trends do not distort understanding of actual trends. As noted, human rights crises often feature significant security concerns and multiple, sometimes conflicting reporting entities that create significant challenges for researchers trying to develop an accurate picture of the crisis.[61] Using MSE, researchers have been able to use the limited and overlapping data that is available to estimate the magnitude of violations that were missed, often finding that official estimates of atrocities severely undercounted victims.[62] Researchers have used MSE for casualty and victim-counting purposes in a number of contexts, from better estimating the number of deaths in the 1993 Srebrenica massacre[63] to more accurately estimating the number of

---

probabilistic calculations required to apply MSE. For more complete discussions of MSE in human rights settings, see also Manrique-Vallier et al. (n 54) 165, 169–170.

[57] Lum et al. (n 51).

[58] De-duplication, or 'matching', may be done manually, but is more likely to be done with automated data processing software. For a discussion of the de-duplication process and the use of 'automated matching', see Amelia Hoover Green, 'Multiple Systems Estimation: The Matching Process, Human Rights Data Analysis Group' (13 March 2013) <http://www.hrdag.org/2013/03/15/mse-matching-process/>.

[59] Manrique-Valler et al. (n 54) 167.

[60] Todd Landman and Anita Gohdes, 'A Matter of Convenience: Challenge of Non-random Data in Analyzing Human Rights Violations During Conflicts in Peru and Sierra Leone', in Taylor B. Seybolt et al. (eds), *Counting Civilian Casualties: An Introduction to Recording and Estimating Nonmilitary Deaths in Conflict* (OUP 2013).

[61] See, e.g., Seybolt et al. (n 53) and Manrique-Valler et al. (n 54).

[62] Graduate Institute of International Studies, Geneva, 'Small Arms Survey 2005: Weapons at War' (2005) 242–243 (noting that MSE estimates of conflict deaths in Guatemala and Peru were significantly higher than official counts).

[63] Helge Brunborg, Torkild Hovde Lyngstad and Henrik Urdal, 'Accounting for Genocide: How Many Were Killed in Srebrenica?' (2003) 19(2) Eur. J. Population 229.

persons who are currently victims of human trafficking or slavery.[64] The Human Rights Data Analysis Group ('HRDAG'), led by Patrick Ball and Megan Price, has been at the forefront of this application of MSE. HRDAG and its members have employed MSE to identify, among other examples, the number of conflict-related deaths as part of the Truth and Reconciliation process in Timor Leste,[65] disappearances and deaths linked to armed conflict in Peru[66] and homicide patterns in Colombia.[67] By providing MSE computer models for use by others, HRDAG aims to make these MSE-related methods more available for human rights researchers.[68]

Researchers interested in MSE, however, must be aware of the method's limitations. Notably, MSE models rely on assumptions that may not be reasonable to make in every context. The technique assumes that specific incidents may be recorded in multiple data sources, but this may not be true in all scenarios, especially where data collection efforts were limited or did not overlap geographically or temporally.[69] Data quality is also a significant concern as de-duplication is critical to MSE techniques. De-duplication

---

[64]   Kevin Bales, Olivia Kesketh and Bernard Silverman, 'Modern Slavery in the UK: How Many Victims?' (2015) 12(3) Significance 16.

[65]   Romesh Silva and Patrick Ball, 'The Demography of Large Scale Human Rights Atrocities: Integrating demographic and Statistical Analysis into Post-conflict Historical Clarification in Timor-Leste' (2006) 4 <http://hrdag.org/wp-content/uploads/2013/02/60827.pdf>.

[66]   Patrick Ball, Jana Asher, David Slumont and Daniel Manrique, 'How Many Peruvians Have Died? An Estimate of the Total Number of Victims Killed or Disappeared in the Armed Internal Conflict Between 1980 and 2000', American Association for the Advancement of Science (28 August 2003) <https://hrdag.org/wp-content/uploads/2013/02/aaas_peru_5.pdf>.

[67]   Patrick Ball and Michael Reed Hurtado, 'Cuentas y Mediciones de la Criminalidad y de la Violencia: Exploración y Análisis de los Datos para Comprender la Realidad', in *Instituto Nacional de Medicina Legal y Ciencias Forenses, 2014 Forensis Datos para la Vida* (2015) 529. Since 2012, HRDAG has provided estimates of fully documented conflict-related killings in Syria. It contends that MSE should be used on databases of reported killings to provide a better sense of the total number of deaths in that conflict than estimates based on simple tallies of reported cases. See Megan Price, Anita Gohdes and Patrick Ball, 'Updated Statistical Analysis of Documentation of Killings in the Syrian Arab Republic' (August 2014) 2 <https://hrdag.org/wp-content/uploads/2014/08/HRDAG-SY-UpdatedReportAug2014.pdf>.

[68]   See, e.g., Megan Price, 'HRDAG Offers New R Package – dga, Human Rights Data Analysis Group' (24 April 2015) <https://hrdag.org/2015/04/24/hrdag-offers-new-r-package-dga/>.

[69]   Lum et al. (n 51) 192 (noting that the 'homogeneity assumption' that all violations will be recorded is 'usually wrong'); Todd Landman and Anita Gohdes, 'A Matter of Convenience: Challenge of Non-Random Data in Analyzing Human Rights Violations During Conflicts in Peru and Sierra Leone', in Taylor B. Seybolt,

requires that individual records be specific enough to compare and match them against records from other datasets.[70] This means that all of the datasets must be sufficiently consistent and robust so that matches can be made, or else a capture pattern will not be discernible.[71] More fundamentally, MSE techniques can produce estimates from which only limited conclusions can be drawn. At its core, MSE is a tool to estimate under- or over-counting, but it does not provide causal insights. An MSE analysis, for example, can estimate that internally displaced persons are being undercounted in a given country but it cannot explain the fundamental cause of the undercount.[72] Previous human rights MSE applications, such as the victim and casualty estimates discussed here, provided more accurate numbers but could not show who was responsible for those deaths or why they were undercounted.[73] At least one court has rejected MSE analyses on this basis: the International Criminal Tribunal for the Former Yugoslavia rejected an MSE-based analysis offered to show common causes behind killings and refugee migration in Kosovo because the analysis left open 'a number of potentially plausible options' for the migrations.[74]

Revealing inequalities, exploring trends: rights-based analysis of development data

Advocates working to improve the enjoyment of economic and social rights frequently make use of data gathered to guide development programming and track the progress of populations on issues such as health and education. The data in these development datasets, discussed above, are drawn from RSS like the MICS and the DHS. Such datasets include rich information about the health status, use of health facilities, access to water and sanitation facilities, and poverty levels in developing countries. For example, the DHS and MICS include questions about sources and types of water sources the household uses, and what kind of toilet

---

Jay D. Aronson and Baruch Fischhoff (eds), *Counting Civilian Casualties: An Introduction to Recording and Estimating Nonmilitary Deaths in Conflict* (OUP 2013).

[70]   Lum et al. (n 51) 194.

[71]   See Rob van Hest, A. Grant and I. Abubakar, 'Quality Assessment of Capture–Recapture Studies in Resource Limited Countries' (2011) 16(8) Trop. Med. Int'l Health 1019, 1036 (noting that in the health context data from resource-poor countries is often 'inaccurate and incomplete', preventing sufficient de-duplication).

[72]   See Landman et al. (n 69) 166 (noting that MSE allows a means to estimate an undercounted population).

[73]   See, e.g., nn 62–64.

[74]   *Prosecutor v. Milan Milutinovic et al.*, Case No. IT-05-87, T.Ch. III, Vol. 3, para. 21 (Int'l Crim. Trib. for the Fmr. Yugoslavia, 26 February 2009).

members of the household use. They collect information about the ownership of household goods and amenities, which is used to estimate poverty levels. The surveys also contain demographic information about the households surveyed. This demographic information includes data about the gender and age of household members, as well as their educational status and information about their residence (e.g. urban vs rural).

Human rights advocates interested in economic and social rights fulfilment query these databases using human rights questions. For example, advocates concerned about the right to water can ask where discrimination and inequalities lie by disaggregating data on access to water using rights-relevant variables contained in the surveys such as ethnicity, language and migration status.[75] Comparisons between groups identified on these bases can reveal disparities in the enjoyment of human rights and point to deprivations that may be grouped along lines of discrimination. Tracking changes – and lack thereof – among identified groups can be enlightening for rights advocates, who can use evidence of plateaus or backsliding as prima facie evidence of human rights violations such as discrimination, retrogression and failure to meet the minimum core obligations. Coupled with analysis of relevant government policies, budgets and programs, this kind of data can help make the case for changes targeted at improving the status of those groups.[76]

Organizations such as the Center for Economic and Social Rights (CESR) have made great use of development data. For example, CESR has developed a systematic approach – called 'OPERA' – to using quantitative data alongside qualitative assessments of government efforts. CESR's Visualizing Rights series contains specific country studies in which development data is queried using human rights questions.[77] For example, a 2013 fact sheet about Egypt highlights unequal access to skilled birth attendants using DHS data.[78] Human rights economists Sakiko Fukuda-Parr, Terra Lawson-Remer and Susan Randolph have created the Social and Economic Rights Fulfillment Index (SERF Index), which uses such development data 'to measure the performance of countries and sub-national units on the fulfillment of economic and social rights obligations'.[79] The SERF Index uses key development indicators as

---

[75]   See Winkler et al. (n 34).

[76]   See CESR, 'OPERA' <http://cesr.org/section.php?id=179>.

[77]   See CESR, Visualizing Rights, series http://www.cesr.org/section.php?id=43.

[78]   CESR, 'Visualizing Rights – Egypt: Fact Sheet No. 13' (2013) <http://www.cesr.org/downloads/Egypt.Factsheet.web.pdf?preview=1>.

[79]   Economic and Social Rights Empowerment Initiative, 'About' http://www.serfindex.org/about/.

proxies for the fulfilment of economic and social rights.[80] For example, the under-five survival rate is used as a core indicator for the right to health.[81] This indicator is tracked by country and analyzed against the 'achievement possibilities frontier', which is a benchmark meant to represent the possible value of an indicator if the maximum available resources were used.[82] The achievement possibilities frontier is calculated using actual outcomes in states with comparable resources, as measured by per capita GDP.[83] Edward Anderson and Malcolm Langford have gone further in investigating state capacity, using six different measures of resources when considering the design of appropriate targets for water and sanitation.[84]

These approaches have the virtue of allowing applied researchers to identify specific values they can use as a benchmark for states to work toward, based on a solid, transparent method. However, they also have a limit shared by all quantitative methods asking human rights questions of development data: the analyses are dependent on the underlying data, which is often inadequate to the most pressing analyses desired – such as analysis of human rights fulfillment disaggregated along the lines of sex, disability, sexual orientation and other prohibited grounds of discrimination, which may be evident in differential outcomes at the individual, not household, level.[85] The kinds of sources used for this type of analysis are often limited in terms of the unit sampled (often the household), underlying demographic variables they capture, and/or in the sample sizes used, which can be too small to allow for meaningful disaggregation even when equality-related variables are present.[86]

---

[80] Ibid.

[81] Sakiko Fukuda-Parr, Terra Lawson-Remer and Susan Randolph, 'SERF Index Methodology: Version 2011.1, Technical Note' (2011) http://www.serfindex.org/data/.

[82] Ibid.

[83] Ibid.

[84] Edward Anderson and Malcolm Langford, 'A Distorted Metric: The MDGs and State Capacity', University of Oslo Faculty of Law Legal Studies Research Paper Series No. 2013-10 (2014) http://papers.ssrn.com/sol3/papers.cfm?abstract_id=2217772.

[85] For a discussion of the benefits and limitations of rights-based analyses in the economic, social and cultural rights contexts, see Allison Corkery, 'Investigating Economic, Social, and Cultural Rights Violations', in Philip Alston and Sarah Knuckey (eds), *The Transformation of Human Rights Fact-Finding* (OUP 2015) 377, 384–388.

[86] For a discussion, see JMP END Working Group, Final Report http://www.wssinfo.org/fileadmin/user_upload/resources/JMP-END-WG-Final-Report-20120821.pdf.

Finding patterns: using big data for human rights research

The primary use of big data analysis by human rights practitioners is to identify trends or other patterns in human behavior.[87] However, there is no broadly accepted definition of the term 'big data analysis'.[88] Even advocates for its promise for human rights acknowledge the lack of fixed definition of 'big data'.[89] The term has been used to refer to large structured datasets collected using traditional means, such as national census data, but it has also referred to large unstructured datasets created as a by-product of recent technological innovations.[90] Structured sources include mobile phone call records and metadata, financial transaction data and GPS device location data.[91] Unstructured sources include online searches, human-produced documents such as newspaper articles or blog posts, and social media interactions.[92] The only consensus definition of big data is that there is a lot of it: 2.5 exabytes, or 25,000,000 gigabytes, of new unstructured data is created in online searches, social media interactions, and human-produced documents, every single day.[93] For the purposes of

---

[87]   Emmanuel Letouze and Patrick Vinck, 'Draft, The Politics and Ethics of CDR Analytics', Data-Pop Alliance White Papers Series 1 (10 December 2014).

[88]   Kenneth Neil Cukier and Victor Mayer-Schoenberger, 'The Rise of Big Data' (May/June 2013) 92(3) Foreign. Aff. 28–40.

[89]   United Nations Global Pulse, 'Big Data for Development: A Primer' (2013).

[90]   Patrick Ball acknowledges that '[b]ig data has been defined many ways', noting the differing uses of the term. See Patrick Ball, 'The Bigness of Big Data' in Philip Alston and Sarah Knuckey (eds), *The Transformation of Human Rights Fact-Finding* (OUP 2015) 427. He then proposes a new definition of the term based on the size of capture of a given population, claiming that a 'big data' set is one that includes all possibly observable data for that population. Ibid. This definition, however, is starkly different than the other uses of the term that primarily focus on the nature of the data itself, rather than the coverage of the dataset. See infra, notes 91–94. While acknowledging the unsettled definition of 'big data', this chapter uses the more widely adopted understanding: 'big data' refers to unstructured or poorly structured information not collected for analytic purposes, created as a by-product of a service or system and potentially requiring processing before analysis, which would be difficult to analyze using traditional methods. Ibid.

[91]   World Economic Forum, 'Big Data, Big Impact: New Possibilities for International Development' (2012) 1.

[92]   Key Resources, 'Data-Pop Alliance' <http://www.datapopalliance.org/resources#key-resources>.

[93]   World Economic Forum (n 91). It should be noted that this amount is nearly equivalent to the total amount of digital storage that was available worldwide in 1986. See Martin Hilbert and Priscila Lopez, 'The World's Technological Capacity to Store, Communicate, and Compute Information' (2011) 332:6025 Science 60.

this chapter, we use 'big data analysis' to refer to techniques or systems for analyzing datasets that were not specifically collected for analysis and that are otherwise difficult to process or analyze owing to their size, structure or both.[94]

Advocates of big data analysis contend that such analysis allows practitioners to identify patterns that would be difficult, if not impossible, to identify using traditional methods of statistical or empirical analysis.[95] The United Nations in particular has latched onto the potential of big data analysis as one way to promote and monitor sustainable development goals.[96] Actual application of big data analysis by human rights practitioners, however, is limited. One application is the creation of monitoring tools to track, or even predict, a specific human rights issue based on big data analysis. For example, DataKind, an NGO that provides data engineers to social organizations on a pro bono basis, partnered with Amnesty International to develop a monitoring tool for the 'Urgent Action Alerts' that it generates on a daily basis.[97] The alerts are created using a number of sources, including email and individual reporting, and are not processed or structured into a searchable database. DataKind created a tool that, by parsing the alerts in real time for keywords related to specific human rights abuses, could predict the location of likely future human rights violations.[98] While this seems an exciting potential development, it must be kept in

---

[94]   SAS Institute Inc., 'What Is Big Data' <http://www.sas.com/en_us/insights/big-data/what-is-big-data.html>.

[95]   See The Information Accountability Foundation, 'A Unified Ethical Framework for Big Data Analysis' (2014) 3. Cf. Ball (n 90) 425 (arguing that 'the notion of big data is misleading in most human rights work').

[96]   United Nations Secretary General's Independent Expert Advisory Group on a Data Revolution for Sustainable Development, 'A World That Counts: Mobilizing the Data Revolution for Sustainable Development' (2014) 4. It should be noted that big data is only one of multiple proposals by the UN Data Revolution Group, including promoting platforms to analyze and visualize sustainable development goals. Ibid. 27.

[97]   DataKind, 'Predicting and Preventing Human Rights Abuses' <http://www.datakind.org/projects/using-predictive-analytics-to-prevent-human-rights-abuses/>.

[98]   Ibid. The model used an algorithm which identified keywords associated with specific violations (such as the relationship of the word clemency to the issue of executions) to predict future violations. The tool, the Urgent Action Globe, also produced a dashboard to track the status of alerts in real time; however, it appears that Amnesty has not been maintaining real-time updates as the available data goes only through 2013. The tool is available at http://www.jrsandbox.com/amnesty/map/. DataKind has also produced a similar mapping tool for Benetech to process human rights violations received through its Martus tool; however, this mapping tool is not available to the public. See DataKind 'Strengthening

mind that AI's Urgent Actions are not representative of the universe of grave human rights violations, and the database contains a large number of known and unknown biases, such as path dependencies for reporting of abuses, efficiencies in reporting in specific languages and the location and resources of frontline monitors. For all of these reasons, it is likely that big data predictions could be better at predicting where the next *report* of a violation will take place, instead of where the next violation might occur.

Most other information about big data use by human rights practitioners refers to potential, not actual, uses. For example, the United Nations Global Pulse initiative proposed uses for big data including tracking mobile phone activity to assist with disaster management or to estimate food security[99] and searching internet search traffic to determine risk factors for non-communicable diseases.[100] However, only a limited number of projects have resulted in any product beyond a research paper, and even then, the actual product is often limited.[101] Some private companies have proposed using their data for a variety of human rights-related projects, but few have advanced past the proposal stage. The mobile phone operator Orange, for example, sponsored the Data for Development challenge in 2012 that sought proposals for the use of call data record analytics in the development sphere.[102] Teams were given access to anonymized CDR records from 5 million customers from December 2011 to April 2012, from which researchers could see overall traffic flows on the network (e.g. call volume), physical movement of customers and records of calls made.[103] Proposals from the challenge

---

Global Human Rights Through Mapping' <http://www.datakind.org/projects/strengthening-global-human-rights-through-mapping/> accessed 11 March 2015.

[99]   United Nations Global Pulse, 'Using Mobile Phone Activity for Disaster Management During Floods' <http://www.unglobalpulse.org/tabasco-floods-CDRs> accessed 10 March 2015; United Nations Global Pulse, 'Using Mobile Phone Data and Airtime Credit Purchases to Estimate Food Security' <http://www.unglobalpulse.org/mobile-CDRs-food-security> accessed 10 March 2015.

[100]   United Nations Global Pulse, 'Online Signals for Risk Factors of Non-Communicable Diseases (NCDs)' <http://www.unglobalpulse.org/non-communicable-diseases> accessed 10 March 2015.

[101]   See, e.g. United Nations Global Pulse, 'Analyzing Attitudes Towards Contraception and Teenage Pregnancy Using Social Data' <http://www.unglobalpulse.org/UNFPA-social-data> accessed 10 March 2015. This project resulted in an online dashboard tool to monitor keywords related to teenage pregnancy in Uganda, but not any specific action beyond this tool. The tool is available at http://pulselabkampala.ug/dashboard/family_planning/.

[102]   Emmanuel Letouze and Patrick Vinck, 'Draft, The Politics and Ethics of CDR Analytics', Data-Pop Alliance White Papers Series 3 (10 December 2014).

[103]   Ibid.

BOX 12.2   BIG DATA FOR THE PROSECUTION OF
PERPETRATORS OF HUMAN RIGHTS
VIOLATIONS

Big data analysis is also being used to help identify perpetrators of human rights violations and hold them accountable. In a first of its kind case, prosecutors at the Special Tribunal for Lebanon are relying on analysis of call records to prove their case against the alleged assassins of former Lebanese Prime Minister Rafiq Hariri. Big data analysis techniques have been used to identify networks of phones in possession of the accused in use at specific times and places linked to the attack, which they argue shows that the accused conspired to kill Hariri. Whether or not the prosecution will succeed in this argument is an open question. However, the promise of big data is clearly shown from this analysis.

Source: Prosecutor v. Ayyash et al., Case No. STL-11-01/T/TC, Decision on Three Prosecution Motions for the Admission Into Evidence of Mobile Telephone Documents, ¶ 2 (Special Trib. for Leb. Mar. 6, 2015).

---

included using CDR data to develop strategies for epidemic containment and to identify social divisions.[104] However, none of the proposals have been implemented.[105] Other uses for big data in the human rights context have been proposed by academics, but the real-world applications appear limited thus far, including mining Twitter posts to track changes in global well-being[106] and behavioral risk factors for public health[107] and using anonymized cell phone GPS data to view migration patterns in real time.[108]

Although big data analysis may be viewed as a panacea for a world full of information, it is still vulnerable to bias and is limited in its conclusory power. First, although big data analysis can show otherwise invisible trends, such patterns may be rendered meaningless by hidden biases in

---

[104]   Ibid. at 4.

[105]   Ibid. at 5. Another mobile operator gave researchers access to CDR data within their facilities, but has not broadly distributed the data or implemented any projects using the data. Ibid. 4.

[106]   H. Andrew Schwartz et al., 'Characterizing Geographic Variation in Well-Being Using Tweets' (2013) <https://www.aaai.org/ocs/index.php/ICWSM/ICWSM13/paper/view/6138/6398>.

[107]   Michael J. Paul and Mark Drezde, 'You Are What You Tweet: Analyzing Twitter for Public Health' (2011) <https://www.aaai.org/ocs/index.php/ICWSM/ICWSM11/paper/view/2880/3264>.

[108]   See, e.g., Martin Adolph, *Big Data: Big Today, Normal Tomorrow* (ITU 2013) ITU-T Technology Watch 8 (noting that volume of big data produces an 'immediate challenge to conventional resources' for analysis).

the underlying data.[109] These biases are likely to be worst in relation to issues most relevant to human rights research, such as the documented gaps in big data in relation to low-income and marginalized communities. Second, confirmation bias – the tendency to interpret patterns consistently with our own beliefs, regardless of whether the pattern supports such a conclusion[110] – is a particularly acute risk when using big data analysis in the human rights context. Because big data analysis cannot specifically tell researchers which correlations are meaningful, it is particularly important for researchers to approach any correlation with skepticism.[111] As put by IBM's 'Big Data Evangelist', James Kobielus: '[t]he sexier the correlation, the more likely any of us is to accept it uncritically'.[112] In the human rights context, this means that researchers, when evaluating correlations identified through big data analysis, must ensure not only that any conclusions drawn are supported by the data, taking into account their biases, but that the conclusions also make sense alongside qualitative information about the context. Finally, as is frequently mentioned in discussions regarding big data, the correlations that can be identified through big data analysis do not equal causation.[113] While this may appear to be an obvious limit of many research tools, it is a particular problem for human rights practitioners wishing to use big data analysis. A focus on correlates to human rights violations may allow practitioners to expand their understanding of human rights issues and potentially to forecast future violations, but it does not in itself lead to the identification of or solutions for the underlying causes of those violations.[114]

---

[109]   For a brief overview of bias in data and data collection, see Root (n 2) 363–364.

[110]   Kim H. Pries and Robert Dunnigan, *Big Data Analytics: A Practical Guide for Managers* (CRC Press 2015) 473–474; see also Raymond S. Nickerson, 'Confirmation Bias: a Ubiquitous Phenomenon in Many Guises' (1998) 2(2) R. Gen. Psych. 175.

[111]   Gary Marcus and Ernest Davis, 'Nine Large Problems With Big Data', Bus. Rev. Week., 10 April 2014 <http://www.brw.com.au/p/tech-gadgets/nine_large_problems_with_big_data_BOkbvT5G7f6Y2Jc2qiMgGM> accessed 26 August 2015.

[112]   James Kobielus, 'Big Data's Bogus Correlations', IBM Big Data and Analytics Hub, 22 May 2014 <http://www.ibmbigdatahub.com/blog/big-datas-bogus-correlations>.

[113]   See, e.g. Chris Taylor, 'Big Data's Slippery Issue of Causation vs. Correlation', Wired, 15 July 2013 <http://insights.wired.com/profiles/blogs/big-data-s-slippery-issue-of-causation-versus-correlation#axzz3k98PZyW6>.

[114]   See, e.g. Cukier and Mayer-Schoenberger (n 88) (noting the focus on big data is a 'move away from . . . trying to understand the deeper reasons behind how

CONCLUSION

Quantitative methods hold real promise for human rights research, but they also pose risks. As Patrick Ball has warned, 'statistics without a rigorous foundation are more confusing than helpful: weak statistics can be worse than having no statistics'.[115] In many human rights contexts, data problems – from missing and biased data to hidden or falsified data – are insurmountable. Yet in other cases, it is possible to use well-chosen methods, with great care. In the end, researchers must consider the objectives of their research; potential sources of relevant data and the biases, omissions and limits of such data; and the methods most suitable for the available data. Quantitative methods should be considered alongside qualitative methods and mixed methods models.[116] Only when the objectives, data and methods match, and when the perils can be obviated or limited to an acceptable level, should practitioners choose quantitative methods.

---

the world works to . . . learning about an association among phenomena . . . to get things done').

[115]   Ball (n 90) 425.
[116]   For a discussion, see Malcolm Langford in Chapter 8.

13. Challenges of human rights measurement

*Simon Walker**

STATE OF THE DEBATE

The measurement of human rights has grown steadily over recent decades and is today an important element of human rights work. Initial attempts began over a century ago with some key initiatives such as the measurement of lynching in the United States[1] and a study of quasi-judicial executions carried out during the height of the French Revolution.[2] Since the adoption of the Human Rights Covenants in 1966,[3] human rights measurement has grown considerably, documenting human rights violations, assessing the perceptions and opinions of the general public about human rights and measuring government compliance with their treaty obligations. Some well-known attempts include the global survey 'Freedom in the world', prepared by Freedom House',[4] and Cingranelli and Richards's Human Rights Data Project,[5] which provides comprehensive country rankings in relation to performance of specific human rights. Other projects have supported truth commissions in the Americas, Africa and Asia-Pacific by identifying violations,

* The views expressed in this chapter are those of the author and do not necessarily reflect those of the United Nations. I would like to thank Nicolas Fasel and Hans-Otto Sano for their insightful comments on earlier drafts.
[1] Richard Claude and Thomas Jabine, 'Exploring Human Rights Issues with Statistics' in Richard Claude and Thomas Jabine (eds), *Human Rights and Statistics* (University of Pennsylvania Press 1992) 5.
[2] Todd Landman, *Studying Human Rights* (Routledge 2006) 82.
[3] International Covenant on Civil and Political Rights, adopted 16 December 1966, entry into force 23 March 1976, United Nations Treaty Series, vol. 999, p. 171 (ICCPR); and International Covenant on Economic, Social and Cultural Rights, 16 December 1966, entry into force 3 January 1976, United Nations, Treaty Series, vol. 993, p. 3 (ICESCR).
[4] See Methodology Fact Sheet at (2014) <https://www.freedomhouse.org/report/methodology-fact-sheet#.UuDsGhAo51t> accessed 16 December 2014.
[5] See Human Rights Data Project at (2014) <http://www.humanrightsdata.com/> accessed 16 December 2014.

victims, and perpetrators of human rights abuse.[6] Global surveys such as the Afrobarometer, the Eurobarometer and the Latinobarometer, as well as surveys by academic and non-governmental organizations such as Physicians for Human Rights have helped measure public perceptions and opinions on aspects of human rights and related issues.[7]

Measurement has been important for diverse reasons from reporting to treaty bodies to informing decisions on whether human rights should condition trade preferences. The need for more accurate measurement has intensified recently with the expansion of human rights monitoring through commissions of inquiry, truth commissions and protection work in conflict and post-conflict zones, as well as prosecutions before international courts. Governments, business enterprises and civil society organizations are increasingly undertaking human rights impact assessments of laws, policies and practices, spurred on in particular by the United Nations Guiding Principles on Business and Human Rights of 2010 and its requirement of human rights due diligence prior to investing.[8]

While human rights measurement offers many opportunities for human rights protection and improving human rights analysis, it also faces several challenges. Some challenges, such as lack of infrastructure and resources to collect and analyze data, confront most fields of measurement. However, human rights measurement has to confront several specific challenges, not least the fact that measurement focuses on some concepts that are at times unclear, complex and understood in different ways, and much human rights measurement takes place in contexts which are highly sensitive, such as conflicts and post-conflict zones or in countries in transition, making measurement difficult and even risky. Human rights measurement also requires cross-disciplinary knowledge, spanning law, political and social science and even economics, which is not always available.

The purpose of this chapter is to outline the main approaches to human rights measurement and examine some of the challenges to ensuring measurement is reliable and valid. The notion of 'measurement' is understood narrowly, focusing principally on quantitative rather than qualitative

---

[6] Landman refers to human rights measurement project supporting truth commissions in Argentina, Chile, El Salvador, Guatemala, Haiti, Peru, South Africa, Sierra Leone and Timor Leste: Landman (n 2) 83.

[7] Office of the High Commissioner for Human Rights, *Human Rights Indicators: A Guide to Measurement and Implementation*, United Nations 2012 (H/PUB/12/5) 65. Landman (n 2) 85.

[8] United Nations Guiding Principles on Business and Human Rights: Implementing the United Nations 'Protect, Respect and Remedy' Framework, United Nations 2011 (HR/PUB/11/04).

research. This is intended as a means of introducing some of the challenges to the reliability and validity of measurement by reference to a specific area of research. This is not to indicate any preference for quantitative research, nor should this chapter be understood as proposing that researchers focus on quantitative methods over qualitative methods. Indeed, I have indicated in other writing that a mixed methods approach – one that combines both quantitative and qualitative methods – is preferable, at least in the area of human rights impact assessment.[9] Nor should the chapter's focus be misconstrued to suggest that qualitative measurement does not face its own challenges of reliability and validity. The reader is encouraged to turn to the chapter in this edition by Sally Engle Merry for a deeper discussion of the potential for ethnographic methods for qualitative human rights research.

The next section sets out the four main approaches to human rights measurement and provides examples of each. The following section identifies the main challenges to achieving valid, reliable and meaningful measurements facing these four approaches. These challenges need to be taken into account when choosing approaches to measure human rights and, where possible, methodologies should be adapted to minimize them. The next section makes some propositions to improve human rights measurement initiatives. The final section sets out conclusions and provides some sources for further reading.

METHODOLOGICAL TOOLS FOR HUMAN RIGHTS RESEARCH

Measuring human rights should follow a sound methodology that helps those doing the measurement to move from the human rights norm being analyzed to valid and reliable measurements.[10] The process should begin with the *identification and specification of the norm* to be measured. For example, a human rights measurement project examining conditions in detention would identify the relevant human rights standards – in particular, the prohibition of torture and ill-treatment – and then elaborate upon those norms by reference to international and national human rights

---

[9]   See e.g. Simon Walker, *The Future of Human Rights Impact Assessment of Trade Agreements* (Intersentia 2009). See also Malcolm Langford and Sakiko Fakuda-Parr, 'The Turn to Metrics' (2012) 30(3) Nordic Journal of Human Rights 238.

[10]   These steps have been adapted from: Todd Landman and Edzia Carvalho, *Measuring Human Rights* (Routledge 2010) 32.

standards, such as treaty law, internationally accepted guidelines and standards, general comments of treaty bodies and national legislation. The second step is the *operationalization of the norm* into meaningful, valid and reliable indicators. Those indicators should be grounded in the norms specified in the first step. Thus, indicators relevant to measuring conditions in detention might be grounded in the Convention against Torture and the Standard Minimum Rules for Treatment of Prisoners (the Mandela Rules) and include, for example, the existence of an up-to-date register, the percentage of adult and juvenile prisoners in separate parts of the institution, cubic metres of floor space per cell and per prisoner and so on.[11] Finally, the process moves to the *provision of scores* for the indicators – in other words, the actual measurement.[12]

There are four main approaches to measuring human rights which are relevant to the measurement process: events-based approaches, expert-scoring approaches, official data approaches and survey approaches. The rest of this section sets out these four approaches and provides examples of each.

First, an 'events-based approach' collects qualitative and quantitative data to record specific human rights violations and identify victims and perpetrators.[13] The main sources of data are 'found' data – such as data from archives, borders, morgues and so on – narrative data from victims, perpetrators and others, and official statements such as statements from Truth Commissions.[14] The data collected helps to understand the types and levels of violations in particular situations, such as during conflicts or demonstrations or during particular episodes such as forced evictions; it helps to provide descriptive and numerical answers to questions of what happened, when it happened and who was involved – also referred to as the 'who did what to whom' model.[15] This approach is popular in human rights monitoring work, particularly work related to monitoring of conflicts and post-conflict situations and to supporting Truth Commissions.[16] The data collected may be both quantitative and qualitative information collated through direct interviews with alleged victims and their friends and families, through observation such as during a political demonstration, or

---

[11]   United Nations Standard Minimum Rules for Treatment of Prisoners, United Nations Commission on Crime Prevention and Criminal Justice, (21 May 2015, resolution E/CN.15/2015/L.6/Rev.1).

[12]   Ibid. 32–33.

[13]   OHCHR (n 7) 52.

[14]   Landman and Carvalho (n 10) 51.

[15]   Landman (n 2) 81; and Landman and Carvalho (n 10) 48.

[16]   Landman and Carvalho (n 10) 59–61.

through review of events recorded in newspapers, court cases, state reports to treaty bodies and so on. Researchers record the information using standardized formats, according to agreed definitions and classifications drawn from the national and international human rights framework. The measurement generally appears as the incidence of alleged violations and the number of victims, for example, 'the number of reports of enforced disappearance' or 'the number of individuals foregoing access to HIV treatments due to cost'.

An example of the 'events-based approach' is a study of the forced migration and deaths of ethnic Albanians in Kosovo between 24 March and 22 June 1999 and whether this was a result of a systematic Yugoslav Government campaign.[17] The study gathered data on the migration patterns and patterns of death of ethnic Albanians over the period, as well as information on the NATO bombing, the activity of the Kosovo Liberation Army (KLA) and the Yugoslav army to identify whether the killings and migration could be attributed to the government. To identify the volume of migration flows and the reasons for the migrations, the researchers built a dataset combining the data compiled by the border guards in Albania, data supplied by the United Nations High Commissioner for Refugees and surveys of refugee camps. To identify the number and cause of deaths, the researchers relied on information from secondary sources gained through interviews with survivors as well as information gained from exhumations of Kosovars killed during the period undertaken by international teams on behalf of the International Criminal Tribunal for the Former Yugoslavia. These four datasets were compared to identify overlaps (people mentioned in more than one list) and to analyze gaps in the lists in order to indicate an overall number and pattern of deaths. With the volumes and timing of migration and killings identified, the researchers examined patterns of KLA activities and NATO bombings to exclude these as having responsibility for the killings and migration. This helped to undermine claims by Slobodan Milosevic's defense that the KLA and NATO bombings were responsible for the deaths and migration, even though, in the absence of detailed data on Yugoslav troop movements, it was not possible to establish Yugoslav troop responsibility. More recently, in 2014, the Human Rights Data Analysis Group published a report, commissioned by the Office of the High Commissioner for Human Rights, documenting conflict-related killings in Syria between March 2011 and April 2014. This is notable as

---

[17]   Patrick Ball and Jana Asher, 'Statistics and Slobodan: Using Data Analysis and Statistics in the War Crimes Trial of Former President Milosevic' (2002) 15(4) Chance 17.

the first major events-based monitoring project taking place during an ongoing conflict.[18]

Secondly, the 'expert-scoring approach'[19] compiles data on human rights violations into a standardized scale with a view to arriving at a generalized understanding of a country's human rights practice, answering questions of how often and to what degree violations occur.[20] The 'expert-scoring approach' relies on the recorded data of human rights violations from a range of reports and articles from media, governments and non-governmental organizations, which independent experts evaluate and translate into quantitative form through the use of coding. The measurement often appears as a ranking across a quantitative scale. In contrast to the 'events-based approach', which focuses on a particular event or events, the 'expert-scoring approach' seeks to measure the overall practice of a country that in turn allows for comparison with the practice other countries assessed according to the same standard. Researchers may repeat the same measurement at different periods, which allows for inter-temporal comparisons.

The Human Rights Data Project of Cingranelli and Richards (CIRI project) provides an example of the 'expert-scoring approach' to measurement. The CIRI project was established in 1994 and now measures human rights practice in 195 countries, covering 15 separate human rights practices, making it one of the largest human rights datasets in the world.[21] Specifically, the project measures government respect for physical integrity rights, civil rights and liberties, workers' rights and women's rights. The project relies on secondary qualitative sources setting out the human rights situations in countries – principally the annual US State Department

---

[18]   Megan Price, Anita Gohdes and Patrick Ball, *Updated Statistical Analysis of Documentation of Killings in the Syrian Arab Republic* (Commissioned by the Office of the UN High Commissioner for Human Rights, Human Rights Data Analysis Group August 2014).

[19]   The term 'expert-scoring approach' is used here to refer to what is commonly referred to as a 'standards-based approach'. The term 'standards-based approach' refers to the fact that information about human rights standards is coded according to a standardized scale, typically ordinal and limited in range (see Landman and Carvalho (n 10) 64). In a human rights context, the term 'standards' recalls human rights 'standards'. However, the standard referred to in the term 'standards-based approach' is more a one-to-10 scale or equivalent rather than the prohibition of torture. Moreover, standards-based approaches do not always rely on internationally agreed human rights standards when coding information along the ordinal scale.

[20]   OHCHR (n 7) 66 and Landman (n 2) 82.

[21]   David Cingranelli and David Richards, 'The Cingranelli and Richards (CIRI) Human Rights Data Project' (2010) 32 Human Rights Quarterly 395.

Country Reports and the annual reports of Amnesty International – which are turned into quantitative indicators through the use of codes. The indicators are ordinal; for example, they indicate whether torture is frequent in a country rather than identifying how many people were tortured. The project assesses human rights practices relative to international human rights standards (an absolute standard) but does not seek to rank countries relative to one another. In this way, the measurement helps to identify human rights that are most and least respected by governments and why that is so as well as demonstrate patterns of respect for various human rights over time. The project is an independent non-government organization and promotes transparency of its data and methodology.[22]

It is also relevant to refer to another manifestation of the 'expert-scoring approach' which examines the extent to which the actions of a state or other entity, such as a business enterprise, comply with human rights standards. The process similarly relies on the use of experts who assess the extent to which laws, policies and practices of an entity comply with human rights standards. An example is the Human Rights Compliance Assessment (HRCA), which comprises a series of 350 questions and 1000 indicators to help companies detect potential human rights violations against employees, local residents and others as a result of their operations and policies. A shortened version of HRCA, known as the Quick Check, comprises 28 questions and 240 corresponding indicators. Each question includes a narrative description of the human rights norm under analysis, and suggested indicators with answer boxes covering 'yes', 'no', 'further attention required', 'not applicable' and 'unknown'.[23]

Thirdly, the 'official data approach', sometimes referred to as the 'proxy-data approach' relies on existing socio-economic data and statistics – instead of directly collected data – as an input for human rights measurement.[24] Socio-economic data includes administrative data – such as birth and death rates – socio-economic statistics drawn from statistical surveys – such as surveys undertaken to measure implementation of the Millennium Development Goals – and census data.[25] Administrative data are information generated by government authorities according to standardized methodologies and tend to cover the whole population. In contrast, statistical surveys identify sample populations with a view to inferring the situation of the entire population. A census relates to the entire population of a

22   Ibid. 395–404.
23   Danish Institute for Human Rights, *Human Rights Compliance Assessment (HRCA): Quick Check* (DIHR 2006).
24   OHCHR (n 7) 56.
25   OHCHR (n 7) 56f.

country undertaken periodically, often at 10-year intervals, and focuses on specific issues such as the housing situation, agriculture, and religious affiliation.

The United Nations Development Program's (UNDP) Human Development Index (HDI) provides an example of official socio-economic statistics which have been used to measure human development achievements that are also used as a proxy for human rights measurement. The HDI aggregates indicators related to life expectancy, literacy, gross enrolment ratio and per capita GDP using special weights to calculate a score for all countries ranging from 0 to 1, with 1 representing good performance. The HDI has been used as a proxy measure to help measure enjoyment of the right to education and the right to health as two of the indicators relate to these rights.[26] The HDI has also provided the basis for more complex human rights measurement. For example, Kimenyi uses the HDI to understand the effort that states have made to fulfill economic and social rights.[27] He subtracts the income index from the HDI to obtain an adjusted income-free HDI and then compares the adjusted index against income. By doing so, it is possible to observe that some countries are achieving good human development results even with lower income, while other countries with higher income are not achieving the human development results that would be expected. This provides a ranking referred to as the Human Development Effort Rankings. The ranking illustrates how socio-economic and administrative data can provide insights into the efforts states parties are making to achieve the progressive realization of economic, social and cultural rights. The Social and Economic Rights Fulfilment Index (SERF Index) also uses official data to help understand the extent to which countries and sub-national units meet the obligation to use the maximum available resources to fulfill economic and social rights.[28] The chapter of Margaret Satterthwaite and Daniel Kacinski in this volume provides further information on this index.

Finally, the 'opinions and perceptions survey approach' draws information from a representative population sample by asking a set of standard questions relating to issues such as human rights violations or their knowledge of and attitudes to human rights. As much of this information

---

[26] Landman and Cavalho (n 10) 113.

[27] Mwangi Kimenyi, 'Economic Rights, Human Development Effort, and Institutions' in Shareen Hertel and Lanse Minkler (eds), *Economic Rights: Conceptual, Measurement, and Policy Issues* (CUP 2007) 192.

[28] Economic and Social Rights Empowerment Initiative, 'About' (n.d.) <http://www.serfindex.org/about/> accessed 29 November 2015.

is qualitative and subjective in nature, researchers transform responses according to numerical scales – such as a 1–10 opinion scale, where 1 is fully positive and 10 is fully negative – or according to yes/no/unsure formats. The information is then aggregated to arrive at a quantitative measurement. Surveys might also include or be supplemented by qualitative methodologies such as case studies or in-depth opinion interviews. The 'survey-based approach' is distinguished from statistics surveys used for the 'official data approach'; the latter – as referred to above – are generally undertaken by non-governmental and academic bodies rather than governmental authorities. Further, the purpose of statistics surveys is to gauge perceptions and opinions rather than to collate official statistics. However, governmental statistical bodies are increasingly using opinion and perception surveys to complement official statistics so that official data can better inform governmental policy-making.[29]

Physicians for Human Rights undertook a population-based survey of the prevalence and impact of sexual violence and other human rights violations among internally displaced persons (IDP) in Sierra Leone during the country's decade-long conflict.[30] The project sampled 1048 households in three IDP camps and in a community with a significant number of IDPs, representing a pool of around 91% of the registered IDP population in the country. Of the sampled households, 991 female heads of household participated in the survey, representing a response rate of 95%. This enabled reporting on the experiences of 9166 household members. The survey had 49 questions covering issues such as demographics, perceptions of physical and mental health, experience of human rights abuses among household members and experiences of sexual violence. In addition, the survey covered issues of assistance needs, opinions on punishment and justice for perpetrators, and attitudes on women's roles in society and on women's human rights.[31] Qualitative measurement supplemented the quantitative measurement: first, by including some qualitative open questions in the survey; and, secondly, by undertaking longer semi-structured interviews

---

[29]   For example, in Australia, the Australian Bureau of Statistics uses opinion surveys to supplement official crime statistics to give a fuller understanding of crime victimization and the overall crime situation, including through opinion surveys measuring women's safety at home and in the community (2004) <http://www.abs.gov.au/ausstats/abs@.nsf/mf/4522.0.55.001> accessed 8 December 2015.

[30]   Physicians for Human Rights, *War Related Violence in Sierra Leone: A Population-Based Assessment*, A report for Physicians for Human Rights with the support of the United Nations Assistance Mission in Sierra Leone, United States of America (2002).

[31]   Ibid. p. 5.

with some survivors.[32] On the basis of the results of the quantitative and qualitative assessment, the organization set out a series of recommendations to the government and armed groups. The recommendation also included a proposal to bilateral donors and the United Nations to hold perpetrators to account for violations, to provide justice to victims, to prevent future violations and to promote international humanitarian and justice-sector assistance.[33]

A human rights research project might combine two or more of these measurement approaches. For example, a human rights impact assessment might rely on expert-scoring as an indication of the current human rights context in a country and then use official data and opinion surveys to assess the impact of the law, policy or practice under examination. These human rights measurement approaches might, in some cases, be combined with other approaches such as economic modeling, particularly where the law or policy being assessed is not explicitly related to human rights, such as a trade agreement.

CHALLENGES TO HUMAN RIGHTS MEASUREMENT

Human rights measurement offers many benefits, from clarifying important information about human rights violations, victims and perpetrators to understanding public perceptions and opinions of human rights and testing theories about the effectiveness of human rights laws and policies. This in turn can assist in making better policies, remedying past injustices and clarifying the relationship between human rights protection and other areas of policy such as development and peace and security. Nonetheless, in a field such as quantitative measurement that generally seeks rigor and precision, human rights measurement faces uncertainties, such as the availability of data and the definition of what needs to be measured. Definitional challenges in turn lead to challenges to making valid, reliable and meaningful measurements of human rights. This section examines some of these challenges in more detail.

---

[32]   Ibid.
[33]   Ibid. 10–14.

Definitional Challenges

Many issues subject to human rights measurement can defy easy definition. For example, some terms associated with human rights, such as 'freedom', 'democracy', 'political terror', 'torture', 'health' or 'poverty' are highly subjective and therefore difficult to define objectively with great accuracy.[34] Their subjective nature means that each individual has a different experience and understanding of the terms and that each country and culture is also likely to consider these terms according to culturally specific norms or in relation to the national economy. It is therefore important to ground human rights measurement in internationally agreed norms as the starting point for analysis (even if contextual factors might still be relevant depending on the level of analysis).

Much has been achieved over the last 70 years in the definition of human rights. Not only treaty law, but also the work of human rights treaty bodies, such as regional courts and commissions, and the United Nations treaty bodies and special procedures have developed rich jurisprudence that is indispensable to achieving reliable and valid measurement of human rights norms and standards. Measurement exercises should start with relevant treaty provisions, and then consider their interpretation and application by reference to the general comments of treaty bodies and decisions on individual petitions before courts and other bodies.

For example, the experience of being tortured is highly personal. However, the Convention against Torture defines torture. The definition requires the presence of four factors: *severity* of physical or mental pain or suffering; *intention* to inflict such pain; a specific *purpose* of obtaining a confession or to punish, intimidate or coerce or to discriminate; and infliction or instigation of the pain with *the consent or acquiescence of a public official* or a person acting in an official capacity.[35]

The Committee on Economic, Social and Cultural Rights has developed General Comments that have identified a framework for understanding and implementing social rights and obligations. The normative content of social rights is divided into four elements: availability, accessibility, acceptability and quality. State responsibility is divided into three elements: the responsibilities to respect rights, to protect rights and to fulfill rights. This can help with measuring social rights. Thus, when

---

[34]   Russel Lawrence Barsh, 'Measuring Human Rights: Problems of Methodology and Purpose' (1993) 15 Human Rights Quarterly 87, 107–109.

[35]   Convention Against Torture and Other Cruel, Inhuman or Degrading Treatment or Punishment, 10 December 1984, United Nations, Treaty Series, Vol. 1465, p. 85, article 1.

measuring enjoyment of the right to water, the exercise should examine the 'affordability' of certain goods and services as well as what the state has done and is doing to 'fulfil' its obligation to ensure affordable access to water and related services.[36]

Basing measurement on international treaties and the work of treaty bodies still of course leaves room for uncertainty. Approaches across treaties to certain issues are not always identical.[37] In practice, human rights experts can and do disagree on definitions and also on the application of those definitions to particular factual situations, such as in determining whether a person was or was not tortured.[38] Further, relying on objective definitions has its limitations: depending on the underlying reason for research, it might be more appropriate to explore individuals' subjective beliefs and impressions on whether they were tortured and the impact it had on them through the use of qualitative techniques rather than relying on an objective definition of torture to identify numbers of cases.

Data Availability

Human rights data are sometimes non-existent, incomplete or inaccessible. Historical data prior to the First World War often does not exist or is highly unreliable.[39] Contemporary data are often incomplete, with more data generally available for developed as opposed to developing countries as well as for economic and social rights in comparison to civil and political rights.[40] Many states do not have adequately funded national statistics offices, sufficient numbers of trained statisticians or the required

---

[36] See e.g. Mads Jensen, Marie Villumsen and Thomas Petersen, 'The AAAQ Framework and the Right to Water: International Indicators for Availability, Accessibility, Acceptability and Quality', Issue Paper for the AAAQ Toolbox, (2014) Danish Institute for Human Rights.

[37] Consider the absolute ban on the deprivation of liberty on the basis of the existence of a disability in the Convention on the Rights of Persons with Disabilities (article 14) as opposed to the understanding of the Human Rights Committee of ICCPR (article 9) which permits deprivation of liberty on the basis of disability in certain limited situations.

[38] Goldstein provides the example of the European Commission on Human Rights unanimous decision in 1976 on British use of torture in Northern Ireland in 1976 which was subsequently rejected by the European Court of Human Rights in 1978 by a 13 to four vote. Robert Justin Goldstein, 'The Limitations of Using Quantitative Data in Studying Human Rights Abuses' in Richard Claude and Thomas Jabine (eds), *Human Rights and Statistics*, (University of Pennsylvania Press 1992) 35, 39.

[39] Ibid. 41–49.

[40] Ibid. 41–49.

technology and infrastructure to collect and manage data.[41] When undertaking cross-country comparisons, comprehensive data might not be available on a particular aspect of a right in a sufficient number of countries to warrant the comparison.[42]

With controversial issues such as torture and enforced disappearance, many victims might never tell their story, witnesses might be harassed or killed, information might be censored, reported information might be incomplete owing, for example, to the editorial policies of newspapers, or the specific conflict or post-conflict situation might make it very difficult for researchers to access information and potential informants at all.[43] Similarly, governments have incentives to hide, misrepresent or simply not count statistical data that relates to human rights, particularly given that human rights touch very sensitive issues.[44]

Similarly, existing data might be insufficiently disaggregated to allow measurement of discrimination and equality, which in turn could hide human rights challenges from view. Aggregated data can misrepresent the human rights situation, for example, by hiding differences between the access of boys and girls to primary and secondary education, potentially exacerbating existing patterns of discrimination in society. While some socio-economic and administrative data are disaggregated by sex (such as UNDP's Gender-related Development Index),[45] they are often not disaggregated by other categories.[46] Data disaggregated by categories such as sex, nationality, race, language, religion, disability and minority status can underline differences in enjoyment of human rights between individuals and reveal patterns of discrimination and inequality.

Validity

A valid measure can be described as 'one that measures exactly what it is supposed to measure, no more and no less'.[47] The unemployment rate

---

[41]   Landman and Carvalho (n 10) 125.

[42]   C. Apodaca, 'Measuring the Progressive Realization of Economic and Social Rights' in Shareen Hertel and Lanse Minkler (eds), *Economic Rights: Conceptual, Measurement, and Policy Issues* (CUP 2007) 172.

[43]   Cingranelli and Richards (n 21) 400; and Kenneth Bollen, 'Political Rights and Political Liberties in Nations: An Evaluation of Human Rights Measures, 1950 to 1984' in Richard Claude and Thomas Jabine (eds), *Human Rights and Statistics* (University of Pennsylvania Press 1992) 198 and 201.

[44]   Landman and Carvalho (n 10) 122.

[45]   <http://hdr.undp.org/en/content/gender-development-index-gdi> accessed 7 January 2015.

[46]   Landman and Carvalho (n 10) 40.

might be an indicator of the state of the economy; however, it does not measure the economy as such as the two are not synonymous.[48] 'Universal suffrage' might be an indicator of 'democracy', yet if the indicator for 'universal suffrage' measures only 'male suffrage', the indicator omits an important aspect of universal suffrage and is therefore not a valid measurement.[49]

The validity of measurement depends in large part on the extent to which the methodology clearly defines the human rights terms under investigation and reflects this definition in the methodology for data collection and analysis and the identification of indicators. As noted above, human rights measurement often relates to subjective and unobservable concepts such as 'democracy' and 'freedom', which are difficult to measure. Relying on clear definitions based in human rights law and admitting conceptual challenges are therefore essential to ensure valid measurement.[50] In order to transform a considerable amount of subjective, qualitative information into quantitative form, controlled vocabularies and coding processes can help define the violations under investigation and provide rules on how to count violations.[51]

Box 13.1 provides an example of controlled vocabularies in relation to events-based research in Sri Lanka. If the controlled vocabulary and coding procedures link with the right or rights being measured, the validity of the measurement is improved. Validity can be enhanced by subjecting controlled vocabulary and coding procedures to experts for review and critique.[52]

Controlled vocabularies and coding procedures also apply to expert-scoring measurement. However, the level of generality required to produce inter-country comparisons typical of expert-scoring measurement means that meticulous coding procedures such as those in Box 13.1 are not

---

[47]   Barsh (n 34) 95.

[48]   Gary King, Robert Keohane and Sidney Verba, *Designing Social Inquiry: Scientific Inference in Qualitative Research* (Princeton University Press 1994) 25.

[49]   Robert Adcock and David Collier, 'Measurement Validity: A Shared Standard for Qualitative and Quantitative Research' (2001) 95 *American Political Science Review* 529, 539.

[50]   Cingranelli and Richards (n 21) 413.

[51]   Romesh Silva, 'On Ensuring a High Level of Data Quality when Documenting Human Rights Violations to Support Research in the Origin and Cause of Human Rights Violations' (2002) Joint Statistical Meetings – Social Statistics Section 3242–3251, 3243.

[52]   Ted Gurr and Barbara Harff, 'The Rights of Collectivities: Principles and Procedures in measuring the Human Rights Status of Communal and Political Groups' in Richard Claude and Thomas Jabine (eds), *Human Rights and Statistics* (University of Pennsylvania Press 1992) 183.

BOX 13.1   CONTROLLED VOCABULARY FOR VALID AND RELIABLE COUNTING OF INCIDENCE OF 'RAPE'

Fieldwork conducted in Sri Lanka with the Human Rights Documentation Coalition examined human rights violations using controlled vocabularies. The category of 'rape' provides an example of the methodology to turn qualitative descriptions of acts into quantitative measures.

The category 'rape' is subject to a definition, a clarification of what acts are included and excluded within the definition (boundary condition), counting rules and an example designed to help researchers understand the application of the standard.

- *Definition* – forceful/unwilling intercourse/penetration on any individual by another individual's genitals regardless of gender under intimidation, threat, fraud, lies, intoxication or while in custody.
- *Definition of perpetrators* – the act must be committed by a person or persons identified on the list of perpetrators which includes government agents, members of political parties, armed groups and organizations.
- *Boundary condition* – act must consist of vaginal or anal intercourse/ penetration. Definition excludes acts which are covered by terms 'sexual abuse' and 'genital abuse' which the controlled vocabulary defines separately.
- *Counting rule* – continuous and one perpetrator is one violation; continuous and multiple perpetrators is one violation; non-continuous and different perpetrators comprise multiple violations (each separate act of penetration constituting one violation).
- *Example* – a woman is gang-raped by three army personnel behind a security checkpoint; this is one violation.

The controlled vocabulary attempts to provide greater validity by defining with some clarity perpetrators of violations and acts that should be counted as 'rape' as well as those that should be excluded, namely acts falling within similar but different violation categories such as 'sexual abuse' or 'genital abuse'. While some terms in the definition remain unclear, such as 'forceful' and 'unwilling', the controlled vocabulary and coding process help to clarify and count what amounts to rape while excluding acts that might be confused with rape and, in this way, help to improve the validity of measurement.

Further, by defining 'rape' and other acts which should not be measured as 'rape' and by providing rules on counting, this helps coders standardize their quantification of qualitative data.

Source: Silva, R., 'On Ensuring a High Level of Data Quality when Documenting Human Rights Violations to Support Research in the Origin and Cause of Human Rights Violations' (2002) Joint Statistical Meetings – Social Statistics Section 3242, 3242–3251.

possible.[53] As coding procedures become more generalized, the risk of omitting violations or of including acts that would not amount to violations if a strict coding procedure applied, increases. This might lead to an inexact national measurement of the rights situation and, in turn, to an inexact and invalid inter-country measurement.

In relation to opinion and perception survey approaches, data validity relies considerably on the design of the survey – the identification of its purpose, relevant definitions, questions and structure – which occurs primarily prior to the data collection stage. For example, the survey must identify common ground as a starting point for the measurement exercise so that the context is clear to respondents, and the content of the survey must cover all dimensions of a particular right.[54] The right to a fair trial or the right to health are dense and include several freedoms and entitlements as well as a range of obligations on the state. To be valid, the survey should cover all dimensions of the right as defined in human rights law or alternatively those dimensions which are specifically of relevance to the survey.[55]

Data from secondary sources is very important for much human rights measurement, particularly for 'expert-scoring' and 'official data' approaches. Yet this raises significant data validity challenges. First, some data relevant to human rights, such as prison data, might rely on different classifications than those relied upon under human rights law. Secondly, most socio-economic indicators have been developed to measure the provision of public goods and services – not human rights – and so do not rely on human rights definitions in the collection of data.[56] In relation to 'expert-scoring approaches', human rights data might have been collected according to different definitions from country-to-country. To ensure validity of measurement in such cases, researchers would have to undertake tedious re-analysis and application of definitions to ensure data validity which might not be possible.[57] In some cases, researches must balance measurement validity with other concerns such as comprehensive coverage of countries.[58] Transparency in the concepts being measured and

---

[53]   Landman and Carvalho (n 10) 89.
[54]   Ibid. 97.
[55]   Ibid. 97.
[56]   For example, the Human Development Index measures human development by reference to life expectancy, literacy, gross enrolment ratio and per capita GDP while the United Nations Declaration on the Right to Development includes not only economic, social and cultural development but also political development as an aspect of human development (article 1). See also Landman and Cavalho (n 10) 111–112.
[57]   Goldstein (n 38) 47.
[58]   Landman and Carvalho (n 10) 89.

their definitions, the data sources, as well as the methodology for data analysis are particularly important to demonstrate the extent to which measurement is valid.[59]

The choice of indicators is also important in ensuring measurement validity. For example, the Freedom House 'Freedom in the World' index claims to evaluate 'freedom' in 195 countries and 15 territories on a 1–7 scale through a methodology derived from the Universal Declaration of Human Rights.[60] The methodology clarifies that the measurement of freedom covers only civil and political liberties. However, this restricted definition of 'freedom' is fundamentally inconsistent with the Universal Declaration, which clearly understands 'freedom' broadly to cover not only freedom from fear but also freedom from want. This choice of freedom-related indicators calls into question the validity of its measure of 'freedom' which, if it did include measures of freedom from want, might result in quite different findings. Comparative scales such as the Political Terror Scale or the Societal Violence Scale might improve validity by focusing measurement explicitly on human rights terms such as 'liberty and security of the person', 'enforced disappearance' or 'torture', thus connecting measurement more clearly to human rights and universally accepted definitions.[61]

Reliability

A measure is reliable if 'measurements are consistent when repeated by the same observer or by different observers using the same instrument' and is often tested through repetition of the measurement.[62] Reliability can relate to two aspects of the measurement: the observer (the person doing the measuring) and the measurement instrument. The same observer repeating a measurement helps to test the reliability of the measurement instrument. Having two observers repeat the measurement helps to test whether the observers are reliable.

Reliability is closely related to validity. For example, the greater the

---

[59]   Cingranelli and Richards (n 21) 413.

[60]   See 'Methodology' (2015) <https://freedomhouse.org/report/freedom-world-2015/methodology> accessed 23 September 2015.

[61]   See Political Terror Scale (n.d.) <http://www.politicalterrorscale.org> accessed 29 November 2015.

[62]   Barsh (n 34) 94. Cingranelli and Richards define a reliable indicator as 'one whereupon different people apply an identical measurement procedure to identical information and come up with identical scores'. Cingranelli and Richards (n 21) 403.

number of categories of acts in the controlled vocabulary – such as rape, physical assault, torture, sexual abuse – the more precise the measurement. Yet this poses a higher risk to the reliability of the measurement, as the likelihood of inter-coder testing leading to coder disagreement is higher.[63] Where the categories of violations are fewer, the margin of coding error is probably lower; however the measurement precision suffers. Similarly, where ordinal or cardinal scales include more score points, the reliability of indicators risks being lower.[64]

For events-based and expert-scoring approaches, reliability is generally tested using inter-coder testing. If two or more observers code the qualitative data using the controlled vocabulary in the same way, the measurement is reliable. Using the example referred to in Box 13.1, if two coders apply the controlled vocabulary to the same testimonies and arrive at the same number of cases of rape, the measurement is more likely to be reliable. If the coders arrive at different results, there could be an issue of either observer or instrument reliability.

In comparison with events-based approaches, expert-scoring approaches tend to have less developed coding procedures.[65] Further, inter-reliability testing in practice tends to be uneven although there are exceptions such as the CIRI Human Rights Project.[66] Box 13.2 provides an illustration of reliability testing for the CIRI Human Rights Project.

Expert-scoring measurements face particular challenges to the reliability of measurement, as the measurement often depends on highly subjective expert judgment based on secondary data in order to ascertain a score. Bollen illustrates the range of implicit and explicit influences that can play on assessors. For example, an assessor might be physically threatened by government agents for having participated in a rating process which might affect his or her judgment for subsequent measurement exercises. Alternatively, an assessor might have political biases that could influence ratings or an economic interest that could affect an evaluation (for example, where he or she is funded by an organization with an interest in the rating). Or the relationship of the assessor's country to the country whose rights compliance is being measured could also subconsciously influence the assessor's ratings.

Beyond the technical reliability of expert-scoring approaches, the

---

[63]   Silva (n 51) 3245.
[64]   Cingranelli and Richards (n 21) 404.
[65]   Landman and Carvalho (n 10) 89.
[66]   Cingranelli and Richards (n 21) 403, 404.
[67]   Bollen (n 43) 201.
[68]   Ibid.

BOX 13.2   TESTING FOR RELIABILITY OF EXPERT-
SCORING MEASUREMENTS

The CIRI project provides an example of reliability testing for expert-scoring measurement. The project has a coding guide which is over 100 pages. Each indicator
in the guide includes a definition of the concept being measured, the process for
measurement, instructions on how to transform the qualitative data from the source
(such as the US State Department reports) to numeric scores, and directions on
where to find information for each indicator under consideration as well as country
examples.[67] At least two trained coders examine each indicator. If no agreement
exists, the CIRI project staff decides on the score.[68] Inter-coder reliability is publicly
reported.

---

question arises whether the ranking of countries according to scales can
really result in a reliable measurement of something as complex and
country-specific as human rights. For example, does the ranking of '2'
to Australia, '3' to Albania and '5' to Algeria for societal violence really
provide a reliable, meaningful or indeed useful indication to help analyze
human rights problems and identify human rights strategies related to
security of the person?[69]

For 'official data approaches' and 'opinion and perception surveys',
reliability depends significantly on the structure of the data collection
instrument, generally a survey. When the questions used in a survey elicit
the same type of information each time they are used under the same
conditions, the survey demonstrates a high degree of reliability.[70] If the
wrong questions are asked over again and provide the same answers, this
demonstrates high reliability but low validity. If the questions are closely
linked to the concept being measured, but yield highly varying responses,
there could be high validity but low reliability.[71] One way to check for
reliability of official data and survey results is to combine measurement
approaches. The Human Rights Measurement Project in the UK has supplemented official data on domestic abuse and sexual violence – known to
have underestimated its prevalence – with a general population survey.[72]

Transparency is very important as a means of promoting reliable human

---

[69]   See e.g. The Societal Violence Scale on the website of the Political Terror
Scale <http://www.politicalterrorscale.org/Data/Download.html> accessed 23
September 2015.
[70]   <http://www.relevantinsights.com/validity-and-reliability> accessed 30
December 2014.
[71]   Ibid.
[72]   Langford and Fukuda-Par (n 9) 235.

rights measurement in relation to all four measurement approaches. Transparency of the data sources, the data collection instrument and the results of reliability testing can help demonstrate reliability.

ANALYSIS, ARGUMENTS, PROPOSITIONS

Ensuring Indicators Reflect the Complexity of Human Rights

The choice of indicators is an important step to ensure that data, once collected, can be used for a valid, reliable and meaningful measurement. As noted above, it is important, particularly for reasons of validity, to adopt a framework for human rights indicators that reflects the complexity of human rights and is based in internationally agreed human rights norms.

The OHCHR indicator framework provides an example which seeks to measure state commitment to human rights, the effort made to fulfill those rights and the extent to which rights are enjoyed – the commitment, effort, results framework.[73] At the conceptual level, the framework links the indicator to the legal standard by identifying the 'attributes' of the indicator, thus encouraging measurement validity.[74] For example, the attributes of the indicator framework on the right to health are: reproductive health; child mortality and health care; natural and occupational environment; prevention treatment and control of disease; and accessibility of health facilities and essential medicines. With minor adaptations, these attributes flow directly from the sub-articles of article 12 of the International Covenant on Economic, Social and Cultural Rights.

At the level of implementation of the right, the framework identifies three categories to measure the extent to which states are meeting their human rights obligations. These are:

(1)   *Structural indicators* – reflect the institutional framework relevant to the right in question and measure the commitment of states to human rights. Structural indicators might range from ratification of treaties to recognition of rights in national laws to the institutional framework for protecting the right.[75]

(2)   *Process indicators* – illustrate the effort that states put into meeting their obligations to respect, protect and fulfill the right. Process

---

[73]   OHCHR (n 7) 33.
[74]   Ibid. 30.
[75]   Ibid. 34.

indicators help to bridge the gap between commitment and result as, without effort, commitments rarely translate into improved enjoyment of human rights.[76]

(3)   *Outcome indicators* – reflect the actual enjoyment of human rights – the results or outcome. Socio-economic data can be useful as proxy measures for outcome indicators.[77]

These three levels of indicators are intrinsically linked and reflect important aspects of the human rights treaty framework. It is understandable if measurement exercises focus on outcome indicators as these provide an illustration of the level of rights enjoyment, giving the impression of getting to the heart of the matter. However, human rights treaties not only identify rights but also the duty-bearers who have obligations to respect, protect, and fulfill rights. Duty-bearers must be committed to meeting their responsibilities – measured through structural indicators – and they must also meet these commitments by taking certain steps or avoiding certain actions. Understanding rights enjoyment as well as the commitments and actions of duty-bearers provides a fuller picture of the human rights situation.

The OHCHR framework is not without its critics. Sally Engle Merry's contribution to this volume warns that the structure/process/outcome framework adopted by the OHCHR displaces the respect/protect/fulfill framework which was developed in the context of economic, social and cultural rights but which today is widely applied to help understand obligations in relation to all rights. Langford and Fukuda-Par have noted that the structural/process/outcome framework may overlook the relationship between these indicator categories, noting that obligations of progressive realization of economic, social and cultural rights are properly categorized as both a process and result.[78]

As human rights analysis should identify not only rights-holders' enjoyment of their rights but also the extent to which duty-bearers are meeting their obligations, those applying the OHCHR framework should be conscious of choosing indicators adapted to the research task at hand and appropriate to reflect states' respect for the three levels of obligations, respect/protect/fulfill. Thus, a structural indicator on the existence of budget allocations to support the policy framework related to detention provides information on the extent to which the State is meeting its obliga-

---

[76]   Ibid. 36.
[77]   Ibid. 37.
[78]   Langford and Fukuda-Par (n 9) 229.

tion to *fulfill* the right to liberty and security of person. The outcome indicator on number of detentions per 100,000 based on a court order can help draw conclusions as to whether the state is *respecting* the right to liberty and security of person. Indicators might have to be analyzed together in order to understand state compliance with some obligations.

Moreover, the OHCHR indicator framework need not be treated as a one-size-fits all framework but one that can be adapted to the legal requirements and available data sources. Langford and Fuduka-Par note how the Human Rights Measurement Framework has used the OHCHR's indicator framework in building up a quantitative evidence database in England, Scotland and Wales on human rights. The project used the OHCHR framework as illustrative indicators but engaged in extensive consultation with national actors to map laws and data sources to adopt better-fitting indicators.[79]

Connecting with the Data Revolution of the Post-2015 Development Agenda

Given the important role of socio-economic and administrative data as a source of information to assess human rights situations, one means of improving human rights measurement could be through the improvement of this data, making it more relevant and reliable for human rights research. The post-2015 development agenda provides an opportunity for such an endeavor.

In preparation for implementation of the new Sustainable Development agenda, the United Nations Secretary-General established an Independent Expert Advisory Group on the Data Revolution for Sustainable Development, which launched its report in November 2014.[80] The report proposed a UN-led effort to mobilize the data for sustainable development and set out basic principles for a data revolution, including data quality and integrity, data disaggregation, data timeliness, data transparency, data usability, data protection, data governance and independence, data resources and capacity, and data rights (the right to be counted, the right to due process and the right to privacy).[81] To move the data revolution

---

[79]   Ibid. 233.

[80]   United Nations, *A World that Counts: Mobilising the Data Revolution for Sustainable Development.* Report of the Independent Expert Advisory Group on a Data Revolution for Sustainable Development (November 2014).

[81]   IEAG launches report on data revolution for sustainable development <http://sd.iisd.org/news/ieag-launches-report-on-data-revolution-for-sustainable-development/> accessed 21 January 2015.

forward, the Secretary-General proposed the establishment of a comprehensive program of action on data including a global data partnership for sustainable development data that would mobilize and coordinate actions required to make the data revolution serve sustainable development.[82]

The inclusion of the data revolution in the new development agenda provides important opportunities to advance human rights measurement. Human rights practitioners can contribute to the call to build capacities to collect disaggregated data, and in doing so, help improve data to measure respect for the principles of non-discrimination and equality. As specific goals and targets relate to human rights – such as achieving gender equality;[83] ending abuse, exploitation, trafficking, violence, and torture against children; and ensuring equal access to justice for all[84] – human rights practitioners can use the monitoring of goals to engage development actors in collecting explicitly human rights data which can be relevant for other human rights measurement exercises. More broadly, human rights practitioners can promote a rights-based approach to statistics that not only produces more human rights relevant data but also promotes respect for human rights in the collection and analysis of data – including the right to be counted, the right to an identity, the right to information, the right to privacy, due process and principles of non-discrimination, equality and free and informed consent, as well as respect for the rights of statisticians.[85]

Standing National Coordination Bodies for Reporting and Follow-up

The various monitoring functions included in regional and United Nations treaties and the broader human rights protection machinery require the generation of a significant amount of human rights data. For example, the United Nations treaties require state parties to report periodically to committees of independent experts, and all states must subject their human rights performance by submitting reports to the Human Rights Council under its Universal Periodic Review procedure. The Human Rights Council also appoints Special Rapporteurs on particular themes – such as health or extra-judicial killings – as well as on particular countries.

---

[82]   United Nations, *The Road to Dignity by 2030: Ending Poverty, Transforming all Lives and Protecting the Planet*, Synthesis Report of the Secretary-General on the post-2015 Sustainable Development Agenda (December 2014, A/69/700) paras 143–144.

[83]   Ibid. goal 5.

[84]   Ibid. goal 17.

[85]   United Nations (n 82) 23.

Regional human rights systems include similar mechanisms and procedures requiring measurement and reporting.

As a result, all states have a significant role in collecting and analyzing human rights data and publishing the results of this analysis. In order to professionalize and streamline efforts at national data collection and analysis, some states have established standing national bodies on reporting and follow-up to human rights recommendations.[86] Through the establishment of such permanent bodies, human rights knowledge can be better managed, sustainable systems of data collection and analysis can be put in place and coordination between government departments and with civil society can be optimized.

Improving Validity and Reliability Though Transparency and Training

Transparency in methodology design and implementation can be an important way to encourage reliability – by knowing that methodology design and implementation is subject to public scrutiny – and to promote validity. In particular, public disclosure of coding methods for events and expert-scoring approaches promotes accountability, demonstrates that the measure does actually measure the norm it is meant to measure and promotes reliability for others wishing to replicate data.[87] The CIRI project provides an example of transparency as set out in Box 13.2.[88] The project has placed its coding guide and publicly available source material on-line so that users can check the reliability of scores.[89]

Training of human rights professionals in research methods is another way to improve reliability and validity of measurement. Human rights practice tends to cover many fields, from law to political and social sciences and increasingly to economics. Practitioners generally do not have experience across all these fields. There is a need to develop the competencies of human rights practitioners, by encouraging a broader range of professionals to work in the field of human rights such as social scientists and economists, but also by broadening human rights education through the encouragement of interdisciplinary training. As Sano and Thelle indicate, there is a need for evidence-based human rights research to help bring greater attention to the economic and social realities of people living in

---

[86]   United Nations, *OHCHR Office Management Plan 2014–17: Working for Your Rights* <http://www2.ohchr.org/english/ohchrreport2014_2017/omp_web_version/index.html#/changing-the-lives-of-people> accessed 23 September 2015.

[87]   Landman and Carvalho (n 10) 50.

[88]   Cingranelli and Richards (n 21) 413.

[89]   Ibid.

vulnerable or marginalized situations. This requires the development of the competencies of human rights scholars so that they are equipped with social science techniques to collect and analyze data beyond the current focus on secondary sources and legal texts.[90]

CONCLUSION

Human rights measurement is an integral part of human rights monitoring and its importance to the human rights agenda is only growing, whether to assist the work of international courts and commissions of inquiry, to give voice to those who have suffered violations, or to examine the impacts of laws and policies on human rights. However, for measurement to be meaningful, reliable and valid, it must be methodologically sound. Many concepts related to human rights, such as 'democracy' or 'poverty', can be subjective and open to many and varied meanings. By grounding measurement in the internationally and regionally agreed human rights norms, this helps provide a level of objectivity to definitions and a better structure for analysis. The use of clear coding procedures can help strengthen the reliability and validity of measurement as can testing data through the use of reliability testing or by supplementing data with data from other sources. Professionalizing human rights measurement, such as through the establishment of permanent coordination bodies at national level, can also assist. To move forward, it will be important that professionals with knowledge of human rights norms and mechanisms such as treaty bodies become more involved in measurement exercises. This requires the broadening of cross-disciplinary dialogue – between law, political and social science, and economics – as well as across professional areas – between human rights, development, and peace and security.

FURTHER READING

Barsh, R.L., 'Measuring Human Rights: Problems of Methodology and Purpose' (1993) 15 Human Rights Quarterly 87
Claude, R. and Thomas Jabine (eds), *Human Rights and Statistics* (University of Pennsylvania Press 1992)
Coomans, F., Fred Grünfeld and Menno Kamminga (eds), *Methods of Human Rights Research* (Intersentia 2009)

---

[90]   Hans-Otto Sano and Hatla Thelle, 'The Need for Evidence-based Human Rights Research' in Fons Coomans, Fred Grünfeld and Menno Kamminga (eds), *Methods of Human Rights Research* (Intersentia 2009) 109.

King, G., Robert Keohane and Sidney Verba, *Designing Social Inquiry, Scientific Inference in Qualitative Research* (Princeton University Press 1994)

Landman, T., *Studying Human Rights* (Routledge 2006)

Landman, T. and Edzia Carvalho, *Measuring Human Rights* (Routledge 2010)

Office of the High Commissioner for Human Rights, *Human Rights Indicators: A Guide to Measurement and Implementation*, United Nations 2012 (H/PUB/12/5)

Sano, O. and Hatla Thelle, 'The Need for Evidence-based Human Rights Research' in Fons Coomans, Fred Grünfeld and Menno Kamminga (eds), *Methods of Human Rights Research* (Intersentia 2009)

BIBLIOGRAPHY

Adcock, R. and David Collier, 'Measurement Validity: A Shared Standard for Qualitative and Quantitative Research' (2001) 95 American Political Science Review 529

Apodaca, C., 'Measuring the Progressive Realization of Economic and Social Rights' in Shareen Hertel and Lanse Minkler (eds), *Economic Rights: Conceptual, Measurement, and Policy Issues* (CUP 2007)

Ball, P. and Jana Asher, 'Statistics and Slobodan: Using Data Analysis and Statistics in the War Crimes Trial of Former President Milosevic' (2002) 15 Chance 17

Barsh, R.L. 'Measuring Human Rights: Problems of Methodology and Purpose' (1993) 15 Human Rights Quarterly 87

Bollen, K. 'Political Rights and Political Liberties in Nations: An Evaluation of Human Rights Measures, 1950 to 1984' in Richard Claude and Thomas Jabine (eds), *Human Rights and Statistics* (University of Pennsylvania Press 1992)

Cingranelli, D. and David Richards, 'The Cingranelli and Richards (CIRI) Human Rights Data Project' (2010) 32 Human Rights Quarterly 395

Claude, R. and Thomas Jabine, 'Exploring Human Rights Issues with Statistics' in Richard Claude and Thomas Jabine (eds), *Human Rights and Statistics* (University of Pennsylvania Press 1992) 5

Danish Institute for Human Rights, *Human Rights Compliance Assessment (HRCA): Quick Check* (DIHR June 2006)

Goldstein, R.J. 'The Limitations of Using Quantitative Data in Studying Human Rights Abuses' in Richard Claude and Thomas Jabine (eds), *Human Rights and Statistics* (University of Pennsylvania Press 1992)

Gurr, T. and Barbara Harff, 'The Rights of Collectivities: Principles and Procedures in measuring the Human Rights Status of Communal and Political Groups' in Richard Claude and Thomas Jabine (eds), *Human Rights and Statistics* (University of Pennsylvania Press 1992)

Jensen, M., Marie Villumsen and Thomas Petersen, *The AAAQ Framework and the Right to Water: International Indicators for Availability, Accessibility, Acceptability and Quality*, Issue Paper for the AAAQ Toolbox (2014) Danish Institute for Human Rights

Kimenyi, M., 'Economic Rights, Human Development Effort, and Institutions' in Shareen Hertel and Lanse Minkler (eds), *Economic Rights: Conceptual, Measurement, and Policy Issues* (CUP 2007)

King, G., Robert Keohane and Sidney Verba, *Designing Social Inquiry: Scientific Inference in Qualitative Research* (Princeton University Press 1994)

Landman, T., *Studying Human Rights* (Routledge 2006)

Landman, T. and Edzia Carvalho, *Measuring Human Rights* (Routledge 2010)

Langford, M. and Sakiko Fakuda-Parr, 'The Turn to Metrics' (2012) 30 Nordic Journal of Human Rights 222

Office of the High Commissioner for Human Rights, *Human Rights Indicators: A Guide to Measurement and Implementation*, United Nations 2012 (H/PUB/12/5)

Physicians for Human Rights, *War Related Violence in Sierra Leone: A Population-Based*

Assessment, A Report for Physicians for Human Rights with the Support of the United Nations Assistance Mission in Sierra Leone, United States of America (2002)

Price, M., Anita Gohdes and Patrick Ball, *Updated Statistical Analysis of Documentation of Killings in the Syrian Arab Republic*, Commissioned by the Office of the UN High Commissioner for Human Rights, Human Rights Data Analysis Group, August 2014

Silva, R., 'On Ensuring a High Level of Data Quality when Documenting Human Rights Violations to Support Research in the Origin and Cause of Human Rights Violations' (2002) Joint Statistical Meetings – Social Statistics Section 3242

Sano, H.O. and Hatla Thelle, 'The Need for Evidence-based Human Rights Research', in Fons Coomans, Fred Grünfeld and Menno Kamminga (eds), *Methods of Human Rights Research* (Intersentia 2009)

United Nations, *A World that Counts: Mobilising the Data Revolution for Sustainable Development*. Report of the Independent Expert Advisory Group on a Data Revolution for Sustainable Development (November 2014)

United Nations, *The Road to Dignity by 2030: Ending Poverty, Transforming all Lives and Protecting the Planet*. Synthesis Report of the Secretary-General on the post-2015 Sustainable Development Agenda, December 2014, A/69/700

United Nations, *Transforming Our World: The 2030 Agenda for Sustainable Development* <https://sustainabledevelopment.un.org/content/documents/7891Transforming%20Our%20World.pdf>, accessed on 23 September 2015

Walker, S., *The Future of Human Rights Impact Assessment of Trade Agreements* (Intersentia 2009)

14. Methods of monitoring the right to food
Kirsteen Shields

INTRODUCTION

Just as geographers have set out to measure the world, human rights theorists set out to 'monitor' human rights. Human rights monitoring is an imprecise science, however, and rights evade definition let alone measurement. There are several inherent challenges associated with human rights monitoring that relate more broadly to data gathering generally. There are also specific challenges attached to each particular right. This chapter focuses on the methods attached to monitoring that right corporeal, intimate and essential to all of life: the right to food.

Across all rights monitoring, a general distinction can be made between monitoring for compliance and monitoring for performance, the latter being potentially broader and 'looser' than a focus on legal compliance. Specifically, in relation to the right to food, the practice of monitoring for performance can rely on and reinforce definitions of the right to food that vary in nature, ranging from an expansive right that is economic, social and cultural in nature to a narrow right that is essentially economic in scope. This chapter considers the methodological choices made when measuring the right to food and the relationship between these choices and the emergent definition of the right to food. The hypothesis that indicators may simplify complex rights situations to numerical figures is central to the analysis.

The chapter details the approach of the UN Food and Agriculture Organization (FAO) to monitoring the right to food as the most widespread and well-developed approach to monitoring. The chapter finds particular strength in the human rights-based approach to monitoring advocated by the FAO, which focuses on assessing the adequacy of structures surrounding the production of and access to food, rather than a focus on the more easily satisfied metrics of physical access and consumption. However, the chapter also highlights certain problems of existing approaches: the lack of legal obligations attached to monitoring and the potential for monitoring to inform and change the definition of the right. The chapter makes recommendations for improvement. The chapter also considers *how* to research monitoring practices in human rights – and secondly, how research knowledge can be essential to complement the blind spots in monitoring.

LOCATING THE RIGHT TO FOOD

The right to food stems from the Universal Declaration of Human Rights 1948, article 25, which recognizes the right to an adequate standard of living, including food. Subsequently, the International Covenant on Economic, Social and Cultural Rights (ICESCR) came into force in 1976 and contains a fundamental right of freedom from hunger[1] and a right to an adequate standard of living, incorporating a right to adequate food (widely shortened to 'a right to food'). General Comment No. 12 of the Committee on Economic, Social and Cultural Rights established that the right to food contained in the ICESCR covered two fundamental concepts: availability and accessibility.[2] As the General Comment explains, 'the right to food is realized when every man, woman and child, alone or in community with others has physical and economic access at all times to adequate food or means for its procurement'.[3] Asbjørn Eide has highlighted that the right to food is much more than a right to be fed, though this mistake is often made and serves to impede implementation.[4]

Monitoring takes on a special significance in relation to the right to food (and economic, social and cultural rights generally), as the right to food is essentially non-justiciable at the international level. In 2013, Uruguay became the tenth state to ratify the Optional Protocol to the International Covenant on Economic, Social and Cultural Rights,[5] which establishes complaint and inquiry mechanisms for the ICESCR for those states that have ratified the Protocol. This means that, for the vast majority of states who have not signed the Optional Protocol, the international provisions on the right to food cannot be relied upon as binding legal obligations in domestic courts. Some states have integrated the right to food into national

---

[1]   International Covenant on Economic, Social and Cultural Rights, 16 December 1966, United Nations, Treaty Series, Vol. 993, p. 3, article 11, para 2.

[2]   Committee on Economic, Social and Cultural Rights, 'General Comment 12: The Right to Adequate Food' (E/C.12/1999/5 1999), para 8.

[3]   Ibid. para 6.

[4]   Asbjørn Eide, *The Human Right to Adequate Food and Freedom from Hunger* (Food and Agriculture Organization (FAO) 1998).

[5]   Optional Protocol to the International Covenant on Economic, Social and Cultural Rights, resolution/adopted by the General Assembly, 5 March 2009, A/RES/63/117.

constitutions, creating domestic avenues of justiciability, but the majority of states have not. Some states have creatively interpreted other provisions in the national constitution to integrate the right to food, for example the right to life clause in the Constitution of India (article 21) was used as an instrument to ensure that school children were entitled to one hot meal per day.[6] The non-justiciable nature of these provisions creates a lack of enforcement, which is compounded by a lack of accountability. Lack of accountability derives from the fact that the UN ICESCR applies directly only to states. Corporations and international institutions are not directly subject to the provisions. In the absence of enforcement and accountability mechanisms, monitoring therefore serves as an important substitute mechanism that supports advocacy of the right to food, rather than enforcement or accountability directly.

PROBLEMS OF MONITORING: GENERAL AND SPECIFIC TO THE RIGHT TO FOOD

As demonstrated elsewhere in this volume, there are several general challenges associated with human rights monitoring. Most generally, researchers are still often slow to acknowledge their own internal and inevitable ideological leanings and constraints. Human rights researchers in particular do not always acknowledge their own research methodology, and in some cases try to deny the inherently political nature of human rights work.[7] This blind-spot can skew vision at the level of individual researchers, but the impact is all the more pervasive when it concerns large-scale monitoring of human rights situations undertaken by human rights and development institutions.

There are several difficulties specifically associated with the methodology of monitoring the right to food. These may be divided into broad categories: who monitors and what is the object being monitored. First, *who monitors?* In states where the right is non-justiciable (which remains to be the majority of states) there is little direct incentive for states to do so as violations will not result in remedial legal action. Consequently, advocacy is the key means of redress. It is often civil

---

[6]   *People's Union for Civil Liberties v Union of India, Writ Petition (Civil) No. 196 of 2001 (India)* (28 November 2001 interim order).

[7]   As discussed in Fons Coomans, Fred Grunfeld and Menno T. Kamminga, 'Methods of Human Rights Research: A Primer' (2010) 32 Human Rights Quarterly 179, 179–186. See further Fons Coomans, Fred Grunfeld and Menno T., Kamminga (eds), *Methods of Human Rights Research* (Intersentia 2009).

society organizations that take on responsibility for monitoring the right to food bringing problems of reliability and more acutely, in a time of austerity, consistency.

Secondly, *who and what is monitored?* There are general and specific problems of data gathering that affect the right to food. In spite of poverty reduction strategies and policies in many countries, the food-insecure and vulnerable are often poorly identified, and the reasons for their food insecurity are not reflected in policy and program designs. An FAO reports that, 'Pro-poor policies and strategies often lack well-defined target groups mainly because the development paradigms that are used to shape such policies are not people-centred'.[8] Arguably, even where people-centered paradigms are at play, efforts to address marginality and vulnerability in representation are generally limited and not sufficient to create consultations that are genuinely representative. Thirdly, barriers to food access are often implicated in other legal structures and not readily identified. Fourthly, and relatedly, in identifying obstacles, responsibility may be attributed to unaccountable actors.[9]

USE OF INDICATORS

More generally, as stated previously, ideological blind-spots can have a pervasive impact when it concerns large-scale monitoring by human rights and development institutions of human rights situations. In the search to find metrics to attach to international development programs, the methodological choices made are critical. This is particularly so when qualitative and quantitative data on human rights are combined to generate statistical '*indicators*'. In a general sense, indicators hold potential to be useful, but they can also be misleading. Meg Davis, senior human rights advisor at The Global Fund to Fight Aids, Tuberculosis and Malaria comments:

> Human rights indicators don't fix problems. They often bring bad news. But they do focus the mind on action. A good human rights indicator is an advocacy

---

[8]   FAO, 'Book 2: Methods to Monitor the Human Right to Adequate Food' (Volume I) (2009) 27.

[9]   Jean-Martin Bauer, Koffi Akakpo, Marie Enlund and Silvia Passeri, 'A New Tool in the Toolbox: Using Mobile Text for Food Security Surveys in a Conflict Setting' (2014) 20 February 2014. Humanitarian Practice Network blog <http://odihpn.org/blog/a-new-tool-in-the-toolbox-using-mobile-text-for-food-security-surveys-in-a-conflict-setting/>.

tool that promotes transparency, accountability and action – globally, region-ally, and nationally. A weak human rights indicator – or a good one that is under-resourced and buried in noise – is actually a barrier to accountability.[10]

By using indicators, entrenched inequalities may be presented as isolated statistics and not the result of relationships in which we are implicit.[11] A key problem that pervades monitoring is the loss of qualitative contextual data that occurs when complex economic, social and cultural situations are reduced to statistics. In this respect, indicators do more than translate experience into numerical representations; they also filter and simplify the lived experience in the process.[12] Situations that may be comparable in numerical form may differ wildly in reality, and so might the appropriate solution therefore. The presentation of complex rights situations in numer-ical form can be effective, 'seductive'[13] even, as it may assert the evidence as objective fact which carries a certain authority.[14] Their purpose being to

---

[10] Meg Davis, 'UNAIDS: Bold Human Rights Targets Need Better Monitoring' <https://www.opendemocracy.net/openglobalrights/meg-davis/unaids-bold-human-rights-targets-need-better-monitoring> accessed 27 July 2015.

[11] Drawing on a survey in the *New York Times*, the *Washington Post* and the *Economist* of four major indicators – Human Development Index, Transparency International's Corruption Perception Index, Freedom House's Freedom in the World indicator and the World Bank's Doing Business Index – Davis, Kingsbury and Merry concluded that, 'after a few years, the indicator is presented simply as a fact that describes a country's situation, with virtually no discussion about the source of the data or the nature of the indicator itself'. In Kevin E. Davis, Benedict Kingsbury and Sally Engle Merry, 'Indicators as a Technology of Global Governance' (2010) 2 IILJ Working Paper 1, 20.

[12] Mary Poovey explains: 'Numbers have become the bedrock of systematic knowledge because they seem neutral and descriptive. The reality that numbers are not free of interpretation but instead embody theoretical assumptions about what should be counted, how to understand material reality, and how quantifica-tion contributes to systematic knowledge about the world, has been obscured. It is a distinctive feature of modernity that numbers appear as an objective descrip-tion of reality outside interpretation.' Mary Poovey, *A History of the Modern Fact: Problems of Knowledge in the Sciences of Wealth and Society* (University of Chicago Press 1998) xii. Cited in Benedict Kingsbury, Sally Engle Merry and Kevin E. Davis (eds), *The Quiet Power of Indicators: Measuring Governance, Corruption, and Rule of Law* (CUP 2015) 2.

[13] Sally Engle Merry, *The Seductions of Quantification: Measuring Human Rights, Gender Violence and Sex Trafficking* (Chicago Series in Law and Society 2016).

[14] For example, Davis, Kingsbury and Merry elaborate, 'In this numerical form, such knowledge carries a distinctive authority that shifts configurations and uses of power and of counter-power. This transformation reflects, but also con-tributes to, changes in decision-making structures and processes. Simplification

simplify, indicators do not generally support variation and particulariza-
tion of context-specific responses.

An example of the manipulation of statistics is the revision of hunger estimates to accelerate apparent progress towards the Millennial Development
Goals, as researched and represented by Colin David Butler.[15] Between
1990 and 1996 the target for reducing global hunger set by the Millennium
Development Goals was revised from reducing a 'fixed number' of the
hungry people in the world to 'halving' the number of hungry people globally. This has had the effect of changing the reduction target of 420 million
(reduction by fixed number) to a more easily achieved reduction target of
569 million, the equivalent of 'halving' the world's population living in
hunger. This was combined with a revision in 2012 of the 1990 baseline
hunger estimate to 21% higher than had been previously estimated, in so
doing shifting the target of halving world hunger from 569 to 687 million.
This 'two way revision' in estimates created an 'easier to reach' target.
Butler's graph demonstrating the revision in statistics is reproduced below.
Butler also points out that there has been not only quantitative but also
qualitative reformulation of world hunger, 'The redefinition of hunger
used by the FAO since 2011 has made progress towards the MDG target
appear better than was the case in the years leading to 2011. This progress
has been widely reported, even celebrated.'[16]

Such 'moving of goalposts' is pervasive across the human rights and
development field. The Human Development Index has encountered
similar criticism and its creator has responded that the index's simplicity
makes it a useful measure for some policy purposes but that it should be
supplemented by other, more detailed socio-economic indicators.[17] Davis,
Kingsbury and Merry claim that the trend of production of indicators,
that they describe as 'technologies of global governance',[18] can result in
public law and political principles such as transparency and accountability

---

(or reductionism) is central to the appeal (and probably the impact) of indicators'.
In Davis et al. (n 11) 4.

[15]   Colin David Butler, 'Revised Hunger Estimates Accelerate Apparent
Progress Towards the MDG Hunger Target' (2015) 5 Global Food Security 19
19–24.

[16]   Ibid. 24: 'Revised hunger estimates accelerate apparent progress towards
the MDG hunger target'. As Butler predicts, a new set of nutritional development
targets to be captured in the Sustainable Development Goals has since been established; see The UN Report of the High Level Panel of Eminent Persons on the
Post-2015 Development Agenda, *A New Global Partnership: Eradicate Poverty and
Transform Economies Through Sustainable Development* (United Nations 2013).

[17]   Davis et al. (n 11) 24.

[18]   See generally Kingsbury et al. (n 12).

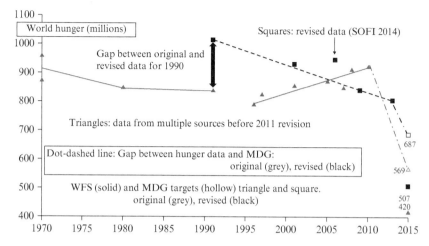

Notes: The small triangles show global hunger numbers and targets using data reported by the FAO in its SOFI (State of Food Insecurity) reports between 1999 and 2010. The small square points refer to FAO data reported in 2014. The datapoints reported in SOFI 2012 and 2013 are similar to these but not shown for simplicity. The solid line connects key datapoints reported before 2011. A decline in hunger between 1970 and 1996 is evident, followed by an obvious increase until 2010, the last year for which data using the pre-2011 method are available. The spike in hunger to over a billion in 2009 (reported in SOFI 2009 and 2010) is not shown, for simplicity. In contrast, the dashed line shows a declining trend between 1990 and 2013 (the most recent point for which revised data are available).

Figure 14.1   World hunger (millions) and 2015 hunger targets, 1970–2015

being lost in the statistics. The extent to which this represents a clash of public and private law values is an increasingly recurrent question. Space prevents a proper exploration of that angle here, but it will probably be a subject of further research.

THE RELATIONSHIP BETWEEN INDICATORS, MONITORING AND DEFINITION OF THE RIGHT TO FOOD

Sally Engle Merry succinctly demonstrates the role of indicators in producing knowledge and shaping definitions:

One of the critical ways an indicator produces knowledge is by announcing what it measures, such as 'rule of law' or 'poverty.' Neither of these categories is self-evident. . ...How indicators are named and who decides what they represent are fundamental to the way an indicator produces knowledge.[19]

Variation in methods of measuring the right to adequate food can be appropriate in response to the varied contexts to be measured but this variation or lack of standardization also creates risk and opportunity. This is particularly significant since variations in measurement of the right to food can have implications for the market and market actors. For example, if food is understood purely as a commodity, the right to food is subject to similar commodification. If the wider dimensions of culture, environment and identity are included in the analysis, the right to food becomes a richer entitlement with potential to impact power structures.

To demonstrate what is meant by the commodification of the right to food, FIAN International, the Food and Information Action Network based in Geneva and Heidelberg, provides useful documentation. In 2013 FIAN published three key case studies on the privatization of food and nutrition projects.[20] It presents the World Bank's 'Scaling Up Nutrition' (SUN) project, designed to create policy to combat malnutrition. One member of the SUN's Lead Group is 'The Global Alliance for Improved Nutrition' (GAIN). GAIN claims to address malnutrition but FIAN also reported that it states that it 'strives to facilitate the opening up of markets for its 600 partner companies (among others, Danone, Pepsico, Coca Cola, Britannia)'.[21] FIAN reports that 'together with its baby food company members, GAIN has been pushing for WHO/FAO global food standards to be weakened so as to allow marketing of a whole new range of fortified products for infants and young children'.[22]

Former Special Rapporteur on the right to food, Olivier De Schutter, has

---

[19]   Sally Engle Merry, 'Measuring the World: Indicators, Human Rights, and Global Governance' (2011) 52(Supplementary Issue 3) Current Anthropology s83.

[20]   *Right to Food and Nutrition Watch 2013: Alternatives and Resistant to Policies that Generate Hunger* (FIAN 2013).

[21]   See GAIN's 'Business Alliance Members' <www.gainhealth.org/partner ships/businessalliance/member> accessed 27 July 2015.

[22]   FIAN (n 20) 22. Consequently GAIN's application for NGO status at the WHO was subject to scrutiny and apparently reorganization of GAIN has been undertaken, or at least of their website. FIAN reports that the WHO's Executive Board decided to, 'postpone consideration of the application for admission into official relations from The Global Alliance for Improved Nutrition to the Executive Board's 134th session, and requested that the following information be provided to the Board through its Standing Committee on Nongovernmental Organizations: information concerning the nature and extent of the Alliance's links with the global food industry, and the position of the Alliance with regard to its support and advocacy of WHO's nutrition policies, including infant feeding

warned SUN that it must not dismiss explicitly aligning its initiatives with human rights, including the right to food, i.e. SUN must not 'overlook the entitlements that have been established under international law for women, children, minorities, refugees and internally displaced persons, and other groups that may be subjected to marginalization and discrimination'.[23] In so doing, De Schutter directly addresses the risk that new indicators may present as progress or successes developments that do not integrate human rights and which operate under different principles altogether.

That the right to food does not consist purely of the satisfaction of hunger or the fulfillment of a certain level of nutrition is reflected in the codification of the right. The original codification of the right to food has been interpreted to incorporate an understanding of the right to include qualitative values of nutrition and culture in the nature of food. The United Nations Committee on Economic, Social and Cultural Rights in General Comment No. 12 on the Right to Food, states that:

> Food is considered 'adequate' when three conditions are fulfilled. These are:
>
> - Daily food intake meets all nutritional requirements, quantitatively (energy content) and qualitatively (protein, vitamins and minerals content).
> - The food is safe for human beings to eat and does not cause any disease.
> - The food is culturally acceptable by those who consume it.[24]

Without certain safeguards around the monitoring process the opportunity for right to food violations to translate into quick markets for 'fake foods' increases. In particular, a key safeguard should be that monitoring applies to the full scope of the right to food, comprising the social, cultural and economic dimensions of the right to produce culturally appropriate food. A focus on monitoring the right to food only as the right to consume or as an economic right misses opportunities to address the root causes which lead to food insecurity. Just as distributing food aid and food banks signify a failure of food security, so too in relation to monitoring the right to food, monitoring access to food aid signifies that the right to food has already been violated.

---

and marketing of complementary foods'. Claudio Schuftan and Ted Greiner, 'The Scaling Up Nutrition (SUN) Initiative' in FIAN (n 20) 22.

[23] United Nations General Assembly, *Compilation Prepared by the Office of the United Nations High Commissioner for Human Rights, in Accordance with Paragraph 10 of Human Rights Council Resolution 16/22*, (26 December 2011) cited in FIAN (n 20).

[24] Committee on Economic, Social and Cultural Rights, 'General Comment 12' (n 2).

The following analysis seeks to establish to what extent the FAO's approach to monitoring is inclusive of these three aspects of the right to food (of nutrition, safety and culture) and how it meets the challenges of 'who monitors?' and 'what and who is monitored?' before considering 'what is not monitored?' in this approach.

CASE STUDY: THE FAO METHOD OF MONITORING THE RIGHT TO FOOD

The most developed literature on the monitoring of the right to food comes from FAO, a UN specialized agency, which has published extensive guides on right to food monitoring as 'The FAO Right to Food Methodological Toolbox' from 2009 to 2014.[25] The six guides cover diverse aspects of monitoring and integrating the right to food in national legislation, policies and programs, and are intended to provide guidance to FAO agents and to all parties and organizations engaged in right to food research, policy and monitoring. The following section explains and describes the FAO approach before considering how it may develop.

The *FAO Voluntary Guidelines to Support the Progressive Realization of the Right to Adequate Food in the Context of National Food Security* (now referred to as 'Right to Food Guidelines') were adopted by the FAO Council in November 2004.[26] Formulation of the Right to Food Guidelines followed a two-year process that included the establishment of an intergovernmental working group by the Council in 2002 following a recommendation by the World Food Summit. The Guidelines do not constitute obligations but are a useful resource in advocating responsibility to monitor the right to food.

The key guideline on monitoring the realization of the right to food, and with evaluating the impacts of these measures, is Guideline 17. Guideline

---

[25] The FAO *Right to Food Methodological Toolbox* contains the following guides: 'Book 1: Guide on Legislating for the Right to Food' (FAO 2009); 'Book 2: Methods to Monitor the Human Right to Adequate Food (Volume I)' (FAO 2009); 'Book 2: Methods to Monitor the Human Right to Adequate Food (Volume II) (FAO 2009); 'Book 3: Guide to Conducting a Right to Food Assessment' (FAO 2009); 'Book 4: Right to Food Curriculum Outline' (FAO 2009); 'Book 5: Budget Work to Advance the Right to Food' (FAO 2009); 'Book 6: Integrating the right to adequate food in national food and nutrition security policies and programmes' (FAO 2014).

[26] FAO, *Voluntary Guidelines to Support the Progressive Realization of the Right to Adequate Food in the Context of National Food Security*, adopted by the 127th Session of the FAO Council November 2004 (FAO 2005).

17 develops an analytical and methodological agenda to monitor the realization of the right to food, recommending that states:

- Establish mechanisms to monitor and evaluate the implementation of the FAO Guidelines (Guideline 17.1).
- Conduct 'Right to Food Impact Assessments' in order to identify the impact of domestic policies, programs and projects on the progressive realization of the right to adequate food of the population at large and vulnerable groups in particular, and as a basis for the adoption of the necessary corrective measures (Guideline 17.2).
- Develop a set of process, impact and outcome indicators, relying on indicators already in use and monitoring systems such as FIVIMS, so as to assess the implementation of the progressive realization of the right to adequate food. They may wish to establish appropriate benchmarks to be achieved in the short, medium and long term, which relate directly to meeting poverty and hunger reduction targets as a minimum, as well as other national and international goals including those adopted at the World Food Summit and the Millennium Summit (Guideline 17.3).
- Identify or design process indicators so that they explicitly relate and reflect the use of specific policy instruments and interventions with outcomes consistent with the progressive realization of the right to adequate food in the context of national food security. Such indicators could enable States to implement legal, policy and administrative measures, detect discriminatory practices and outcomes, and ascertain the extent of political and social participation in the process of realizing that right (Guideline 17.4).
- Monitor the food-security situation of vulnerable groups, especially women, children and the elderly, and their nutritional status, including the prevalence of micronutrient deficiencies (Guideline 17.5).
- Ensure a participatory approach to information gathering, management, analysis, interpretation and dissemination (Guideline 17.6).

Additional relevant aspects related to monitoring include, for example, (a) undertaking right to food assessments to formulate a national human-rights-based strategy (Guideline 3.2), (b) establishing national inter-sectoral coordination mechanisms to monitor and evaluate policies, plans and programs (Guideline 5.2), (c) involving stakeholders, particularly communities and local government in monitoring and evaluating food production and consumption programs (Guidelines 10.3), (d) undertaking disaggregated food insecurity, nutrition and vulnerability analysis to assess forms of discrimination (Guideline 13.2), and (e) encouraging participation by civil society organizations and individuals in the monitoring activities of human rights institutions (Guideline 18.1).

HOW DO THE FAO'S GUIDELINES ADDRESS IDENTIFIED PROBLEMS OF MONITORING?

In this instance, the subject of analysis is the monitoring (particularly the human process of monitoring) and not the monitored (the right to food). Attention will be paid to the FAO's directions on methodology of measurement. In particular monitoring is considered from the two angles already identified: (a) *who monitors*; and (b) *who and what is monitored?*

Who Undertakes the Monitoring?

As the right to food is often non-justiciable it brings particular challenges to monitoring, specifically in incentivizing monitoring. As explained above, the absence of effective monitoring is doubly significant where the right is non-justiciable, as monitoring and reporting the implementation of the right become central to advocacy and protection of the right at stake. Motivation behind monitoring may be critical to the outcome of the monitoring, and therefore a key distinction arises between public and private monitoring.

The FAO guidelines are voluntary and leave a high degree of discretion to states as to the actors that are used and the models they employ. There is a diverse food security mandate among various institutions. Institutional situations vary with respect to responsibilities to generate monitoring information, to monitor progress and to implement 'pro right to food' measures. To overcome some of these inter-institutional gaps, the FAO advocates an 'inter- institutional network' to monitor the right to adequate food, with some institutional members identified as primary or leading monitoring institutions or organizations, and others as associated institutions that may undertake specialized and highly technical tasks, the results of which feed into the overall monitoring function.

Several scenarios are considered by the FAO:

- One scenario would be where a human rights institution assumes a central monitoring role, relying largely on information generated by associated institutions, such as line and planning ministries, statistical offices, poverty monitoring units and non-governmental organizations. Technical monitoring expertise may have to be seconded to the human rights institution.

- A second scenario may be where monitoring is part of the mandate of an inter-ministry body, like a national food security and nutrition council, which relies on information from various sources. The human rights institution should be a member of this body. Such a council would need a technical secretariat, with capacity to analyze information including from a human rights perspective. For example, staff from a human rights institution can be seconded to this technical secretariat.
- A third scenario is where most of the monitoring of the realization of human rights is undertaken by a network of non-governmental agencies, in the first instance, monitoring government efforts to realize human rights. Civil society organizations often rely on government statistics to monitor the realization of human rights, although they may have means to generate additional information and/or to verify government statistics. Rather than being an antagonistic relationship, efforts should be made for this to eventually lead to a government–civil society partnership in monitoring and ultimately the implementation of pro-right-to-adequate food measures.[27]

The guidelines apply to the full range of actors (including international non-governmental organizations, state bodies, domestic charities and community actors); however, the FAO advocates that a *rights-based approach* is best achieved by '*community-led monitoring*'.[28] A 'rights-based approach' looks to protect rights involved in the process of obtaining rights. It pays attention to rights in the means used to obtain rights as opposed to focusing on the ends. This is particularly relevant with regard to the right to food given the growth of nutritionally deficient pre-prepared foodstuffs. In many areas of the world, 'therapeutic food stuffs' are used to satiate hunger, but the satiation of hunger does not equate to the realization of the right to food. If applying a rights-based approach,[29] the right to food does

---

[27] FAO, 'Book 2: Methods to Monitor the Human Right to Adequate Food (Volume I) (n 25) 36.
[28] FAO, 'Book 2: Methods to Monitor the Human Right to Adequate Food (Volume II) (n 25) 89.
[29] This chapter does not consider the shortcomings of the rights-based approach, but a pervasive critique of rights-based approaches is made by Jethro Pettit and Joanna Wheeler, who argue that emphasis on empowerment 'fails to address the structural causes of marginalization and the power relations that perpetuate those. The assumption is that one sector of society can be empowered without necessarily challenging the power of other sectors. Jethro Pettit and Joanna Wheeler, 'Developing Rights? Relating Discourse to Context and Practice' (2005) 6(1) International Development Studies Bulletin 1, 1–8.

not relate purely to the satisfaction of hunger; it also applies to the means used to reach that end.

'Community monitoring' is more commonly referred to as participatory monitoring and draws from various participatory traditions that have evolved over the past 20 years, such as participatory action research spearheaded by Paulo Freire[30] and others.[31] Participatory monitoring has been advocated since the 1980s by large development organizations such as UK Department of the International Development, the Swedish International Development Authority, the Norwegian Agency for International Development and, the World Bank, amongst others. The approach is described by Robert Chambers in *Whose Reality Counts?*[32] as starting with people's knowledge as the basis for planning and change. As Estrella and Gaventa point out, as a result of greater participatory approaches by institutions, questions of 'who measures' results and 'who decides' success become more critical; '"Who counts reality?" may prove as significant a question as "whose reality counts?"'[33]

Who and What is Monitored?

The choice of indicators is directly related to what is monitored. As barriers to food access are often implicated in other legal structures and are not readily identified, to what extent does the FAO methodology address punitive legal structures as root causes of food insecurity? Recall that 'food aid' is a sign of food security systemic failure, and, as such, regulatory environments should prevent systemic and widespread food insecurity (i.e. outside of war and natural disasters). In order to do so the analysis must go beyond analyzing access to food and consider the economic, historical or legal structural causes preventing access to food.

---

[30]   Paulo Freire, *Cultural Action for Freedom* (Penguin 1972). Cited in Marisol Estrella and John Gaventa, *Who Counts Reality? Participatory Monitoring and Evaluation: A Literature Review*, Working Paper 70 (1998) Institute of Development Studies.

[31]   In particular, farming systems research developed by Amanor, Farrington and Martin as foundations of participatory monitoring. Kojo Amanor, *Analytical Abstracts on Farmer Participatory Research*, Occasional Paper 10 (Agricultural Administration Unit 1990). John Farrington and Adrienne Martin, *Farmer Participation in Agricultural Research: A Review of Concepts and Practices*, Occasional Paper 9 (Agricultural Administration Unit 1993), cited in Estrella and Gaventa (n 30).

[32]   Robert Chambers, *Whose Reality Counts? Putting the First Last* (2nd edn, ITDG 1997).

[33]   Estrella and Gaventa (n 30) 3.

In terms of analyzing the process of monitoring, a rights-based approach to monitoring as described above is of particular interest. Beyond seeking to be particularly inclusive of the food insecure, the human rights approach is useful in pursuing the *root causes* of food insecurity. A rights-based approach to monitoring should include an assessment of legal structures and legal cultures surrounding access to food and it may extend the analysis to budgets. FAO elaborates: 'It means, for example, monitoring of public budgets from a rights perspective by asking: do budget allocations and expenditures reflect the principle that states should take measures "to the maximum of their available resources" for the realisation of economic, social and cultural rights?'[34]

The incorporation of state budgets in the right to food audit renders right to food monitoring more relevant, as policy decisions clearly shape the food cultures within a state. Yet arguably the net should be cast wider yet to include those factors that limit or influence the state's capacity to implement food security policies. In this respect, the interdependence of states on trade in agriculture is particularly relevant. Ultimately, comprehensive monitoring of the right to food should include an analysis of food policies and inclusivity of those policies, an examination of how those policies are limited by state budgets and, in turn, an examination of how budgets are limited by external factors such as international trade agreements.

The FAO delineates the choices of indicators that monitoring bodies may choose from. The FAO distinguishes between three types of indicators: 'structural (or contextual) indicators', 'process indicators' and 'outcome indicators'. According to the FAO: 'Structural indicators seek to measure different dimensions of legal, regulatory, institutional frameworks and socio-economic development priorities, and poverty reduction strategies and policies that bear on the implementation of policy measures, and condition the outcomes of those measures'.[35]

Whereas structural indicators are used in right to food assessments and program assessment and monitoring, '*process indicators*' or '*indicators of conduct*' capture different dimensions of the design and implementation processes of policy measures and programs. The third set of indicators, outcome indicators, monitor, in conjunction with targets and benchmarks, progress with respect to the realization of the right to food. These are

---

[34] FAO, 'Book 2: Methods to Monitor the Human Right to Adequate Food (Volume II) (n 25) 12.

[35] Ibid. 18. See also OHCHR, *Guide, Human Rights Indicators: A Guide to Measurement and Implementation* (United Nations 2012).

linked to process and structural indicators in order to inform the remedial action to be taken.[36]

Furthermore the FAO stipulates two types of criteria to guide the development of indicators: (a) practical criteria that reflect human rights principles and approaches; and (b) technical or statistical criteria. Ideally a hybrid approach would be employed in selecting the criteria; nonetheless the choice of criteria can generate results which differ dramatically.

> Particular rights-related process indicators still need to be identified. Process indicators to monitor the appropriateness and effectiveness of policy, legal and administrative institutional frameworks that correspond to and reflect the realisation of the right to adequate food still need to be developed and agreed upon. Other process indicators that can be used to monitor budgetary practices, public participation, public service delivery and the implementation of food security, nutrition and poverty reduction programmes are also needed.[37]

What is Not Monitored? The Missing Links

The 2008 UN Food security report, Declaration of the High-level Conference on World Food Security: the Challenges of Climate Change and Bioenergy,[38] identified that the root causes of food insecurity often lie beyond the national government, as have many other reports. To not include international trade agreements in right to food monitoring is to overlook a significant factor affecting of the realization of the right to food in exporter states. Further, a right to food audit should not be limited to examining policies and programs and should include the legal structures behind food production, such as land law, company law and intellectual property law.

Susan Randolph and Shareen Hertel trace the root causes to 'the devastating impact of debt burdens on poor countries as well as the adverse impact of classic stabilization and structural adjustment programs was widely acknowledged, even by the International Monetary Fund (IMF)

---

[36]   FAO, 'Book 2: Methods to Monitor the Human Right to Adequate Food (Volume II) (n 25) 20.

[37]   FAO, 'Book 2: Methods to Monitor the Human Right to Adequate Food (Volume I) (n 25) 58. Here, FAO 'acknowledge that the Office of the High Commissioner for Human Rights (OHCHR) in Geneva, and FIAN International in Heidelberg joined the collaboration and provided valuable inputs' to the guide (8).

[38]   Conference on World Food Security (2008), 'Declaration of the High-level Conference on World Food Security: the Challenges of Climate Change and Bioenergy'.

and World Bank (WB)'.[39] Their study shows that states have been far more effective at putting in place normative commitments, i.e. structural indicators of progress, than they have been at affecting policy that would change the reality of pervasive and increasing hunger, i.e. measuring the right to food using process and outcome indicators. They also critique the discourse on obligations to ensure adequate access to food as state-centric at the expense of the identification and pursuit of both extraterritorial obligations and the responsibility and impact of non-state actors with the power to significantly affect food policy.

In this regard, the FAOs 'causality analysis' is very useful, and this links to the third challenge, accountability of actors. According to FAO:

> The causality analysis is singly the most important factor of a right to food assessment and completes the trend and causes of food insecurity assessment. Only when the factors that hinder individuals to realize their right to food are known can a targeted right to food strategy be pursued.[40]

The proposed structure for such a causality analysis is based on UNICEF's conceptual framework that distinguishes three causality levels:

- Immediate causes of malnutrition are those that are directly related to food intake and the possibility of the body to adequately use these food items.
- Underlying causes analyze what determines the food intake and body functions, i.e. the extent to which the environment where an individual lives supports or hinders adequate nutrition intake.
- Root causes are addressed at the macro-level in addition to an assessment of the system at subnational, national and international level that affects the potential of an individual to realize the right to food. [41]

---

[39]   Susan Randolph and Shareen Hertel, 'The Right to Food: A Global Overview' in Lanse P. Minkler (eds) *The State of Economic and Social Rights* (CUP 2013) 44. More recently in Ladawn Haglund and Robin Stryker (eds) *Closing the Rights Gap. From Human Rights to Social Transformation* (UCLA 2015), the authors shift the spotlight from global actors to focus on the power of states to maximize their available resources in pursuit of rights realization, with a case study on India. See further Susan Randolph and Shareen Hertel, 'The Challenge of Ensuring Food Security: Global Perspectives on Evidence from India' in Ladawn Haglund and Robin Stryker (eds), *Closing the Rights Gap. From Human Rights to Social Transformation* (UCLA 2015).

[40]   FAO, 'Book 3: Guide to Conducting a Right to Food Assessment' (n 25) 20.

[41]   UNICEF, *Strategy for Improved Nutrition of Children and Women in Developing Countries* (UNICEF policy review 1990). Cited in FAO, 'Book 3: Guide to Conducting a Right to Food Assessment (n 25).

The causality analysis is widely used through the UN development agencies in determining the major causes of these violations and the key actors involved. The significant downfall of this approach, however, is that it is often limited to operating *within* the context of the state as an 'island' of policy-making. It considers how the state uses its policy space and resources without seeking to question the limitations on policy space and resources generated by external factors, such as international trade and investment agreements.[42] In this way the analysis of a violation of the right to food could go further to consider (a) the extent to which general socio-economic and political conditions of a country influence the determinants of nutrition[43] and (b) relatedly, to identify the role that external actors (other states, corporations, and international institutions) play in creating those socio-economic and political constraints on a states' food policy.

The identification of the effects on the right to food that are beyond the direct influence of the national government may strengthen inter-governmental negotiations helping to address harmful contractual relationships choose a different path for development in which the international constraints are no longer harmful. In a subsequent step the constraints that have the greatest influence and the most negative impact on the realization of the right to food of the individual or group in question must be related to a government action. This could lead to laws, rules, or even the constitution being adapted through policies, strategies or programs, strengthening of institutions, strengthening the implementation of policies, reallocation of national budget, etc.[44]

CONCLUSIONS AND RECOMMENDATIONS

As a relatively 'new' right, researchers and civil society organizations play a key role in developing the definition of the right to food. There are a number of ways that both actors can improve the efficacy of monitoring. First, monitoring should extend to include both the full scope of the right to food and to the causes – not merely the effects – of right to food violations. On the full scope of the right to food, monitoring should comprise the social, cultural and economic dimensions of the right to produce culturally appropriate food. A focus on monitoring the right to food only as

---

[42]   FAO, 'Book 3: Guide to Conducting a Right to Food Assessment (n 25).
[43]   Ibid. 62.
[44]   Ibid. 66.

right to consume misses opportunities to address the root causes, which leads to food insecurity. Just as distributing food aid and food banks signify a failure of food security, the same holds true in relation to monitoring the right to food: if we are monitoring access to food aid it is too late – the right to food has already been violated. The monitoring is therefore only monitoring the effect and not the cause.

Secondly, community monitoring should be resourced and incentivized. Establishing a stronger ethnographic base behind monitoring will help identify what exactly is being measured, by whom, and will thus inform statistics with ideological contextualization. Monitoring the right to food demands much more than monitoring patterns of consumption and therefore the inclusion of culturally diverse actors and communities within the monitoring process brings a far stronger knowledge base. Thirdly, both accountability mechanisms and the links between food poverty and government policy require strengthening. Without appropriate accountability mechanisms, the monitoring process may embed market approaches to the right to food rather than addressing structural arrangements through which market forces may profit from food insecurity.

On all of these points the FAO's recommendation to establish national food security councils holds merit. The recommendation is to set up:

> a stand-alone national authority for the right to food or food security at the highest level of government or transforming existing structures into such a national authority (in the president's or the prime minister's office) is a better strategy for ensuring a clear view across ministries and divisions, and the authority needed to guarantee collaboration by all relevant state and nonstate actors. The high hierarchical position of the authority and its exclusive focus on the realization of the right to food would facilitate systematic consideration of the right to food or of its relevant components when decisions are made on economic, social, financial, agricultural, trade and other state policies.[45]

This also serves the function of building stronger visibility of the causal relation between state policy, trade and food governance.

Yet, even once established, national food security councils do not automatically ameliorate right to food situations and much work remains in the realm of 'civil society'. The 'public' values of objectivity once attributed to the state and state institutions no longer hold firm, however, and it is not immediately evident that national food security councils would have the remit or resources to establish strong ethnographic backgrounds to monitoring. Any new institutions established may be subject to increasing pressure for econometrics, as are other government departments and

---

[45]   FAO, 'Book 1: Guide on Legislating for the Right to Food' (n 25) 139.

public institutions worldwide. It then falls to human rights researchers to continually challenge definitions and metrics that seek to isolate the right to food from the root causes and the responsible actors, often located 'elsewhere' and out of reach.

REFERENCES

Amanor, K., *Analytical Abstracts on Farmer Participatory Research*, Occasional Paper 10 (Agricultural Administration Unit 1990)

Bauer, J.-M., Koffi Akakpo, Marie Enlund and Silvia Passeri, 'A New Tool in the Toolbox: Using Mobile Text for Food Security Surveys in a Conflict Setting', Humanitarian Practice Network blog, 20 February 2014, http://odihpn.org/blog/a-new-tool-in-the-toolbox-using-mobile-text-for-food-security-surveys-in-a-conflict-setting/

Butler, C.D., 'Revised Hunger Estimates Accelerate Apparent Progress Towards the MDG Hunger Target' (2015) 5 Global Food Security 19.

Chambers, R., *Whose Reality Counts? Putting the First Last* (2nd edn, ITDG 1997)

Committee on Economic, Social and Cultural Rights, 'General Comment 12: The Right to Adequate Food' (E/C.12/1999/5 1999)

Coomans, F., Fred Grunfeld and Menno T. Kamminga (eds), *Methods of Human Rights Research* (Intersentia 2009)

Coomans, F., Fred Grunfeld and Menno T. Kamminga, 'Methods of Human Rights Research: A Primer' (2010) 32 Human Rights Quarterly 179

Davis, K.E., Benedict Kingsbury, Sally Engle Merry, 'Indicators as a Technology of Global Governance' (2010) 2 IILJ Working Paper 1

Davis, M., 'UNAIDS: Bold Human Rights Targets Need Better Monitoring', <opendemon cracy.net> accessed 27 July 2015

Eide, A., *The Human Right to Adequate Food and Freedom from Hunger* (FAO 1998)

Estrella, M. and John Gaventa, *Who Counts Reality? Participatory Monitoring and Evaluation: A Literature Review*, Working Paper 70 (Institute of Development Studies 1998)

Farrington, J. and Adrienne Martin, *Farmer Participation in Agricultural Research: A Review of Concepts and Practices*, Occasional Paper 9 (Agricultural Administration Unit 1993)

Food and Agriculture Organization, *Voluntary Guidelines to Support the Progressive Realization of the Right to Adequate Food in the Context of National Food Security*, adopted by the 127th Session of the FAO Council November 2004

Food and Agriculture Organization, *Methods to Monitor the Human Right to Adequate Food: Making the Case for Rights-Focused and Rights-Based Monitoring*, Vol. 1 (FAO 2009a)

Food and Agriculture Organization, *Methods to Monitor the Human Right to Adequate Food: Making the Case for Rights-Focused and Rights-Based Monitoring*, Vol. 1, Book 2 (FAO 2009b)

Food and Agriculture Organization, *Guide to Conducting a Right to Food Assessment*, Book 3 (FAO 2009c)

Freire, P., *Cultural Action for Freedom* (Penguin 1972)

International Covenant on Economic, Social and Cultural Rights, 16 December 1966, United Nations, Treaty Series, Vol. 993, 3

Kingsbury, B., Sally Engle Merry and Kevin E. Davis (eds), *The Quiet Power of Indicators: Measuring Governance, Corruption, and Rule of Law* (CUP 2015)

Merry, S.E., 'Measuring the World: Indicators, Human Rights, and Global Governance' (2011) 52(Supplementary Issue 3: Current Anthropology) s83

Merry, S.E., *The Seductions of Quantification: Measuring Human Rights, Gender Violence and Sex Trafficking* (Chicago Series in Law and Society 2016)

OHCHR, *Human Rights Indicators: A Guide to Measurement and Implementation* (United Nations 2012)

Optional Protocol to the International Covenant on Economic, Social and Cultural Rights, resolution/adopted by the General Assembly, 5 March 2009, A/RES/63/117

People's Union for Civil Liberties v Union of India, Writ Petition (Civil) No. 196 of 2001 (India) (28 November 2001 interim order)

Pettit, J. and Joanna Wheeler, 'Developing Rights? Relating Discourse to Context and Practice' (2005) 6(1) International Development Studies Bulletin 1

Poovey, M., *A History of the Modern Fact: Problems of Knowledge in the Sciences of Wealth and Society* (University of Chicago Press 1998)

Randolph, S. and Shareen Hertel, 'The Challenge of Ensuring Food Security: Global Perspectives on Evidence from India' in Ladawn Haglund and Robin Stryker (eds), *Closing the Rights Gap. From Human Rights to Social Transformation* (UCLA 2015)

Right to Food and Nutrition Watch 2013: Alternatives and Resistant to Policies that Generate Hunger (FIAN 2013)

Schuftan, C. and Ted Greiner, 'The Scaling Up Nutrition (SUN) Initiative' in *Right to Food and Nutrition Watch 2013: Alternatives and Resistance to Policies that Generate Hunger* (FIAN 2013)

UNICEF, *Strategy for Improved Nutrition of Children and Women in Developing Countries* (UNICEF policy review 1990)

United Nations General Assembly, 'Compilation Prepared by the Office of the United Nations High Commissioner for Human Rights, in Accordance with Paragraph 10 of Human Rights Council' Resolution 16/22 (26 December 2011)

The UN Report of the High Level Panel of Eminent Persons on the Post-2015 Development Agenda, *A New Global Partnership: Eradicate Poverty And Transform Economies Through Sustainable Development* (United Nations 2013)

15. Social network analysis in human rights research

*Anna-Luise Chané and Arjun Sharma**

INTRODUCTION

As human rights research continues to expand its use of social science methodologies – especially those employing quantitative data, or data quantitatively – there has been an ongoing debate about the appropriateness and effectiveness of such approaches in capturing the multidimensional nature of human rights issues.[1] Significant advances in statistical methods and technology allow researchers to detect patterns underlying various social phenomena. Within human rights research, there are an increasing number of studies that examine the attributes of countries (e.g. economic development, form of government or institutional structure) and their correlation with variables of interest, such as the degree of compliance with human rights conventions.[2] Skeptics of this approach contend that, while it may allow researchers to understand to some extent *why* a phenomenon may occur, it does not necessarily shed light on the underlying processes that cause it to occur.[3]

Another issue associated with studies employing traditional statistical methods is the often-used assumption that complex social phenomena can be explained by aggregating the actions of self-interested – often rational –

---

* All websites were last accessed on 30 May 2016.

[1] See also in the present volume Simon Walker, Chapter 13; Margaret L. Satterthwaite and Justin Simeone, 'A Conceptual Roadmap for Social Science Methods in Human Rights Fact-Finding' in Philip Alston and Sarah Knuckey (eds), *The Transformation of Human Rights Fact-Finding* (OUP 2016).

[2] See e.g. AnnJanette Rosga and Margaret L. Satterthwaite, 'The Trust in Indicators: Measuring Human Rights' (2009) 27 Berkeley Journal of International Law 253; see also the annotated bibliography of quantitative human rights studies in David L. Cingranelli and David L. Richards, 'Quantitative Studies' in David P. Forsythe (ed.), *Encyclopedia of Human Rights* (OUP 2009), Vol 4, 293–296.

[3] See Russel Lawrence Barsh, 'Measuring Human Rights: Problems of Methodology and Purpose' (1993) 15 Human Rights Quarterly 87. See also Alexandra Marin and Barry Wellman, 'Social Network Analysis: An Introduction' in John Scott and Peter J. Carrington (eds), *The SAGE Handbook of Social Network Analysis* (Sage 2011).

actors (e.g. countries or individuals), endowed with fixed capacities, values and motivations. This view tends to neglect how interactions between actors can change capacities and generate new values. Since most human rights research begins from normative assumptions about what constitutes rights, it could be argued that a narrow focus on explaining events by comparing the material endowments of actors may obfuscate how perceptions of human rights are inherited, transmitted and contested within and between social networks operating in different cultural contexts.

Social network analysis is a set of tools and methods developed around a theoretical orientation that aims to examine the relational dynamics between actors, rather than merely their attributes.[4] This emphasis on structure is sometimes interpreted as a sign of the agnosticism of social network analysis towards individual agency; however, there is enough scope within its methods to consider the impact of individual actions on networks as well as the salience of structures in constraining or enabling actors' behavior.[5] Combining analysis of relationships using social network analysis with statistical and qualitative methods provides human rights researchers with an opportunity not only to delve into how certain phenomena are created from interactions between actors, but also to identify the specific mechanisms, or forces, that shape these interactions.[6]

The purpose of this chapter is to introduce the reader to some of the key features of social network analysis along with the opportunities and challenges in applying them to human rights research. To illustrate, we use examples from our research on co-sponsorship patterns at the UN Human Rights Council.[7]

---

[4]   For a concise overview of the use of network analysis in the social sciences see Stephen P. Borgatti and others, 'Network Analysis in the Social Sciences' (2009) 323 Science 892. On the development of social network analysis see for example Linton C. Freeman, *The Development of Social Network Analysis: A Study in the Sociology of Science* (Empirical Press 2004); and same author, 'The Development of Social Network Analysis – with an Emphasis on Recent Events' in John Scott and Peter J. Carrington (eds), *The SAGE Handbook of Social Network Analysis* (Sage 2011). On social network theory see for example Martin Kilduff and Wenpin Tsai, *Social Networks and Organizations* (Sage 2003) 35–65; and Stephen P. Borgatti and Virginie Lopez-Kidwell, 'Network Theory' in John Scott and Peter J. Carrington (eds), *The SAGE Handbook of Social Network Analysis* (Sage 2011).

[5]   Patrick Doreian, 'Causality in Social Network Analysis' (2001) 30 Sociological Methods and Research 81.

[6]   See also in the present volume Malcolm Langford, Chapter 8.

[7]   Anna-Luise Chané and Arjun Sharma, 'Universal Human Rights? Exploring Contestation and Consensus in the UN Human Rights Council' (2016) 10 Human Rights & International Legal Discourse 219 and Anna-Luise Chané and Arjun

KEY CONCEPTS OF SOCIAL NETWORK ANALYSIS

The increasing popularity of *networks*, as a term and as a concept, indicates a convergence of academic and public interest in understanding the processes underlying diverse issues including crime, terrorism, biology and even social interactions on the Internet. At its most basic level, a network is a dataset comprising entities (*nodes*) and the relations between them (*ties* or *edges*). In a network graph, nodes are displayed as dots or similar symbols, whereas ties are depicted as lines connecting the dots. A node can represent almost anything, from actors (e.g. individual persons,[8] countries,[9] courts,[10] companies or organizations[11]), to concepts or objects (e.g. legal instruments or judgments)[12] and events (e.g. international summits or ses-

---

Sharma, 'The European Union in the Human Rights Council: A Social Network Analysis of (Co-)Sponsorship Patterns' (forthcoming).

[8]   See e.g. Daniel M. Katz and Derek K. Stafford, 'Hustle and Flow: A Social Network Analysis of the American Federal Judiciary' (2010) 71 Ohio State Law Journal 457; Emmanuel Lazega, 'Mapping Judicial Dialogue Across National Borders: An Exploratory Network Study of Learning from Lobbying Among European Intellectual Property Judges' (2012) 8 Utrecht Law Review 115.

[9]   See e.g. Kevin T. Macon, Peter J. Mucha and Mason A. Porter, 'Community Structure in the United Nations General Assembly' (2011) 391 Physica A: Statistical Mechanics and its Applications 1; Jang Hyun Kim and George A. Barnett, 'A Structural Analysis of International Conflict: From a Communication Perspective' (2007) 33 International Interactions 135; and Emilie M. Hafner-Burton and Alexander H. Montgomery, 'Power Positions: International Organizations, Social Networks, and Conflict' (2006) 50 Journal of Conflict Resolution 3.

[10]   See e.g. Martin Gelter and Mathias Siems, 'Networks, Dialogue or One-way Traffic? An Empirical Analysis of Cross-citations between Ten of Europe's Highest Courts' (2012) 8 Utrecht Law Review 88.

[11]   See e.g. Spencer Moore, Eugenia Eng and Mark Daniel, 'International NGOs and the Role of Network Centrality in Humanitarian Aid Operations: A Case Study of Coordination During the 2000 Mozambique Floods' (2003) 27 Disasters 305.

[12]   See e.g. Kyounghee Kwon, George A. Barnett and Hao Chen, 'Assessing Cultural Differences in Translations: A Semantic Network Analysis of the Universal Declaration of Human Rights' (2009) 2 Journal of International and Intercultural Communication 107. See also the network analyses of the citation practice of the United States Supreme Court, James H. Fowler and others, 'Network Analysis and the Law: Measuring the Legal Importance of Precedents at the U.S. Supreme Court' (2007) 15 Political Analysis 324; Frank B. Cross and others, 'Citations in the U.S. Supreme Court: An Empirical Study of Their Use and Significance' [2010] University of Illinois Law Review 489; and more generally on the United States judiciary, Thomas A. Smith, 'The Web of Law' (2007) 44 San Diego Law Review 309. See also Pauwelyn on the network of WTO Appellate Body reports, Joost Pauwelyn, 'Minority Rules: Precedent and Participation

sions of international organizations). Although it may be more obvious to consider only actors as nodes in a network, everything that can form relations can, in fact, be conceived as a node.

In the same vein, ties can capture any possible relation that can exist between two nodes. Countries, for example, can be linked by trading with each other, by being members of the same international organization or by engaging in diplomatic relations.[13] Documents, such as legal instruments or judicial decisions, can be linked by containing references to one another.[14] Events can be related by attracting the same participants. The multitude of possible relations between nodes equals a multitude of possible networks: for every set of nodes, it is possible to build a large number of networks, depending on which class of relations one focuses on. Selecting the network that best answers the research question is consequently not only of utmost importance but can also constitute a significant challenge.

Ties can be further defined by determining their *directionality* and *value*. *Directed* ties indicate asymmetric relations, originating in one node and going to another, whereas *undirected* ties capture symmetric relations, in which the link exists mutually between both nodes without a specific orientation. Cross-references in court judgments, for example, form an asymmetric network: the citation of an earlier judgment is necessarily a one-way relation. Countries engaging in human rights dialogues, on the contrary, form a symmetric network: the mutual exchange between them is a two-way relation. In a network graph, directed ties would be depicted as arrows, pointing from one node to another. Furthermore, ties can be either *binary* or *valued*. Binary ties indicate only the existence or absence of a relation, whereas valued ties indicate the strength of the link between two nodes. For example, a network of state parties to international human rights treaties can only have binary ties: either states are a party to a treaty or they are not.[15] A network of judicial dialogue between courts, however,

---

before the WTO Appellate Body' in Joanna Jemielniak, Laura Nielsen and Henrik Palmer Olsen (eds), *Establishing Judicial Authority in International Economic Law* (CUP 2016).

[13]   Macon, Mucha and Porter focus on the voting behavior of the UN member states in the General Assembly (n 9); Kim and Barnett use a variety of data on bilateral relationships in their study, e.g. alliance pacts, joint membership in international organizations, telecommunication, air traffic and foreign aid (n 9).

[14]   See n 12.

[15]   See e.g. the network graphs of the signatories to major human rights treaties by Kyounghee Kwon and George A. Barnett, 'Mapping International Agreement on Human Rights Treaties, 1980–2006: An Application of Network Analysis', paper presented at the Sunbelt Social Networks Conference, January 2008, cited in Skye Bender-deMoll, 'Potential Human Rights Uses of Network Analysis and

could indicate the number of cross-references using valued ties.[16] In a network graph, valued ties can be represented using different tie strengths or a color code. Finally, ties can be assigned a positive or negative value. This is used in studies that examine the 'transitivity' or 'structural balance' within a network.[17] Transitivity aims at studying patterns of positive or negative ties and the 'tension' they cause. In essence, it is concerned with evaluating theories such as 'the friend of my friend is my friend, and the enemy of my enemy is my friend'.[18] Within the field of international relations, for example, there is a body of social network research that attempts to map the extent to which antagonistic or amicable relations between groups of countries impact their relations with other countries or regional groups.

APPLYING SOCIAL NETWORK ANALYSIS

In applying social network analysis to a concrete research project, researchers encounter a number of challenges ranging from boundary setting to collecting data, preparing data for analysis and, finally, selecting the appropriate measures for analyzing the resulting network. We highlight some of the key opportunities and challenges that these steps entail.[19]

Research Design

At the beginning of a research project involving social network analysis, the design of the study – which includes selecting the units of analysis, establishing a sampling frame and developing strategies to collect and analyze data – is determined by whether the researcher adopts a *whole*

Mapping: A Report to the Science and Human Rights Program of the American Association for the Advancement of Science' (2008) 17.

[16]   See e.g. the network graph of the cross-citations between ten European high courts in Gelter and Siems (n 10) 95.

[17]   See for more detail Stanley Wasserman and Katherine Faust, *Social Network Analysis: Methods and Applications* (CUP 1994) 220–248.

[18]   Emilie M. Hafner-Burton, Miles Kahler and Alexander H. Montgomery, 'Network Analysis for International Relations' (2009) 63 International Organization 559.

[19]   For a more detailed introduction to social network analysis see Peter J. Carrington, John Scott and Stanley Wasserman (eds) *Models and Methods in Social Network Analysis* (CUP 2005); John Scott, *Social Network Analysis* (3rd edn, Sage 2013); John Scott and Peter J. Carrington, *The SAGE Handbook of Social Network Analysis* (Sage 2011); and Wasserman and Faust (n 17).

network or an *egocentric network* approach. A whole network approach is broader than the egocentric network approach, in that it examines the relations between all nodes that are considered to belong to a 'bounded social collective'.[20] The egocentric network approach, instead, focuses on one entity (ego) and studies only its local network. For example, a study of non-governmental organizations (NGOs) active in a particular geographic and thematic area could include all NGOs that match these criteria (whole network) or focus on one of them (egocentric network).[21] The latter approach may be useful in cases of large networks, to avoid dealing with unfeasible amounts of data. Here, the focus on one actor may allow for sampling.

CASE STUDY: THE EUROPEAN UNION IN THE UN HUMAN RIGHTS COUNCIL

1.   Introduction and Basic Research Design

As part of a large-scale research project on the human rights policies of the European Union, we studied the European Union's engagement in the UN Human Rights Council.[22] Specifically, our aim was to assess the extent to which the European Union's internal co-ordination among its member states allows it to act cohesively to achieve its human rights agenda in the face of political opposition and priorities of other countries in the Human Rights Council. Existing research on the subject tends to study the cohesion of the European Union in multilateral fora by analyzing whether its member states vote cohesively on contested resolutions. Such studies implicitly assume that the European Union's success in realizing its agenda is contingent on its members 'speaking with one voice', ignoring the agency of other countries and groups in constraining the European Union's ability to do so. Moreover, these studies focus only on a select sample of resolutions rather than trying to determine patterns based on the entire population of available resolutions. Social network analysis allowed us to address these gaps by providing a set of methods to assess not only whether the European Union acts cohesively within the Human Rights Council but also to identify how other countries or groups influence the European Union's ability to achieve its human rights agenda. We

---

[20]   Peter V. Marsden, 'Recent Developments in Network Measurement' in Peter J. Carrington, John Scott and Stanley Wasserman (eds), *Models and Methods in Social Network Analysis* (CUP 2005).

[21]   Moore, Eng and Daniel, for example, use a whole network approach to study the coordination between NGOs which provided humanitarian aid during the 2000 Mozambique floods (n 11).

[22]   European Commission, Seventh Framework Programme (FP7/2007-2013): FRAME – Fostering Human Rights Among European Policies (project no. 320000) <www.fp7-frame.eu>.

complemented our analysis with statistical and qualitative methods in order to identify the processes that shape co-sponsorship patterns and to test the veracity of our results.

For our research purposes it could have made sense to opt for an egocentric network, in order to study the local network of the member states of the European Union. This would have enabled us to examine the European Union's cohesiveness and the extent to which it cooperates with countries from other regions. However, we decided to choose the whole network approach instead in order to obtain a more complete picture of the overall structure of the Human Rights Council network and to determine how other countries and groups affect the behavior of the European Union. The size of the network was not a constraining factor in our case.

Boundary Setting

The research design informs the identification and selection of nodes and relations that are necessary for answering the research question. The omission of entities or the focus on relations that do not capture the social phenomenon, which is the object of the study, will invariably distort the outcome of the analysis and limit the conclusions that can be reliably drawn from it. Boundary setting can be challenging, partly because entities may belong to different networks and play different roles in these networks, and partly also because networks can influence each other. For example countries belonging to the same trade networks may develop similar networks in other foreign policy forums.

Three approaches are commonly recognized for boundary setting.[23] The *positional approach* selects entities based on common characteristics of interest or formal membership criteria. Individuals, for example, could be selected based on their professional position, countries based on their status in an international organization. The *event-based approach* includes entities based on their participation in events considered relevant for the research question, for example international conferences or the sessions of international institutions. The *relation-based approach* identifies networks based on the degree of connectedness between entities. Here, researchers would first identify a small number of actors that are considered to be part of the network, and then expand the group by identifying other actors with whom they are connected. For example, researchers

---

[23]   Edward O. Laumann, Peter V. Marsden and David Prensky, 'The Boundary Specification Problem in Network Analysis' in Linton C. Freeman, Douglas R. White and A. Kimball Romney (eds), *Research Methods in Social Network Analysis* (Transaction 1982).

could select a number of NGOs that work in a particular region on a particular human rights issue, and then gradually include other NGOs with whom they cooperate.[24] These approaches are not mutually exclusive and studies may employ a combination of various approaches to define the network.

---

2. Boundary Setting

To address our research question using social network analysis, we first determined the boundary of our network to identify the relevant nodes and relations, which we aimed to include in our analysis. Adopting the positional approach we could have limited our focus to the 47 member states of the Human Rights Council. However, this approach would not have allowed us to capture a large range of the dynamics that we considered important for our research. It would have excluded other UN and non-UN member states that very frequently participate in the Human Rights Council as observers. While only members have voting rights, both member and observer states may actively engage in the negotiations at the Human Rights Council, for example by sponsoring or co-sponsoring resolutions. Consequently, adopting the positional approach described above, we established a network boundary encompassing 193 UN member states comprising both member and observer states and two non-UN member states represented by observers (Palestine and the Holy See).

Once the appropriate actors, or nodes, have been identified, the relations between them need to be defined. Given the multitude of possible connections between the selected entities, determining the relation that corresponds to the research question is of crucial importance. Generally, four different types of relations are distinguished: *similarities* (e.g. shared characteristics, such as membership or political system), *social relations* (e.g. family ties), *interactions* (e.g. diplomatic relations) and *flows* (e.g. transfer of resources or information).[25] To be useful, a relation should include both the frequency (the intensity of interactions between actors) and the magnitude (whether the relation is actually significant).

---

[24] See Marin and Wellman (n 3) 12.
[25] Wasserman and Faust (n 17) 37–38; and Borgatti and others (n 4) 893 (with a table illustrating the typology of ties on p. 894).

3. Defining Relations between Nodes

There are many ways in which member and observer states at the Human Rights Council enter into relations with one another. They may, for example, refer to each other in their statements, they may negotiate with each other, co-host side events or make recommendations in the framework of the Universal Periodic Review. For every type of interaction, a different network could be constructed. Confronted with the multitude of possible interactions, we have to choose the one that responds best to our research question.

We decided to focus on the adoption of resolutions by the Human Rights Council. The negotiation, co-sponsorship and voting on resolutions is the primary mechanism through which a country or a group of countries at the Human Rights Council can signal their agreement or disagreement with a particular initiative or the interpretation of a human rights issue. Traditionally, voting behavior has been used as a proxy to indicate ideological preferences and political dynamics within similar networks.[26] In the framework of the Human Rights Council, however, this approach has the disadvantage that it only captures the positions of the 47 Council members and only those resolutions on which a vote has been called. This approach limits analysis because it omits the significant involvement of the observer states prior to the adoption process, and it would omit all resolutions which are adopted by consensus. Studying the negotiations between states on the content of a resolution might yield a more comprehensive picture of the dynamics at the Human Rights Council; however, collecting data on interactions, which often take place in informal meetings and behind closed doors, would have been impractical if not impossible.

Consequently, and in line with other recent studies,[27] we opted for co-sponsorship as a proxy. In the Human Rights Council, the main sponsor or sponsors of a resolution are usually responsible for drafting the text and initiating the negotiations. They may invite the support of co-sponsors – other Council members or observers who endorse the proposal before the Council members decide on its adoption. Sponsorship is an important tool at the Human Rights Council because it indicates the strength of a proposal and can be used as a bargaining chip by member and observer states. Co-sponsoring a resolution is a sound indicator for policy support.

---

[26]   See e.g. Simon Hug and Richard Lukacs, 'Preferences or Blocs? Voting in the United Nations Human Rights Council' (2014) 9 Review of International Organizations 83; Xi Jin and Madeleine O. Hosli, 'Pre- and Post-Lisbon: European Union Voting in the United Nations General Assembly' (2013) 36 West European Politics 1274; Helen Young and Nicholas Rees, 'EU Voting Behaviour in the UN General Assembly, 1990–2002: the EU's Europeanising Tendencies' (2005) 16 Irish Studies in International Affairs 193; James E. Todd, 'An Analysis of Security Council Voting Behavior' (1969) 22 The Western Political Quarterly 61; and see also Macon, Mucha and Porter (n 9).

[27]   See e.g. James E. Campbell, 'Cosponsoring Legislation in the U.S. Congress' (1982) 7 Legislative Studies Quarterly 415; Daniel Kessler and Keith Krehbiel, 'Dynamics of Cosponsorship' (1996) 90 American Political Science Review 555; Rick K. Wilson and Cheryl D. Young, 'Cosponsorship in the U.S. Congress'

Data Collection

Although the methods to collect data are not unique to social network analysis, there are certain inherent challenges associated with collecting network data. Compared with standard approaches, which collect data about individual attributes such as name, age, nationality, etc., network data must establish relations between individuals. Since relations, unlike specific attributes, are often subjective and dynamic, social network researchers have to ensure the reliability of their data. To collect relational data, researchers can use traditional data collection methods, such as documentary sources, participant observation, surveys and questionnaires.[28] The use of documentary sources (e.g. reports, yearbooks, judgments, newspapers) has increased in the past decades with the growing amount of publicly and electronically available data.[29] Digital databases and archival sources allow for the use of electronic data mining techniques, which facilitate the handling of large-scale data. Observational data, gained through fieldwork, played an important role in earlier social network studies, but is used less today.[30] It presents the researcher with a range of practical problems, including the capacities required to observe larger scale networks and the difficulty of adequately capturing the relevant behavior.[31] Instead, today many network researchers rely on surveys to collect relational data. The design of these approaches is crucial and can entail considerable challenges.[32] For example, respondents could be provided with a list of all actors in a network and asked to indicate with whom they share certain defined relations. While this technique limits the risk that respondents overlook actors and their relations with them, it is unfeasible in cases of very large networks or if information on the complete network is not available. In those cases, researchers could consider wording their survey in a more open manner and asking respondents to provide lists of all actors

---

(1997) 22 Legislative Studies Quarterly 25; Gregory Kogler, 'Position Taking and Cosponsorship in the U.S. Congress' (2003) 28 Legislative Studies Quarterly 225; James H. Fowler, 'Connecting the Congress: A Study of Cosponsorship Networks' (2006) 14 Political Analysis 456.

[28]   See e.g. Marsden (n 20); Scott (n 19) 41–43; and Wasserman and Faust (n 17) 45–59.

[29]   For example, studies on cross-citations between courts and on the use of precedents (n 12) have been facilitated by the development of legal databases such as LexisNexis.

[30]   Marsden (n 20) 25.

[31]   Ibid.

[32]   Marin and Wellman (n 3) 21. See e.g. Lazega (n 8), who uses surveys to collect data on the discussion network between European intellectual property judges.

with whom they share the particular relation. As indicated, however, this approach could decrease the reliability of the obtained data. An additional problem is that the perception of relations can be very subjective, thus leading to diverging assessments of the respondents. To avoid this, researchers could consider using objective criteria as a proxy to capture the relation. Finally, researchers need to be aware of the particularly detrimental effect of data gaps. Missing nodes or relations can severely distort the network and lead to inaccurate conclusions.

In addition, the collection of relational data can raise ethical concerns.[33] These are particularly pressing when surveys require respondents to provide personal information, but they also have to be considered when drawing data from publicly available documents. Individuals whose data is contained in these documents may not foresee or have consented to the use of this data. It is the nature of social network analysis that makes dealing with sensitive data particularly challenging. Other than in traditional statistical methods, where respondents can be anonymously grouped together, social network analysis treats every actor individually and determines their position in the network conspicuously. Consequently, anonymity of the participants at the stages of data collection and analysis is not possible because the individual actors and their relations need to be identified. Even if names or other personal identifiers are redacted in the published results, it will often be possible to identify the participants through 'reverse engineering' based on existing information.[34] Researchers should also consider how to deal with non-participants who – while not having consented to the study – could nevertheless be identified by participants as actors with whom they share relations.

Data Storage and Preparation

Another important factor to consider when collecting data for social network analysis is data storage and preparation. The method for storing

---

[33]   For a more detailed discussion of the ethical aspects of social network analysis see Stephen P. Borgatti and José Luis Molina, 'Ethical and Strategic Issues in Organizational Social Network Analysis' (2003) 39 The Journal of Applied Behavioral Science 337; Charles Kadushin, 'Who Benefits from Network Analysis: Ethics of Social Network Research' (2005) 27 Social Networks 139. More generally on ethical concerns in human rights research see also in this volume George Ulrich, Chapter 9.

[34]   Bender-deMoll (n 15) 36.

[35]   Session reports can be downloaded from the website of the Human Rights Council <www.ohchr.org/EN/HRBodies/HRC/Pages/Sessions.aspx>.

4. Data Collection

Collecting data on co-sponsorship behavior in the Human Rights Council required extraction of information about (co-)sponsors listed in the session reports of the Human Rights Council, which are publicly and electronically available on the website of the Council.[35] The public nature of the sponsorship or co-sponsorship of resolutions and the fact that we were dealing with states, rather than individual persons, limited the ethical concerns in our study.

data has to be based on whether the researcher has the appropriate tools at his disposal to manipulate the data according to the requirements of the network analysis software used. While small datasets may be manageable using simple word processors or spreadsheets, for large datasets it may be advisable to use a relational database management system such as SQL or MS Access. It is not only important to ensure a complete and clean database (e.g. avoiding duplicates, ensuring that all entities are consistently labeled) but also to ensure from the start that all factors that are relevant for the analysis are coded.

5. Building a Database

For the purpose of our study, we used MS Access to create a database containing a record of 691 thematic and country-specific draft resolutions tabled during the 28 regular and 22 special sessions of the Human Rights Council held between 2006 and 2015.[36] For each draft resolution, the database records the sponsors and co-sponsors, along with the title of the draft resolution and the date it was submitted. Additionally, we labeled each draft resolution according to the thematic or country-specific human rights issue it addressed.[37] This would allow us later to conduct issue-specific analyses. Finally, we indicated for each resolution whether it was sponsored or co-sponsored by a regional group or international organization.[38] In such cases, the database identifies both the groups (as individual actors) as well as their members as (co-)sponsors.

---

[36]   We omitted draft amendments to resolutions and draft resolutions on institutional matters.

[37]   We initially labeled the resolutions in line with the thematic human rights areas identified by the Office of the High Commissioner for Human Rights, see 'List of Human Rights Issues, <www.ohchr.org/EN/Issues/Pages/ListOfIssues. aspx>. Subsequently we expanded the list to include additional thematic issues that were frequently addressed in draft resolutions.

Representing Network Data

Matrices are the primary way to represent network data.[39] One particularly useful feature of social network analysis software is its ability to visualize these matrices so that relations are more intuitively grasped. Figure 15.1A illustrates how, when using standard statistical methods, data is organized based on attributes of a specific case or actor. In contrast, a relational (one-mode) network matrix (Figure 15.1B) depicts the relations between two actors. The 1 or 0 in this case indicates the presence or absence of a relation between actors. The adjacent graph then translates matrix data into a visual format.

In social network studies it is not always possible to establish direct relations between two actors, as illustrated in Figure 15.1B. Often, a relation is contingent on the status of actors in particular organizations (e.g. being a member of an international organization or a party to an international convention) or participation in a common activity (e.g. attending an international conference). In such cases, relations are depicted in a two-mode form as shown in Figure 15.1C. Nodes in a two-mode network belong to two classes of entities and ties can only be formed between nodes that belong to different classes. For ease of analysis, however, these two-mode matrices can be simplified into one-mode form by defining the common affiliation with the nodes of the latter class as the connection between the nodes of the former class (e.g. co-membership).

---

6.   Representing Network Data

For the purposes of our study of the Human Rights Council co-sponsorship network, we generated a rectangular – two-mode – matrix, in which each country is assigned a column and their co-sponsorship of a resolution is either a 1 or 0, indicating whether a country did (1) or did not (0) co-sponsor a particular resolution. Subsequently, we transformed this matrix into two separate one-mode matrices (Figure 15.1C). One matrix (country × country) shows the co-sponsorship relations between two countries, whereas the other (resolution × resolution) shows how many countries any two resolutions have in common. More specifically, in the case of the country × country matrix, the value of 2 between A and C indicates that these countries co-sponsored two resolutions together. Similarly, a value of two between resolutions 1 and 3 indicates that these resolutions had two countries in common. In a social network analysis, both matrices can be analyzed separately

---

[38]   The session reports indicate whether a country (co-)sponsored a resolution 'on behalf of' a regional group or international organization.

[39]   On organizing network data see also Scott (n 19) 52–62.

or jointly. However, since our primary focus was on the relations between countries in the Human Rights Council, we mainly employed the country × country matrix.

Furthermore, when we present the network as a graph (Figure 15.2), relations are shown as undirected, valued ties. Joint sponsorship of a resolution is a mutual relationship that does not originate in one particular actor. It is valued because repeated (co-)sponsorship will increase the strength of the relation.

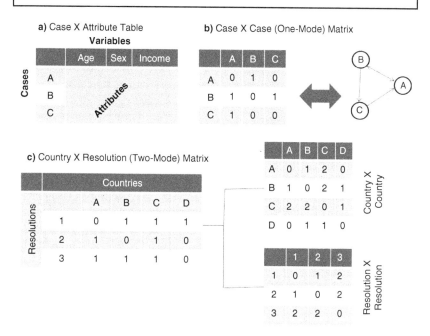

Figure 15.1   Data representation as matrices and graphs

Analyzing Networks

Social network analysis provides a set of tools that allow researchers to analyze networks at different levels. Network level measures allow researchers to determine the overall topology, or 'lay of the land' of the network, while other measures focus on how actors are positioned within the network (actor level), and how actors interact as members of sub-groups (subgroup level).[40]

---

[40]   For the analysis of dyads and triads see for example Christina Prell, *Social Network Analysis: History, Theory and Methodology* (Sage 2012) 134–150; and Wasserman and Faust (n 17) 503–602.

Network level

Density and *centralization* are two common measures used to examine whole network characteristics.[41] Both measures provide an indication of the basic structure of the network and can be useful for the comparison of different networks.

The *density* of a network is measured by comparing the number of possible ties with the number of actual ties between the nodes. Density is measured on a scale of 0–1, with 0 indicating no connections between nodes and 1 indicating a graph where all nodes are connected to each other. In a dense network (see e.g. Figure 15.2), most nodes are connected to each other, whereas in sparse networks most nodes are only tied to few or to no other nodes (*isolates*). The density of a network can be a helpful measure for example in studies of epidemics, where dense networks can increase the probability and rate of disease spread. However, dense networks can also have counter-intuitive effects. For example, it has been demonstrated that sparser networks can be more effective than denser networks.[42]

Centralization is a complementary whole-network measure that indicates the extent to which a graph focuses on specific nodes. Centralization, like density, is measured on a scale of 0–1, with 1 representing a completely centralized network where the network activity is organized around a specific node and 0 indicating a completely decentralized network, where all nodes have equal centrality scores (see Figure 15.2 for an example of a decentralized network).[43]

---

7. Density and Centralization

The Human Rights Council is a highly dense network (0.96), with very low centralization (0.037). However, these values need to be interpreted with caution for two reasons: first, the network graph does not distinguish between strong and weak relations – countries that only co-sponsored with another country once are represented along with those countries that have consistently co-sponsored together. Secondly, the graph only represents the network at a point in time. It is possible that the (co-)sponsorship patterns of some countries varied from session to session.

---

[41]   On density see Wasserman and Faust (n 17) 101–103; Scott (n 19) 69–82; and on centralization see Scott (n 19) 89–94.

[42]   Kilduff and Tsai (n 4) 31–32, referring to Keith G. Provan and Juliann G. Sebastian, 'Networks within Networks: Service Link Overlap, Organizational Cliques, and Network Effectiveness' (1998) 41 The Academy of Management Journal 453.

[43]   See e.g. the network graphs representing a star, a centralized and an equal network in Cédric Sueur, Jean-Louis Deneubourg and Odile Petit, 'From Social Network (Centralized vs. Decentralized) to Collective Decision-Making (Unshared vs. Shared Consensus)' (2012) 7 PLoS One 1, 4.

Actor level

Besides determining the overall structure of the network, social network analysis allows researchers also to focus on individual actors and to draw conclusions on their roles and positions. Two common measures are the *centrality* and the *connectedness* of a node.

Centrality is a positional variable, used to determine the prominence of a node in the network. It has been captured in a variety of different measures. Researchers distinguish between measures such as *degree centrality*, *closeness centrality* or *betweenness centrality. Degree centrality* measures an entity's influence within the network by quantifying the number of ties it has with others. A higher total – or degree – indicates that the node is closely linked with other network members. *Closeness centrality* measures the geodesic distance of a node to all other nodes in the network. A geodesic distance may be understood as the number of links (ties/relationships) between any two nodes of interest. Within a personal network, immediate relatives, for instance, would be at a geodesic distance of 1, whereas friends of these relatives would be at a distance of 2 and so forth. The 'six degree of separation' hypothesis popularized by Stanley Milgram used the concept of geodesic distances to conjecture that all Americans are separated by a maximum geodesic length of 6.[44] *Betweenness centrality* measures whether an entity holds a brokerage position in the network. The degree of *betweenness* is measured using an algorithm that determines how many shortest geodesic paths go through a particular actor.

Connectedness, which is the weighted form of traditional betweenness centrality, measures not only how well a node is connected to others but also who it is connected to.[45] In a network, nodes with high centrality scores act as bridges or gatekeepers. Without them, the network would become disjointed. Depending on the context, these nodes could be crucial in relaying or creating a bottleneck for information, material or other objects of interest.

---

8. Degree Centrality

For our study, we calculated the degree centrality of all nodes in the network, to identify which nodes participate actively and closely with other countries in co-sponsoring resolutions. The distribution of degree centrality scores in the Human Rights Council network shows that 110 countries have a centrality degree between

---

[44] Stanley Milgram, 'The Small World Problem' (1967) 2 Psychology Today 60.
[45] Adapted from the approach described in Mark E.J. Newman, 'Scientific Collaboration Networks: I. Network Construction and Fundamental Results' (2001) Physical Review E 64(016131); and Fowler (n 27) 456.

200 and 400, implying that they (co-)sponsored roughly between 30 and 60% of the resolutions tabled. Zooming in on the scores of individual countries, we can identify those that take central positions in the network and those that are located more towards the periphery. This allows us to compare the results obtained for the member states of the European Union with those of third states and to detect divergences within the European Union.

Cohesive subgroups

As with the determination of power and position, network researchers have devised a host of methods to characterize and analyze cohesive subgroups. Subgroups can be analyzed as *blocks*, *cliques*, *clusters*, *components*, *cores*, *circles* and *factions*. Each of these approaches comes with its own theoretical concerns and methods for evaluation.[46]

9. Cohesive Subgroups

For the purpose of our study, we were interested in identifying whether the member and observer states at Human Rights Council are acting as blocks and how these groups are placed in relation to each other. One way to achieve this would be to organize countries into clusters based on the similarity or density of the (co-)sponsorship ties between them. We used the FACTION algorithm in UCINET to perform a similar operation on the Human Rights Council network.[47] One important point to note is that the identification of subgroups usually requires a process of trial and error. It is best to use different techniques and then compare the output to check for consistent as well as divergent patterns.[48]

The resulting graph (Figure 15.2) shows the four subgroups that were identified by running the FACTION algorithm. As part of our subgroup identification routine, we eliminated ties that were insignificant, or below 2.0; as a result, countries with very low participation and close ties were also eliminated. In order to arrive at this threshold, we ran the NETDRAW FACTION algorithm multiple times starting at the

---

[46]   See e.g. Ulrik Brandes and Thomas Erlebach (eds), *Network Analysis: Methodological Foundations* (Springer 2005) 112–292; Wouter de Nooy, Andrej Mrvar and Vladimir Batagelj, *Exploratory Social Network Analysis with Pajek* (CUP 2005) 59–83; Prell (n 40) 151–165; and Scott (n 19) 99–138; Wasserman and Faust (n 17) 249–290.

[47]   Stephen P. Borgatti, Martin G. Everett and Linton C. Freeman, *Ucinet for Windows: Software for Social Network Analysis* (Analytic Technologies, 2002). For an overview of various visualization methods and techniques see Sean F. Everton, 'A Guide for the Visually Perplexed: Visually Representing Social Networks' (Stanford University 2004) <http://web.stanford.edu/group/esrg/sili convalley/docs/networkmemo.pdf>.

[48]   See Sean F. Everton, *Disrupting Dark Networks* (CUP 2012) 170–205.

lowest tie strength of 0.5 up to a maximum of 6.0. At each threshold, we determined the level of fitness.[49] At a threshold of 2.0, we find the best fit at 0.69 when we segment the network into four blocks. By network analysis standards this is a significant score, suggesting that (co-)sponsorship in the Human Rights Council is predicated on membership in different blocks.

The network graph in Figure 15.2 shows the division of the Human Rights Council network into four blocks. Each of the symbols represents a different block. We can observe that the block division largely corresponds to geographic or cultural attributes. Studying each block individually, we can then again measure the density and centralization of each block.

For our research purposes, these results are highly informative. First, the graph appears to confirm the fact that co-sponsorship in the Human Rights Council is driven by group rather than individual country agendas. The graph also allows us to identify the European Union's closest allies, to measure its overall cohesiveness and to determine the extent to which it cooperates with actors from other regions. Finally, the graph confirms our findings about the centrality and connectedness of individual nodes, given that high-scoring countries take more central positions in the graph.

In a next step, we take a more macro view of our network in order to examine how the European Union is placed vis-à-vis other groups. Regional groups (African States, the Arab states, the Asian States, and GRULAC) and international organizations (European Union, the Non-Aligned Movement, Mercosur and the Organization of Islamic Cooperation) regularly sponsor and co-sponsor draft resolutions at the Human Rights Council.

Figure 15.3 shows the network graph at the level of regional groups/international organizations. The position of the nodes and the tie strength are determined by the similarity of the respective (co-)sponsorship patterns. Based on this, we can detect convergences and divergences in the (co-)sponsorship patterns of the different groups, keeping in mind, that some of these results are due to overlapping memberships.

Going Beyond Social Network Analysis

As discussed previously, social network analysis is not a comprehensive theory but a set of tools built on the premise that structures (i.e. networks) play an important role in shaping the agency of actors.[50] Although not always stated explicitly, most research employing social network analysis attempts to examine the causal link between two objects, namely, the patterns of individual interactions and the structural properties of the networks within which they occur. Examining the link between the structure of

---

[49]   This procedure was outlined by Stephen P. Borgatti, Martin G. Everett and Linton C. Freeman in the technical manual for UCINET.

[50]   See Marin and Wellman (n 3) 13.

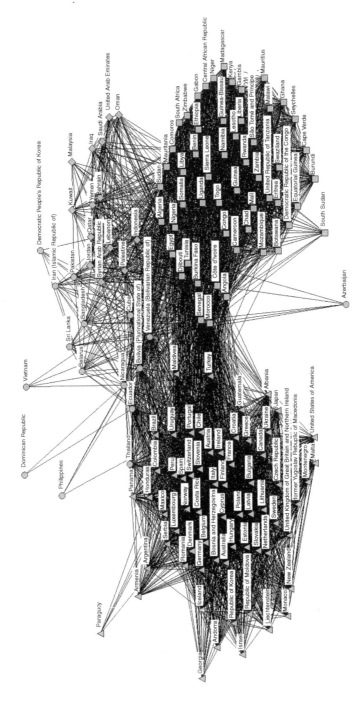

Figure 15.2 Blocks at the Human Rights Council

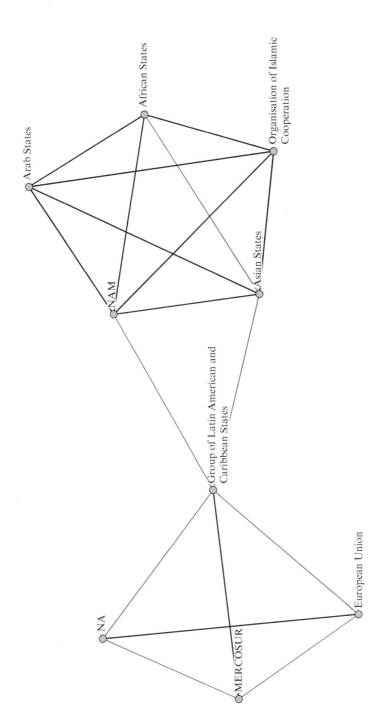

Figure 15.3   Inter-group co-operation in the Human Rights Council network

a network and actions of actors often requires researchers to incorporate information about the *relationships* as well as the *attributes* of individual actors. Moreover, networks themselves need to be contextualized according to the broader socio-economic, cultural and political environment in which they operate. This opens up the possibility, even necessity, of complementing social network measures with statistical methods and qualitative approaches.[51]

CONCLUDING PERSPECTIVES: OPPORTUNITIES AND CHALLENGES

Social network analysis can be a useful tool for understanding social processes by examining the interaction of actors through the flow of resources, ideas and power relationships between them. Consequently, social network analysis has considerable potential for the analysis of human rights related subjects, ranging from the development, interpretation, implementation and impact of human rights, to human rights violations or advocacy. As demonstrated in the case study above, analyzing networks of states in multilateral human rights fora can yield new insights about the processes that underlie the development of human rights norms and identify areas of contestation. Similarly, applying social network analysis to interactions between human rights courts can reveal the dynamics that shape the legal interpretation of human rights norms. Network studies can also help map the structures of transnational advocacy networks or social movements; they can contribute to understanding the constraints that human rights defenders face, or detect key players in illegal arms, human trafficking or other criminal networks.

Despite its usefulness researchers must also be aware of the challenges and limitations of incorporating social network analysis. As we have indicated above, delineating appropriate relationships and network boundaries in the real world where such boundaries are highly porous and networks are nested within each other can present considerable difficulties. Furthermore, selecting the appropriate values to measure the power and significance of relationships requires experimentation, which makes results vulnerable to misinterpretation by researchers and other stakeholders. Collecting data about relationships poses additional challenges, not only because it can be a complicated and subjective process, but also because it may in some cases raise ethical concerns. Finally, researchers need to be aware of the general risk of oversimplifying relationships when conduct-

---

[51]   See Langford (n 6).

ing social network analysis. These shortcomings can often be mitigated by complementing social network analysis with suitable qualitative and quantitative tools. Ethnographic methods, discourse analysis and interviews may be useful in helping researchers understand the broader context to improve their accuracy in delineating network boundaries and selecting the appropriate relationships.[52] Statistical methods can similarly complement social network analysis measures by testing the validity of the obtained results or modeling the behavior of actors and networks over time.

REFERENCES

Introductory Texts

Brandes, Ulrik and Thomas Erlebach (eds), *Network Analysis: Methodological Foundations* (Springer 2005)

Carrington, Peter J., John Scott and Stanley Wasserman (eds), *Models and Methods in Social Network Analysis* (CUP 2005)

Degenne, Alain and Michel Forsé, *Introducing Social Networks* (Sage 1999)

de Nooy, Wouter, Andrej Mrvar and Vladimir Batagelj, *Exploratory Social Network Analysis with Pajek* (CUP 2005)

Everton, Sean F., *Disrupting Dark Networks* (CUP 2012)

Prell, Christina, *Social Network Analysis: History, Theory and Methodology* (Sage 2012)

Scott, John, *Social Network Analysis* (3rd edn, Sage 2013)

Scott, John and Peter J. Carrington, *The SAGE Handbook of Social Network Analysis* (Sage 2011)

Wasserman, Stanley and Katherine Faust, *Social Network Analysis: Methods and Applications* (CUP 1994)

Selected Texts on Social Network Analysis and Human Rights

Carpenter, R. Charli, 'Studying Issue (Non)-adoption in Transnational Advocacy Networks' (2007) 61 International Organization 643

Etling, Bruce, Rob Faris and John Palfrey, 'Mapping the Arabic Blogosphere: Politics and Dissent Online' (2010) 12 New Media and Society 1225

Keck, Margaret E. and Kathryn Sikkink, *Activists beyond Borders: Advocacy Networks in International Politics* (Cornell University Press 1998)

Kwon, Kyounghee, George A. Barnett and Hao Chen, 'Assessing Cultural Differences in Translations: A Semantic Network Analysis of the Universal Declaration of Human Rights' (2009) 2 Journal of International and Intercultural Communication 107

Lake, David A. and Wendy Wong, 'The Politics of Networks: Interests, Power, and Human Rights Norms' in Miles Kahler (ed.), *Networked Politics: Agency, Power, and Governance* (Cornell University Press 2009)

Lazer, David, 'Networks and Politics: The Case of Human Rights' in Ryan Goodman, Derek Jinks and Andrew K. Woods (eds), *Understanding Social Action, Promoting Human Rights* (OUP 2012)

Lupu, Yonatan and Erik Voeten, 'Precedent in International Courts: A Network Analysis

---

[52] See e.g. in the present volume Sally Engle Merry, Chapter 7.

of Case Citations by the European Court of Human Rights' (2011) 42 British Journal of Political Science 413
Macon, Kevin T., Peter J. Mucha and Mason A. Porter, 'Community Structure in the United Nations General Assembly' (2011) 391 Physica A: Statistical Mechanics and its Applications 1
Murdie, Amanda, 'The Ties that Bind: A Network Analysis of Human Rights International Nongovernmental Organizations' (2014) 44 British Journal of Political Science 1
Roter, Petra, Anuska Ferligoj and Andrej Mrvar, 'State Support for Human Rights Treaties' in Thomas J. Volgy, Zlatko Šabič, Petra Roter, Andrea K. Gerlak (eds), *Mapping the New World Order* (Wiley-Blackwell 2009)

BIBLIOGRAPHY

Barsh, Russel Lawrence, 'Measuring Human Rights: Problems of Methodology and Purpose' (1993) 15 Human Rights Quarterly 87
Bender-deMoll, Skye, 'Potential Human Rights Uses of Network Analysis and Mapping: A Report to the Science and Human Rights Program of the American Association for the Advancement of Science' (2008) 17
Borgatti, Stephen P. and Virginie Lopez-Kidwell, 'Network Theory' in John Scott and Peter J. Carrington (eds), *The SAGE Handbook of Social Network Analysis* (Sage 2011)
Borgatti, Stephen P. and José Luis Molina, 'Ethical and Strategic Issues in Organizational Social Network Analysis' (2003) 39 The Journal of Applied Behavioral Science 337
Borgatti, Stephen P., Ajay Mehra, Daniel J. Brass and Guiseppe Labianca, 'Network Analysis in the Social Sciences' (2009) 323 Science 892
Borgatti, Stephen P., Martin G. Everett and Linton C. Freeman, *Ucinet for Windows: Software for Social Network Analysis* (Analytic Technologies 2002)
Brandes, Ulrik and Thomas Erlebach (eds), *Network Analysis: Methodological Foundations* (Springer 2005)
Campbell, James E., 'Cosponsoring Legislation in the U.S. Congress' (1982) 7 Legislative Studies Quarterly 415
Carrington, Peter J., John Scott and Stanley Wasserman (eds) *Models and Methods in Social Network Analysis* (CUP 2005)
Chané, Anna-Luise and Arjun Sharma,'Universal Human Rights? Exploring Contestation and Consensus in the UN Human Rights Council' (2016) 10 Human Rights & International Legal Discourse 219
Chané, Anna-Luise and Arjun Sharma, 'The European Union in the Human Rights Council: A Social Network Analysis of (Co-)sponsorship Patterns' (forthcoming)
Cingranelli, David L. and David L. Richards, 'Quantitative Studies' in David P. Forsythe (ed.), *Encyclopedia of Human Rights* (OUP 2009), Vol. 4, 293–296
Cross, Frank B., James E. Spriggs II, Timothy R. Johnson and Paul J. Wahlbeck, 'Citations in the U.S. Supreme Court: An Empirical Study of Their Use and Significance' [2010] University of Illinois Law Review 489
de Nooy, Wouter, Andrej Mrvar and Vladimir Batagelj, *Exploratory Social Network Analysis with Pajek* (CUP 2005)
Doreian, Patrick, 'Causality in Social Network Analysis' (2001) 30 *Sociological Methods and Research* 81
Everton, Sean F., 'A Guide for the Visually Perplexed: Visually Representing Social Networks' (Stanford University 2004) <http://web.stanford.edu/group/esrg/siliconvalley/docs/network memo.pdf>
Everton, Sean F., *Disrupting Dark Networks* (CUP 2012)
Fowler, James H., 'Connecting the Congress: A Study of Cosponsorship Networks' (2006) 14 Political Analysis 456

Fowler, James H., Timothy R. Johnson, James F. Spriggs II, Sangick Jeon and Paul J. Wahlbeck, 'Network Analysis and the Law: Measuring the Legal Importance of Precedents at the U.S. Supreme Court' (2007) 15 Political Analysis 324

Freeman, Linton C., *The Development of Social Network Analysis: A Study in the Sociology of Science* (Empirical Press 2004)

Freeman, Linton C., 'The Development of Social Network Analysis – with an Emphasis on Recent Events' in John Scott and Peter J. Carrington (eds), *The SAGE Handbook of Social Network Analysis* (Sage 2011)

Gelter, Martin and Mathias Siems, 'Networks, Dialogue or One-way Traffic? An Empirical Analysis of Cross-citations between Ten of Europe's Highest Courts' (2012) 8 Utrecht Law Review 88

Hafner-Burton, Emilie M. and Alexander H. Montgomery, 'Power Positions: International Organizations, Social Networks, and Conflict' (2006) 50 Journal of Conflict Resolution 3

Hafner-Burton, Emilie M., Miles Kahler and Alexander H. Montgomery, 'Network Analysis for International Relations' (2009) 63 International Organization 559

Hug, Simon and Richard Lukacs, 'Preferences or Blocs? Voting in the United Nations Human Rights Council' (2014) 9 Review of International Organizations 83

Jin, Xi and Madeleine O. Hosli, 'Pre- and Post-Lisbon: European Union Voting in the United Nations General Assembly' (2013) 36 West European Politics 1274

Kadushin, Charles, 'Who Benefits from Network Analysis: Ethics of Social Network Research' (2005) 27 Social Networks 139

Katz, Daniel M. and Derek K. Stafford, 'Hustle and Flow: A Social Network Analysis of the American Federal Judiciary' (2010) 71 Ohio State Law Journal 457

Kessler, Daniel and Keith Krehbiel, 'Dynamics of Cosponsorship' (1996) 90 American Political Science Review 555

Kilduff, Martin and Wenpin Tsai, *Social Networks and Organizations* (Sage 2003)

Kim, Jang Hyun and George A. Barnett, 'A Structural Analysis of International Conflict: From a Communication Perspective' (2007) 33 International Interactions 135

Kogler, Gregory, 'Position Taking and Cosponsorship in the U.S. Congress' (2003) 28 Legislative Studies Quarterly 225

Kwon, Kyounghee, George A. Barnett and Hao Chen, 'Assessing Cultural Differences in Translations: A Semantic Network Analysis of the Universal Declaration of Human Rights' (2009) 2 Journal of International and Intercultural Communication 107

Laumann, Edward O., Peter V. Marsden and David Prensky, 'The Boundary Specification Problem in Network Analysis' in Linton C. Freeman, Douglas R. White and A. Kimball Romney (eds), *Research Methods in Social Network Analysis* (Transaction 1982)

Lazega, Emmanuel, 'Mapping Judicial Dialogue across National Borders: An Exploratory Network Study of Learning from Lobbying Among European Intellectual Property Judges' (2012) 8 Utrecht Law Review 115

Macon, Kevin T., Peter J. Mucha and Mason A. Porter, 'Community Structure in the United Nations General Assembly' (2011) 391 Physica A: Statistical Mechanics and its Applications 1

Marin, Alexandra and Barry Wellman, 'Social Network Analysis: An Introduction' in John Scott and Peter J. Carrington (eds), *The SAGE Handbook of Social Network Analysis* (Sage 2011)

Marsden, Peter V., 'Recent Developments in Network Measurement' in Peter J. Carrington, John Scott and Stanley Wasserman (eds), *Models and Methods in Social Network Analysis* (CUP 2005)

Milgram, Stanley, 'The Small World Problem' (1967) 2 Psychology Today 60

Moore, Spencer, Eugenia Eng and Mark Daniel, 'International NGOs and the Role of Network Centrality in Humanitarian Aid Operations: A Case Study of Coordination During the 2000 Mozambique Floods' (2003) 27 Disasters 305

Newman, Mark E.J., 'Scientific Collaboration Networks: I. Network Construction and Fundamental Results' (2001) Physical Review E 64 (016131)

Pauwelyn, Joost, 'Minority Rules: Precedent and Participation before the WTO Appellate

Body' in Joanna Jemielniak, Laura Nielsen and Henrik Palmer Olsen (eds), *Establishing Judicial Authority in International Economic Law* (CUP 2016)

Prell, Christina, *Social Network Analysis: History, Theory and Methodology* (Sage 2012)

Provan, Keith G. and Juliann G. Sebastian, 'Networks within Networks: Service Link Overlap, Organizational Cliques, and Network Effectiveness' (1998) 41 The Academy of Management Journal 453

Rosga, AnnJanette and Margaret L. Satterthwaite, 'The Trust in Indicators: Measuring Human Rights' (2009) 27 Berkeley Journal of International Law 253

Satterthwaite, Margaret L. and Justin Simeone, 'A Conceptual Roadmap for Social Science Methods in Human Rights Fact-Finding' in Philip Alston and Sarah Knuckey (eds), *The Transformation of Human Rights Fact-Finding* (OUP 2016)

Scott, John, *Social Network Analysis* (3rd edn, Sage 2013)

Scott, John and Peter J. Carrington, *The SAGE Handbook of Social Network Analysis* (Sage 2011)

Smith, Thomas A., 'The Web of Law' (2007) 44 San Diego Law Review 309

Sueur, Cédric, Jean-Louis Deneubourg and Odile Petit, 'From Social Network (Centralized vs. Decentralized) to Collective Decision-Making (Unshared vs. Shared Consensus)' (2012) 7 PLoS One 1

Todd, James E., 'An Analysis of Security Council Voting Behavior' (1969) 22 The Western Political Quarterly 61

Wasserman, Stanley and Katherine Faust, *Social Network Analysis: Methods and Applications* (CUP 1994)

Wilson, Rick K. and Cheryl D. Young, 'Cosponsorship in the U.S. Congress' (1997) 22 Legislative Studies Quarterly 25

Young, Helen and Nicholas Rees, 'EU Voting Behaviour in the UN General Assembly, 1990–2002: the EU's Europeanising Tendencies' (2005) 16 Irish Studies in International Affairs 193

16. Researching discrimination
Dimitrina Petrova

Discrimination on a number of grounds,[1] despite being prohibited under certain international and domestic laws, is a pervasive social evil and source of injustice. It deserves to be addressed urgently. It also deserves to be the subject of research, be it for academic or practical purposes.

Research on discrimination rarely rests on a rigorous and explicit methodology and is often driven by civil society advocacy, political concerns or movements for justice and equality. This chapter seeks to contribute to filling this gap by focusing on the methodology of researching discrimination.

The focus of the chapter is on mapping out relevant methods and its purpose is essentially practical: to help potential researchers of discrimination develop better methods. It regards discrimination as a violation of human rights and therefore takes as a point of departure a number of assumptions that are intrinsic to the project of international human rights law. These assumptions have been the subject of a growing body of critical literature.[2] This chapter assumes familiarity with and an acceptance – however critical – of the discursive framework of international human rights law and of the continued relevance of the legal construction contained therein of 'discrimination'.

WHAT IS DISCRIMINATION?

Before we turn to the methods of researching discrimination, it is necessary to recall the status and normative content of the right to non-discrimination,

---

[1] See e.g. the UN International Covenant on Civil and Political Rights, article 2(1), prohibiting discrimination on any ground such as sex, race, colour, language, religion, political or other opinion, national or social origin, property, birth or other status. International Covenant on Civil and Political Rights, 16 December 1966, United Nations, Treaty Series, Vol. 999, p. 171 (ICCPR).

[2] Unsettling as some of the academic deconstructions of human rights are, they are of little concern compared with the global massive assault on human rights by a growing number of states and the shrinking space for human rights work, including research.

and place the methodological approaches to researching discrimination on the firm basis of a legal definition of discrimination.

Non-discrimination and Equality

The emerging global consensus among experts is that non-discrimination and equality are two distinct rights, whereby the right to non-discrimination is narrower in content and subsumed under the right to equality.[3] This understanding justifies the re-invention of discrimination law as equality law, of which discrimination law is an essential but not exclusive part.[4]

This chapter focuses only on non-discrimination, but one should be conscious that any research which ignores more general inequalities while researching the phenomena of discrimination is limited and at risk of being much less relevant to the context and the lived experiences of people. The research of discrimination, in other words, should be regarded as a necessary but not exclusive element of the study of inequalities.

Status of the Right to Non-discrimination

Non-discrimination has a triple status in the United Nations human rights instruments: it is (1) a general principle, (2) an autonomous right and (3) an accessory right.

(1)   *General principle*: in the Universal Declaration of Human Rights (UDHR),[5] equality (and non-discrimination subsumed in it) – 'equal

---

[3]   See e.g. Declaration of Principles on Equality, Equal Rights Trust (December 2008), Principle 4, p. 6. This document was signed initially by 128 experts and subsequently by hundreds of further experts and activists on equality and human rights from all over the world. The principles formulated and agreed by the experts are based on concepts and jurisprudence developed in international, regional and national legal contexts. Since its adoption, the Declaration has guided efforts to develop equality legislation in a number of countries. In 2011, the Parliamentary Assembly of the Council of Europe adopted a Recommendation calling on the 47 Council of Europe member states to take the Declaration into account when developing equality law and policy (Parliamentary Assembly of the Council of Europe, *Resolution and Recommendation: The Declaration of Principles on Equality and activities of the Council of Europe,* REC 1986 (2011), 25 November 2011).
[4]   B. Hepple, *Equality: The New Legal Framework* (Hart 2011), p.1. This shift can be seen in the UK's legislative terminology, with the move from the Sex Discrimination Act 1975 and further non-discrimination laws to the Equality Act 2010.
[5]   Universal Declaration of Human Rights, 10 December 1948, 217 A (III).

and inalienable rights' of 'all members of the human family' – is a *general principle*, the recognition of which is the 'foundation of freedom, justice and peace in the world'.[6] 'Equal rights of men and women' in particular are reaffirmed in the fifth recital. Article 1 then proclaims: 'All human beings are born free and equal in dignity and rights'. Article 1 can be regarded as expressing both a general principle of the human rights framework and an accessory right to be equal in respect of the enjoyment of rights (see below).

(2) *Autonomous right*: the first sentence of article 7 UDHR reads: 'All are equal before the law and are entitled without any discrimination to equal protection of the law'. This provision enshrines an independent (autonomous, free-standing) right to non-discrimination with two discernible elements of its content; namely, equality before the law and equal protection of the law.

(3) *Accessory right*: article 2 UDHR provides a right to non-discrimination attaching to all other human rights recognized within UDHR. The article reads:

> Everyone is entitled to all the rights and freedoms set forth in this Declaration, without distinction of any kind, such as race, colour, sex, language, religion, political or other opinion, national or social origin, property, birth or other status. Furthermore, no distinction shall be made on the basis of the political, jurisdictional or international status of the country or territory to which a person belongs, whether it be independent, trust, non-self-governing or under any other limitation of sovereignty.[7]

This provision introduces an accessory (subsidiary) right to non-discrimination, or, to be more precise, it creates as many separate accessory rights to non-discrimination as there are human rights recognized in UDHR (e.g. a right to non-discrimination in respect to the enjoyment of the right to life; a right to non-discrimination in respect to liberty and security of person, a right to non-discrimination in respect to freedom of expression, etc.).

The second sentence of article 7 of UDHR also affirms non-discrimination as an accessory right: 'All are entitled to equal protection against any discrimination in violation of this Declaration and against any incitement to such discrimination'.

Following the UDHR, subsequent international human rights law has

---

6 Ibid. preamble, first recital.
7 Universal Declaration of Human Rights (n 5) article 2.

retained and developed non-discrimination as a fundamental principle underlying the entire system, an autonomous right, and accessory right coupled with each of the rights recognized in it.

Legal Instruments which Provide the Right to Non-discrimination

The key *international human rights law instruments* which provide the right to non-discrimination include:

(1) general treaties – the International Covenant on Civil and Political Rights (ICCPR)[8] and the International Covenant on Economic, Social and Cultural Rights (ICESCR);[9]
(2) special group treaties;[10] and
(3) thematic treaties, such as the Convention against Torture and Other Cruel, Inhuman or Degrading Treatment or Punishment.[11]

Each of the general treaties contains relevant anti-discrimination provisions, although these differ in scope.[12] Notably, the ICCPR contains a free-standing equality clause in article 26:

> All persons are equal before the law and are entitled without any discrimination to the equal protection of the law. In this respect, the law shall prohibit any discrimination and guarantee to all persons equal and effective protection against discrimination on any ground such as race, colour, sex, language, religion, political or other opinion, national or social origin, property, birth or other status.

Here, non-discrimination is construed as an autonomous civil right, in addition to the accessory right provided in article 2(1) of the same Covenant, which reads:

---

[8]   See n 1.

[9]   16 December 1966, United Nations, Treaty Series, Vol. 993, p. 3.

[10]   The special group treaties include the International Convention on the Elimination of All Forms of Racial Discrimination (ICERD), 21 December 1965, United Nations, Treaty Series, Vol. 660, p. 195; the Convention on the Elimination of All Forms of Discrimination against Women (CEDAW), 18 December 1979, United Nations, Treaty Series, Vol. 1249, p. 13; the Convention on the Rights of the Child (CRC), 20 November 1989, United Nations, Treaty Series, Vol. 1577, p. 3; and the Convention on the Rights of Persons with Disabilities (CRPD), resolution/adopted by the General Assembly, 24 January 2007, A/RES/61/106.

[11]   10 December 1984, United Nations, Treaty Series, Vol. 1465, p. 85.

[12]   See, e.g. W. Vandenhole, *Non-discrimination and Equality in the View of the UN Human Rights Treaty Bodies* (Intersentia 2005).

Each State Party to the present Covenant undertakes to respect and to ensure to all individuals within its territory and subject to its jurisdiction the rights recognized in the present Covenant, without distinction of any kind, such as race, colour, sex, language, religion, political or other opinion, national or social origin, property, birth or other status.

An accessory right to non-discrimination is also found in ICESCR, article 2(2), which obliges states to ensure that 'the rights enunciated in the present Covenant will be exercised without discrimination of any kind'. The article goes on to reference an open-ended list of protected characteristics identical to the one contained in article 2(1) ICCPR.[13]

The UN special group treaties prohibit discrimination in respect to certain categories of people defined by race, sex, age (children) and disability. Unlike the general treaties, these contain definitions of discrimination related to the particular protected characteristics they cover.

In addition, numerous *regional human rights instruments* prohibit discrimination, including treaties in the framework of the African Union, the Organization of American States, the European Union and the Council of Europe.

Definition of Discrimination

The research of discrimination in the conceptual framework of human rights law requires the researcher to operate from a certain definition of discrimination, in order to seek answers to the right questions when investigating cases and patterns of suspected discrimination. However, it should be noted that, while a certain definition of discrimination guides the researcher, the respondent/provider of testimony should not be assumed to know what discrimination is, or to correctly characterize events and circumstances as 'discrimination'. Moreover, among the general public, 'discrimination' is understood very broadly, usually as being synonymous with any human rights violation generally, or even as broadly as to cover any injustice whatsoever.

The international human rights law treaties do not contain a general definition of discrimination.[14] The definition of discrimination provided

---

[13] See n 1.

[14] General definitions extrapolating from the group-specific definitions have been offered however by treaty bodies. See UN Human Rights Committee, 'General Comment 18, Non-discrimination', U.N. Doc. HRI/GEN/1/Rev.1 Para 7 (1994); UN Committee on Economic, Social and Cultural Rights, 'General Comment No. 20: Non-discrimination in Economic, Social and Cultural Rights (art. 2, para. 2, of the International Covenant on Economic, Social and Cultural

here is from the 2008 Declaration of principles on Equality,[15] an instrument of international best practice which brings together the scattered concepts and approaches found in international human rights law and reflects the modern understanding of equality (see Box 16.1). It is not the only one that can be applied – there can be certain variations – but it is important that the reseach methods be based on some kind of definition that orientates the identification of the essential elements of discrimination in real-life situations and the assessment of national laws and policies.

BOX 16.1 THE DEFINITION OF DISCRIMINATION IN THE DECLARATION OF PRINCIPLES ON EQUALITY

Discrimination must be prohibited where it is on grounds of race, colour, ethnicity, descent, sex, pregnancy, maternity, civil, family or carer status, language, religion or belief, political or other opinion, birth, national or social origin, nationality, economic status, association with a national minority, sexual orientation, gender identity, age, disability, health status, genetic or other predisposition toward illness or a combination of any of these grounds, or on the basis of characteristics associated with any of these grounds.

Discrimination based on any other ground must be prohibited where such discrimination (i) causes or perpetuates systemic disadvantage; (ii) undermines human dignity; or (iii) adversely affects the equal enjoyment of a person's rights and freedoms in a serious manner that is comparable to discrimination on the prohibited grounds stated above.

Discrimination must also be prohibited when it is on the ground of the association of a person with other persons to whom a prohibited ground applies or the perception, whether accurate or otherwise, of a person as having a characteristic associated with a prohibited ground.

Discrimination may be direct or indirect.

Direct discrimination occurs when for a reason related to one or more prohibited grounds a person or group of persons is treated less favourably than another person or another group of persons is, has been, or would be treated in a comparable situation; or when for a reason related to one or more prohibited grounds a person or group of persons is subjected to a detriment. Direct discrimination may be permitted only very exceptionally, when it can be justified against strictly defined criteria.

Indirect discrimination occurs when a provision, criterion or practice would put persons having a status or a characteristic associated with one or more prohibited grounds at a particular disadvantage compared with other persons, unless that provision, criterion or practice is objectively justified by a legitimate aim, and the means of achieving that aim are appropriate and necessary.

Rights)', 2 July 2009, E/C.12/GC/20, Para 7ff. These definitions are subsumed in the more useful and detailed definition provided in the 2008 Declaration of Principles on Equality used here.

[15] See n 3.

Harassment constitutes discrimination when unwanted conduct related to any prohibited ground takes place with the purpose or effect of violating the dignity of a person or of creating an intimidating, hostile, degrading, humiliating or offensive environment.

An act of discrimination may be committed intentionally or unintentionally.

Source: Declaration of Principles on Equality (Equal Rights Trust 2008) Principle 5.

This definition takes a broad view regarding the *personal scope* of the prohibition of discrimination, containing a long list of *protected characteristics* (*prohibited grounds of discrimination*). It features both a list of explicitly prohibited grounds and criteria for the inclusion of further grounds, according to which 'candidate grounds' should meet at least one of three listed conditions.[16] It recognizes that a person may experience discrimination on a combination of grounds, and therefore covers both the cumulative and intersectional forms of multiple discrimination.[17] Thus, the definition provides a foundation for tackling the full complexity of the problem to be addressed: people's lived experience of discrimination.

Regarding the *material scope* of the prohibition, discrimination must

---

[16] The definition of discrimination in Principle 5 includes an extended list of prohibited grounds of discrimination, omitting the expression 'or other status' which follows the list of characteristics in article 2 of the Universal Declaration of Human Rights. While intending to avoid abuse of anti-discrimination law by claiming discrimination on any number of irrelevant or spurious grounds, the definition nonetheless contains the possibility of extending the list of prohibited grounds and includes three criteria, each of which would be sufficient to recognize a further characteristic as a prohibited ground. This approach is inspired by the solution to the open vs closed list of grounds dilemma provided by the South African Promotion of Equality and Prevention of Unfair Discrimination Act (2000). See D. Petrova, 'The Declaration of Principles on Equality: A Contribution to International Human Rights' in *Declaration of Principles on Equality* (Equal Rights Trust 2008).

[17] *Multiple* discrimination is *cumulative* when the perpetrator discriminates on both grounds separately, and *intersectional* when the perpetrator does not discriminate on either ground separately but only the combination of grounds triggers discrimination. In the latter case, unless the law prohibits multiple discrimination, an ethnic minority woman, for example, will be unable to make a successful claim of either sex or race discrimination if her employer can show that they do not discriminate against either women or ethnic minority members as such. See P. Uccellari, 'Multiple Discrimination: How Law Can Reflect Reality' [2008] 1 Equal Rights Review. See also the special issue devoted to intersectionality of the Equal Rights Review, Vol. 16 (March 2016).

be prohibited in all areas of life regulated by law.[18] A research project can cover all such areas in a certain geographic context or only specified areas, e.g. criminal justice, administrative or other services, employment, education, healthcare or political participation. It must be stressed that discrimination should be prohibited in both the public sphere and in the private sector, and that only those areas of life that are not regulated by law remain outside the remit of the prohibition – for example, the choice of friends on Facebook or decisions regarding who to include in one's will. While states are the principal duty-bearer, and as such have a duty to respect, protect and fulfill the right to non-discrimination for all persons present within their territory or subject to their jurisdiction, non-state actors, including transnational corporations and other non-national legal entities, should respect the right to non-discrimination in all areas of their activity regulated by law.

The definition covers three major forms of *prohibited conduct* which constitute discrimination: *direct discrimination, indirect discrimination* and *harassment*. All three concepts reflect current expert opinion on the definitions of the different forms of discrimination in international human rights and equality law.[19] An example of direct gender discrimination would be a provision in a labour code that bans women from taking jobs with night shifts on the basis of their alleged vulnerabilities. An example of indirect age discrimination would be a case in which the government introduces a new policy requiring all persons who are self-employed to complete their tax returns online and there is no option to file one's tax declaration on paper. Some older persons do not have computers or are unfamiliar with how to use the internet. In addition, the *denial of reasonable accommodation* is increasingly recognized as a distinct form of discimination.[20] An

---

[18]   See ICCPR (n 1) article 26.

[19]   See e.g. United Nations Committee on Economic, Social and Cultural Rights, 'General Comment No. 20: Non-discrimination in Economic, Social and Cultural Rights' (n 14) para 10.

[20]   Reasonable accommodation is defined in Principle 13 of the Declaration: 'To achieve full and effective equality it may be necessary to require public and private sector organizations to provide reasonable accommodation for different capabilities of individuals related to one or more prohibited grounds. Accommodation means the necessary and appropriate modifications and adjustments, including anticipatory measures, to facilitate the ability of every individual to participate in any area of economic, social, political, cultural or civil life on an equal basis with others. It should not be an obligation to accommodate difference where this would impose a disproportionate or undue burden on the provider' (note 3) Principle 13, 10–11. See also Convention on the Rights of Persons with Disabilities, resolution/ adopted by the General Assembly, 24 January 2007, A/RES/61/106, article 2.

example of this denial would be the failure to provide wheelchair access to a public building when this would not amount to an undue burden on the relevant authority.

Positive Action

The research of discrimination should also contain among its definitional assumptions an understanding of the relationship between discrimination and *positive action* (also known as *affirmative action*). The understanding of positive action in the Declaration of Principles on Equality is in line with emerging approaches in international and regional human rights law, in this case with regard to the concepts of special measures in the various human rights law instruments.[21] It should be noted that the Declaration captures the growing tendency of interpreting special measures as part of, rather than an exception to, equal treatment.[22] Principle 3 states:

> To be effective, the right to equality requires positive action. Positive action, which includes a range of legislative, administrative and policy measures to overcome past disadvantage and to accelerate progress towards equality of particular groups, is a necessary element within the right to equality.[23]

The right to equality extends beyond a right to be free from discrimination and contains an element of participation on an equal basis with others in all areas of life regulated by law. Positive action is key to addressing those inequalities which are not attributable solely to discrimination. A clear understanding of the relationship between equality, discrimination and positive action is necessary to avoid confusion by the researcher of discrimination. The importance of the notion of positive action in the research on discrimination is in that without it we are at risk of documenting grievances by non-beneficiaries of positive action as instances of alleged discrimination. For example, people may complain that children from a disadvantaged ethnic minority receive additional support for attending pre-school while other children do not. This in fact should be characterized as positive action aimed at achieving equality.

---

[21] See e.g. International Convention on the Elimination of All Forms of Racial Discrimination, G.A. Res. 2106 (XX), 1965, article 1(4); Convention on the Elimination of All Forms of Discrimination against Women, G.A. Res. 34/180, 1979, article 4(1); and Organization of African Unity, Protocol to the African Charter on Human and Peoples' Rights on the Rights of Women in Africa, OAU Doc. CAB/LEG/66.6, 2000, article 2(1)(d).
[22] See Petrova (n 16) p. 32.
[23] Declaration of Principles on Equality (n 3) Principle 3, 5.

RESEARCH METHODOLOGIES

Research methodology depends on the *purpose* of the research and the research questions, both of which should be clearly defined. This chapter is limited to examining only some of the *main types of research* within the study of discrimination, based on the *subject* of the research, i.e. the answer to the question on *what* do we research: (a) individual discrimination cases; (b) patterns of discrimination; (c) perceptions about discrimination; (d) legal and policy framework related to discrimination; (e) discrimination jurisprudence; or (f) other subjects which may include the effectiveness of enforcement of anti-discrimination laws and policies, best practices in addressing discrimination, best practices (affirmative action, awareness raising, capacity building, etc.) for preventing discrimination,

A study's subject can combine any of the above types. For example, one can study the effectiveness of a national normative framework that would contain elements of (a), (c), (e) and (f) above. Most studies in practice will have a combined subject and will need to make use of a combination of empirical and normative research methods.

Apart from the subject of the research we wish to undertake, the methodology will also depend on the *thematic scope* of the research. This can be limited by (a) grounds of discrimination (gender, race, religion, etc,); (b) areas of life to be covered (discrimination in the area of employment, education, the administration of justice, public functions such as policing, provision of goods and services, etc.); and (c) relatedness to certain human rights, e.g. we may want to study discrimination in respect to the prohibition of torture and ill-treatment, the right to freedom of expression or freedom of religion, the right to education, health, work, etc.

In determining the research methodology, we should also take into account the *geographic scope* of the study, which can be conducted at a national or sub-national level, or be a comparative or combined study covering several countries, or a global study covering a certain discrimination topic at a global level. Further, it is important to specify clearly the *time-frame* of the study as it will make a methodological difference whether we aim to explore individual cases, patterns or jurisprudence in the last 5–10 years, the last 12 months, or the last three months.

The sections that follow will briefly present the most frequently used research methods, structured by the subject of the study of discrimination.

Researching Individual Discrimination Cases

When the purpose of a study is to document individual discrimination cases, we use observation, in the form of direct observation, review of recorded complaints or different types of interviews. The reliability and accuracy of these methods vary, moving from direct observation, which is the most reliable and accurate, to focus group interviews, which may be accepted as context mapping or starting points but demand caution as they can be highly misleading. Interview reliability depends on whether the respondents shared personal experience, were eye-witnesses, had other direct participation in a reported case or had only indirect knowledge of the case gleaned from different sources, ranging from direct victims to hearsay. To use any of the research methods relevant to studying individual cases of discrimination, researchers should be provided with training and guidance, and their work should be accompanied by a monitoring and evaluation plan.

Direct observation and review of records

Direct observation is more adequate, reliable and easier when we are dealing with repetitive, routine discriminatory practices, e.g. systematic racial profiling in public places.

Review of recorded complaints is a method of research used when public bodies (such as human rights or equality commissions, ombudsmen, etc.), non-governmental organizations, community services or legal aid bodies can be enlisted to provide access to their databases of recorded complaints of discrimination. These may include letters from victims or information sheets filled in by paralegals and others registering oral complaints by visitors.

Face-to-face interviews: general issues

Face-to-face interviews are a major method of documentation of individual cases. There are various kinds of interview: structured (based on a rigorous questionnaire), semi-structured (following pre-ordered themes but allowing for deviation based on respondent's answers) and exploratory (investigating a certain issue and lacking a preliminary plan, guided by the need to establish facts, as when researching a specific incident). Each has its own limitations and strengths.[24] Face-to-face interviews can be conducted with *individuals* or *focus groups*, the latter being a widely used method of collecting evidence and opinions from a group of similar respondents, usually six to 12 persons, who are presumed to have similar

---

[24]   For more on interview methods, see e.g. C.L. Briggs, *Learning How To Ask: A Sociolinguistic Appraisal of the Role of the Interview in Social Science Research* (CUP 1986); J.A. Gubrium and J.A. Holstein, *Handbook of Interview Research: Context and Method* (Sage 2001), especially part 1: 'Forms of Interviewing'.

experience as they share a protected characteristic and/or demographics (by age, occupation, residence, health status, etc.). Interviews and evidence provided by focus group participants can vary in content: they can be an account of personal experience of discrimination or knowledge of discrimination affecting others.

The *method of face-to-face interview* is the one which is most widely used in researching individual discrimination cases (as well as patterns of discrimination – see below). The guidelines for interviewers should contain two types of instructions: (a) non-specific to investigating discrimination cases; and (b) specific to investigating direct and indirect discrimination, harassment, denial of reasonable accommodation and other forms of discrimination. Non-specific guidelines are broadly applicable in the investigation of a large number of human rights violations including discrimination, and cover, *inter alia*:

- compliance with local laws and regulations, with a strict security protocol if needed;
- instructions about acceptable locations for the interview;
- issues of informed consent to be provided by the respondents;[25]
- issues of sensitivity and discomfort caused by possibly upsetting questions;
- risks and benefits for the respondent;
- confidentiality in handling of interview information;
- recording of personal details relevant to the object and purpose of the research;
- safeguards for children;[26]
- the effect of the interviewer's identity, personality, dress and conduct.

---

[25]   Consent can be given verbally or in writing. Bearing in mind that it may not always be appropriate to ask the respondent to sign a statement to confirm consent (for example because of the sensitivity of the issue or security considerations), it may be preferable to request that the interviewer signs a statement to the effect that all information on the consent sheet has been read to the respondent (see e.g. World Health Organization, *Ethical and Safety Recommendations for Researching, Documenting and Monitoring Sexual Violence in Emergencies* (2007) 23 <http://www.who.int/reproductivehealth/publications/violence/9789241595681/en/> accessed 14 May 2016.

[26]   The research institution should not condone practices that are illegal or harmful to children and should alert the authorities where such practices are discovered. These include child marriages, female genital mutilation and ritual abuse. While remaining aware and respectful of cultural and religious diversity, interviewers should in all cases advocate respect for the core rights of children above any other cultural or religious considerations.

While indispensable in the research of human rights abuses, interviews have methodological limitations even in respect to what seems like the most trusted type of evidence – *eye-witness testimony*. The perils of eye witness testimony have been pointed out by psychologists, and there is a body of literature analysing the multitude of factors undermining its value. The cultural context and the differing group psychologies functioning in it cannot be overestimated. Researchers should be aware that factual truth is not necessarily equivalent to the testimony of bona fide eye witnesses and should always seek to corroborate every detail of fact.

Face-to-face interviews: issues specific to documenting discrimination

The guidelines specific to the research of individual discrimination cases through face-to-face interviews should explain what facts and circumstances would constitute the elements allowing us to allege that discrimination has occurred.[27] In this regard, the researcher would be guided by the definition of discrimination adopted in the study's methodology. If the definition is the one provided above (see Box 16.1), the researcher would be trying to establish whether all of the following elements are in place in order to properly describe certain conduct, policy or practice as *direct discrimination*:

(1)   less favourable treatment;
(2)   a causal link between the treatment and a protected characteristic;
(3)   a comparable situation of the treatment caused by the protected characteristic and the treatment of a person unrelated to that characteristic.[28]

Similarly, identifying *indirect discrimination* on a certain ground would involve establishing the presence of:

(1)   a provision, criterion or practice that is neutral in respect to that ground;
(2)   the fact that the said provision, criterion or practice would put persons having a status or a characteristic associated with that ground at a particular disadvantage;

---

[27]   Note that these guidelines, insofar as they focus on how to identify discrimination, would be similar in respect to focus group interviews, as well as to analysing records of complaints filed by victims at different institutions.

[28]   However, if the definition of direct discrimination one has accepted contains a second hypothesis of a 'detriment' (as in the one cited above), in certain cases, e.g. pregnancy, one may not require the element of comparison.

(3)   a comparison between persons associated with the ground in question and persons not associated with it;

(4)   a lack of objective justification, which itself would require (a) a legitimate aim, (b) strict necessity of the means (the provision, criterion or practice) such that the aim could not have been achieved with less restrictive means and (c) proportionality between the means and the legitimate aim.

It is important to note that the aim in this type of research is by definition limited to presenting factual circumstances or conducts in which discrimination *may be presumed*. By virtue of the nature of proof that applies in discrimination cases, in many cases we cannot determine whether discrimination really occurred as we cannot perform proof procedures typical of discrimination law during the field research. Whilst in some cases the proof will be easy to obtain already during the research process, and we can ascertain that discrimination has occurred as all elements needed for the proof are in place,[29] in most cases we would be able to document only presumed discrimination. These will be cases in which a court would have to act on the presumption and proceed to prove the discrimination, for example through forensic investigation or by reversing the burden of proof in civil proceedings. In respect to the latter, the following principle of procedural equality law is well established:

> Legal rules related to evidence and proof must be adapted to ensure that victims of discrimination are not unduly inhibited in obtaining redress. In particular, the rules on proof in civil proceedings should be adapted to ensure that when persons who allege that they have been subjected to discrimination establish, before a court or other competent authority, facts from which it may be presumed that there has been discrimination (*prima facie* case), it shall be for the respondent to prove that there has been no breach of the right to equality.[30]

In many discrimination cases described in human rights reports the discrimination, strictly speaking, is not proven as the causation is not definitively established, the causation being the link between the protected

---

[29]   For example, a member of a religious minority is dismissed and the employer states to her in writing that the reason is her religion, while the job is such that belonging to a certain religion different from hers is not a genuine and determining occupational requirement, and the victim is in possession of the written statement; or a well-documented statement by a policeman who has beaten an ethnic minority person saying that what he has done was because of the ethnicity of the victim.

[30]   See above, n 3, Principle 21, p.13. See also, *inter alia*, Council Directive 2000/43/EC implementing the principle of equal treatment between persons irrespective of racial or ethnic origin, article 8.

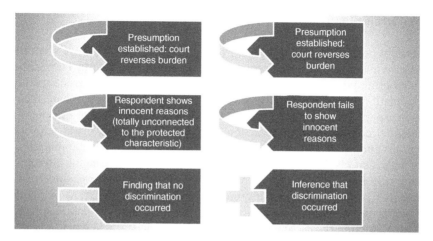

Figure 16.1   The logic of the reversal of the burden of proof

characteristic and the less favourable treatment. Frequently, all we can do in our research into such individual cases is limited to establishing a *prima facie* case. Based on this stage, a competent body would be able to follow the logic of proof and reach a positive or negative conclusion, depending on whether the respondent would be able to demonstrate that the treatment complained of had nothing to do with the protected characteristic (see Figure 16.1).

Further, as in any observation, the challenge is to not allow the act of researching itself to pollute the information collected. In observation, we should try to control for variables – for example, if race discrimination is alleged, we should try to establish whether race is really the reason for the less favourable treatment we are describing by exploring whether the same treatment is also afforded to persons with other suspect characteristics, e.g. variables such as religion or place of residence. Issues to be mindful of include whether the comparator (which in our case plays the role of the control group) is adequate and representative. For example, if we establish ethnic discrimination by law enforcement bodies against a certain ethnic minority group, are we comparing with a representative sample of the general population, rather than, for example, with an atypically affluent surrounding community that is treated better whilst most other groups in the country are threated in a way similar to that of the ethnic minority group in question?

Researching Patterns of Discrimination

It is not possible for any research project to provide an exhaustive account of discrimination in a given geographic or thematic framework. The reality of discrimination is such that experiences are as many and varied as the population of the territory we want to cover. Each person will have their own experiences of discrimination, arising in different areas of life, in different circumstances, in interaction with different persons, institutions or groups and as a result of any aspect of their identity, or any combination of these aspects. It has been acknowledged that the measuring of discrimination in any society is not easy.[31] Hence, it may be useful to undertake research on the patterns of discrimination in a given context, as opposed to reporting on individual cases, in order to understand the depth, spread and interaction of discriminatory practices in a society. When patterns are the subject of the research, individual cases would still be very useful as illustrations of the patterns.

Developing a hypothesis

At the start of this type of research, we should formulate a hypothesis about the prevailing patterns of discrimination in the chosen geographic, jurisdictional, demographic and/or temporal framework, and the research in this case would aim at falsifying or verifying the hypothesis. The hypothesis can be arrived at through a baseline study reviewing the available literature as well as consultations with stakeholders or experts. It is advisable to start with *desk research*, which contains both legal/normative and interdisciplinary social science components before launching field research into discrimination patterns. The desk research may help formulate a hypothesis which the field research will seek to falsify or verify.

In terms of sources to look at, UN monitoring and review mechanisms and some regional mechanisms have generated an abundance of reports which can be assessed during the desk research phase. Each UN human rights instrument is monitored by an expert committee following treaty-based procedures including country reviews, issuing of general comments and recommendations and considering individual complaints. The country review documentation is of the greatest value in establishing a baseline. For example, the Human Rights Committee in its Concluding Observations on Austria (December 2015) referred to the 'rise of advocacy of racial or

---

[31]   See e.g. Office of the High Commissioner, *Human Rights Indicators: A Guide to Measurement and Implementation* (United Nations Human Rights Office of the High Commissioner 2012) 82.

religious hatred against Roma, Muslims, Jews, minorities, migrants and asylum seekers, including political hate speech', 'advocacy of hatred against persons of a different faith by some radical Islamist preachers' and 'hate speech on the Internet and online forums'.[32] If we convert this to the language of equality law, we may formulate a number of suspected patterns, for example, 'political hate speech amounting to race discrimination against Roma', 'incitement to hatred by Islamist preachers amounting to religious discrimination', etc. However, only someone who is trained in equality law can perform this task, as not all suggested patterns would be valid in an equality law framework.

A certain amount of additional information about patterns of discrimination can be gleaned from the individual complaints submitted to treaty bodies. However, one should be cautioned that, while country-specific concluding observations can indeed be suggestive of patterns of discrimination, individual cases are not necessarily indicative of typical practices. As such, they can only be used as initial clues in baseline research aimed at identification of patterns.

UN special procedures, including the over 40 thematic mandates and the more than a dozen country mandates, have also generated a large number of reports that contain a wealth of information useful to the identification of discrimination patterns. Further, the Universal Periodic Review (UPR) has also generated a wealth of recommendations related to combating various forms of discrimination in UN member states. However, as there is no category capturing non-discrimination as a distinct issue in the UPR information database,[33] it is difficult to generate the relevant statistics. This difficulty of categorization reflects the permeating, cross-cutting and truly ubiquitous nature of equality rights in the UN system; it is challenging, for example, to unravel the overlap of 'non-discrimination' with thematic entries such as 'racial discrimination', 'women's rights', 'sexual orientation and gender identity' or indeed the more general categories of 'civil and political rights – general' and 'economic, social and cultural rights – general' which are featured in the UPR data base.

Further sources include reports by human rights organizations, group-specific or thematic NGOs, academic literature, jurisprudence and media stories. One should bear in mind that information on the existence of discrimination may be found in a range of different forms, including direct testimony from victims of abuse, statistics indicating socio-economic

---

[32]   Human Rights Committee, 'Concluding Observations on the 5th Periodic Report of Austria', CCPR/C/AUT/CO/5, 3 (December 2015) para 15.

[33]   UPR Info Database <http://www.upr-info.org/database/>.

disparities between different groups, reports or information on other human rights abuses overlapping with discrimination and reports on the availability of basic services in a given country. The researcher should be open minded in terms of the types of sources at this stage.

Following an initial desk research, depending on the magnitude of the study and the available resources, the researcher may conduct a *scoping field research*, the objective of which would be to collect a small number of samples/stories/cases, as diverse as possible, illustrating suspected patterns of discrimination, and to refine the list of patterns we would be dealing with in the chosen context.

Documentation of discrimination patterns

Once the hypothesis of the study is in place, we can launch proper *field research* – the empirical research aimed at the collection of as much relevant information as possible within our resources about discrimination cases and practices, through detailed documentation of victims' and witnesses' testimonies, and comments by duty bearers and other stakeholders. In this type of reseach, we can apply the observational methods described above related to the research of individual cases but accommodate them to the purpose of the patterns research.

A more powerful tool compared with observational methods is the construction of *experimental methods* for identifying patterns of discrimination. While observation does not contain intervention, and is limited to only retrospective gathering of information, experimental approaches allow us to intervene and 'cause' the discrimination. One such method may be termed *testing survey*. For example, a study in several French cities identified discrimination against ethnic minority persons in access to employment. It presented 2400 pairs of applications to employers in response to recruitment announcements. Regarding the job requirements, all applications were the same, and differed solely in respect to the applicant's name; one name was indicative of 'metropolitan' French ancestry and the other indicated origin from former French colonies. Eighty per cent of the recruitment choices gave preference to the 'metropolitan' French candidate.[34] This quantitative research method is an excellent tool for revealing the bias that underlies discriminatory practices.

A rarely used but most powerful method in researching discrimination

---

[34]   E. Cediey and F. Foroni, 'Discrimination in Access to Employment on Grounds of Foreign Origin in France: A National Survey of Discrimination based on the Testing Methodology of the International Labor Office' (International Labor Office 2008).

patterns is the conducting of an *experiment* known as *situation testing*. In situation testing, researchers provoke the discriminatory conduct whilst documenting it. For example, we may send testers to an establishment which – we suspect – excludes homosexuals from entering but denies doing this. We send a couple of testers who play the role of a gay couple, for example through displaying visible signs of affection. As they are refused entry, we document the situation discreetly. They may, for example, be told that the establishment is overbooked. Our testers would then leave, but just a few minutes later a second couple of testers, this time heterosexual, would appear at the door and be waved in without issue.

There are many forms of discrimination which can be documented through similar creative experiments, particularly in the areas of employment and access to goods and services. Situation testing has been used mainly by organizations involved in strategic litigation, but there is no reason why it cannot be used in research projects, bringing to the research all the rigour of prospective experiment over retrospective observation.[35]

Alongside observational and experimental field research, further in-depth *literature review* should continue. This involves further review of relevant literature on discrimination in the given jurisdiction, including reports by government and non-governmental organizations (NGOs) to UN treaty bodies and the UPR process, government and intergovernmental data and reports, and research published by international and national NGOs, academic studies and media reports. Given the scattered and cross-cutting nature of the right to non-discrimination and the frequent overlaps of discrimination with other abuses, the literature review should cover relevant aspects of human rights and equality, as well as a number of related issues in fields such as development studies, economics and conflict studies. As the approach to discrimination should be contextual, traditional methods of human rights documentation should be complemented by sociological research, in particular related to the study of discrimination patterns in employment, education and healthcare. In the interests of objectivity and balance, we should also seek to include the government's perspective on the issues discussed in the report.

Wherever possible, socio-demographic *statistical data* should be relied on to improve understanding of discrimination patterns.[36] We should look at census data, data found in reports and publications produced

---

[35] For more information, see e.g. Isabelle Rorive, *Proving Discrimination Cases: The Role of Situation Testing* (Centre for Equal Rights and Migration Policy Group 2009).

[36] However, as Andrew Lang once said, an unsophisticated researcher 'uses statistics as a drunken man uses lamp posts – for support rather than illumination'.

by authoritative sources, such as the World Bank,[37] the World Health Organization, the United Nations Development Program and the United Nations Educational, Scientific and Cultural Organization. It should be stressed, however, that the availability of statistical data relevant to discrimination is usually very limited in respect to most countries. The scarcity of relevant statistical data – in particular data disaggregated by protected characteristics such as gender, ethnicity, age or religion – presents a challenge to effective quantitative research on discrimination. This in itself is a cause for concern, as government should ensure collection of disaggregated data, allowing it to assess and address discrimination and inequalities.[38]

The obligation to gather statistical data notwithstanding, the identification of group categories may be a sensitive issue:

> Although many population groups call for more visibility (for themselves) in statistics to inform on prevalent discrimination or disparities and to support targeted policy measures, being identified as a distinct group may be a politically sensitive issue, which may discourage disaggregation of data.[39]

High-quality research on discrimination patterns will be based on a critical analysis of all available social statistics, factoring in any relevant sensitivities that may have led to lacking or flawed statistics.

Validation and presenting the findings

In order to strengthen the accuracy and legitimacy of the research findings and conclusions regarding discrimination patterns, the draft report can be exposed to a *validation process*. It is always a good idea to present the draft to interested parties from civil society, government, academia, the legal profession, the media and others. In face-to-face meetings, group

---

Quoted in Steven Novella, *Your Deceptive Mind: A Scientific Guide to Critical Thinking Skills* (The Teaching Company 2012).

[37]   See in particular the World Bank Human Opportunity Index, which is a good proxy for studying possible patterns of discrimination.

[38]   States have an obligation to collect data on different groups in certain areas of life under the ICERD, CEDAW and CRPD, an obligation which is frequently invoked by treaty bodies when reviewing state compliance. Under the Declaration of Principles of Equality, the obligation to collect disaggregated data covers all characteristics relevant to identifying structural disadvantage. Principle 24 states: 'To give full effect to the right to equality States must collect and publicise information, including relevant statistical data, in order to identify inequalities, discriminatory practices and patterns of disadvantage, and to analyse the effectiveness of measures to promote equality' (see above, n 3, p. 14).

[39]   United Nations Human Rights Office of the High Commissioner (n 31) 34.

consultations and remote communications, the draft report would be subjected to critique by a range of stakeholders, with the aim of validating and fine-tuning its findings and conclusions. The feedback received throughout this phase of the research should be incorporated in the draft prior to publication.

It is particularly useful, although not always possible, to *engage the relevant authorities* in the validation process, through consultation with representatives of government ministries and other governmental bodies. They should be given an opportunity to review and comment on the findings and conclusions of the research, provide updates, correct inaccuracies or add additional relevant facts or comments. The government response should be taken into account during the finalization of the report. If the authorities have neglected or denied the findings, this should be mentioned in the report itself.

In terms of *presenting the results* of the research on discrimination patterns, we should try to describe each discrimination pattern in turn, by reference to the vulnerable group affected (e.g. women, an ethnic minority). In each case, we should describe the major forms of discrimination affecting this group. Yet we should give more attention to patterns we consider more important, and present different discrimination patterns in order of importance within the political, economic and social context that is our reference framework. Criteria to decide which the more important patterns are may include:

- the severity of the consequences of the discriminatory acts or practices;
- the number of the people affected;
- the geographic extent of the discriminatory acts or practices;
- the direct involvement of state actors as perpetrators.

Methodological challenges

A couple of methodological comments are necessary here. When the purpose of a study is to reveal patterns of discrimination in a certain context, we use *inductive logic* – generalizing from a number of similar cases and estimating the numbers of victims and/or instances and/or the spread of the discriminatory practice. The limitations of induction as a knowledge generator are well known, and they are more pronounced in the frequent practice by human rights researchers of relying on *case studies* (namely taking a certain – often rather limited – type of cases and building on the findings to arrive at more or less convincing generalizations). It stands to reason that the smaller the study in scope, the greater the so-called 'noise-to-signal ratio'. Small studies may be useful, but we should attempt to follow them up by studies on a scale big enough to reduce the 'noise'.

Case studies are less problematic when they reveal patterns that are based on discrimination contained in the laws of a country (i.e. when we are dealing with discriminatory legal provisions) as opposed to discrimination in fact. For example, the denial of equal rights to homosexuals in a number of countries is enshrined in national legislation criminalizing same-sex sexual relationships, pointing at a pattern of sexual orientation discrimination in areas like family life, housing, health, etc.

Further, we should be conscious of the well-established fact on which cognitive sciences insist, namely that humans are generally very good at pattern recognition – so 'good' that *we often see patterns that are not actually there.*[40] Therefore, we need to subject all our hypotheses regarding patterns to a critical examination to ensure that our patterns stand for real phenomena of discrimination that have a certain spread and uniformity of occurrence in the given context.

In the study of patterns of discrimination, it should be remembered that the lists of *protected characteristics* and *areas* of civil, cultural, economic, political and social life in which discrimination is prohibited featured in various jurisdictions should not be regarded as the limits of legitimate research. Discrimination can be related to other characteristics and can exist in other areas of life not specified in the national law. It should be recalled that the major international human rights law instruments contain open lists of grounds of discrimination, while best practice suggests the use of a test for the inclusion of new characteristics in closed lists (see above), and that discrimination should be prohibited in all areas of life regulated by law.[41]

Researching Perceptions of Discrimination

This type of research falls within the field of sociological research on opinions and attitudes, and it follows methodologies elaborated by the professional community conducting attitudinal surveys or opinion polls. The rules of validity here are not specific to the study of discrimination. As

---

[40]   Novella (n 36) 2.

[41]   Article 26 ICCPR (n 1) construing non-discrimination as an autonomous right defines the material scope as covering 'any' discrimination. The Human Rights Committee clarified that: 'It prohibits discrimination in law or in fact in any field regulated and protected by public authorities' (Human Rights Committee, 'General Comment 18, Non-discrimination' (Thirty-seventh session, 1989), U.N. Doc. HRI/GEN/1/Rev.1 at 26 (1994)).

with any such research, the quality of the procedures and thus the reliability of the findings are a function of the representativeness of the sample, the objectivity (lack of bias) of the questionnaire, the rules of the field-work, including the characteristics and conduct of the interviewers, the quality of the data entry, the quality of the data analysis, etc.

What is important to remember in respect to this kind of study is that the results should not be confused with a picture of the reality of discrimination; they describe perceptions, and the relationship between perceptions and reality is rarely straightforward. For example, a rise in perceptions that discrimination occurred may be the result of actual negative developments, but it may also reflect an improved awareness of discrimination or a trend in the public discourse propelled by the media.

Surveys on perceptions of discrimination are of reduced value to the extent that the survey respondents can opt in or out. We will learn the opinions of only those who chose to respond: this is one of the methodological limitations of self-selecting surveys, particularly through online platforms.[42]

Needless to say, there are numerous methodological challenges in every survey of perceptions as opposed to the collection of objective data, and a survey of perceptions of discrimination carries, if anything, an amplified risk. For example, asking marginalized groups whether they have experienced discrimination may produce a false negative result in cases where the group has not made significant steps to self-emancipation and has strongly internalized stereotypical societal views. Women in certain contexts still believe that it is only natural for husbands to discipline their wives in cases of disobedience, so they would not perceive as an unjust offence what the researcher – and the law – would consider gender-based discrimination.[43]

---

[42] For research on perceptions of discrimination across European Union member states, see the work of the Fundamental Rights Agency <www.fra.europa.eu>. In particular, see European Union Agency for Fundamental Rights, *EU-MIDIS: European Union Minorities and Discrimination Survey* (2009). See also OECD Journal of Development, Measuring Human Rights and Democratic Governance: Experiences and Lessons from Metagora (2008) 9(2), which contains some perception studies of poverty, human rights and corruption that are relevant to discrimination.

[43] On the structural differences in the perceptions of minority groups of discrimination in federal employment, see K. Naff, 'Perceptions of Discrimination' (1995) 23(3) Policy Studies Journal 483.

Normative Research on Protection Frameworks

The purpose of this kind of research is to assess a legal and policy framework related to the protection against discrimination within a chosen jurisdiction. The subject of this type of research would typically focus on the *legal framework* as it pertains to *protection* against discrimination.[44] When the research targets the jurisdiction of an individual state, it may cover, *inter alia*, the following matters:

(1)   Binding international and regional law relevant to non-discrimination,[45] including declarations, reservations and derogations, if any, and an analysis of the status of international legal provisions in the domestic legal order;
(2)   constitutional protections from discrimination – a legal critique;
(3)   specific anti-discrimination laws, be they comprehensive laws covering both numerous grounds and numerous areas of life, or group-specific or area-specific laws;
(4)   non-discrimination provisions in other fields of law, such as criminal and civil codes, family laws, education, health, employment, citizenship laws, etc.[46]

The purpose of this research is to provide a critical assessment of the state's legal framework, against the backdrop of international standards and best legislative practice. An assessment should be made of the comprehensiveness, as well as the strengths and weaknesses, of both the substantive and procedural elements of the system of national anti-discrimination laws. The researcher should identify areas where legislative protections are absent, inadequate, insufficient or otherwise weak.

Further to laws, this type of research may focus on governmental and/or

---

[44]   Note that laws and provisions which are themselves discriminatory or are frequently applied in a discriminatory manner should be studied as part of the research on patterns or individual cases of discrimination as they do not belong to the *protective* framework.

[45]   To identify a state's international legal obligations, one might use the United Nations Treaty Collection database: United Nations, *United Nations Treaty Series Online Collection* <http://treaties.un.org/pages/UNTSOnline.aspx?id=1>; or the website of the Office of the High Commissioner for Human Rights: Office of the High Commissioner for Human Rights <http://www.ohchr.org/EN/Pages/WelcomePage.aspx>.

[46]   Research on national laws, including the Constitution and national legislation, relies on reviewing primary sources, accessed via online databases or print material.

private sector organizations' policies related to preventing and protecting against discrimination. Most states have policies related to gender equality, persons with disabilities and persons living with HIV/AIDS. Research on government policies can be undertaken through a review of state reports to UN treaty bodies and documents gathered from government websites.[47]

The review of laws and policies should be assessed against international and regional normative standards related to discrimination and best practice documents, such as the Declaration of Principles on Equality discussed above. It is necessary to be clear about the allocation of responsibilities for preventing and eliminating discrimination. The *obligations of the state* in this regard are analogous to those confirmed in regard to the ICCPR and the ICESCR as explained, *inter alia*, in General Comment 3 of the CESCR and General Comment 31 of the UN Human Rights Committee.[48]

Research on Discrimination Jurisprudence

In this type of study, we look at any significant cases in which courts have ruled on discrimination matters. One might address the following issues:

- How have *constitutional provisions prohibiting discrimination* been interpreted in decisions of the state's supreme or constitutional court?
- How have *discriminatory provisions* in the constitution and other legislation been interpreted by the courts? Have they been challenged?
- How have any *specific anti-discrimination laws* been interpreted, if at all, by the courts?
- How have *non-discrimination provisions in other areas of law* been interpreted, if at all, by the courts?
- Have there been any other cases which have dealt with issues of equal treatment or the rights of particular vulnerable groups, even if they have not been litigated in terms of discrimination?

---

[47] For comprehensive country reports on the legal and policy framework related to discrimination in a number of countries, including, for example, Belarus, Kenya, Malaysia, Solomon Islands, Sudan and Ukraine, see the work of the Equal Rights Trust, Country Report Series, part 3 of each report <www.equalrightstrust.org>.

[48] States are required to take all necessary steps, including legislation, to give effect to the right to non-discrimination in the domestic order and in their international cooperation programs. While the broader right to *full and effective equality* may be difficult to fulfill, the requirement to take steps to *eliminate discrimination* is unqualified and of immediate effect. A failure to comply with this obligation cannot be justified by reference to cultural, economic, political, security, social or other factors.

When writing about jurisprudence, one should provide a brief description of the facts of each case, sum up the arguments made by the parties and quote the key words of the decision. Full citation for all cases should be included.

To be able to assess the quality of court decisions, the legal research in this type should be orientated by *authoritative interpretation* of international, regional and best practice legal and policy standards, e.g. by UN treaty bodies, and international, regional and national courts, as well as academic legal commentary.

One of the *challenges* in assessing jurisprudence related to discrimination is to consider court decisions in the light of the conflict of rights (a conflict between non-discrimination and other rights) and a conflict between rights and other interests. Courts are called upon to weigh and strike a balance between the effects of discrimination and those of restriction or violation of other rights and against other public interests. In fact, a large part of court reasoning related to discrimination is about defining such balances.

METHODOLOGICAL RISKS COMMON TO ALL METHODS IN RESEARCHING DISCRIMINATION

The following risks need to be reflected upon and mitigated across all of the research methods described in the above section.

First, we should be conscious of the risks related to the uncritical acceptance of implicit normative, political and philosophical *choices embodied in laws* themselves which appear to be benign and neutral on their face. A good rule of thumb for the researcher on how to go behind the norms and look critically at their content is to always ask whether the norms are used in practice to entrench existing power hierarchies and political influence. Norms that do not appear to improve the position of vulnerable and marginalized groups in society should be suspect and examined for discriminatory application, even if they are neutral on their face. The trend in modern equality law is a departure from a formal, procedural and symmetrical notion of equality and an acceptance of a transformative role for equality law, in that we refuse to be neutral between the powerful and the powerless, and aim to shift the power balance on the fabric of society towards empowerment of the weaker. We see the essence of discrimination as an assault on the dignity of those who are less powerful, and equality law is currently undergoing a slow, incremental evolution towards an asymmetrical interpretation of its principal dyad of the person with the protected characteristic and the comparator.

Secondly, discrimination law relies on identity categories, meaning that there is a risk of *fetishizing the 'grounds' of discrimination* and miss the opportunity to highlight serious cases that do not fall into familiar identity boxes. Arguably, this is in part due to the influence of liberalism on equality law,[49] with its approach to the legal subject as an atomistic, abstract individual. One should be reassured that intersectionality approaches are currently developing within discrimination law, which has been trying to re-think itself in order to better reflect reality.[50] As Claire L'Heureux-Dube put it in 1995 while sitting on the Supreme Court of Canada, discrimination law requires that courts focus 'on the issue of whether [individuals] are victims of discrimination, rather than becoming distracted by ancillary issues such as "grounds"'.[51]

Thirdly, the so called *publication bias*[52] is a high risk in the research of discrimination, as well as in human rights research generally. This risk arises from the fact that the authors compare their findings with the published sources and tend to amplify their generalizations in cases of alignment with the latter. To make matters worse, in the area of human rights research, including discrimination, negative studies – those that do not reveal violations – are as a rule not publicized, resulting in an even stronger publication bias.

Fourthly, discrimination research is also at a high risk of so-called *confirmation bias*: the tendency to look for confirming evidence and to avoid or disregard negative evidence. Focus group research and interviews in the context of patterns research are especially 'suspect', as they often amount to anecdotal evidence (i.e. uncontrolled or *ad hoc* observations). However, even more rigorous systematic research based on random samples can be plagued with confirmation bias.

Fifthly, a *qui bono (who benefits) bias* is another very high risk in discrimination research – as researchers are usually on the side of the potential or real victims of discrimination, despite a wish to be neutral. To mitigate this, we could present our findings to the stakeholders who are on the side of the alleged perpetrators and account for their side of the story.

Sixthly, a risk is created by the desire of the researcher to demonstrate

---

[49]   See R. Hunter (ed.), *Rethinking Equality Projects in Law: Feminist Challenges* (Hart 2008).

[50]   See e.g., the seminal work of K. Crenshaw, 'Demarginalizing the Intersection of Race and Sex: A Black Feminist Critique of Anti-discrimination Doctrine, Feminist Theory, and Anti-racist Policies' (1989) 4 University of Chicago Legal Forum 139.

[51]   *Egan v Canada* [1995] 2 S.C.R. 513, p. 563.

[52]   Novella (n 36).

legal technical competence at an expert level – an *aspiration bias*. The researcher may eliminate facts and cases, thinking that they do not meet some element of what he understands to be 'discrimination' – which admittedly is not an easy concept to master (in particular indirect discrimination). To mitigate this, we should instruct empirical researchers to not disregard cases or patterns of discrimination or examples illustrating patterns even if they are unsure if they constitute 'discrimination' in a strict legal sense.

CONCLUSION

Human rights research in general and the research of discrimination in particular is a methodological minefield. To pass muster, the methodology of discrimination research needs to be clear, explicit about its limitations, conscious of the many risks and containing strategies mitigating these risks. Otherwise, the research may end up being discarded as 'not even wrong' – the worst possible indictment for anyone who has invested their time and effort in creating new knowledge.

BIBLIOGRAPHY

Briggs, C.L., *Learning How To Ask: A Sociolinguistic Appraisal of the Role of the Interview in Social Science Research* (CUP 1986)

Cediey, E. and F. Foroni, 'Discrimination in Access to Employment on Grounds of Foreign Origin in France: A National Survey of Discrimination Based on the Testing Methodology of the International Labor Office' (International Labor Office 2008)

Convention on the Rights of Persons with Disabilities, resolution/adopted by the General Assembly, 24 January 2007, A/RES/61/106

Convention on the Rights of the Child, 20 November 1989, United Nations, Treaty Series, Vol. 1577

Crenshaw, K., 'Demarginalizing the Intersection of Race and Sex: A Black Feminist Critique of Anti-discrimination Doctrine, Feminist Theory, and Anti-racist Policies' [1989] University of Chicago Legal Forum 4

Declaration of Principles on Equality, Equal Rights Trust (December 2008)

Egan v Canada [1995] 2 S.C.R. 513

EU Council Directive 2000/43/EC implementing the principle of equal treatment between persons irrespective of racial or ethnic origin

European Union Agency for Fundamental Rights, *EU-MIDIS: European Union Minorities and Discrimination Survey* (2009)

Equal Rights Trust, Country Report Series, part 3 of each report <www.equalrightstrust.org>

Gubrium, J.A. and J.A. Holstein, *Handbook of Interview Research: Context and Method* (Sage 2001)

Hepple, B., *Equality: The New Legal Framework* (Hart 2011)

Human Rights Committee, 'Concluding Observations on the 5th Periodic Report of Austria', CCPR/C/AUT/CO/5, 3 (December 2015)

Human Rights Committee, 'General Comment 18, Non-discrimination' (Thirty-seventh session, 1989), U.N. Doc. HRI/GEN/1/Rev.1 at 26 (1994)

Hunter, R. (ed.), *Rethinking Equality Projects in Law: Feminist Challenges* (Hart 2008)

International Convention on the Elimination of All Forms of Discrimination against Women, G.A. Res. 34/180, 1979

International Convention on the Elimination of All Forms of Racial Discrimination, G.A. Res. 2106 (XX), 1965

International Convention on the Rights of Persons with Disabilities, resolution/adopted by the General Assembly, 24 January 2007, A/RES/61/106

Naff, K., 'Perceptions of Discrimination' [1995] Policy Studies Journal 23(3)

Novella, S., *Your Deceptive Mind: A Scientific Guide to Critical Thinking Skills* (The Teaching Company 2012)

OECD Journal of Development, Measuring Human Rights and Democratic Governance: Experiences and Lessons from Metagora (2008) 9

Office of the High Commissioner, *Human Rights Indicators: A Guide to Measurement and Implementation* (United Nations Human Rights Office of the High Commissioner 2012) 82

Office of the High Commissioner for Human Rights: Office of the High Commissioner for Human Rights <http://www.ohchr.org/EN/Pages/WelcomePage.aspx>

Organization of African Unity, Protocol to the African Charter on Human and Peoples' Rights on the Rights of Women in Africa, OAU Doc. CAB/LEG/66.6, 2000

Parliamentary Assembly of the Council of Europe, *Resolution and Recommendation: The Declaration of Principles on Equality and activities of the Council of Europe*, REC 1986 (2011), 25 November 2011

Petrova, D., 'The Declaration of Principles on Equality: A Contribution to International Human Rights' in *Declaration of Principles on Equality* (Equal Rights Trust 2008)

Rorive, I., *Proving Discrimination Cases: The Role of Situation Testing* (Centre for Equal Rights and Migration Policy Group 2009)

Uccellari, P., 'Multiple Discrimination: How Law Can Reflect Reality' [2008] Equal Rights Review 1

UN Committee on Economic, Social and Cultural Rights, 'General Comment No. 20: Non-Discrimination in Economic, Social and Cultural Rights (art. 2, para. 2, of the International Covenant on Economic, Social and Cultural Rights)', 2 July 2009, E/C.12/GC/20

UN Human Rights Committee, 'General Comment 18, Non-discrimination', U.N. Doc. HRI/GEN/1/Rev.1 Para 7 (1994)

UN International Covenant on Civil and Political Rights, 16 December 1966, United Nations, Treaty Series, Vol. 999

United Nations Treaty Collection Database: United Nations, *United Nations Treaty Series Online Collection* <http://treaties.un.org/pages/UNTSOnline.aspx?id=1>

UPR Info Database <http://www.upr-info.org/database/>

Vandenhole, W., *Non-discrimination and Equality in the View of the UN Human Rights Treaty Bodies* (Intersentia 2005)

World Health Organization, *Ethical and Safety Recommendations for Researching, Documenting and Monitoring Sexual Violence in Emergencies* (2007)23 <http://www.who.int/reproductivehealth/publications/violence/9789241595681/en/> (accessed 14 May 2016)

17. Assessing work at the intersection of health and human rights: why, how and who?

Laura Ferguson

INTRODUCTION

The relevance of human rights to the field of public health came into sharp focus thanks to the pioneering work of Jonathan Mann and his colleagues in the early days of the global response to the HIV epidemic.[1] Slowly, there has been increasing recognition of the applicability of human rights to other areas of health including, perhaps most recently, non-communicable diseases.[2]

Human rights are grounded in international law so there is a legal requirement for action by duty-bearers towards their realization, including within the field of health. Furthermore, work in public health is increasingly driven by evidence, which has created a need for an evidence base around the effectiveness of using human rights to shape health interventions that goes beyond the legal imperative for attention to these norms and standards. Work to generate this evidence has started, and even as methodological challenges remain, useful documentation of the impact of human rights-based approaches to health is emerging.[3]

This chapter will explore some of the methodological challenges inherent in seeking to assess health-related human rights from both a human rights perspective and a public health perspective. In trying to assess the impact of any work at the intersection of human rights and health, what

---

[1] Jonathan Mann and Daniel Tarantola, 'Responding to HIV/AIDS: A Historical Perspective' (1998) 2(4) Health and Human Rights 5.

[2] Sofia Gruskin, Laura Ferguson, Daniel Tarantola and Robert Beaglehole, 'Noncommunicable Diseases and Human Rights: A Promising Synergy' (2014) 104(5) American Journal of Public Health 773.

[3] Flavia Bustreo, Paul Hunt, Sofia Gruskin, Asbjørn Eide, Linsey McGoey, Sujatha Rao, Francisco Songane, Daniel Tarantola, Maya Unnithan, Alicia Yamin, Annemiek van Bolhuis, Laura Ferguson, Emma Halliday, Shyama Kuruvilla, Jennie Popay and Genevieve Sander, *Women's and Children's Health: Evidence of Impact of Human Rights* (World Health Organization, Geneva, 2013).

should we be trying to measure? What data, tools and mechanisms exist that can be used as the basis of assessments of health-related human rights? What political or normative choices underpin particular tools or the use of particular tools and mechanisms? What are the challenges inherent in these types of assessments and how might they be overcome? These are some of the questions that I seek to address in this chapter.

Throughout the chapter, illustrative examples are drawn from different areas of health. These should not be understood to be '*the*' way to assess human rights in each of these different areas of health; they are merely examples of relevant datasets, mechanisms for action, or work that has been carried out. Bringing together experts on human rights and public health will be necessary for determining the best approach for any given assessment of human rights in health.

The focus of this chapter is on assessing human rights in public health laws, policies, programs and services. Even as litigating health-related human rights can be a useful strategy for improving health and the realization of rights, this chapter does not extend to the assessment of such strategies.

The chapter provides a brief introduction to the relevance of human rights to health, and how to think about assessment in this context. It then provides an overview of some human rights mechanisms through which countries' compliance with health-related human rights can be assessed, noting strengths and weaknesses of these mechanisms. Attention then turns to the public health field where examples are provided of mechanisms and datasets that can provide additional, complementary information relevant to assessing health-related rights. Two tools designed to elicit information about health-related human rights are presented: one starting from a human rights perspective and another starting from a public health perspective. Finally, some key challenges relating to assessing health-related human rights are explored. The aim is to provide an overview of some of the different methods that can be used for assessing human rights in health, noting their respective pitfalls and advantages, with a view to informing the selection and further development of methods for future work in this area.

WORKING AT THE INTERSECTION OF HEALTH AND HUMAN RIGHTS: THE ENTRY POINT MATTERS

Work at the intersection of health and human rights is expanding and the entry point from which this work is approached is not always the same: largely based on disciplinary training and background, some people use human rights as their starting point while others start from health. All may end up working in 'health and human rights', looking at health-related human rights, but why and how this is done may still be very different. While health and human rights should not be set up as conflicting paradigms, it is important to understand the differences that exist between them.

Grounded in international law, human rights rely on legal norms and obligations. Health is relevant only because governmental obligations encompass actions that affect health. From a human rights perspective, assessing health-related human rights is critical for understanding the extent to which States Parties are compliant with these obligations. Traditional sources of data might be human rights indicators as well as reports through structures such as United Nations treaty monitoring bodies, special procedures and the Universal Periodic Review.

From a public health perspective, the purpose of assessing human rights in health is to demonstrate the impact on health of realizing human rights. Moving beyond compliance with international obligations, does the realization of rights relevant to health also lead to better health outcomes? In this case, not only does the extent to which a government has fulfilled its health-related human rights obligations matter, but this must also be tied to health indicators such as health outcomes or uptake of health services. Routine health statistics and health-related data collected for international and global reporting purposes are commonly used for these types of assessment.

HOW AND WHY ARE HUMAN RIGHTS RELEVANT TO HEALTH?

Human rights outline state obligations for action across many different areas, including health. State commitments regarding the right to the highest attainable standard of health specifically are outlined in article 12 of the International Covenant on Economic, Social and Cultural Rights (ICESCR)[4] and have been further clarified by General Comments. General Comment 14 on the right to health makes explicit the substantive content and monitoring requirements of the right to health and underscores that this right is 'an inclusive right extending not only to timely and appropriate health care but also to the underlying determinants of health'.[5] Regional instruments, such as the African Charter on Human and Peoples' Rights

---

[4]   United Nations. International Covenant on Economic, Social and Cultural Rights (1966).

[5]   'General Comment No. 14: The Right to the Highest Attainable Standard of Health (Art. 12 of the Covenant)' (11 August 2000) E/C.12/2000/4.

and the European Social Charter, also contain provisions relevant to health.[6]

Other health topics, broader issues that are relevant to health and health related to specific populations are addressed in a range of rights across the body of human rights law. Examples include, but are not limited to, the rights to non-discrimination, education, information and privacy. Assessment of all of these rights could be relevant to work at the intersection of health and human rights, and specificity about what is included in any given assessment, as well as justification for these decisions, is important.

The child's right to health is expanded upon below to illustrate some of the different sources available to guide understanding of a health-related right. The child's right to health is article 24 in the Convention on the Rights of the Child (CRC),[7] and it is elaborated upon in General Comment 15 of the Committee on the Rights of the Child, which helps elucidate state obligations.[8] The General Comment includes a section entitled 'The action cycle', which is designed to guide states in operationalizing the child's right to health through the development, implementation and monitoring of relevant policies, programs and services.[9] Two key points are made with regard to monitoring and evaluation. First, the Committee notes that 'A well-structured and appropriately disaggregated set of indicators should be established for monitoring and evaluation to meet the requirements under the performance criteria above [availability, accessibility, acceptability and quality of health services and programmes]'.[10] States parties are advised that they should have in place a functional health information system that produces reliable data, that the data should be used to inform policies, programs and services, and that the quality of the system itself should be regularly reviewed. Secondly, 'National accountability mechanisms should monitor, review and act on their findings', which also highlights the need for regular use of available data, placing responsibility on national accountability mechanisms for ensuring that this occurs.[11] This points to a range of things that can be assessed to monitor state compli-

---

[6] African Charter on Human and Peoples' Rights ('Banjul Charter'), 27 June 1981 OAU Doc. CAB/LEG/67/3 rev. 5, 21 I.L.M. 58 (1982); ETS 163 – European Social Charter (Revised), 3 May 1996.

[7] United Nations, Convention on the Rights of the Child (1989).

[8] UN Committee on the Rights of the Child (CRC), 'General Comment No. 15 (2013) on the Right of the Child to the Enjoyment of the Highest Attainable Standard of Health (Art. 24)', 17 April 2013, CRC/C/GC/15.

[9] Ibid.

[10] Ibid.

[11] Ibid.

ance with realizing the child's right to health such as the availability, disaggregation and appropriate use of routinely collected data.

Technical Guidance on implementing a human rights-based approach to different areas of health has recently been passed by the Human Rights Council and can also usefully inform implementation and assessment efforts. Building on the example of the child's right to health above, the Technical Guidance on Implementing a Human Rights Based Approach to Under-Five Mortality and Morbidity includes a list of actions that states are required to undertake regularly as part of effective self-assessment.[12] This includes: monitoring and evaluating the effects of the national legal and policy framework on child mortality and morbidity; monitoring budget allocations and expenditure for child health; and ensuring the functionality and monitoring the use of mechanisms for reporting, remedy and redress in the case of violations of human rights relating to child mortality and morbidity.[13] All of these constitute additional points of assessment to help elucidate states' progress towards fulfilling their human rights obligations in relation to child health.

So, even just looking at one illustrative right – the child's right to health – a lot of guidance exists on how States Parties should understand, implement and monitor their obligations. Whether seeking to understand compliance with these obligations or the impact of human rights on health, this guidance is useful for determining what should be assessed.

TRANSLATING INTERNATIONAL HUMAN RIGHTS COMMITMENTS INTO PUBLIC HEALTH ACTION

Upon ratification of an international human rights treaty, governments are bound to incorporate its provisions into their national legal framework. This, in turn, shapes national and sub-national policies, programs and services. Thus, upon ratification of the ICESCR, for example, a government should ensure that its obligations under article 12 on the right to health are incorporated into all health-related legislation at the national level. This includes amending any laws that conflict with these obligations. Furthermore, all health services and programs should be implemented

---

[12]   Human Rights Council, 'Technical Guidance on the Application of a Human Rights-based Approach to the Implementation of Policies and Programmes to Reduce and Eliminate Preventable Mortality and Morbidity of Children under 5 Years of Age: Report of the Office of the United Nations High Commissioner for Human Rights' (30 June 2014) A/HRC/27/31.

[13]   Ibid.

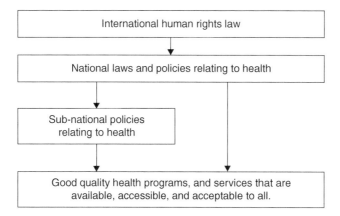

Figure 17.1 Translating international human rights commitments into public health action

within this legal framework so that the commitments made under the ICESCR permeate government structures through to the interface with the population.

Human rights are enshrined in international law, but their true value is felt at the individual level. For this value to be realized, therefore, rights must filter down from the level of international law, through national and sub-national structures, to people's lived realities. It is at this point that public health professionals are interested in human rights: what difference do rights make to people's lives through their incorporation into laws, policies, programs and services? Figure 17.1 illustrates how this should occur in relation to health.

The goal of ensuring that laws, policies, programs and services are consistent with international human rights law relevant to health is to contribute to the fulfillment of human rights, but this obviously requires assessment.[14] It is assumed that this will also improve health outcomes, but given the demand for evidence of effectiveness in public health, it is critical that this assumption be tested and that assessments illustrate to public health experts how human rights can contribute to health.[15]

---

[14] UN Office of the High Commissioner for Human Rights (OHCHR), 'Principles and Guidelines for a Human Rights Approach to Poverty Reduction Strategies' (2006) HR/PUB/06/12; World Health Organization, 'Health and Human Rights: Factsheet No. 323' <www.who.int/mediacentre/factsheets/fs323/en/> accessed 27 February 2016.

[15] Paul Hunt, 'The Human Right to the Highest Attainable Standard of Health: New Opportunities and Challenges' (2000) 100(7) Transactions of

To assess compliance with human rights, we have to understand the extent to which these international obligations have been incorporated not only into national laws and policies but also health programs and services. This also constitutes an important step towards understanding the impact of human rights on health.

WHAT DOES 'ASSESSMENT' MEAN?

Before we turn to how to generate evidence relating to human rights in health work, we first need to clarify what we mean by this. A challenge of working at the intersection of different fields is that terms can be used very differently in each one. 'Evidence', for example, carries different connotations in a court of law than in the context of health policies and programs. Thus, before we can explore how best to create an evidence base for 'health and human rights', better understanding is required of the types of evidence needed.

Within the field of law, rules of evidence are the rules by which a court determines what evidence is admissible at trial, but no globally recognized rules exist: they vary by type of court (criminal, civil, family, etc.) and by jurisdiction. Furthermore, in this context, 'evidence' is often considered for relevance to an adversarial legal proceeding in which it will be assessed by legal counsels, a judge and a jury. Something that is considered 'evidence' is not understood to be definitive proof.

Within public health, a different standard is set for 'evidence', as this is generally understood to mean that the strength of evidence has already been ascertained and found to be acceptable. The 'gold standard' for evidence has traditionally been the results of randomized controlled trials in which study participants are randomly assigned to the treatment and control arms of the study and outcomes of interest compared. This is absolutely appropriate in many instances such as clinical trials of new drugs, but this methodology does not lend itself equally to all public health interventions. While randomized controlled trials can give a definitive answer as to which of two interventions performed better, they cannot tease apart why or elucidate the pathways of change. Furthermore, these designs cannot be considered ethical with respect to human rights: it would not be appropriate to randomize people to receive an intervention designed to help realize their human rights as this

---

the Royal Society of Tropical Medicine and Hygiene 603; J.K. Hansen and H. Sano, 'The Implications and Value Added of a Rights Based Approach' in B.A. Andreassen and S.P. Marks (eds), *Development as a Human Right: Legal, Political, and Economic Dimensions* (CUP 2006).

would imply randomizing some people to receive an intervention that was not designed to help realize their rights. Yet certain other forms of 'evidence', such as qualitative data, have often been considered inferior and inappropriate as a basis for informing public health policies or resource allocation.

Assessing a country's compliance with its human rights commitments can be done based on both quantitative and qualitative evidence produced through studies and reports. Assessing how human rights impact health also requires a mix of quantitative and qualitative data. Thus, for both of these types of assessment, there is a need to go beyond either field's 'traditional' understanding of evidence to accord equal value to the types of data that are most appropriate for assessment in these contexts.

Neither definition of 'evidence' is right or wrong; they exist equally but are appropriate in different instances. Thus, for work at the intersection of health and human rights, it is important that clarity exist around which definition is being used and why it is appropriate in a given situation. In work around litigating health-related rights, a legal understanding of 'evidence' may be required. However, in work that focuses on bringing human rights into public health laws, policies, programs and services, different definitions are required that will best be determined by the exact nature of the work and through collaboration between human rights lawyers and public health experts.

HEALTH-RELATED HUMAN RIGHTS: WHAT TO ASSESS

This section provides a brief overview of what to assess in the context of work at the intersection of health and human rights. It is divided into two sub-sections: the first examines how to assess human rights in health-related laws and policies, while the second is concerned with assessing human rights in health programs, interventions and services. These constitute different types of assessment, each with its own specific challenges. The issues raised in this section will be re-visited throughout subsequent sections of the chapter as specific assessment mechanisms and initiatives are explored.

Assessing Human Rights in Health-related Laws and Policies

As described above, in assessing health-related human rights, it is important to assess the congruence of national laws and policies with international human rights commitments. General Comments provide detailed interpretations of rights that are useful for this purpose. The first level of assessment is of the existence and content of national laws and policies:

do these reflect international human rights law and, if not, what has to change to ensure that they do? Moving beyond this, assessment of the degree to which health-related laws and policies are implemented is also required: laws and policies only serve their purpose if they are duly implemented. This is harder to do but, as seen in the Technical Guidance on Implementing a Human Rights-Based Approach to Under-Five Mortality and Morbidity, it can be approached by looking at issues such as budget allocations and expenditures, coverage of health services among different populations and use of mechanisms for complaints and/or redress. These issues will be explored further below.

Assessing Human Rights in Health Programs, Interventions and Services

Assessing human rights in health programs, interventions and services involves assessing the extent to which human rights obligations are reflected not only in the objectives of programs, interventions and services but also in their processes of implementation. Distinct from simply looking at the outcomes of any work (whether the fulfillment of a human right or a change in health outcome), a human rights-based approach (HRBA) to health also requires attention to the processes through which work is implemented.

An HRBA to health requires the adoption of a process explicitly shaped by human rights principles, norms and standards, and specific attention to the key elements of the right to health.[16] In particular, participation, equality and non-discrimination, attention to the legal and policy environment, and accountability are of critical importance to the implementation of the right to health. Further, the right to health encompasses standards requiring health facilities, goods and services to be available, accessible, acceptable and of sufficient and measurable quality as these attributes can crucially impact health.

Figure 17.2 illustrates how the different elements of a HRBA to health can be conceptualized as feeding into the planning, design, implementation and monitoring and evaluation of health programs, interventions and services.

Before any intervention begins, an understanding of the legal and policy context is required as well as a decision about how the health issue of

---

[16]   Peter Uvin, *Human Rights and Development* (Kumarian Press 2004); Office of the High Commissioner for Human Rights, *Frequently Asked Questions on a Human Rights-based Approach to Development Cooperation* (United Nations 2006).

[17]   Sofia Gruskin, Dina Bogecho and Laura Ferguson, '"Rights-based Approaches" to Health: Articulations, Ambiguities and Assessment' (2010) 31(2) Journal of Public Health Policy 129.

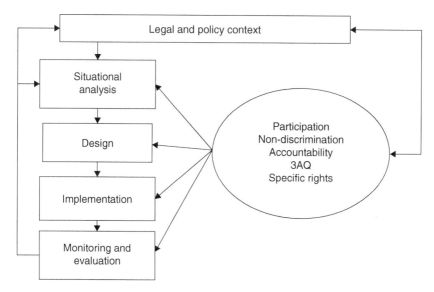

Source: Sofia Gruskin, Shahira Ahmed and Laura Ferguson. 'An Introduction to Rights-based Approaches: Focusing on the Design, Implementation, and Evaluation of Effective HIV and AIDS Programmes' (2006) submitted to UNAIDS, unpublished.

Figure 17.2   A human rights-based approach to health[17]

concern should be addressed. Both of these preliminary phases should include consideration of all the relevant human rights norms and standards listed. The latter then also help inform the design, implementation and monitoring and evaluation of any intervention.

Of primary interest for this chapter is the small box at the bottom of Figure 17.2 – 'Monitoring and evaluation': how do we assess human rights in health efforts? How can work be planned to ensure adequate attention to assessment of these human rights norms and standards throughout all stages of an intervention? This is relevant to our understanding of states' overall fulfillment of their health-related human rights obligations as well as exploration of how their actions in relation to human rights might impact health.

Whether or not rights are explicitly invoked in health programs, interventions and services also impacts how they should be assessed. An HRBA to health has a lot in common with good public health practice, but it also goes beyond this in large part owing to its legal foundation. So how do you assess health-related rights in programs that are, for example, participatory and focused on access to health services? Unless participation is framed as a human right or human rights principle and access to health services is situated within the 'availability, accessibility, acceptability, and quality' framework of the right to health, it might be inappropriate to assume that the program intended to improve the realization of these rights.

Questions arise about the validity of retroactively fitting human rights into the assessment of policies, programs and services that were not explicitly designed around rights. It may be that convergence exists between what these interventions do and the realization of human rights that it is entirely appropriate to assess, but this is not the same as assessing interventions that were designed from the outset to contribute to the realization of health-related human rights. This, again, is a place where specificity is important: what is the intervention being assessed? Did its original design explicitly include attention to human rights? Which human rights? How is this visible in the initial design, implementation and routine monitoring and evaluation efforts? All of this provides key context for any subsequent assessment of human rights in these interventions.

Incorporating and assessing human rights in health interventions is context-specific work, so no step-by-step 'how-to' guide exists for how best this might be done. However, recognizing the principles, norms and standards of a HRBA to health, guiding questions can be put forward to assist those designing interventions and how to monitor them to incorporate rights appropriately (Box 17.1).[18]

SECONDARY DATA ANALYSIS: CHOOSING DATA SOURCES AND COMMUNICATING FINDINGS

It can be both useful and practical to use existing data to carry out assessments at the intersection of health and human rights, but this must be done appropriately. Whatever their source, no data should be taken at face value nor assumed to be objective. It is key to understand the context within which they were collected: for what purpose were they collected? On what basis was the selection of data to be collected made (and what was excluded)? How were axes of disaggregation decided upon? None of this suggests that the data are not 'correct' (assuming that they were rigorously and appropriately collected and analyzed), but it provides a framework

---

[18]   Allison Smith-Estelle, Laura Ferguson and Sofia Gruskin. 'Incorporating Human Rights Principles in Health Programming' (2015) (12) Knowledge Matters. Concern Worldwide. <https://doj19z5hov92o.cloudfront.net/sites/default/files/media/resource/knowledge_matters_-_innovations_for_maternalnewborn_and_child_health.pdf > accessed 26 May 2016.

BOX 17.1 ILLUSTRATIVE QUESTIONS TO HELP DETERMINE THE EXTENT TO WHICH HEALTH PROGRAMS, INTERVENTIONS, AND SERVICES ARE HUMAN RIGHTS BASED

The key elements of a human rights based approach to health were outlined in Figure 17.2. Below are illustrative lists of questions that can usefully be asked during design, implementation, monitoring, and evaluation to help assess the extent to which health programs, interventions and services are grounded in human rights. The lists are sub-divided by human rights and rights standards.

(1) The right to health, encompassing the availability, accessibility, acceptability and quality of health facilities, goods and services
    (a) Are laws, policies and interventions relevant to the program consistent with international human rights norms and standards?
    (b) Can the national policy environment help frame/support program activities? Is it problematic in any way?
    (c) What mechanisms are in place to determine the degree to which existing relevant goods, services and information are provided in a manner that is available, accessible, acceptable and of high quality?
    (d) How does the health facility or program capture client perspectives on the availability, accessibility, acceptability and quality of its interventions?

(2) Participation
    (a) Who are the relevant duty-bearers and rights-holders?
    (b) What is their capacity to participate and how might this need to be built?
    (c) How are relevant actors participating in program design, implementation, monitoring and evaluation?
    (d) How is the participation of women and marginalized groups being ensured?
    (e) How is meaningful participation of different stakeholders monitored and evaluated?

(3) Non-discrimination
    (a) Do policies refer to excluded populations? In what ways? What impact might this have on programmatic efforts to ensure non-discrimination?
    (b) How will considerations of non-discrimination and equality of rights-holders be integrated in programs and services?
    (c) Do assessments of marginalization and vulnerability take into account the analysis of data disaggregated by, as relevant, race, color, ethnicity, gender, religion, language, political opinion, disability, nationality, birth or other status, and other bases of discrimination?

(4) Transparency and accountability
    (a) For all services and interventions, including those provided by the government, are there monitoring, claims and redress mechanisms in place and accessible?
    (b) How will impediments to accountability be identified and addressed?
    (c) What mechanisms is the program putting in place to ensure transparency in decision-making and accountability of all stakeholders?
    (d) How are clients' comments and complaints documented, including the outcomes arising from any such comments/complaints?

within which they can be interpreted. This is equally true for quantitative, qualitative and policy data.

All three of these types of data, particularly in combination, are needed to fully assess human rights in health, which impacts choices around data sources as well as how findings are communicated. Data analysis and evidence generation are not as 'clean' as the pure quantitative work often favored by public health where a *p*-value can indicate 'significance' in a single number. Capturing the attention of public health policy-makers and programmers requires succinct and clear messages, which can be challenging to produce when concurrent analysis of quantitative, qualitative and policy data is required.

The UN Office of the High Commissioner for Human Rights (OHCHR) has done substantial work on human rights indicators, including in relation to health. Their approach has been to illustrate how data on ratification and domestication of relevant treaties can be examined alongside frequently reported quantitative health indicators to create an understanding of realization of the right to health. They propose 55 illustrative indicators, all of which 'should be disaggregated by prohibited grounds of discrimination, as applicable'.[19] While many of the indicators proposed are widely collected, few are available at the level of disaggregation suggested. This combination of indicators might, therefore, provide some insight into monitoring realization of the right to health but additional sources will be needed to supplement them such as the Treaty Monitoring Bodies' reports, reports by the Special Rapporteur on the Right to Health, and reports submitted under the Universal Periodic Review mechanism.

GLOBAL REPORTING MECHANISMS AND DATA FOR ASSESSMENT AT THE INTERSECTION OF HEALTH AND HUMAN RIGHTS

Assessing work at the intersection of health and human rights requires the use of multidisciplinary approaches in which different methods and types of data can be concurrently examined to create an understanding of invariably complex situations.

At the global level, monitoring mechanisms exist both for human rights and public health. Some of these can be used for monitoring work at the health and human rights intersection; two examples from

---

[19]   Human Rights Council (n 12).

global human rights structures and one example from global health structures are explored below. They illustrate how existing mechanisms and the data produced through these mechanisms can be used to shed light on human rights in health. Disciplinary background and training make each of us more familiar with one set of structures or the other, highlighting again why collaboration between lawyers and public health experts can help maximize the effectiveness of health and human rights assessments.

Using Human Rights Mechanisms and Data to Assess Health-related Human Rights

Human rights mechanisms capture information relevant to health and can be useful for raising awareness of health issues and trying to effect change. These mechanisms can be used to assess human rights in health-related laws, policies, programs, interventions and services, with reporting usually focused on national level actions. Two such mechanisms are discussed below: treaty monitoring bodies and the Universal Periodic Review mechanism. A brief overview is provided of each mechanism and how attention can be brought to health in its processes, and then analysis is presented of the degree to which health has been considered by the mechanism in recent years.

Treaty monitoring bodies

Treaty monitoring bodies are a key mechanism within the international human rights system and are known to have generated positive results in health. States that ratify a treaty willingly subscribe to an obligation to report their progress with implementation to the relevant monitoring body every few years, following which the committee in question highlights areas of concern and where additional efforts are needed to promote the realization of relevant rights. Although the effectiveness of treaty monitoring bodies' recommendations is still subject to debate, positive changes have been effected in different countries. As an example of how this process can work, in Peru sexual abuse laws were strengthened as a result of concerns raised by the Human Rights Committee about the inadequacy of the national law to protect teenagers from sexual abuse.[20]

The reporting guidelines for both the Committee on Economic, Social

---

[20] Isfahan Merali, 'Advancing Women's Reproductive and Sexual Health Rights: Using the International Human Rights System' (2000) 10(5) Development in Practice 609.

and Cultural Rights (CESC) and the Committee on the Rights of the Child include some detail on the type of information relevant to health that States Parties should include in their reports. Both the ICESCR and the CRC include multiple rights that are relevant to health and are key to include in any assessment of health-related human rights. For the sake of simplicity, I will focus only on the rights to health in the ICESCR and the CRC to illustrate the information requested by the Committees. The section of the reporting guidelines specific to the right to health in the ICESCR draws heavily on the content of General Comment 14 on the right to health and requests that states:

> 55. Indicate whether the State party has adopted a national health policy and whether a national health system with universal access to primary health care is in place.
>
> 56. Provide information on the measures taken to ensure:
> (a) That preventive, curative, and rehabilitative health facilities, goods and services are within safe reach and physically accessible for everyone, including older persons and persons with disabilities;
> (b) That the costs of health-care services and health insurance, whether privately or publicly provided, are affordable for everyone, including for socially disadvantaged groups;
> (c) That drugs and medical equipment are scientifically approved and have not expired or become ineffective; and
> (d) Adequate training of health personnel, including on health and human rights.
>
> 57. Provide information on the measures taken:
> (a) To improve child and maternal health, as well as sexual and reproductive health services and programmes, including through education, awareness-raising, and access to family planning, pre- and post-natal care and emergency obstetric services, in particular in rural areas and for women belonging to disadvantaged and marginalized groups;
> (b) To prevent, treat and control diseases linked to water and ensure access to adequate sanitation;
> (c) To implement and enhance immunization programmes and other strategies of infectious disease control;
> (d) To prevent the abuse of alcohol and tobacco, and the use of illicit drugs and other harmful substances, in particular among children and adolescents, ensure adequate treatment and rehabilitation of drug users, and support their families;
> (e) To prevent HIV/AIDS and other sexually transmitted diseases, educate high-risk groups, children and adolescents as well as the general public on their transmission, provide support to persons with HIV/AIDS and their families, and reduce social stigma and discrimination;
> (f) To ensure affordable access to essential drugs, as defined by the WHO, including anti-retroviral medicines and medicines for chronic diseases; and

(g) To ensure adequate treatment and care in psychiatric facilities for mental health patients, as well as periodic review and effective judicial control of confinement.[21]

While this guidance comprises a relatively long list of areas of health on which States Parties should report, the focus is squarely on reporting on the steps that states have taken to address these different areas of health. There is no request for data to highlight which areas of health might require most attention. Nor is information requested on any special efforts made to reach particular vulnerable or disadvantaged populations. Furthermore, as the global burden of disease has evolved, additional priority health topics have emerged that are not included in these guidelines but that warrant government action in order to fully realize the right to health.

Despite these shortcomings, the Committee requests that States Parties provide a wide range of information relevant to health, suggesting that reports and corresponding concluding observations should provide useful data for assessing human rights in health.

The reporting guidelines for the CRC also include a fairly detailed request for information relating to the child's right to health such as the rates of infant and under-five child mortality and the number/percentage of children infected and affected by HIV/AIDS.[22] In contrast to the information requested by CESC, the CRC requests purely quantitative data to provide an overview of the state of children's health. These data do not provide insight into governmental action to address ill-health. Thus the approach of these two Committees to monitoring the right to health is very different, with CESC focused entirely on governmental actions to address health and the CRC purely focused on understanding the health situation.

Despite the differences in the type of information requested, both Committees ask States Parties to provide substantial information that they hope will help them assess health-related human rights. Yet a search of documents (including General Comments, States Parties' reports and Concluding Observations) relating to CESC and CRC reporting processes yielded relatively few documents that mention health.[23]

---

[21] Economic and Social Council, 'Guidelines on Treaty-specific Documents to be Submitted by States Parties under Articles 16 and 17 of the International Covenant on Economic, Social and Cultural Rights' (24 March 2009) E/C.12/2008/2.

[22] CRC, 'General Guidelines Regarding the Form and Contents of Periodic Reports – CRC' (13 September to 1 October 2010) CRC/C/58/Rev.3.

[23] The United Nations Refugee Agency, 'Refworld' <www.refworld.org/cgi-bin/texis/vtx/rwmain> accessed 18 February 2016.

During the period 1991–2015, the right to health was mentioned 18 and 19 times under CESC and CRC, respectively. Further teasing this apart, under CESC reporting, this constituted one General Comment, three States Parties' reports and 14 Concluding Observations; under CRC it was one General Comment, two States Parties' reports and 16 Concluding Observations. Very few states reported directly on the right to health in their reports to these Committees and relatively few reported on the range of health topics explored. This raises a very obvious question: why not?

At the national level, political decision-making underlies the final content of reports to these Committees. The higher up the political agenda health is, the more likely it is to be included in States Parties' reports. These findings suggest that, in many countries, little priority is accorded to health by those responsible for compiling reports for the CESC and CRC.

Civil society organizations can play an important role in bringing attention to health issues through the treaty monitoring body reporting mechanisms by submitting shadow reports to the committees highlighting areas of concern in a specific country. There are varying levels of shadow reporting to each committee, with notable engagement in reporting to the Committee on the Rights of the Child, for example, but much less to CESC.

Of note, for the treaty monitoring bodies mechanism to be effective for assessing human rights in health, sufficient capacity has to exist within each of the relevant treaty monitoring bodies to request or analyze information relevant to health. Given the breadth of many of the treaties and the relatively small size of each treaty monitoring body, this may not always be the case. This may be a contributing factor to the small number of Concluding Observations issued by the CESC and CRC that directly address health.

Sometimes, rather than relying on indexing in easily accessible databases such as Refworld (which formed the basis for the analysis above), it can be preferable to carry out primary research into how health has been addressed in the work of a specific treaty monitoring body. Steps for carrying out this work are outlined in Box 17.2. An analysis of attention to non-communicable diseases (including cancers, diabetes, cardiovascular diseases, and chronic respiratory diseases) in recent reporting under the ICESCR and CRC found very little attention to these diseases or their primary risk factors that require state action under the right to health.[24]

[24]   Laura Ferguson, Daniel Tarantola, Michael Hoffman and Sofia Gruskin, 'Non-communicable Diseases and Human Rights: Assessing the Links' (2016) Global Public Health; doi: 10.1080/17441692.2016.1158847.

BOX 17.2   HOW TO ASSESS TREATY MONITORING
BODY REPORTS AND RECOMMENDATIONS
FOR ATTENTION TO HEALTH-RELATED
HUMAN RIGHTS

1. Identify the area of health you are interested in.
2. List appropriate search terms relating to this area of health.
3. Search through state reports to treaty monitoring bodies as well as the responses to these reports.
4. It can be useful to track these over time for the same country and/or across countries at a given moment in time and/or across treaty monitoring bodies.

The Universal Periodic Review mechanism

The Universal Period Review (UPR) mechanism is 'a State-driven process, under the auspices of the Human Rights Council, which provides the opportunity for each State to declare what actions they have taken to improve the human rights situations in their countries and to fulfil their human rights obligations'.[25] As such, it constitutes an additional mechanism through which health-related human rights can be assessed. States can choose to report on health issues and, equally, the Human Rights Council can request information and/or issue recommendations in relation to health in the country.

National reports submitted through the UPR are meant to cover all human rights commitments, which means that there is very little space available for any given topic. The reporting guidelines are generic and do not provide any details on the type of information that countries should provide to illustrate their progress towards realizing health-related human rights.[26]

An assessment was recently carried out of attention to sexual and reproductive health and rights and gender equality in UPR reporting, and provides useful insight into the degree to which this particular health topic has been addressed through this reporting mechanism. It found that 21,956 recommendations and voluntary commitments were made by states at the completion of the first cycle of reporting, 26% of which related to sexual and reproductive health and rights and gender equality; 77% of these were

---

[25]   OHCHR, 'Universal Periodic Review' <www.ohchr.org/EN/HRBodies/UPR/Pages/UPRMain.aspx> accessed 27 February 2015.
[26]   Human Rights Council, 'Decision of the Human Rights Council: Follow-up to the Human Rights Council resolution 16/21 with Regard to the Universal Periodic Review' (19 July 2011) A/HRC/DEC/17/119.

formally accepted by states.[27] The levels of state action in response to these recommendations could now usefully be assessed. Thus, despite the lack of specific guidance for reporting on health through this mechanism, one in four of the recommendations and voluntary commitments made during the first reporting cycle related to sexual and reproductive health and rights or gender equality. Attention to other areas of health has not yet been assessed.

Similar to the situation with the treaty monitoring bodies, the capacity of all those involved in the UPR process (those submitting country reports, those submitting shadow reports and those reviewing the reports), and the political priority accorded to health, and different areas within health, influence the extent to which the UPR mechanism is, and could be, used to assess health-related human rights.

Maximizing synergies moving forward
Neither the treaty monitoring bodies nor the UPR are specific to health, but they can be used for reviewing states' actions towards realizing health-related human rights if this is instigated by states, civil society actors or members of the relevant human rights committee. Capacity building of public health professionals to engage with these human rights mechanisms might help increase their use for the purposes of assessing health-related human rights. This would include building capacity on the normative content of health-related rights, how to assess and document the realization of health-related human rights and how to form strategic alliances within the human rights community to advocate for these issues.

If this could all be achieved and more systematic use of these mechanisms instituted, state reports and Committees' responses could constitute a valuable dataset for assessing health-related human rights in countries around the world. Reports submitted by the Special Rapporteur on the Right to Health constitute an additional useful source of data that might also be considered.

Using Public Health Mechanisms to Assess Health-related Human Rights

Given the limitations of the above-mentioned human rights mechanisms for assessing human rights in health, it can also be useful to turn to public

---

[27]   Kate Gilmore, Luis Mora, Alfonso Barragues and Ida Krogh Mikkelsen, 'The Universal Periodic Review: A Platform for Dialogue, Accountability, and Change on Sexual and Reproductive Health and Rights' (2015) 17/2 Health and Human Rights E167.

health for additional sources of data for understanding the degree to which health-related rights are being realized. Some of these mechanisms also allow for preliminary insight into how the realization of these rights might contribute to improving health. As mentioned above, in seeking to assess the operationalization of human rights in health-related laws and policies, two levels of analyses are required: the existence and content of relevant laws and policies should be assessed for consonance with human rights (whether or not they align with international human rights standards); and the degree of implementation of relevant laws should be assessed.

Attention to human rights in a global reporting mechanism focused on national-level responses to the HIV epidemic is analyzed below as an example of one such mechanism from which useful lessons can be learnt.

Monitoring human rights in the global HIV response

Every two years, countries submit reports to the Joint United Nations Programme on HIV/AIDS (UNAIDS) on their progress toward fulfilling global commitments on addressing HIV, including in relation to human rights. The National Commitments and Policies Instrument (NCPI, formerly the National Composite Policy Index) forms part of this reporting process. The NCPI is a globally standardized questionnaire that 'measures progress in the development and implementation of national-level HIV and AIDS policies, strategies and laws'.[28] Some of the human rights questions in the NCPI are asked twice: once to governments and once to a variety of civil society stakeholders, including non-governmental organizations, people living with HIV, national human rights commissions, United Nations agencies and private sector representatives. This allows for comparison of government and civil society responses.

One such question provides a useful example of how this tool seeks to assess the existence, content and level of implementation of laws relevant to HIV and human rights. The question, with its sub-questions, reads: 'Does the country have a general (i.e., not specific to HIV-related discrimination) law on non-discrimination? IF YES, briefly describe the content of the/laws; Briefly explain what mechanisms are in place to ensure these laws are implemented; Briefly comment on the degree to which they are currently implemented'.[29]

The answer to the initial question provides quantitative data about the

---

[28] UNAIDS, 'Indicator Registry' www.indicatorregistry.org/?q=node/862> accessed 28 February 2016.
[29] UNAIDS, WHO and UNICEF, *Global AIDS Response Progress Reporting 2014: Construction of Core Indicators for Monitoring the 2011 UN Political Declaration on HIV/AIDS* (UNAIDS 2014).

existence of laws on non-discrimination in every country that submits a report (180 countries submitted reports through this mechanism in 2014).[30] Answers to the follow-up questions provide qualitative data that help to understand the potential effectiveness of such laws for realizing rights and impacting health in each country: the existence of such a law might seem positive, but if its content is problematic (e.g. by excluding certain key populations) or no mechanisms exist through which it can be implemented, its potential to contribute to the realization of rights and to positively impact health is severely constrained. For example, in Malawi's most recent report through this mechanism, in its comments on the degree to which non-discrimination protections are currently implemented, civil society responded:

> In general most people do not claim their rights when violated and they are not aware of the laws. Judiciary has not delivered decisive judgments especially for key populations (mandatory testing of sex workers and convicted gay couple). Legal aid system is not accessible to people in the rural areas. The Malawi Police Services has the Victims Support Units [VSU], which are not well developed. However it is a good start but there is a need to equip the VSU and capacitate the police officers.[31]

This contextualizes their report that there are good legal protections to ensure non-discrimination. It highlights the insufficiency of merely analyzing quantitative data on the existence of legal protections: without a deeper understanding of the content and implementation of these laws, little can be ascertained about their potential effectiveness.

Of course, a law on non-discrimination constitutes only one law in an entire legal framework and caution must be exercised in examining any law or policy in isolation from its broader context. Again, its impact on rights and health might be affected by conflicting laws or policies that co-exist so a picture of the broader legal and policy framework is needed. The NCPI includes questions about a range of laws and policies relevant to HIV (see Box 17.3)[32] so it is possible to build up such a picture by looking across the responses to all of these questions. This is, of course, time-consuming work, as it involves not only looking at summary statistics but also reading the qualitative responses that help elucidate the

---

[30]   WHO and UNAIDS, *Global AIDS Response Progress Reporting 2015* (World Health Organization 2015).

[31]   UNAIDS, 'Malawi Report NCPI' <www.unaids.org/sites/default/files/en/dataanalysis/knowyourresponse/ncpi/2014countries/Malawi%20NCPI%202013.pdf> accessed 28 February 2016.

[32]   UNAIDS, WHO and UNICEF (n 29).

BOX 17.3　EXAMPLE QUESTIONS RELEVANT TO HUMAN RIGHTS IN THE NCPI

Does the country have non-discrimination laws or regulations which specify protections for specific key populations and other vulnerable groups?

Does the country have laws, regulations or policies that present obstacles to effective HIV prevention, treatment, care and support for key populations and vulnerable groups?

- IF YES, for which key populations and vulnerable groups?
- Briefly describe the content of these laws, regulations or policies:
- Briefly comment on how they pose barriers:

Is the promotion and protection of human rights explicitly mentioned in any HIV policy or strategy? IF YES, briefly describe how human rights are mentioned in this HIV policy or strategy:

Is there a mechanism to record, document and address cases of discrimination experienced by people living with HIV, key populations and other vulnerable populations?
IF YES, briefly describe this mechanism:

Does the country have a policy or law prohibiting HIV screening for general employment purposes (recruitment, assignment/relocation, appointment, promotion, termination)?
IF YES, briefly describe the content of the policy or law:

Does the country have the following human rights monitoring and enforcement mechanisms?
(a)　Existence of independent national institutions for the promotion and protection of human rights, including human rights commissions, law reform commissions, watchdogs and ombudspersons which consider HIV-related issues within their work;
(b)　Performance indicators or benchmarks for compliance with human rights standards in the context of HIV efforts.
IF YES on any of the above questions, describe some examples:

quantitative data. However, this is precisely the type of data and analysis that is needed to help strengthen the evidence base of how laws and policies impact health. Where laws have changed since NCPI reporting began, longitudinal analysis of these data can yield particularly interesting findings.

TOOLS FOR ASSESSING WORK AT THE INTERSECTION OF HEALTH AND HUMAN RIGHTS

The previous section analyzed how existing reporting mechanisms and the datasets that result from their use can be used in assessments of health-related human rights. An alternative approach is to use tools that have been designed for carrying out assessments of work at the intersection of health and human rights to generate new data. Some of these tools emanate from the human rights community while others have been produced by organizations whose primary mandate is public health. One example of each of these is presented below to illustrate how existing tools can be used to carry out relevant assessments.

A Tool for Assessing Corporate Compliance with Human Rights

The responsibilities of private sector actors in respecting human rights have been clarified in the United Nations Guiding Principles on Business and Human Rights.[33] The United Nations Global Compact is a voluntary corporate citizenship initiative that seeks to promote responsible corporate citizenship with due attention to human rights principles, drawing from the International Bill of Human Rights as well as relevant International Labour Organization core conventions. A self-assessment tool has been created that is in line with the Guiding Principles on Business and Human Rights to help businesses assess their performance in the context of the Global Compact.[34]

The tool 'unpacks the substantive content of what it means for a business to respect each human right through business relevant questions and

---

[33] 'Guiding Principles on Business and Human Rights: Implementing the United Nations "Protect, Respect and Remedy" Framework' (2011) HR/PUB/11/04.

[34] Confederation of Danish Industry, the Industrialization Fund for Developing Countries, the Danish Business Authority, Danish Institute for Human Rights and the UN Global Compact Office 'Global Compact Self Assessment Tool' <www.globalcompactselfassessment.org/> accessed 23 February 2016.

indicators'.[35] The right to health is encompassed in this tool, with attention given to health and safety systems, protective equipment and training, leave, impact assessments and product stewardship. Grounded in human rights commitments, a series of questions covers these different aspects relating to health, each with sub-questions to provide additional detail. This can identify areas of strong and weak performance, and if the 'comments' section of the tool is completed, it can provide useful guidance for how to improve corporate performance in each area.

The findings from these assessments often remain unpublished so there is no 'dataset' of completed assessments that can be used for secondary analysis for assessing human rights in health. However, for corporations that are interested in fulfilling their human rights responsibilities, including those in relation to health, this tool can help them understand their commitments, assess current performance and target their efforts to where they are most needed.

A Tool for Strengthening Legal and Regulatory Frameworks for Sexual and Reproductive Health

The WHO has published a tool designed to improve understanding of states' human rights obligations as a means to improving sexual and reproductive health and the realization of relevant rights.[36] The tool brings together readily available data on laws, regulations, and policies as well as health systems and health outcomes. These data are analyzed alongside a country's human rights commitments to identify discrepancies or gaps that need addressing. The tool is structured by health topic rather than by rights to ensure its accessibility for public health researchers who are most likely to implement it.

Where the tool has been used, it has highlighted critical gaps in data for understanding the health status of marginalized groups, and it has drawn attention to 'the (lack of) responsiveness of the legal and policy framework to address the needs of identified groups, and whether the laws were in and of themselves discriminatory'.[37] Presenting data within the context of

---

[35]   Ibid.

[36]   World Health Organization, *Reproductive, Maternal, Newborn and Child Health and Human Rights: A Toolbox for Examining Laws, Regulations and Policies* (World Health Organization 2014).

[37]   Jane Cottingham, Eszter Kismodi, Adriane Martin Hilber, Ornella Lincetto, Marcus Stahlhofer and Sofia Gruskin, 'Using Human Rights for Sexual and Reproductive Health: Improving Legal and Regulatory Frameworks' (2010) 88(7) Bulletin of the World Health Organization 551.

human rights commitments has also helped to elevate discussions beyond politically or ideologically based positions on topics such as sex work, abortion and access to information and services.[38]

This tool constitutes a useful example of using public health as an entry point to bring together existing information in novel ways to draw attention to where gaps exist between a country's health-related human rights commitments and their related actions. Implementing the tool is a comprehensive and time-consuming process, but the reward is new insight into the complex intersection of sexual and reproductive health and human rights at the national level. This tool could be adapted for use in other areas of health.

GENERAL CHALLENGES

The sections above have highlighted a diverse range of mechanisms and efforts to assess human rights in health, many of which use innovative mixes of methods to try to capture the complexity of work at this intersection. However, this work is undoubtedly challenging. Work can take place in various domains, e.g. laws, policies, programs and services, and at different levels, e.g. national, sub-national and community. These different levels and types of intervention each raise specific methodological challenges with regard to measurement.

From a human rights perspective, it is challenging to capture information on activities at the level of interventions and service delivery as these can occur at a very micro level, and thus require assessment throughout any given country setting. Human rights apply everywhere yet the specificity of interventions required to ensure the realization of rights is critical to success and varies enormously by location. This is as true for health-related rights as all others, which creates a challenge for the creation of generic indicators for measuring human rights in health. While human rights are universal, their realization is dependent upon national and sub-national structures. Given the interdependence of rights, assessing health-related rights does not preclude attention to structures in sectors beyond health that will impact health outcomes as well as the realization of health-related rights. In all cases, specificity about which human rights are being assessed, in what interventions, and at what levels is critically important to maintaining the rigor of the evidence base of why rights matter to health.

From a public health perspective, there are challenges around attributing changes in health to changes in the national legal and policy environment

---

[38]   Ibid.

given how many other factors may also influence health. Acknowledging these complexities and being transparent in how they are addressed in any given assessment is key: obfuscating their existence serves only to devalue the rigor of this work.

Assessing human rights in health brings together two different fields, which, as explored above, brings challenges with regard to definitions and values attached to single words or concepts. This highlights the need for precision and specificity in presenting findings so as to prevent misunderstandings and ensure that, despite the complexity of this work, clarity exists as to what has been assessed, how, to what end and with what implications.

A recent publication on assessing the evidence of impact of human rights-based approaches on women's and children's health underscores the complexity of this work, emphasizing the need for a multidisciplinary and multi-method approach and stating that 'it is necessary to be alert to (a) the historical, political, social, cultural and environmental context; (b) laws, policies, and programs; and (c) health-related outcomes and impacts, including health gains, individuals' well-being and community empowerment'.[39]

CONCLUSIONS

This chapter has provided a brief introduction to some existing data, mechanisms, and tools relevant to work assessing health-related human rights. This work can be approached using either human rights or public health as the entry point, and it can occur at different (or multiple) levels. The examples presented were designed to illustrate some of the resources available to people seeking to address human rights in health. I have highlighted a few ways in which these resources can be used to advance our assessment of health-related human rights while also drawing attention to the inadequacy of any single effort for covering the broad range of assessments required at the intersection of health and rights.

The overarching message of this chapter is that the range of ways in which human rights are brought into public health work necessitates a variety of methods for assessing work at this intersection. There is no single methodology for assessing health-related human rights; choice of methods must be made based on the nature of the work to be assessed and the purposes for which assessment is being done. As with any other assessment, appropriate rigor in data collection and analysis is fundamental to

---

[39] Bustreo et al. (n 3).

ensure the validity and credibility of the evidence base being created. I hope that recognition of these methodological challenges as well as some of the recommendations advanced for how to address them might improve the quality of future assessments in this area.

REFERENCES

Center for Reproductive Rights and UNFPA, *Reproductive Rights: A Tool for Monitoring State Obligations* (Center for Reproductive Rights)

Gruskin, S. and Laura Ferguson, 'Using Indicators to Determine the Contribution of Human Rights to Public Health Efforts. What? Why? And How?' (2009) 87 WHO Bulletin 714

Gruskin, S., Laura Ferguson, Tobias Alfven, Deborah Rugg and Greet Peersman, 'Identifying Structural Barriers to an Effective HIV Response: Using 2010 National Composite Policy Index Data to Evaluate the Human Rights, Legal and Policy Environment' (2013) 16 Journal of the International AIDS Society 18000

Human Rights Council, 'Technical Guidance on a Human Rights-based Approach to Reducing Preventable Maternal Morbidity and Mortality' A/HRC/21/22 and Corr .1 and 2.

Hunt, P. and Judith Buena de Mesquita, 'Reducing Maternal Mortality: The Contribution of the Right to the Highest Attainable Standard of Health. Project Report' (Colchester: Human Rights Centre 2010)

Lawyers Collective and O'Neill Institute for National and Global Health Law, 'Global Health and Human Rights Database: A Free Online Database of Health and Human Rights Law' <www.globalhealthrights.org>

National Economic and Social Rights Initiative, *Human Rights Assessment Tool for Health Care Reform* (National Economic and Social Rights Initiative 2011)

OHCHR, 'Human Rights Indicators: A Guide to Measurement and Implementation' HR/PUB/12/5 (United Nations 2012)

OHCHR, Harvard FXB Center, The Partnership for Maternal, Newborn and Child Health, UNFPA and WHO, *Summary Reflection Guide on a Human Rights-based Approach to Health: Application to Sexual and Reproductive Health, Maternal Health and Under-5 Child Health – National Human Rights Institutions* (United Nations 2015)

United Nations Development Programme, *Legal Environment Assessment for HIV: An Operational Guide to Conducting National Legal, Regulatory and Policy Assessments for HIV* (United Nations Development Programme 2014)

United Nations Evaluation Group, *Integrating Human Rights and Gender Equality in Evaluations* (UNEG 2014).

WHO, *Reproductive, Maternal, Newborn and Child Health and Human Rights: A Toolbox for Examining Laws, Regulations and Policies* (WHO 2014a) <http://apps.who.int/iris/bitstream/10665/126383/1/9789241507424_eng.pdf?ua=1>

WHO, *Ensuring Human Rights within Contraceptive Programmes: A Human Rights Analysis of Existing Quantitative Indicators* (WHO 2014b) <http://apps.who.int/iris/bitstream/10665/126799/1/9789241507493_eng.pdf?ua=1>

18. How to study human rights in plural legal contexts: an exploration of plural water laws in Zimbabwe
Anne Hellum

INTRODUCTION

Human rights, in all parts of the world, operate in a terrain were a plurality of normative orders coexist, interact and sometimes conflict.[1] State-law does not, in spite of the nation-state's formal status as the main duty-bearer under international law, provide the sole means of regulating social behaviour. This socio-legal phenomenon, termed legal pluralism, is a characteristic feature of modern nation-states in all parts of the world. To come to grips with the complex legal situations that legal pluralities give rise to in an increasingly transnational world, many human rights scholars have started to cross disciplines like anthropology, law and political science.[2] There is today a growing body of interdisciplinary human rights research, exploring the interaction between international, national and local norms at different levels of law and in different social contexts.

Research from this burgeoning field of study indicates that formal state justice, in most parts of the world, is not readily accessible for vulnerable

---

[1] S.F. Moore, 'Law and Social Change: The Semi-Autonomous Field as an Appropriate Subject of Study' (1973) 7 Law and Society Review 719–746; J. Griffiths, 'What is Legal Pluralism?' (1986) 24 Journal of Legal Pluralism 1–50.

[2] Key analytical contributions to anthropological theory of legal pluralism are: Moore (n 1), Griffiths (n 1); S.E. Merry, 'Legal Pluralism' (1988) 22(5) Law and Society Review 869–896; A. Griffiths, 'Legal Pluralism' in R. Banakar and M. Travers (eds), *An Introduction to Law and Social Theory* (Hart 2002) 289–310. How anthropological theory on legal pluralism may be integrated in legal studies that seek an understanding of law in a gendered context is addressed in A.W. Bentzon, A. Hellum, J. Stewart, W. Ncube and T. Agersnap, *Pursuing Grounded Theory in Law. South-North Experiences in Developing Women's Law* (TANO/ Mond Books 1998); A. Hellum, J. Stewart, S. Sardar Ali and A. Tsanga, 'Paths are Made by Walking: Introductory Thoughts' in A. Hellum, J. Stewart, S. Sardar Ali and A. Tsanga (eds), *Human Rights, Plural Legalities and Gendered Realities: Paths are made by walking* (Weaver Press 2007) ii–xi; and R. Sieder and J.A. McNeish (eds), 'Introduction' in *Gender Justice and Legal Pluralities: Latin American and African Perspectives* (Routledge 2013) 1–31.

groups and individuals within these groups, most importantly women and children.[3] This has prompted a series of international policy initiatives suggesting that the plurality of alternative norms and institutions people turn to for justice be considered as a tool to promote human rights.[4] International political and economic agencies like The Commission on Legal Empowerment of the Poor (CLEP) and the World Bank have recommended justice sector initiatives that include non-state legal services and informal justice systems. Seeing poverty and disadvantage as a result of legal exclusion, CLEP concludes that most human rights and development initiatives fail because they 'tend to focus on the official economy, the formal legal system and the national rather than the local level'.[5]

Human rights scholars and practitioners have seen such initiatives as a two-edged sword. As a pathway to the realization of human rights, legal pluralist approaches may, on the one hand, expand the spaces for the exercise of local autonomy by different social, ethnic and religious groups. Such approaches may, on the other hand, reinforce unequal power relations based on gender, age and class within different groups.[6] Legal pluralities, as emphasized by UN Women, often constitute an obstacle for women's rights since local customary and religious forums often rely on traditional norms that are discriminatory.[7] The former UN Special Rapporteur in the field of cultural rights, Fareda Shaheed, has in her report to the UN emphasized the need to strengthen women's agency within such groups because: 'the critical issue, from the human rights perspective, is not whether and how religion, culture and tradition prevail over women's human rights, but how to arrive at a point at which women own their culture (and religion and tradition) and their human rights'.[8]

A key question is, in the light of these developments and discussions,

---

[3]   G. Corradi, 'Justice Sector Aid in Plurally Legal Africa' in Eva Brems, Giselle Corradi and Martien Schotsmans (eds), *On Tradition and Justice: The Role of International Actors in Africa* (Intersentia 2013).

[4]   World Bank, 'Customary Justice and Legal Pluralism in Post-Conflict and Fragile Societies', conference hosted by United States Institute of Peace, George Washington University, Washington, DC, 17–18 November 2009; Commission on Legal Empowerment of the Poor. *Making the Law Work for Everyone* Vol. 1 (United Nations Development Program 2008); and DANIDA, *Informal Justice Systems* (Ministry of Foreign Affairs of Denmark 2010).

[5]   Commission on Legal Empowerment of the Poor (n 4) 2.

[6]   International Council on Human Rights Policy, *When Legal Orders Overlap, Human Rights, State and Non-State Law* (ICHRP 2009).

[7]   UN Women, *Progress of the World's Women* (United Nations 2011).

[8]   United Nations General Assembly, 'Report of the Special Rapporteur in the Field of Cultural Rights, Farida Shaheed' (10 August 2012) AA/67/287, para 3.

whether and under what conditions legal pluralities as a socio-legal phenomenon constitute a factor that prevents or promotes human rights for different groups and for differently positioned individuals within them. This broad research question gives rise to a series of closely interrelated phenomenological, evaluative and normative sub-questions that require an approach that cuts across law and social science.[9]

Firstly, it poses research problems that call for analytical tools which facilitate analysis of human rights as part of a process of overlapping, intersecting and sometimes conflicting norms that are invoked by differently positioned actors in terms of gender, ethnicity or social status. A phenomenological approach, which sees human rights as socially constructed, is needed to transcend the longstanding normative debate between human rights universalists and cultural relativists within law and anthropology on whether it is possible to define common values and principles across different societies and cultures.[10] The theory of law as a semi-autonomous social field, proposed by Sally Falk Moore, constitutes a useful analytical starting point to describe and understand the process of interaction between international, national and local norms in different social, political and legal contexts.[11]

Secondly, the options and limits of an anthropology of law's purely descriptive approach to the plurality of norms that have a bearing on the realization of the human rights of different groups and individuals need to be considered. From a human rights perspective methods that can assess the outcome of the interaction between international, national and local norms with a view to whether and how they promote or prevent the realization of human rights standards are needed. This evaluative research task requires a vertical comparative approach addressing both similarities and differences between existing human rights, national law and the living local law. To assess how different groups and vulnerable individuals within them in terms of gender, age or social status are able to invoke international, national and local norms towards their own ends and goals a horizontal comparison is needed.

A third and closely related challenge that the question whether and under what circumstances legal pluralities promote or constrain human rights is

---

[9]   On these three dimensions on interdisciplinary human rights research see Malcolm Langford, Chapter 8.

[10]   B. Derman, A. Hellum and K. Sandvik, 'Ethnographic and Historical Perspectives on Rights Claiming on the African Continent' in B. Derman, A. Hellum and K. Sandvik (eds), *Worlds of Human Rights: Ambiguities of Rights Claiming in Africa* (Brill 2013) 18–21.

[11]   Moore (n 1).

how to handle the gap between the dominant human rights discourses and the norms and values that are evolving through human interaction in different social fields. While local norms in certain respects may be more responsive to local needs than existing human rights, they may in other respects fall short of human rights standards. A difficult question from a social science perspective is whether abolition or formalization of the living law would be the most promising way to promote human rights.[12] From a jurisprudential perspective the question of how human rights should be interpreted in order to respond to local demands represents a challenge.

To address these closely related phenomenological, evaluative and normative dimensions of this broad research question this chapter presents an interdisciplinary research design that constitutes a cross-fertilization of law and anthropology. The aim is to demonstrate how human rights analysis that is contextually specific and sensitive to different layers of legal norms, the interaction between them and possible conflicts may be carried out. While legal pluralism is a characteristic feature of all modern nation-states there are considerable regional, national and local differences as to how existing relations of domination, inequality and control are affected by emerging constellations of governance shaped by history, power structures and legal pluralism.[13] To offer insight into some of the context-specific methodological challenges and considerations associated with empirical, evaluative and normative explorations of the relationship between human rights and legal pluralism, this chapter uses empirical research from a former Western colony in Southern Africa, Zimbabwe.

The aim of the Zimbabwean case is to show how a study of the interplay between the human right to water, national water laws and local community-based water norms in rural and urban areas may be designed. The ratification of the human right to water in the context of a political, legal and economic crisis that led to breakdown of rule of law and rural and urban public water supply makes Zimbabwe an interesting case

---

[12] F. Von Benda-Beckmann and K. von Benda-Beckmann, '"Living Law" as Political and Analytical Concept' in K. Papendorf, S. Machura and A. Hellum (eds), *Ehrlich's Sociology of Law* (Litt 2014) 69–95.

[13] For a thorough discussion of the different historical origins of legal pluralism in Latin America and Africa see Sieder and McNeish (n 2). For a study of women's rights and legal pluralism in the Danish labour market see H. Petersen, *Home Knitted Law. Norms and Values in Gendered Rule-making* (Dartmouth 1996). For a study of human rights gender, islam and legal pluralism in Norway see A. Hellum and F. Taj, 'Taking What Law Where and to Whom? Legal Literacy as Transcultural "Law-Making" in Oslo' in A. Hellum, S.S. Ali and A. Griffiths (eds), *From Transnational Relation to Transnational Laws. Northern European Laws at the Crossroads* (Ashgate 2011) 93–117.

study. The legal system in Zimbabwe constitutes 'weak' legal pluralism. It is made up of a mixture of inherited Western law, formal customary laws developed by the colonial and post-colonial courts and post-independence legislation. In practice access to water for domestic, livelihood and productive purposes is regulated by a mixture of statutory law, municipal by-laws and the living local norms expressed in the Shona proverb 'water is life'.[14] This proverb, which is based on the idea that to deny water is to deny life, forms part of a broad right to water for livelihood: for humans, animals and nature.[15] This phenomenon constitutes 'strong' legal pluralism.[16]

This chapter unfolds in five sections. Following this introduction an analytical framework is set out for the study of human rights and legal pluralism with focus on Sally Falk Moore's theory of law as a semi-autonomous social field. The next two sections show what this analytical framework may yield through a brief presentation of my own academic journey accompanied by a longitudinal study of the interplay between international human rights, national law and community-based water norms in Zimbabwe. By way of conclusion the final section discusses the broader normative and evaluative implications that the interpretation and implementation of the human right to water give rise to in the context of complex power relations and social inequalities that today shape the existing multiplicity of coexisting, overlapping and conflicting water governance systems in Zimbabwe.

LEGAL PLURALISM AS A DESCRIPTIVE, ANALYTICAL TOOL: LAW'S SEMI-AUTONOMY

Analysis of the relationship between human rights and different normative orders raises questions about social science methodology and how law is framed. In post-colonial anthropological theory legal pluralism has been

---

[14]   The Shona is the largest ethnic group in Zimbabwe.

[15]   B. Sithole, 'Use and Access to Dambos in Communal Lands in Zimbabwe: Institutional Considerations', PhD thesis, Centre for Applied Social Sciences, University of Zimbabwe (1999); P. Matondi, 'The Struggle for Access to Land and Water Resources in Zimbabwe: The Case of Shamva District'. PhD thesis, Swedish University of Agricultural Sciences (Uppsala 2001); B. Derman and A. Hellum, 'Neither Tragedy nor Enclosure: Are There Inherent Human Rights in Water Management in Zimbabwe's Communal Lands' (2002) 14(2) The European Journal of Development Research 31–50.

[16]   The concepts 'weak' and 'strong' legal pluralism are elaborated in the next section.

defined as 'the presence in one social field of more than one legal order'.[17] It distinguishes between 'weak' and 'strong' legal pluralism.[18] 'Weak legal pluralism' refers to situations where the state legal order recognizes a plurality of normative orders. An example of 'weak legal pluralism' is the legal systems in former British colonies where imported Western law applied to the settlers while the customary and religious laws of the different ethnic and religious groups applied to the native population. 'Strong legal pluralism' refers to situations where regulatory and normative orders other than the formal state law (statutory, customary or religious) affect and control people's lives.

Post-colonial anthropological theory constitutes a descriptive socio-legal theory which focuses on 'strong legal pluralism'. Addressing the co-existence of several normative orders in different social fields, legal pluralism is not seen as a product of the colonial legal systems in former Western colonies. It is a socio-legal phenomenon to be found in all states, whether situated in the North or South, in the 'developed' or 'underdeveloped' world. This body of theory offers different conceptual frameworks that can be used to describe and analyse various aspects of the interaction between international human rights, state-law and local norms that are inherent in human interaction in different social fora. The anthropologist Sally Engle Merry has focused on ways in which women's human rights, particularly the right to a life free from domestic violence, travel between the international and the local. She uses the concept of 'vernacularization' and 'indigenization' to analyse the process whereby human rights are adopted, translated or resisted in different local contexts.[19] Describing how, in the era of globalization, law is constituted in an intersection of different legal orders, the sociologist Boaventura de Sousa Santos uses the term 'interlegality' to characterize the mixed and porous character of law at this point in time.[20] The aim of this theory is to explore how organized grass-roots resistance to neo-liberal globalization that invokes human rights can translate into emerging counter-hegemonic socio-legal discourses.[21]

---

[17]   Griffiths (n 1).

[18]   Ibid.

[19]   S.E. Merry, *Human Rights and Gender Violence* (University of Chicago Press 2006).

[20]   Moore (n 1); B. Sousa Santos, 'Law a Map of Misreading: Towards a Post-modern Conception of Law' (1987) 14(3) Journal of Law and Society 279–299; Merry (n 19); Von Benda-Beckmann (n 12).

[21]   B. Sousa Santos and C.A. Rodriguez-Garavito, *Law and Globalization from Below. Towards a Cosmopolitan Legality* (CUP 2005).

Drawing attention to the fact that the same social space and the same activities often are subject to other regulatory regimes than state-law, the legal anthropologist Sally Falk Moore has suggested that we approach law as a semi-autonomous social field.[22] Law, as suggested by Sally Falk Moore, should be studied as a process, observable to the researchers, in small social fields 'in terms of its semi-autonomy – the fact that it can generate rules and customs and symbols internally, but that it is vulnerable to rules and decisions and other forces emanating from the larger world it is surrounded by'.[23] Semi-autonomy offers a framework that enable the researcher to identify those arenas where actions and decisions informed by different international, national and local norms invoked by different actors are taken. The boundary of the semi-autonomous social field is defined by a processual characteristic – namely a social arena made up by actors that have the capacity to generate rules and the power to induce compliance with them. Compliance is not limited to norms that are sanctioned through the state-legal system but includes various forms of social sanctions such as shaming and blaming and social stigmatization and exclusion.

The concept of the semi-autonomous social field, in other words, is a tool that can be used to draw initial boundaries around the social fields where the researcher assumes that encounters between international, national and local norms take place.[24] The different actors that participate in the process of norm generation define the social field of investigation. Semi-autonomous social fields, in a global world, often involve women and men embedded in relationships that extend beyond geographic and national boundaries. Examples of norm-generating entities are families or clans, workplaces, companies, religious communities, epistemic communities, national or international donor agencies, national or international humanitarian agencies and non-governmental organizations.

The norm-generating processes that take place within such social fields can be observed through fieldwork where participant observation is supplemented with qualitative interviews to get insight in different actors' sense of obligations and duties and those on which different actors base their claims and decisions. The case study method is well suited to explore claims-making processes where differently situated actors invoke different norms with different outcomes. 'Trouble cases' and 'trouble-less cases' constitute two main roads into norm-generating and norm-upholding

---

[22]   Moore (n 1).
[23]   Ibid. 55–56.
[24]   See Bentzon et al. (n 2) 146–148.

activities.[25] 'Trouble cases' are cases that are handled by formal and informal dispute resolution agencies. They offer an opportunity to study how different norms invoked by different actors are dealt with by different courts. 'Trouble-less cases' offer insight in the norms which are evolving through arrangements or agreements in everyday life, and different actors' participation in these processes. The inclusion of 'trouble-less cases' has proved particularly valuable from a gender perspective because it indicates how women and men on a day-to-day basis negotiate access, use and control of resources in the family and in the local community.[26]

Questions of power are pertinent in plural legal constellations where different state and non-state actors are 'engaged in contestations over who has the power to generate law and construct its meaning'.[27] Most importantly, these processes include questions of power where norm-generation can be dominated by a relatively powerful group who define and use rights for their own narrow purposes.[28] Local communities have often been seen as undifferentiated, having similar interests, and therefore little account has been taken of their complexities and divided interests.[29] To come to grips with the complex struggles of power and resources that shape the way in which the relationship between international, national and local norms is negotiated, the notion of common community interests requires unpacking. As regards the study of access to resources, such as the human right to water, a framework that addresses women as members of a group and as differently situated individuals within the group is needed.[30]

---

[25]   John F. Holleman, 'Trouble-cases and Trouble-less in the Study of Customary Law and Legal Reform' (1973) 7(4) Law and Society Review 585–609.

[26]   Bentzon et al. (n 2) 60–61.

[27]   K. Von Benda-Beckmann, F. von Benda-Beckmann and A. Griffiths (eds), *Mobile People, Mobile Law. Expanding Legal Relations in a Changing World* (Ashgate 2005) 11–14.

[28]   H. Englund, *Prisoners of Freedom: Human Rights and the African Poor* (University of California Press 2006). Englund's analysis shows how elements of the Malawian middle class have turned the language of human rights to their advantage.

[29]   Sieder and McNeish (n 2); B. Derman, A. Hellum and K. Sandvik 'Ethnographic and Historical Perspectives on Rights Claiming on the African Continent' in *Worlds of Human Rights: Ambiguities of Rights Claiming in Africa* (Brill 2013) 7–9.

[30]   A. Hellum, 'Human Rights in a Gendered, Relational and Plural Legal Landscape. Introduction' in B. Derman, A. Hellum and K. Sandvik (eds) *Worlds of Human Rights: Ambiguities of Rights Claiming in Africa* (Brill 2013) 131–143; A. Hellum, P. Kameri-Mbote and B. van Koppen (eds), 'The Human Right to Water and Sanitation in a Legal Pluralist Landscape: Perspectives of Southern and

FROM THEORY TO EMPIRICAL RESEARCH: EXPLORING THE HUMAN RIGHT TO WATER IN ZIMBABWE

The formulation of research problems raises questions about the choice of theory which in turn calls for considerations about what kind of activities, what actors and what geographic, social and institutional areas should be studied. To illustrate the various steps in the research process and to demonstrate what kind of knowledge the above described approach may yield I will use my own research on the relationship between the human right to water and plural water norms in Zimbabwe, which was carried out between 1999 and 2014.

My Own Research Journey: From Lived Realities to Legal Pluralities

As a background to the study of plural water laws in Zimbabwe, which will be presented below, I will briefly share my own research history. I was trained as a lawyer at the Faculty of Law at the University of Oslo. Research in women's law, a legal discipline that sets out to describe, understand and improve the position of women in law and society, led me to further studies in anthropology and anthropology of law.[31] Anthropology, particularly Marianne Gullestad's[32] conception of the family as a kitchen-table society and the legal anthropologist Sally Falk Moore's concept of law as a semi-autonomous social field, attracted my interest because it facilitated studies of women as actors in the process of law.[33]

A turning point in my understanding of human rights as process was my encounter with post-colonial African law through a joint teaching and research program between the Faculty of Law at the University of Oslo and the University of Zimbabwe. In the 1990s, Zimbabwe, like a number of other Southern and Eastern African states that was part of this cooperation, ratified the Convention on the Elimination of All Forms of Discrimination against Women (CEDAW). As a researcher with a background in the Scandinavian women's law tradition, which took women's lived realities as a starting point, I was puzzled by the disjuncture between

---

Eastern African Women' in *Water is Life: Women's Human Rights in Local Water Governance in Southern and Eastern Africa* (Weaver Press 2015) 1–32.

[31]   T.S. Dahl, *Feminist Jurisprudence* (Norwegian University Press 1986).

[32]   M. Gullestad, *Kitchen Table Society* (Norwegian University Press 2002).

[33]   A. Hellum, 'Legal Pluralist Perspectives in Scandinavian and African Women's Law' in K. Papendorf, S. Machura and A. Hellum (eds), *Ehrlich's Sociology of Law* (Litt 2014) 95–115.

the customary laws that were applied by the post-colonial courts and the living customary norms that evolved through social life. I was curious how the CEDAW's demand for gender-equal marriage laws was reconciled with women's experiences of the legal pluralities that had a bearing on their marriage and family relationships in everyday life.[34]

To bring the concept of gender equality down from the plane of abstract international principles I embarked on a study of how different groups of Zimbabwean women and their families dealt with problems associated with childlessness. To explore these questions I carried out fieldwork in urban middle-class areas in Harare, a lower-class high-density area in Harare and in a peri-urban area. To describe and understand the circumstances under which the promotion of women's human rights, particularly the right to equality in marriage and family life, was promoted or hindered I turned the concept of law as a semi-autonomous social field. This framework facilitated analysis of decision-making in the family, consultations with traditional healers, church leaders, traditional leaders and local courts, and as such the complex process in which human rights were adopted or resisted by various actors invoking different norms. The study showed how different communities responded to the new family and marriage laws at different rates and in different ways, and with different effects for different groups of women. I was puzzled by insight in the process whereby the living law, under certain circumstances, was more receptive to the ongoing process of social and economic change than statutory law and state-court customary law. Regarding the disjunction between international human rights and the uneven normative development taking place on the ground, I concluded that it was an important task for legal sciences to provide a nuanced picture of custom and local law as a site of diverse and contested practices.

An opportunity to further explore these questions arose when in 1999, I was invited to join an interdisciplinary research project hosted by the Center for Applied Social Studies at the University of Zimbabwe.[35] The overall aim of the research project was to study the Zimbabwean water reform. The reform was partly informed by the World Bank's quest for a more efficient water management system and partly by the quest for greater racial justice regarding the distribution of water for productive

---

[34] Hellum, A., *Women's Human Rights and Legal Pluralism in Africa: Mixed Norms and Identities in Infertility Management in Zimbabwe* (TANO Aschehoug/ Mond Books 1999).

[35] The project, which was funded by USAID, was a cooperation between Michigan State University (MSU) and the University of Zimbabwe (UoZ). It was led by Francis Gonese from UoZ and Bill Derman from MSU.

purposes. Empirical research that I carried out in Mhondoro communal land with my colleague Bill Derman uncovered community-based norms which imposed a duty to share clean drinking water and land with accessible water to grow food. To our great surprise, these local norms had much in common with the bundle of human rights that forms the right to an adequate living standard.[36] They were embedded in the Shona proverb 'water is life', which saw the right to water as deriving from the right to life, livelihood and dignity. These norms, which we termed 'living customary law', were not described in legal textbooks that addressed the customary laws applied by the formal courts. As the main regulation of the way in which local communities managed and shared water, these norms were important for new and innovative forms of commercial cropping in the communal areas. They were particularly important for the role women, through home gardens, played with regard to food security, health and education. However, the Zimbabwean water reform of 2000, we observed, failed to recognize the community-based norms and institutions that guided the use of water for domestic and productive uses in the communal areas. We thus concluded that the right to water for personal, domestic, livelihood and productive purposes was by far better protected by 'the living customary norms' than by state-law and international human rights law. The human right to water was, at that point in time, not fully recognized by the UN.

The Human Right to Water in Zimbabwe: Problems, Concepts, Field Sites and Actors

In 2010 I embarked on a study of the incorporation and implementation of the human right to water in Zimbabwe.[37] In this year the Zimbabwean Government of National Unity (GNU) signed the UN General Assembly Resolution 64/292 on the Human Right to Water and Sanitation in the aftermath of the political and economic crisis that culminated after the Fast Track Land Reform Program (FTLRP). In an attempt to cope with the water crisis the GNU included the right to clean drinking water in Section 77 of the new Zimbabwean Constitution and in the new water policy. We were interested in a broader comparative study of the plurality

---

[36] Derman and Hellum (n 15).

[37] Members of the research team were Dr Ellen Sithole, PhD scholar Elizabeth Rutsate, Professor Bill Derman and myself. The research, which was part of a study of four Southern and Eastern African countries, is compiled in the book A. Hellum, P. Kameri-Mbote and B. van Koppen (eds), *Water is Life: Women's Human Rights in Local Water Governance in Southern and Eastern Africa* (Weaver Press 2015).

of norms and institutions that people in different rural and urban contexts were turning to in order to access water for production, livelihood and domestic uses. Taking account of the multiplicity of state and non-state actors, norms and institutions that were involved in the governance of water in Zimbabwe, we decided to approach water governance as the system of actors, resources, and processes which mediate society's access to water.[38] We thus moved beyond a statist conception of law and governance, which is limited to the exercise of state authority through institutions, laws, policies and procedures.

Through this pluralist definition of law and governance we set out to explore how national and local government agencies, development agencies, humanitarian organizations, traditional leaders, local communities, families and individual women and men navigated a terrain where international and national law coexist and interact with local norms and practices. Underlying this research strategy was the assumption that different rural and urban communities would be affected by both national water laws and the human right to water, but that they also had the capacity to uphold and generate norms internally. We were interested in how the norms that guided the management and distribution of water were negotiated in different rural, peri-urban and urban communities. We were also interested in how the existing pluralities of norms and institutions were shaped by political and economic power relations on a larger scale. We were particularly interested in the effects of the politicization of water governance, for example how the ZANU PF party used water as a source of political control in the struggle against the competing Movement for Democratic Change (MDC) party. What norms were invoked by different actors and with what outcome? Who in the different urban and rural communities had the power to interpret and enforce the norms that guided people's access to different water sources? In the light of earlier research in communal land areas we were curious what norms would be applied by the new farmers in the Fast Track Resettlement Areas. We were also curious as to what the norms that guided urban citizens' use of groundwater and open sources were. Whether and to what extent did the human right to water make a mark on the way in which water was negotiated in different rural and urban contexts?

The overall methodological challenge, as regards the choice of field sites, was to lay an empirical foundation for a comparative study that could demonstrate how legal pluralities under certain conditions may promote

---

[38]   T. Franks and F. Cleaver, 'Water Governance and Poverty: A Framework for Analysis', (2007) 7(4) Progress in Development Studies, 291–306.

the realization of the human right to water for some groups while preventing the human rights of other groups. We were also interested in the situation of vulnerable individuals within the group, such as women in poor households and widows looking after children and grandchildren. Towards this end a research strategy that encompassed a communal lands area, an urban high-density area and a Fast Track Resettlement Area (A1) was designed. The sites selected were three villages in Domboshawa Communal Land Area, three A1 resettlement farms in Mazowe Catchment and three high-density areas in Harare.[39]

Domboshawa Communal Area is a water-rich area with good soils 20 km outside Harare.[40] The growing and marketing of vegetables and fruits in combination with non-farm employment in Harare has led to economic growth among many families. Owing to informal sale of communal land there is an increasing competition of access to land and water in the area. Small-scale farmers in Domboshawa, as in other communal areas, have through the digging of canals, small dams and wells made significant investments in water infrastructure, operation and maintenance. These irrigation systems establish relations between water users and form the basis of norms that govern the ways in which water is shared. In these three villages we charted the different water sources that women and men made use of for productive and domestic purposes. We were particularly interested in how the interests of poor users, particularly widows in charge of children and grandchildren, were affected by the breakdown of public water services and the increasing competition over water for agricultural production in the area. In-depth interviews were carried out with women in three villages, including wealthy, middle-income and poor households.[41] To gain insight into the formal and informal water governance structures in place in the selected areas we interviewed staff from women's non-governmental organizations operating in the area, chiefs, sub-chiefs, headmen and elected councillors from the Rural District Council.

In Zimbabwe, the FTLRP, which involved the invasion and redistribution of white-owned large-scale commercial farms, resulted in a dramatic

---

[39]   A1 resettlement farm is a small land allocation under the Fast Track Land Resettlement Program.

[40]   See Chapter 12 in *Water is Life* (n 37).

[41]   The structures of the buildings at the homestead were the main indicator of a household's economic status. For instance, the wealthy had a modern brick house with at least three rooms while the middle had the same structure with at least two rooms. The poor had one or two round huts in their homestead. Additional factors used to determine status included the type of building material used, the roofing, availability and type of toilet, and possessions such as vehicles.

change of circumstances for farm workers. As a result of violent evictions, more than 200,000 workers with families lost their jobs and homes, including access to sanitation and water for domestic and livelihood use. The farm workers' right to water and sanitation had, before the occupations, been part of the work contract with the commercial farmer. To explore how the new farmers and the displaced farm workers negotiated access to the different water sources on the former commercial farms, three A1 resettlement farms in Mazowe Catchment were studied.[42] The politicization of land and water made it difficult to do research in the area. For security reasons the white team members visited the area only once because it potentially could have jeopardized the research. The Zimbabwean researcher explored how the new farmer's and displaced farm worker's urgent need for clean water and water to grow food was responded to by international and national actors in the aftermath of the cholera outbreaks in 2008. Both new farmers and displaced farm workers were interviewed with a focus on women's access to water for personal, domestic and livelihood uses. Key informant interviews were carried out with UNICEF officials, employees and members of rural district council, municipal health workers, chiefs, village heads and leaders of local irrigation committees.

To explore the relationship between formal and informal water governance systems in an urban context we choose three high-density areas in Harare: Mabvuku, Tafara and Glen Norah.[43] We were interested in how women from middle- and low-income households coped with the breakdown of public water delivery.[44] The aim was to establish what water sources people in these areas were using to supplement municipal water and what the norms and institutions governing access, use and control of these sources were. Towards this end, we focused on public provision of water by the City of Harare, provision of water through humanitarian assistance by UNICEF and self-provision at the household level. We interviewed employed, high- and low-income women, married women with employed

---

[42]   These farms were studied by Elizabeth Rutsate who was a PhD fellow participating in the Zimbabwean country study. See Chapter 13 in *Water is Life* (n 37).

[43]   The low-density suburbs have found private solutions. These include private boreholes, bottled drinking water and/or the purchase of water from private water vendors who bring a weekly or monthly quantity of water to a place in large elevated water containers. There are currently large numbers of water delivery trucks carrying water to those who can afford to pay; L. Mangwanya, 'A Study of Individual and Collective Responses to Domestic Water Scarcity in the City of Harare', MA thesis, University of Zimbabwe (2011) and personal observations.

[44]   See Chapter 11 in *Water is Life* (n 37).

and unemployed husbands, female-headed households and female renters, as well as elderly and disabled women. Key informant interviews were conducted with officials in international humanitarian organizations, city councillors from the area, administrative staff from the area and the city of Harare, borehole committee members and representatives of Mabvuku, Tafara and Glen Norah resident associations. Our discussions with people at boreholes in the areas were several times interrupted by ZANU PF supporters who accused us of being foreign infiltrators and the people talking to us of being traitors.

STUDYING NORMATIVE INTERPLAY: THE HUMAN RIGHT TO WATER, NATIONAL WATER LAW AND LOCAL NORMS

In Zimbabwe community-based water governance systems anchored in unwritten customary norms and values are widespread, in spite of efforts by both colonial and independent African governments to redefine citizens' relationship to water through state laws and policies. We were, as already mentioned, curious as to how different actors in different rural and urban contexts negotiated access to water in the face of the breakdown of the public water governance system and the adaptation of the human right to water. An overall aim was to gain insight in whether and to what extent different actors in different communities had the capacity to invoke or generate norms that overruled the formal laws employed by the official water governance institutions.

Domboshawa Communal Land: How Villagers Generate, Uphold and Enforce Norms

In Domboshawa communal land the formal legal responsibility for provision of primary water, which according to the Zimbabwean Water Act includes both drinking water and water for cattle, brick-making and family food, lies with the Rural District Council.[45] The maintenance of water infrastructure is with the District Development Fund. On paper national legislation – particularly the right to primary water in rural areas – is in consonance with Zimbabwe's human rights obligations.

Field work observations combined with interviews with villagers and councillors showed that public water service provision, as a result of

---

[45] See Chapter 12 in *Water is Life* (n 37).

the political and economic crisis, had broken down. Those who did not have groundwater on their land, those who could not afford to invest in a private well and those whose wells dried up in the 'winter season' were hard hit by the lack of functioning boreholes. Our study showed that women, who were responsible for fetching water for domestic needs, accessed water from their neighbour's wells dug by family members. This practice was described by the first female sub-chief in the area, who had just returned from the UK where she had lived for many years, in the following way:

> When I returned from the UK, I dug this well here in our compound for my mum. I was surprised when women from the surrounding area, when their wells dried up at the end of the dry season, started flocking here to fetch water. I said to myself, 'Look, no one assisted me in buying cement and bricks to build the well as well as pay for labour for its digging.' I used to become furious about the whole issue and sometimes I would not even greet some of the people who came here to fetch water. Some would come as early as 4 a.m. My mother then sat me down and said to me, 'Look here, you can't deny people access to water in your well because if you do that people are bound to get angry with you such that they may dump a dead dog into the well or even put poison into the well'.[46]

The obligation to share, according to the women we interviewed and local leaders, arose from good neighbourliness and the fact that water is a basic need that can be denied no one. In Domboshawa communal land, like other communal areas we had studied, the Shona proverb 'water is life' formed part of a broad right to water for livelihood entailing corresponding rights and duties.[47] Local authorities tried to ensure that urban dwellers who had bought land in the area followed these rules:

> Those with privately dug wells share with neighbours who don't have with the exception of this new guy called Tsatsa. He locks up his well so that neighbours cannot access it. He is a civil servant working in Harare but his wife lives here all the time. He is a newcomer who settled here recently. I will have to go and talk to him about it because it's not acceptable in our community for an African to deny others access to drinking water which belongs to God.

Yet the community-based institutions often lacked the power to enforce these norms when they were not adhered to by wealthy and well-connected actors in the community. In one of the villages, about seven households who all belonged to the same family regularly blocked the water on the river from flowing downstream to the rest of the villagers. These farmers,

---

[46]   Interview with the first female Sub-Chief in Domboshawa, July 2012.
[47]   Sithole (n 15), Matondi (n 15), Derman and Hellum (n 36).

who were engaged in large-scale vegetable production, were blocking water in order to produce enough to meet the demands of their markets. According to one of the family members:

> We will be thinking about them [downstream users] but in Shona there is a saying that you can't stop eating just because someone you know has a problem. So I understand their situation but I have a family to feed and that comes first.[48]

This and many other conflicts between large- and small-scale farmers remained unresolved. The offenders did not adhere to the agreed resolutions because they came from more powerful families and were strategically located in terms of water resources. In some instances the local leaders, who came from the wealthiest families in the area, were also protecting their own interests as large-scale water users. The national water governance institutions that formally are charged with regulating and allocating water were not present in the area. Poor women, producing food and other items for livelihood, were the ones who suffered most in a situation where the national water governance institutions were absent and the local institutions tended to side with larger and more powerful water users.

This demonstrates the need to analyse the outcome of the interaction between international, national and local norms with a view to whether and how they promote or prevent the realization of human rights standards. A methodological challenge is to uncover how these processes include questions of power where norm-generation can be dominated by a relatively powerful group who define and use rights for their own narrow purposes. To come to grips with the consequences of legal pluralities from the perspective of differently positioned groups and individuals, the combination of an actor perspective and a comparative research strategy involving gender, ethnicity and social status is helpful.

New Farmers and Displaced Farm Workers on A1 Resettlement Farms: The Limit of Local Customary Norms

Both national water governance institutions and international humanitarian organizations were conspicuous by their absence in the Fast Track Land Reform Areas. On the three A1 farms we studied in the Mazowe there was, with the exception of intervention by one local health official, no state

---

[48] Makonde villager, September 2012; however, it isn't just about feeding a family but continuing to provide more income for a range of purposes.

intervention to ensure clean drinking water for the new farmers and the displaced farm workers. International humanitarian organizations, coordinated by UNICEF, would not step in on resettlement farms because the farms were taken illegally and without compensation of the former owners.

Owing to the breakdown of water infrastructure on the former commercial farms, the lack of clean drinking water and sanitation was a problem for everyone living in these areas. It was not just farm workers who suffered from insufficient access to clean drinking water but also most of the A1 settlers. The displaced farm workers' access to basic resources, such as housing, land, water and sanitation, relied on their ability to negotiate with the few remaining commercial farmers and the new A1 farmers. Generally the displaced farm workers felt insecure about voicing their complaints over unclean drinking water to the white commercial farmers who were still farming. They were afraid any complaints could endanger their job security. They were also reluctant to approach the new farmers on the A1 irrigation committees. They feared they would be regarded as rebellious elements of the worker community, which could lead to their eviction from the farms as traitors who were against land reform.

Common pool water sources like river water or water from shallow wells in the wetlands were generally shared between the new A1 farmers and the farm workers. However, the Shona customary norm providing a duty to share clean drinking water and land with water to grow food proved to be highly problematic in the context of resettled farms. In the resettlement areas access to resources was, to our surprise, to a large extent decided on the basis of group membership. Viewing the farm workers as foreigners without citizenship, most of the new settlers who had taken over the formerly white-owned farms did not see themselves as obliged to share available sources of clean drinking water with them. Most village heads did not allow farm worker access to land to grow food along the rivers, referring to the statutory requirement that no cultivation should be done within a 30 metre distance from a river bank. Despite denying women farm workers the opportunity to have riparian gardens, these village heads allowed women A1 farmers to have such gardens. There were, however, instances where women from the farm worker communities, owing to a longstanding amicable relationship with the people who had taken over the farms, were allowed access to clean drinking water and land to grow food close to the rivers.

This study, by comparing the way in which different social and ethnic groups accessed water, showed the multiple forms of exclusion and marginalization experienced by displaced farm workers in relation to the customary, national and international obligations of the different actors involved in the governance of water on the A1 farms. Because farms had been taken through a process that fell short of rule of law standards, international donors did not see themselves as obliged to address the basic needs of the displaced farm workers and their children, still living in the FTLRP areas.[49] The Shona customary norm entailing a duty to share clean drinking water with those in need was in most instances not extended to the displaced farm workers, mainly owing to the perception that farm workers were of foreign origin, and as such outsiders to the group.

Harare's High-density Areas – Customary Norms Overrule State-law

The city council of Harare, where the MDC at the time of the study was in majority, is in accordance with existing legislation tasked with provision of treated potable water services. Since there is no clear legislative obligation to ensure affordable water to consumers in under-privileged communities, the existing legal framework falls short of human rights standards. The City of Harare, which is economically dependent on fees from water users, has, in order to increase its water revenue, stepped up the number of water disconnections. Water and property revenues are, overwhelmingly, the largest income of Harare City Council.[50]

Owing to the irregular supply of water from the municipality caused by mismanagement, the disconnection of people who could not afford to pay and the breakdown of the public boreholes provided by humanitarians, the inhabitants in these areas had dug wells next to their houses or in surrounding wetlands. We were surprised to find a widespread application of the customary principle, 'water is life', implying a duty to share clean drinking water. As these customary norms have so far been associated with rural Zimbabwe, we did not expect to find that many owners of private wells in these high-density areas freely shared water with their poorer neighbours or people who did not have groundwater on their property. The duty to share in Harare's high-density areas was, like in the communal lands, based on the belief that water is an essential, God-given resource which cannot be denied anyone. As a woman stated: 'water is something

---

[49]   CESCR, 'General Comment No. 15. The Right to Water' (2002) E/C.12/200 2/11, para. 16.

[50]   Interviews with Harare City Council Councilors, October 2013; 'Water: Council's Cash Cow Causes Concern', *The Zimbabwean*, 12 May 2012 <http://www.thezimbabwean.co/news/zimbabwe/62655/water-councils-cash-cow-causes.html> accessed 7 October 2013. Quoted from 'Troubled Water. Burst Pipes, Contaminated Wells, and Open Defecation in Zimbabwe's Capital' (Human Rights Watch 2013) 45.

that you cannot deny another person'.[51] In one neighbourhood almost all the women we interviewed reported that when the taps ran dry they would fetch water in a well in a garden in the wetlands about one kilometre away. There was also a belief that those who did not share their water with those who need it would be punished:

> There is one man who did not want to share water from his well with others but he has since had his well filled up with earth. Some people say the well's walls were not reinforced with bricks and so the walls collapsed. But well, God is not a fool! God punishes you if you do things out of the expected. How can a person charge a fee for water which he did not create?[52]

The existing plurality of norms were not recognized by municipal authorities and national government who sought a centralized legal framework. The widespread practice of sinking wells in backyards for water supply or drilling private boreholes has put residents in conflict with City of Harare by-laws on issues of environmental and health concerns. The municipality, with reference to the by-laws, ordered that the wells be closed and that a penalty be charged against those who have a well. The citizens were of the view that the city was forcing them to resort to alternative water sources since it did not fulfil its duty to provide safe, available and affordable water for domestic, sanitary and livelihood needs. In their view, water in the urban areas, as in the rural areas, 'is life' and the municipality should not deny their use of groundwater for such basic needs. Within this struggle the local norms have so far taken precedence. The citizens in these areas have also contested the widespread water disconnections on legal grounds. Many of them are active members of local resident's associations that, with the support of organizations such as Zimbabwe Lawyers for Human Rights, have challenged the legality of the City of Harare's water cuts through litigation. Litigation invoking Section 77 of the new Zimbabwean constitution, which recognizes the right to clean water, has been successful. In a decision of April 2014 the High Court outlawed the City of Harare's by-laws, which empowers the City Council to cut off water from residents arbitrarily without a court order, with reference to the constitution.

In defiance of this court order the City of Harare has, however, cut off the water supplies of thousands of defaulters without a court order.[53] The continued disconnections must, however, be understood in the light of the bitter conflict over water governance between ZANU-PF and the

---

[51]   Harare North resident, December 2011.
[52]   Elderly widow in Mabvuku, January 2011.
[53]   <http://www.sundaymail.co.zw/?p=19919#.VHGudoj6ojI.gmail>.

MDC. Owing to the fact that the MDC has had majority representation in Harare and other cities since 2000, there has been continuous contestation for power and interference in local governance structures, including water, by the ZANU-PF-controlled Ministry of Local Government, Rural and Urban Development (the Ministry of Local Government). During the campaign for the 2013 elections the ZANU-PF Minister of Local Government passed a Directive to Write off Debts by all Local Authorities. The Directive, which addressed all provincial administrators, town clerks and chief executive officers, was used by ZANU-PF, including Robert Mugabe, as one of the key points in their election campaign. The directive undermined the MDC-dominated council's need for revenue to fund the city's water and sanitation system and specific measures directed at those public and private institutions and citizens who had not paid their water bills which mounted to millions of US dollars. In response to the dire economic situation, partly caused by political interventions by the ZANU PF government, the City of Harare has stepped up the number of illegal water disconnections and introduced reconnection fees and, in spite of resistance from civil rights organizations, is planning to install water meters.

All in all this study from Harare's high-density areas demonstrates the importance of linking the understanding of law's semi-autonomy and legal pluralism in small-scale social fields to political, economic and legal events on a larger scale. Clearly the breakdown of the physical water infrastructure along with the lack of independent and transparent governance institutions has created a situation of legal impunity where both state-law and customary norms are reconfigured and manipulated through the dominant political networks. This underscores the need to study legal pluralities as a process of constantly changing and interacting normative constellations and power relations taking place in a shifting legal, political and economic terrain.

CONCLUDING REMARKS: DESCRIPTIVE, EVALUATIVE AND NORMATIVE RESEARCH CHALLENGES

All in all the case study from Zimbabwe demonstrates how an analytical approach seeing law as a semi-autonomous social field, an actor perspective involving gender, ethnicity and class and comparisons between different social fields and levels of law may be combined to explore how legal pluralities may be an enabling or constraining factor regarding the realization of human rights. This discussion entails interrelated phenomenological, evaluative and normative challenges that this interdisciplinary human rights approach poses.

Descriptive and Evaluative Dimensions

The empirical study of how norms were generated in the three different social fields provided a window into the way in which differently situated actors negotiated access to water in the context of a conflict-ridden and fragmenting national and municipal water governance system. A finding that cut across the three field sites was that the human right to water and the right to primary water in the Zimbabwean Water Act played a modest role in ensuring people access to water in comparison to local customary norms expressed in the proverb 'water is life'. These living customary norms were in many instances so strong that they overruled state-law that, to protect the environment or people's health, restricted people's use of common pool water sources.

A vertical comparison between the content of international, national and local norms revealed that the living customary law was more responsive to the needs of vulnerable groups and women within them than the dominant legal understanding of the human right to water. An observation that cut across the three sub-cases was that the community-based water norms not were confined to water for personal and domestic uses, but included water for growing, preparing and selling food and other products that were vital for family welfare. Both rural and urban women's access to water for domestic, livelihood and productive purposes relied heavily on these local norms. They formed part of a broader cluster of norms that defined their rights and duties as members of a family and of a local community. These small-scale studies thus point to a disjuncture between the community-based water norms and the ambiguities that are inherent in human rights water discourse. The CESCR General Comment No. 15 states that priority in the allocation of water must be given to such personal and domestic uses. Defining the human right to water through its link to the right to life, the right to food and the right to health, it also demonstrates a wider understanding. On this background General Comment No. 15 also recognizes that priority should be given to water resources required to prevent malnutrition, starvation and disease. UN General Assembly Resolution 64/292 on the Human Right to Water and Sanitation, however, remains silent on water for broader livelihood needs. The UNGA resolution, which has become the dominant paradigm in international human rights discourse, does not fully respond to the holistic way in which rural, peri-urban and urban women access water, not only for personal and domestic uses, but also for growing nutritious food.

A horizontal comparison, however, displayed differences in terms of gender, social status and ethnic background with a view to differently positioned actors' capacity to invoke different layers of law to their own advantage. Local norms and practices, on the one hand, ensured women from the ethnic majority groups' access to water for domestic, livelihood and productive purposes. These norms, on the other hand, imposed a series of water-related duties on lower middle class and poor women. These deep-seated gender stereotypes undermined other rights, such as the right to education, work and participation. Another limitation of the community-based water norms is that they were not seen as universal but limited to group members. Research conducted in the FTLRP resettlement areas clearly showed that the duty to share drinking water and land with water to grow food in most instances did not apply to the displaced farm workers. Owing to their lack of recognized citizenship and the claims that they had 'foreign' backgrounds, they were not in a position to assert their rights either under state law[54] or under the living customary law.

The Normative Dimension – And So What?

An overall normative question is what social science and human rights theory has to offer with regard to consider measures that may be taken to improve the situation for weak and vulnerable groups.

A key question is whether formalization or abolition of the living customary law would be the most promising way to attain the human right to water for different social groups.[55] From a social science perspective this question calls for careful consideration of the political, economic and legal power relations that shape legal pluralities. As demonstrated by the Zimbabwean case study, the legal pluralities that inform the fragmenting national water governance system were closely linked to the autocratic ZANU PF government's efforts to control both national and local water governance institutions. In this situation, both state-law and the living norms are shaped by broader political and economic power structures. Rather than a return to the customary, this contextual understanding points to the need to strengthen the normative and institutional protection of vulnerable groups' access to water, not only for personal and domestic uses, but also for livelihood purposes.

---

[54] Namely under section 77 of the 2013 Zimbabwe Constitution, the right to free primary water for rural households provisions under the Water Act Chapter 20:24 and the 2012 National Water Policy.

[55] Von Benda Beckmann (n 12) 69–95.

Furthermore, the small-scale studies point to the need of a human rights framework that responds to the holistic way in which rural, peri-urban and urban women access water, not only for personal and domestic uses, but also for growing, preparing and selling food and other products that are vital for family welfare and food security. From this perspective a dynamic and context sensitive mode of human rights interpretation that takes into account the normative diversity that exists in law and society should be considered.[56] From this perspective mechanisms that can assist poor water users in holding the plurality of coexisting water governance institutions accountable should be explored.

Towards an Empirically Informed Dialogue Between International, National and Local Norms

In view of human rights methods, this chapter illustrates how the role of legal pluralities as an enabling and constraining factor to human rights realization can be studied empirically in local contexts. The use of law as a semi-autonomous social field is demonstrated in comparative case studies of the interplay between international, national and local water norms in three social and geographically distinct localities in Zimbabwe. This case study and the embedded sub-cases, underscore the need for human rights analysis that is contextually specific and sensitive to different layers of legal norms, the interaction between them and possible conflicts that may arise. From a social science perspective the need to situate the norm-generating processes that take place in small social fields into long-run historical processes, changing political power relations and paradigms of governance is emphasized.[57] From a normative human rights perspective the need for an empirically informed dialogue between international, national and local norms with a view to better integration and harmonization is pointed out.[58]

---

[56]   E. Brems, 'The Unesco Convention for the Promotion and Protection of Diversity of Cultural Expressions: A Table of Fragmentation in International Law' (2012) 9 International Law 183–200; M. Langford and M. Woodhouse, 'There is no human right to water for livelihoods', (2009) Waterlines Vol. 28 No.1 1–12.

[57]   Sieder and McNeish (n 2).

[58]   E. Brems, G. Corradi and M. Goodale, *Human Rights Encounter Legal Pluralism, Normative and Empirical Approaches* (Hart 2017).

REFERENCES

Bentzon, A.W., A. Hellum, J. Stewart, W. Ncube and T. Agersnap, *Pursuing Grounded Theory in Law. South-North Experiences in Developing Women's Law* (TANO/Mond Books 1998)

Brems, E., 'Should Pluriform Human Rights Become One? Exploring the Benefits of Human Rights Integration' (2014) (4) *European Journal of Human Rights* 447–470

Brems, E., Corradi, G. and Goodale, M., *Human Rights Encounter Legal Pluralism, Normative and Empirical Approaches* (Hart 2017).

CESCR, 'General Comment No. 14. The Right to the Highest Attainable Standard of Health' (2000) E/C12/2000/4

CESCR, 'General Comment No. 15. The Right to Water' (2002) E/C.12/2002/11

Commission on Legal Empowerment of the Poor. *Making the Law Work for Everyone* Vol. 1 (United Nations Development Program 2008)

Constitution of Zimbabwe (2013)

Corradi, G., 'An Emerging Challenge for Justice Sector Aid in Africa: Lessons from Mozambique on Legal Pluralism and Human Rights' (2012) 4(3) *Journal of Human Rights Practice* 289–311

Corradi, G., 'Justice Sector Aid in Legally Plural Africa' in E. Brems et al. (eds), *International Actors and Traditional Justice in Sub-Saharan Africa* (Antwerp, Intersentia 2015)

Dahl, T.S., *Feminist Jurisprudence* (Norwegian University Press 1986)

DANIDA, *Informal Justice Systems* (Ministry of Foreign Affairs of Denmark 2010)

Derman, B. and A. Hellum, 'Neither Tragedy nor Enclosure: Are There Inherent Human Rights in Water Management in Zimbabwe's Communal Lands' (2002) 14(2) The European Journal of Development Research 31–50

Derman, B., A. Hellum and K. Sandvik 'Ethnographic and Historical Perspectives on Rights Claiming on the African Continent' in B. Derman, A. Hellum and K. Sandvik (eds), *Worlds of Human Rights: Ambiguities of Rights Claiming in Africa* (Brill 2013) 1–35

Dublin Principles, 'The Dublin Statement on Water and Sustainable Development, International Conference on Water and the Environment: Development Issues for the 21st Century', organized by the World Meteorological Organization in Dublin, 26–31 January 1992

Englund, H., *Prisoners of Freedom: Human Rights and the African Poor* (University of California Press 2006)

Franks, T. and F. Cleaver, 'Water Governance and Poverty: A Framework for Analysis', (2007) 7(4) Progress in Development Studies 291–306

Government of Zimbabwe, 'Towards Integrated Water Resources Management: Water Resources Management Strategy for Zimbabwe' (2000)

Government of Zimbabwe, National Water Policy, Ministry of Water Resources, Development and Management (2012)

Griffiths, A., 'Legal Pluralism' in R. Banakar and M. Travers (eds), *An Introduction to Law and Social Theory* (Hart 2002) 289–310

Griffiths, J., 'What is Legal Pluralism?' (1986) 24 Journal of Legal Pluralism 1–50

Gullestad, M., *Kitchen Table Society* (Norwegian University Press 2002)

Hellum, A., *Women's Human Rights and Legal Pluralism in Africa: Mixed Norms and Identities in Infertility Management in Zimbabwe* (TANO Aschehoug/Mond Books 1999)

Hellum, A., 'Human Rights in a Gendered, Relational and Plural Legal Landscape. Introduction' in *Worlds of Human Rights: Ambiguities of Rights Claiming in Africa* (Brill 2013) 131–143

Hellum, A., 'Legal Pluralist Perspectives in Scandinavian and African Women's Law' in K. Papendorf, S. Machura and A. Hellum (eds), *Ehrlich's Sociology of Law* (Litt 2014) 95–115

Hellum, A. and F. Taj, 'Taking What Law Where and to Whom? Legal Literacy as Transcultural "Law-Making" in Oslo' in A. Hellum, S.S. Ali and A. Griffiths (eds), *From Transnational Relation to Transnational Laws. Northern European Laws at the Crossroads* (Ashgate 2011) 93–117

Hellum, A., J. Stewart, S. Sardar Ali and A. Tsanga, 'Paths are Made by Walking: Introductory Thoughts' in A. Hellum et al. (eds), *Human Rights, Plural Legalities and Gendered Realities: Paths are made by walking* (Weaver Press 2007) ii–xi

Hellum, A., P. Kameri-Mbote and B. van Koppen (eds), 'The Human Right to Water and Sanitation in a Legal Pluralist Landscape: Perspectives of Southern and Eastern African Women' in *Water is Life: Women's Human Rights in Local Water Governance in Southern and Eastern Africa* (Weaver Press 2015) 1–32

Holleman, John F., 'Trouble-cases and Trouble-less in the Study of Customary Law and Legal Reform' (1973) Law and Society Review 585–609

International Council on Human Rights Policy, *When Legal Orders Overlap, Human Rights, State and Non-State Law* (ICHRP 2009)

Langford, M. and M. Woodhouse, 'There is no human right to water for livelihoods' (2009), Waterlines Vol. 28 No.1 1–12

Matondi, P., 'The Struggle for Access to Land and Water Resources in Zimbabwe: The Case of Shamva District'. PhD thesis, Swedish University of Agricultural Sciences (Uppsala 2001)

Merry, S.E., 'Legal Pluralism' (1988) 22(5) Law and Society Review 869–896

Merry, S.E., *Human Rights and Gender Violence* (University of Chicago Press 2006)

Moore, S.F. 'Law and Social Change: The Semi-Autonomous Field as an Appropriate Subject of Study' (1973) 7 Law and Society Review 719–746

Petersen, H., *Home Knitted Law. Norms and Values in Gendered Rule-making* (Dartmouth 1996)

Sieder, R. and J.A. McNeish (eds), 'Introduction' in *Gender Justice and Legal Pluralities: Latin American and African Perspectives* (Routledge 2013) 1–31

Sithole, B., 'Use and Access to Dambos in Communal Lands in Zimbabwe: Institutional Considerations', PhD thesis, Centre for Applied Social Sciences, University of Zimbabwe (1999)

Sousa Santos, B., 'Law a Map of Misreading: Towards a Post-modern Conception of Law' (1987) 14(3) Journal of Law and Society 279–299

Sousa Santos, B. and C.A. Rodriguez-Garavito, *Law and Globalization from Below. Towards a Cosmopolitan Legality* (CUP 2005)

United Nations General Assembly, 'Report of the Special Rapporteur in the Field of Cultural Rights, Farida Shaheed' (10 August 2012) AA/67/287

UN Women, *Progress of the World's Women* (United Nations 2011)

Van Koppen, B., M. Giordano and J. Butterworth (eds), *Community-based Water Law and Water Resource Management* (CABI International 2007)

Von Benda-Beckmann, F. and K. von Benda-Beckmann, '"Living Law" as Political and Analytical Concept' in K. Papendorf, S. Machura and A. Hellum (eds), *Ehrlich's Sociology of Law* (Litt 2014) 69–95

Von Benda-Beckmann, K., F. von Benda-Beckmann and A. Griffiths (eds), *Mobile People, Mobile Law. Expanding Legal Relations in a Changing World* (Ashgate 2005) 11–14

World Bank, 'Customary Justice and Legal Pluralism in Post-Conflict and Fragile Societies', conference hosted by United States Institute of Peace, George Washington University, Washington, DC, 17–18 November 2009

Zimbabwe National Water Authority Act No.11/98

Zimbabwean Water Act No. 31/98

Index